Anti-Inflammatory Diet Cookbook

900 Quick, Easy and Delicious Recipes to Reduce Inflammation and Boost Autoimmune System. Includes a 21-Day No-Stress Meal Plan.

© Copyright 2021 by Taste Academy -
All rights reserved.

Table of Contents

INTRODUCTION 7

CHAPTER 1: TRACING CHRONIC INFLAMMATION 8

CHAPTER 2: HEALTHY LIVING VIA EMPOWERED EATING 14

CHAPTER 3: BREAKFAST RECIPES 18

CHAPTER 4: LUNCH RECIPES 56

CHAPTER 5: DINNER RECIPES 91

CHAPTER 6: SEAFOOD RECIPES 123

CHAPTER 7: MEATS RECIPES 151

CHAPTER 8: SNACKS AND SIDES RECIPES 189

CHAPTER 9: DESSERTS RECIPES 216

CHAPTER 10: MEAL PLAN 231

CHAPTER 11: CONVERSION UNITS OF MEASURE 233

CHAPTER 12: RECIPE INDEX 235

<u>Do you want to take a look at our recipes?</u>

Then just turn on your phone's camera, and you'll be automatically head over to our official Instagram page and follow us!

INTRODUCTION

It is well acknowledged that chronic inflammation is the root of most health problems. The recent explosion of studies on inflammation has opened up a whole new field of study for health professionals. For example, high levels of inflammation have been linked to more than 50 different diseases. There are countless diets that you can follow to lower your risk for many chronic illnesses, but only one diet can reduce your risk of more than 50 different diseases at once! That diet is the Anti-Inflammatory Diet.

Research suggests that certain foods can trigger an inflammatory response in the body. Foods that promote inflammation include sugar, trans fats, soy, dairy, eggs, and processed foods in general. Many studies suggest that if you can avoid these inflammatory foods, you may reduce your risk of chronic disease. By doing away with such foods from your daily diet for an extended period, you can lower your body's production of inflammation-causing agents known as cytokines.

This book is here to educate you on the tips of preparing delicious recipes designed to fight inflammation. I am a person who has experienced the benefits of this diet for myself. Suppose you are already following an anti-inflammatory diet by itself. In that case, this book will offer you further insight to improve the health of your body by strengthening it with specific nutrients that have been shown to have anti-inflammatory benefits. If you're already following a nutrient-rich diet, adding these recipes to your healthy eating experience will take your health to the next level.

Are you on an anti-inflammatory diet already? How can you ensure you are getting all of the nutrients your body needs without gaining weight? The answer is simple. Eat more of the foods that are rich in nutrients, avoiding processed foods as much as possible. These higher-quality foods are also rich in fiber, which means they are bulky and filling.

I created this book to give you easy-to-follow recipes that will help you eat more delicious foods while keeping inflammation under control. In addition, if your lifestyle is more sedentary (e.g., desk job or watching TV), this book will give you tips on incorporating exercise into your daily routine while still eating healthy foods.

So what are you waiting for? Read on to learn more about the anti-inflammatory diet and then start planning your meals. You can even come up with your own recipes based on the recipes that I provide if you like!

CHAPTER 1:
TRACING CHRONIC INFLAMMATION

What exactly is inflammation? Inflammation is a protective response that happens as a result of injury or infection. However, if the body's immune system goes into overdrive and starts attacking healthy tissue, inflammation can become a pathological reaction. In such a case, your body is fighting to protect itself from damage but is overreacting and damaging the tissues that they are protecting. This type of inflammation can be caused by infections or disease or can be caused by damage to tissues due to injury, surgery, or aging. For example, if you cut yourself, your body will send white blood cells to the area to heal the wound and remove debris. If you burn yourself, your body will swell and try to protect the damaged tissue from further damage. There are many causes of inflammation (bacterial and viral infections, trauma, and environmental toxins, among others). Inflammation is a process acting as a natural immune response that keeps us alive and healthy.

How does inflammation occur in the body?

We have two kinds of inflammation, the acute type, and chronic. Acute inflammation usually involves a single episode of swelling and pain, which goes away when the injury heals itself. Chronic inflammation is a more serious condition that can damage cells and tissues in the body. The most known root for chronic inflammation is the overactive immune system, which leads to the production of cytokines. Cytokines are powerful chemicals that have been linked to nearly every disease known to man. Several diseases and disorders are caused by inflammation. Inflammation is present in any condition that ends in "itis": arthritis, endocarditis, appendicitis, bronchitis, colitis, and laryngitis, to mention a few. Inflammation affects everyone, but persons with lower immune systems, such as youngsters, elderly people, and those experiencing autoimmune diseases, are more vulnerable.

Inflammation has no visible signs, which is why it's difficult to diagnose the condition. In addition, the inflammation affects everyone differently and can range from mild to severe, according to the individual. Some people even appear "normal" before suffering from an inflammatory reaction (i.e., chronic low-level but constant inflammation). The major difference between acute and chronic inflammation is that acute inflammation resolves within a few days or weeks, while chronic inflammation may last months or years.

What are cytokines?

We define cytokines as chemicals used by our immune systems to fight infections. They are released by white blood cells called lymphocytes. Cytokines have also been linked to many different diseases, including asthma, diabetes, obesity, and cancer. Cytokines are related to most chronic diseases because most chronic diseases share one common feature: An overactive immune response. Researchers have found that cytokines are present in people who have suffered from most chronic diseases. For such a reason, the presence of cytokines in the body is one of the strongest indicators of chronic disease.

Inflammation is linked to several health conditions like:

Several studies have shown that chronic inflammation is the root cause behind a wide variety of illnesses. Inflammation is especially suspected in heart disease, diabetes, Alzheimer's disease, and cancer, although many other illnesses have a correlation with inflammation.

Health conditions linked to inflammation include:

Asthma: This disease of the lungs is one of a number of symptoms that involve shortness of breath, coughing, and chest tightness. Asthma can be a result of the airways being attacked by chronic inflammation; it is also closely linked to allergies.

Heart disease: Chronic inflammation leads to the formation of plaque in the arteries, which leads to heart attacks and strokes.

Diabetes: The immune system is called upon to regulate blood sugar levels throughout the day. This can lead to an inflammatory response during periods of high blood sugar, which further increases the risk of diabetes.

Cancer: Although the link is not fully understood, research suggests that inflammation in the body can hike the likelihood of cancer attacks like prostate, colon, or breast cancers.

Inflammatory Bowel Disease (IBD): IBD can lead to inflammation of the stomach and intestines, which causes abdominal pain and bleeding. It includes Crohn's disease and colitis.

Allergy: Allergic reactions involve immune system hypersensitivity. When a person is exposed to a certain allergen, the body releases histamines that cause his or her nose to run, eyes to water, and throat or chest to tighten.

Alzheimer's disease: The link between Alzheimer's disease and inflammation is not completely understood. However, studies show that people at risk for Alzheimer's commonly had chronic inflammation before developing the illness.

Rheumatoid Arthritis: This condition causes pain, swelling, stiffness, stiffness, muscle weakness, and reduced mobility.

Osteoarthritis: Osteoarthritis results in continuing joint pain along with the early stages of arthritis. It's usually caused by wear-and-tear on the joints due to overuse. Cartilage located in joints is susceptible to inflammation. Damage to joint cartilage leads to joint inflammation, pain, and swelling (especially after exercising).

Lupus: Lupus affects the whole body. Symptoms include joint and muscle pain and fatigue.

Hashimoto's Disease: Hashimoto's is a type of thyroid disease that involves inflammation in the thyroid gland. It's associated with a reduced immune system, which leaves the body vulnerable to infection.

Chronic Fatigue & Fibromyalgia: These conditions are characterized by extreme fatigue and pain. Chronic fatigue syndrome affects 60-80% of people with Lyme Disease. In chronic fatigue, inflammation occurs in the muscles and joints, resulting in pain and stiffness. Fibromyalgia is associated with muscle pain/soreness and tenderness, as well as sleep difficulties and depression.

Celiac Disease: A disorder is known to affect the small intestine and can lead to chronic inflammation in the body. It is caused by an inherited protein called gliadin, which goes undigested by the body. Therefore, when gluten enters the bloodstream, it triggers an immune response that damages the small intestine and causes inflammation.

Multiple Sclerosis (MS): MS causes inflammation in the brain and spinal cord, leading to dizziness, vision problems, difficulty walking, and coordination problems.

Skin Diseases: Inflammation on the skin occurs in a wide variety of diseases, including acne, psoriasis, and eczema.

Headaches: Inflammation can also cause headaches, which may be a sign of a more serious illness. Headaches may be due to inflammation in the tissues surrounding the brain or in the blood vessels that supply blood to the brain.

Brain Disorders: Inflammation can affect the brain, causing seizures, weakness, or numbness. Chronic brain disorders like Parkinson's disease and multiple sclerosis can be caused by inflammation, which can damage nerves.

SHOULD I VISIT A DOCTOR?

Chronic inflammation can be a serious cause for concern. Because it is often symptomless, it may be overlooked. By the time symptoms are detected, the condition could be well underway. If you have any signs of inflammation or autoimmune disease, always see your doctor so that it can be tracked and treated early on.

What are the tests to request?

Chronic inflammation can be hard to diagnose. It is usually discovered when there is an obvious cause, like an infection or disease. However, if you have consistent signs and/or symptoms of inflammation, your doctor may order a variety of tests. The most common tests for chronic inflammation include:

C-Reactive Protein (CRP): CRP is a protein found in the blood produced by the liver. During an infection or injury, CRP is released in the blood to decrease inflammation in the body. Plasma C-reactive protein (CRP) is a test that measures CRP in your whole bloodstream, including white blood cells.

Cortisol test: The cortisol test measures the amount of cortisol in your blood after you wake up in the morning. Adrenal glands produce cortisol used to mobilize fat stores, which is important for energy production. High amounts of cortisol in the bloodstream are associated with chronic inflammation.

Practitioners that you can consult

There is a couple of wellness and health practitioner that provide advice and help regarding inflammatory conditions.

Naturopathic Doctor: Naturopaths are alternative, natural practitioners who focus on preventing and treating disease by supporting our immune system and capability to heal itself. They will investigate all potential causes for inflammation and create a holistic treatment plan to heal your body from infection and disease. Practitioners in this sector combine natural and traditional medicine, intending to efficiently identify health issues at their main root. Neuropathy spends a lot of time with their patients; some can even be under a health benefits plan.

Acupuncturist: Maybe you have seen Chinese people use needles to try and heal diseases by inserting them into specific body points. Well, this type of therapy is called Acupuncture. Research from the internal medicines Archives states that Acupuncture helps to manage chronic pains. Acupuncturists believe that symptoms and pain result from blockages in the meridians, which are channels of energy throughout the body. By releasing the blockages, symptoms and pain will disappear. Acupuncture is a safe treatment with no known side effects. It is very relaxing and helps to balance the body's energy systems.

Nutritionist: Nutritionists help to control inflammation by focusing on the diet. They will help you learn to eat properly and suggest supplements for specific conditions, such as arthritis. Great and informed dieting choices are pretty crucial when it comes to dealing with inflammation. Nutritionists can develop a special menu that is anti-inflammatory to implement to soothe your pain and improve as per your symptoms.

Yoga teacher: Yoga is a holistic practice that can help to reduce stress and calm the body. It is wonderful to stretch and strengthen muscles and improve balance. Exercise and stress management is crucial as per inflammation management. Yoga's gentle movement and deep breathing can ultimately help you feel relaxed, which reduces muscle tension, anxiety, blood pressure, depression, and chronic pain.

Mental health counselor: Chronic Diseases can be emotionally and physically debilitating. When you talk to an objective, qualified professional, you can ultimately reduce emotional anxiety, plus you get to feel supported and relaxed.

Common inflammation symptoms

The symptoms associated with acute inflammation are generally short-term (e.g., pain, swelling). In contrast, symptoms associated with chronic inflammation include slow to develop symptoms (e.g., high blood pressure, which can lead to heart disease). Although it is still not fully understood, most studies suggest that chronic inflammation may be the root of many diseases. This is because inflammation can manifest itself in so many ways in the human body. In this section, you will get to discover the not-pretty-obvious and obvious inflammation signs.

Normal

Most often, the symptoms of inflammation are pretty obvious, and they demand your undivided attention. These symptoms include:

- Heat
- Redness
- Soreness and pain
- Swelling

Silent

Inflammation signs are not always obvious. Most people do not realize that the symptoms they are going through are directly linked to chronic inflammation. Some pretty common signs of inflammation are:

Disease	Possible symptoms
Heart disease	Fatigue, high blood pressure, chest fluttering, sweating, and dizziness
Inflammatory bowel disease	Constipation, poor appetite, mucus or blood in stool, fatigue, night sweating, diarrhea, nausea
Obesity	Blood sugar imbalance, sweating, snoring, excess weight
Rheumatoid Arthritis	Joint stiffness, weight loss, weakness, fatigue
Osteoarthritis	Morning stiffness
Allergies	Digestive issues, food intolerance, dizziness, bedwetting, watery eyes, runny nose, mental fogginess
Asthma	Mucus, coughing

Lupus	Fever, fatigue, light sensitivity, anemia, hair loss
Hashimoto diseases	Cold sensitivity, weight gain, thinning hair, fatigue, depression, dry skin
Diabetes	Increased urination, thirst, and hunger
Cancer	Fever, fatigue, weight loss
Celiac disease	Fever, fatigue, weight loss
Multiple sclerosis	Weakness, tingling, dizziness, blurred vision
Skin condition	Family allergen history, digestive issues
Headaches	Dull acne, blurred vision, nausea
Brain disorder	Behavioral changes, decreased cognitive functioning, anxiety, insulin resistance, memory loss.

Medical and lifestyle intervention

Inflammation is addressed in the world's medical community with a wide range of lifestyle practices and medication. Therefore, it is crucial to know your options and work for hand in hand with a personal doctor to identify the best type of treatment that can work for you efficiently.

There are several ways to reduce your risk of chronic inflammation. Some people find that creating a good lifestyle is the key to reducing the signs of inflammation from chronic disease. Some lifestyle modifications to undertake include:

- Eat a healthy diet rich in fruits and vegetables.
- Avoid junk food and fast, processed food.
- Have a regular exercise routine that includes at least 30-minutes of physical activity each day.
- Get enough sleep for your body; experts recommend at least 8 hours of sleep per night.

Once you've done the things you can to avoid chronic inflammation, it's time to get tested for signs of inflammation. To determine if you are suffering from inflammation by getting tested for high levels of white blood cells or high levels of C-Reactive Protein (CRP). Your doctor can help you with this step, but make sure they are not overmedicating you. You can also try to get blood work done by a nutritionist or alternative doctor to get more objective results.

Some inflammation treatments include:

Nonsteroidal Anti-inflammatory Drugs (NSAIDs) – NSAIDs drug group works by blocking specific enzyme groups hence preventing the creation of chemicals that cause inflammation. Ibuprofen and aspirin are two pretty popular NSAIDs. However, long-term consumption of this drug can ultimately increase getting stomach ulcers; hence you should be careful.

Corticosteroids – Some genes are activated during an inflammation process, so this drug simply deactivates these genes, hence reducing inflammation.

Acetaminophen –Acetaminophen, also called paracetamol and Tylenol, helps to manage pain caused by chronic conditions. However, it does not address or prevent inflammation.

Some lifestyle practices that your doctor might recommend to keep inflammation under control:

Rest – Getting an excellent night's sleep helps reduce inflammation, boost memory repairs, and heal tissue. Plus, it keeps your appetite under control. It would help if you hence aimed to sleep for a minimum of 8 hours every night. Consider staying off any electronic device, screens an hour before your bedtime.

Anti-inflammatory diets – A tremendous and nutritious diet loaded with fruits, vegetables, healthy fats, fiber, antioxidants, clean water, and proteins play a massive role in managing inflammation.

Consult a medical practitioner to gain more information on targeted and specific strategies that you can apply to fight inflammation.

CHAPTER 2:
HEALTHY LIVING VIA EMPOWERED EATING

Our lives bear a lot of things that are ultimately beyond our own control. However, if you are lucky, what you eat does not fall under this category. Good nutrition is pretty crucial in the management, development, and prevention of inflammatory conditions. Knowing about food types that cause or worsen inflammation, inflammatory fares that you can implement in your usual diet, plus how one can follow an anti-inflammatory diet is pretty crucial. You can now make efficient and intelligent grocery choices to enhance and fuel a pretty healthy lifestyle when you gain these details.

Food-types that ultimately worsen inflammation

When discussing inflammation, you will find yourself mentioning a lot about food and diets because meals are crucial when it comes to inflammation. This section will go through some food types that you should avoid when implementing an anti-inflammatory diet.

Gluten

Farina, triticale, semolina, bulgur, farro, Kamut, spelt, rye, barley, wheat germ, and wheat all have one thing in common, they contain a protein known as gluten. Since gluten is pretty challenging to digest efficiently, it ends up causing digestive and intestinal problems. Individuals suffering from celiac usually have an unusual immune reaction to a specific protein contained in gluten known as gliadin. The body's immune cells respond to this protein by destroying microvilli used by the small intestine to absorb nutrients. However, gluten does not stop at that point in terms of causing bodily harm. Gluten can also cause blood sugar imbalance, joint pain, sinus problems, brain fog, skin condition, and hormonal imbalance. Even though media reports state that a gluten-free diet is necessary for individuals suffering from celiac conditions only, gluten intake can ultimately worsen the symptoms of so many chronic diseases. Any person suffering from an inflammatory illness can ultimately benefit from gluten-free diets.

Focusing on whole, natural, and fresh gluten-free meals can help you implement a gluten-free diet efficiently. Therefore, you should substitute gluten-free bagels and cookies with fresh fruits, gluten-free grains, nuts, legumes, seeds, fish, and lean meat. Following a diet packed with this foodstuff provides sufficient nutrients for your body and leaves you feeling pretty satisfied.

Foods containing gluten that you should avoid:

Gluten primarily acts as a thickener or binder in food. Therefore, the following foods can act as hidden gluten sources. Ensure you read the food labels to identify these major sources:

Cookies	Beer	Crouton	Bread	Soy sauce	Noodles and past
Cereals	Soup	Sauce	Gravies	Flour	Salad dressings
Deli meat	Candy	Cakes	Breadcrumbs	Pastries	Pasta sauce

Dairy

While growing, kids are told that to grow bigger and stronger, they should consume dairy products. However, most people do not produce lactase enzymes essential for the digestion of lactose sugar contained in milk. Due to this, many people get diarrhea, a bloated stomach, and ultimately being gassy. Other than just lactose intolerance, most people suffer from milk allergies. According to the American College of allergy immunology and Asthma and FARE, milk allergies fall under the topmost allergies experienced by children in North America (Food Allergy Research and Education). Milk is categorized as a foodstuff that causes mucus formation; the issue with this type of food is that when mucus coats digestive tracts, nutrient absorption becomes an issue. In addition, dairy cows that are raised to produce milk are fed antibiotics and hormones for growth. These antibiotics and hormones can ultimately interfere with the hormones of the human body leading to inflammation.

What's more, some dairy products (convectional) contain preservatives and sugar in high contents, increasing the risk of inflammation. While these details apply to a vast number of people, you should also know that some individuals can eat dairy products even though they fall under the category of foods that you should avoid. To learn more on this topic, refer to the foods with sensitivity alerts.

Food from the dairy category that you should avoid:

Cheese	Butter	Yogurt
Cream and milk	Kefir	Ice cream
Frozen yogurt	Cream cheese	Cottage cheese

Corn

Since many corns in the 21st century are extensively modified genetically, it falls under the category of foods that you should avoid. In the US, out of the overall corn content, ninety percent has been genetically engineered. GMOs (Genetically modified organisms) or foods that have been genetically modified are pretty new to the human body food system. They hence pose pretty serious health issues. The modifications applied to these food-stuffs can ultimately promote inflammation by suppressing the bodies' immune system. Corn is pretty ubiquitous as per processed foods: take, for instance, corn syrup that contains high fructose content; this foodstuff is pretty prevalent as per the many processed foods. Vegetable oils such as corn oil contain high levels of omega-six fatty acids; this fatty acid is also inflammatory hence not good for your health.

Foods containing corn that you should avoid

Xanthan gum	Corn sugar	Maltose	Golden syrup
Corn starch	Maize	Dextrin	Corn oil
Cornmeal	Maltodextrin	Corn syrup	High fructose
Tortillas made from corn	Corn syrup	Corn flour	Corn

Soy

Just like corn, soy is a pretty common allergen. Research carried out United states department of Agriculture's Economic Research shows that ninety-three percent of United States soy plants are genetically modified. What's more, soy contains high amounts of goitrogen, a compound that quickly suppresses thyroid functioning. Soy also has anti-nutrients, for example, oxalates and phytates. These anti-nutrients mess up the digestive process and also disrupt the system of endocrine.

Soy foods that you should avoid

Tofu	Protein (TVP)	Textured vegetables	Tempeh	Tamari	Soy Yogurt	Soy sauce
Soy protein	Soy oil	Soy nuts	Soy nut butter	Milk made via soy	Soy lecithin	Soy isolate
Soy ice cream	Soy flour	Soy flakes	Soybeans	Miso	Edamame	Bean curd

Peanuts

Peanuts are another pretty common allergen. It contains aflatoxin, which is a mold carcinogen that affects individuals with candida or liver conditions. In addition, peanut plantations are treated heavily with pesticides which can ultimately increase the chances of an allergic reaction and inflammation. Peanuts also contain high amounts of omega-six fatty acid acids, which is an inflammation-causing fat. Conventional peanut butter is also packed with high levels of trans fats and sugars, which also ultimately cause inflammation.

Caffeine

Many people use caffeine to start up their morning or gain an afternoon boost. However, if you're suffering from any chronic inflammatory disease, it would be good to stop your regular caffeine intake habit. Caffeine cause premature release of content by your stomach, which in turn leads to the injection of undigested foods into your small intestine. Once in the small intestine, these foods can significantly aggravate your digestion tract. What's more, caffeine raises blood sugar levels, heart rates, and blood pressure immensely. It also suppresses your appetite and ultimately disrupts sleeping patterns. To finalize why caffeine is pretty bad for your health, it stresses your nervous system and eventually interferes with cortisol levels. Health practitioners mostly recommend avoiding cocoa powder that is raw since when raw cocoa contains caffeine, it is not good for your health.

Alcohol

Even though the intake of a glass of white or red wine occasionally offers a significant boost in antioxidant content. Excessive alcohol consumption increases C-reactive protein production, an inflammation marker. What's more, many alcoholic drinks contain high levels of sugar. Alcohol messes up the gut floral, which is a pretty crucial digestive system part. A dis-functioning gut can cause leaky guts whereby small food particles break through intestinal barriers, which activates the immune cells; this activation stimulates allergies and inflammation.

Citrus Foods

The majority of citrus food-stuffs are pretty acidic, which can trigger inflammation in individuals with illnesses such as citrus sensitivities, arthritis, and gastroesophageal reflux disease (GERD). To shield itself from this acidic content, the human body utilizes its alkaline minerals, for example, potassium, magnesium, and calcium. If this buffer is not present, then acid contents from citrus foods can cause severe damage. However, when utilized in moderation, lime and lemons can be pretty helpful in an anti-inflammatory diet as they enhance the liver's detoxification and kick-start the digestion process. Once citrus foods are utilized by the human body, they eventually leave some alkaline minerals that the body can use. Some citrus foods even contain nutrients that are anti-inflammatory and antioxidants. Overall, however, avoiding citrus foods is the best option.

Citrus foods you should either avoid or limit

Tangelos	Pomelos	Oranges
Limes	Lemons	Grapefruits
Clementine	Satsumas	Tangerine

Feedlot Animal products

Animal products (convectional) from large-scale industrial animal farms end up causing inflammation due to a couple of reasons. For starters, the animal raised for convectional animal product purposes are fed anti-biotics and hormones. Due to this reason, many people have now developed antibiotic resistance worldwide. FDA (Food and drug administration) has determined that eighty percent of antibiotics sold in the USA are fed to animals; bacteria have hence begun to adjust and adapt to antibiotics. As a result, antibiotics are becoming more and more inefficient in terms of treatment. Animals are mostly fed fare, which is pretty different compared to their natural diets. GMOs corns, wheat, and GMO soy are some foodstuffs fed to animals in the feedlot. All these foods stuff cause inflammation. Animals that feed on grains also ultimately yield meat high in omega-six fatty acids. To avoid falling victim to this unhealthy animal product, you should only consume organic animal products from those animals that are raised without antibiotics and hormones, with access to the outdoors, and fed grain and grass simultaneously. Suppose you find a hard time accessing organic meat. In that case, you can always consult local farmers- sometimes local farmers follow strict organic practices but lack the funds to be certified as organic farmers. If you want organic animal products, ask, and you shall receive them, it's that simple, and you get to live a healthy life.

Feedlot animal products that you should avoid

Turkey	Sheep	Pork	Lamb
Goat	Gelatin	Eggs	Dairy
Chicken	Broth	Beef	

CHAPTER 3: ## BREAKFAST RECIPES

1. Turkey Burgers

Prep Time: 15 mins | Total Time: 23mins | Yield: 5-servings

Ingredients:

2 minced garlic cloves	1 peeled and cored ripe pear, roughly chopped
1 lb. lean ground turkey	1 tsp. fresh ginger, finely grated
1 tsp. fresh rosemary, minced	1 tsp. fresh sage, minced
A dash of Salt to taste	¼ tsp. Freshly ground black pepper, to taste
2 tbsps. coconut oil	

Directions:

Pulse the pear using a blender to get a smooth consistency. Set in a bowl and mix with the rest of the ingredients except the oil. From the mixture into 10 patties. Using a frying pan, add coconut oil and heat using medium high heat. Arrange your patties and allow them to cook for 5-minutes on one side. Flip the patties and cook for 3 more-minutes.

Nutritional Information: Calories: 477 |Fat: 15g |Carbohydrates: 26g |Fiber: 11g |Protein: 35g

2. Root Vegetable Egg Casserole

Prep Time: 12-minutes | Total Time: 45-minutes | Yield: 4-servings

Ingredients:

1 tbsp. avocado oil	1 small yellow onion, peeled and diced
1 small turnip, peeled and diced	1 medium parsnip, peeled and diced
2 small carrots, peeled and diced	1 tsp. kosher Salt
8 large eggs	1 tbsp. lemon juice
1 tbsp. fresh thyme leaves	

Directions:

To the inner pot, add in oil and allow to Sauté for 1 minute. Add the onion, turnip, parsnip, carrots, and Salt. Cook until the vegetables are softened, 10-minutes. Press the Cancel button. In a bowl, add the lemon-juice and eggs. Add the thyme and vegetable mixture and stir to combine. Spray the inside of a 7-cup glass bowl with cooking spray. Transfer the egg mixture to the bowl. To your inner pot, add a cup of and set the steam rack inside. Set your bowl on the steam rack. Secure the lid. Pressure cook for about 18-minutes. Quick release pressure and unlock the lid. Set bowl aside and let cool for 5-minutes before slicing and serving.

Nutritional Information: Calories: 221 Fat: 12g Protein: 14g Fiber: 3g Carbs: 12g Sugar: 3g

3. Egg Porridge

Prep Time: 14-minutes | Total Time: 15-minutes | Yield: 2-servings

Ingredients:

2 eggs	2 tbsps. ghee; melted
1/3 c. heavy cream	1 tbsp. stevia
A pinch of cinnamon	

Directions:

In a bowl, mix eggs with stevia and heavy cream and whisk well. Using a pan over medium heat, add ghee and heat; add egg mixture and cook until they are done. Transfer to 2 bowls, sprinkle cinnamon on top, and serve

Nutritional Information: Calories: 340 Fat: 12 g Fiber: 10g; Carbs: 3 g

4. Huevos Rancheros

Prep Time: 8-minutes | Total Time: 15-minutes | Yield: 2-servings

Ingredients:

2 (8-inch) whole wheat tortillas	2 hard-boiled eggs, sliced
2 slices Canadian bacon or ham	1 oz. slice cheddar cheese
2 tbsps. salsa	

Directions:

Prepare the hardboiled eggs. Get a plate, add 1 tortilla, then add a slice of bacon/ham on top followed by sliced egg and the cheddar cheese. Roll your tortilla. Do the same procedure for the rest of the ingredients for your second burrito. Serve along with the Salsa.

Nutritional Information: Calories: 741| Protein: 36.12 g| Fat: 30.75 g |Carbohydrates: 79.37 g

5. Herb and Avocado Omelet

Prep Time: 2-minutes | Total Time: 15-minutes | Yield: 2-servings

Ingredients:

3 large free-range eggs	½ medium avocado, sliced
½ c. almonds, sliced	¼ tsp. each Salt and pepper as needed

Directions:

Over medium high source of heat set your non-stick skillet. Take a bowl and add eggs, beat the eggs. Pour into the skillet and cook for 1 minute. Lower heat to low and cook for 4-minutes. Top the omelet with almonds and avocado. Sprinkle Salt and pepper and serve. Enjoy!

Nutritional Information: Calories: 193 Fat: 15g Carbohydrates: 5g Protein: 10g

6. Cherry Smoothie

Prep Time: 6-minutes | Total Time: 7-minutes | Yield: 1 serving

Ingredients:

½ c. Cherries, pitted & frozen	½ Banana, frozen
10 oz. Almond Milk, unsweetened	1 tbsp. Almonds
1 Beet, small & quartered	

Directions:

To make this delightful smoothie, you need to blend all the ingredients in a high-speed blender for 3-minutes or until smooth. Pour into a serving glass and enjoy it.

Nutritional Information: Calories: 208 Proteins: 5.2g Carbohydrates: 34.4g Fat: 7.1g

7. Strawberry Yogurt treat

Prep Time: 13-minutes | Total Time: 15-minutes | Yield: 2-servings

Ingredients:

1 c. cut strawberries	4 c. 0% Fat plain yogurt
4 tbsps. honey	8 tbsps. flax meal
8 tbsps. Walnuts, chopped	

Directions:

Set 2 cups of yogurt in bowls. Layer walnut and flax meal in the middle. Put in a sprinkle of half of the honey before covering with the final layer of yogurt. Put in the honey on top of the yogurt to put in color when you serve.

Nutritional Information: Calories: 733 , Protein: 38.42 g, Fat: 30.57 g, Carbohydrates: 83.44 g

8. Pumpkin Is for More than Just Pie

Prep Time: 8-minutes | Total Time: 13-minutes | Yield: 4-servings

Ingredients:

2 c. old fashioned rolled oats	1 tsp. baking powder
2 tbsps. erythritol	1 tbsp. poppy seeds
¼ tsp. salt	1 large egg
Juice and zest from 1 Meyer lemon	1 c. unsweetened vanilla almond milk

Directions:

Lightly grease four (8 oz.) ramekin dishes. Set aside.
In a bowl, combine the erythritol, oats, poppy seeds, baking powder, and Salt. Add the egg, juice, and zest from the lemon and the almond milk and stir to combine. Divide the oatmeal mixture into the four dishes.
Pour ½ cup water into the inner pot of your Instant Pot. To the inner pot, set in your steam rack and place ramekins onto the top of your rack. Secure the lid.
Pressure cook for about 5-minutes. Quick release pressure and unlock the lid. The ramekins will be hot when you open the lid, so be sure to use your mini oven mitts to lift them out of the Instant Pot and let them cool before serving.

Nutritional Information: Calories: 229 Fat,: 6g Protein:9g Sodium: 330mg Fiber: 9g Carbs: 40g Sugar: 1g

9. Sun-Dried Tomato Garlic Bruschetta

Prep Time: 13-minutes | Total Time: 18-minutes | Yield: 6-servings

Ingredients:

1 garlic clove, peeled	1 tsp. chives, minced
1 tsp. olive oil	2 slices sourdough bread, toasted
2 tsp. sun-dried tomatoes in olive oil, minced	

Directions:

To your bread slices, rub the garlic clove. Spread equivalent portions of sun-dried tomatoes on the garlic side of the bread. Drizzle chives and sprinkle olive oil on top. Set the slices in your oven toaster, and allow to cook until done. Set the bruschetta on a serving plate. Serve warm.

Nutritional Information: Calories: 149, Protein: 6.12 g, Fat: 2.99 g, Carbohydrates: 24.39 g

10. Walnut and Banana Bowl

Prep Time: 13-minutes | Total Time: 30-minutes | Yield: 4

Ingredients:

2 c. water	1 c. steel-cut oats

1 c. almond milk	1 tsp. vanilla flavoring
¼ c. walnuts, chopped	2 tbsps. chia seeds
2 bananas	

Directions:

Toss all ingredients in a pot. Cook on simmer over medium high heat for about 15-minutes. Serve and enjoy!

Nutritional Information: Calories: 162 Fat: 4g Carbohydrates: 11g Protein: 4g

11. Breakfast Shakshuka

Prep time: 7-minutes | Total time: 17-minutes; Yield: 6-servings

Ingredients:

1 tbsp. olive oil	½ onion, chopped
1 clove garlic, minced	1 red bell pepper
4 c. tomatoes, diced	1 tsp. chili powder
1 tsp. paprika	6 eggs, pasture-raised
½ tbsp. freshly chopped parsley	salt and pepper

Directions:

Use medium heat and set a skillet in place. Add oil and heat. Sauté the onion and garlic for 30 seconds or until fragrant. Add in tomatoes and red bell pepper. Season with Salt and pepper to taste. Stir in the chili powder and paprika. Allow simmering until the tomatoes are soft. Reduce the heat and create 6 wells in the skillet. Crack in one egg in each well and increase the heat. Cover and allow to simmer for 5-minutes. Garnish with parsley last.

Nutritional Information: Calories 177, Total Fat 12g, Saturated Fat 3g, Carbs 5g, Protein 10g, Sugar: 2g

12. Swiss Chard and Spinach with Egg

Prep Time: 8-minutes | Total Time: 18-minutes | Yield: 4

Ingredients:

1 tsp. olive oil	20 pieces spinach leaves
20 pieces Swiss chard leaves	4 egg whites
4 pieces rice bread	4 tbsps. parsley (fresh)
Sea salt, ground pepper, and dried mint	

Directions:

Add 2 cups water to a pan and allow to boil. Split 1 egg and set yolks and the whites apart. Set whites in a container and lower towards the boiled water, and gently pour in the pan. Place the whites in a small container. Lower the container towards the heated water and gently pour the egg into the pan. Pouch your egg for 4-minutes. Set to a plate and do the same for the other eggs. Cut your parsley and sauté alongside the leaves in a pan for 6-minutes. Meanwhile, toast your bread. Once done, arrange a layer of chopped parsley and sautéed greens to the top of the toasted bread. Add an egg. To each serving, sprinkle with sea salt, mint, and pepper.

Nutritional Information: Calories: 49 , Protein: 5.31 g, Fat: 2.73 g, Carbohydrates: 0.48 g

13. Zucchini and Carrot Combo

Prep Time: 12-minutes | Total Time: 8 h 12-minutes | Yield: 3-servings

Ingredients:

½ c. steel cut oats	1 c. coconut milk
1 carrot, grated	¼ zucchini, grated
Pinch of nutmeg	½ tsp. cinnamon powder
2 tbsps. brown sugar	¼ c. pecans, chopped

Directions:

Grease the Slow Cooker well. Add oats, zucchini, milk, carrot, nutmeg, cloves, sugar, cinnamon, and stir well. Set the lid in place and allow it to cook for about 8 hours on LOW. Divide among bowls to serve!

Nutritional Information: Calories: 200 Fat: 4g Carbohydrates: 11g Protein: 5g

14. Carrot Cake Overnight Oats

Prep Time: 5-minutes + overnight | Total time: 5-minutes + overnight | Yield: 1 serving

Ingredients:

1 c. Coconut or almond milk	1 tbsp. Chia seeds
1 tsp. Cinnamon, ground	½ c. Raisins
2 tbsp. Cream cheese, low fat	1 Large Carrot, peel, and shred
2 tbsps. Honey	1 tsp. Vanilla

Directions:

Combine all ingredients and refrigerate overnight. Enjoy in the morning while cold. If you need it warm, set it in the microwave to warm for about a minute and stir.

Nutritional Information: Calories 340 |32 gr sugar| 4 gr protein |4 gr fat| 9 gr fiber | 70 gr carbs

15. Scrambled Eggs with Smoked Salmon

Prep time: 11-minutes | Total time: 12-minutes | Yield: 2-servings

Ingredients:

4 eggs	2 tbsps. coconut milk

Fresh chives, chopped	4 slices of wild-caught smoked salmon, chopped
salt to taste	

Directions:

In a bowl, whisk the egg, coconut milk, and chives. Grease the skillet with oil and heat over medium low heat. Pour your egg mixture and scramble the eggs while cooking. When the eggs start to settle, add in the smoked salmon and cook for 2 more-minutes.

Nutritional Information: Calories 349, Saturated Fat 4g, Net Carbs 1g, Protein 29g, Sugar: 2g, Fiber: 2g

16. Healthy Zucchini Stir Fry

Prep Time: 13-minutes | Total time: 13-minutes | Yield: 4-servings

Ingredients:

2 tbsps. heaping olive oil	1 whole medium-sized onion, sliced thinly
2 whole medium-sized zucchini, cut up into thin sized strips	2 heaping tbsps. flavored teriyaki sauce, low sodium
1 whole tbsp. coconut aminos	1 whole tbsp. a sesame seed, toasted
Ground pepper (black) as much as needed	

Directions:

Set a skillet on medium level heat. Add onions and stir cook for 5-minutes. Add your zucchini and stir cook for 1 minute more. Gently add the sauces alongside the sesame seeds. Cook for 5-minutes more until the zucchini is soft. Finally, add in pepper and enjoy!

Nutritional Information: Calories: 110 Fat: 9g Carbohydrates: 8g Protein: 3g

17. Avocado Cup with Egg

Prep Time: 8-minutes | Total time: 33-minutes | Yield: 4-servings

Ingredients:

4 tsp. parmesan cheese	1 chopped stalk scallion
4 dashes pepper	4 dashes paprika
2 ripe avocados, halved and deseeded	4 medium eggs

Directions:

Preheat your oven to attain 375 degrees F. Slice avocado rounded portions for better leveling and set well on the baking sheet. Crack one egg and set it in each of the avocado's holes. Appy paprika and pepper for seasoning. Put in preheated oven. Let bake until well-cooked for 25-minutes. Sprinkle the parmesan before serving.

Nutritional Information: Calories: 206 Cal Fat: 15.4 g Carbs: 11.3 g Protein: 8.5 g Sugars: 0.4 g

18. Healthy Breakfast Chocolate Donuts

Prep time: 13-minutes | Total time: 28-minutes | Yield: 12-servings

Ingredients:

1 c. coconut flour	¼ c. raw cacao powder
½ tsp. baking soda	4 eggs, pasture-raised
¼ c. coconut oil, melted	¼ c. unsweetened applesauce
1 tsp. vanilla	¼ c. honey
¼ tsp. salt	

Directions:

Preheat the oven to 350 degrees F. In a mixing bowl, mix the coconut flour, cacao, baking soda, and Salt. Set aside. In another bowl, combine the eggs, coconut oil, and applesauce. Stir in the vanilla and honey. Fold the dry ingredients gradually into the wet ingredients until well-combined. Grease the donut pan with coconut oil. Press down the dough into the pan. Bake for 15-minutes or until the dough is cooked through. Set from your oven and let cool before removing from the donut pan.

Nutritional Information: Calories 115, Saturated Fat 4g, Net Carbs 8.2g, Protein 4g, Sugar: 4g, Fiber: 0.8g

19. Roasted Pumpkin Seeds

Prep Time: 10-minutes | Total time: 30 | Yield: 4-servings

Ingredients:

1 c. pumpkin seeds, washed and dried	2 tsp. garam masala
1/3 tsp. red chili powder	¼ tsp. ground turmeric
Salt, to taste	3 tbsps. coconut oil, meted
½ tbsp. fresh lemon juice	

Directions:

Preheat the oven to 350 degrees F. In a bowl, add all ingredients except lemon juice and toss to coat well. Transfer the almond mixture right into a baking sheet. Roast approximately twenty or so minutes, flipping occasionally. Remove from oven and make aside to cool completely before serving. Add drizzles of lemon juice before serving.

Nutritional Information: Calories: 136 Fat: 4g Carbohydrates: 15g, Fiber: 9g, Protein: 25g

20. Breakfast Stir Fry

Prep Time: 23-minutes | Total time: 44-minutes | Yield: 2-servings

Ingredients:

1/2 lbs. beef meat; minced	1 tbsp. tamari sauce

2 bell peppers; chopped.	2 tsp. red chili flakes
1 tsp. chili powder	1 tbsp. coconut oil
Salt and black pepper to the taste.	For the bok choy:
6 bunches bok choy; trimmed and chopped.	1 tsp. ginger; grated
1 tbsp. coconut oil	Salt to the taste.
For the eggs:	2 eggs
1 tbsp. coconut oil	

Directions:

Heat up a pan with 1 tbsp. coconut oil over medium high heat; add beef and bell peppers; stir and cook for 10-minutes. Add Salt, pepper, tamari sauce, chili flakes, and chili powder; stir, cook for 4-minutes more and take off the heat. Heat up another pan with 1 tbsp. oil over medium heat; add bok choy; stir, and cook for 3-minutes. Add Salt and ginger; stir, cook for 2-minutes more and take off the heat. Heat up the third pan with 1 tbsp. oil over medium heat; crack eggs and fry them. Divide beef and bell peppers mix into 2 bowls. Divide bok choy and top with eggs

Nutritional Information: Calories: 248 Cal Fat: 14 g Fiber: 4 g Carbs: 10 g Protein: 14 g

21. Banana with Cashew Toast

Prep Time: 11-minutes | Total time: 12-minutes | Yield: 3-servings

Ingredients:

1 c. unsalted cashews, roasted	2 tsp. flax meals
4 slices of oat bread	2 peeled ripe bananas, sliced to 1/2" pieces
¼ tsp. salt	¼ tsp. cinnamon
2 tsp. honey	

Directions:

Toast your bread. Add cashews and Salt to a food processor and puree until smooth. Spread the puree on the toasts. Set a layer of bananas on the spread.
Add a topping of flax meals, cinnamon, and honey before serving.

Nutritional Information: Calories: 633 |Protein: 13.32 g|Fat: 48.6 g |Carbohydrates: 47.02g

22. Blueberry Hemp Seed Smoothie

Prep time: 8-minutes | Total time: 10-minutes | Yield: 1 serving

Ingredients:

1 ¼ c. frozen blueberries	2 tbsps. hemp seeds
1 serving vanilla plant-based protein powder	½ c. packed fresh spinach
1 tsp. spirulina powder	1 ¼ unsweetened plant-based milk
¼ tsp. holy basil leaves, chopped	

Directions:

Place all ingredients in a blender. Blend until smooth.

Nutritional Information: Calories:442, Saturated Fat 5g, Net Carbs:43g, Protein:27g, Fiber:7g

23. Brown Sugar Cinnamon Oatmeal

Prep Time: 1 Minute| Total time: 4-minutes | Yield: 4-servings

Ingredients:

½ tsp. ground cinnamon	1 ½ tsps. pure vanilla extract
¼ c. light brown sugar	2 c. low-fat milk
1 1/3 c. quick oats	

Directions:

Set vanilla and milk in a saucepan over the medium high source of heat and allow to boil. Lower to medium heat. Add in sugar, oats, and cinnamon as you stir. Cook for about 3-minutes. Serve with an extra sprinkle of cinnamon if preferred.

Nutritional Information: Calories: 208 Cal Fat: 3 g Carbs:38 g Protein:8 g Sugars: 6 g

24. Tuna & Sweet Potato Croquettes

Prep Time: 18-minutes | Total time: 30-minutes | Yield: 8-servings

Ingredients:

1 tbsp. coconut oil	½ large onion, chopped
1 (1-inch piece fresh ginger, minced	3 garlic cloves, minced
1 Serrano pepper, seeded and minced	½ tsp. ground coriander
¼ tsp. ground turmeric	¼ tsp. red chili powder
¼ tsp. garam masala	Salt, to taste
Freshly ground black pepper, to taste	2 (5 oz.) cans of tuna
1 c. sweet potato, peeled and mashed	1 egg
¼ c. tapioca flour	¼ c. almond flour
Olive oil, as required	

Directions:

Set your frying pan over medium heat. Add coconut oil and warm. Add garlic, onion, Serrano pepper, and ginger. Sauté for 5-minutes. Add in the spices as you stir and allow to sauté for 1 more minute. Take a bowl and add in this mixture. Mix in sweet potato and tuna.

Form oblong shaped patties of equal size from your mixture. Set croquettes in one layer on a baking sheet and put them in the refrigerator overnight. Beat the 1 egg in a shallow dish. In a separate dish, combine your flours. Add oil to a skillet and heat. Layer croquettes in batches and allow to shallow fry each side for 3-minutes.

Nutritional Information: Calories: 404 | Fat: 9g | Carbohydrates: 20g | Fiber: 4g | Protein: 30g

25. Coconut Chocolate Oatmeal

Prep Time: 7-minutes | Total time: 14-minutes | Yield: 4-servings

Ingredients:

1 c. steel cut oats	1 (13.25 oz.) can full-fat unsweetened coconut milk
2 c. water	½ c. cacao powder
½ c. erythritol	1/8 tsp. sea salt

Directions:

Place the oats, coconut milk, water, cacao powder, erythritol, and Salt in the inner pot and stir to combine. Secure the lid. Pressure cook for about 6-minutes. Quick release pressure and unlock the lid. Allow the oatmeal to cool slightly before spooning into bowls to serve.

Nutritional Information: Calories: 394 Fat: 23g Protein: 11g Sodium: 60mg Fiber: 7g: Carbs: 62g

26. Crepes with Coconut Cream & Strawberry Sauce

Prep Time: 18-minutes | Total time: 27-minutes | Yield 4

Ingredients:
For Sauce:

12 oz. frozen strawberries, thawed and liquid reserved	1½ tsps. tapioca starch
1 tbsp. honey	

For the Coconut cream:

1 (13½ oz.) can chilled coconut milk	1 tsp. organic vanilla flavoring
1 tbsp. organic honey	

For Crepes:

2 tbsps. tapioca starch	2 tbsps. coconut flour
¼ c. almond milk	2 organic eggs
Pinch of Salt	Avocado oil, as required

Directions:

To prepare the sauce: Use a bowl to combine tapioca starch and some frozen strawberry. Add in the remaining sauce ingredients and ensure you thoroughly mix. Set your mix in a pan and place on medium high source

f heat. Allow boiling as you stir. Let cook until sauce thickens for 3-minutes. Set aside and cover until you need to serve.

Prepare coconut cream: Scoop cream of the coconut milk. Mix vanilla flavoring, coconut cream, and honey in a mixer. Pulse until fluffy for 8-minutes.

Prepare crepes: set all crêpe ingredients in a blender and pulse until smooth. Set a nonstick skillet on medium low heat and grease using avocado oil. Set some of the mixtures to the pan and tilt to spread out. Allow cooking for 2-minutes. Flip and let the other side cook for 1 ½ more minutes. Do the same for the rest of the mix. Evenly divide coconut cream into every crepe and fold neatly into quarters. Add strawberry sauce and serve.

Nutritional information: Calories: 36 | Fat: 9g | Carbohydrates: 26g | Fiber: 7g | Protein: 15g

27. Oat Porridge with Cherry & Coconut

Prep Time: 13-minutes | Total time: 13 | Yield: 3-servings

Ingredients:

1 ½ c. regular oats	3 c. coconut milk
4 tbsps. chia seed	3 tbsps. raw cacao
Coconut shavings	Dark chocolate shavings
Fresh tart cherries	Pinch stevia, optional
Maple syrup	

Directions:

Using a saucepan, combine the milk, cacao, oats, and stevia and boil over medium high heat. Reduce the heat, simmer until your oats cook well to the required doneness. Set the mixture in 3 serving bowls and apply a topping of cherries, coconut shavings, and dark chocolate. Drizzle with maple syrup.

Nutritional Information: Calories: 343 | Protein: 15.64 g | Fat: 12.78 g | Carbohydrates: 41.63 g

28. Savory Pancake Blast

Prep Time: 5-minutes | Total time: 11 | Yield: 4-servings

Ingredients:

¼ tsp. turmeric powder	1 c. of coconut milk
½ c. tapioca flour	½ c. almond flour
1 red onion, chopped	1 cilantro leaves, chopped
½ inch ginger, chopped	1 tsp. salt
¼ tsp. black pepper, ground	

Directions:

Take a bowl and mix all ingredients until well-combined. Heat a pan on low, medium heat, and grease with oil. Pour ¼ cup batter onto the pan and spread the mixture to create a pancake. Fry 3-minutes for each side. Repeat the process. Serve and enjoy!

Nutritional Information: Calories: 340 Fat: 30g Carbohydrates: 40g Protein: 17g

29. Oats with Berries

Prep Time: 13-minutes | Total time: 43-minutes | Yield: 4-servings

Ingredients:

1 c. Steel Cut Oats	Dash of Salt
3 c. Water	For toppings:
½ c. Berries of your choice	¼ c. almonds or hemp seeds

Directions:

To begin with, place the oats in a small saucepan and heat it over medium-high heat. Now, toast it for 3-minutes while stirring the pan frequently. Next, pour water into the saucepan and mix well. Allow the mixture to boil. Lower the heat. Allow it to cook for 23 to 25-minutes or until the oats are cooked and tender. Once done cooking, transfer the mixture to the serving bowl and top it with the berries and seeds. Serve it warm or cold.

Tip: If you desire, you can add sweeteners like maple syrup or coconut sugar, or stevia to it.

Nutritional Information: Calories: 118 Proteins: 4.1g Carbohydrates: 16.5g Fat: 4.4g

30. Sautéed Veggies on Hot Bagels

Prep Time: 12-minutes | Total time: 28-minutes | Yield: 2-servings

Ingredients:

1 diced yellow squash	1 thinly sliced zucchini
½ sliced onion	2 pcs. Sliced tomatoes
vegan butter	1 chopped clove garlic
Salt and pepper	1 tbsp. olive oil
2 pcs. vegan bagels	

Directions:

Set a skillet over medium heat. Add oil and heat. Reduce heat to medium low. Add onions and sauté until they start becoming brown for about 10-minutes. Switch the heat back to medium. Add in zucchini and diced squash and allow 5-minutes to cook. Add your garlic and continue cooking for 1 more minute. Add in tomato slices and cook for an extra 11 minutes. Add Salt and pepper for seasoning. Toast your bagels and slice them in half. Take the butter and spread it over the bagels. Serve alongside sautéed vegetables.

Nutritional information: Calories: 375 |Protein: 14.69 |Fat: 11.46 g |Carbohydrates: 54.61 g

31. Breakfast Spinach Mushroom Tomato Fry Up

Prep Time: 7-minutes | Total time: 17-minutes | Yield 2

Ingredients:

1 tsp. olive oil	1 red onion, sliced
6 button mushrooms, sliced	½ c. cherry tomatoes halved
½ tsp. diced lemon rind	3 large handfuls of baby spinach
salt and pepper to taste	

Directions:

In a skillet, heat oil over medium low heat. Sauté the onion until fragrant. Add in the mushrooms and tomatoes. Season with lemon rind, Salt, and pepper. Cook for another 5-minutes. Stir in the baby spinach until wilted.

Nutritional Information: Calories 38, Saturated Fat 1g, Net Carbs 1.5g, Protein 2g, Sugar: 1g, Fiber: 1.5g

32. Breakfast Pitas

Prep Time: 4-minutes | Total time: 10-minutes | Yield: 4-servings

Ingredients:

2 c. chopped bell peppers	1 tsp. fine garlic powder
8 egg whites	1 tsp. onion powder
1 c. raw or cooked spinach	2 tsp. olive oil
4 pita pockets, whole-wheat	

Directions:

Set a sauté pan to a medium source of heat. Add the olive oil and heat. When hot, add bell pepper. Toss well and sauté till tender for 3-minutes. Toss in your spinach and allow to sauté until it wilts for 33-minutes. Using a bowl, whisk together your egg whites. Whisk in your spices. Set egg mix in the pan, place together. Set away from heat and stuff 1 cup of the mixture into your pita pocket. Enjoy.

Nutritional Information: Calories: 153 |Protein: 12.4 g|Fat: 3.41 g |Carbohydrates: 19.32 g

33. Granola

Prep Time: 12-minutes | Total time: 1 hour 12-minutes | Yield: 2-servings

Ingredients:

½ c. Flax Seeds, grounded	1 c. Almonds, whole & raw
½ c. Ginger, grated	1 c. Pumpkin Seeds, raw

½ tsp. Salt	1 c. Shredded Coconut, unsweetened
¾ c. Water	1 c. Oat Bran
½ c. Coconut Oil, melted	1 c. Dried Cherries, pitted
4 tsp. Turmeric Powder	

Directions:

Preheat your oven to attain 300 degrees F. Next, combine dried cherries, almonds, grounded flax, pumpkin seeds, coconut, Salt, and turmeric in a large mixing bowl until mixed well. After that, mix ginger, coconut oil, and water in the blender and blend for 30 to 40 seconds or until well incorporated. Now, spoon in the coconut oil mixture to the nut mixture. Mix well. Then, transfer the mixture to a parchment paper-lined baking sheet and spread it across evenly. Bake for 50 to 60-minutes while checking on it once or twice. Allow it to cool completely and enjoy it.

Tip: Substitute dried cherries with raisins if preferred.

Nutritional Information: Calories: 225 Proteins: 6g Carbohydrates: 18g Fat: 16g

34. Golden Milk

Prep Time: 7-minutes | Total time: 12-minutes | Yield: 2-servings

Ingredients:

1 tbsp. Coconut Oil	1 ½ c. Coconut Milk, light
Pinch of Pepper	1 ½ c. Almond Milk, unsweetened
¼ tsp. Ginger, grated	1 ½ tsp. Turmeric, grounded
¼ tsp. Cinnamon, grounded	Sweetener of your choice, as needed

Directions:

To make this healthy beverage, you need to place all the ingredients in a medium-sized saucepan and mix it well. After that, heat it over medium heat for 3 to 4-minutes or until it is hot but not boiling. Stir continuously. Taste for seasoning. Add more sweetener or spice as required by you. Finally, transfer the milk to the serving glass and enjoy it.

Tip: Instead of cinnamon powder, you can also use the cinnamon stick, which can be discarded at the end if you prefer a much more intense flavor.

Nutritional Information: Calories: 205 Proteins: 3.2g Carbohydrates: 8.9g Fat: 19.5g

35. Coco-Tapioca Bowl

Prep Time: 12-minutes | Total time: 32-minutes | Yield: 2-servings

Ingredients:

¼ c. tapioca pearls, small sized	1 can light coconut milk
¼ c. maple syrup	1 ½ tsp. lemon juice
½ c. unsweetened coconut flakes, toasted	2 c. water

Directions:

Using a saucepan, add tapioca and top with water. Set aside for ½ an hour. Add in syrup and coconut milk. Allow heating until boiling over medium heat. Stir in lemon juice. Add coconut flakes for garnishing.

Nutritional information: Calories: 309 |Protein: 3.93 |Fat: 9.02 g |Carbohydrates: 54.55 g

36. No Cook Overnight Oats

Prep Time: 9-minutes | Total time: 9-minutes | Yield: 1 serving

Ingredients:

2 tbsps. Oats	1 ½ c. milk, low fat
5 almond pieces, whole	1 tsp. each of chia and sunflower seeds
1 tbsp. Craisins	

Directions:

Add all the above ingredients to a jar and mix well. Set in the refrigerator overnight. Serve as breakfast.

Nutritional Information: Calories: 271 Cal Fat: 9.8 g Carbs: 35.4 g Protein: 16.7 g Sugars: 4 g

37. Spinach Fritters

Prep Time: 17-minutes| Total time: 22-minutes | Yield: 2-3-servings

Ingredients:

2 c. chickpea flour	¾ tsps. white sesame seeds
½ tsp. garam masala powder	½ tsp. red chili powder
¼ tsp. ground cumin	2 pinches of baking soda
Salt, to taste	1 c. water
12-14 fresh spinach leaves	Olive oil, for frying

Directions:

Using a bowl, mix all ingredients to get an easy mixture except for oil and spinach. In a sizable skillet, heat oil on medium heat. Dip each spinach leaf in the chickpea flour mixture evenly and place in the hot oil in batches. Cook, occasionally flipping for about 3-5-minutes or till

golden brown from each side. Transfer the fritters onto a paper towel lined plate.
Nutritional Information: Calories: 211 Fat: 2g, Carbohydrates: 13g, Fiber: 11g, Protein: 9g

38. Savory Breakfast Pancakes
Prep Time: 9-minutes | Total time: 16-minutes | Yield: 4-servings

Ingredients:

½ c. almond flour	½ c. tapioca flour
1 c. coconut milk	½ tsp. chili powder
¼ tsp. turmeric powder	½ red onion, chopped
1 handful cilantro leaves, chopped	½ inch ginger, grated
1 tsp. salt	¼ tsp. ground black pepper

Directions:
Set all the above ingredients in a bowl and thoroughly mix. Grease a pan with some oil and set over low, medium heat. Pour ¼ cup of batter onto the pan and spread the mixture to create a pancake. Fry for 3-minutes per side. Repeat until the batter is done.
Nutritional Information: Calories 108, Saturated Fat 1g, Net Carbs 12.5g, Protein 2g, Sugar: 2g, Fiber: 0.5g

39. Anti-Inflammatory Crepes
Prep Time: 8-minutes | Total time: 12-minutes | Yield: 4-servings

Ingredients:

2 tbsp. coconut flour	4 large eggs, pasture-raised
1 tbsp. coconut oil	1 c. hazelnuts, soaked in water overnight
2/3 c. dark chocolates	½ tsp. vanilla extract
2 tbsp. maple syrup	½ c. water

Directions:
Preheat your oven to 350 degrees F. In a bowl, mix the coconut flour, eggs, and water until well-combined. Using a skillet, add oil and heat over medium heat, and grease the skillet with coconut oil. Scoop 1/3 cup of the crepe mixture into the skillet and cook for 4-minutes while flipping halfway through the cooking time. Repeat until all batter is made into crepes. Make the hazelnut sauce by combining the hazelnuts, dark chocolates, vanilla extract, and maple syrup in a blender. Pulse until smooth. Spread the Nutella sauce over the crepes before serving.
Nutritional Information: Calories 465, Total Fat 29g, Saturated Fat 6g, Total Carbs 46g, Net Carbs g, Protein 9g, Sugar: 11g, Fiber: 5g, Sodium: 53mg

40. Spiced Morning Chia Pudding
Prep Time: 12-minutes | Total time: 17-minutes | Yield: 1 serving

Ingredients:

½ tsp. Cinnamon	1 ½ c. Cashew Milk
1/8 tsp. Cardamom, grounded	1/3 c. Chia Seeds
1/8 tsp. Cloves, grounded	2 tbsp. Maple Syrup
1 tsp. Turmeric	

Directions:
To begin with, combine all the ingredients in a medium bowl until well mixed. Next, spoon the mixture into a container and allow it to sit overnight. In the morning, transfer to a cup and serve with toppings of your choice.
Tip: You can top it with toppings of your choice like coconut flakes or seeds etc.
Nutritional Information: Calories: 237 Proteins: 8.1g Carbohydrates: 28.9g Fat: 8.1g

41. Gluten-Free Crepes
Prep Time: 12-minutes | Total time: 16-minutes | Yield: 6-servings

Ingredients:

2 organic pasture-raised eggs	1 tsp. of pure vanilla flavoring
½ c. of unsweetened almond milk	½ c. of water
¼ tsp. of Salt	1 tbsp. of pure maple syrup
1 c. of gluten-free all-purpose flour	2 tbsps. of coconut oil, melted
1 tbsp. of coconut oil for cooking	

Filling Options:

Strawberries, blueberries, and honey	Nut butter with bananas

Directions:
Using a saucepan, add 2tbsps. of coconut oil and warm using low heat. Set this aside. Using a bowl, mix the eggs, vanilla, unsweetened nut milk, water, Salt, and pure maple syrup in a mixing bowl. Add flour and whisk again. Add the melted oil to the batter and stir. Heat a tsp. of coconut oil in a large frying pan over medium-high heat. Pour a third cup of batter into the frying pan. Quickly, tilt and swirl the pan in a circular motion to allow the batter to coat evenly. Cook each crepe for two-minutes. Ensure that it does not scorch. Flip to the second side and cook the other side for two-minutes. Repeat the procedure while cooking the other

crepes. Once the crepes get cooked, add your fillings (either berry with honey or nut butter with bananas.)
Nutritional Information: Carbohydrates: 14g, Dietary Fiber: 1g, Protein: 4g, Total Fat: 8g, Calories: 143

42. No-Bake Frittata

Prep Time: 12-minutes | Total time: 32-minutes | Yield: 6-servings

Ingredients:

2 tbsps. of extra-virgin olive oil	10 oz. of fresh button mushrooms, sliced
2 garlic cloves, minced	6 oz. of fresh baby spinach
8 organic eggs	2 tbsps. of unsweetened almond milk
Salt and ground black pepper	

Directions:

Put some oil in a sizable skillet and heat it over medium-high. Cook the mushrooms for 4-5-minutes while stirring occasionally. Add garlic, Salt, and black pepper and cook for 1 minute. Add spinach and cook for around 3-4-minutes. Meanwhile, combine eggs with almond milk, Salt, and pepper in a bowl. Add the egg mixture to the spinach combination and cook for around 2-minutes. Shake the pan to spread the eggs evenly and cook for 4-5-minutes. Cut it into 6 wedges and serve immediately.

Nutritional Information: Calories: 143, Fats: 10.8g, Carbs: 3.4g, Sugar: 1.4g, Proteins: 9.8g

43. Berry Coconut Porridge

Prep Time: 7-minutes | Total time: 17-minutes | Yield: 3-servings

Ingredients:

1 ½ glasses gluten-free rolled oats	2 tbsps. Chia seeds
3 c. almond milk	2 tbsps. raw cocoa nibs
2 tbsps. shredded coconut	1 c. blueberries (frozen or fresh)

Directions:

Cook the rolled oats with almond milk and Chia seeds over medium heat. Simmer before the oats get cooked. Transfer the mixture to three serving bowls and top with shredded coconut, raw cocoa nibs, and berries. Serve warm.

Nutritional Information: Total Carbohydrates: 56g, Fiber: 15g, Protein: 11g, Total Fat: 18g, Calories: 416

44. Cucumber Bites

Prep Time: 18-minutes | Total time: 18-minutes | Yield: 4-servings

Ingredients:

½ c. prepared hummus	2 tsp. nutritional yeast
¼-½ tsp. ground turmeric	Pinch of red pepper cayenne
Pinch of Salt	1 cucumber, cut diagonally into ¼-½-inch thick slices
1 tsp. black sesame seeds	Fresh mint leaves for garnishing

Directions:

In a bowl, mix together hummus, turmeric, cayenne, and Salt. Transfer the hummus mixture to the pastry bag and pipe on each cucumber slice. Serve while using garnishing of sesame seeds and mint leaves.

Nutritional Information: Calories: 203 Fat: 4g, Carbohydrates: 20g, Fiber: 3g, Protein: 8g

45. Breakfast Sausage and Mushroom Casserole

Prep Time: 22-minutes | Total time: 1 hour 7-minutes | Yield: 4-servings

Ingredients:

450g Italian sausage, cooked and crumbled	¾ c. coconut milk
8 oz. white mushrooms, sliced	1 medium onion, finely diced
2 Tbsps. ghee, organic	6 eggs, free-range
600g sweet potatoes, peeled, shredded, and soaked	1 peeled and roasted red bell pepper, deseeded, and diced
3/4 tsp. divided black pepper, ground	1 ½ tsp. divided sea salt

Directions:

Preheat your oven to attain 375°F. Grease a baking dish using ghee. Using a medium source of heat, set a skillet in place and cook your mushrooms until browned. Take them from the skillet and combine them with sausage. Using the same skillet, add in onions and sauté until golden and soft for approximately 5-minutes. Mix the mushroom-sausage mix with onions. Mix in bell pepper and mix properly. Drain your soaked potatoes and pat dry with the use of a paper towel. Set them in a bowl and mix with ½ tsp. Each of black pepper and Salt. Crack eggs in a separate bowl and blend in your coconut milk. Mix in the remaining Salt and black pepper. Evenly spread sweet potatoes in the casserole dish. Spread with sausage mix followed by the egg mixture. Use aluminum foil to cover the dish. Allow baking for

30-minutes. Remove cover from a dish and bake for 10 more-minutes until golden at the top. Set it to cool for about 10-minutes. Serve and enjoy.

Nutritional Information: Calories: 598 |Protein: 28.65 g|Fat: 36.75 g |Carbohydrates: 48.01 g

46. Blueberry & Cashew Waffles

Prep Time: 15-minutes | Total time: 19 – 20-minutes | Yield: 5-servings

Ingredients:

1 c. raw cashews	3 tbsps. coconut flour
1 tsp baking soda	Salt, to taste
½ c. unsweetened almond milk	3 organic eggs
¼ c. coconut oil, melted	3 tbsps. organic honey
½ tsp. organic vanilla flavor	1 c. fresh blueberries

Directions:

Preheat your waffle iron and grease. Pulse cashews using a mixer to form a flour-like consistency. Set in a bowl. Mix in salt, baking soda, and almond flour. In a separate bowl, add the remaining ingredients and mix well. Combine flour mixture and egg mixture. Fold in your blueberries. Set enough amount of your mixture in your prepared waffle iron. Allow cooking for 5-minutes. Do the same thing for the rest of the mix.

Nutritional Information: Calories: 432|Fat: 32|Carbohydrates: 32g|Protein: 13g

47. Bake Apple Turnover

Prep Time: 32-minutes | Total time: 57-minutes | Yield: 4-servings

Ingredients:

For your turnovers :

All-purpose flour to help roll out your dough	4 peeled and cored apples, diced
1 Tbsp. almond flour	1 puff pastry, frozen and thawed
½ c. crumbled palm sugar	½ tsp. cinnamon powder

For egg wash :

1 whisked in egg white	2 Tbsps. water

Directions:

To prepare the filling: mix sugar, cinnamon powder, and almond flour. Add in apple pieces and toss to coat. Place aside. Lightly flour a surface, roll puff pastry to attain ¼ inch thinness. Cut into 8 equal pieces. Divide apples equally and set them to the pastry slices. Fold halfway diagonally and seal by pressing the edges. Line a parchment paper on your baking tray and set it on

your pastries. Allow freezing for 20-minutes. Preheat your oven to attain 400 degrees F for about 10-minutes. Brush the pastries using the egg wash. Set in the oven and bake until browned for 15-minutes. Allow to cool and set one apple turnover to a serving platter and enjoy.

Nutritional Information: Calories: 203 |Protein: 5.29 g|Fat: 4.4 g |Carbohydrates: 38.25 g

48. Oatmeal-Apple sauce Muffins

Prep Time: 17-minutes | Total time: 42-minutes | Yield: 12-servings

Ingredients:
Topping:

1/4 c. rolled oats, presoaked in advance for 1 hour	1/8 tsp. ground cinnamon
1 tbsp. brown sugar	1 tbsp. melted butter, unsalted

Muffins:

1 c. old fashioned oats, rolled	1 c. milk, nonfat
1 c. flour, whole wheat	½ c. brown sugar
1 tsp. Baking powder	½ c. applesauce, unsweetened
2 egg whites	½ tsp. Baking soda
½ tsp. Salt	½ tsp. Cinnamon
½ tsp. sugar	Raisins

Directions:

Set oven to preheat and attain 400°F, then use cooking spray to grease a 12-cup muffin pan. Use a mixing bowl to mix applesauce, oat-milk mix, and egg whites. Set aside. Mix sugar, baking powder, Salt, brown sugar, cinnamon, baking soda, and flour in a different bowl. Blend dry and wet ingredients. You may add in nuts or raisins if preferred. For the topping: Use a bowl to mix brown sugar, oats, and cinnamon. Toss in melted butter to ensure even coating. Set the batter to each of your muffin cups to be 2/3 full. Add the topping and tap to even out your butter. Set in the oven and cook until done for 25-minutes. Set aside to cool for 5-minutes, then serve.

Nutritional Information: Calories: 115 |Protein: 5.06 g| Fat: 2.57 g| Carbohydrates: 22.33 g

49. Banana Baked Oatmeal

Prep Time: 7-minutes | Total time: 14-minutes | Yield: 6-servings

Ingredients:

3 c. old fashioned rolled oats	¼ tsp. salt
2 large bananas, mashed (1 heaping cup)	2 large eggs, lightly beaten

1/3 c. xylitol

Directions:
Place the oats, Salt, bananas, eggs, and xylitol in a medium bowl and stir to combine well. Lightly spray a 6" cake pan with cooking spray. Transfer the oat mixture to the pan. To your inner pot, add 1½ c. water. Place a steam rack in the inner pot and place the pan on the steam rack. Secure the lid. Pressure cook for about 7-minutes. Quick release pressure and unlock the lid. Allow the oatmeal to cool 5-minutes before serving.
Nutritional Information: Calories: 280; Fat: 5g Protein: 10g Sodium: 120mg Fiber: 6g Carbs: 53g

50. Maple Oatmeal
Prep Time: 7-minutes | Total time: 27-minutes | Yield: 4-servings

Ingredients:

1 tsp. Maple flavoring	1 tsp. Cinnamon
3 tbsps. Sunflower seeds	½ c. Pecans, chopped
¼ c. unsweetened coconut flakes	½ c. Walnuts, chopped
½ c. Milk, almond, or coconut	4 tbsps. Chia seeds

Directions:
Using a food processor, add in pecans, walnuts, and sunflower seeds. Process until well crumbled. Combine crumbled nuts with the remaining ingredients and set in a pot. Set your heat source to low and allow the mix to simmer for approximately 30-minutes. You can add cinnamon or use fresh fruit to garnish before serving.
Nutritional Information: Calories 374|3.2 grams' carbs|9.25 grams' protein|4.59 grams' fat

51. Waffles
Prep Time: 22-minutes | Total time: 32-minutes | Yield: 5-servings

Ingredients:

5 eggs separated	4 oz. ghee; melted
3 tbsps. almond milk	1 tsp. baking powder
4 tbsps. coconut flour	2 tsp. vanilla
3 tbsps. stevia	

Directions:
Using a bowl, add in the egg white and whisk well. Add the baking powder, egg yolks, stevia, and flour in a separate bowl. Mix well. Stir in milk, ghee, egg white, and vanilla. Transfer part of your mixture to a waffle maker and allow to cook until it turns golden. Perform the same process for the remaining batter.

Nutritional Information: Calories: 240 Cal Fat: 23 g Fiber: 2 g Carbs: 4 g Protein: 7 g

52. Breakfast Burgers with Avocado Buns
Prep Time: 12-minutes | Total time: 17-minutes | Yield: 5-servings

Ingredients:

1 ripe avocado	1 egg, pasture-raised
1 red onion slice	1 tomato slice
1 lettuce leaf	Sesame seed for garnish
Salt to taste	

Directions:
Peel the avocado and remove the seed. Slice the avocado in half. This will serve as the bun. Set aside. Grease a skillet over medium flame and fry the sunny egg side up for 5-minutes or until set. Assemble the breakfast burger by placing on top of one avocado half with the egg, red onion, tomato, and lettuce leaf. Top with the remaining avocado bun. Garnish with sesame seeds on top and season with Salt to taste.
Nutritional Information: Calories 458, Saturated Fat: 4g, Net Carbs:6g, Protein:13g, Sugar:4g

53. Almond Butter-Banana Smoothie
Prep Time: 7-minutes | Total time: 8-minutes | Yield: 1 serving

Ingredients:

1 tbsp. almond butter	½ c. spinach, packed
½ c. ice cubes	1 peeled and frozen banana
1 c. milk, fat-free	

Directions:
Sett all the above ingredients in a blender. Process well to get a creamy and smooth mixture.
Nutritional Information: Calories: 293 Cal Fat: 9.8 g Carbs: 42.5 g Protein: 13.5 g Sugars: 7 g

54. Sweet Potato Cranberry Breakfast bars
Prep Time: 11-minutes | Total time: 52-minutes | Yield: 8-servings

Ingredients:

1 ½ c. sweet potato puree	2 tbsps. coconut oil, melted
2 tbsps. maple syrup	2 eggs, pasture-raised
1 c. almond meal	1/3 c. coconut flour
1 ½ tsp. baking soda	1 c. fresh cranberry, pitted and chopped
¼ c. water	

Directions:
Preheat your oven to attain 350 degrees F. Apply coconut oil to grease a baking pan (9-inch). Set aside. In a mixing bowl. Combine the sweet potato puree, water, coconut oil, maple syrup, and eggs. In another bowl, sift

the almond flour, coconut flour, and baking soda. Gradually add the dry ingredients to the wet ingredients and mix well. Move to the prepared baking pan and top with cranberries. Place in the oven and bake for 40-minutes or until a toothpick inserted in the middle comes out clean. Allow to rest or cool before removing from the pan.

Nutritional Information: Calories 98, Saturated Fat 1g, Net Carbs 8.5g, Protein 3g, Sugar: 5g, Fiber: 0.5g

55. Spinach and Artichoke Egg Casserole

Prep Time: 11-minutes | Total time: 29-minutes | Yield: 8-servings

Ingredients:

12 large eggs	¼ c. water
4 c. baby spinach, roughly chopped	1 (14 oz.) can baby artichoke hearts, drained, and roughly chopped
1 tbsp. chopped fresh chives	1 tbsp. fresh lemon juice
¾ tsp. table salt	½ tsp. black pepper
¼ tsp. garlic salt	

Directions:

Use a cooking spray to coat a 6" round pan. Whisk the eggs and water together in a medium mixing dish. Combine the spinach, artichokes, chives, lemon juice, table salt, pepper, and garlic salt in a large mixing bowl. Place the mixture in the pan that has been prepared. Fill the inner pot halfway with water and insert the steam rack inside. Placing the pan on top of the steam rack is a good idea. Close the lid. Cook for 18-minutes on high pressure. Release the pressure quickly and open the lid. Allow 5-minutes for the egg casserole to cool. Slice.

Nutritional Information: Calories 122 Fat: 7g Protein: 10g Sodium: 603mg Fiber: 1g Carbs: 3g Sugar: 1g

56. Banana Pancake Bites

Prep Time: 10-minutes | Total time: 16-minutes | Yield: 3-servings

Ingredients:

1 ¾ c. old fashioned rolled oats	3 small ripe bananas
3 large eggs	2 tbsps. erythritol
1 tsp. ground cinnamon	1 tsp. pure vanilla extract
1 tsp. baking powder	

Directions:

Place the oats, bananas, eggs, erythritol, cinnamon, vanilla, and baking powder in a blender and process for 1 minute to get a smooth mix. In seven wells of Silicon Mold, pour the mixture into them. Top with a paper towel followed by aluminum foil. Tighten the edges to prevent extra moisture from getting inside. Place the mold on top of your steam rack with handles. Pour 1 cup of water into the inner pot. Place the steam rack and mold inside. Secure the lid. Pressure cook for about 6-minutes. Quick release pressure and unlock the lid. Pull the steam rack and mold out of the Instant Pot® and remove the aluminum foil and paper towel. Allow the pancake bites to cool completely, and then use a knife to pull the edges of the bites away from the mold. Press the mold's bottom to pop out the pancake bites.

Nutritional Information: Calories 389 Fat 9g Protein 16g Sodium 234mg Fiber 9g Carbs 70g Sugar 7g

57. Ginger Turmeric Shake Meal

Prep Time: 7-minutes | Total time: 9-minutes | Yield: 1 serving

Ingredients:

1 blood orange	½ c. of frozen mango
1/3 c. of coconut water	½ tsp. of ground ginger
1 tsp. of ground turmeric	½ tsp. of ground cinnamon
1 pinch of cayenne pepper	

Directions:

Put all ingredients into a high-speed blender. Pulse until it smoothens.

Pour your shake into a glass, drink immediately.

Nutritional information: Carbohydrates: 34g, Dietary Fiber: 6g, Protein: 3g, Total Fat: 1g, Calories: 138

58. Anti-Inflammatory Muffins

Prep Time: 16-minutes | Total time: 42-minutes | Yield: 12-servings

Ingredients:

2 glasses of almond flour	½ tsp. of sea salt
2 tsp. of aluminum-free baking powder	4 organic pasture-raised eggs
2 ripe bananas, mashed	1 c. of organic-canned sweet potatoes
¼ c. of essential olive oil	1 tsp. of ground turmeric
1 tsp. of ground ginger	1 tsp. of ground cinnamon

Directions:

Preheat your oven to attain 400°F. Use 12 muffin liners to line a muffin pan. Mix olive oil with eggs and bananas. Mix in sweet potatoes. Using a bowl, stir and mix baking powder, almond flour spices, and sea salt.

Stir together wet ingredients and flour mixture. Divide and set in the muffin liners. Allow baking for 25-minutes.

Nutritional Information: Carbohydrates: 14g, Dietary Fiber: 4g, Protein: 7g, Fat: 18g, Calories: 235

59. Pumpkin Quinoa Porridge

Prep Time: 2.5-minutes | Total time: 4-minutes | Yield: 4-servings

Ingredients:

¾ c. dry quinoa	2 c. water
¾ c. pumpkin purée	¼ c. monk fruit sweetener
1½ tsp. pumpkin pie spice	1 tsp. pure vanilla extract
¼ tsp. salt	

Directions:

Using a fine-mesh strainer, rinse the quinoa very well until the water runs clear. Add the quinoa, water, pumpkin purée, sweetener, pumpkin pie spice, vanilla, and salt to the inner pot. Stir to combine. Secure the lid. Pressure Cook for 1 minute. Quick-release pressure then unlocks the lid. Allow the quinoa to cool slightly before spooning into bowls to serve.

Nutritional Information: Calories 141 Fat: 2g Protein: 5g Sodium: 148mg Fiber: 3g Carbs: 37g Sugar: 2g

60. Chicken Muffins

Prep Time: 1 hour 10-minutes | Total time: 1 hour 40-minutes | Yield: 3-servings

Ingredients:

3/4 lb. chicken breast; boneless	1/2 tsp. garlic powder
2 tbsps. green onions; chopped.	3 tbsps. hot sauce mixed with 3 tbsps. melted coconut oil
6 eggs	Salt and black pepper

Directions:

Apply pepper, salt, and garlic powder to the chicken breast to season. Set on a parchment paper-lined baking sheet. Place your oven preheated at 425 degrees F and bake for 25-minutes. Transfer to a mixing bowl and use a fork to shred as you mix with coconut oil and half the sauce. Toss well to coat before setting aside. Using a bowl, add in the remaining sauce, green onions, eggs, pepper, oil, and salt and mix well. Apportion the mixture in a muffin tray, add a topping of the chicken, then bake in the oven preset at 350 degrees F for 30-minutes. Enjoy while warm.

Nutritional Information: Calories: 140 | Fat: 8 | Fiber: 1 | Carbs: 2 | Protein: 13

61. Coconut and Cinnamon Pancakes

Prep Time: 6-minutes | Total time: 25-minutes | Yield: 2-servings

Ingredients:

2 eggs, organic	1 tbsp. Almond flour
¼ c. coconut, shredded and more to garnish	½ tbsp. erythritol
A dash salt	1 tsp. ground cinnamon
4 tbsps. stevia	2 oz. cream cheese
1 tbsp. olive oil	

Directions:

Using a bowl, crack and beat your eggs until fluffy. Add in the cream cheese and flour and beat to smoothen. Add the rest of the ingredients as you stir to combine. Set your heat to medium high and place a frying pan on top. Grease the pan with oil. Take half your batter and put it in your pan. Let each side cook for 4-minutes until they become golden brown. Transfer to a serving platter and do the same for the rest of the batter. Top with coconut before serving.

Nutritional Information: Calories 575 | Total Fat 51g | Total Carbs 3.5g | Protein 19g

62. Mediterranean toast

Prep Time: 10-minutes | Total time: 10-minutes | Yield: 2-servings

Ingredients:

1 ½ tsp. crumbled feta, reduced-fat	3 Greek olives, sliced
¼ avocado, mashed	1 slice bread, whole wheat
1 tbsp. red pepper hummus, roasted	3 cherry tomatoes, sliced
1 sliced egg, hardboiled	

Directions:

Toast your bread and add a topping of hummus and avocado. Add in olives, feta, egg, and cherry tomatoes. Add in pepper and salt for seasoning if desired.

Nutritional Information: Calories: 333.7 Cal Fat: 17 g, Carbs: 3 3.3 g Protein: 16.3 g Sugars: 1 g

63. Oven-Poached Eggs

Prep Time: 2minutes | Total time: 13-minutes | Yield: 4-servings

Ingredients:

6 eggs, at room temperature	Water
Ice bath	2 c. water, chilled
2 c. ice cubes	

Directions:
Preheat your oven to preheat at 350°F. Using a deep roasting tin, add 2 cups water, and set on the oven's lower rack. In each muffin tin, add 1 egg and 1 tbsp. Water and set in the middle rack. Allow your eggs to bake for about 45-minutes. Transfer to your cake rack to allow for cooling before you extract the eggs. In a bowl, add the ice bath ingredients. Set your eggs into the ice bath to ensure the cooking stops. Drain your eggs after 10-minutes.

Nutritional Information: Calories: 357 | Protein: 17.14 g | Fat: 24.36 g | Carbohydrates: 16.19 g

64. Pineapple Ginger Smoothie

Prep Time: 6-minutes | Total time: 9-minutes | Yield: 1 serving

Ingredients:

1 c. pineapple slice	½ inch thick ginger, sliced
1 c. coconut milk	

Directions:
Place all ingredients in a blender. Pulse until smooth. Chill before serving.

Nutritional Information: Calories 258, Saturated Fat 5g, Carbs 51g, Net Carbs 49g, Protein 9g, Sugar: 13g,

65. Baked Eggs with Portobello Mushrooms

Prep Time: 13-minutes | Total time: 32-minutes | Yield: 4-servings

Ingredients:

4 portobello mushroom caps	1 c. arugula
1 medium tomato, chopped	4 large eggs, pasture-raised
salt and pepper to taste	

Directions:
Preheat the oven to 3500F and line a baking sheet with parchment paper. Scoop out the gills from the mushrooms using a spoon. Discard the gills and set them aside. Place the mushrooms on the baking sheet inverted (gill side up) and fill each cap with arugula and tomato. Carefully crack an egg on each mushroom cap. Bake in the oven for about 20-minutes or until the eggs have set.

Nutritional Information: Calories 82, Saturated Fat 2.2g, Net Carbs 3.2g, Protein 5g, Sugar: 3g, Fiber: 2g

66. Almond Scones

Prep Time: 12-minutes | Total time: 32-minutes | Yield: 6 servings

Ingredients:

1 c. almonds	1 1/3 c. almond flour
¼ c. arrowroot flour	1 tbsp. coconut flour
1 tsp. ground turmeric	Salt, to taste
Freshly ground black pepper, to taste	1 egg
¼ c. essential olive oil	3 tbsps. raw honey
1 tsp. vanilla flavoring	

Directions:
Set almonds in a mixer and pulse to have them roughly chopped. Transfer to a bowl. Mix in spices and flour.
In a different bowl, add the rest of the ingredients and mix well. Mix in your flour mixture. Set a plastic wrap on a cutting board. Spread over the dough and pat into circles of 1-inch thickness. Slice into 6 wedges.
Place your scones in one layer onto the cookie sheet and allow to bake for 20-minutes.

Nutritional Information: Calories: 304 | Fat: 3g | Carbohydrates: 22g | Fiber: 6g | Protein: 20g

67. Shirataki Pasta with Avocado and Cream

Prep Time: 10-minutes | Total time: 16 | Yield: 2-servings

Ingredients:

½ packet cooked shirataki noodles	½ avocado
½ tsp. black pepper, cracked	½ tsp. salt
½ tsp. basil, dried	1/8 c. cream, heavy

Directions:
In a medium pot, add water until half full. Set over medium heat and allow to boil. Add in noodles and let cook for about 2-minutes. Drain noodles and place them aside. Add avocado to a bowl and mash using a fork. Set in a blender alongside the other ingredients. Process well to get a smooth consistency. Set your heat to medium. Add noodles and avocado, mix in a frying pan and cook over heat for 2-minutes. Serve.

Nutritional Information: Calories 131 | Total Fat 12.6g | Total Carbs 4.9g | Protein 1.2g | Sugar 0.3g

68. Tomato and Avocado Omelet

Prep Time: 5-minutes | Total time: 10-minutes | Yield: 1 serving

Ingredients:

2 eggs	¼ avocado, diced
4 cherry tomatoes, halved	1 tbsp. cilantro, chopped
A squeeze of lime juice	Pinch of salt

Directions:
Mix lime juice, avocado, salt, cilantro, and tomatoes and place aside in a bowl. Place a nonstick skillet over medium heat. Form a frothy by whisking the eggs and

transferring them to the skillet. Use a spatula to move the eggs around. Over half your omelet, scatter with the avocado mixture. Transfer from heat and set on the serving platter as you fold in half. Enjoy.

Nutritional Information: Calories: 433 | Protein: 25.55 | Fat: 32.75 | Carbohydrates: 10.06 g

69. Spiced Popcorn

Prep Time: 5 ½-minutes | Total time: 7-minutes | Yield: 2-3-servings

Ingredients:

3 tbsps. coconut oil	½ c. popping corn
1 tbsp. olive oil	1 tsp. ground turmeric
¼ tsp. garlic powder	Salt, to taste

Directions:

In a pan, melt coconut oil on medium-high heat. Add popping corn and cover the pan tightly. Cook, shaking the pan occasionally for around 1-2-minutes or till corn kernels begin to pop. Remove from heat and transfer right into a large heatproof bowl. Add essential olive oil and spices and mix well. Serve immediately

Nutritional Information: Calories: 200, Fat: 4g, Carbohydrates: 12g, Fiber: 1g, Protein: 6g

70. Banana Steel Oats

Prep Time: 11-minutes | Total time: 27-minutes | Yield: 3-servings

Ingredients:

1 small banana	1 c. almond milk
¼ tsp. cinnamon, ground	½ c. rolled oats
1 tbsp. honey	

Directions:

Using a saucepan, mix almond milk, ½ banana, and ground cinnamon. Add sunflower seeds for seasoning. Stir well to ensure the banana is thoroughly mashed and allowed to boil. Add in the oats and stir. Set your heat to medium low and let simmer for about 7-minutes. The remaining ½ banana should be diced and topped with oatmeal. Serve.

Nutritional information: Calories: 358 Fat: 6g Carbohydrates: 76g Protein: 7g

71. Spicy Ginger Crepes

Prep Time: 15-minutes | Total time: 35 – 45-minutes | Yield: 8-servings

Ingredients:

1 1/3 c. chickpea flour	½ tsp. red chili powder
Salt, to taste	1 (1-inch) fresh ginger piece, grated finely

1 c. fresh cilantro leaves, chopped	1 green chili, seeded and chopped finely
1 c. water	Cooking spray, as required

Directions:

In a sizable bowl, mix together flour, chili powder, and salt. Add ginger, cilantro, and chili and mix well.

Add water and mix till a consistent mixture form.

Keep aside, covered for approximately ½-120-minutes. Lightly grease a substantial nonstick skillet with cooking spray and heat on medium-high heat. Add the desired volume of the mixture and tilt the pan to spread it evenly inside the skillet. Cook approximately 10-15 seconds per side. Repeat while using the remaining mixture.

Nutritional Information: Calories: 73 | Fat: 1.3 | Carbohydrates: 11g | Fiber: 2.1g, | Protein: 4.3g

72. Buckwheat Ginger Granola

Prep Time: 13-minutes | Total time: 22-minutes | Yield: 8-servings

Ingredients:

1½ c. raw buckwheat groats	1½ c. old fashioned rolled oats
1/3 c. walnuts, coarsely chopped	1/3 c. unsweetened shredded coconut
¼ c. coconut oil, melted	1" piece fresh ginger, peeled and grated
3 tbsps. date syrup	1 tsp. ground cinnamon
¼ tsp. salt	

Directions:

In a bowl, combine oats, shredded coconut, buckwheat groats, and walnuts. Stir in coconut oil, salt, date syrup, cinnamon, and ginger. Transfer your mixture to a 6-inch cake pan. To the inner pot, add a cup of water and set a steam rack to the inside. Close the pan and put it on your rack. Allow to Pressure Cook for about 10-minutes. Quick release pressure and remove the lid.

Using a sheet pan, take your granola and spread it over the pan to cool, undisturbed, for about 1 hour. It becomes crisp while it cools.

Nutritional Information: Calories: 311 Fat: 13g Protein: 7g Sodium: 78mg Fiber: 6g Carbohydrates: 42g

73. Blue Cheese, Fig and Arugula Salad

Prep Time: 10-minutes | Total time: 10-minutes | Yield: 4-servings

Ingredients:

¼ c. cashew cheese	2 bags arugula
1-pint figs, quartered	3 tbsps. balsamic vinegar
3 tbsps. olive oil	1 tsp. Dijon mustard

Salt and pepper, to taste	

Directions:
Take a bowl and add Dijon mustard, balsamic, vinegar, olive oil, salt, and pepper. Whisk them thoroughly, and then set them aside for 30-minutes to marinate. Take 4 serving plates and add cheese and figs on top. Drizzle with 1 ½ tbsp for each. Serve and enjoy!

Nutritional Information: Calories: 143 Fat: 13g Carbohydrates: 5g Protein: 3g

---

74. Spicy Pineapple Smoothie

Prep Time: 6 ½-minutes | Total time: 8-minutes | Yield: 1 serving

Ingredients:

1 tbsp. chia seeds	1 tsp. black pepper powder
1 orange, peeled	1 ½ c. frozen pineapple chunks
1 c. coconut water	1 tsp. ground turmeric

Directions:
Place all ingredients in a blender. Pulse until smooth. Serve chilled.

Nutritional Information: Calories 378, Saturated Fat 2g, Carbs 47g, Protein 9g, Fiber: 20g, Sodium: 261mg

---

75. Turmeric Protein Donuts

Prep Time: 50-minutes | Total time: 50-minutes | Yield: 8-servings

Ingredients:

1 ½ c. cashews, raw	2 tbsps. maple syrup
¼ tsp. vanilla extract	1 tbsp. vanilla protein powder
½ c. Medjool dates pitted	¼ c. dark chocolate
½ c. coconut, shredded	1 tsp. turmeric powder

Directions:
Using a food processor, add in all the above ingredients except for chocolate. Process until you obtain a smooth consistency. Roll batter 8 balls and press into silicone mold. Place into the refrigerator for 30-minutes. Make the chocolate topping. Once done, remove the donuts from the mold. Then drizzle with chocolate. Serve.

Nutritional Information: Calories: 320 Fat: 26g Carbohydrates: 20g Protein: 11g

---

76. Apple Bruschetta with Blackberries and Almonds

Prep Time: 22-minutes | Total time: 50-minutes | Yield: 5-servings

Ingredients:

1 sliced apple	¼ c. thawed blackberries, mash lightly
½ tsp. lemon juice, fresh	1/8 c. toasted almond slivers
¼ tsp. Sea salt, to taste	

Directions:
Line a parchment paper on a tray. Drizzle your apple slices with lemon juice and set them on the tray. To the top of each slice, spread a small number of mashed berries. Top off with almond slivers. Sprinkle "bruschetta" with sea salt before serving.

Nutritional Information: Calories: 56 |Protein: 1.53 g|Fat: 1.43 g |Carbohydrates: 9.87 g

---

77. Apple, Ginger, and Rhubarb Muffins

Prep Time: 15-minutes | Total time: 40-minutes | Yield: 4-servings

Ingredients:

½ c. finely ground almonds	¼ c. brown rice flour
½ c. buckwheat flour	1/8 c. unrefined raw sugar
2 tbsp. arrowroot flour	1 tbsp. linseed meal
2 tbsp. Crystallized ginger, finely chopped	½ tsp. ground ginger
½ tsp. ground cinnamon	2 tsp. gluten-free baking powder
A pinch of fine sea salt	1 small apple, peeled and finely diced
1 c. finely chopped rhubarb	1/3 c. almond/ rice milk
1 large egg	¼ c. extra virgin olive oil
1 tsp. pure vanilla extract	

Directions:
Set oven to preheat at 350F. Grease an eight-cup muffin tin and use paper cases to line it. Mix the linseed meal, sugar, ginger, and almond four in a mixing bowl using a bowl. Sieve the mix over the other spices, flours, and baking powder. Add in rhubarb and apple to evenly coat. Mix the vanilla, milk, and egg in a different bowl, then transfer into a dry mixture. Stir well to combine. Scoop the mixture and set in the muffin tin and add rhubarb as a topping. Allow baking for 25-minutes, till turn golden. Set aside to cool for about 5-minutes. Enjoy alongside squeezed juice.

Nutritional Information: Calories: 325 |Protein: 6.32 g|Fat: 9.82 g |Carbohydrates: 55.71 g

---

78. Fruity Bowl

Prep Time: 10-minutes | Total time: 10-minutes | Yield: 2-servings

Ingredients:

2 c. of frozen cherries (pitted)	4 dates (pitted and chopped)
1 large apple (peeled, cored, and chopped)	A c. of fresh cherries pitted
2 tbsps. of Chia seeds	

Directions:

Put frozen cherries and dates in a high-speed blender and pulse. Mix the chopped apple with fresh cherries and Chia seeds in a bowl. Add cherry sauce to the puree and stir. Cover and refrigerate them overnight before serving.

Nutritional Information: Calories: 211, Fats: 3.2g, Carbs: 49.7g, Sugar: 11g, Proteins: 3.8g, Sodium: 6mg

79. Breakfast Cherry Muffins

Prep Time: 12-minutes | Total time: 42-minutes | Yield: 6-servings

Ingredients:

1 ½ c. almond flour	¼ c. arrowroot flour
¼ c. coconut oil	¼ c. maple syrup
3 whole eggs	2 tsp. vanilla extract
1 ½ tsp. almond extract	1 tsp. baking powder
1 c. fresh cherry, pitted and chopped	¼ tsp. salt

Directions:

Preheat your oven to attain 350 degrees F. Using a mixing bowl, add in and mix all the ingredients except for cherries. Once combined completely, add in your cherries. Add batter to fill the muffin liners and allow to bake until done for 30-minutes.

Nutritional Information: Calories 528, Saturated Fat 5g, Net Carbs 29g, Protein 13g, Sugar: 8g, Fiber: 7g

80. Peanut Butter-Banana Muffins

Prep Time: 16-minutes | Total time: 42-minutes | Yield: 12-servings

Ingredients:

1½ c. all-purpose flour	1 c. old-fashioned oats
1 tsp. Baking powder	½ tsp. Baking soda
½ tsp. salt	2 tbsp. Applesauce
¾ c. light brown sugar	2 large eggs
1 c. mashed banana (about 3 bananas)	6 tbsp. creamy peanut butter
1 c. low-fat buttermilk	

Directions:

Bring a small nonstick skillet on medium heat and spray lightly with cooking spray. Add in the bell pepper and onion and sauté for 1 to 2-minutes, or until both are tender and the onion translucent. In a small bowl, crack in eggs and whisk. Add in milk; whisk until well-blended. Pour eggs into the pan and cook, frequently stirring until eggs are scrambled to your liking.

To serve, spoon half the egg mixture into each tortilla, wrap, and serve. Try serving with a side of fresh fruit for a complete meal.

Nutritional Information: Calories: 187 | Protein: 8.12 g | Fat: 6.25 g | Carbohydrates: 27.82 g

81. Anti-Inflammatory Porridge

Prep Time: 12-minutes | Total time: 17-minutes | Yield: 2-servings

Ingredients:

¼ c. walnuts, chopped and toasted	2 tbsps. hemp seeds, toasted
2 tbsps. chia seeds	1 c. almond milk, unsweetened
¼ c. coconut milk, unsweetened	¼ c. coconut, shredded and toasted
¼ c. almond butter	1 tbsp. coconut oil, melted
½ tsp. turmeric powder	1 tsp. bee pollen
A pinch of black pepper	

Directions:

Add coconut milk and almond in a pot and heat using medium heat. Stir in black pepper, coconut, walnuts, bee pollen, hemp seeds, turmeric, and chia seeds and allow to cook for about 5-minutes. Remove from heat and mix in almond butter and coconut oil. Allow to sit for about 10-minutes and divide into 2 and enjoy.

Nutritional Information: Calories 152, Fat 11, Fiber 6, Carbs 15, Protein 11

82. Dairy-Free Antioxidant Yogurt Parfait

Prep Time: 6-1/2-minutes | Total time: 6-1/2-minutes | Yield: 2-servings

Ingredients:

1 c. of full-fat, unsweetened coconut yogurt	1 c. of wild blueberries
2 tbsps. of ground flaxseeds	2 tbsps. of hemp seeds
2 tbsps. of chopped walnuts	2 tsp. of raw honey

Directions:

Divide the coconut milk yogurt between two serving bowls or cups. Top each bowl with a half mug of wild berries, 1 tbsp. Of ground flaxseeds, 1 tbsp. Of hemp seeds, 1 tbsp. Of chopped walnuts, and 1 tsp. Of raw honey.

Nutritional Information: Carbohydrates: 28g, Fiber: 7g, Protein: 9g, Total Fat: 16g, Calories: 275

83. Choco-Nana Pancakes

Prep Time: 6-minutes | Total time: 11-minutes | Yield: 2-servings

Ingredients:

2 large eggs, pasture-raised	2 large bananas, peeled and mashed
1 tsp. pure vanilla extract	2 tbsps. almond butter
3 tbsps. cacao powder	1/8 tsp. salt
Coconut oil, for greasing	

Directions:

Pre-heat a skillet over medium-low heat. Coconut oil should be used to grease the pan. In a food processor, combine all ingredients and pulse until smooth. Make the pancake by pouring the batter into a skillet. Cook each side for 3-minutes. Serve and have fun!

Nutritional Information: Calories: 303 Fat: 17g Carbohydrates: 36g Protein: 5g

84. Quick Burrito

Prep Time: 13-minutes | Total time: 24-minutes | Yield: 1 serving

Ingredients:

1/4 lb. beef meat; ground	1 tsp. sweet paprika
1 tsp. cumin; ground	1 tsp. onion powder
1 small red onion; julienned 3 eggs	1 tsp. coconut oil
1 tsp. garlic powder	1 tsp. cilantro; chopped.
Salt and black pepper to the taste.	

Directions:

Heat a skillet over a medium heat source, then add your beef and cook until browned. Stir in salt, cumin, onion powder, garlic, pepper, and paprika; allow to cook for another 4-minutes, then remove from heat. Whisk eggs, pepper, and salt in a mixing bowl. Heat the oil in a pan over medium-heat; add in the eggs, and cook for about 6-minutes. Place the egg burrito on a dish, divide the beef mixture, top with cilantro and onion, and roll up to serve.

Nutritional Information: Calories: 280 Cal Fat: 12 g Fiber: 4 g Carbs: 7 g Protein: 14 g

85. Cauliflower and Chorizo

Prep Time: 16-minutes | Total time: 56-minutes | Yield: 4-servings

Ingredients:

1 cauliflower head; florets separated	4 eggs; whisked
1/2 tsp. garlic powder	2 tbsps. green onions; chopped.
1 lb. chorizo; chopped.	12 oz. canned green chilies; chopped.
1 yellow onion; chopped.	Salt and black pepper to the taste

Directions:

Using a medium heat source, heat up a pan. Stir in onion and chorizo and cook until browned. Stir in the green chiles, cook for some-minutes, then remove from the heat. Blend cauliflower with a pinch of salt and pepper in a food processor. Transfer to a mixing bowl and whisk in the salt, garlic powder, pepper, and eggs. Whisk in the chorizo mixture, then transfer the mixture to a baking dish that is greased. Preheat your oven to 375°F and let bake until done for 40-minutes. Allow it cool before sprinkling green onions on top, slicing, and serving.

Nutritional Information: Calories: 350 Cal Fat: 12 g Fiber: 4 g Carbs: 6 g Protein: 20 g

86. Beet and Cherry Smoothie

Prep Time: 7.5-minutes | Total time: 8-minutes | Yield: 4-servings

Ingredients:

10 oz. almond milk, unsweetened	2 small beets, peeled and cut into quarters
½ c. frozen cherries, pitted	½ tsp. frozen banana
1 tbsp. almond butter	

Directions:

Add all ingredients to a blender. Blend until smooth.

Nutritional Information: Calories 470, Saturated Fat 6g, Net Carbs 14g, Protein 16g, Fiber: 10g

87. Blueberry-Bran Breakfast Sundae

Prep Time: 10-minutes | Total time: 10-minutes | Yield: 2-servings

Ingredients:

2 c. vanilla or lemon-flavored low-fat yogurt or flavor of choice.	2 c. bran flakes
1/4 c. fresh blueberries	2 tbsp. sliced almonds
2 tbsp. dried cranberries (or dried or fresh fruit of choice)	

Directions:

In a bowl, place 1 c. yogurt and one c. bran flakes. Top with 1/8 c. fresh blueberries, followed by 1 tbsp. Each of sliced almonds, chopped pecans, and dried cranberries. Repeat using the remaining ingredients to make a second serving. Serve immediately.

Nutritional Information: Calories: 420 | Protein: 21.12 g | Fat: 13.58 g | Carbohydrates: 59.8 g

88. Cinnamon-Apple Granola with Greek Yogurt

Prep Time: 7-minutes | Total time: 17-minutes | Yield: 2-servings

Ingredients:

1/2 c. raw almonds, chopped	1/2 c. raw walnuts, chopped (or raw nuts of choice)
1/2 apple, peeled and diced	1 tbsp. almond flour
2 tbsp. vanilla protein powder	1 tsp. ground cinnamon
1/8 c. applesauce, unsweetened preferred	2 tsp. honey
2 tsp. almond butter	1/16 tsp. vanilla extract
dash of sea salt	1 c. Greek plain or vanilla yogurt (or flavor of choice)

Directions:

In a mixing bowl, combine the chopped almonds, chopped walnuts (or preferred raw nuts), diced apple, vanilla protein powder, almond flour, Lucuma (opt), and cinnamon and salt in a bowl. Mix well. In a second bowl, combine the apple sauce, almond butter, honey, and vanilla extract. Mix well. Pour the bowl with the nuts into the bowl with the wet ingredients and blend together thoroughly. Make sure all dry ingredients get coated. Place the granola mixture onto a parchment paper lined baking sheet and bake until the desired crunch is obtained, approximately 8 to 10-minutes. Take off from the oven and let cool or eat hot. Place 1/2 cup of each Greek yogurt into two bowls. Divide the granola and sprinkle over the yogurt in each bowl. Serve immediately.

Nutritional Information: Calories: 312 | Protein: 11.72 g | Fat: 22.37 g | Carbohydrates: 19.92 g

89. Coconut Almond Granola

Prep Time: 6-minutes | Total time: 13-minutes | Yield: 8-servings

Ingredients:

1½ c. old fashioned rolled oats	½ c. unsweetened shredded coconut
¼ c. monk fruit sweetener	1/8 tsp. salt
¾ c. almond butter	¼ c. coconut oil

Directions:

Combine the salt, sweetener, coconut, and oats in a medium mixing bowl. Mix in the oil and almond butter until everything is thoroughly mixed. Using nonstick cooking oil, grease a 6" cake pan. Fill the pan with the oat mixture. Ensure the inner pot of your Instant Pot is filled with 1 cup of water. Sett the steam rack inside the oven and the pan on top of it. Close the lid. Cook for 7-minutes on high pressure. Release the pressure quickly and open the lid. Remove the pan and spread the granola out on a baking sheet to cool thoroughly before serving (at least 30-minutes).

Nutritional Information: Calories: 307 Fat: 22g Protein: 8g Sodium: 37mg Fiber: 5g Carbohydrates: 24g Sugar: 2g

90. Anti-Inflammatory Berry Smoothie

Prep Time: 10-minutes | Total time: 10-minutes | Yield: 2-servings

Ingredients:

½ c. of raspberries	½ c. of blueberries
½ frozen banana(ripe)	1 c. of dairy-free unsweetened milk
1 tbsp. of flaxseeds	1 couple of fresh spinach
1 tbsp. of almond butter	

Directions:

Add all the listed ingredients to your blender and puree. Serve immediately.

Nutritional Information: Carbohydrates: 26g, Dietary Fiber: 8g, Protein: 4g, Total Fat: 9g, Calories: 185

91. Apple Cinnamon Steel Cut Oats

Prep Time: 12-minutes: Total time: 16-minutes | Yield: 6-servings

Ingredients:

2 c. steel cut oats	3 c. unsweetened vanilla almond milk
3 c. water	3 peeled and cored apples, cut into 1"-thick chunks
2 tsp. ground cinnamon	¼ c. date syrup
¼ tsp. salt	

Directions:

Add the steel cut oats, almond milk, water, apple chunks, cinnamon, date syrup, and salt to the Instant Pot and stir to combine. Secure the lid. Pressure cook for about 4-minutes. When the timer beeps, let the pressure release naturally for 15-minutes, quick-release any remaining pressure until the float valve drops, and unlock the lid. Serve warm.

Nutritional Information: Calories: 311 Fat,: 6g Protein: 10g Sodium: 193mg Fiber: 8g Carbohydrats: 57g Sugar: 8g

92. Hearty Pineapple Oatmeal

Prep Time: 11-minutes | Total time: 4-8 hours + 11-minutes | Yield: 5-servings

Ingredients:

1 c. steel-cut oats	4 c. unsweetened almond milk
2 medium apples, slashed	1 tsp. coconut oil
1 tsp. cinnamon	¼ tsp. nutmeg
2 tbsps. maple syrup, unsweetened	A drizzle of lemon juice

Directions:

Set a cooking pan on low heat and mix in all ingredients. Cook for 8 hours, or you can adjust to 4 hours if on high heat. Gently stir. Add toppings of your preference and enjoy.

Nutritional Information: Calories: 180 Fat: 5g Carbohydrates: 31g Protein: 5g

93. Overnight Muesli

Prep Time: 10-minutes | Total time: 10-minutes | Yield: 2-servings

Ingredients:

1 c. of gluten-free rolled oats	1 c. of coconut milk
1/4 c. of no-added-sugar apple juice	1 tbsp. of apple cider vinegar (optional)
1/2 cored and chopped apple	Dash ground cinnamon

Directions:

Combine the oats, apple juice, coconut milk, and vinegar in a medium mixing dish. Refrigerate overnight, covered. The following day, add the sliced apple and a pinch of cinnamon to the muesli.

Nutritional Information: Calories: 213, Fat: 4g, Carbs: 39g, Sugar: 6g, Fiber: 6g, Protein: 6g, Sodium: 74mg

94. Lovely Pumpkin Oats

Prep Time: 6-minutes | Total time: 14-minutes | Yield: 3-servings

Ingredients:

1 c. quick-cooking rolled oats	¾ c. almond milk
½ c. canned pumpkin puree	¼ tsp. pumpkin pie spice
1 tsp. cinnamon, ground	

Directions:

Microwave the oats and almond milk in a microwave-safe bowl for 2-minutes on high. If necessary, add more almond milk to get the required consistency. Cook for another 30 seconds. Combine pumpkin pie spice, pumpkin puree, and ground cinnamon in a mixing bowl. Gently heat and enjoy!

Nutritional information: Calories: 229 Fat: 4g Carbohydrates: 38g Protein: 10g

95. Green Smoothie Bowl

Prep Time: 10-minutes | Total time: 10-minutes | Yield: 2-servings

Ingredients:

1 c. of fresh strawberries, hulled	2 medium ripe bananas (previously sliced and frozen)
1/4 of a ripe avocado (peeled, pitted, and chopped)	1 c. of fresh spinach
1 c. of fresh kale, trimmed	1 tbsp. of flaxseed meal
11/2 c. of unsweetened almond milk	1/4 c. of almonds
1/4 c. of unsweetened coconut, shredded	

Direction:

Put all ingredients into a high-speed blender except almonds and coconut. Pulse to smoothen. Transfer the puree to bowls and serve immediately with almonds and coconut toppings.

Nutritional Information: Calories: 352, Fats: 18.6g, Carbs: 45.3g, Sugar: 8.3g, Proteins: 7.9g

96. Gingerbread Oatmeal Breakfast

Prep Time: 10-minutes | Total time: 10-minutes | Yield: 4-servings

Ingredients:

1 c. steel-cut oats	4 c. drinking water
Organic Maple syrup, to taste	1 tsp ground cloves
1 ½ tbsp. ground cinnamon	1/8 tsp nutmeg
¼ tsp ground ginger	¼ tsp ground coriander
¼ tsp ground allspice	¼ tsp ground cardamom
Fresh mixed berries	

Directions:

Cook the oats based on the package instructions. When it comes to a boil, reduce heat and simmer. Add in all spices as you stir and continue cooking until cooked to desired doneness. Serve in four serving bowls and drizzle with maple syrup and top with fresh berries.

Nutritional Information: Calories: 87 | Protein: 5.82 g | Fat: 3.26 g

97. Mango Granola
Prep Time: 12-minutes | Total time: 43-minutes | Yield 4-servings

Ingredients:

2 c. rolled oats	1 c. dried mango, chopped
½ c. almonds, roughly chopped	½ c. dates, roughly chopped
3 tbsp. sesame seeds	2 tsp. cinnamon
2/3 c. agave nectar	2 tbsp. coconut oil
2 tbsp. water	

Directions:

Set your oven to preheat at 320F. In a bowl, add the oats, sesame seeds, cinnamon, dates, almonds, and mix properly. Meanwhile, heat a saucepan over medium heat, pour in the agave syrup, coconut oil, and water. Stir and let it cook for at least 3-minutes or until the coconut oil has melted. Gradually pour the syrup mixture into the bowl with the oats and stir well, ensuring the syrup coats all ingredients. Transfer the granola to a baking sheet lined with parchment paper and place it in the oven to bake for 20-minutes. After 20-minutes, take off the tray from the oven and lay the chopped dried mango on top. Put back in the oven, then bake again for another 5-minutes. Before serving, let the granola cool to room temperature or place it in an airtight container for storage. The shelf life of the granola will last up to 2-3 weeks.

Nutritional Information: Calories: 434 | Protein: 13.16 | Fat: 28.3 g | Carbohydrates: 55.19 g

98. Tomato Bruschetta with Basil
Prep Time: 10-minutes | Total time: 10-minutes | Yield: 8-servings

Ingredients:

½ c. basil, chopped	2 garlic cloves, minced
1 tbsp. balsamic vinegar	2 tbsps. Extra virgin Olive oil
½ tsp. black pepper, cracked	1 sliced baguette, whole wheat – 18 slices
8 ripe Roma tomatoes, diced	1 tsp. sea salt

Directions:

Preheat your oven to attain 375 degrees F. Combine tomatoes, pepper, basil, salt, vinegar, olive oil, and garlic using a mixing bowl. Set aside. Set baguette slices in a baking pan to bake for 10-minutes. Serve your meal with warm bread slices.

Nutritional Information: Calories: 57 Cal Fat: 2.5 g Carbs: 7.9 g Protein: 1.4 g Sugars: 0.2 g

99. Instant Banana Oatmeal
Prep Time: 1 Minute | Total time: 3-minutes | Yield: 1 serving

Ingredients:

1 ripe banana, mashed	½ c. quick oats
½ c. water	

Directions:

Using a bowl, mix water and oats and set in a microwave. Allow to heat for about 2-minutes on high mode. Take from microwave and add in banana as you stir.

Nutritional Information: Calories: 243 Cal Fat: 3 g Carbs: 50 g Protein: 6 g Sugars: 10 g

100. Overnight Coconut Chia Oats
Prep Time: 10-minutes | Total time: 1 hour 10-minutes | Yield: 1-2-servings

Ingredients:

½ c. Coconut Milk, unsweetened	2 tsp. Chia Seeds
1 ½ c. Old Fashioned Oats, whole grain	½ tsp. Cinnamon, grounded
1 c. Almond Milk, unsweetened	½ tsp. Cinnamon, grounded
2 tsp. Date Syrup	½ tsp. Black Pepper, grounded
1 tsp. Turmeric, grounded	

Directions:

To start with, keep the oats in the mason jar. After that, mix the rest of the ingredients in a medium bowl until combined well. Then, pour the mixture into the jars and stir well. Now, close the pot and place it in the refrigerator overnight. In the morning, stir the mixture and then enjoy it.

Tip: You can top it with toasted nuts or berries.

Nutritional Information: Calories: 335 Proteins: 8g Carbohydrates: 34.1g Fat: 19.9g

101. Egg Casserole with Kale
Prep Time: 1-minutes | Total time: 27-minutes | Yield: 6-servings

Ingredients:

1 tbsp. avocado oil	1 small yellow onion, peeled and chopped
5 large kale leaves, tough stems removed, and finely chopped	1 clove garlic, diced
2 tbsp. lemon juice	½ tsp. salt, divided
9 large eggs	2 tbsps. water

| 1½ tsp. dried rosemary | 1 tsp. dried oregano |
| ¼ tsp. black pepper | ½ c. nutritional yeast |

Directions:

Add the oil to the pot, press the Sauté button, and heat the oil for 1 minute. Add the onion and sauté for 2-minutes until just softened. Add the kale, garlic, lemon juice, and ¼ tsp. Salt. Stir and allow to cook 2-minutes more. Press the Cancel button. Meanwhile, whisk together the eggs, water, rosemary, oregano, ¼ tsp in a medium bowl. Salts, pepper, and nutritional yeast.

Add the kale mixture and onion to the egg mixture and stir to combine. Rinse the inner pot, add 2 cups water, and place a steam rack inside.

Spray a 7" springform pan with cooking spray. Transfer the egg mixture to the springform pan. Set the pan on a steam rack and close the lid. Allow pressuring to cook for about 12-minutes. Quick release pressure and unlock the lid. Remove the pan from the pot and allow to cool 5-minutes before slicing and serving.

Nutritional Information: Calories: 157 Fat: 9g Protein: 13g Sodium: 311mg Fiber: 2g Carbs: 5g Sugar: 1g

102. Veggie Balls

Prep Time: 17-minutes | Total time: 43-minutes | Yield: 5-6-servings

Ingredients:

2 medium sweet potatoes, cubed into ½-inch size	2 tbsps. coconut milk
1 c. fresh kale leaves, trimmed and chopped	1 medium shallot, chopped finely
1 tsp. ground cumin	½ tsp. granulated garlic
¼ tsp. ground turmeric	Salt, to taste
Freshly ground black pepper, to taste	Ground flax seeds, as required

Directions:

Set the oven to 400°F. Line a baking sheet with parchment paper. In a pan of water, arrange a steamer basket. Bring the sweet potato to a steamer basket and steam for approximately 10-15-minutes. In a sizable bowl, put the sweet potato. Add coconut milk and mash well. Add remaining ingredients except for flax seeds and mix till well combined. Make about 1½-2-inch balls from your mixture. Arrange the balls onto the prepared baking sheet inside a single layer. Sprinkle with flax seeds. Bake for around 20-25-minutes.

Nutritional Information: Calories: 464 | Fat: 12g | Carbohydrates: 20g | Fiber: 8g | Protein: 27g

103. Zucchini Pancakes

Prep Time: 15-minutes | Total time: 21 – 25-minutes | Yield: 8-servings

Ingredients:

1 c. chickpea flour	1½ c. water, divided
¼ tsp. cumin seeds	¼ tsp cayenne
¼ tsp. ground turmeric	Salt, to taste
½ c. zucchini, shredded	½ c. red onion, chopped finely
1 green chili, seeded and chopped finely	¼ c. fresh cilantro, chopped

Directions:

In a large bowl, add flour and ¾ cup with the water and beat till smooth. Add remaining water and beat till a thin. Fold inside the onion, ginger, Serrano pepper, and cilantro. Lightly grease a substantial nonstick skillet with oil and heat on medium-low heat. Add about ¼ cup of mixture and tilt the pan to spread it evenly in the skillet. Cook for around 4-6-minutes. Carefully alter the side and cook for approximately 2-4-minutes. Repeat while using the remaining mixture. Serve together with your desired topping.

Nutritional Information: Calories: 389 | Fat: 13g | Carbohydrates: 25g | Fiber: 4g | Protein: 21g

104. Honey Pancakes

Prep Time: 12-minutes | Total time: 16-minutes | Yield: 2-servings

Ingredients:

½ c. almond flour	2 tbsps. coconut flour
1 tbsp. ground flaxseeds	¼ tsp baking soda
½ tbsp. ground ginger	½ tbsp. ground nutmeg
½ tbsp. ground cinnamon	½ tsp. ground cloves
Pinch of salt	2 tbsps. organic honey
¾ c. organic egg whites	½ tsp. organic vanilla extract
Coconut oil, as required	

Directions:

Mix together flours, flax seeds, baking soda, spices, and salt in a big bowl. In another bowl, add honey, egg whites, and vanilla and beat till well combined. Put the egg mixture into the flour mixture, then mix till well combined. Lightly grease a big nonstick skillet with oil and heat on medium-low heat. Add about ¼ cup of mixture and tilt the pan to spread it evenly inside the skillet. Cook for about 3-4-minutes. Carefully customize the side and cook approximately 1 minute more. Repeat with the remaining mixture. Serve along with your desired topping.

Nutritional Information: Calories: 29 | Fat: 8 | Carbo-hydrates: 26g | Fiber: 4g | Protein: 23g

105. Cheddar and Chive Souffles

Prep Time: 10-minutes | Total time: 35-minutes | Yield: 8-servings

Ingredients:

½ c. almond flour	¼ c. chopped chives
1 tsp salt	½ tsp xanthan gum
1 tsp ground mustard	¼ tsp cayenne pepper
½ tsp cracked black pepper	¾ c. heavy cream
2 c. shredded cheddar cheese	½ c. baking powder
6 organic eggs, separated	

Directions:

Switch on the oven, then set its temperature to 350°F and let it preheat. Take a medium bowl, add flour, add remaining ingredients, except for baking powder and eggs, and whisk until combined. Separate egg yolks and egg whites between two bowls, add egg yolks in the flour mixture, and whisk until incorporated.

Add baking powder into the egg whites and beat with an electric mixer until stiff peaks form, and then stir egg whites into the flour mixture until well mixed. Divide the batter evenly between eight ramekins and then bake for 25-minutes until done. Serve straight away or store in the refrigerator until ready to eat.

Nutritional Information: Calories 288 | Total Fat 21g | Total Carbs 3g | Protein 14g

106. Quinoa & Pumpkin Porridge

Prep Time: 10 minutes | Total time: 22-minutes | Yield: 4-servings

Ingredients:

3½ c. of filtered water	1¾ c. of quinoa (soaked for fifteen-minutes and rinsed)
14 oz. of unsweetened coconut milk	1¾ c. of sugar-free pumpkin puree
2 tsp. of ground cinnamon	1 tsp. of ground ginger
A pinch of ground cloves	A pinch of ground nutmeg
Salt	3 tbsps. of extra-virgin coconut oil
4-6 drops of liquid stevia	1 tsp. of organic vanilla flavor

Directions:

Pour water and quinoa into a pan and cook on high heat. Cover the pan and let the produce boil. Adjust your heat to low and allow to simmer for 12-minutes.

Add the remaining ingredients and stir thoroughly. Immediately, remove switch off the cooker and serve warm.

Nutritional Information: Calories: 561, Fats: 29g, Carbs: 60.3g, Sugar: 6.2g, Proteins: 13g

107. Morning Scrambled Turkey Eggs

Prep Time: 16-minutes | Total time: 31-minutes | Yield: 2-servings

Ingredients:

1 tbsp. coconut oil	1 medium red bell pepper, diced
½ medium yellow onion, diced	¼ tsp. hot pepper sauce
3 large free-range eggs	¼ tsp. black pepper freshly ground
¼ tsp. salt	

Directions:

Add coconut oil to a pan and heat medium-high heat. Add the onions and allow to sauté. Mix in red pepper and turkey. Cook until well done. Take a bowl and beat eggs, stir in salt and pepper. Pour eggs in the pan with turkey and gently cook and scramble eggs. Top with hot sauce and enjoy!

Nutritional Information: Calories: 435 Fat: 30g Carbohydrates: 34g Protein: 16g

108. Cilantro Pancakes

Prep Time: 10-minutes | Total time: 16 – 18-minutes | Yield: 6-servings

Ingredients:

½ c. tapioca flour	½ c. almond flour
½ tsp. chili powder	¼ tsp. ground turmeric
Salt, to taste	Freshly ground black pepper, to taste
1 c. full- fat coconut milk	½ of red onion, chopped
1 (½-inch) fresh ginger piece, grated finely	1 Serrano pepper, minced
½ c. fresh cilantro, chopped	Oil, as required

Directions:

In a big bowl, put together the flours and spices, then mix. Put the coconut milk and mix till well combined. Fold within the onion, ginger, Serrano pepper, and cilantro. Lightly grease a sizable nonstick skillet with oil and warmth on medium-low heat. Add about ¼ cup of mixture and tilt the pan to spread it evenly inside the skillet. Cook for around 3-4-minutes from either side. Repeat with all the remaining mixture. Serve along with your desired topping.

Nutritional Information: Calories: 33 | Fat: 10 | Carbohydrates: 37g | Fiber: 6g | Protein: 28g

109. Spinach Avocado Smoothie

Prep Time: 5-minutes | Total time: 10-minutes | Yield: 1 serving

Ingredients:

¼ of 1 Avocado	1 c. Plain Yoghurt, non-fat
2 tbsp. Water	1 c. Spinach, fresh
1 tsp. Honey	1 Banana, frozen

Directions:

Set all ingredients in a high-speed blender and process for 3-minutes to get a creamy smooth mixture. Divide in glasses and enjoy.

Nutritional Information: Calories: 357 Proteins: 17.7g Carbohydrates: 57.8g Fat: 8.2g

110. Yummy Steak Muffins

Prep Time: 10-minutes | Total time: 30-minutes | Yield: 4-servings

Ingredients:

1 c. red bell pepper, diced	2 Tbsps. of water
8 oz. thin steak, cooked and finely chopped	¼ tsp. of sea salt
Dash of freshly ground black pepper	8 free-range eggs
1 c. of finely diced onion	

Directions:

Set the oven to 350°F. Take 8 muffin tins and line them with parchment paper liners. Get a large bowl and crack all the eggs in it. Beat the eggs well. Blend in all the remaining ingredients. Spoon the batter into the arranged muffin tins. Fill three-fourth of each tin. Put the muffin tins in the preheated oven for about 20-minutes until the muffins are baked and set in the middle.

Nutritional Information: Calories: 151 | Protein: 17.92 g | Fat: 7.32 g | Carbohydrates: 3.75 g

111. Savory Bread

Prep Time: 10-minutes | Total time: 30 – 35-minutes | Yield: 8-10-servings

Ingredients:

½ c. plus 1tbsp. almond flour	1 tsp. baking soda
1 tsp. ground turmeric	Salt, to taste
2 large organic eggs	2 organic egg whites
1 c. raw cashew butter	1 tbsp. water
1 tbsp. apple cider vinegar	

Directions:

Set the oven to 350F. Grease a loaf pan. In a big pan, mix together flour, baking soda, turmeric, and salt. In another bowl, add eggs, egg whites, and cashew butter and beat till smooth. Gradually add water and beat till well combined. Add flour mixture and mix till well combined. Stir in apple cider vinegar treatment. Place a combination into the prepared loaf pan evenly. Bake for around twenty-minutes or till a toothpick inserted within the center is released clean.

Nutritional information: Calories: 347 | Fat: 11g | Carbohydrates: 29gFiber: 6g | Protein: 21g

112. Hash Browns

Prep Time: 15-minutes | Total time: 30-minutes | Yield: 4-servings

Ingredients:

1 lb. Russet potatoes, peeled	Pinch of sea salt
Pinch of black pepper, to taste	3 Tbsp. olive oil

Directions:

Line a microwave safe-dish with paper towels. Spread shredded potatoes on top. Microwave veggies on the highest heat setting for 2-minutes. Remove from heat. Pour 1 tbsp of oil into a skillet placed on medium heat. Cooking in batches, place a generous pinch of potatoes into the hot oil. Use a spatula to press down. Cook for 3-minutes every side, or until brown and crispy. Drain on paper towels. Repeat step for remaining potatoes. Add more oil as needed. Season with salt and pepper.

Nutritional Information: Calories: 200 | Protein: 4.03 g | Fat: 11.73 g | Carbohydrates: 20.49 g

113. Morning Bowl

Prep Time: 7-minutes | Total time: 7-minutes | Yield: 1 serving

Ingredients:

1 c. coconut milk	1 tsp. raw honey
1 tsp. walnuts; chopped.	1 tsp. pistachios; chopped.
1 tsp. almonds; chopped.	1 tsp. pine nuts; raw
1 tsp. pepitas; raw	2 tsp. raspberries
1 tsp. pecans; chopped.	1 tsp. sunflower seeds; raw

Directions:

In a bowl, mix milk with honey and stir. Add pecans, walnuts, almonds, pistachios, sunflower seeds, pine nuts, and pepitas. Stir, top with raspberries, and serve

Nutritional Information: Calories: 100 Cal Fat: 2 g Fiber: 4 g Carbs: 5 g Protein: 6 g

114. Vegan-Friendly Banana Bread

Prep Time: 16-minutes | total time: 56-minutes | Yield: 4-6-servings

Ingredients:

2 ripe bananas, mashed	1/3 c. brewed coffee

½ tsp. salt	3 tbsps. chia seeds
6 tbsps. water	½ c. soft vegan butter
½ c. maple syrup	2 c. flour
2 tsp. baking powder	1 tsp. cinnamon powder
1 tsp. allspice	

Directions:

Set your oven to preheat and attain 350 degrees F. Bring the chia seeds to a small bowl, then soak it with 6 tbsp of water. Stir well and set aside. In a mixing bowl, mix the vegan butter and maple syrup with a hand mixer until it turns fluffy. Add the chia seeds along with the mashed bananas. Mix well, and then add the coffee. Meanwhile, sift all the dry ingredients (flour, baking powder, cinnamon powder, allspice, and salt) and gradually add them to the bowl with the wet ingredients. Combine the ingredients well, and then pour over a baking pan lined with parchment paper. Place in the oven to bake for at least 30-40-minutes, or until the toothpick comes out clean after inserting in the bread. Allow the bread to cool before serving.

Nutritional information: Calories: 371 | Protein: 5.59 | Fat: 16.81 g | Carbohydrates: 49.98 g

115. Strawberry-Oat-Chocolate Chip Muffins

Prep Time: 10-minutes | Total time: 33-minutes | Yield: 12-servings

Ingredients:

1¼ c. whole wheat pastry flour	1 c. rolled oats
¾ tsp. Baking soda	½ tsp. Baking powder
¼ tsp. salt	1 heaping c. bananas (about 2 to 3 large very ripe bananas)
1 tbsp. extra virgin olive oil	1 tbsp. honey or agave nectar
1 tsp. vanilla	1 egg
1 egg white	1/3 c. nonfat plain Greek yogurt
½ c. unsweetened vanilla almond milk	1/3 c. mini chocolate chips
2/3 c. diced strawberries	12 thin slices of strawberries (about 3-4 strawberries) for garnish, if desired

Directions:

Preheat your oven to attain 350 degrees F and lightly grease or line a standard 12-cup muffin pan. Combine baking powder, baking soda, salt, oats, and flour in a large mixing bowl. To combine the ingredients, stir them together. 2 tbsp. Of the mixture should be set aside. Combine the olive oil, vanilla, honey, and mashed banana in a separate large mixing bowl. After that, beat in the egg and egg white until well blended.

Now, with an electric mixer on the low, whip in the almond milk and Greek yogurt until smooth.

Gradually mix the wet and dry ingredients; do not overmix the mixture, or the muffins will become stiff. Add batter to each muffin until 2/3 full. To smooth out the batter, gently tap the pan on the counter. If preferred, top each muffin with a tiny slice of strawberry. Place the pan in the oven. Then bake for about 23-minutes, or until a toothpick inserted in the center comes out clean. Set from oven and allow to cool for 10-minutes, then set to a cooling rack.

Nutritional Information: Calories: 91 | Protein: 4.02 g | Fat: 2.63 g | Carbohydrates: 16.31 g

116. Cinnamon Flaxseed Breakfast Loaf

Prep Time: 12-minutes | Total time: 43-minutes | Yield: 6-servings

Ingredients:

½ c. ground golden flaxseed meal	½ c. almond flour
1 tbsp. ground cinnamon	2 tsp. baking powder
½ tsp. salt	2/3 c. xylitol
4 large eggs	½ c. coconut oil, melted and cooled

Directions:

Mix the flaxseed meal, cinnamon, baking powder, xylitol, flour, and salt in a bowl. Whisk together the eggs and cool coconut oil in a separate medium-bowl. Stir together dry and wet ingredients. Grease a 6" cake pan well, pour the mixture into the pan, and cover with aluminum foil. In the inner pot, add 1½ cups of water and place your steam rack with handles in the pot. The cake pan should sit on the rack. Set lid in place. Pressure Cook for about 30-minutes. Quick-release pressure and unlock the lid. Remove pan from Instant Pot and allow the bread to cool completely before flipping the pan upside down and removing the loaf. Slice and serve.

Nutritional Information: Calories 389 Fat 30g Protein 9g Sodium: 407mg Fiber: 6g Carbs: 29g Sugar: 1g

117. Coconut Flakes and Almond Pancakes

Preparation: Time: 6-minutes | Total time: 17-minutes | Yield: 6-servings

Ingredients:

1 overripe mashed banana	2 eggs, separate yolks, and whites
½ c. applesauce, unsweetened	1 c. finely milled almond flour
¼ c. water	¼ tsp. coconut oil

Garnish	2 Tbsps. almond flakes, blanched
¼ tsp. cinnamon powder	¼ c. sweetened coconut flakes
¼ tsp. sea salt	Pure maple syrup

Directions:

Using a bowl, whisk the egg whites until you form soft peaks. In a separate bowl, combine the other ingredients except for coconut oil and egg whites. Mix well to form a batter. Fold in the egg whites. Do not over mix. Add oil in a nonstick skillet and place over medium heat. Drop-in ½ cup of your batter and cook until every side is set. Bubbles should appear at the center. Turn it over and then cook the second side for 2 more-minutes. Set flapjacks to a serving plate. Do the same for the remaining batter. You should get about 6 pancakes. Stack your pancakes and top with maple syrup. Garnish with coconut-almond cinnamon-flavored flakes before serving. For your garnish, the oven should be preheated to 350°F 10-minutes before use. Line a parchment paper to a baking sheet and set it aside. Using a bowl, combine coconut flakes and almonds and spread them on the baking sheet. Bake for 10-minutes until flakes become golden brown and stir midway. Allow cooling for about 10-minutes. Sprinkle with salt and cinnamon powder and toss well.

Nutritional Information: Calories: 62 | Protein: 2.24 g | Fat: 4.01 g | Carbohydrates: 4.46 g

118. Spicy Marble Eggs

Prep Time: 16-minutes | Total time: 2 hours 16-minutes | Yield: 12-servings

Ingredients:

6 medium-boiled eggs, unpeeled, cooled	For the Marinade
2 oolong black tea bags	3 Tbsp. brown sugar
1 thumb-sized fresh ginger, unpeeled, crushed	3 dried star anise, whole
2 dried bay leaves	3 Tbsp. light soy sauce
4 Tbsp. dark soy sauce	4 c. of water
1 dried cinnamon stick, whole	1 tsp. salt
1 tsp. dried Szechuan peppercorns	

Directions:

Using the back of a metal spoon, crack eggshells in places to create a spider web effect. Do not peel. Set aside until needed. Pour marinade into a large Dutch oven set over high heat. Put lid partially on. Bring water to a rolling boil, about 5-minutes. Turn off heat. Secure lid. Steep ingredients for 10-minutes. Using a slotted spoon, fish out and discard solids. Cool marinade completely to room proceeding. Place eggs into an airtight non-reactive container just small enough to snugly fit all this in. Pour in marinade. Eggs should be completely submerged in liquid. Discard leftover marinade, if any. Line container rim with generous layers of saran wrap. Secure container lid. Chill eggs for 24 hours before using. Extract eggs and drain each piece well before using, but keep the rest submerged in the marinade.

Nutritional Information: Calories: 75 | Protein: 4.05 g | Fat: 4.36 g | Carbohydrates: 4.83 g

119. Awesome Breakfast Parfait

Prep Time: 5-minutes | Total time: 5-minutes | Yield: 2-servings

Ingredients:

1 c. pretzels, broken into small pieces	1 c. strawberries, sliced
2 c. Greek yogurt, non-fat	

Directions:

To the bottom of a glass, and yogurt and top with strawberries and pretzels pieces. You can use more yogurt if desired.

Nutritional Information: Calorie: 304 Fat: 1g Carbohydrates: 58g Protein: 15g

120. Amazing Pesto Egg

Prep Time: 5-minutes | Total time: 10-minutes | Yield: 2-servings

Ingredients:

2 large whole eggs	1/2 tbsp. almond butter
1/2 tbsp. pesto	1 tbsp. creamed coconut almond milk
Sunflower seeds and pepper as needed	

Directions:

Take a bowl and crack open your egg. Add pepper and sunflower seeds for seasoning. Using a pan, add in eggs and almond butter. Allow cooking on low, then add in pesto. Remove from heat once the egg is done. Mix in coconut cream. Set to low heat and cook until you have a creamy mix. Enjoy.

Nutritional Information: Calories: 467 Fat: 41g Carbohydrates: 3g Protein: 20g

121. Savory Veggie Muffins

Prep Time: 15-minutes | Total time: 33- 38-minutes | Yield: 5-servings

Ingredients:

¾ c. almond meal	½ tsp baking soda
¼ c. concentrate powder	2 tsp. fresh dill, chopped

Salt, to taste	4 large organic eggs
1½ tbsps. nutritional yeast	2 tsp. apple cider vinegar
3 tbsps. fresh lemon juice	2 tbsps. coconut oil, melted
1 c. coconut butter, softened	1 bunch scallion, chopped
2 medium carrots, peeled and grated	½ c. fresh parsley, chopped

Directions:

Set your oven to preheat and attain 350F. Grease 10 cups of your large muffin tin. In a bowl, mix baking soda, salt, Protein powder, and flour. In a separate bowl, combine eggs, vinegar, oil, lemon juice, and nutritional yeast. Beat in coconut butter. Mix flour mixture with egg mixture. Fold in carts, scallion, and parsley. Evenly set the amalgamation to your prepared muffin cups. Bake for 23-minutes and enjoy.

Nutritional Information: Calories: 378 | Fat: 13 | Carbohydrates: 32g | Fiber: 11g | Protein: 32g

122. Poached Eggs

Prep Time: 10-minutes | Total time: 50-minutes | Yield: 4-servings

Ingredients:

3 tomatoes; chopped.	3 garlic cloves; minced
1 tbsp. ghee 1/4 tsp. chili powder	1 tbsp. cilantro; chopped. 6 eggs
1 white onion; chopped.	1 red bell pepper; chopped.
1 tsp. paprika	1 tsp. cumin
1 Serrano pepper; chopped.	Salt and black pepper to the taste.

Directions:

Over medium heat, add the ghee to a pan and then heat. Stir in onion and cook for about 10-minutes. Stir in garlic and Serrano pepper and cook for an additional 1 minute. Stir in red bell pepper, cumin, black pepper, tomatoes, paprika, chili powder, and salt. Allow cooking for 20-minutes. Add in eggs and add pepper and salt for seasoning if desired. Cook while covered for 6-minutes. Top with cilantro and enjoy.

Nutritional Information: Calories: 300 Cal Fat: 12 g Fiber: 4 g Carbs: 22 g Protein: 14 g

123. Avocado Eggs with Balsamic Vinegar

Prep Time: 5-minutes | Total time: 10-minutes | Yield: 1 serving

Ingredients:

2 organic pasture-raised eggs	½ avocado, peeled and sliced
1 slice of tomato	A tbsp. of balsamic vinegar

Directions:

Fry the eggs. Set the sliced avocado on a serving plate. Top with tomatoes and cooked eggs. Sprinkle over with vinegar.

Nutritional Information: Carbohydrates: 10g, Fiber: 5g, Protein: 13g, Total Fat: 19g, Calories: 252

124. Mushroom Crepes

Total Time: 25-minutes | Yield: 4-servings

Ingredients:

1 c. whole-wheat flour	1 tsp onion powder
½ tsp baking soda	¼ tsp sea salt
1 c. crumbled tofu	⅓ c. almond milk
¼ c. lemon juice	2 tbsp extra-virgin olive oil
½ c. chopped mushrooms	½ c. finely chopped onion
2 c. collard greens	

Directions:

Combine the flour, onion powder, baking soda, and salt in a bowl. Place the tofu, almond milk, lemon juice, and oil in your food processor. Blitz until everything is well combined. Mix with flour mixture. Stir in mushrooms, onion, and collard greens. Grease cooking spray to a skillet and heat. Lower the heat and spread a ladleful of the batter across the surface of the skillet. Cook both sides for 4-minutes. Remove to a plate. Do the same with the remaining batter, greasing with a little more oil, if needed. Serve.

Nutritional Information: Cal 282; Fat 15g; Carbs 30g; Protein 10g

125. Blueberry Vanilla Quinoa Porridge

Prep Time: 2-minutes | Total time: 3-minutes | Yield: 6-servings

Ingredients:

1½ c. dry quinoa	3 c. water
1 c. frozen wild blueberries	½ tsp. pure stevia powder
1 tsp. pure vanilla extract	

Directions:

Using a fine-mesh strainer, rinse the quinoa very well until the water runs clear. Add the quinoa, water, blueberries, stevia, and vanilla to your inner pot. Stir to combine. Secure the lid. Pressure cook for about 1 minute. Quick release pressure and unlock the lid.
Allow the quinoa to cool slightly before spooning into bowls to serve.

Nutritional Information: Calories: 181 Fat: 3g Protein: 6g Sodium: 9mg Fiber: 5g Carbs: 33g Sugar: 3g

126. Omega-3-rich Cold Banana Breakfast

Prep Time: 10-minutes | Total time: 10-minutes | Yield: 2-servings

Ingredients:

½ c. cold milk	4 tbsp. sesame seeds
2 tbsp. flaxseeds	4 tbsp. sunflower seeds
2 tbsp. ground coconut	1 large sliced Banana

Directions:

Mix the milk and honey in your breakfast bowl. Use your coffee grinder to grind all the seeds. Add the ground seeds to the honey and milk mixture. Place the sliced bananas neatly on top. Sprinkle the ground coconuts for added flavor.

Nutritional Information: Calories: 393 | Protein: 14.85 g | Fat: 27.63 g | Carbohydrates: 27.37 g

127. Banana Date Porridge

Prep Time: 5-minutes | Total time: 9-minutes | Yield: 4-servings

Ingredients:

1 c. buckwheat groats	1½ c. unsweetened vanilla almond milk
1 c. water	1 large banana, mashed
5 pitted dates, chopped	¾ tsp. ground cinnamon
¾ tsp. pure vanilla extract	

Directions:

Place the buckwheat groats, almond milk, water, banana, dates, cinnamon, and vanilla in the inner pot and stir. Secure the lid. Pressure Cook for 4-minutes. Quick-release pressure and unlock the lid. Allow the porridge to cool slightly before spooning into bowls to serve.

Nutritional Information: Calories: 211 Fat 2g Protein: 6g Sodium: 72mg Fiber: 6g Carbs: 46g Sugar: 10g

128. Oatmeal Pancakes

Prep Time: 10-minutes | Total time: 35-minutes | Yield: 2-servings

Ingredients:

1 ½ c. Rolled Oats, whole-grain	2 Eggs, large & pastured
2 tsp. Baking Powder	1 Banana, ripe
2 tbsp. Water	¼ c. Maple Syrup
1 tsp. Vanilla Extract	2 tbsp. Extra Virgin Olive Oil

Directions:

To make this delicious breakfast dish, you need to first blend all the ingredients in a high-speed blender for a minute or two or until you get a smooth batter. Tip: To blend easily, pour egg, banana, and all other liquid ingredients first and finally add oats at the end. Set a skillet and heat over medium-low heat. Once the skillet is hot, put ¼ cup of the batter into it and cook it for 3 to 4-minutes per side or until bubbles start appearing in the middle portion. Turn the pancake and cook the other side also. Serve warm.

Tip: You can pair it with maple syrup and fruits.

Nutritional Information: Calories: 201 Proteins: 5g Carbohydrates: 28g Fat: 8g

129. Gingerbread Buckwheat Cereal

Prep Time: 6-minutes | Total time: 9-minutes | Yield: 3-servings

Ingredients:

1 c. of buckwheat grouts	1 ½ c. of full-fat canned coconut milk
½ tsp. of ground ginger	1 tsp. of ground cinnamon
1 tbsp. of raw cocoa powder	2 tbsps. of pumpkin seeds
2 tbsps. of pure maple syrup	

Directions:

Place the buckwheat grouts and coconut milk in a pot and cook over medium heat. Add ginger, cinnamon, and raw cocoa. Stir. Allow the ingredients to boil and then simmer them for around 2-3-minutes or until the buckwheat grouts are cooked. Subdivide the gingerbread between three bowls. Top each serving with a tbsp of pumpkin seeds and that of pure maple syrup.

Nutritional Information: Carbohydrates: 487g, Fiber: 8g, Protein: 10g, Total Fat: 31g, Calories: 487

130. Coconut and Cinnamon Bowl

Prep Time: 5-minutes | Total time: 10-minutes | Yield: 4-servings

Ingredients:

1 c. water	1/2 c. cashew cream
½ c. shredded dried coconut, unsweetened	1 tbsp. oat bran
1 tbsp. flaxseed meal	1/2 tbsp. almond butter
1 ½ tsps. stevia	½ tsp. cinnamon
Toppings like banana slices or blueberries	

Directions:

In a pot, add all ingredients, mix well until fully incorporated. Set the pot over medium-low heat and allow to boil. Stir well and remove the heat. Divide the mix into equal-servings and allow to sit for about 10-minutes. Add your preferred toppings and enjoy!

Nutritional Information: Calories: 171 Fat: 16g Protein: 2g Carbohydrates: 8g

131. Coconut & Banana Cookies

Prep Time: 17-minutes | Total time: 42-minutes | Yield: 7-servings

Ingredients:

2 c. unsweetened coconut, shredded	3 medium bananas, peeled
½ tsp. ground cinnamon	½ tsp. ground turmeric
Pinch of salt, to taste	Freshly ground black pepper

Directions:

Set the oven to 350°F. Line a cookie sheet a lightly greased parchment paper. In a mixer, put all together ingredients and pulse till a dough-like mixture forms. Form small balls through the mixture and set them onto a prepared cookie sheet in a single layer. Using your fingers, press along the balls to create the cookies.
Bake for at least 15-20-minutes or till golden brown.
Nutritional Information: Calories: 370 | Fat: 4g | Carbohydrates: 28g | Fiber: 11g | Protein: 33g

132. Perfect Barley Porridge

Prep Time: 5-minutes | Total time: 30-minutes | Yield: 4-servings

Ingredients:

1 c. barley	1 c. of wheat berries
2 c. unsweetened almond milk	2 c. of water
Toppings, like berry, hazelnuts, etc.	

Directions:

Take a medium saucepan and place it over medium-high heat. Place barley, almond milk, wheat berries, water and bring to a boil. Ensure heat is reduced to low and simmer for about 25-minutes. Divide amongst serving bowls and top with your desired toppings.
Nutritional Information: Calories: 295 Fat: 8g Carbohydrates: 56g Protein: 6g

133. No-Bake Turmeric Protein Donuts

Prep Time: 50-minutes | Total time: 50-minutes | Yield: 8-servings

Ingredients:

1 ½ c. raw cashews	½ c. medjool dates, pitted
1 tbsp. vanilla protein powder	½ c. shredded coconut
2 tbsps. maple syrup	¼ tsp. vanilla extract
1 tsp. turmeric powder	¼ c. dark chocolate

Directions:

Combine all the ingredients except for chocolate in a food processor. Pulse until smooth. Roll batter into 8 balls and press into a silicone donut mold. Freeze for 30-minutes until set. Meanwhile, use a double boiler to melt chocolate to form a chocolate topping. Once the donuts have been set, remove the donuts from the mold and drizzle with chocolate.
Nutritional Information: Calories 320, Saturated Fat 5g, Net Carbs 12g, Protein 7g, Sugar: 9g, Fiber: 2g

134. Mediterranean Frittata

Prep Time: 7-minutes | Total time: 27-minutes | Yield: 6-servings

Ingredients:

6 Eggs	¼ c. Feta cheese crumbled
¼ tsp. Black pepper	Oil, spray, or olive
1 tsp. Oregano	¼ c. Milk, almond, or coconut
1 tsp. Sea salt	¼ c. Black olives, chopped
¼ c. Green olives, chopped	¼ c. Tomatoes, diced

Directions:

Heat oven to 400. Oil one eight by eight-inch baking dish.
Beat the milk into the eggs, and then add other ingredients.
Pour all of this mixture into the baking dish and bake for twenty minutes.
Nutritional Information: Calories 107 | 2 g sugars | 3g carb | 7 g fat | 7 g protein

135. Salmon Burgers

Prep Time: 16-minutes | Total time: 24-minutes | Yield: 3-servings

Ingredients:

1 (6-oz. can) skinless, boneless salmon, drained	1 celery rib, chopped
½ of a medium onion, chopped	2 large eggs
1 tbsp. Plus 1 tsp. coconut flour	1 tbsp. dried dill, crushed
1 tsp. lemon	Salt, to taste
Freshly ground black pepper, to taste	3 tbsps. coconut oil

Directions:

In a substantial bowl, add salmon and which has a fork, break it into small pieces. Add remaining ingredients, excluding the oil, and mix till well combined. Make 6 equal sized small patties from the mixture. In a substantial skillet, melt coconut oil on medium-high heat. Cook the patties for around 3-4-minutes per side.

Nutritional Information: Calories: 393 | Fat: 12g | Carbohydrates: 19g | Fiber: 5g | Protein: 24g

136. Spinach Breakfast

Prep Time: 12-minutes | Total time: 47-minutes | Yield: 4-servings

Ingredients:

2 sweet potatoes, peeled and diced	2 tbsps. olive oil
½ tsp. onion powder	½ tsp. garlic powder
¼ tsp. paprika	4 eggs, pasture-raised
½ onion, sliced	½ c. mushrooms, sliced
2 c. baby spinach, fresh	salt and pepper
Coconut oil for greasing	

Directions:

Preheat the oven to 425 degrees F. Using a baking dish, add potatoes and drizzle with olive oil. Season using onion powder, paprika, pepper, salt, and garlic powder. Once cooked, set aside. Bake for 30-minutes while turning the sweet potatoes halfway through the cooking time. Grease a skillet using coconut oil and heat. Add in onions and saute for until fragrant 30 seconds. Mix in egg, pepper, salt, and mushrooms. Scramble your eggs and stir in baby spinach. Cook until spinach wilts. Divide potatoes among plates and add egg mixture as a topping.

Nutritional Information: Calories 252, Saturated Fat 4g, Net Carbs 13g, Protein 11g, Fiber: 2g

137. Ham and Veggie Frittata Muffins

Prep Time: 10-minutes | Total time: 35-minutes | Yield: 12-servings

Ingredients:

5 oz. thinly sliced ham	8 large eggs
4 tbsps. coconut oil	½ yellow onion, finely diced
8 oz. frozen spinach, thawed and drained	8 oz. mushrooms, thinly sliced
1 c. cherry tomatoes, halved	¼ c. coconut milk (canned)
2 tbsps. coconut flour	Sea salt and pepper to taste

Directions:

Preheat oven to 375 degrees Fahrenheit. In a medium skillet, warm the coconut oil on medium heat. Add the onion and cook until softened. Add the mushrooms, spinach, and cherry tomatoes. Season with salt and pepper. Cook until the mushrooms have softened. About 5-minutes. Remove from heat and set aside.

In a huge bowl, beat the eggs together with coconut milk and coconut flour. Stir in the cooled veggie mixture. Line each cavity of a 12 cavity muffin tin with the thinly sliced ham. Pour the egg mixture into each one and bake for 20-minutes. Remove from oven. Then allow cooling for about 5-minutes before transferring to a wire rack.

To maximize the benefit of a vegetable-rich diet, it's essential to eat a variety of colors, and these veggie-packed frittata muffins do just that. The onion, spinach, mushrooms, and cherry tomatoes provide a wide range of vitamins and nutrients and a healthy dose of fiber.

Nutritional Information: Calories: 125 | Protein: 5.96 g | Fat: 9.84 g | Carbohydrates: 4.48 g

138. Buckwheat Pancakes with Vanilla Almond Milk

Prep Time: 10-minutes | Total time: 14-minutes | Yield: 1 serving

Ingredients:

½ c. unsweetened vanilla almond milk	2-4 packets of natural sweetener
1/8 tsp. salt	½ c. buckwheat flour
½ tsp. baking powder, double-acting	

Directions:

Use cooking spray to grease a nonstick pancake griddle. Set it over medium heat. In a bowl, mix baking powder, flour, stevia, and salt. Add in almond milk and stir. Scoop a spoonful of the batter and set it to the pan. Allow cooking for 4-minutes until dried and bubbles are no longer popping out. Turn to the second-side and then cook for about 4 more-minutes. Do the same process for the rest of the batter.

Nutritional Information: Calories: 240 Cal Fat: 4.5 g Carbs: 2 g Protein: 11 g Sugars: 9 g

139. Crispy Chicken Fingers

Prep Time: 15-minutes | Total time: 33-minutes | Yield: 4-6-servings

Ingredients:

2/3 c. almond meal	½ tsp. ground turmeric
½ tsp. red pepper cayenne	½ tsp. paprika
½ tsp. garlic powder	Salt
black pepper, freshly ground	1 egg
1 lb. chicken breasts, cut into strips (skinless and boneless)	

Directions:

Preheat your oven to attain 375 degrees F. Line a substantial baking sheet with parchment paper. In a shallow dish, beat the egg. In another shallow dish, mix together almond meal and spices. Coat each chicken strip with egg, after which roll into spice mixture evenly. Arrange the chicken strips onto the prepared baking sheet in a single layer. Bake for approximately 16-18-minutes.

Nutritional Information: Calories: 236 Fat: 10g, Carbohydrates: 26g, Fiber: 5g, Protein: 37g

140. Apple Omelet

Prep Time: 7-minutes | Total time: 17-minutes | Yield: 1 serving

Ingredients:

2 large organic eggs	1/8 tsp. of organic vanilla flavoring
A Pinch of salt	2 tsp. of coconut oil, divided
½ apple fruit (cored and sliced)	¼ tsp. of ground cinnamon
1/8 tsp. of ground ginger	1/8 tsp. of ground nutmeg

Directions:

Combine eggs with vanilla flavoring and salt in a bowl. Stir the mixture to obtain a fluffy texture and set aside. Melt one tsp. of coconut oil in a non-stick pan over medium-low heat. Sprinkle the apple slices and spices in a layered manner. Cook for around 4-5-minutes while flipping. Add the residual oil to the skillet. Add the egg mixture over apple slices evenly. Tilt the pan to spread the egg-mixture evenly. Cook for around 3-4-minutes. Transfer the omelet to a wide plate and serve.

Nutritional Information: Calories:284, Fats:19.3g, Carbs:17g,Sugar:7.5g,Proteins:12.9g,Sodium:296mg

141. Pumpkin & Banana Waffles

Prep Time: 15-minutes | Total time: 20-minutes | Yield: 4-servings

Ingredients:

½ c. almond flour	½ c. coconut flour
1 tsp baking soda	1½ tsps. ground cinnamon
¾ tsp. ground ginger	½ tsp. ground cloves
½ tsp. ground nutmeg	Salt, to taste
2 tbsps. olive oil	5 large organic eggs
¾ c. almond milk	½ c. pumpkin puree
2 medium bananas, peeled and sliced	

Directions:

Preheat the waffle iron, and after that, grease it. In a sizable bowl, mix together flours, baking soda, and spices. In a blender, put the remaining ingredients and pulse till smooth. Add flour mixture and pulse till. In preheated waffle iron, add the required quantity of mixture. Cook approximately 4-5-minutes. Repeat using the remaining mixture.

Nutritional Information: Calories: 357.2 | Fat: 28.5g | Carbohydrates: 19.7g | Fiber: 4g | Protein: 14g

142. Power Pancakes

Prep Time: 17-minutes | Total time: 43-minutes | Yield: 6-servings

Ingredients:

4 organic pasture-raised eggs	1/4 c. of organic orange juice
1 ¼ c. of organic unsweetened almond milk	2 glasses of gluten-free white rice flour
1 tsp. of aluminum-free baking powder	Coconut oil

Toppings:

1 ½ c. sliced bananas	6 tbsps. crushed walnuts
1 ½ glasses pure maple syrup	

Directions:

Whisk the eggs. Add orange juice and almond milk to it and whisk cautiously. Be careful not to over whisk. Mix dry ingredients in a separate bowl. Add the wet ingredients and stir. Heat a skillet with one tbsp of coconut oil. Pour three tbsps. of batter to the pan and cook both of its sides for 2-minutes. Transfer the pancake to flatter and repeat the procedure when preparing the other pancakes. Top each serving with a ¼ cup of sliced bananas, one tbsp. of crushed walnuts and ¼ cup of pure maple syrup.

Nutritional Information: Carbohydrates: 109g, Dietary Fiber: 3g, Protein: 8g, Total Fat: 8g, Calories: 538

143. Choco-Banana Oats

Prep Time: 5-minutes | Total time: 13-minutes | Yield: 2-servings

Ingredients:

2 c. oats	2 c. almond milk
¾ c. water	2 ripe bananas, sliced
¼ tsp. Vanilla	¼ tsp. almond extract
2 tbsp. cocoa powder, unsweetened	2 tbsp. agave nectar
1/8 tsp. cinnamon	1/8 tsp. salt
1/3 c. toasted walnuts, chopped	2 tbsp. vegan chocolate chips, semisweet

Directions:
Stir in the almond milk, salt, water, vanilla, bananas, and almond extract in a saucepan. Set over high heat and heat. Using a pan, mix cocoa powder, oats, and a tablespoon of agave nectar. Set heat to medium and cook for 8-minutes. Scoop the cooked oats into serving plates and garnish with the drizzles of the remaining agave nectar, chocolate chips, and walnuts.
Nutritional information: Calories: 522 |Protein: 30.17 |Fat: 27.01 g |Carbohydrates: 79.09 g

144. Cheesy Hemp Seeds and Flax Muffins

Prep Time: 7-minutes | Total time: 37-minutes | Yield: 2-servings

Ingredients:

1/8 c. flax seeds meal	¼ c. hemp seeds, raw
¼ c. almond meal	¼ tsp. Salt
¼ tsp. baking powder	1/8 c. nutritional yeast flakes
3 beaten eggs	¼ c. low-fat cottage cheese
1 tbsp. olive oil	¼ c. parmesan cheese, grated
¼ c. sliced scallion	

Directions:
Preheat your oven to 360°F. Grease two ramekins with oil. Set aside. Using a medium bowl, mix hemp seeds, flax seeds, and almond meal. Stir in salt and baking powder. In a separate bowl, crack the eggs. Stir in parmesan, cottage cheese, and yeast. Mix this mixture with the almond meal mix. Fold in the scallions, divide the mixture between your ramekins and allow to bake for until firm 30-minutes and top becomes golden brown. Once done, remove muffins from ramekins and allow them to cool.
Nutritional Information: Calories 178.5|Fat 11g| Carbs 8g|Protein 16g|Sugar 3g|Sodium 313mg

145. Almond Syrup with Greek Yogurt Parfait

Prep Time: 25-minutes | Total time: 30-minutes | Yield: 2-servings

Ingredients:

1 c. fresh pitted red or black cherries	2 tbsps. almond syrup
2 tbsps. coconut palm sugar	2 tbsps. almonds, sliced for garnishing
1 tsp. lemon juice, freshly squeezed	2 c. Greek plain yogurt
4 tbsps. granola for garnishing	

Directions:
Using a medium high source of heat, set a saucepan in place. Stir in lemon juice, almond syrup, a tbsp of water, sugar, and cherries. Allow simmering until the sugar dissolves. Simmer for 5 more-minutes until it starts becoming syrupy. Transfer the mix to a bowl. Allow to cool for about 5-minutes and then refrigerate until cold. In 2 bowls, add 1 cup Greek yogurt and spoon ½ the cherry mix over the yogurt. Add granola or almond slices for garnishing and serving.
Nutritional Information: Calories: 186 |Protein: 4.87 g|Fat: 5.10 g |Carbohydrates: 34.03 g

146. Raisins and Cranberry Granola

Prep Time: 15-minutes | Total time: 35-minutes | Yield: 4-servings

Ingredients:

4 c. old-fashioned rolled oats	1/4 c. sesame seeds
1 c. dried cranberries	1 c. golden raisins
1/8 tsp. nutmeg	2 tbsps. olive oil
1/2 c. almonds, slivered	2 tbsps. warm water
1 tsp. vanilla extract	1 tsp. cinnamon
1/4 tsp. of salt	6 tbsps. maple syrup
1/3 c. of honey	

Directions:
Add in the sesame seeds, salt, almonds, oats, nutmeg, and cinnamon using a bowl. In a separate bowl, combine vanilla, oil, honey, water, and syrup. Slowly pour the vanilla mix into oats mix. Toss well to combine. Add the mixture in a jelly-roll pan that is greased and spread well. Set oven to 350 degrees F and bake for about 55-minutes. Stir well after every 10-minutes to ensure no clumps form. Remove from oven and add in raisins and cranberries. Let cool and serve.
Nutritional Information: Calories: 698 |Protein: 21.34 g |Fat: 20.99 g Carbohydrates: 148.59 g

147. Tofu Scramble with Veggies

Prep time: 50-minutes | Total time: 50-minutes | Yield: 4-servings

Ingredients:

8 oz. extra firm tofu	2 tbsps. olive oil
1 red bell pepper, chopped	1 tomato, finely chopped
2 tbsps. chopped scallions	Sea salt and pepper to taste
1 tsp. red chili powder	3 tsp. grated Parmesan cheese

Directions:
Place the tofu in between two parchment papers to drain liquid for about 30-minutes. Warm the olive oil in

a large nonstick skillet until no longer foaming. Crumble the tofu into the skillet and fry until golden brown, stirring occasionally, making sure not to break the tofu into tiny pieces, about 4 to 6-minutes.

Stir in the bell pepper, tomato, scallions, and cook until the vegetables are soft, about 4-minutes. Season with chili powder, pepper, salt, and stir in the Parmesan cheese to incorporate and melt for about 2-minutes. Spoon the scrambled into a serving platter and serve.

Nutritional Information: Cal 130; Fat 11g; Carbs 4.8g; Protein 7g

148. Avocado Toast with Spinach Leaves

Prep time: 5-minutes | Total time: 9-minutes | Yield: 1 serving

Ingredients:

1 ripe avocado, halved and pitted	2 slices gluten-free bread
1 ½ tbsps. lemon juice, freshly squeezed plus extra as needed	⅛ tsp. salt, plus additional as needed
2 c. lightly packed spinach leaves	

Directions:

Toast the bread. In a medium pot, fill with 2 inches of water and insert a steamer basket. The water must be boiled over high heat. Use a spoon to scoop the avocado flesh from the peel into a small bowl.

Add the salt and lemon juice. Using a fork, mash it together. Taste it, then adjust the seasoning with more salt or lemon juice, if necessary. Add the spinach to the steamer basket when the water boils. Cover and steam it for at least 3 to 4-minutes, or until wilted. Between the two pieces of toast, divide the avocado mixture. Top each with half of the wilted greens.

Nutritional Information:Calories: 486 Fat: 44g Carbs: 46g Sugar: 8g Fiber: 2g Protein: 6g Sodium 219mg

149. Appetizing Quinoa Breakfast Stew

Prep time: 5-minutes | Total time: 22-minutes | Yield: 1 serving

Ingredients:

¼ c. quinoa, rinsed	¾ c. water, plus additional as needed
½ small, finely chopped broccoli head	1 grated carrot
¼ tsp. salt	1 tbsp. chopped fresh dill

Directions:

Set a small pot over high heat, then stir the quinoa and water together. Bring to a boil. Reduce the heat to low. For 5-minutes, cover and cook it. Add the broccoli, carrot, and salt. For 10 to 12-minutes more, cook it or until

the quinoa is fully cooked and tender. Add more water if desired to ensure the stew doesn't become too dry. This should be on the liquid side as opposed to the drier consistency of a pilaf. Fold in the dill and serve.

Nutritional Information: Calories: 220 Fat: 3g Carbs: 41g Sugar: 5g Fiber: 7g Protein: 10g Sodium 667mg

150. Warm Oatmeal with Ginger and Honey

Prep time: 2-minutes | Total time: 10-minutes | Yield: 2-servings

Ingredients:

3 c. water or soy milk	2 c. oats, wholemeal, or steel cut
1 tbsp. cinnamon, ground	1 tsp. cloves, ground
¼ tsp. ginger, fresh, or grated	¼ tsp. ground allspice
¼ tsp. nutmeg	¼ tsp. cardamom
1 tsp. honey, to taste	

Directions:

In a saucepan, combine water and oats. For 5 to 8-minutes, gently heat on medium heat until cooked through. While cooking, stir in the spices.

Pour into the bowl when it is hot and cooked.

Drizzle honey over the top if you prefer it.

Nutritional Information: Calories: 423 | Fat: 14g | Carbs: 88g | Sugar: 11g | Fiber: 17g | Protein: 22g |

151. Healthy and Tasty Vanilla Crepes

Prep time: 7-minutes | Total time: 17-minutes | Yield: 2-servings

Ingredients:

2 free range eggs	1 tsp. vanilla
½ c. nut milk	½ c. water
1 tsp. maple syrup	1 c. all-purpose flour, gluten-free
3 tbsps. coconut oil	

Directions:

Add the eggs, vanilla, nut milk, water, and syrup together until combined in a medium bowl. Add the mix in the flour to form a smooth paste. Take 2 tablespoons of the coconut oil and melt in a pan over medium heat. Add ½ crepe mixture and tilt. To form a round crepe shape, swirl the pan. For 2-minutes, cook until the bottom is light brown and comes away from the pan with the spatula. Flip and let cook for 2 extra-minutes. Serve and repeat with the mixture left.

Nutritional Information:Calories: 556 Fat: 35g Carbs: 54g Sugar: 4g Fiber: 3g Protein: 8g Sodium: 12mg

152. Wonderful Breakfast Salad with Grapefruit, Oranges, and Berries

Prep time: 2-minutes | Total time: 2-minutes | Yield: 2-servings

Ingredients:

1 c. oats, steel cut	1 pink grapefruit, peeled and sliced
2 oranges, peeled and sliced	454 g low fat Greek yogurt
A handful of cranberries or cherries, fresh	

Directions:

Mix the oats and fruit with the yogurt. Allow soaking overnight. Serve and top with honey and cranberries or cherries. The oats should be nice and mushy and will soak up the flavors of the fruit.

Nutritional Information: Calories: 302 Fat: 7g Carbs: 58g Sugar: 12g Fiber: 9g Protein: 21g Sodium: 161mg

153. Cold Oatmeal with Apple and Cinnamon

Prep time: 10-minutes | Total time: 10-minutes | Yield: 4-6-servings

Ingredients:

2 c. rolled oats, gluten-free	1 ¾ c. coconut milk
¼ c. no-added-sugar apple juice	1 tbsp. apple cider vinegar
1 apple, cored and chopped	Dash ground cinnamon

Directions:

Stir together the oats, coconut milk, apple juice, and vinegar in a medium bowl. Cover and refrigerate overnight. Stir in the chopped apple and season the cold oatmeal with cinnamon the next morning.

Nutritional Information: Calories: 213 Fat: 4g Carbs: 39g Sugar: 8g Fiber: 6g Protein: 6g Sodium: 74mg

154. Yummy Parfait with Yogurt, Berry, and Walnut

Prep time: 2-minutes | Total time: 2-minutes | Yield: 2-servings

Ingredients:

2 c. plain unsweetened yogurt (coconut or almond yogurt)	2 tbsps. honey
1 c. blueberries, fresh	1 c. raspberries, fresh
½ c. walnut pieces	

Directions:

Whisk the yogurt and honey in a medium bowl. Spoon into 2 serving bowls. Top each with ½ cup blueberries, ½ cup raspberries, and ¼ cup walnut pieces.

Nutritional information: Calories: 505 Fat: 22g Carbs: 56g Sugar: 13g Fiber: 8g Protein: 23g Sodium: 174mg

155. Anti-Inflammatory Breakfast Oatmeal

Prep time: 5minutes | Total time: 13-minutes | Yield: 1 serving

Ingredients:

2/3 c. coconut milk	1 egg white, pasture-raised
½ c. gluten-free quick cooking oats	½ tsp. turmeric powder
½ tsp. cinnamon	¼ tsp. ginger

Directions:

In a saucepan, set over medium-heat, heat the non-dairy milk. Add in egg white and mix well until smooth. Cook for 3-minutes extra after adding the other ingredients.

Nutritional Information: Calories 395, Saturated Fat 7g, Carbs 16g, Protein 10g, Sugar: 2g, Sodium: 76mg,

156. Tropical Carrot Ginger and Turmeric Smoothie

Prep time: 7.5-minutes | Total time: 7.5-minutes | Yield: 1-servings

Ingredients:

1 blood orange, peeled and seeded	1 large carrot, peeled and chopped
½ c. frozen mango chunks	2/3 c. coconut water
1 tbsp. raw hemp seeds	¾ tsp. grated ginger
1 ½ tsps. peeled and grated turmeric	A pinch of cayenne pepper
A pinch salt	

Directions:

In a blender, place each and every ingredient and then blend until smooth. Chill before serving.

Nutritional Information: Calories 259, Saturated Fat 0.9g, Carbs 40g Protein 7g Fiber:11g, Sodium: 225mg,

157. Sweet Cherry Almond Chia Pudding

Prep time: 3-hours | Total time: 3-hours | Yield: 4-servings

Ingredients:

2 c. whole sweet cherries, pitted	2 c. coconut milk
¼ c. maple syrup, organic	1 tsp. vanilla extract
¾ c. chia seeds	½ c. hemp seeds
1/8 tsp. salt	

Directions:

In the blender, combine the cherries, coconut milk, maple syrup, and vanilla extract. Season with salt. Pulse until smooth. Distribute the chia seeds and hemp seeds in four glasses and pour in the cherry and milk mixture. Allow cooling for 3 hours while in the refrigerator before serving.

Nutritional Information: Calories 302, Saturated Fat 4g, Carbs 22g, Protein 10g, Fiber: 7g, Sodium: 59mg,

158. Omega-3 Chocolate Chia Hemp Pudding

Prep time: 7.5-minutes | Total time: 7.5-minutes | Yield: 1 serving

Ingredients:

2 tbsps. chia seeds	2 tbsps. hemp seeds
1 tbsp. cacao powder	6 small pitted dates, chopped
½ c. unsweetened almond milk	½ tsp. pure vanilla extract
1 tbsp. Chocolate protein powder	¼ tsp. salt

Directions:

Using a blender, set in all ingredients. Process until you get a smooth consistency.

Divide into containers, and you can refrigerate for 2 hours before you serve.

Nutritional Information: Calories 367, Total Fat 13g, Saturated Fat 1g, Total Carbs 55 g, Net Carbs 47g, Protein 12g, Sugar: 13g, Fiber: 8g, Sodium: 129mg, Potassium 686mg

159. Quinoa Bowls Avocado Egg

Prep time: 12-minutes | Total time: 22-minutes | Yield: 1 serving

Ingredients:

2 tsp. extra virgin olive oil	2 large eggs, pasture-raised
1 c. grape tomatoes, halved	1 tsp. red wine vinegar
1 c. cooked quinoa	½ c. black beans, cooked
2 tbsps. chopped cilantro	½ ripe avocado, sliced
¼ tsp. salt	

Directions:

Set a skillet on medium heat and heat oil. Fry the eggs for 3-minutes. Set aside. Using the same skillet, sauté the tomatoes for 3-minutes until wilted. Add in the red wine vinegar and season with salt and pepper to taste. Set aside. Assemble the bowl by putting the quinoa in a bowl and top with beans and tomatoes. Add in the eggs and avocado. Garnish with avocado slices.

Nutritional Information: Calories 343, Saturated Fat 3.1 g Net Carbs 26g, Protein 15g, Sodium: 332mg

160. Coconut Rice with Berries

Prep Time: 12-minutes | Total time: 43-minutes | Yield: 4-servings

Ingredients:

1 c. brown basmati rice	1 c. water
1 c. coconut milk	1 tsp. salt
2 dates, pitted and chopped	1 c. fresh blueberries, or raspberries, divided
¼ c. toasted slivered almonds, divided	½ c. shaved coconut, divided

Directions:

In a saucepan set over a high heat source, add basmati rice, coconut milk, date pieces, salt, and water. Stir properly and allow the mixture to boil. Reduce the heat to simmer and cook for 20 to 30-minutes, without stirring, or until the rice is tender. Equally, divide your rice into four serving bowls and top with 2 tbsps. Coconut, a tablespoon of almonds, and ¼ c. blueberries.

Nutritional information: Calories: 281 Fat: 8g Protein: 6g carbs: 49g fiber: 5g sugar: 7g sodium: 623mg

161. Fruit-and-Seed Breakfast Bars

Prep time: 15-minutes | Total time: 45-minutes | Yield: 6-servings

Ingredients:

½ c. pitted dates	¾ c. toasted sunflower seeds
¾ c. toasted pumpkin seeds	¾ c. white sesame seeds
½ c. dried blueberries	½ c. dried cherries
¼ c. flaxseed	½ c. almond butter

Directions:

Preheat your oven to attain 325°F (165°C). Line a parchment paper on a baking dish. Pulse the dates until it's chopped into a paste inside a food processor. Add the sunflower seeds, pumpkin seeds, sesame seeds, blueberries, cherries, and flaxseed, and pulse to combine. Scoop the mixture into a medium bowl. Stir in the almond butter. In the prepared-dish, transfer the mixture and press it down firmly. Bake for about 30-minutes, or until firm and golden brown. Cool for about 1 hour until it is at room temperature. Remove from the baking dish and cut into 12 squares. 8. You may refrigerate for 1 week.

Nutritional information: Calories: 312 fat: 22g protein: 10g carbs: 24g fiber: 6g sugar: 13g sodium: 16mg

162. Simple Steel-Cut Oats

Prep time: 15-minutes | Total time: 6-8 hours + 15-minutes | Yield: 4-6-servings

Ingredients:

1 tbsp. coconut oil	4 c. boiling water
½ tsp. sea salt	1 c. steel-cut oats
2 tbsps. blueberries	

Directions:

Coat the slow cooker with coconut oil. In your slow cooker, combine the boiling water, salt, and oats. Cover the cooker and set to warm (or low if there is no warm setting). Cook for 6 to 8 hours, blueberry decorations, and serve.

Nutritional information: Calories: 172 fat: 6g protein: 6g carbs: 27g fiber: 4g sugar: 0g sodium: 291mg

163. Cinnamon Granola

Prep time: 16-minutes | Total time: 56-minutes | Yield: 8-servings

Ingredients:

4 c. gluten-free rolled oats	1½ c. sunflower seeds
½ c. maple syrup	½ c. coconut oil
1½ tsps. ground cinnamon	

Directions:

Preheat your oven to attain 325ºF (165ºC). Line parchment paper to two baking sheets. Add in oats, maple syrup, cinnamon, coconut oil, and sunflower seeds in a bowl and mix well to ensure maximum coating. Divide your mixture between your two sheets and set them in the oven. Allow baking until evenly browned for 40-minutes. Allow cooling before serving.

Nutritional information: Calories: 400 fat: 22g protein: 9g carbs: 47g fiber: 6g sugar: 9g sodium: 3mg

164. Squash with Broccoli

Prep time: 12-minutes | Total time: 27-minutes | Yield: 4-servings

Ingredients:

4 c. spaghetti squash, peeled, cooked, and flesh scraped out	1½ c. broccoli florets
1 tbsp. olive oil	1 c. coconut milk, unsweetened
1 egg, whisked	1 tsp. garlic powder
A pinch of salt and black pepper	

Directions:

Over medium-high heat, heat the oil in a pan and add the broccoli and spaghetti squash. Cook for 6-minutes, stirring occasionally. Combine the salt, egg, garlic powder, and pepper in a mixing bowl. Cook for another 5-minutes, stirring occasionally. Cook for extra 5-minutes

once you add in the coconut milk, then divide among your bowls and enjoy the breakfast.

Nutritional Information: Calories 207, Fat 5, Fiber 8, Carbs 14, Protein 7

165. Spinach and Blackberries Smoothie

Prep time: 10-minutes | Total time: 10-minutes | Yield: 2-servings

Ingredients:

1 c. blackberries	1 avocado, pitted, peeled, and chopped
1 banana, peeled and roughly chopped	1 c. baby spinach
1 tbsp. hemp seeds	1 c. water
½ c. almond milk, unsweetened	

Directions:

In your blender, add all ingredients. Process well until smooth. Divide into 2 glasses and enjoy.

Nutritional Information: Calories 160, Fat 3, Fiber 4, Carbs 6, Protein 3

166. Breakfast Corn Salad

Prep time: 10-minutes | Total time: 10-minutes | Yield: 4-servings

Ingredients:

2 avocados, pitted, peeled, and cubed	1-pint mixed cherry tomatoes halved
2 c. fresh corn kernels	1 red onion, chopped
For the salad dressing:	2 tbsps. olive oil
1 tbsp. lime juice	½ tsp. grated lime zest
A pinch of salt and black pepper	¼ c. chopped cilantro

Directions:

In a salad bowl, add corn, avocados, onion, and tomatoes. Mix well. Toss in the remaining ingredients and enjoy.

Nutrition Information: Calories 140, Fat 3, Fiber 2, Carbs 6, Protein 9

167. Mushroom Frittata

Prep Time: 12-minutes | Total time: 43-minutes | Yield: 4-servings

Ingredients:

¼ c. coconut milk, unsweetened	6 eggs

1 yellow onion, chopped	4 oz. white mushrooms, sliced
2 tbsps. olive oil	2 c. baby spinach
A pinch of salt and black pepper	

Directions:
Add oil to a pan and heat using medium-high heat, add the onion, stir and cook for 3-minutes. Stir in pepper, mushrooms, and salt and cook for 2 additional-minutes. Mix the eggs with salt and pepper in a bowl, stir well, and pour over the mushrooms. Add the spinach, mix a bit, place in the oven, and bake at 360 degrees F for 25-minutes. Slice the frittata and serve it for breakfast. Enjoy!
Nutritional Information: Calories 200, Fat 3, Fiber 6, Carbs 14, Protein 6

168. Apple Muesli
Prep time: 10-minutes | Total time: 10-minutes | Yield: 4-servings

Ingredients:

2 apples, peeled, cored, and grated	1 c. rolled oats
3 tbsps. flax seeds	1¼ c. coconut cream
1¼ c. coconut water	½ c. goji berries
2 tbsps. chopped mint	3 tbsps. raw honey

Directions:
Mix the apples with oats, flax seeds, coconut cream, coconut water, goji berries, mint, and honey in a bowl. Stir well, divide into smaller bowls and serve for breakfast.
Nutritional Information: Calories 171, Fat 2, Fiber 6, Carbs 14, Protein 5

169. Yogurt, Berry, and Walnut Parfait
Prep time: 10-minutes | Total time: 10-minutes | Yield: 2-servings

Ingredients:

2 tbsps. of honey	2 c. Plain unsweetened coconut yogurt or almond yogurt
1 c. fresh blueberries	1/2 c. walnut pieces
1 c. fresh raspberries	

Directions:
Stir the yogurt and honey together. Divide into two bowls. Sprinkle in blueberries and raspberries along with A quarter cup of chopped walnuts
Nutritional Information: Calories: 505   Total Carbs: 56g Sugar: 14g Fiber: 8g Protein: 23g Sodium: 174mg

170. Warm Chia-Berry Non-dairy Yogurt
Prep time: 11-minutes | Total time: 17-minutes | Yield: 2-servings

Ingredients:

1 tbsp. maple syrup	1/2 vanilla bean halved lengthwise
2 c. unsweetened almond yogurt or coconut yogurt	1 (10 oz.) package frozen mixed berries, thawed
1 tbsp. freshly squeezed lemon juice	1/2 tbsp. chia seeds

Directions:
Combine the berries, lemon juice, maple syrup, and vanilla bean in a medium saucepan over medium-high flame. Get the mixture to a boil, continuously stirring. Reduce the heat to low heat and continue to cook for 3-minutes. Switch off the heat from the pan. Detach the vanilla bean from the mixture and discard it. Add the chia seeds and mix well. Allow 5 to 10-minutes for the seeds to thicken. Cover each bowl with one cup of yogurt and divide the fruit mixture among both of them.
Nutritional Information:Calories: 246 Fat: 10g Carbs: 35g Sugar: 11g Fiber: 5g Protein: 5g Sodium: 2mg

171. Turkey with Thyme and Sage Sausage
Prep time: 42-minutes | Total time: 1 hour 7-minutes | Yield: 4-servings

Ingredients:

1 lb. ground turkey	½ tsp. cinnamon
½ tsp. garlic powder	1 tsp. fresh rosemary
1 tsp. fresh thyme	1 tsp. sea salt
2- tsp. fresh sage	2 Tbsps. coconut oil

Directions:
Stir in all the ingredients, except for the oil, in a mixing bowl. Refrigerate overnight or for 30-minutes.
Pour the oil into the mixture. Form the mixture into four patties.
In a lightly greased skillet placed over medium heat, cook the patties for 5-minutes on each side or until their middle portions are no longer pink. You can also cook them by baking in the oven for 25-minutes at 400F.
Nutritional Information: Calories: 284 | Fat: 9.4g | Protein: 14.2g | Sodium: 290mg | Total Carbs: 36.9g

CHAPTER 4:
<u>LUNCH RECIPES</u>

172. Beets Gazpacho
Prep Time: 10-minutes | Total time: 20-minutes | Yield: 4-servings
Ingredients:

1× 20oz. Can Great North-ern Beans, rinsed and drained	¼ tsp. Kosher Salt
1 tbsp. Extra-Virgin Olive Oil	½ tsp. Garlic, fresh and minced
1× 6oz. pouch Pink Salmon flaked	2 tbsp. Lemon juice, freshly squeezed
4 Green Onions, sliced thinly	½ tsp. Ground Black Pepper
½ tsp. Lemon rind grated	¼ c. Flat-leaf Parsley, fresh and chopped

Directions:
First, place lemon rind, olive oil, lemon juice, black pepper, and garlic in a medium-sized mixing bowl and mix them with a whisker. Combine beans, onions, salmon, and parsley in another medium-sized bowl and toss them well. Then, spoon in the lemon juice dressing over the bean's mixture. Mix well `until the dressing coats the beans mixture. Serve and enjoy.
Nutritional Information: Calories 131, Proteins: 1.9g Carbohydrates: 14.8g Fat: 8.5g

173. Strawberries and Cream Trifle
Prep Time: 10-minutes | Total time: 55-minutes | Yield: 12-servings
Ingredients:

6 oz. packaged cream cheese softened	1 ½ c. condensed milk
12 oz. frozen whipped cream, thawed	1 angel food cake, cubed
3 pints fresh strawberries, hulled and sliced	

Directions:
In a bowl, put together the cream cheese, sweetened condensed milk, and whip in until smooth. In a bowl, put a layer of angel food cake cubes. Add a layer of strawberries and cream on top. Repeat the layers.
Bring it in the refrigerator to cool for at least 35-minutes.

Nutritional Information: Calories: 378 | Fat: 17g | Carbs: 51g | Protein: 7g

174. Edamame Omelet
Prep Time: 5-minutes | Total time: 10-minutes | Yield: 2-servings

Ingredients:

3 tbsp. olive oil, divided	1 tsp. minced garlic
1 bunch scallions, cut into 1-inch pieces	½ c. shelled edamame
1 tbsp. low-sodium soy sauce, or to taste	3 large eggs or ¾ c. egg substitute
½ c. shredded regular or soy Cheddar cheese	Snips of fresh cilantro for garnish

Directions:
Using a skillet set over medium heat, warm 2 tbsps. Oil and sauté the garlic and scallion for about 2-minutes. Add the edamame and soy sauce and sauté 1 minute more. Remove from the skillet and set aside. Warm the other 1 tbsp. Oil in the same skillet. Whisk the eggs until mixed and pour into the hot oil. Scatter the shredded cheese on top. Lift up the omelet's edges, tipping the skillet back and forth to cook the uncooked eggs.
Once the top looks firm, sprinkle the scallion mixture over one half of the omelet and fold the other half over the top. Lift the omelet out of the skillet. Divide it in half, sprinkle with the cilantro, and serve.
Nutritional Information: Calories: 416 Fat: 31 g Protein: 27 g Sodium: 640 Fiber: 3 g Carbohydrate: 7.5 g

175. Pineapple Three Bean Salad
Prep Time: 11-minutes plus 2 hours chilling time | Total time: 2 hours 11-minutes | Yield: 6-servings

Ingredients:

1 (15 oz.) can drain black beans, rinsed	1 (15 oz.) can drained chickpeas, rinsed
1 ½ c. cherry tomatoes, halved	1 c. shelled edamame, thawed if frozen
1 c. corn kernels	1 c. pineapple, finely chopped
½ c. cilantro, finely minced	3 cloves garlic, minced
2 tbsps. extra-virgin olive oil	2 tbsps. apple cider vinegar
1 tsp. chili powder	½ tsp. salt
½ tsp. red pepper flakes	½ tsp. cumin

Chips for serving (optional)

Directions:
Combine cilantro, black beans, tomatoes, pineapple, edamame, chickpeas, corn, and garlic using a mixing bowl. Mix well. Mix olive oil, chili powder, red pepper flakes, salt, apple cider vinegar, and cumin in a different bowl. Drizzle this over the beans and veggies, and fold it in. Refrigerate for 2 hours, stirring occasionally. Serve with chips or make lettuce wraps.
Nutritional Information: Calories 287, Fat 8 g, carbs 43 g, Protein 14 g, sodium 209 mg

176. Instant Pot Black Beans
Prep Time: 15-minutes | Total time: 30-minutes | Yield: 8-servings

Ingredients:

2 c. of black beans, rinsed & dried	1 yellow onion, chopped
2 tbsps. of extra virgin olive oil	2 garlic cloves, smashed
1 sliced jalapeno pepper	1 red or yellow bell-pepper, seeded & stemmed
1 handful of cilantro	½ tsp. of red pepper flakes
2 tsp. cumin, ground	2 tsp. kosher salt

Directions:
Keep the black beans in your saucepan. Cover with cold water for 6 hours. Drain and rinse. Heat oil and add garlic, onions, and salt. Sauté for 5-minutes. Add the jalapeno, bell pepper, red pepper flakes, black pepper, and cumin. Sauté for another 3-minutes. Stir frequently. Now include the cilantro stems, beans, water, and some more salt. Combine well by stirring. Cook for 7-minutes. Release naturally.
Nutritional Information: Calories 144 Fat 8g Carbs 14g Protein 4g Sugar 1g Fiber 4g Sodium 606mg

177. Baked Butternut Squash Rigatoni
Prep Time: 10-minutes | Total time: 1-hour 40-minutes | Yield: 4-servings

Ingredients:

1 enormous butternut squash	3 clove garlic
2 tbsp. olive oil	1 lb. rigatoni
1/2 c. substantial cream	3 c. destroyed fontina
2 tbsp. slashed crisp sage	1 tbsp. salt
1 tsp. naturally, ground pepper	1 c. panko breadcrumbs

Directions:
Preheat broiler to 425 degrees F. In the meantime, in a huge bowl, hurl squash, garlic, and olive oil to cover. Spot on a huge rimmed preparing sheet and dish until delicate, around 60-minutes. Set your container on a wire rack to allow for cooling, around 10-minutes. Decrease stove to 350 degrees F. In the meantime, heat a huge pot of salted water to the point of boiling and cook rigatoni as per bundle bearings. Channel and put in a safe spot. Utilizing a blender or nourishment processor, purée held squash with overwhelming cream until smooth. In a huge bowl, hurl squash puree withheld rigatoni, 2 cups fontina, savvy, salt, and pepper. Brush base and sides of a 9-by 13-inch preparing dish with olive oil. Move rigatoni-squash blend to a dish.
In a little bowl, consolidate the remaining fontina and panko. Sprinkle over pasta and heat until brilliant darker, 20 to 25-minutes.
Nutritional Information: Calories: 654 , Protein: 34.43 g, Fat: 47.92 g, Carbohydrates: 23.17 g

178. Creamy Sweet Potato Mash
Prep Time: 15-minutes | Total time: 36-minutes | Yield: 4-servings

Ingredients:

1 tbsp. olive oil	2 large sweet potatoes, peeled and chopped
2 tsp. ground turmeric	1 garlic clove, minced
2 c. vegetable broth	2 tbsps. unsweetened coconut milk
Freshly ground black pepper & salt, to taste	Chopped pistachios for garnishing

Directions:
Heat oil on medium-high heat inside a large skillet. Add sweet potato and stir fry for bout 2-3-minutes. Add turmeric and stir fry for about 1 minute. Add garlic and stir fry for about 2-minutes. Add broth and allow to boil. Reduce the heat to low. Then cook for about 10-15-minutes or till all the liquid is absorbed. Transfer the sweet potato mixture into a bowl. Add coconut milk, salt, and black pepper and mash it completely. Garnish with pistachio and serve.
Nutritional Information: Calories: 110 Fat: 5g Carbohydrates: 16g Protein: 1g

179. Fruity Muffins
Prep Time: 10-minutes | Total time: 12 – 13-minutes | Yield: 8-servings

Ingredients:

½ c. almond meal	1 tbsp. linseed meal
¼ c. raw sugar	2 tbsps. crystallized ginger, chopped finely
½ c. buckwheat flour	¼ c. brown rice flour
2 tbsps. arrowroot flour	2 tbsps. organic baking powder

½ tsp. ground ginger	12 tsp. ground cinnamon
Pinch of salt	1 large organic egg
7 tbsps. almond milk	¼ c. extra-virgin olive oil
1 tsp. organic vanilla extract	1 peeled and cored apple, finely chopped
1 c. rhubarb, finely sliced	

Directions:

Set oven to preheat at 350F. Grease 8 cups that fit in a muffin tin (large enough). In a bowl, mix linseed meal crystallized ginger, sugar, and almond meal. In a separate bowl, mix spices, flour, salt, and baking powder. Transfer flour mixture to almond meal mixture to combine well. In a third bowl, mix milk, vanilla, oil, and egg. Add egg mixture into the flour mixture and mix till well combined. Fold in apple and rhubarb. Place the mixture into prepared muffin cups equally. Bake for about 20-25-minutes or till a toothpick inserted in the center comes out clean.

Nutritional Information: Calories: 227 Fat: 4.2g | Carbs: 26.9g Fiber: 4.9g Sugars: 10.4g Protein: 4.1g

180. Puttanesca-Style Greens and Beans

Prep Time: 15-minutes | Total time: 1-hour 15-minutes | Yield: 6-servings

Ingredients:

3 c. water	1 c. baby lima beans, dried (soaked overnight)
¾ c. kalamata olives, pitted	½ c. green olives pitted
½ c. tomatoes in olive oil, sundried (optional)	1 yellow onion
2 cloves garlic	2 tsp. capers
2 tbsps. olive oil	2 c. greens, shredded (kale or beet greens)
4 anchovies	½ tsp. ground black pepper

Directions:

Mix the water and lima beans in a large saucepan and allow to boil over medium-high heat. After it boils, set heat to low, and simmer for 45-minutes while covered. You want the beans to be tender. When they are, drain well. In a food processor, combine sundried tomatoes, olives, onion, garlic, and capers and pulse well until roughly chopped. Heat 2 tbsps. Of oil set over medium-high heat in a large skillet. When hot, add your olive mixture and allow to cook until onions soften for 5-minutes. Add the anchovies, greens, and black pepper. Stir and cook about 4 more-minutes, and then stir in beans. Heat through, and serve.

Nutritional Information: Calories 314, fat 19 g, carbs 28 g, protein 8 g, sodium 927 mg

181. Chicken Breasts and Mushrooms

Prep Time: 5-minutes | Total time: 30-minutes | Yield: 6-servings

Ingredients:

3 lbs. chicken breasts, skin-less and boneless	1 yellow onion, chopped
1 garlic clove, minced	A pinch of salt and black pepper
10 mushrooms, chopped	1 tbsp. olive oil
2 red bell peppers, chopped	

Directions:

Put the chicken in a baking dish, add onion, garlic, salt, pepper, mushrooms, oil, and bell peppers. Mix briefly and bake in the oven at 425°F for 25-minutes.
Divide between plates and serve. Enjoy!

Nutritional Information: Calories 285 Total Fat 11g Carbs 13g Protein 16g Fiber 1g

182. White Bean Chili

Prep Time: 10-minutes | Total time: 30-minutes | Yield: 4-servings

Ingredients:

¼ c. extra-virgin olive oil	2 small onions, cut into ¼-inch dice
2 celery stalks, thinly sliced	2 small carrots, peeled and thinly sliced
2 garlic cloves, minced	2 tsp. ground cumin
1½ tsp. dried oregano	1 tsp. salt
¼ tsp. freshly ground black pepper	3 c. vegetable-broth
1 (15½ oz.) can drain & rinsed white beans	¼ finely chopped fresh flat-leaf parsley
2 tsp. grated or minced lemon zest	

Directions:

Heat-up the oil over high heat in a Dutch oven. Add the onions, celery, carrots, and garlic and sauté until softened, 5 to 8-minutes. Add the cumin, oregano, salt, and pepper and sauté to toast the spices, about 1 minute.
Put the broth and boil. Simmer the mix before adding in the beans. Cook while partially covered to obtain the flavors for 5-minutes. Mix in the parsley and lemon zest and serve.

Nutritional Information: Calories 300 Total Fat: 15g Total Carbohydrates: 32g Sugar: 4g Fiber: 12g Protein: 12g Sodium: 1183mg

183. Sweet Onion and Egg Pie

Prep Time: 20-minutes | Total time: 55-minutes | Yield: 10-servings

Ingredients:

2 sweet onions, halved and sliced	1 tbsps. butter
6 eggs	1 c. evaporated milk
11 frozen deep-dish pie crust	Salt and pepper to taste

Directions:

Preheat the oven to 4000F. Melt the butter in a non-stick skillet. Sauté the onions over medium-low heat until very tender. Place the onions in a bowl. Add in eggs and evaporated milk. Season with salt and pepper to taste. Pour egg & onion mixture into the pie crust. Bake in the oven for 35-minutes.

Nutritional Information: Calories: 169 | Fat: 7g | Carbs: 21g

184. Sesame Wings with Cauliflower

Prep Time: 5-minutes | Total time: 35-minutes | Yield: 4-servings

Ingredients:

2 ½ tbsps. soy sauce	2 tbsps. sesame oil
1 ½ tsps. balsamic vinegar	1 tsp. minced garlic
1 tsp. grated ginger	Salt
1 lb. chicken wing, the wings itself	2 c. cauliflower florets

Directions:

Mix the soy sauce, sesame oil, balsamic vinegar, garlic, ginger, and salt in a freezer bag, then add the chicken wings. Coat flip then chills for 2 to 3 hours. Preheat the oven to 400 F and line a foil-based baking sheet. Spread the wings along with the cauliflower onto the baking sheet. Bake for 35-minutes, then sprinkle on to serve with sesame seeds.

Nutritional Information: Calories: 400 | Fats: 15 | Protein: 5 | Carbohydrates: 3

185. Lentil Stew

Prep Time: 10minutes | Total time: 40-minutes | Yield: 4-servings

Ingredients:

1 Tbsp. Olive Oil	8 Brussels Sprouts, Halved
3 Carrots, Peeled & Sliced	1 Onion, Chopped
1 Turnip, Peeled, Quartered & Sliced	6 C. Vegetable Broth
1 Clove Garlic, Sliced	15 Oz. Can Lentils, Drained & Rinsed
1 C. Corn, Frozen	1 Tbsp. Parsley, Fresh & Chopped
Sea Salt & Black Pepper to Taste	

Directions:

Get out a Dutch oven and heat your oil over high heat, adding in your onion. Cook for three-minutes. Your onions should soften. Add in your carrots, turnip, garlic, and Brussels sprouts. Cook for three more-minutes. Throw in your broth, allow to boil, then reduce it to a simmer. Cook for extra 5-minutes. Add in your pepper, corn, parsley, salt, and lentils. Cook until well done and serve warm.

Nutritional Information: Calories: 240 Protein: 10 Grams Fat: 4 Grams Carbs: 42 Grams

186. Hearty Beef and Bacon Casserole

Prep Time: 26-minutes | Total time: 56-servings | Yield: 8-servings

Ingredients:

8 slices uncooked bacon	1 medium head cauliflower, chopped
¼ c. canned coconut milk	Salt and pepper
2 lbs. ground beef (80% lean)	8 oz. mushrooms, sliced
1 large yellow onion, chopped	2 cloves garlic, minced

Direction:

Preheat to 375 F on the oven. Cook bacon in the skillet until crispy, then drain and chop on paper towels. Bring to boil a pot of salted water, then add the cauliflower. Boil until tender for 6 to 8-minutes, then drain and add the coconut milk to a food processor. Mix until smooth, then sprinkle with salt and pepper. Cook the beef until browned in a pan, then wash the fat away. Remove the mushrooms, onion, and garlic, then move to a baking platter. Place on top of the cauliflower mixture and bake for 30-minutes. Broil for 5-minutes on high heat, then sprinkle with bacon to serve.

Nutritional Information: Calories: 410 | Fats: 25 | Protein: 37 | Carbohydrates: 6

187. Balsamic Chicken and Vegetables

Prep Time: 15-minutes | Total time: 25-minutes | Yield: 4-servings

Ingredients:

4 chicken thigh, boneless and skinless	5 stalks of asparagus, halved

1 bell pepper, cut in chunks	1/2 red onion, diced
1 garlic cloves, minced	2 oz. mushrooms, diced
¼ c. balsamic vinegar	1 tbsp. olive oil
½ tsp. stevia	½ tbsp. oregano
Salt and pepper, as needed	

Directions:

Preheat your oven to 425 degrees Fahrenheit. Mix the spices, olive oil, and vinegar. Combine the vegetables and mushrooms in a bowl. Season with spices and sprinkle with oil. Dip the chicken pieces into a spice mix and coat them thoroughly. Place the veggies and chicken onto a pan in a single layer. Cook for 25-minutes. Serve and enjoy!

Nutritional Information: Calories: 401 | Fat: 17g | Net Carbohydrates: 11g | Protein: 48g | Fiber: 3g |

188. Apple Bread

Prep Time: 25-minutes | Total time: 1-hour 35-minutes | Yield: 8-servings

Ingredients:

1 packet yeast	3 tbsp. sugar
11/3 c. warm water	3 tbsp. soft butter
1 tsp. Salt	¼ tsp. baking powder
1¾ c. all-purpose flour	1¾ c. flour, whole-wheat
1 c. chopped apples, peeled	1 tbsp. cinnamon mixed with 1 tbsp. sugar

Directions:

Using a bowl, mix ½ tsp. sugar, yeast, and 1/3 cup water. Allow sitting for about 5-minutes. Using a bowl, add in the remaining water, remaining sugar, baking powder, salt, and butter and mix well. Add in all-purpose flour and yeast as you stir. Add in whole-wheat flour and knead your dough hook for 10-minutes. Set dough in an oiled bowl. Set in a warm place for 2 hours while covered to rise and double in bulk. Punch down your dough, and form a rectangle. To the dough, scatter over the apples and dust with cinnamon sugar. Roll to form a cylinder and transfer in an oiled loaf pan. Allow rising while covered for 90-minutes in a warm place until it doubles in size.Preheat your oven to 350°F. Uncover your bread and allow it to bake for about 50-minutes.

Nutritional Information: Calories:256 | Fat:5.3 g | Protein: 7.4 g | Sodium: 293 mg | Fiber: 4.9 g | Carbs: 47 g

189. Sautéed Shrimp Jambalaya Jumble

Prep Time: 15-minutes | Total time: 45-minutes | Yield: 4-servings

Ingredients:

10-oz. medium shrimp, peeled	¼-c. celery, chopped ½-c. onion, chopped
1 tbsp. oil or butter ¼-tsp garlic, minced	¼-tsp onion salt or sea salt
1/3-c. tomato sauce ½-tsp smoked paprika	½-tsp Worcestershire sauce
2/3-c. carrots, chopped	1¼-c. chicken sausage, precooked and diced
2-c. lentils, soaked overnight and precooked	2-c. okra, chopped
A dash of crushed red pepper and black pepper	Parmesan cheese, grated for topping (optional)

Directions:

Sauté the shrimp, celery, and onion with oil in a pan placed over medium-high heat for five-minutes, or until the shrimp turn pinkish. Add in the rest of the ingredients, and sauté further for 10-minutes, or until the veggies are tender. To serve, divide the jambalaya mixture equally among four serving bowls. Top with pepper and cheese, if desired.

Nutritional Information: Calories: 529 Fat: 17.6g Protein: 26.4g Carbs: 98.4g Fiber: 32.3g

190. Green Soup

Prep Time: 10-minutes | Total time: 15-minutes | Yield: 2-servings

Ingredients:

1 c. Water	1 c. Spinach, fresh & packed
½ of 1 Lemon, peeled	1 Zucchini, small & chopped
2 tbsp. Parsley, fresh & chopped	1 Celery Stalk, chopped
Sea Salt & Black Pepper, as needed	½ of 1 Avocado, ripe
¼ c. Basil	2 tbsp. Chia Seeds
1 Garlic clove, minced	

Directions:

To make this easy blended soup, place all the ingredients in a high-speed blender and blend for 3-minutes or until smooth. Next, you can serve it cold or warm it up on low heat for a few minutes.

Nutritional Information: Calories: 250Proteins: 6.9gCarbohydrates: 18.4gFat: 18.1g

191. Maple Toast and Eggs

Prep Time: 20-minutes | Total time: 40-minutes | Yield: 6-servings

Ingredients:

12 bacon strips, diced	½ c. maple syrup
¼ c. butter	12 slices white bread
12 large eggs	Salt and pepper to taste

Directions:

Fry the bacon on a skillet on medium heat until the fat has been rendered. Take the bacon out and place it on paper towels to drain excess Fat. Warm the maple syrup and butter until melted in a saucepan. Set aside. Trim the edges of the bread and flatten the slices with a rolling pin. Brush one side with the syrup mixture and press the slices into greased muffin cups. Divide the bacon into the muffin cups. Break one egg into each cup. Sprinkle with salt and pepper to taste. Cover using foil, then bake in the oven at 4000F for 20-minutes or until the eggs have set.

Nutritional Information: Calories: 671 | Fat: 46g | Carbs: 44g | Protein: 21g

192. Yogurt Cheese and Fruit

Prep Time: 10-minutes | Total time: 10-minutes | Yield: 6-servings

Ingredients:

3 c. plain nonfat yogurt	1 tsp. fresh lemon juice
½ c. orange juice	½ c. water
1 fresh Golden Delicious apple	1 fresh pear
¼ c. honey	¼ c. dried cranberries or raisins

Directions:

Prepare the yogurt cheese the day before by lining a colander or strainer with cheesecloth. Scoop the yogurt into the cheesecloth, place the strainer over a pot or bowl to catch the whey, and refrigerate for at least 8 hours before serving. In a huge mixing bowl, mix together the juices and water. Cut the apple than pear into wedges, place the wedges in the juice mixture, let sit for at least 5-minutes. Strain off the liquid.

When the yogurt is firm, remove it from the refrigerator, slice, and place on plates. Arrange the fruit wedges around the yogurt. Drizzle with honey and sprinkle with cranberries or raisins just before serving.

Nutritional Information: Calories: 177 | Fat: 1 g | Protein: 6.5 g | Sodium: 87 mg | Fiber: 2 g | Carbohydrate: 35 g

193. Classic Guacamole Dip

Prep Time: 15-minutes | Total time: 15-minutes | Yield: 4-servings

Ingredients:

2 mediums avocado, pitted	1 small yellow onion, diced
1 small tomato, diced	¼ c. fresh chopped cilantro
1 tbsp. fresh lime juice	1 jalapeno, seeded and minced
1 clove garlic, minced	Salt
Sliced veggies to serve	

Directions:

Mash avocado flesh into a bowl. Stir the onion, tomato, cilantro, lime juice, garlic, and jalapeno in a bowl. Season lightly with salt and spoon into a bowl – serve with sliced veggies.

Nutritional Information: Calories: 225 | Fats: 20 | Protein: 12 | Carbohydrates: 3

194. Lemony Mackerel

Prep Time: 10-minutes | Total time: 25-minutes | Yield: 4-servings

Ingredients:

Juice of 1 lemon	Zest of 1 lemon
4 mackerels	1 tbsp. minced chives
Pinch of sea salt	Pinch black pepper
2 tbsps. olive oil	

Directions:

Warm a pan with the oil on medium-high heat, add the mackerel and cook for 6-minutes on each side. Add the lemon zest, lemon juice, chives, salt, and pepper, then cook for 2 more-minutes on each side. Divide everything between plates and serve.

Nutritional Information: Calories: 289 Cal | Fat: 20 g | Fiber: 0 g | Carbs: 1 g | Protein: 21 g

195. Onion Bacon Pork Chops

Prep Time: 10-minutes | Total time: 55-minutes | Yield: 2-servings

Ingredients:

1 onion, peeled and chopped	3 bacon slices, chopped
1/4 c. chicken stock	Salt and pepper to taste
2 pork chops	

Directions:

Heat a pan over medium heat and then add bacon. Stir and cook until crispy. Transfer to a bowl. Return pan to medium heat. Then add the onions, season with salt and pepper. Stir and cook for 15-minutes. Transfer to the same bowl with bacon. Return the pan to heat (medium-high) and add pork chops. Season with salt, pepper, and brown for 3-minutes. Flip and lower heat to medium. Cook for 7-minutes more. Add stock and stir cook for 2-minutes. Return the bacon and onions to the pan and stir cook for 1 minute. Serve and enjoy!

Nutritional Information: Calories: 325 | Fat: 18g | Protein: 36g | Fiber: 2g | Net Carbohydrates: 4g

196. Lemon-Caper Trout with Caramelized Shallots

Prep Time: 10-minutes | Total time: 30-minutes | Yield: 2-servings

Ingredients:
For the Shallots:

2 shallots, thinly sliced	1 tsp. ghee
Dash salt	

For the Trout:

1 tbsp. plus 1 tsp. ghee, divided	2 (4 oz.) trout fillets
¼ c. freshly squeezed lemon juice	3 tbsps. capers
¼ tsp. salt	Dash freshly ground black pepper
1 lemon, thinly sliced	

Directions:
To make the Shallot:
In a huge skillet on medium heat, cook the shallots, ghee, and salt for 20-minutes, stirring every 5-minutes, until the shallots have fully wilted and caramelized.

To make the Trout:
While the shallots cook, in another large skillet over medium heat, heat 1 tsp. of ghee.
Add the trout fillets. Cook for at least 3-minutes on each side, or until the center is flaky. Transfer to a plate and set aside.
In the skillet used for the trout, add lemon juice, capers, salt, and pepper. Bring it to a simmer. Whisk in the remaining 1 tbsp of ghee. Spoon the sauce over the fish. Garnish the fish using the lemon slices and caramelized shallots before serving.

Nutritional Information: Calories: 399|Saturated Fat: 10g |Carbs: 17g|Fiber: 2g|Protein: 21g

197. Quinoa with Apricots

Prep Time: 15-minutes | Total time: 27-minutes | Yield: 4-servings

Ingredients:

2 c. water	1 c. quinoa
½ tsp. fresh ginger, grated finely	½ c. dried apricots, chopped roughly
Salt and freshly ground black-pepper, to taste	

Directions:
In a pan, add water on high heat and bring to a boil. Add quinoa and reduce the heat to medium. Cover and reduce the heat to low. Simmer for about 12-minutes. Remove from heat and immediately stir in ginger and apricots. Keep aside, covered for about 15-minutes before serving.

Nutritional Information: Calories: 196 Protein: 6.56 g Fat: 2.66 g Carbohydrates: 37.49 g

198. Cabbage with Apple

Prep Time: 15-minutes | Total time: 24-minutes | Yield: 2-4-servings

Ingredients:

2 tsp. coconut oil	1 large apple, cored and sliced thinly
1 onion, sliced thinly	1½ lbs. cabbage, chopped finely
1 tbsp. fresh thyme, chopped	1 red chili, chopped
1 tbsp. apple cider vinegar	2/3 c. almonds, chopped

Directions:
In a nonstick skillet, melt 1 tsp. of coconut oil on medium heat. Add apple and stir fry for about 2-3-minutes. Transfer the apple into a bowl. In the same skillet, melt 1 tsp. of coconut oil on medium heat. Add onion and sauté for about 1-2-minutes. Add cabbage and stir fry for about 3-minutes. Add apple, thyme, and vinegar and cook, covered for about 1 minute. Serve warm with the garnishing of almonds.

Nutritional Information: Calories: 106 Protein: 2.68 g Fat: 2.73 g Carbohydrates: 21.07 g

199. Tzatziki Dip with Cauliflower

Prep Time: 10-minutes | Total time: 10-minutes | Yield: 6-servings

Ingredients:

½ (8 oz.) package cream cheese, softened	1 c. sour cream
1 tbsp. ranch seasoning	1 English cucumber, diced
2 tbsps. chopped chives	2 c. cauliflower florets

Directions:
Pound the cream cheese until smooth using an electric-mixer. Stir in the sour cream and ranch seasoning beat

until smooth. Fold in the cucumbers and chives, then chill with cauliflower florets for dipping before serving.
Nutritional Information: Calories: 125 |Fats: 10 |Protein: 5 |Carbohydrates: 3

200. Curried Shrimp and Vegetables
Prep Time: 10-minutes | Total time: 25-minutes | Yield: 4-servings

Ingredients:

3 tbsps. coconut oil	1 onion, sliced
2 c. cauliflower, cut into florets	1 c. of coconut milk
1 tbsp. curry powder	¼ c. fresh parsley, chopped
1 lb. shrimp, tails removed	

Directions:
In a large skillet over medium high-heat, and melt the coconut oil. Add the onion and cauliflower and cook until they are softened. Add coconut milk, curry, and parsley to the skillet. (Feel free to add any other spices you like. Turmeric will give you an even bigger anti-inflammatory boost.) Cook for 2–3 more-minutes. Stir the shrimp inside the skillet and cook until it is opaque.
Nutritional Information: Calories 332 Total Fat 22g Carbs 11g Protein 24g Sodium 309 mg

201. Shrimp Cakes
Prep Time: 10-minutes | Total time: 20-minutes | Yield: 24-servings

Ingredients:

½ lb. tiger shrimp, peeled, deveined, and chopped	A little sea salt and black pepper
2 tbsps. olive oil	½ lb. ground pork
1 egg, whisked	2 tbsps. coconut flour
2 tbsps. chicken stock	1 tsp. coconut aminos
1 green onion stalk, chopped	1 tsp. freshly grated ginger

Directions:
Mix the shrimp with the pork, salt, pepper, egg, stock, amino, onion, ginger, and flour in a bowl. Stir well and shape medium cakes out of this mix. Heat up a pan using the oil over medium-high heat, add the cakes and cook for 5-minutes on each side. Divide between plates and serve with a side salad.

Nutritional Information: calories 281, fat 8, fiber 7, carbs 19, protein 8

202. Keto Salmon Tandoori with Cucumber Sauce
Prep Time: 15-minutes | Total time: 35-minutes | Yield: 4-servings

Ingredients:

½ shredded cucumber (squeeze out the water completely)	½ tsp. salt (not necessary)
1 1/4 c. sour cream or mayonnaise	1 tbsp. tandoori seasoning
1 yellow bell pepper (diced)	2 avocados (cubed)
2 minced garlic cloves	2 tbsps. coconut oil
25 oz. salmon (bite-sized pieces)	3 ½ oz. lettuce (torn)
3 scallions (finely chopped)	For the crunchy salad
For the cucumber sauce	Juice of ½ lime

Directions:
Preheat your oven to 350 degrees Fahrenheit. Combine the tandoori seasoning with oil in a small container and coat the salmon pieces with this mixture. Coat the baking tray using parchment paper and spread the coated salmon pieces in it. Bake for about twenty-minutes until tender, and the salmon flakes using a fork. Take another container and put the shredded cucumber in it. Put in the mayonnaise, minced garlic, and salt (if the mayonnaise doesn't have salt) to the shredded cucumber. Mix thoroughly. Squeeze the lime juice at the top and set the cucumber sauce aside. Combine the lettuce, scallions, avocados, and bell pepper in a different container. Sprinkle the contents with lime juice. Move the veggie salad to a plate and put the baked salmon over it. Top the veggies and salmon with cucumber sauce. Serve instantly and enjoy!
Nutritional Information: Calories 847, Fat: 73 g, Protein: 35 g Net carb: 6 g

203. Caramelized Pork Chops
Prep Time: 5-minutes | Total time: 35-minutes | Yield: 2-servings

Ingredients:

2 lbs. chuck roast, sliced	2 oz. green chili, chopped
1 tbsp. chili powder	1/4 tsp. dried oregano
1/4 tsp. ground cumin	1 garlic cloves, minced
2 tbsps. olive oil	Salt as needed

Directions:
Rub up your chop with 1 tsp. of pepper and 2 tsp. of seasoning salt. In a skillet, heat a little oil over medium heat. Brown your pork chops on each side. Add some water and chili to the pan. Cover it up and lower down the heat, simmer it for about 20-minutes. Turn your

chops over and add the rest of the pepper and salt. Cover it up, cook until the water evaporates, and the chili turns tender. Remove the chops from your pan and serve with some peppers on top.

Nutritional Information: Calories: 271 | Fat: 19g | Carbohydrates: 4g | Protein: 27g | Fiber: 2g

204. Zucchini Bread

Prep Time: 10-minutes | Total time: 1-hour 10-minutes | Yield: 16-servings

Ingredients:

1½ c. flour, all-purpose	1½ c. 100% whole-wheat flour
1 tsp. salt	1 tsp. baking soda
1 tbsp. cinnamon	3 eggs, beaten, or ¾ c. of egg substitute
1 c. canola oil	2 c. sugar
¼ tsp. baking powder	2 c. grated zucchini
1 c. chopped pecans	1 c. raisins

Directions:

Preheat your oven to attain 350°F. Oil 2 loaf pans and set aside. Put the baking powder, flour, salt, baking soda, and cinnamon in a bowl. Mix the oil, eggs, and sugar in another bowl. Add the zucchini and dry ingredients alternately until fully incorporated into a smooth batter. Fold in the pecans and raisins and scrape the batter into the loaf pans. Bake for 60-minutes, cool on a rack and wrap when cool.

Nutritional Information: Calories: 396 | Fat: 20 | Protein: 5 g | Sodium: 237 mg | Fiber: 3 g | Carbw: 52 g

205. Dill Haddock

Prep Time: 10-minutes | Total time: 40-minutes | Yield: 4-servings

Ingredients:

1 lb. haddock fillets	3 tsp. veggie stock
2 tbsps. lemon juice	Salt and black pepper to the taste
2 tbsps. mayonnaise	2 tsp. chopped dill
A drizzle of olive oil	

Directions:

Grease a baking dish with the oil, add the fish, and add stock mixed with lemon juice, salt, pepper, mayo, and dill. Toss a bit and place in the oven at 350 degrees F to bake for 30-minutes. Divide between plates and serve. Enjoy!

Nutritional Information: Calories: 214 | Fat: 12 Cal | Fiber: 4 g | Carbs: 7 g Protein: 17 g

206. Rosemary Garlic Lamb Chops

Prep Time: 3-minutes | Total time: 13-minutes | Yield: 2-servings

Ingredients:

4 chops of lamb	1 tsp. olive oil
2 tsp. garlic puree	Fresh garlic
Fresh rosemary	

Directions:

Keep your lamb chops in the fryer grill pan. Season the chops with pepper and salt. Brush some olive oil. Add some garlic puree to each chop. Cover the grill pan gaps with garlic cloves and rosemary sprigs. Refrigerate to marinate. Take out after 1 hour. Keep in the fryer and cook for 5-minutes. Use your spatula to turn the chops over. Add some olive oil and cook for another 5-minutes. Set aside for a minute. Take out the rosemary and garlic before serving.

Nutritional information: Calories 678, Carbs 1g, Total Fat 38g, Protein 83g, Sugar 0g, Sodium 200mg

207. Keto Zoodles with White Clam Sauce

Prep Time: ten-minutes | Total time: 20-minutes | Yield: 4-servings

Ingredients:

½ c. dry white wine	1 tbsp. garlic (minced)
1 tsp. kosher salt	1 tsp. lemon zest (grated)
1/4 c. butter	1/4 c. fresh parsley (chopped)
1/4 tsp. black pepper (ground)	2 lbs. small clams
2 tbsps. lemon juice	2 tbsps. olive oil
8 c. zucchini noodles	

Directions:

In a pan at moderate heat, put the olive oil, butter, pepper, and salt. Stir to melt the butter.

Put in the garlic. Sautee the garlic until aromatic for a minimum of 2-minutes

Set in the lemon juice and wine. Cook for a minimum of 2-minutes, until the liquid, is slightly reduced

Put in the clams. Cook the clams until they are all opened (about three-minutes). Discard any clam that does not open after three-minutes.

Take away the pan from the heat. Put in the zucchini noodles. Toss the mixture to blend well. Allow the zoodles to rest for about 2-minutes to tenderize them.

Put in the lemon zest and parsley. Stir and serve.

Nutritional Information: Calories: 311, Carbohydrates: 9 g, Fat: 19 g, Protein: 13 g, Fiber: 2 g

208. Seared Tuna with Vinaigrette and Salad

Prep Time: 22-minutes | Total time: 2 hour 8-minutes | Yield: 6-servings

Ingredients:
Seared Ahi Tuna Poke ingredients:

20 wonton wrappers, square and in strips	2 tbsps. olive oil
¼ c. soy sauce	1 tsp. cornstarch
¼ c. pineapple juice	¼ c. honey
1 tsp. sriracha or chili garlic sauce	2 tbsps. toasted sesame oil
6 (4 oz.) ahi tuna steaks	2 tbsps. toasted sesame seeds, black and white

For the salad:

8 c. spring greens	½ c. fresh cilantro
1 c. diced pineapple, fresh	1 sliced avocado
1 jalapeño or red chili, sliced	Vinaigrette - Hula Ginger (makes 1 ½ cups)
½ c. hot chili sesame oil	¼ c. soy sauce
2 tbsps. pineapple juice	2 tbsps. rice vinegar
1 tsp. sriracha	1 tbsp. tahini
1 zested and juiced lime	2 tsp. grated ginger, fresh
1 minced clove garlic	1 tbsp. toasted sesame seeds, black and white

Directions:
Preheat your oven to attain 400°F. Grease a baking sheet using olive oil and lay the wonton strips on it in a single layer. Sprinkle them with salt. Bake the strips for about 5-minutes, or until they are golden brown and crispy. Set the finished strips to the side for now. Pour the soy sauce into a small saucepan, then whisk in the cornstarch until incorporated. Stir in the pineapple juice, honey, and chili sauce. Over medium-high heat, allow the mixture to boil, then reduce the temperature and simmer for 3–5-minutes, or until your sauce begins to thicken. Set the thickened sauce aside. Pour the sesame oil into a large skillet, and heat over high-heat. Sear tuna steaks for about 2-minutes on each side. Brush the thickened soy sauce mixture over each side and cook another 1–2-minutes. Baste with sauce, so each side is well covered. When the steaks are done, sprinkle each side with sesame seeds. Prepare the salad. In a salad bowl, combine the avocado, cilantro, greens, pineapple, and jalapeño pepper. Toss to combine. Prepare vinaigrette by combining all the ingredients and whisking well. Plate the greens, top with seared tuna, and your wonton crisps. Top with some of the vinaigrette and serve.
Nutritional Information: (before adding vinaigrette) Calories 447, fat 18 g, carbs 45 g, protein 32 g

209. Brown Rice and Chicken Mix

Prep Time: 10-minutes | Total time: 20-minutes | Yield: 4-servings

Ingredients:

1½ c. brown rice, cooked	1½ tbsps. coconut sugar
1 c. chicken stock	2 tbsps. coconut aminos
4 oz. chicken breast boneless, skinless, and cut into small pieces	1 egg
2 egg whites	2 scallions, chopped

Directions:
Put stock in a pot, heat up over medium-low heat, add coconut aminos and sugar, stir, bring to a boil, add the chicken, and toss. Mix the egg with egg whites, whisk well, and then add over the chicken mix in a bowl. Sprinkle the scallions on top and cook for 3-minutes without stirring. Divide the rice into 4 bowls, add the chicken mix on top and serve. Enjoy!
Nutritional Information: Calories 231 Total Fat 11g Carbs 8g Protein 9g Fiber 7g

210. Grilled Salmon and Zucchini with Mango Sauce

Prep Time: 5-minutes | Total time: 15-minutes | Yield: 4-servings

Ingredients:

4 (6 oz.) boneless salmon fillets	1 tbsp. olive oil
Salt and pepper	1 large zucchini, sliced in coins
2 tbsps. fresh lemon juice	½ c. chopped mango
¼ c. fresh chopped cilantro	1 tsp. lemon zest
½ c. canned coconut milk	

Directions:
Preheat a grill pan to heat, and sprinkle with cooking spray liberally.
Brush with olive oil to the salmon and season with salt and pepper.
Apply lemon juice to the zucchini, and season with salt and pepper.
Put the zucchini and salmon fillets on the grill pan.
Cook for 5-minutes, then turn all over and cook for another 5-minutes.
Combine the ingredients remaining in a blender and combine to create a sauce.
Serve the side-drizzled salmon filets with mango sauce and zucchini.
Nutritional Information: Calories: 350 |Fats: 23 |Protein: 7 |Carbohydrates: 6

211. Almond Mascarpone Dumplings

Prep Time: 10-minutes | Total time: 20-minutes | Yield: 6-servings

Ingredients:

1 c. whole-wheat flour	1 c. all-purpose un-bleached flour
¼ c. ground almonds	4 egg whites
3 oz. mascarpone cheese	1 tsp. extra-virgin olive oil
2 tsp. apple juice	1 tbsp. butter
¼ c. honey	

Directions:

Strain together both types of flour in a large bowl. Mix in the almonds. Mix egg whites, oil, cheese, and juice using an electric mixer on medium speed in a different bowl. Put the egg white and flour mixture with a dough hook on medium speed or by hand until a dough forms. Boil 1-gallon water in a medium-size saucepot. Take a scoop of dough and use a second spoon to push it into the boiling water. Cook up to the dumpling floats to the top, at least 5 to 10-minutes. You can cook several dumplings at once — just take care not to crowd the pot. Take off with a slotted spoon and drain on paper towels. Warm a medium-size sauté pan on medium-high heat. Add the butter, then put the dumplings in the pan and cook until light brown. Set on serving plates and drizzle with honey.

Nutritional Information: Calories:254 | Fat:6.4 g | Protein: 7 g | Sodium: 20 mg | Fiber: 3.5 g | Carbs: 44 g

212. Roasted Brussels Sprouts & Sweet Potato

Prep Time: 15-minutes | Total time: 1-hour | Yield: 6-8-servings

Ingredients:

1 large sweet-potato, peeled and cut into 1-2-inch pieces	1 lb. Brussels sprouts, trimmed and halved
2 minced garlic cloves	1 tsp. ground cumin
½ tsp. garlic salt	Freshly ground black pepper & salt, to taste
1/3 c. olive oil	1 tbsp. apple cider vinegar
Chopped fresh thyme for garnishing	

Directions:

Preheat your oven to 400-degrees F. Grease a sheet pan. In a large bowl, add all ingredients except vinegar and thyme and toss to coat well. Transfer the mixture into a prepared baking pan. Roast for 40-45-minutes more. Transfer the vegetable mixture to a serving plate and drizzle with vinegar. Garnish with thyme and serve.

Nutritional Information: Calories: 127 Protein: 2.48 g Fat: 9.18 g Carbohydrates: 10.38 g

213. Simple Brown Rice

Prep Time: 10-minutes | Total time: 1-hour | Yield: 4-servings

Ingredients:

1 c. brown rice	2 c. chicken broth
1 tbsp. ground turmeric	1 tbsp. olive oil

Directions:

In a pan, add rice, broth, and turmeric and bring to a boil. Reduce the heat to low. Simmer, covered for about 50-minutes. Add the olive-oil and then fluff using a fork. Keep aside, covered for about 10-minutes before serving.

Nutritional Information: Calories: 227 Protein: 26.16 g Fat: 11.75 g Carbohydrates: 2.5 g

214. Spicy Cauliflower Rice

Prep Time: 15-minutes | Total time: 25 minutes | Yield: 4-servings

Ingredients:

3 tbsps. coconut oil	1 small white onion, chopped
3 garlic cloves, minced	1 large head cauliflower, trimmed and processed into a rice consistency
½ tsp. ground cumin	½ tsp. paprika
Freshly ground black pepper and salt, to taste	1 large tomato, chopped
¼ c. tomato paste	¼ c. fresh cilantro, chopped
Chopped fresh cilantro for garnishing	2 limes, quarters

Directions:

In a large skillet, melt coconut-oil on medium-high heat. Add onion and sauté for about 2-minutes. Add garlic & sauté for about a minute. Stir in cauliflower rice. Add cumin, paprika, salt, and black pepper and cook, occasionally stirring for about 2-3-minutes. Stir in tomato, tomato paste, and cilantro and cook for about 2-3-minutes. Garnish with cilantro and serve alongside lime.

Nutritional Information: Calories: 137 Protein: 2.73 g Fat: 10.69 g Carbohydrates: 11.1 g

215. Italian Halibut Chowder

Prep Time: five-minutes | Total time: 25-minutes | Yield: 8-servings

Ingredients:

½ c. apple juice, organic and unsweetened	½ tsp. dried basil

1 c. tomato juice	1 onion, chopped
1 red bell pepper, seeded and chopped	1/8 tsp. dried thyme
2 ½ lbs. halibut steaks, cubed	2 tbsps. olive oil
3 cloves of garlic, minced	3 stalks of celery, chopped
Salt and pepper to taste	

Directions:

Put a heavy-bottomed pot on moderate to high fire and heat pot for a couple of minutes. Put in oil and heat for one minute. Sauté the onion, celery, and garlic until aromatic. Mix in the halibut steaks and bell pepper. Sauté for about three-minutes. Pour in the remaining ingredients and mix thoroughly. Cover and bring to its boiling point. Once boiling, lower the fire to a simmer and simmer for about ten minutes. Tweak seasoning to taste. Serve and enjoy.

Nutritional Information: Calories: 318 Cal, Fat: 23g, Carbohydrates: 6g, Protein: 21g, Fiber: 1g

216. Anti-Inflammatory Buddha Bowl

Prep Time: 10-minutes | Total time: 40-minutes | Yield: 4-servings

Ingredients:

2 lbs. cauliflower florets, stems removed	1 tbsp. plus one tsp. extra-virgin olive oil, divided
1 tsp. turmeric	Salt and pepper
10 oz. kale, chopped	1 clove garlic, minced
8 medium beets, cooked, peeled, and chopped	2 avocados, cubed
2 c. fresh blueberries	1/3 c. raw walnuts, chopped

Directions:

Preheat the oven to 425°F. Cover a baking tray using foil and spray the foil with either coconut or olive oil. Toss the cut cauliflower with 1 tbsp of olive oil and turmeric. Arrange it on the prepared baking tray. Season with salt and pepper and transfer the tray to the oven. Bake for about 30-minutes.

When the cauliflower is almost done, heat 1 tsp. of olive oil in a large skillet. Add the kale and cook until it starts to wilt, then add the garlic.

When the cauliflower and kale are done, assemble the bowls. Start with kale, then top with cauliflower, beets, avocado, blueberries, and walnuts.

Serve, and enjoy!

Nutritional Information: Calories 450, fat 27 g, carbs 49 g, protein 13 g

217. Simply Sautéed Flaky Fillet

Prep Time: 2-minutes | Total time: 10-minutes | Yield: 6-servings

Ingredients:

6-fillets tilapia	2-Tbsp.s olive oil
1-pc lemon, juice	Salt and pepper to taste
¼-c. parsley or cilantro, chopped	

Directions:

Sauté tilapia fillets with olive oil in a medium-sized skillet placed over medium heat. Cook for 4-minutes on each side until the fish flakes easily with a fork. Add salt and pepper to taste. Pour the lemon juice into each fillet. To serve, sprinkle the cooked fillets with chopped parsley or cilantro.

Nutritional Information: Calories: 249 Cal Fat: 8.3 g Protein: 18.6 g Carbs: 25.9 g Fiber: 1 g

218. Curried Beef Meatballs

Prep Time: 4-minutes | Total time: 26-minutes | Yield: 6-servings

Ingredients:

For Meatballs:

1 lb. lean ground beef	2 organic eggs, beaten
3 tbsps. red onion, minced	¼ c. fresh basil leaves, chopped
The 1-inch fresh ginger piece, chopped finely	4 garlic cloves, chopped finely
3 Thai bird's eye chilies, minced	1 tsp. coconut sugar
1 tbsp. red curry paste	Salt, to taste
1 tbsp. fish sauce	2 tbsps. coconut oil

For Curry:

1 red onion, chopped	Salt, to taste
4 garlic cloves, minced	The 1-inch fresh ginger piece, minced
2 Thai bird's eye chilies, minced	2 tbsps. red curry paste
14 oz. coconut milk	Freshly ground black pepper & salt, to taste
Lime wedges	

Directions:

In a large bowl, add each and every ingredient except oil and mix till well combined. Make small balls from the mixture. In a large skillet, melt the coconut oil on medium heat. Add meatballs and cook for about 3-5-minutes or till golden brown on all sides. Transfer the meatballs right into a bowl. In the same skillet, add onion and a pinch of salt and sauté for around 5-minutes.

Add garlic, ginger, and chilies, and sauté for about 1 minute. Add curry paste and sauté for around 1 minute. Add coconut milk and meatballs and convey to some gentle simmer. Reduce the warmth to low and simmer, covered for around 10-minutes. Serve using the topping of lime wedges.

Nutritional Information: Calories 444 Total Fat 15g Carbs 20g Protein 37g Fiber 2

219. Raisin Bran Muffins

Prep Time: 15-minutes | Total time: 45-minutes | Yield: 36-servings

Ingredients:

1 c. boiling water	2½ c. All-Bran cereal
2½ c. all-purpose flour	2½ tsps. baking soda
1 tsp. salt	½ c. vegetable oil
1 c. sugar	2 eggs, beaten
2 c. buttermilk	1½ c. raisins
1 c. bran flakes	

Directions:

Set the oven to 400°F. Grease a muffin tin. Put the boiling water over 1 cup All-Bran, and let sit for 10-minutes. Place the baking soda, flour, and salt in a mixing bowl, then mix, set aside. Stir the oil into the bran and water mixture, then put the remaining bran, sugar, eggs, and buttermilk. Put the flour mixture into the bran mixture and mix to combine. Stir in the raisins, bran flakes, then fill the muffin c. ¾ full with the batter. Bake muffins for 20-minutes.

Nutritional Information: Calories: 104 | Fat: 4 g | Protein: 2.5 g | Sodium: 187 mg | Fiber: 2 g | Carbs: 17 g

220. Pumpkin Spiced Almonds

Prep Time: 5-minutes | Total time: 30-minutes | Yield: 4-servings

Ingredients:

1 tbsp. olive oil	1 ¼ tsp. pumpkin pie spice
Pinch salt	1 c. whole almonds, raw

Direction:

Preheat the oven to 300 ° F and then line a parchment baking sheet.

In a mixing bowl, whisk together the olive oil, pumpkin pie spice, and salt.

Toss in the almonds until coated evenly, then scatter onto the baking sheet.

Bake and place in an airtight container for 25-minutes, then cool down completely.

Nutritional Information: Calories: 170 | Fats: 15 | Protein: 5 | Carbohydrates: 3

221. Leek and Chard Frittata

Prep Time: 5-minutes | Total time: 40-minutes | Yield: 5-servings

Ingredients:

1 tbsp. olive or avocado oil, more as needed	1 leek, finely chopped
1 ½ c. potatoes, diced	1 c. chard, chopped
1 tsp. fine sea salt, divided	1 clove garlic, minced
½ c. cherry tomatoes	10 large eggs
½ tsp. black pepper	½ tsp. paprika
½ tsp. turmeric	

Directions:

Preheat the oven to 375°F. Heat the oil in an ovenproof skillet. When it is hot, cook the leeks for 1–2-minutes, and then add the potatoes and cook 5 more-minutes. Add the chard into the skillet, and then cook until it is soft. Sprinkle with half of the salt and add the garlic and tomatoes. Whisk together the eggs, remaining salt, pepper, paprika, and turmeric, and pour the mixture into the skillet. Move the skillet to the oven and bake for about 25-minutes, or until set.

Nutritional Information: Calories 224, fat 12 g, carbs 13 g, protein 14 g, sodium 684 mg

222. Chickpea Stuffed Butternut Squash

Prep Time: 10-minutes | Total time: 1-hour 25-minutes | Yield: 4-servings

Ingredients:

For the squash:

2 small butternut squashes, cut in half lengthwise and seeds removed	2 ½ tbsps. olive oil
1 ¼ c. fresh corn kernels	

For the filling:

1 c. quinoa, cooked inside 2 cups of water or vegetable broth	1 (14 oz.) can chickpeas, drained
¼ c. red onion, diced	1 c. roasted red peppers, diced
½ c. fresh parsley, chopped	¾ c. pine nuts
1/3 c. olive oil	¼ c. apple cider vinegar
Salt and freshly ground black pepper	½ c. shredded Gruyère cheese

Directions:

Preheat the oven to 400°F. Line 2 baking trays using aluminum foil and spray with non-stick cooking spray. Rub the squash halves with some olive oil, and season them with salt and pepper. Arrange the squash (cut side down) on one of the prepared trays. Bake until the squash just begins to get tender (about 20–25-minutes). Spread the corn kernels on the other baking tray and drizzle them with the remaining olive oil. Bake for 8–10-minutes, or until the corn starts to brown.

Prepare the filling. Place the cooked quinoa in a mixing bowl and toss the roasted corn, chickpeas, red onion, red peppers, parsley, and pine nuts.

In a bowl, combine together the olive oil and apple cider vinegar. Season using salt & pepper to taste, and add it to the corn and chickpea mixture. Stir so that everything is well covered with the dressing.

Fill each squash half with some fillings, sprinkle with shredded cheese, and place it back in the oven. Cook until your cheese melts.

Nutritional Information: Calories 201, fat 9 g, carbs 29 g, protein 3 g, sodium 110 mg

223. Cabbage Orange Salad with Citrusy Vinaigrette

Prep Time: 10-minutes | Total time: 10-minutes | Yield: 8-servings

Ingredients:

1 tsp. orange zest, grated	2 tbsps. vegetable stock, reduced-sodium
1 tsp. each cider vinegar	4 c. red cabbage, shredded
1 tsp. lemon juice	1 fennel bulb, sliced thinly
1 tsp. balsamic vinegar	1 tsp. raspberry vinegar
2 tbsps. fresh orange juice	2 oranges, peeled, cut into pieces
1 tbsp. of honey	1/4 tsp. salt
Freshly ground pepper	4 tsp. olive oil

Directions:

Put lemon juice, orange zest, cider vinegar, salt and pepper, broth, oil, honey, orange juice, balsamic vinegar, and raspberry in a bowl and whisk.

Extract the oranges, fennel, and cabbage. Toss to coat.

Nutritional Information: Calories 70 Carbs: 14g Fat: 0g Protein: 1g

224. Grapefruit-Pomegranate Salad

Prep Time: 10-minutes | Total time: 10-minutes | Yield: 6-servings

Ingredients:

2 ruby red grapefruits	3 oz. Parmesan cheese
1 pomegranate	6 c. mesclun leaves
¼ c. Basic Vegetable Stock	

Directions:

Peel the grapefruit using a knife, take off all the pith. (The white layer under the skin). Cut out every section with the knife, ensure that no pith remains. Shave Parmesan using a vegetable peeler to form curls. Peel the pomegranate using a paring knife; take off the berries/seeds. Toss the mesclun greens in the stock.

To serve, mound the greens on plates and arrange the grapefruit sections, cheese, and pomegranate on top.

Nutritional Information: Calories: 84 | Fat: 2 g | Protein: 4 g | Sodium: 102 mg | Fiber: 2 g | Carbs: 14 g

225. Fried Coconut Shrimp with Asparagus

Prep Time: 15-minutes | Total time: 25-minutes | Yield: 6-servings

Ingredients:

1 ½ c. shredded unsweetened coconut	2 large eggs
Salt and pepper	1 ½ lbs. large shrimp, peeled and deveined
½ c. canned coconut milk	1 lb. asparagus, cut into 2-inch pieces

Directions:

Pour the coconut onto a shallow platter. Beat the eggs using a little salt and pepper. Dip the shrimp into the egg first, then dredge with coconut. Heat up coconut oil over medium-high heat in a large skillet. Add the shrimp and fry over each side for 1 to 2-minutes until browned. Remove the paper towels from the shrimp and heat the skillet again. Remove the asparagus and sauté to tender-crisp with salt and pepper, then serve with the shrimp.

Nutritional Information: Calories: 535 | Fats: 38 | Protein: 16 | Carbohydrates: 3

226. Honey Ginger Shrimp Bowls

Prep Time: 20-minutes | Total time: 26-minutes | Yield: 2-servings

Ingredients:
For the shrimp:

2 tbsps. honey	2 tbsps. coconut aminos or soy sauce
1 tsp. fresh ginger, minced	2 cloves garlic, minced
12 oz. large uncooked shrimp, peeled and deveined	2 tsp. avocado oil
Lime, sea salt, and pepper	

For the salad:

4 c. greens of your choice	½ c. shredded carrots
½ c. shredded radishes	4 green onions, sliced
¼ c. cilantro, chopped	1 avocado, sliced

For the dressing:

2 tbsps. lime juice	2 tbsps. extra-virgin olive oil

2 tsp. coconut aminos	1 tbsp. honey
1 clove garlic, minced	½ tsp. ginger powder
Sea salt and pepper to taste	

Directions:

Combine the honey, coconut aminos (or soy sauce), ginger, and garlic as listed under shrimp ingredients in a bowl. Set your shrimp in a resealable bag and add the marinade mixture. Manipulate the bag to make sure all the shrimp are covered. Refrigerate while you are preparing the salad and dressing. Over medium-high heat, heat the avocado oil inside a skillet. Add in marinade and shrimp and cook for 3-minutes. Flip the shrimp and cook for additional 3-minutes. Season with salt, lime juice, and pepper. Prepare salad in a bowl by mixing the salad ingredients. Divide the salad into 2-servings, and top each with half the shrimp. Prepare your dressing by mixing all dressing ingredients.

Top the salad with dressing, and serve.

Nutritional Information: Calories 516, fat 32 g, carbs 47 g, protein 12 g, sodium 636 mg

227. Coconut Chicken Curry with Cauliflower Rice

Prep Time: 15-minutes | Total time: 45-minutes | Yield: 6-servings

Ingredients:

1 tbsp. olive oil	1 medium yellow onion, chopped
1 ½ lbs. boneless chicken thighs, chopped	Salt and pepper
1 (14 oz.) can coconut milk	1 tbsp. curry powder
1 ¼ tsp. ground turmeric	3 c. riced cauliflower

Directions:

Heat the oil over medium-heat in a large skillet.

Add the onions, and cook for about 5-minutes, until translucent.

Stir in chicken and pat with pepper and salt to season. Cook for 8-minutes, stirring frequently until all sides are browned.

Pour coconut milk into your pan, then whisk in the curry and turmeric powder.

Simmer until hot and bubbling, for 15 to 20-minutes.

Meanwhile, steam the cauliflower rice until tender with a few tbsp of water.

Serve the cauliflower rice over the curry.

Nutritional Information: Calories: 430 |Fats: 29 |Protein: 9 |Carbohydrates: 3

228. Potato Mash

Prep Time: 15-minutes | Total time: 35-minutes | Yield: 32-servings

Ingredients:

10 large baking potatoes, peeled and cubed	3 tbsps. olive oil, divided
1 onion, chopped	1 tbsp. ground turmeric
½ tsp. ground cumin	Freshly ground black pepper & salt, to taste

Directions:

In a large pan of water, add potatoes and bring to a boil on medium-high heat. Cook for about 20-minutes. Drain and set into a bowl. With a potato masher, mash the potatoes. Meanwhile, in a skillet, heat 1 tbsp. of oil on medium-high heat. Add onion and sauté for about 6-minutes. Add onion mixture into the bowl with mashed potatoes. Add turmeric, cumin, salt, and black pepper and mash till well combined. Stir in remaining oil and serve.

Nutritional Information: Calories: 103 Sat Fat: 2g Carbs: 23g Fiber: 2g Sugar: 1g Protein: 8g

229. Spicy Chicken and Cauliflower

Prep Time: 5-minutes | Total time: 30-minutes | Yield: 4-servings

Ingredients:

2 lbs. chicken breasts, skinless, boneless, and cubed	1 tbsp. rice vinegar
4 tbsps. raw honey	6 tbsps. coconut aminos
2 garlic cloves, minced	2 lbs. cauliflower, florets separated
½ c. of water	1 tbsp. whole wheat flour
2 tbsps. olive oil	3 green onions, chopped
2 tbsps. sesame seeds	

Directions:

In a bowl, mix 3 tbsps. honey with 3 tbsps. coconut aminos, garlic, vinegar, and chicken. Heat a pan with ½ of the oil over medium heat, add cauliflower, stir, then cook for 5-minutes and set in a bowl. Heat the pan with the rest of the oil over medium heat, Drain the chicken, reserve the marinade, then add it to the pan. Toss and cook for 6-minutes. In a separate bowl, whisk together the rest of the amino with the remaining honey, water, whole wheat flour, and the reserved marinade. Add over the chicken, cover the pan and cook on low heat for 10-minutes, take off the heat, add the cauliflower and toss. Divide between plates, sprinkle green onions and sesame seeds on top, and serve. Enjoy!

Nutritional Information: Calories 250 Total Fat 4g Carbs 10g Protein 12g

230. Lemony Trout

Prep Time: ten-minutes | Total time: 30-minutes | Yield: 2-servings

Ingredients:

1 lemon	1 tsp. rosemary
2 garlic cloves	2 tbsp. capers
5 oz. trout fillets	5 tbsp. ghee butter
Salt and pepper to taste	

Directions:

Preheat your oven to 400F. Peel the lemon, mince the garlic cloves, and cut the capers. Flavor the trout fillets with salt, rosemary, and pepper. Grease a baking dish with the oil and put the fish onto it. Warm the butter in a frying pan on moderate heat. Put in the garlic and cook for 4-5-minutes until golden. Turn off the heat, put in the lemon zest and 2 tbsps. of lemon juice, stir thoroughly. Pour the lemon-butter sauce over the fish. Then top with the capers. Bake for 14-fifteen-minutes. Serve hot

Nutritional Information: Carbohydrates: 3,1 g , Fat: 25 g , Protein: 15,8 g , Calories: 302

231. Lime Cod Mix

Prep Time: 10-minutes | Total time: 25-minutes | Yield: 4-servings

Ingredients:

½ c. chicken stock	½ tsp. cumin, ground
1 tbsp. olive oil	2 tbsps. lime juice
2 tsp. lime zest, grated	3 tbsps. cilantro, chopped
4 cod fillets, boneless	A pinch of salt and black pepper

Directions:

Set the instant-pot on sauté mode, put oil, heats it, put it in the cod, and cook for a minute on each side. Put in the rest of the ingredients, put the lid on, and cook on High for 13-minutes. Release the pressure naturally for around ten-minutes, split the mix between plates before you serve.

Nutritional Information: Calories 187, Fat: 13.1, Fiber: 0.2, Carbohydrates: 1.6, Protein: 16.1

232. Bake Chicken Top-up with Olives, Tomatoes, And Basil

Prep Time: 10-minutes | Total time: 55-minutes | Yield: 4-servings

Ingredients:

8 Chicken thighs	Small Italian tomatoes
1tbsp Black pepper & salt	1tbsp Olive oil
15 Basil leaves (large)	Small black olives
1-2 Fresh red chili flakes	

Directions:

Marinate chicken pieces with all spices & olive oil and leave it for some time. Assemble chicken pieces in a rimmed pan with top-up with tomatoes, basil leaves, olives, and chili flakes. Bake this chicken in an already preheated oven (at 220C) for 40-minutes. Bake until the chicken is tender, tomatoes, basil, and olives are cooked. Garnish it with fresh parsley and lemon zest.

Nutritional Information: Calories 304 Carbs: 18g Fat: 7g Protein: 41g

233. Italian Calamari

Prep Time: 10-minutes | Total time: 40-minutes | Yield: 6-servings

Ingredients:

15 oz. canned tomatoes, chopped	1 ½ lbs. calamari, cleaned, tentacles separated and cut into thin strips
1 garlic clove, minced	½ c. veggie stock
1 bunch chopped parsley	A pinch of red pepper flakes
Juice of lemon	A drizzle of olive oil
A pinch of sea salt & black pepper	

Directions:

Add oil in a pan, and then heat over medium-high heat. Stir in pepper flakes and garlic and cook for 3-minutes. Add calamari, stir and cook for 3-minutes more. Add tomatoes, stock, lemon juice, salt, and pepper, bring to a simmer, then reduce heat to medium and cook for 25-minutes. Add the parsley, stir, divide into bowls and serve.

Nutritional Information: calories 228, fat 2, fiber 4, carbs 11, protein 39

234. Rosemary Roasted Pork with Cauliflower

Prep Time: 12-minutes | Total time: 32-minutes | Yield: 4-servings

Ingredients:

1 ½ lbs. boneless pork tenderloin	1 tbsp. coconut oil
1 tbsp. fresh chopped rosemary	Salt and pepper
1 tbsp. olive oil	2 c. cauliflower florets

Directions:

Rub the coconut oil into the pork, then season with rosemary, salt, and pepper. Heat up the olive oil over medium to high heat in a large skillet. Add the pork on each side and cook until browned for 2 to 3-minutes. Sprinkle the cauliflower over the pork in the skillet. Adjust to low heat, cover the skillet, and cook until the pork is cooked through for 8 to 10-minutes. Slice the pork with cauliflower and eat.

Nutritional Information: Calories: |320 Fats | 37 Protein: 3 |Carbohydrates: 1

235. Chili Snapper

Prep Time: 15-minutes | Total time: 35-minutes | Yield: 2-servings

Ingredients:

2 red snapper fillets, boneless and skinless	3 tbsps. chili paste
A pinch of sea salt	Black pepper
1 tbsp. coconut aminos	1 garlic clove, minced
½ tsp. freshly grated ginger	2 tsp. sesame seeds, toasted
2 tbsps. olive oil	1 green onion, chopped
2 tbsps. chicken stock	

Directions:

Warm a pan with the oil on medium-high heat, add the ginger, onion, and garlic, stir and cook for 2-minutes. Add chili paste, amino, salt, pepper, and the stock stir and cook for 3-minutes more. Add the fish fillets, toss gently, and cook for 5-6-minutes on each side.

Divide into plates, sprinkle sesame seeds on top, and serve.

Nutritional Information: Calories 261 |Fat: 10 g| Fiber: 7 g |Carbs: 15 g| Protein: 16 g

236. Kale Salad

Prep Time: 12-minutes | Total time: 42-minutes | Yield: 6-servings

Ingredients:

2 Tbsps. Apple Cider Vinegar	1 Tsp. Sea Salt, Fine
½ Tsp. Red Pepper Flakes	¼ Tsp. Black Pepper
2 Sweet Potatoes Small & Peeled	1 Leek, Small
1 Apple, Peeled	¼ C. Pine Nuts
1 Tbsp. Avocado Oil	3 Tbsps. Olive Oil
15 Oz. Kale, Stemmed & Chopped	

Directions:

Start by heating your oven to 350. Get the baking sheet, then line it with parchment paper. Combine your kale, olive oil, red pepper flakes, black pepper, and vinegar. Knead these spices and oil into your kale for a minute. Transfer three quarters of this mixture to your baking pan, spreading it out. Bake for twenty-minutes, tossing halfway through. Add it back to your remaining kale. Chop your leeks, sweet potatoes, and apple into bite sized pieces, and then throw your avocado oil in a skillet. Place your skillet over medium heat, cooking the mixture for ten-minutes. Your sweet potatoes should be soft. Remove the kale from the oven, and then top your sweet potato mixture with it and pine nuts. Mix well before serving.

Nutritional Information: Calories: 213 Protein: 5 Grams Fat: 14 Grams Carbs: 22 Grams

237. Healthy Chicken Marsala

Prep Time: 20-minutes | Total time: 50-minutes | Yield: 4-servings

Ingredients:

1-1/2 chicken breasts, boneless and skinless	2 tbsps. of dairy-free margarine
1/2 lb. shiitake mushrooms, sliced and stemmed	1 lb. baby Bella mushrooms, sliced and stemmed
2 tbsps. of extra virgin olive oil	3 cloves of garlic, chopped
1 c. shallot, chopped	2 c. of chicken broth, low-sodium
3/4 c. dry marsala wine	Black pepper, kosher salt, chopped parsley leaves

Directions:

Dry your chicken breasts using a paper towel. Slice them horizontally into half. Keep each piece between parchment paper. Use your meat mallet to pound until you have 1/4 inch thickness. Season all sides with black pepper and kosher salt. Dredge in some whole wheat flour. Keep aside. Heat your skillet over medium temperature. Pour olive oil and margarine into your pan. Sauté the chicken for 5-minutes. Work in batches, not overcrowding your pan. Transfer to a baking sheet. Set aside. Wipe off excess cooking fat from your pan. Bring back to heat. Add the remaining margarine and the mushrooms. Sauté over high temperature. Season with black pepper and salt. Add the garlic and chopped shallot to your pan. Sauté 3-minutes. Include the marsala wine. Bring down the heat for a minute. Include the chicken broth and cook for 5-minutes. Transfer chicken cutlets to the pan. Spoon over the sauce.

Garnish with parsley.

Nutritional information: Calories 546, Carbohydrates 41g, Cholesterol 31mg, Total Fat 38g , Protein 10g , Sugar 6g , Fiber 5g , Sodium 535mg

238. Sheet Pan Rosemary Mushrooms

Prep Time: 15-minutes | Total time: 30-minutes | Yield: 2-servings

Ingredients:

1 c. mushrooms	1 tsp. minced rosemary
½ tsp. of sea salt	1 tbsp. sesame oil

Directions:

Line the baking tray with baking paper. Slice the mushrooms roughly and put them in the baking tray. Sprinkle mushrooms with minced rosemary, sea salt, and sesame oil. Mix up the vegetables well with the help of the hand palms. Preheat the oven to 360°F. Cook mushrooms for 15-minutes.

Nutritional Information: Calories 70 Total Fat 7g Carbs 1.5g Protein 1.1g Fiber 4g

239. Clean Eating Egg Salad

Prep Time: 15-minutes | Total time: 15-minutes | Yield: 2-servings

Ingredients:

6 organic pasture-raised eggs, hard-boiled	1 avocado
¼ c. of Greek yogurt	2 tbsps. of olive oil mayonnaise
1 tsp. of fresh dill	Sea salt to taste
Lettuce for serving	

Directions:

Mash the hard-boiled eggs and avocado together. Add in the Greek yogurt, olive oil mayonnaise, and fresh dill. Season with sea salt. Serve on a bed of lettuce.

Nutritional Information: Carbohydrates 18g Dietary Fiber: 10g Protein: 23g Total Fat: 38g Calories: 486

240. Chicken Chili

Prep Time: 12-minutes | Total time: 42-minutes | Yield: 4-servings

Ingredients:

8 Oz. Can Green Chilies, Mild, Diced & With Liquid	4 C. White Beans, Cooked & Drained
4 C. Chicken Broth	4 Tsp. Cumin, Ground
1 Tsp. Chili Powder	2 Tsp. Oregano, Dried
4 C. Chicken, Shredded & Cooked	¼ Tsp. Cayenne Pepper
2 Scallions, Sliced	1 Tbsp. Ghee
6 Cloves Garlic, Minced	2 Onions, Small & Chopped
1 Tbsp. Ghee	

Directions:

Get out a soup pot, placing it over medium heat. Melt your ghee in it before adding your garlic and onion in. sauté for five-minutes, stirring well. Add in your chilies, cooking for another two-minutes. Remember to stir. Stir in your oregano, chili, cayenne, cumin, beans, and broth. Bring the mixture to a simmer. Add in your chicken, letting it come to a simmer again. Adjust to low medium, and cook for another ten-minutes. Top with scallions before serving warm.

Nutritional Information: Calories: 304 Protein: 21 Grams Fat: 4 Grams Carbs: 46 Grams

241. Air Fryer Salmon

Prep Time: 10minutes | Total time: 15-minutes | Yield: 2-servings

Ingredients:

1/3 lb. filets of salmon	1/4 c. of margarine
1/4 c. of pistachios, chopped finely	1-1/2 tbsps. of minced dill
2 tbsps. of lemon juice	

Directions:

Warm your air fryer to 400 degrees F. Spray olive oil on the basket. Season your salmon with pepper to taste. You can also apply all-purpose seasoning. Combine the margarine, lemon juice, and dill in a bowl. Pour a spoonful on the fillets. Top the fillets with chopped pistachios. Be generous. Spray olive oil on the salmon lightly. Air fry your fillets now for 5-minutes. Take out the salmon carefully with a spatula from your air fryer. Keep on a plate. Garnish with dill.

Nutritional information: Calories 305, Carbs 1g, Fat 21g, Protein 28g, Fiber 2g, Sugar 3g, Sodium 92mg

242. Carrot Bread

Prep Time: 12-minutes | Total time: 1 hour 12-minutes | Yield: 8-servings

Ingredients:

2 c. almond meal	1 tsp. organic baking powder
1 tbsp. cumin seeds	Salt, to taste
3 organic eggs	2 tbsps. macadamia nut oil
1 tbsp. apple cider vinegar	3 c. carrot, peeled and grated
½-inch piece of fresh-ginger (peeled & grated)	¼ c. sultanas

Directions:

Set the oven to 35 F, then line a loaf pan with parchment paper. Put together the almond meal, baking powder, cumin seeds, and salt and mix in a large bowl. In another bowl, add eggs, nut oil, and vinegar and beat till well combined. Put the egg mixture into the flour mixture and mix till well combined. Fold in the remaining ingredients. Place the mixture into the prepared loaf pan equally. Bake for about 1 hour.

Nutritional Information: Calories: 215 | Fat: 17.1g | Carbs:10.8g | Sugars: 3.9g | Protein: 7.6g

243. Simple Carrots Mix

Prep Time: 12-minutes | Total time: 52-minutes | Yield: 6-servings

Ingredients:

15 carrots, halved lengthwise	2 tbsps. coconut sugar
¼ c. extra virgin organic olive oil	½ tsp. rosemary, dried
½ tsp. garlic powder	A pinch of black pepper

Directions:

In a bowl, combine the carrots with the sugar, oil, rosemary, garlic powder, and black pepper, toss well, spread with a lined baking sheet, introduce in the oven and bake at 400 degrees F for 42-minutes. Divide it between plates, then serve as a side dish.

Nutritional Information: calories 211, fat 2, fiber 6, carbs 14, protein 8

244. Greek Turkey Burgers with Tzatziki

Prep Time: 22-minutes | Total time: 57-minutes | Yield: 4-servings

Ingredients:

Turkey Burgers	1 tbsp. extra-virgin olive oil
½ c. sweet onion, minced	2 cloves garlic, minced
1 egg	½ c. chopped fresh parsley
½ tsp. dried oregano	¼ tsp. red pepper flakes
1 lb. ground turkey	¾ c. breadcrumbs
black pepper (Salt and freshly ground) for taste	1 batch tzatziki sauce for serving
4 hamburger buns for serving	

Directions:

Preheat the oven to 375°F. In a small skillet over medium, heat oil and sauté the onions and garlic until soft. Set aside until they are cool. Once cooled, mix the aromatics together with the egg, parsley, oregano, red pepper flakes, and ground turkey. Stir in the breadcrumbs, season with salt and pepper, and mix gently until completely combined. Form the mixture into four patties.

Use a non-stick cooking spray to spray an ovenproof skillet with, then heat it over medium-high heat. Place the patties in the skillet, then sear them on both sides, about 2-minutes on each side. Transfer the skillet to the oven, then cook for about 15-minutes, or until the burgers are cooked through. While waiting for the burgers to cook, prepare the tzatziki sauce by mixing together all the ingredients. When burgers are done, top with tzatziki sauce and whatever other toppings you desire.

Nutritional Information: Calories 326, fat 14 g, carbs 22 g, protein 27 g, sodium 109

245. Roasted Summer Squash & Fennel Bulb

Prep Time: 22-minutes | Total time: 42-minutes | Yield: 4-servings

Ingredients:

2 small summer squash, cubed into 1-inch size	1½ c. fennel bulb, sliced
1 tbsp. fresh thyme, chopped	1 tbsp. extra-virgin olive oil
ground black pepper (Salt and freshly) to taste	¼ c. garlic, sliced thinly
1 tbsp. fennel fronds, chopped	

Directions:

Preheat the oven to 450-degrees F. Mix all of the ingredients in a large-bowl, except garlic and fennel fronds, and toss to coat well. Transfer the mixture into a large, rimmed baking sheet. Roast for about 10-minutes. Remove from oven and stir in the sliced garlic. Roast for 5-minutes more. Remove from oven and stir in the fennel fronds. Serve immediately.

Nutritional Information: Calories: 66 Fat: 4g Sat Fat: 1g Carbs: 8g Fiber: 2g Sugar: 0g Protein: 2g

246. Grilled Avocado Sandwich

Prep Time: 12-minutes | Total time: 27-minutes | Yield: 4-servings

Ingredients:

8 slices of pumpernickel bread	1 c. sauerkraut, drained and rinsed
1 c. hummus	1 tsp. dairy-free margarine
1 avocado sliced into 16 pieces	

Directions:

Preheat your oven to 450 degrees F. Apply margarine on one side of your bread slices. Keep 4 slices on your baking sheet. The margarine side should be down. Distribute half of the hummus over the bread slices. Place sauerkraut on the hummus. Keep avocado slices over your sauerkraut. Spread hummus on the remaining slices. Keep the hummus side down on your slices of avocado. Bake for 7-minutes. Set over and bake for another 6-minutes.

Nutritional information: Calories 340, Carbs 39g, T Fat 16g, Protein 10g, Fiber 11g, Sugar 1g

247. Crispy Cheese-Crusted Fish Fillet

Prep Time: 5-minutes | Total time: 15-minutes | Yield: 4-servings

Ingredients:

¼-c.whole-wheat bread-crumbs	¼-c.Parmesan cheese, grated
¼-tsp sea salt	¼-tsp ground pepper
1 tbsp. olive oil	4-pcs tilapia fillets

Directions:

Preheat the oven to 375°F. In a mixing bowl, stir in the breadcrumbs, Parmesan cheese, salt, pepper, and olive oil. Mix well until blended thoroughly. Coat the fillets with the mixture, and lay each on a lightly sprayed baking sheet. Place the sheet in the oven. Bake for 10-minutes until the fillets cook through and turn brownish.

Nutritional Information: Calories: 255 Fat: 7g Protein: 15.9g Carbs: 34g Fiber: 2.6g

248. Mango & Avocado Salad

Prep Time: 12-minutes | Total time: 22-minutes | Yield: 2-servings

Ingredients:

1 Romaine Lettuce Heart, Chopped	¼ C. Dressing
¼ C. Almonds, Toasted	1 Tbsp. Chives, Fresh & Chopped
1 Avocado, Peeled, Pitted & Sliced	1 Mango, Sliced

Directions:

Divide your lettuce between bowls, topping with mango and avocado. Sprinkle with chives, and drizzle with the salad dressing of your choice. Top with almonds before serving.

Nutritional Information: Calories: 500 Protein: 8 Grams Fat: 39 Grams Carbs: 40 Grams

249. Salmon and Sweet Potato Mix

Prep Time: 10-minutes | Total time: 10 minutes | Yield: 4-servings

Ingredients:

1½ lbs. sweet potatoes, baked and cubed	1 tbsp. olive oil
4 oz. smoked salmon, chopped	1 tbsp. chopped chives
2 tsp. horseradish	¼ c. coconut cream
Salt and black pepper to the taste	

Directions:

In a bowl, whisk together the coconut cream with salt, pepper, horseradish, and chives. Add salmon and potatoes, toss to coat, and serve right away.

Nutritional Information: Calories 233 Total Fat 6g Carbs 37g Protein 9g Fiber 5g

250. Cornmeal Grits

Prep Time: 5-minutes | Total time: 20-minutes | Yield: 4-servings

Ingredients:

4 c. water	1 tsp. salt
1 c. polenta meal	2 tbsps. butter

Directions:

Put water and salt in a saucepan, then place it to a boil. Gradually add polenta and constantly stir over medium-low heat until it has thickened, about 15-minutes. Stir in butter. Serve immediately for soft grits or pour into a greased loaf pan and let cool. Once cool, grits can be sliced and fried, or grilled.

Nutritional Information: Calories: 177 | Fat: 6 g | Protein: 3 g | Sodium: 641 mg | Fiber: 2.5 g | Carbs: 27 g

251. Lemon Buttery Shrimp Rice

Prep Time: 13-minutes | Total time: 23-minutes | Yield: 3-servings

Ingredients:

¼ c. cooked wild rice	½ tsp. Butter divided
¼ tsp. olive oil	1 c. raw shrimps, shelled, deveined, drained
¼ c. frozen peas, thawed, rinsed, drained	1 Tbsp. lemon juice, freshly squeezed
1 Tbsp. chives, minced	Pinch of sea salt, to taste

Directions:

Pour ¼ tsp. Butter and oil into wok set over medium heat. Add in shrimps and peas. Sauté until shrimps are coral pink, about 5 to 7-minutes. Add in wild rice and cook until well heated season with salt and butter. Transfer to a plate. Sprinkle chives and lemon juice on top. Serve.

Nutritional Information: Calories 510 Carbs: 36g Sat Fat: 2g Protein: 40g

252. Spicy Ramen Soup

Prep Time: 15-minutes | Total time: 30-minutes | Yield: 4-servings

Ingredients:

2 Tbsps. Sesame Seeds	8 Oz. Rice Noodles, Cooked
¼ C. Cucumber, Sliced Thin	¼ C. Scallion, Sliced
¼ C. Cilantro, Fresh & chopped	2 Tbsps. Sesame Oil
1 Tbsp. Coconut Aminos	1 Tbsp. Ginger, Fresh, Grated & Peeled
2 Tbsps. Rice vinegar	1 Tbsps. Honey, Raw
1 Tbsp. Lime Juice, Fresh	1 Tsp. Chili Powder

Directions:

Mix your sesame seeds, cucumber, scallion, noodles, cilantro, sesame oil, ginger, coconut aminos, vinegar, honey, chili powder, and lime juice together.

Dive amount four soup bowls and serve at room temperature.

Nutritional Information: Calories: 663 Protein: 21 Grams Fat: 28 Grams Carbs: 115 Grams

253. Ratatouille

Prep Time: 10-minutes | Total time: 25-minutes | Yield: 4-servings

Ingredients:

1 c. Water	3 tbsp. Olive oil
2 Zucchinis, sliced in rings	2 Eggplants, sliced in rings
3 large Tomatoes, sliced in thick rings	1 medium Red-Onion (sliced in thin-rings)
3 cloves Garlic, minced	2 sprigs Fresh Thyme
Salt to taste	Black Pepper to taste
4 tsp Plain Vinegar	

Directions:

Place all veggies in a bowl, sprinkle with salt and pepper, toss. Line foil in a springform tin and arrange 1 slice each of the vegetables in, one after the other, in a tight circular arrangement. Fill the entire tin. Sprinkle the garlic over, some more black pepper and salt, and arrange the thyme sprigs on top. Drizzle olive oil and vinegar over the veggies. Place a trivet to fit in the Instant Pot, pour the water in, and place the veggies on the trivet. Seal the lid, secure the pressure valve, and select Manual mode on High Pressure for 6-minutes. Once ready, quickly release the pressure. Carefully remove the tin and serve ratatouille.

Nutritional Information: Calories 152, |Protein 2g, |Net Carbs 4g, |Fat 12g

254. Gingered Cauliflower Rice

Prep Time: 15-minutes | Total time: 25-minutes | Yield: 3-4-servings

Ingredients:

3 tbsps. coconut oil	4 (1/8-inch thick) fresh ginger slices
1 small head cauliflower, trimmed and processed into a rice consistency	3 garlic cloves, crushed
1 tbsp. chives, chopped	1 tbsp. coconut vinegar
Salt, to taste	

Directions:

In a skillet, melt coconut oil on medium-high heat. Add ginger and sauté for about 2-3-minutes. Discard the ginger slices and stir in cauliflower and garlic. Cook, occasionally stirring for about 7-8 min. Stir in remaining ingredients and remove from heat.

Nutritional Information: Calories: 111 Protein: 1.48 g Fat: 10.42 g Carbohydrates: 4.49 g

255. Capellini Soup with Tofu and Shrimp

Prep Time: 11minutes | Total time: 31-minutes | Yield: 8-servings

Ingredients:

4 c. of bok choy, sliced	1/4 lb. shrimp, peeled, deveined
1 block firm tofu, sliced into squares	1 can sliced water chestnuts, drained
1 bunch scallions, sliced	2 c. reduced-sodium chicken broth
2 tsp. soy sauce, reduced-sodium	2 c. capellini
2 tsp. of sesame oil	Freshly ground white pepper
1 tsp. of rice wine vinegar	

Directions:

Pour the broth in a saucepan over medium-high heat. Bring to a boil. Add the shrimp, bok choy, oil, and sauce. Allow to boil and turn the heat to low. Simmer for 5-minutes. Add the water chestnuts, pepper, vinegar, tofu, capellini, and scallions. Cook for 5-minutes or until the capellini is barely tender. Serve while hot.

Nutritional Information: Calories 205 Carbs: 20g Fat: 9g Protein: 9g

256. Beef and Broccoli Stir-Fry

Prep Time: 22-minutes | Total time: 37-minutes | Yield: 4-servings

Ingredients:

¼ c. soy sauce	1 tbsp. sesame oil

1 tsp. garlic chili paste	1 lb. beef sirloin
2 tbsps. almond flour	2 tbsps. coconut oil
2 c. chopped broccoli florets	1 tbsp. grated ginger
3 cloves garlic, minced	

Directions:
Whisk the soy sauce in a small bowl, sesame oil, and chili paste together. In a plastic freezer bag, slice the beef and mix with the almond flour. Pour in the sauce and toss to coat for 20-minutes, then let rest. Heat up the oil over medium to high heat in a large skillet. In the pan, add the beef and sauce and cook until the beef is browned. Move the beef to the skillet sides, then add the broccoli, ginger, and garlic. Sauté until tender-crisp broccoli, then throw it all together and serve hot.

Nutritional Information: Calories: 350 |Fats: 19 |Protein: 37 |Carbohydrates: 6

257. Herb Butter Scallops
Prep Time: 20-minutes | Total time: 30minutes | Yield: 3-servings

Ingredients:

1 lb. sea scallops, cleaned	Freshly ground black pepper
8 tbsps. butter, divided	2 tsp. minced garlic
Juice of 1 lemon	2 tsp. chopped fresh basil
1 tsp. chopped fresh thyme	

Directions:
Pat the scallops dry using paper towels and season them lightly with pepper. Over medium heat, place a large skillet and add 2 tbsp of butter. Arrange the scallops in the skillet, evenly spaced but not too close together, and sear each side until they turn golden brown, about 2½-minutes per side.Remove the scallops to a plate and set them aside. Add the remaining 6 tbsps. of butter to the skillet and sauté the garlic until translucent, about 3-minutes. Stir in the lemon juice, basil, and thyme and return the scallops to the skillet, turning to coat them in the sauce.
Serve immediately.

Nutritional Information: Calories: 306 |Fat: 24g |Protein: 19g |carbohydrates: 4g |Fiber: 0g

258. Sweetened Brown Rice
Prep Time: 10-minutes | 55 - 70-minutes | Yield: 8-servings

Ingredients:

1½ c. soy milk	1½ c. water
1 c. brown rice	1 tbsp. honey

¼ tsp. nutmeg	Fresh fruit (optional)

Directions:
Put all the ingredients, excluding the fresh fruit, in a medium-size saucepan; place the mixture to a slow simmer, then cover using a tight-fitting lid.
Simmer for at least 45-60-minutes, up to the rice is tender and done. Serve in bowls, topped with your favorite fresh fruit.

Nutritional Information: Calories: 155 |Fat: 1.5 g Protein: 3.5 g |Sodium: 35 mg |Fiber: 1.5 g |Carbs: 13 g

259. Whitefish Curry
Prep Time: 12-minutes | Total time: 27minutes | Yield: 6-servings

Ingredients:

1 chopped onion	1 lb. Firm white fish fillets
¼ c. chopped fresh cilantro	1 c. vegetable broth
2 minced garlic cloves	1 tbsp. Minced fresh ginger
1 tsp. Salt	¼ tsp. ground black pepper
Lemon wedges	1 bruised lemongrass
2 c. cubed butternut squash	2 tsp. curry powder
2 tbsps. coconut oil	2 c. chopped broccoli
oz. coconut milk	1 thinly sliced scallion

Directions:
In a pot, add coconut oil and melt. Add onion, curry powder, ginger, garlic, and seasonings, then sauté for 5-minutes. Add broccoli, lemongrass and butternut squash and sauté for two more-minutes. Stir in broth and coconut milk and bring to a boil. Lower the heat to simmer and add the fish. Cover the pot, then simmer for 5-minutes, then discard the lemongrass. Spoon the curry into a medium serving bowl. Add scallion and cilantro to garnish before serving with lemon wedges.

Nutritional Information: Calories: 218 |Protein: 18.1 g|Fat: 8.57 g |Carbohydrates: 18.2 g

260. Creamy Queso Dip
Prep Time: 17-minutes | Total time: 22-minutes | Yield: 8-servings

Ingredients:

4 oz. chorizo, crumbled	1 minced clove garlic
¼ c. heavy cream	6 oz. white cheddar cheese, shredded
2 oz. pepper jack cheese, shredded	¼ tsp. xanthan gum
Pinch salt	1 seeded jalapeno, minced
1 diced tomato	

Directions:
Using a skillet, let your chorizo cook until browned evenly, then scatter in a dish. At medium-low, pressure the skillet and add in the garlic and let cook for a further 30 seconds. Add in heavy cream and cheese as you stir until the cheese melts. Apply sprinkles of salt and xanthan gum, then mix thoroughly and cook until well thickened. Add jalapeno and tomato. Stir well, then serve, dipping with vegetables.
Nutritional Information: Calories: 195 | Fats: 16 | Protein: 12 | Carbohydrates: 1

---

261. Popcorn Chicken

Prep Time: 17-minutes | Total time: 27-minutes | Yield: 4-servings

Ingredients:

1/5 lb. chicken breast halves, boneless and skinless	1/2 tsp. paprika
1/4 tsp. mustard, ground	1/4 tsp. of garlic powder
3 tbsps. of arrowroot	

Directions:
Divide the chicken into small pieces and keep it in a bowl. Combine the paprika, garlic powder, mustard, salt, and pepper in another bowl. Reserve a tsp. of your seasoning mixture. Sprinkle the other portion on the chicken. Coat evenly by tossing. Combine the reserved seasoning and arrowroot in a plastic bag. Combine well by shaking. Keep your chicken pieces in the bag. Seal it and shake for coating evenly. Now transfer the chicken to a mesh strainer. Shake the excess arrowroot. Keep aside for 5-10-minutes. The arrowroot should start to get absorbed into your chicken. Warm your air fryer to 390 degrees F. Apply some oil to the air fryer basket. Keep the chicken pieces inside. They should not overlap. Apply cooking spray. Cook until the chicken isn't pink anymore.
Nutritional information: Calories 156, Carbs 6g, Total Fat 4g, Protein 24g, Sugar 0g, Fiber 1g

---

262. Chicken & Cabbage Platter

Prep Time: 9-minutes | Total time: 23-minutes | Yield: 2-servings

Ingredients:

½ c. onion, sliced	1 tbsp. sesame garlic-flavored oil
2 c. Bok-Choy/Spinach, shredded	1/2 c. fresh bean sprouts
1½ stalks celery, chopped	1½ tsp. garlic, minced
1/2 tsp. stevia	1/2 c. chicken broth
1 tbsp. coconut aminos	1/2 tbsp. freshly minced ginger
2 boneless chicken breast salt, to taste	pepper, to taste

Directions:
Cut chicken breasts into pieces, season with salt and pepper. Fry it in the pan with garlic. Add chicken broth and sauté for a while. Shred the cabbage with a knife. Add onion, bean sprouts, celery, and sauté it until tender. Add stevia, coconut aminos, and ginger. Season with salt and pepper in preference to your taste.
Place the braised cabbage on your platter alongside the rotisserie chicken.
Nutritional Information: Calories: 368 | Fat: 18g | Net Carbohydrates: 8g | Protein: 42g | Fiber: 3g |

---

263. Irish Style Clams

Prep Time: five-minutes | Total time: 20-minutes | Yield: 4-servings

Ingredients:

1 bottle infused cider	1 small green apple; chopped.
1 tbsp. olive oil	2 garlic cloves; minced
2 lbs. clams; scrubbed	2 thyme springs; chopped.
3 oz. pancetta	3 tbsps. ghee
Juice of ½ lemon	Salt and black pepper to the taste.

Directions:
Heat a pan with the oil on moderate to high heat; put in pancetta, brown for about three-minutes, and decrease the temperature to moderate. Put in ghee, garlic, salt, pepper, and shallot; stir and cook for about three-minutes. Raise the heat again, put in cider; stir thoroughly, and cook for a minute. Put in clams and thyme, cover the pan and simmer for five-minutes.
Discard unopened clams, put in lemon juice and apple pieces; stir and split into bowls. Serve hot.
Nutritional Information: Calories: 100, Fat: 2, Fiber: 1, Carbohydrates: 1, Protein: 20

---

264. Pepperoni Pizza Loaf

Prep Time: 22-minutes | Total time: 1 hour 2 min | Yield: 4-servings

Ingredients:

1 portion (1 lb.) solidified bread mixture, defrosted	2 enormous eggs, isolated
1 tbsp. ground Parmesan cheddar	1 tbsp. olive oil
1 tsp. minced crisp parsley	1 tsp. dried oregano
1/2 tsp. garlic powder	1/4 tsp. pepper

8 oz. cut pepperoni	2 c. destroyed part-skim mozzarella cheddar
1 can (4 oz.) mushroom stems and pieces, depleted	1/2 c. cured pepper rings
1 medium green pepper, diced	1 can (2-1/4 oz.) cut ready olives
1 can (15 oz.) pizza sauce	

Directions:

Preheat stove to 350°. On a lubed preparing sheet, turn out batter into a 15x10-in. square shape. Consolidate the egg yolks, Parmesan cheddar, oil, parsley, oregano, garlic powder, and pepper in a little bowl. Brush over the mixture. Sprinkle with pepperoni, mozzarella cheddar, mushrooms, pepper rings, green pepper, and olives. Move up, jam move style, beginning with a long side, squeeze crease to seal and fold finishes under. Position portion with crease side down; brush with egg whites. Try not to let rise. Prepare until brilliant dark colored and mixture are cooked through, 35-40-minutes. Warm the pizza sauce, present with cut portion.

Nutritional Information: Calories: 387, Protein: 18.15 g, Fat: 33.14 g, Carbohydrates: 2.79 g

265. Lemon Onion Mash

Prep Time: 17-minutes | Total time: 32-minutes | Yield: 4-servings

Ingredients:

2 white onions	4 oz. cauliflower
¼ c. heavy cream	4 oz. Cheddar cheese, shredded
½ tsp. Pink salt	1 tsp. white pepper
½ tsp. lemon zest	1 tsp. lemon juice
1 tsp. butter	

Directions:

Peel the onion and grind it. Put ground onion and butter in the saucepan. Blend cauliflower until you get cauliflower rice. Add cauliflower rice in the saucepan too. Add Pink salt, white pepper, lemon zest, and lemon juice. Stir it. Close the lid and cook the mass for 5-minutes over medium heat. Then add shredded Cheddar cheese and heavy cream. Mix up well and stir until cheese is melted. Close the lid and simmer mash for 5-minutes more over the low heat. Switch off the heat and close the lid. Let the lemon onion mash chill for 10-minutes.

Nutritional Information: Calories 171 Total Fat 13.5g Carb 6.5g Protein 8.1g Fiber 4g

266. Mackerel Bombs

Prep Time: 17-minutes | Total time: 27-minutes | Yield: 4-servings

Ingredients:

¼ c. spinach, chopped	½ tsp. thyme
1 egg, beaten	1 tsp. chili flakes
1 tsp. garlic, minced	1 tsp. mustard
1 tsp. salt	1 white onion, peeled and diced
1/3 c. almond flour	10 oz. mackerel, chopped
4 tbsp. coconut oil	

Directions:

Put mackerel in blender or food processor and pulse until texture is smooth. In a container, mix the onion with mackerel. Put in garlic, flour, egg, thyme, salt, and mustard, stir thoroughly. Put in chili flakes and mix up the mixture until you get a homogenous mass. Put in spinach and stir. Heat a pan at moderate heat, then put in oil. Shape fish mixture into bombs 1½ inch in diameter. Put bombs on a pan and cook for five-minutes on all sides. Move to paper towels and drain grease and serve.

Nutritional Information: Calories 318, Carbs: 3.45g, Fat: 26.5g, Protein: 20.1g

267. Salmon Cakes

Prep Time: 36 min | Total time: 1 hour 26 min | Yield: 5-servings

Ingredients:

½ lb. fresh salmon	1 tbsp. olive oil
Freshly ground black pepper and Kosher salt	¼ c. olive oil
¼ c. unsalted butter	1 red onion, diced small
3 stalks celery, diced small	1 small red bell pepper, diced small
1 small yellow bell pepper, diced small	¼ c. minced fresh flat-leaf parsley
1 tbsp. drained capers	½ tsp. hot sauce
½ tsp. Worcestershire sauce	1 tsp. Old Bay seasoning
3 slices stale bread, crusts removed	½ c. mayonnaise
1 tsp. mustard	2 eggs, lightly beaten

Directions:

Preheat your oven to 375°F. Use parchment paper to cover the baking tray and place the salmon skin side down on the paper. Brush it with olive oil and allow to bake for 15–20-minutes, or until it is just done. Cool for 10-minutes, then put it in the fridge until it has cooled completely. Over a medium high, heat half the olive oil and half the butter in a large skillet over medium high heat. Add the onion, celery, peppers, parsley, capers, hot sauce, Worcestershire, Old Bay, and salt and pepper to taste. Allow it to cook for about 15-minutes, or until the vegetables are soft. Remove it from the heat. Then let it cool. Lightly toast the bread and crumble it up. Using a fork, gently shred the cold salmon in a mixing bowl. Add the mayonnaise, mustard, and eggs. Then mix in the breadcrumbs and the cooled vegetables. Refrigerate the mixture for about 20-minutes, then shape it into patties. (It should make about 10 patties.) Heat the rest of the oil & butter in a large-skillet. When it is hot, add the patties and cook for approximately 3–4-minutes on each side until they are a nice golden brown. Take the cooked patties to a paper towel lined plate to drain.

Nutritional Information: Calories 503, fat 43 g, carbs 12 g, protein 17 g, sodium 458 mg

268. Zesty Zucchini & Chicken in Classic Santa Fe Stir-Fry

Prep Time: 15-minutes | Total time: 30-minutes | Yield: 2-servings

Ingredients:

1 tbsp. olive oil	2-pcs chicken breasts, sliced
1-pc onion, small, diced	2-cloves garlic, minced
1-pc zucchini, diced	½- c. carrots, shredded
1-tsp paprika, smoked	1-tsp cumin, ground
½-tsp chili powder	¼-tsp sea salt
2 tbsp. fresh lime juice	¼-c. cilantro, freshly chopped
Brown rice or quinoa, when serving	

Directions:

Sauté the chicken with olive oil for about 3-minutes until the chicken turns brown. Set aside. Use the same wok and add the onion and garlic. Cook until the onion is tender. Add in the carrots and zucchini. Stir the mixture, and cook further for about a minute. Add all the seasonings into the mix, and stir to cook for another minute. Return the chicken to the wok, and pour in the lime juice. Stir to cook until everything cooks through. To serve, place the mixture over cooked rice or quinoa and top with the freshly chopped cilantro.

Nutritional Information: Calories: 191 Fat: 5.3g Protein: 11.9g Carbs: 26.3g Fiber: 2.5g

269. Buttered Sprouts

Prep Time: 7-minutes | Total time: 27-minutes | Yield: 4-servings

Ingredients:

10 oz. Brussel sprouts	2 oz. prosciutto
3 tsp. butter	1 c. of water
1 tsp. salt	

Directions:

Chop prosciutto and place in the saucepan. Roast it until it starts to be crispy. Then add water and Brussel sprouts. Bring the mixture to a boil and close the lid. Boil the vegetables for 15-minutes. After this, drain ½ part of all liquid and add butter. Mix it until the butter is melted and bring the meal to boil one more time in the butter liquid. Serve buttered sprouts with the butter liquid.

Nutritional Information: Calories 76 Total Fat 5g Carbs 6.5g Protein 5.1g Fiber 4g

270. Carrot Salad

Prep Time: 10-minutes | Total time: 20-minutes | Yield: 6-servings

Ingredients:

½ C. Cilantro, Fresh & Chopped Fine	4 Carrots, Shredded
1/3 C. Pistachios, Shelled & Roughly Chopped	¼ Tsp. Red Pepper Flakes
3 Scallions, Sliced	4 Medjool Dates, Pitted & Chopped
½ C. Tahini Lime Dressing	

Directions:

Mix everything together and toss with your dressing before serving.

Nutritional Information: Calories: 101 Protein: 2 Grams Fat: 2 Grams Carbs: 22 Grams

271. Easy Roasted Carrots

Prep Time: 12-minutes | Total time: 42-minutes | Yield: 4-servings

Ingredients:

2 lbs. carrots, quartered	A pinch of black pepper
3 tbsps. olive oil	2 tbsps. parsley, chopped

Directions:

Arrange the carrots with a lined baking sheet, add black pepper and oil, toss, introduce inside the oven and allow it to cook at 400 degrees F to get a half-hour.

Add parsley, toss, divide between plates and serve as a side dish.

Nutritional Information: calories 177, fat 3, fiber 6, carbs 14, protein 6

272. Parmesan-Crusted Halibut with Asparagus

Prep Time: 15-minutes | Total time: 30-minutes | Yield: 4-servings

Ingredients:

2 tbsps. olive oil	¼ c. butter softened
Salt and pepper	¼ c. grated Parmesan
1 lb. asparagus, trimmed	2 tbsps. almond flour
4 (6 oz.) halibut fillets, boneless	1 tsp. garlic powder

Directions:

Ensure you preheat your oven to 400 F and line a foil-based baking sheet. Throw the asparagus in olive oil before scattering it over your baking sheet. Add the butter, almond flour, salt, garlic powder, Parmesan cheese, and pepper in a blender, and mix until smooth. Set fillets with the asparagus on your baking sheet, and spoon Parmesan over the eggs.Bake for 12-minutes, then broil until browned for 2 to 3-minutes.

Nutritional Information: Calories: 415 |Fats: 26 |Protein: 42 |Carbohydrates: 3

273. Open Avocado Tuna Melts

Prep Time: 12-minutes | Total time: 27-minutes | Yield: 4-servings

Ingredients:

4 Slices Sourdough Bread	2 Cans Wild Caught Albacore Tuna, 5 Oz.
¼ C. Paleo Mayonnaise	1 Tsp. Lemon Juice, Fresh Dash Garlic Powder
2 Tbsps. Shallots, Minced	
Dash Paprika	1 Avocado, Cut into 8 Slices
1 Tomato, Cut into 8 Slices	¼ C. Parmesan Cheese, Shredded & Divided

Directions:

Start by preheating your broiler, and then get out a baking sheet. Line it with foil. Arrange your bread in the pan. Get out a bowl, and then mix your mayonnaise, tuna, lemon juice, garlic, shallot, and paprika together. Top each bread slice with the mixture. Use two tomato slices and two avocado slices as a topping on each. Sprinkle with a tbsp. of parmesan, and then broil for three to four-minutes. Serve warm.

Nutritional Information: Calories: 471 Protein: 27 Grams Fat: 27 Grams Carbs: 31 Grams

274. Hot Tuna Steak

Prep Time: 12-minutes | Total time: 37-minutes | Yield: 6-servings

Ingredients:

¼ c. whole black peppercorns	2 tbsps. Extra-virgin olive oil
2 tbsps. Fresh lemon juice Pepper.	6 cut tuna steaks
	Roasted orange garlic mayonnaise
Salt	

Directions:

Bring the tuna in a container to fit. Place the oil, salt, lemon juice & pepper. Turn the tuna to coat well inside the marinade. Rest for a minimum of fifteen to twenty-minutes, flipping over once. Place the peppercorns in a twofold thickness of plastic bags. Tap the peppercorns with a heavy deep cooking pan or small mallet to crush them crudely. Put on a big plate. Once ready to cook the tuna, immerse the edges into the crushed peppercorns. Heat a nonstick frying pan on moderate heat. Sear the tuna steaks, in batches if required, for about four-minutes per side for medium-rare fish, putting in two to three tbsps. of the marinade to the frying pan if required to stop sticking.

Serve dolloped with roasted orange garlic mayonnaise

Nutritional Information: Calories: 124, Fat: 0.4 g, Carbohydrates: 0.6 g, Protein: 28 g Sugars: 0 g

275. Apple and Tomato Dipping Sauce

Prep Time: 12-minutes | Total time: 12-minutes | Yield: 2-4-servings

Ingredients:

¼ c. of cider vinegar	¼ tsp. of freshly ground black pepper
½ tsp. of sea salt	1 garlic clove, finely chopped
1 large-sized shallot, diced	1 tbsp. natural tomato paste
1 tbsp. of extra-virgin olive oil	1 tbsp. of maple syrup
1/8 tsp. of ground cloves	3 moderate-sized apples, roughly chopped
3 moderate-sized tomatoes, roughly chopped	

Directions:

Put oil into a huge deep cooking pan and heat it up on moderate heat. Put in shallot and cook until light brown for approximately 2-minutes. Stir in the tomato paste, garlic, salt, pepper, and cloves for approximately half a minute. Then put in the apples, tomatoes, vinegar, and maple syrup. Bring to its boiling point, then decrease the heat to allow it to simmer for approximately 30-minutes. Allow cooling for twenty additional-minutes before placing the mixture into your blender. Combine the mixture until the desired smoothness is achieved.

Keep in a mason jar or an airtight container; place in your fridge for a maximum of 5 days.

Serve it on a burger or with fries.

Nutritional Information: Calories: 142, Protein: 3 g, Fat: 3.46 g, Carbohydrates: 26.93 g

276. Tasty Grilled Asparagus

Prep Time: 15-minutes | Total time: 21-minutes | Yield: 4-servings

Ingredients:

2 lbs. asparagus, trimmed	2 tbsps. organic olive oil
A pinch of salt and black pepper	

Directions:

In a bowl, combine the asparagus with salt, pepper, and oil and toss well. Place the asparagus on preheated grill over medium-high heat, cook for 3-minutes with them, divide between plates and serve as a side dish.

Nutritional Information: calories 172, fat 4, fiber 7, carbs 14, protein 8

277. Cauliflower Steaks with Tamarind and Beans

Prep Time: 7-minutes | Total time: 42-minutes | Yield: 2-servings

Ingredients:

½ c. of olive oil	1/5 lb. cauliflower head
1 tsp. black pepper, ground	2 tsp. of kosher salt
3 cloves of garlic, chopped	½ lb. green beans, trimmed
1/3 c. parsley, chopped	¾ tsp. lemon zest, grated
1/5 lb. parmesan, grated	¼ lb. panko bread-crumbs
1/3 c. tamarind	1 lb. white beans, rinsed & drained
1 tsp. of Dijon mustard	2 tbsps. of margarine

Directions:

Preheat your oven to 425°F. Take out the leaves and trim the stem ends of your cauliflower. Keep the core side down on your working surface. Slice from the center top to down with a knife. Keep it on a baking sheet.

Apply 1 tbsp. oil on both sides. Season with pepper and salt. Roast for 25-minutes. Turn halfway through.

Toss the green beans in the meantime with 1 tbsp. of oil and pepper. Keep on your baking sheet in a single layer. Whisk the lemon zest, garlic, parsley, salt, pepper, and oil together in a bowl. Keep half of this mix in another bowl. Add Parmesan and panko to the first bowl. Use your hands to mix. Add tamarind and white beans to the second bowl. Coat well by tossing.

Now whisk together the mustard and margarine. Spread your margarine mix over the cauliflower. Sprinkle the panko mixture over the cauliflower. Add the white bean mix to the sheet with beans. Combine. Keep the sheet in the oven and roast for 5-minutes. Divide the beans, cauliflower, and tamarind among plates.

Nutritional Information: Calories 925 Fat 67g Carbs 166g Protein 59g Fiber 41g Sugar 12g

278. Lemon Tuna

Prep Time: 5-minutes | Total time: 23-minutes | Yield: 4-servings

Ingredients:

4 tuna steaks	1 tbsp. olive oil
½ tsp. smoked paprika	¼ tsp. black pepper-corns, crushed
Juice of 1 lemon	4 scallions, chopped
1 tbsp. chives, chopped	

Directions:

Begin by heating up a pan with the oil over medium-high heat, add the scallions and sauté for 2-minutes. Add the tuna steaks, then sear them for 2-minutes on each side. Add the remaining ingredients toss gently, introduce the pan in the oven and bake at 360 degrees F for 12-minutes. Divide everything between plates and serve for lunch.

Nutritional Information: calories 324, fat 1, fiber 2, carbs 17, protein 22

279. Chicken Meatball Soup

Prep Time: 13-minutes | Total time: 43-minutes | Yield: 4-servings

Ingredients:

2 lbs. chicken breast, skin-less, boneless, and minced	2 tbsps. cilantro, chopped
2 eggs, whisked	1 garlic clove, minced
¼ c. green onions, chopped	1 yellow onion, chopped
1 carrot, sliced	1 tbsp. olive oil

5 c. chicken stock	1 tbsp. parsley, chopped
A pinch of salt and black pepper	

Directions:

Take a bowl and combine the meat with the eggs and the other ingredients except for the oil, yellow onion, stock, and parsley. Stir and shape medium meatballs out of this mix. Heat up a pot with the oil on medium heat, add the yellow onion and the meatballs, and brown for 5-minutes. Add the remaining ingredients, toss, bring to a simmer and cook over medium heat for 25-minutes more. Ladle the soup into bowls and serve.

Nutritional Information: calories 200, fat 2, fiber 2, carbs 14, protein 12

280. Chocolate chip

Prep time: 10 | Total time: 30 – 40-minutes | Yield: 12-servings

Ingredients:

150 g Almond meal	40 g macadamia oil or coconut oil
40 g honey	½ tsp. vanilla bean extracts
50g dark chocolate	

Directions:

Combine the almond meal, honey, oil, and vanilla beans. Mix them thoroughly to form a dough. Add in a splash of water 1 – 2 tsp. to help form the dough. Add the chocolate mix in. Using a spoon from 12 cookies. Press the scoops into a baking tray lined with a sheet of baking paper. You can also garnish using a tiny flakes almond before you begin the baking process. Bake in low heat for about 30-minutes until the cookies turn golden brown. Let the cookies cool off completely

Nutritional information:Calories 148 | Fat: 7.4g | Cholesterol: 0 mg | Saturated fat: 2.4g | Sodium: 93 mg

281. Savory White bean soup

Prep time: 5- 10-minutes | Total time: 25 – 30-minutes | Yield: 4-servings

Ingredients:

2 (15 oz.) cans white bean	1 medium yellow onion
4 clove garlics	¼ tsp. red pepper flakes (optional)
2 tbsps. olive oil	4 c. low-sodium chicken or vegetable broth
1 (14 oz) can tomatoes, diced	2 fresh spring rosemary
1 tsp. black pepper, freshly ground	1 parmesan rind (optional)
5 oz. baby spinach	Parmesan cheese, grated

Directions:

Drain & rinse the 2 cans of white beans, then set them aside. Chop 1 medium yellow onion finely and then mince 4 clove garlics. Heat 2 tbsp. olive oil in a large pot or Dutch oven until shimmering. Add the onion and sauté till translucent and softened, this takes about 3-4-minutes. Add ¼ tsp. red pepper flakes and garlic, if using, and the sauté till fragrant, this take about a-minutes Pour in 4 c. low sodium chicken or vegetable broth, 1 can diced tomatoes and their juice, followed by the white beans. Add 2 rosemary springs, fresh, 1 tsp. kosher salt, ¼ tsp. black pepper, and 1 parmesan rind, if using, then stir to combine. Let them boil. Reduce heat to maintain a simmer. Simmer uncovered for about 10-minutes to let t5he flavor meld. Stir in 5 oz baby spinach, a few at a time, until just wilted, this takes 1 – 2-minutes. Serve garnished with grated parmesan cheese.

Nutritional information: Calories 135 | Total fat: 3.16g | Sodium: 758.33 mg | carbs: 13.92 | Sugars: 2.67g

282. Chicken Bacon Quesadilla

Prep time: 5-minutes | Total time: 10-minutes | Yield: 2-servings

Ingredients:

4 (8 inches) flour tortillas	¼ c. ranch dressing
1 c. cooked rotisseries chicken sliced into tiny bite size piece	4 slices of crispy cooked bacon, chopped
2/3 c. shredded Colby jack	2/3 c. shredded queso quesadilla cheese
2 tbsps. butter	

Directions:

Spread 2 tbsp. of ranch dressing over 2 tortillas. Top each tortilla with half of the set bacon, half of the chicken, and half of the set cheese. Top each with another tortilla. Melt 1 tbsp. butter in a large skillet using medium heat. Add 1 quesadilla and cook it till the bottom part is lightly brown. Flip the quesadilla and cook it until the other side is lightly brown too. Add in another tbsp. of butter to the skillet and then repeat the procedure for the second quesadilla.

Nutritional information: Calories: 830 | Total Fat: 50g | Saturated Fat: 20g | Cholesterol: 120 mg | Total Carbohydrates: 48 g

283. Tempeh Wraps with Avocado and Veggies

Prep time: 5-minutes | Total time: 15-minutes | Yield: 1 wrap

Ingredients:

Tempeh logs:

4 oz tempeh, sliced into "logs"	1 tbsp. maple syrup
1 tbsp. tamari	½ tsp. liquid smoke or 1/8 tsp. smoky paprika
Pepper and salt to taste	2 tsp. extra virgin olive oil for the cooking pan

Secret sauce:

2 tbsps. vegan mayo	2 tsp. maple syrup
3 tsp. sriracha or hot sauce	2 big handful veggies
½ avocado, well sliced	1 large tortilla or sandwich wrap

Directions:

Tempeh: Warm your skillet using high heat, add on the olive oil. When oil gets hot, add tempeh logs. Cook the tempeh logs for about 2-minutes, let them brown. Reduce heat to low, then add on the maple syrup and tamari. Toss, so all sides of the tempeh begin to brown. Add the smoky or liquid smoke paprika over the top of the tempeh. Sauté for 1-3-minutes till the edges are caramelized. Turn the heat off and add on a pinch of salt, then pepper on top. Whisk together the secret sauce, then warm the wrap/tortilla. Smash avocado onto the tortilla. Add 1-2 tbsp. of the secret sauce over the top. Add on the greens and tempeh. Roll up, slice.

Nutritional information: Calories:582 | Fat:32 g | Cholesterol: 0 mg | Carbohydrates: 53g | Proteins: 28g

284. Tofu, Chickpeas, and veggie bowl

Prep time: 5-minutes | Total time: 25-minutes | Yield: 4-servings

Ingredients:

1 c. chickpeas, boiled	1 c. long grain brown rice, dry and boiled
½ c. Portobello mushroom	1 clove garlic, minced
1 tbsp. gluten free tamari	1 tbsp. minced ginger roots
½ avocado	1 c. sweet potato
2 c. spinach	2 tbsps. cashew nuts, raw
2 green onion stems, scallion, and ramp (chopped)	¼ c. tahini
1 tsp. garlic powder	1 tbsp. maple syrup
1 tsp. gluten free tamari	1 tsp. hulled hemp seeds, shelled
¼ c. cubes Tofu, silken and firm	

Directions:

Boil rice first and use pre-baked potatoes cut into cubes. Use Buffalo chickpea recipe. Add the cooked rice onto the bottom of a medium size bowl. Using a medium saucepan, reheat the chickpeas, you can add some extra coconut oil or sauce at this stage, it should be a small amount, though. Remove from heat and layer on top of rice, placing close to the edge to create room for other ingredients. Rinse your saucepan and add on a tiny amount of coconut oil. Add garlic, sauté mushroom, and ginger. Add on chopped veggies to the mix at this stage and splash on 1 tbsp. of tamari. Add another splash of coconut oil followed by tofu and cashews. Cook the tofu cubes on all sides till they are slightly brown. Add onto a bowl. Using the same saucepan, add rinsed spinach. Toss them and let them wilt a bit. Remove from heat and add onto the bowl. Add tahini, garlic powder, maple, and tamari onto a separate bowl. Whisk until they form a smooth consistency. Pour over ingredients in the bowl. Slice avocadoes on top. Sprinkle the sesame and/or hemp plus the chopped green onions

Nutritional information: Calories: 459g | Fat: 16.8g | Sodium: 282 mg | Carbs: 66g | Proteins: 15.0 g

285. Almond Butter and Berry Sandwiches

Prep time: 15-minutes | Total time: 15-minutes | Yield: 2-servings

Ingredients:

4 slices whole wheat bread	½ c. almond butter
1 c. fresh blueberries	Pinch sea salt or kosher (optional)
Pinch brown sugar (optional)	

Directions:

Spread the almond butter on all four bread slices. Add one layer of blueberries on two of the four slices of bread. Sprinkle s pinch of brown sugar or sea salt over the blueberries (optional). Top the slices of bread using the remaining two slices. Slice and serve. Enjoy!

Nutritional information: Calories: 261 | Fat: 10g | Cholesterol: 0.0mg | Carbohydrates: 9.2g |

286. Black Bean and Mango Lettuce Wraps

Prep time: 10-minutes | Total time: 15-minutes | Yield: 5-servings

Ingredients:

1 (15 oz.) can black beans, rinsed and drained	1 mango, peeled and diced, then squeezed to provide 1 tbsp. juice
½ red onion, diced	1 medium sized jalapeno pepper

1 large red bell pepper, diced and seeded	2 tbsps. red wine vinegar
1 tbsp. olive oil	1 tbsp. honey
10 Butter lettuce leaves	

Directions:
Combine all the ingredients inside a medium sized bowl leaving out the lettuce. Refrigerate ingredients in the bowl for at least one houR. Arrange the lettuce leaves on a large sized plate, then fill each of them with ¼ c. of salad mixture

Nutritional information: Calories: 150 | Fat: 3.5g | Cholesterol: 0mg | Carbohydrates: 27g | Proteins: 6g

287. Vegan Sweet Potato and Corn Chowder

Prep time: 10-minutes | Total time: 35-minutes | Yield: 6-servings

Ingredients:

1 white onion, diced	4 cloves garlic, minced
4 rib celery, chopped	1 medium sized sweet potato, well peeled and cubed
1 red bell pepper, diced	4 c. frozen corn
4 c. vegetable broth	2 tsp. chili powder
1 tsp. paprika	Fresh cracked black pepper & sea-salt, to taste

Directions:
Add garlic, celery, and onions onto a soup pot, then add a splash of vegetable broth or water. Cook until it starts to soften for about 5-minutes. Add on the sweet potato and broth, bring to a light simmer, and then cook for about 8-minutes. Add the remaining ingredients and let simmer lightly for another 5-10-minutes till the sweet potatoes can be easily pierced using a fork. Scoop about 2/3 of the soup carefully into a blender. Blend until it becomes creamy and smooth. Let the steam escape while you are blending. Pour the blended portion back in the pot with the unblended soup, then stir to combine. Season using pepper and salt and serve. Enjoy!

Nutritional information: Calories: 186 | Fat: 0g | Carbohydrates: 40g | Fiber: 6g | Protein: 6g

288. Ginger-Turmeric Carrot Soup

Prep time: 10-minutes | Total time: 50-minutes | Yield: 4-servings

Ingredients:

1 tbsp. olive oil	1 leek, well cleaned and sliced
1 c. chopped fennel (1 small sized head)	3 c. chopped butternut squash
2 cloves garlic, minced	1 tbsp. grated ginger

1 tbsp. turmeric powder	Pepper and salt to taste
3 c. vegetable broth, low sodium	1 can (14.5 oz) lite coconut milk

Directions:
Heat the olive-oil inside a large sized Dutch oven or using a saucepan. Add leeks, fennel, carrots, and squash. Sauté until the vegetables start to soften, for about 5-minutes. Add the turmeric, pepper, salt, and ginger, then sauté for a few more-minutes. Add the broth then the coconut milk. Let the mixture boil, cover for another 20-minutes. Add it into a blender once the soup is well cooked and blend it till it becomes creamy. You can also alternatively use an immersion blender. Taste and manipulate the seasoning to your preferred taste. Serve immediately with a dollop of coconut yogurt. Enjoy!

Nutritional information: Calories: 210.64 | Carbs: 25.64 g | Protein: 2.11g | Saturated fat: 7.44g |

289. Broiled Lamb Chops

Prep time: 10-minutes | Total time: 20-minutes | Yield: 4-servings

Ingredients:

Cooking spray	8 lamb loin chops, around 4 oz.
¼ tsp. black pepper	½ tsp. salt
1 tbsp. bottled minced garlic	2 tbsps. lemon juice
1 tbsp. dried oregano	

Directions:
Preheat broiler. In a big bowl/dish, combine the black pepper, salt, minced garlic, lemon juice, and oregano. Then rub it equally on all sides of the lamb chops.
Then coat a broiler pan with the cooking spray before placing the lamb chops on the pan and broiling until the desired doneness is reached or for five-minutes per side.

Nutritional Information: Calories 332, Fat 2.3g, Net Carbs 2.7g, Protein 46g, Sugar: 0.6g, Fiber 0.3g,

290. Pepper Steak Taco

Prep time: 10-minutes | Total time: 30-minutes | Yield: 8-servings

Ingredients:

2 tbsps. sliced pickled jalapenos	2 tbsps. chopped fresh cilantro
½ avocado, sliced	8 small whole wheat tortillas, warmed
½ c. fresh frozen corn kernels	3 bell pepper, 1 each red, yellow, and orange, sliced thinly
½ red onion, sliced	3 tsp. vegetable oil

½ tsp. mild chili powder	2 garlic cloves, crushed
1 tsp. salt	Juice of one lime, plus lime wedges for serving
1 pound of flank or hanger steak	

Directions:

In a re-sealable plastic bag, mix chili powder, garlic, salt, and lime juice until salt is dissolved. Add steak and marinate for at least 30-minutes while making sure to flip over or toss around steak halfway through the marinating time. On high fire, place a large saucepan and heat 2 tsp. oil. Once hot, sauté bell peppers and red onion for 5-minutes. Add corn and continue sautéing for another 3 to 5-minutes. Transfer veggies to a bowl and keep warm. With a paper towel, wipe the skillet and return to medium high fire. Heat remaining tsp. of oil. Once hot, add steak to pan in a single layer and cook 4-minutes per side for medium rare. Remove from fire and then let it rest for about 5-minutes on a chopping board before cutting into thin slices. To make a tortilla, layer jalapenos, cilantro, avocado, steak, and veggies. Best serve with a dollop of sour cream.

Nutritional Information: Calories 268, Saturated Fat 2g, Net Carbs 23g, Protein 17g, Sugar: 3g, Fiber 6g, Sodium 539mg, Potassium 514mg

291. Lamb Burger on Arugula

Prep time: 10-minutes | Total time: 16-minutes | Yield: 6-servings

Ingredients:

2 tbsps. shelled and salted Pistachio nuts	½ oz fresh mint, divided
1 tbsp. salt	3 oz dried apricots, diced
2 lbs. ground lamb	4 c. arugula

Directions:

In a bowl, blend salt, ½ of fresh mint (diced), apricots, and ground lamb with your hands. Then form into balls or patties with an ice cream scooper. Press ball in between the palm of hands to flatten to half an inch. Do the same for the remaining patties. In a thick nonstick pan on medium fire, place patties without oil and cook for 3-minutes per side or until lightly browned. Flip over just once and then cook the other side. Meanwhile, arrange 1 cup of arugula per plate. Total of 4 plates. Divide evenly and place cooked patties on top of the arugula. In a food-processor, process until finely chopped the remaining mint leaves and nuts. Sprinkle on top of patties, serve and enjoy.

Nutritional Information: Calories 332, Saturated Fat 4g, Net Carbs 5g, Protein 32g, Sugar: 5g, Fiber 1g, Sodium 1264mg, Potassium 520mg

292. Asian Beef Short Ribs

Prep time: 10-minutes | Total time: 10 hours 10-minutes | Yield: 4-servings

Ingredients:

1 c. water	1 onion, diced
1 tbsp. Szechuan peppercorns	2 lbs. beef short ribs
2 tbsps. curry powder	3 tbsps. coconut aminos
6 pieces star anise	1 tbsp. sesame oil
Salt and pepper to taste	

Directions:

1. Add all ingredients to the slow cooker and mix well.
2. Cook on low settings for 10 hours.
3. Serve and enjoy.

Nutritional information: Calories 442, Saturated Fat 4g, Net Carbs 4g, Protein 47g, Sugar: 2g, Fiber 2g

293. Stir-Fried Mushrooms and Beef

Prep time: 10-minutes | Total time: 35-minutes | Yield: 4-servings

Ingredients:

2 tbsps. olive oil	2 cloves of garlic, minced
1-lb 4 beef steaks, cut into strips	¼ c. water
salt and pepper to taste ½ tsp. salt	2 c. mushrooms, sliced

Directions:

Heat oil & butter in a skillet and sauté the garlic until fragrant. Stir in the beef strips for 3-minutes until lightly golden. Pour in water and season with salt and pepper to taste. Close the lid and allow to simmer for 15-minutes. Stir in the mushrooms and salt. Cook for another 5 more-minutes. Serve and enjoy.

Nutritional information: Calories 226, Saturated Fat 3g, Net Carbs 1.5g, Protein 24g, Sugar: g, Fiber 0.2g

294. Turkey and Quinoa Stuffed Peppers

Prep time: 15-minutes | Total time: 50-minutes | Yield: 6-servings

Ingredients:

3 large red bell peppers	2 tsp. chopped fresh rosemary
2 tbsps. chopped fresh parsley	3 tbsps. chopped pecans, toasted
2 tbsps. extra virgin olive oil	½ c. chicken stock
½ lb. fully cooked smoked turkey sausage, diced	½ tsp. salt
2 c. water	1 c. uncooked quinoa

Directions:
On high fire, place a large saucepan and add salt, water, and quinoa. Bring to a boil. Once boiling, reduce fire to a simmer, cover, and cook until all water is absorbed, around 15-minutes. Uncover quinoa, turn off the fire and let it stand for another 5-minutes. Add rosemary, parsley, pecans, olive oil, chicken stock, and turkey sausage into a pan of quinoa. Mix well. Slice peppers lengthwise in half and discards membranes and seeds. In another boiling pot of water, add peppers, boil for 5-minutes, drain and discard water. Grease a 13 by 9 baking-dish and preheat the oven to 350oF. Place boiled bell pepper onto a prepared baking dish, evenly fill with the quinoa mixture, and pop into the oven. Bake for 15-minutes.
Nutritional Information: Calories 253, Saturated Fat 2g, Net Carbs 19.7g, Protein 14g, Sugar: 1.3g, Fiber 3g

295. Chicken Pasta Parmesan
Prep time: 10-minutes | Total time: 30-minutes | Yield: 1 serving

Ingredients:

½ c. cooked whole wheat spaghetti	1 oz. reduced fat mozzarella cheese, grated
¼ c. prepared marinara sauce	2 tbsps. seasoned dry breadcrumbs
4 oz. skinless chicken breast	1 tbsp. olive oil

Directions:
On medium high fire, place an ovenproof skillet and heat oil. Pan fry chicken for about 3 - 5-minutes per side or until cooked through. Pour marinara sauce, stir and continue cooking for 3-minutes. Turn off fire, add mozzarella and breadcrumbs on top. Pop into a preheated broiler on high and broil for 10-minutes or until breadcrumbs are browned, and mozzarella is melted. Remove from broiler, serve and enjoy.
Nutritional Information: Calories 492, Saturated Fat 3g, Net Carbs 21g, Protein 49g, Sugar: 11g, Fiber 6g

296. Easy Stir-Fried Chicken
Prep time: 10-minutes | Total time: 22-minutes | Yield: 3-servings

Ingredients:

1 tbsp. soy sauce	1 tbsp. virgin coconut oil
¼ medium onion, sliced thinly	¼ lb. brown mushrooms
1 large orange bell pepper	2 (7-oz) skinless and boneless chicken breast

Directions:
On medium high fire, place a nonstick saucepan and heat coconut oil. Add soy sauce, onion powder, mushrooms, bell pepper, and chicken. Stir fry for 8 to 10-minutes. Remove from pan and serve.
Nutritional Information: Calories 277, Saturated Fat 2g, Net Carbs 3g, Protein 44g, Sugar: 2g, Fiber 1g

297. Brussels Sprouts and Paprika Chicken Thighs
Prep time: 10-minutes | Total time: 35-minutes | Yield: 4-servings

Ingredients:

4 large bone-in chicken thighs, skin removed	1 tsp. dried thyme
1 tbsp. smoked paprika	2 cloves garlic, minced
½ tsp. ground pepper, divided	¾ tsp. salt, divided
3 tbsps. extra virgin olive oil, divided	1 lemon, sliced
4 small shallots, quartered	1 lb. Brussels sprouts, trimmed and halved

Directions:
Preheat your oven to 450-degrees F. Position rack to lower third in the oven. On a large and rimmed baking sheet, mix ¼ tsp. pepper, ¼ tsp. salt, 2 tbsp. oil, lemon, shallots, and Brussels sprouts. With a chef's knife, mash ½ tsp. salt and garlic to form a paste. In a small bowl, mix ¼ tsp. pepper, 1 tbsp. oil, thyme, paprika, and garlic paste. Rub all over the chicken and place it around Brussels sprouts in a pan. Pop in the oven and roast for 20 to 25-minutes or until chicken is cooked and juices run clear. Serve and enjoy.
Nutritional information: Calories 293, Saturated Fat 3.2g, Net Carbs 10g, Protein 29g, Sugar: 4g, Fiber 5g,

298. Open-Faced Garden Tuna Sandwich
Prep time: 10-minutes | Total time: 25-minutes | Yield: 2-servings

Ingredients:

2 (5 oz. each) cans of low sodium tuna packed in water, drained	4 green onions, sliced
4 slices hearty multigrain bread	1 tbsp. fresh parsley, chopped
1 tbsp. lemon juice	1 tbsp. extra-virgin olive oil
1/4 c. cherry tomatoes, sliced	A handful of fresh arugulas

2 tbsps. low fat whipped cream cheese - Black pepper powder to taste	

Directions:

Mix oil, lemon juice, parsley, green onion, and pepper. Add tuna to a bowl. Add about 2/3 of the above mixture and mix well. Spread a little of the remaining mixture lightly on both sides of the bread. Heat a nonstick pan over high heat. Place the bread slices and cook until the bottom side is golden brown. Turn and cook the other side. Add the remaining mixture to the arugula and toss well. To make sandwiches: Spread cream cheese on each of the bread slices. Divide and spread the tuna mixture over the slices. Place the arugula over the tuna mixture and finally cherry tomatoes.

Nutritional Information: Calories: 360 Fat: 20g Carbohydrates: 18g; Protein: 24g Sodium: 76mg

299. Spinach Salad with Walnuts and Strawberry

Prep time: 10-minutes | Total time: 25-minutes | Yield: 2-servings

Ingredients:

1/2 c. walnuts	4 c. fresh spinach, loosely trimmed stems
3 tbsps. honey	2 tbsps. spicy brown mustard
1/4 c. balsamic vinegar	1/4 tsp. sea salt
1/4 c. crumbled feta (about 1 oz.) - optional	

Directions:

Heat the oven until 375 ° F.Arrange walnuts on a rimmed baking-sheet and bake for 8-minutes until they are fragrant and toasted. Switch to an excellent plate. Place the spinach in a large container. The honey, mustard, vinegar, and salt are whisked together in a small cup. Drizzle the salad over 3/4 of the dressing and scatter the walnuts on top. Serve sprinkled with both the cheese (if it is used) and the remaining side dressing.

Nutritional Information: Calories: 129 Fat: 8g Carbohydrates: 10g; Protein: 7g Sodium: 120mg

300. Veggie Sushi

Prep time: 10-minutes | Total time: 25-minutes | Yield: 2-servings

Ingredients:

3 c. brown rice	2 tbsps. rice wine vinegar
2 avocados, longitudinally cut	2 carrots, longitudinally sliced

1 cucumber, longitudinally sliced	6 tbsps. cabbage
Ponzu sauce, to taste	

Directions:

Cook brown rice, as indicated in instructions. Fold rice to vinegar rice wine. Let the cooked rice cool down. When cool, spread rice uniformly with a wooden spoon on a bamboo sushi mat, or dip your hands in a cold bowl of water and spread the rice with your fingertips, on the top layer, avocado, cabbage, and slices of cucumber. Using the mat to roll it into a packed rice and vegetable roll, slide the mat out and repeat.

Slice into circles of 1/2 inch. Serve.

Nutrition information: Calories: 135 Fat: 3g Carbohydrates: 22g; Protein: 3g Sodium: 116mg

301. Zucchini Zoodles with Chicken

Prep time: 10-minutes | Total time: 20-minutes | Yield: 2-servings

Ingredients:

2 chicken fillets, cubed	2 tbsps. ghee
1 lb. tomatoes, diced	1/2 c. basil, chopped
1/4 c. almond milk	1 garlic clove, peeled, minced
1 zucchini, shredded	

Directions:

Sauté cubed chicken in ghee until no longer pink. Add tomatoes and season with sunflower seeds. Simmer and reduce the liquid. Prepare your zucchini Zoodles by shredding zucchini in a food processor. Add basil, garlic, coconut almond milk to the chicken and cook for a few-minutes. Add half of the zucchini Zoodles to a bowl and top with creamy tomato basil chicken, and enjoy!

Nutritional information: Calories: 540 Fat: 27g Carbohydrates: 13g Protein: 59g Sodium: 180mg

302. Pasta With Spinach, Garbanzos, And Raisins

Prep time: 10-minutes | Total time: 25-minutes | Yield: 2-servings

Ingredients:

2 tbsps. olive oil	8 oz. farfalle (bowtie) pasta
4 crushed garlic cloves	1/2 (19 oz.) can rinsed garbanzos, drained
1/2 c. chicken broth, unsalted	1/2 c. golden raisins
4 c. spinach, freshly chopped	2 tbsps. Parmesan cheese

black peppercorns (Cracked) to taste	

Directions:
Fill about 75% of a large pot with water and bring to a boil. Put in the pasta and cook until tender 10 to 12-minutes, or according to the package directions. Drain the pasta completely. Warm olive oil and garlic on a skillet with medium heat. Put in the garbanzos and chicken broth. Stir until warmed through. Put raisins and spinach. Cook spinach for about 3-minutes. Do not overcook. Divide the pasta among plates. Put 1/6 of the sauce, 1 tsp. Parmesan cheese and peppercorns on top of each serving to taste. Serve instantly.
Nutritional Information: Calories 283, Carbohydrates 21g, Protein 11g, Fat 7g, Sodium 106mg

303. Broiled White Sea Bass
Prep time: 5-minutes | Total time: 15-minutes | Yield: 2-servings
Ingredients:

1 tbsp. lemon juice	2 (4 oz.) white sea bass fillets
1 tsp. minced garlic	1/4 tsp. herbed seasoning blend, salt-free
Black pepper, ground	

Directions:
Preheat the broiler or grill.
Use a cooking spray to coat your baking pan and set it in the fillets.
Drizzle the herbed seasoning, pepper, garlic, and lemon juice over your fillets.
Broil for 10-minutes until your fish is all opaque once you test using a knife's tip. Serve instantly.
Nutritional information: Calories 114, Carbohydrates 2g, Protein 21g, Fat 2g, Sodium 96mg

304. Creamy Chicken Breast
Prep time: 10-minutes | Total time: 30-minutes | Yield: 4-servings

Ingredients:

1 tbsp. olive oil	A pinch of black pepper
2 lbs. chicken breasts, skinless, boneless, and cubed	4 garlic cloves, minced
2 1/2 c. low-sodium chicken stock	2 c. coconut cream
1/2 c. low-fat parmesan, grated	1 tbsp. basil, chopped

Directions:
Heat-up a pan with the oil over medium-high heat, add chicken cubes and brown them for 3-minutes on each side. Add garlic, black pepper, stock, and cream, toss, cover the pan and cook everything for 10-minutes more. Add cheese and basil, toss, divide between plates and serve for lunch. Enjoy!
Nutritional Information: Calories 221, Carbohydrates 14g, Protein 7g, Fat 6g, Sodium 197mg

305. Salsa Chicken
Prep time: 10-minutes: Total time: 35-minutes | Yield: 4-servings

Ingredients:

1 c. mild salsa, no-salt-added	1/2 tsp. cumin, ground Black pepper to the taste
1 tbsp. chipotle paste	1 lb. chicken thighs, skinless and boneless
2 c. corn	Juice of 1 lime
1 tbsp. olive oil	2 tbsps. cilantro, chopped
1 c. cherry tomatoes, halved	1 small avocado, pitted, peeled, and cubed

Directions:
In a pot, combine the salsa with the cumin, chipotle paste, chicken thighs, black pepper, and corn, toss, bring to a simmer and cook over medium heat for about 25-minutes. Add lime juice, oil, avocado, and cherry tomatoes, toss, divide into bowls, and serve lunch. Enjoy!
Nutritional information: Calories 269, Carbohydrates 18g, Protein 7g, Fat 6g, Sodium 500mg

306. Coconut Turkey Mix
Prep time: 10-minutes | Total time: 40-minutes | Yield: 4-servings

Ingredients:

1 yellow onion, chopped	1 lb. turkey breast, skinless, boneless, and cubed
2 tbsps. olive oil	5 garlic cloves, minced
1 zucchini, sliced	1 c. coconut cream
A pinch of sea salt black pepper	

Directions:
Bring the pan to medium heat, add the onion and the garlic and sauté for 5-minutes. Put the meat and brown within 5-minutes more. Add the ingredients remaining, toss, bring to a simmer. Cook over medium heat for about 20-minutes more. Serve for lunch.

Nutritional information: Calories 200 | Fat 4g | Carbohydrates 14g | Protein 7g | Sodium 111mg

307. Lime Shrimp and Kale

Prep time: 10-minutes | Total time: 30-minutes |
Yield: 4-servings

Ingredients:

1 lb. shrimp, peeled & deveined 4 scallions, chopped	1 tsp. sweet paprika
1 tbsp. olive oil Juice of 1 lime	Zest of 1 lime, grated
A pinch of salt & black pepper 2 tbsps. parsley, chopped	

Directions:

Bring the pan to medium heat, add the scallions & sauté for 5-minutes.

Add other ingredients with the shrimp, toss, cook over medium heat for about 15-minutes more, divide into bowls and serve.

Nutritional information: Calories: 149 Carbohydrates: 12g Fat: 4g Protein: 21g Sodium: 250 mg

CHAPTER 5:
DINNER RECIPES

308. Honey Mustard Grilled Pork

Prep Time: 10-minutes | Total time: 18-minutes | Yield: 6-servings

Ingredients:

1/3 c. honey	1 tsp. hot sauce
3 tsp. lemon juice	1 tbsp. apple cider vinegar
2 tsp. onion powder	1 tsp. Worcestershire sauce
3 tbsp. Dijon mustard	¼ tsp. rosemary
8 pork chops	1 tsp. cranberry sauce

Directions:

Add honey, hot sauce, lemon juice, vinegar, onion powder, Worcestershire sauce, mustard, and rosemary in a resealable bag. Add pork and shake until well coated. Place inside your fridge and let marinate for at least 2 hours. Remove pork from the marinade and grill it for 8-minutes. Discard the marinade. Serve the pork with sauce.

Nutritional Information: Calories 169 Total Fat 7 g Carbs 13 g Protein 14 g

309. Mushroom Pork Chops

Prep Time: 12-minutes | Total time: 52-minutes | Yield: 2-servings

Ingredients:

8 oz. mushrooms, sliced	1 tsp. garlic
1 onion, peeled and chopped	1 c. keto-friendly mayonnaise
3 pork chops, boneless	1 tsp. ground nutmeg
1 tbsp. balsamic vinegar	½ c. of coconut oil

Directions:

Take a pan and then place it over medium-heat. Add oil and let it heat up. Add mushrooms, onions, and stir. Cook for 4-minutes. Add pork chops, season with nutmeg, garlic powder, and brown both sides. Transfer pan into the oven and then bake for 30-minutes at 350 degrees F. Transfer pork chops to plates and keep it warm. Take a pan and then place it over medium-heat. Add vinegar, mayonnaise over the mushroom mixture, and stir for a few-minutes. Drizzle sauce over pork chops

Nutritional Information: Calories: 600 | Fat: 10g | Carbohydrates: 8g | Protein: 30g | Fiber: 2g |

310. Roasted Tofu and Greens

Prep Time: 12-minutes | Total time: 32-minutes | Yield: 4-servings

Ingredients:

3 c. baby spinach or kale	1 tbsp. sesame oil
1 tbsp. ginger, minced	1 garlic clove, minced
1 lb. firm tofu, cut into 1-inch dice	1 tbsp. gluten-free tamari or soy sauce
¼ tsp. red pepper flakes (optional)	1 tsp. rice vinegar
2 scallions, thinly sliced	

Directions:

Preheat the oven to 400°F. Combine the spinach, oil, ginger, and garlic on a large, rimmed baking sheet. Bake until the spinach has wilted, 3 to 5-minutes. Add the tofu, tamari, and red pepper flakes (if using) and toss to combine well. Bake until the tofu is beginning to brown, 10 to 15-minutes. Top with the vinegar and scallions and serve.

Nutritional Information: Calories: 121 Fat: 8g Carbs: 4g Sugar: 1g Fiber: 2g Protein: 10g Sodium: 258mg

311. Mediterranean Pork

Prep Time: 12-minutes | Total time: 47-minutes | Yield: 2-servings

Ingredients:

2 pork chops, bone-in	Salt and pepper, to taste
1/2 tsp. dried rosemary	1 garlic clove, peeled and minced

Directions:

Season pork chops with salt and pepper. Place in a roasting pan. Add rosemary, garlic to the pan. Preheat oven to about 425 degrees F. Bake for 10-minutes. Lower heat to 350 degrees F. Roast for 25-minutes more. Slice pork and divide on plates. Drizzle pan juice all over. Serve and enjoy!

Nutritional Information: Calories: 165 | Fat: 2g | Protein: 26g | Fiber: 1g | Net Carbohydrates: 1g

312. Zucchini Pasta with Avocado Sauce

Prep Time: 12-minutes | Total time: 22-minutes | Yield: 1 serving

Ingredients:

A squeeze of lemon juice	Salt and pepper to taste
1 tbsp. coconut milk	½ ripe avocado
1 medium zucchini cut into noodles	2 tbsp. olive oil

Directions:

Heat oil using a skillet over medium heat and add the zucchini noodles. Sauté for three-minutes or until the noodles have softened. While the zucchini is cooking, mash the avocado with coconut milk, lemon juice, and salt and pepper. Add the sauce to the zucchini noodles and sauté. Serve warm.

Nutritional Information: Calories: 471 Fat: 41g Carbohydrates: 23g Protein: 6g Sugar: 13g Fiber: 7g

313. Easy Shrimp

Prep Time: 6-minutes | Total time: 10-minutes | Yield: 2-servings

Ingredients:

1 lb. Shrimp, peeled and deveined	2 Garlic cloves, crushed
1 tbsp. Butter.	A pinch of red Pepper
Salt and Pepper, to taste	1 c. Parsley, chopped

Directions:

Melt butter on Sauté mode. Add shrimp, garlic, red pepper, salt, and pepper. Cook for 5-minutes, occasionally stirring the shrimp until pink. Serve topped with parsley.

Nutritional Information: Calories 245, |Protein 45g, |Net Carbs 4.8g, |Fat 4g

314. Roasted Vegetables with Polenta

Prep Time: 7-minutes | Total time: 32-minutes | Yield: 6-servings

Ingredients:

2 tsp. oregano	10 ripe olives, chopped
6 dry-packed sun-dried tomatoes, soaked in water to rehydrate, drained, and chopped	2 plum or Roma tomatoes, sliced
10-oz frozen spinach, thawed	¼ tsp. cracked black pepper
2 tsp. trans-free margarine	1 ½ c. coarse polenta
6 c. water	2 tbsp. + 1 tsp. extra virgin olive oil
1 sweet red pepper, seeded, cored, and cut into chunks	6 medium mushrooms, sliced
1 small green zucchini, cut into ¼-inch slices	1 small yellow zucchini, cut into ¼-inch slices
1 small eggplant, peeled and cut into ¼-inch slices	

Directions:

Grease a baking sheet and a 12-inch circle baking dish, position oven rack 4-inches away from a heat source, and preheat broiler. With 1 tbsp. olive oil, brush red pepper, mushrooms, zucchini, and eggplant. Place in a prepared baking sheet in a single layer. Pop in the broiler and broil under a low setting. Turn and brush again with oil the veggies after 5-minutes. Continue broiling until veggies are slightly browned and tender. Wash and drain spinach. Set aside. Preheat oven to 350oF. Bring water to boil using a medium sized pan. Whisk in the polenta and lower fire to a simmer for 5-minutes, cook, and stir. Once polenta no longer sticks to the pan, add 1/8 tsp. pepper and margarine. Mix well and turn off the fire. Evenly spread the polenta on a base of prepped baking dish. Brush tops with olive oil, and for ten-minutes, bake in the oven. When done, remove the polenta from the oven and keep warm.

With paper towels, remove excess water from spinach. Layer spinach on top of polenta, followed by sliced tomatoes, olives, sun-dried tomatoes, and roasted veggies. Season with remaining pepper and bake for another 10-minutes. Remove from oven, cut into equal-servings and enjoy.

Nutritional Information: Calories 135 Fat 2g Carbohydrates: 27g Protein 5g Fiber: 6g

315. Spinach Almond Tortilla

Prep Time: 7-minutes | Total time: 17-minutes | Yield: 3-servings

Ingredients:

1 c. Almond flour + extra for dusting	1 c. Spinach, chopped
¼ tbsp. Chili flakes	¼ c. Mushrooms, sliced
½ tbsp. Salt	2 tbsp. Olive oil

Directions:

In a bowl, combine flour, mushrooms, spinach, salt, and flakes; mix well. Add ¼ cup of water and make a thick batter. Roll out the batter until it is thin. Heat oil on Sauté mode. Cook the tortilla for 5-minutes until golden brown. Serve with cilantro sauce and enjoy.

Nutritional Information: Calories 165, |Protein 5g, |Net Carbs 2.1g, | Fat 9g

316. Gluten-Free Pineapple Burgers

Prep Time: 12-minutes | Total time: 27-minutes | Yield: 3-servings

Ingredients:

2 lbs. lean meat, ground	½ c. gluten-free teri-yaki sauce
8 oz. pineapple slices, re-serve the juice	4 lettuce leaves
4 slices fat-free cheese	4 slices tomato
4 buckwheat burger buns	

Directions:

In a mixing bowl, mix meat, sauce and season with salt and pepper. Divide the meat mixture into 4 patties. Drizzle each patty with pineapple juice, then place the pineapple slices on each patty. Grill patties using medium heat for 7-minutes or until cooked through. Layer the burgers starting with the bottom bun, lettuce, pineapple, cheese, tomato, grilled patty, and the top bun.

Nutritional Information: Calories 714 Total Fat 23 g Carbs 39 g Protein 83 g

317. Spicy baked fish

Prep Time: 6-minutes | Total time: 21-minutes | Yield: 5-servings

Ingredients:

1 tbsp. olive oil	1 tsp. spice salt free seasoning
1 lb. salmon fillet	

Directions:

Preheat the oven to 350F. Sprinkle the fish with olive oil and the seasoning. Bake for 15 min uncovered. Slice and serve.

Nutritional Information: Calories: 192, Fat: 11 g, Carbs: 14.9 g, Protein: 33.1 g, Sugars: 0.3 g

318. Parmesan and Lemon Fish

Prep Time: 17-minutes | Total time: 27-minutes | Yield: 2-servings

Ingredients:

4 tilapia fillets	¼ c. cornflakes, crushed
2 tbsps. of vegan Parmesan, grated	2 tsp. vegan dairy-free butter, melted
1/8 tsp. black pepper, ground	½ tsp. lemon peel, shredded
Lemon wedges	

Directions:

Heat your oven to 450 °F. Rinse and then dry the fish using paper towels. Apply cooking spray on your baking pan. Now roll up your fish fillets. Start from their short ends. Keep in the baking pan. Bring the vegan butter, Parmesan, corn flakes, pepper, and lemon peel in a bowl. Sprinkle the crumb mix on your fish roll-ups. Press the crumbs lightly into the fish. Bake for 6-8-minutes. The fish should flake easily with your fork. Serve with lemon wedges.

Nutritional Information: Calories 191 Cholesterol 71mg Carbs 7g Fat 7g Sugar 1g Fiber 0g Protein 25g

319. Hibiscus Ginger Gelatin

Prep Time: 1 hour 58-minutes | Total time: 2 hours 18-minutes | Yield: 5-servings

Ingredients:

3 tbsps. hibiscus flower, dried	2 tbsps. gelatin powder
1 tsp. ginger juice	1 and ½ tbsps. honey
1 c. of water	

Directions:

Bring water to boil. Once boiled, remove from the heat Add hibiscus flowers to boiled water. Allow infusing for 5-minutes. Remove the flowers and discard. Heat the liquid and add honey, ginger, and gelatin. Dissolve the gelatin. Take a baking sheet and pour the mixture. Place your meal inside the fridge and let it cook. Slice the gelatin and serve. Enjoy!

Nutritional Information: Calories: 27 Fat: 0.06g Carbohydrates: 7g Protein: 0.2g

320. Spiced Broccoli, Cauliflower, and Tofu with Red Onion

Prep Time: 12-minutes | Total time: 37-minutes | Yield: 2-servings

Ingredients:

2 c. broccoli florets	2 c. cauliflower florets
1 medium red onion, diced	3 tbsps. extra-virgin olive oil
1 tsp. salt	¼ tsp. freshly ground black pepper
1 lb. firm tofu, cut into 1-inch dice	1 garlic clove, minced
1 (¼-inch) piece fresh ginger, minced	

Directions:

Preheat the oven to 400°F. Combine the broccoli, cauliflower, onion, oil, salt, and pepper on a large, rimmed baking sheet, and mix well. Roast until the vegetables have softened, 10 to 15-minutes. Add the tofu, garlic, and ginger. Roast within 10-minutes. Gently mix the ingredients on the baking sheet to combine the tofu with the vegetables and serve.

Nutritional Information: Calories: 210 Fat: 15g Carbs: 11g Sugar: 4g Fiber: 4g Protein: 12g Sodium: 626mg

321. Lemonade Broccoli

Prep Time: 7-minutes | Total time: 17-minutes | Yield: 3-servings

Ingredients:

1 lb. Broccoli, cut in bitable sizes	3 Lemon Slices
¼ c. Water	Salt to taste
Pepper to taste	

Directions:

Pour the water into the Instant Pot. Add the broccoli and sprinkle with lemon juice, pepper, and salt.
Seal the lid, secure the pressure valve, and Manual in Low Pressure mode for 3-minutes. Once ready, quickly release the pressure. Drain the broccoli and serve as a side dish.

Nutritional Information: Calories 34, |Protein 2.8g, |Net Carbs 5.6g, |Fat 0.4g

322. Brie-Packed Smoked Salmon

Prep Time: 7-minutes | Total time: 7-minutes | Yield: 4-servings

Ingredients:

4 oz. Brie round	1 tbsp. fresh dill
1 tbsp. lemon juice	2 oz. smoked salmon

Directions:

Slice Brie in half lengthwise. Spread salmon, dill, and lemon juice over the Brie cheese. Place the other half on top. Serve with Celery sticks/ cauliflower bites.

Nutritional Information: Calories: 241 | Fat: 19g | Protein: 18g | Fiber: 2g | Carbohydrates: 3g

323. Cauliflower Tikka Masala with Chickpeas

Prep Time: 12-minutes | Total time: 22-minutes | Yield: 4-servings

Ingredients:

1 tsp. olive oil	4 c. cauliflower florets
¼ tsp. salt	¼ c. of water
1 can (15 oz.)of chickpeas, well, rinsed, and dried	1 ½ c. tikka masala sauce
2 tsp. clarified butter	Fresh cilantro

Directions:

Using a skillet, heat your oil using medium heat.
Add cauliflower and salt to a skillet and cook for 2-minutes, stirring occasionally. Add water to the cauliflower and cook covered for about 5-minutes until the cauliflower gets tender. Add chickpeas and sauce to the cauliflower and cook for 2-minutes, stirring often.
Remove the cauliflower from heat and stir in the butter.

Transfer the cauliflower and chickpeas to a serving platter and garnish with cilantro. This is a healthy dinner recipe.

Nutritional Information: Calories 268 Total fat 16g Carbs 26g Protein 8g

324. Spicy Keto Chicken Wings

Prep Time: 22-minutes | Total time: 52-minutes | Yield: 4-servings

Ingredients:

2 lbs. Chicken Wings	1 tsp. Cajun Spice
2 tsp. Smoked Paprika	½ tsp. Turmeric
A dash Salt	2 tbsps. Baking Powder
A dash Pepper	

Directions:

After commencing the application of a Ketogenic diet, you may find that you won't be eating the traditional foods that may have made up a majority of your diet in the past. While this is a good thing for your health, you may feel you are missing out! The upside of it is that they are super delicious alternatives that aren't lacking in flavor! To start this recipe, you'll want to prep the stove to 400. As these heats up, you will want to take some time to dry your chicken wings with a paper towel. Doing so helps you get rid of any moistures to attain some nice, crispy wings! When you are all set, take out a mixing bowl and place all the seasonings along with the baking powder. If you feel like it, you can adjust the seasoning levels however you would like. Once these are set, go ahead, and throw the chicken wings in and coat evenly. If you have one, you'll want to place the wings on a wire rack over your baking tray. If not, you can just lay them across the baking sheet. Now that your chicken wings are set, you are going to pop them into the stove for thirty-minutes. By the end of this time, the tops of the wings should be crispy. If they are, take them out from the oven and flip them so that you can bake the other side. You will want to cook these for an additional thirty-minutes.
Finally, take the tray from the oven and allow it to cool slightly before serving up your spiced keto wings. For additional flavor, serve with any of your favorite keto-friendly dipping sauces.

Nutritional Information: Fats: 7g |Carbs: 1g |Proteins: 60g

325. Anti-Inflammatory Turmeric Gummies

Prep Time: 4 hours | Total time: 4 hours 10-minutes

Ingredients:

1 tsp. turmeric, grounded	8 tbsps. gelatin powder, unflavored

6 tbsps. maple syrup	3 ½ c. water

Directions:

Take a pot and combine maple syrup, turmeric, and water. Bring it to boil for 5-minutes. Remove from the heat and sprinkle with gelatin powder. Mix to hydrate the gelatin. Then turn on the heat again. Then bring to a boil till the gelatin dissolve properly. Take a dish and pour the mixture. Let it chill for 4 hours in your refrigerator. Once ready, slice and serve

Nutritional Information: Calories: 68 Fat: 0.03g Carbohydrates: 17g Protein: 0.2g

326. Steamed Artichokes

Prep Time: 7-minutes | Total time: 27-minutes | Yield: 3-servings

Ingredients:

2 medium Artichokes	3 Lemon Wedges (for cooking and serving)
1 ½ c. Water	

Directions:

Clean the artichokes by removing all dead leaves, the stem, and the top third of it. Rub the top of the artichokes with the lemon. Set aside. Place a trivet to fit in the Instant Pot, pour in water.

Place the artichokes on the trivet, seal the lid. Select Manual mode on High Pressure for 9-minutes. Once the timer ends, keep the pressure valve for 10-minutes; then quickly release the remaining pressure. Remove artichokes and serve with garlic mayo and lemon wedges.

Nutritional Information: Calories 47, |Protein 3.3g, |Net Carbs 6g, |Fat 0.2g

327. Cheesy Ham Quiche

Prep Time: 12-minutes | Total time: 42-minutes | Yield: 6-servings

Ingredients:

8 Eggs	1 c. Zucchini
½ c. Shredded heavy Cream	1 c. Ham, Diced
1 tsp. Mustard	A dash Salt

Directions:

For this recipe, you can start off by prepping your stove to 375 and getting out a pie plate for your quiche. Next, it is time to prep the zucchini. First, you will want to go ahead and shred it into small pieces. Once this is complete, take a paper towel and gently squeeze out the excess moisture. This will help avoid a soggy quiche.

When the step from above is complete, you will want to place the zucchini into your pie plate along with the cooked ham pieces and your cheese. You will want to whisk the seasonings, cream, and eggs together before pouring them over the top once these items are in place. Now that your quiche is set, you will pop the dish into your stove for about forty-minutes. By the end of this time, the egg should be cooked. Test by inserting a knife into the meal, as you eject it from the meal, it should come out clean. If the quiche is cooked to your liking, take the dish from the oven, and allow it to chill slightly before slicing and serving.

Nutritional Information: Fats: 25g |Carbs: 2g |Proteins: 20g

328. The Almond Breaded Chicken Goodness

Prep Time: 17-minutes | Total time: 32-minutes | Yield: 3-servings

Ingredients:

2 large chicken breasts, boneless and skinless	1/3 c. lemon juice
1 ½ c. seasoned almond meal	2 tbsps. coconut oil
Lemon pepper, to taste	Parsley for decoration

Directions:

Slice chicken breast in half. Pound out each half until ¼ inch thick. Take a pan and place it over medium heat, add oil, and heat it up. Dip each chicken breast slice into lemon juice and let it sit for 2-minutes. Turnover and let the other side sit for 2-minutes as well. Transfer to almond meal and coat both sides. Add your coated chicken into the oil, then fry for 4-minutes per side, making sure to sprinkle lemon pepper liberally. Transfer to a paper-lined sheet and repeat until all chicken is fried. Garnish with parsley and enjoy!

Nutritional Information: Calories: 325 Fat: 24g Carbohydrates: 3g Protein: 16g

329. Spicy Tuna Rolls

Prep Time: 11-minutes | Total time: 11-minutes | Yield: 6-servings

Ingredients:

1 can yellowfin tuna, wild-caught	1 medium cucumber
2 slices avocado, diced	1/8 tsp. salt
1/8 tsp. pepper	

Directions:

Take a cucumber and use a mandolin to thinly slice it lengthwise. Take a mixing bowl and add avocado and tuna. Season with salt and pepper to taste. Spoon the tuna and avocado mixture. Spread it consistently on

cucumber slices. Roll the cucumber slices. Use a toothpick to secure the ends. Serve chilled and enjoy!
Nutritional Information: Calories: 135 Fat: 10g Carbohydrates: 6g Proteins: 9g

330. Mexican Cod Fillets

Prep Time: 12-minutes | Total time: 22-minutes | Yield: 3-servings

Ingredients:

3 Cod fillets	1 Onion, sliced
2 c. Cabbage	Juice from 1 Lemon
1 Jalapeno Pepper	½ tsp Oregano
½ tsp Cumin powder	½ tsp Cayenne Pepper
2 tbsp. Olive oil	Salt and black Pepper to taste

Directions:

Heat the oil on Sauté, add onion, cabbage, lemon juice, jalapeño pepper, cayenne pepper, cumin powder, and oregano, and stir to combine. Cook for 8-10-minutes. Season with salt and black pepper. Arrange the cod fillets in the sauce, using a spoon to cover each piece with some sauce. Seal the lid and press Manual. Cook for 5-minutes on High pressure. When ready, do a quick release and serve.
Nutritional Information: Calories 306, |Protein 21g, |Net Carbs 6.8g, | Fat 19.4g

331. Chicken Marrakesh

Prep Time: 27-minutes | Total time: 4 hours 27-minutes | Yield: 8-servings

Ingredients:

1 slice onion	2 garlic cloves, minced
½ lb. pumpkins	2 carrots, diced & peeled
1 lb. garbanzo beans, drained & rinsed	½ tsp. cumin, ground
2 lbs. chicken breasts, skinless, halved, cut into small pieces	¼ tsp. cinnamon, ground
½ tsp. turmeric, ground	½ tsp. black pepper, ground
1 tsp. salt	1 tsp. parsley, dried
½ lb. tamarind, pulped	

Directions:

Keep the garlic, onion, pumpkin, carrots, chicken breast, and garbanzo beans in your slow cooker. Mix turmeric, cumin, black pepper, cinnamon, salt, and parsley in your bowl. Sprinkle over the vegetables and chicken. Add the tamarind. Combine well by stirring. Keep your cooker covered. Set the heat to high. Cook for 4 hours. The sauce should be thick.

Nutritional Information: Calories 520 Carbs 59g Cholesterol 101mg Fat 15g Fiber 13g Sugar 12g Protein 45g Sodium 424mg

332. Vegan Mushrooms in Broth

Prep Time: 17-minutes | Total time: 27-minutes | Yield: 4-servings

Ingredients:

1 tbsp. extra-virgin olive oil	1 onion, sliced
3 garlic cloves, sliced	1 celery stalk, finely chopped
1 lb. mushrooms, sliced	A pinch of nutmeg
1 tsp. salt	½ tsp. black pepper
4 c. vegetable broth	1 c. cooked chicken
2 tbsp. tarragon, freshly chopped	

Directions:

Using a large pot, heat your olive oil using medium heat. Sauté onions, garlic, and celery for 3-minutes or until the onions are fragrant. Add mushrooms, nutmeg, salt, and pepper. Sauté for an additional 10-minutes. Add broth, then let your soup boil. Reduce heat and simmer for 5-minutes. Stir in chicken and tarragon.
Nutritional Information: Calories 111 Total Fat 5 g Carbs 9 g Protein 9 g

333. Italian Stuffed Peppers

Prep Time: 12-minutes | Total time: 1 hour | Yield: 6-servings

Ingredients:

½ onion, chopped	1 tbsp. olive oil
½ tsp. kosher salt	1 carrot, diced into ¼ inch thickness
1 tsp. of Italian seasoning	3 garlic cloves, minced
3 c. of pumpkin, grated	½ tsp. of red pepper flakes
1-1/4 c. cooked quinoa	1 lb. chickpeas, drained and rinsed
3 red bell pepper, cut, remove the seeds and membrane	¼ c. parsley, minced
¼ c. of vegan Parmesan, grated	

Directions:

Preheat your oven to 350 degrees F. Heat olive oil in your nonstick skillet over medium temperature. Now add the carrots and onions. Season with a little bit of salt. Cook for 5-minutes, stirring occasionally. Stir the Italian seasoning, red pepper flakes, and garlic in. Cook for another minute. Add the chickpeas, pumpkin, and the remaining salt. Boil and simmer for 8-minutes. Remove from heat. Stir 3 tbsp. of parsley and the cooked quinoa in. Keep the pepper in your baking dish. The cut side should be up. Now divide your chickpea mix between the peppers evenly. Pour half of the water into your baking dish. Use a foil to cover tightly for 30-minutes. The peppers should be tender. Sprinkle the parmesan over each pepper. Bake uncovered for 5-minutes. Garnish with the remaining parsley.

Nutritional Information: Calories 276 Carbs 40g Fat 8g Protein 11g Sugar 6g Fiber 8g Sodium 612mg

334. Vegan Coconut Chickpea Curry

Prep Time: 6-minutes | Total time: 22-minutes | Yield: 4-servings

Ingredients:

2 tsp. avocado oil	1 c. chopped onion
1 c. diced bell pepper	1 zucchini, halved and sliced
1(15 oz.) can chickpeas, drained and rinsed	½ c. vegetable broth
4 c. baby spinach	2 c. precooked brown rice

Directions:

Using a skillet, heat your oil using medium heat. Sauté onion, pepper, and zucchini for about 6-minutes, stirring often. Add the chickpeas and broth to the onion mixture and bring to a simmer as you stir. Reduce heat to medium-low heat and let the vegetables simmer for 6-minutes. Stir in the spinach to the chickpeas and remove from heat. Serve the chickpeas over rice.

Nutritional Information: Calories 471 Total fat 18g Carbs 66g Protein 11g

335. Peas Soup

Prep Time: 12-minutes | Total time: 22-minutes | Yield: 4-servings

Ingredients:

1 white onion, chopped	1 tbsp. olive oil
1-quart veggie stock	2 eggs
3 tbsps. lemon juice	2 c. peas
2 tbsps. parmesan, grated	Salt and black pepper to the taste

Directions:

Heat up a pot using the oil over medium-high heat, add the onion and sauté for 4-minutes. Add on the remaining ingredients leaving out the eggs, bring to a simmer, and cook for 4-minutes. Add whisked eggs, stir the soup, cook for 2-minutes more, divide into bowls, and serve.

Nutritional Information: Calories 293, |fat 11.2 |fiber 3.4, |carbs 27, |protein 4.45

336. Fruit Bowl with Yogurt Topping

Prep Time: 16-minutes | Total time: 16-minutes | Yield: 6-servings

Ingredients:

¼ c. golden brown sugar	2/3 c. minced fresh ginger
1 16-oz Greek yogurt	¼ tsp ground cinnamon
2 tbsp. honey	½ c. dried cranberries
3 navel oranges	2 large tangerines
1 pink grapefruit, peeled	

Directions:

Into sections, break tangerines and grapefruit. Slice tangerine sections in half and grapefruit sections into thirds. Place all sliced fruits and its juices in a large bowl. Peel oranges, remove the pith, slice into ¼-inch thick rounds, and then cut into quarters. Transfer to the bowl of fruit along with juices. In a bowl, add cinnamon, honey, and ¼ cup of cranberries. Place in the ref for an hour. In a medium bowl, mix ginger and yogurt. Place on top of the fruit bowl, drizzle with remaining cranberries and brown sugar. Serve and enjoy.

Nutritional Information: Calories 171 Fat 1g |Carbs 35g| Protein 9g| Fiber 3g

337. Steamed fish balls

Prep Time: 7-minutes | Total time: 32-minutes | Yield: 2-servings

Ingredients:

2 whisked eggs	2 tbsps. Rinsed and cooked rice
Salt.	10 oz. minced white fish fillets

Directions:

Combine the minced fish with the rice. Add eggs, season with salt, and stir well. Form the balls. Arrange inside a steaming basket. Place basket inside a pot with 1 inch of water. Steam, covered, for 25-minutes or until soft.

Nutritional Information:Calories:169,Fat:4.3g, Carbs: 1.1 g, Protein: 5.3 g, Sugars: 0 g, Sodium: 173.1 mg

338. Salsa Chicken Bites

Prep Time: 4-minutes | Total time: 18-minutes | Yield: 2-servings

Ingredients:

2 chicken rest	1 c. of salsa
1 taco seasoning mix	1 c. plain Greek yogurt

½ c. cheddar cheese, cubed	

Directions:

Bring a skillet and place it over medium heat. Add chicken breast, a ½ cup of salsa, and taco seasoning. Mix well and cook for 12-15-minutes until the chicken is done. Take the chicken out and cube them. Place the cubes on a toothpick and top with cheddar. Place yogurt and remaining salsa in cups and use them as dips.
Nutritional Information: Calories: 359 | Fat: 14g | Protein: 43g | Fiber: 3g | Carbohydrates: 17g

339. Vegetable and Chicken Stir Fry

Prep Time: 7-minutes | Total time: 22-minutes | Yield: 6-servings

Ingredients:

3 tbsps. olive oil	3 chicken breasts
3 medium zucchini or yellow squash	2 onions
1 tsp. of garlic powder	1 broccoli
1 tsp. basil	1 tsp. of pepper and salt

Directions:

Chop the vegetables and chicken. Heat your skillet over medium temperature. Pour olive oil and add the chicken. Cook while stirring. Include the seasonings if you want. Add the vegetables. Keep cooking until it gets slightly soft. Add the onions first and broccoli last.
Nutritional Information: Calories 183 Carbs 9g Total Fat 11g Protein 12g Sugar 4g Fiber 3g Sodium 468mg

340. Shrimp with Linguine

Prep Time: 12-minutes | Total time: 22-minutes | Yield: 4-servings

Ingredients:

1 lb. Shrimp, cleaned	1 lb. Linguine
1 tbsp. Butter	½ c. Parmesan cheese, shredded
2 Garlic cloves, minced	1 c. Parsley, chopped
Salt and Pepper, to taste	½ c. Coconut Cream, for garnish
½ Avocado, diced, for garnish	2 tbsp. fresh Dill, for garnish

Directions:

Melt the butter on Sauté. Stir in linguine, garlic cloves, and parsley. Cook for 4-minutes until aromatic. Add shrimp; season with salt and pepper, seal the lid.
Select Manual and cook for 5-minutes on High pressure. When ready, quick release the pressure. Unseal and remove the lid. Press Sauté, add the cheese, and stir well until combined, for 30-40 seconds. Serve topped with coconut cream, avocado, and dill.

Nutritional Information: Calories 412, | Protein 48g, | Net Carbs 5.6g, | Fat 21g

341. Tempeh and Root Vegetable Bake

Prep Time: 12-minutes | Total time: 42-minutes | Yield: 4-servings

Ingredients:

1 tbsp. extra-virgin olive oil	1 large, sweet potato, dice
2 carrots, thinly sliced	1 fennel bulb, trimmed and cut into ¼-inch dice
2 tsp. minced fresh ginger	1 garlic clove, minced
12 oz. tempeh, cut into ½-inch dice	½ c. vegetable broth
1 tbsp. gluten-free tamari or soy sauce	2 scallions, thinly sliced

Directions:

Preheat the oven to 400°F. Grease a baking sheet with oil. Arrange the sweet potato, carrots, fennel, ginger, and garlic in a single layer on the baking sheet. Bake until the vegetables have softened, about 15-minutes. Add the tempeh, broth, and tamari. Bake again until the tempeh is heated through and lightly browned for 10 to 15-minutes. Add the scallions, mix well, and serve.
Nutritional Information: Calories: 276 Fat: 13g Carbs: 26g Sugar: 5g Fiber: 4g Protein: 19g Sodium: 397mg

342. Especial Glazed Salmon

Prep Time: 45-minutes | Total time: 55-minutes | Yield: 4-servings

Ingredients:

4 pieces salmon fillets, 5 oz. each	4 tbsps. coconut aminos
4 tsp. olive oil	2 tsp. ginger, minced
4 tsp. garlic, minced	2 tbsp. sugar-free ketchup
4 tbsps. dry white wine	2 tbsps. red boat fish sauce, low sodium

Directions:

Take a bowl and mix in coconut aminos, garlic, ginger, fish sauce, and mix. Add salmon and let it marinate for 15-20-minutes. Take a skillet/pan and place it over medium heat. Add oil and let it heat up. Add salmon fillets and cook on HIGH for 3-4-minutes per side. Remove dish once crispy. Add sauce and wine. Simmer for 5-minutes on low heat. Return salmon to the glaze and flip until both sides are glazed. Serve and enjoy!
Nutritional Information: Calories: 372 Fat: 24g Carbohydrates: 3g Protein: 35g

343. Romesco Sauce with Vegetables and Sheet-Pan Chicken

Prep Time: 26-minutes | Total time: 56-minutes | Yield: 4-servings

Ingredients:

2 cubed Yukon gold potatoes	6 tbsps. olive oil
1 tsp. ground black pepper	½ tsp. salt
4 chicken thighs, bone-in, and skinless	4 c. broccoli florets
1(7 oz.) jarred pepper, roasted	¼ c. slivered almonds
1 crushed garlic clove	1 tsp. paprika
½ tsp. ground cumin	¼ tsp. red pepper, crushed
2 tbsps. fresh cilantro, chopped	

Directions:

Preheat your oven to attain 450°F. Add the 1/8 tbsp. salt, ¼ tbsp. black pepper, 1 tbsp. oil, and potatoes in a bowl and toss to combine. Transfer the potatoes to one side of a rimmed baking sheet. Add the ¼ tsp. pepper, chicken, 1 tbsp. oil, and 1/8 tbsp. salt into the same bowl and toss to coat. Transfer the chicken to the other side of the baking sheet. Roast the chicken and potatoes for 10-minutes. Meanwhile, add the broccoli, 2 tbsps. oil, ¼ tbsp. pepper, and 1/8 tbsp. salt inside a different bowl then tosses to mix. Add broccoli mixture to the potato side of your baking sheet and stir to mix.
Roast the broccoli for 15-minutes. Meanwhile, add the roasted pepper, paprika, red pepper, cumin, almonds, ¼ tbsp. pepper, 2 tbsps. oil,1/8 tbsp. garlic and salt inside a food processor and process until a smooth consistency is achieved. Transfer the vegetables and chicken to a serving platter and sprinkle with the cilantro. Serve with roasted pepper sauce.

Nutritional Information: Calories 499 Total fat 27g Carbs 30g Protein 33g

344. Nutty Pina Colada

Prep Time: 11-minutes | Total time: 11-minutes | Yield: 1 serving

Ingredients:

1/2 banana	1/2 c. fresh pineapple, diced
1/4 tsp. coconut extract	1/4 c. quick-cooking oats
5-6 ice cubes	1 container (6 oz.) Greek yogurt
1 c. almond milk	1 c. Swiss chard
1/4 c. Dandelion Greens	

Directions:

Add all ingredients to your blender. Blend it till you attain a smooth and creamy mixture. Serve chilled.

Nutritional Information: Calories: 321 Fat: 6g Carbohydrates: 16g Protein: 15g

345. Vanilla Turmeric Orange Juice

Prep Time: 1 hours 58-minutes | Total time: 1 hours 58-minutes | Yield: 2-servings

Ingredients:

3 oranges, peeled and quartered	1 tsp. vanilla extract
1 c. almond milk, unsweetened	½tsp. cinnamon
¼ tsp. turmeric	A pinch of pepper

Directions:

Add all ingredients into your blender
Pulse until smooth
Serve chilled and enjoy!

Nutritional Information: Calories: 188 Fat: 5g Carbohydrates: 33g Protein: 5g

346. Lemon-Mint Green Tea

Prep Time: 11-minutes | Total time: 11-minutes | Yield: 1 serving

Ingredients:

2 lemon slices	1 green tea bag
3 mint leaves	1 tbsp. honey
2 c. boiling water	

Directions:

Inside a large mug, add a tea bag, lemon slices, and then hot water. Leave the mixture for 10-minutes. Eject the tea bag and stir in the lemon slices and honey. Mix them well. Stir in mint leaves. Serve and enjoy!

Nutritional Information: Calories: 87 Fat: 0.2g Carbohydrates: 24g Protein: 0.8g

347. Vegan and Mediterranean Mango and Bean stew

Prep Time: 12-minutes | Total time: 22-minutes | Yield: 4-servings

Ingredients:

2 tbsps. coconut oil	1 onion, chopped
2 15oz. beans	1 tbsp. chili powder
1 tsp. salt	¼ tsp. black pepper
1 c. water2 ripe mangoes, thinly sliced	¼ c. cilantro, chopped
¼ c. scallions, sliced	

Directions:

Using a pot, heat your coconut oil over medium heat.

Sauté onions in oil for 5-minutes, then add beans, chili powder, salt, and pepper. Add in some water and bring the mixture to a boil. Reduce heat and simmer for 5-minutes. Remove pot from heat, then stir mangoes. Serve garnished with scallions and cilantro.

Nutritional Information: Calories 431 Total Fat 9 g Carbs 72 g Protein 20 g

348. Honey-Roasted Chicken Thighs with Carrots

Prep Time: 12-minutes | Total time: 1 hour | Yield: 4-servings

Ingredients:

2 tbsps. unsalted butter, at room temperature	3 large carrots, thinly sliced
2 garlic cloves, minced	4 bone-in, skin-on chicken thighs
1 tsp. salt	½ tsp. dried rosemary
¼ tsp. freshly ground black pepper	2 tbsps. honey
1 c. chicken broth or vegetable broth	Lemon wedges, for serving

Directions:
Preheat the oven to 400°F. Grease the baking sheet with butter. Arrange the carrots and garlic in a single layer on the baking sheet. Put the chicken, skin-side up, on the vegetables, and season with the salt, rosemary, and pepper. Put the honey on top and add the broth. Roast within 40 to 45-minutes. Remove, and then let it rest for 5-minutes, and serve with lemon wedges.

Nutritional Information: Calories: 428 Fat: 28g Carbs: 15g Sugar: 11g Fiber: 2g Protein: 30g Sodium: 732mg

349. Sheet Pan Turkey Breast with Golden Vegetables

Prep Time: 17-minutes | Total time: 1 hour | Yield: 4-servings

Ingredients:

2 tbsps. unsalted butter, at room temperature	1 medium acorn squash, seeded and thinly sliced
2 large golden beets, peeled and thinly sliced	½ medium yellow onion, thinly sliced
½ boneless, skin-on turkey breast (1 to 2 lbs.)	2 tbsps. honey
1 tsp. salt	1 tsp. turmeric
¼ tsp. freshly ground black pepper	1 c. chicken broth or vegetable broth

Directions:
Preheat the oven to 400°F. Grease the baking sheet with butter. Arrange the squash, beets, and onion in a single layer on the baking sheet. Put the turkey skin-side up. Drizzle with the honey. Season with salt, turmeric, and pepper, and add the broth. Roast until the turkey registers 165°F in the center with an instant-read thermometer, 35 to 45-minutes. Remove, and let rest for 5-minutes. Slice and serve.

Nutritional Information: Calories: 383 Fat: 15g Carbs: 25g Sugar: 13g Fiber: 3g Protein: 37g Sodium: 748mg

350. Almond Breaded Chicken Goodness

Prep Time: 17-minutes | Total time: 32-minutes | Yield: 2-servings

Ingredients:

2 large chicken breast, boneless and skinless	1/3 c. lemon juice
1½ c. seasoned almond meal	2 tbsps. coconut oil
Lemon pepper, to taste	Parsley for decoration

Directions:
Slice Hicken breast in half. Pound out each half until a ¼ inch thick. Place pan over some medium heat, add in oil, and heat it. Dip each chicken breast slice into lemon juice and let it sit for 2-minutes. Turnover and let the other side sit for 2-minutes as well. Transfer to almond meal and coat both sides. Add your coated chicken inside the oil, then fry for 4-minutes per side, making sure to sprinkle lemon pepper liberally. Transfer to a paper-lined sheet and repeat until all chicken is fried. Garnish with parsley and enjoy.

Nutritional Information: Calories: 325 | Fat: 24g | Carbohydrates: 3g | Protein: 16g | Fiber: 1g |

351. Bacon Cheeseburger

Prep Time: 12-minutes | Total time: 47-minutes | Yield: 12-servings

Ingredients:

Low-sodium bacon (16 oz. pkg.)	Ground beef (3 lb.)
Eggs (2)	Medium chopped onion (half of 1)
Shredded cheddar cheese (8 oz.)	

Directions:
Fry the bacon and chop it to bits. Shred the cheese and diced the onion. Combine the mixture with the beef and blend in the whisked eggs. Prepare 24 burgers and grill them the way you like them. You can make a double-decker since they are small. If you are a big-sized-

burger fan, then you can quickly whip up 12 burgers as a single-decker.

Nutritional Information: Net Carbohydrates: 0.8 g | Protein 27 g | Fats: 41 g | Calories: 489

352. Chicken with Herb Parmesan Spaghetti Squash

Prep Time: 17-minutes | Total time: 37-minutes | Yield: 4-servings

Ingredients:

1 lb. chicken breast, skinless & boneless, cut into small pieces	3 lb. spaghetti squash
2 tsp. of olive oil	3 tbsps. shallots, minced
1 tbsp. of melted coconut oil	½ tsp. rosemary, dried
½ tsp. oregano, dried	½ tsp. thyme, dried
3 cloves of garlic, minced	¼ tsp. of ground pepper
¼ tsp. of kosher salt	2 tbsps. parsley, minced
1/3 c. vegan Parmesan, grated	½ c. of chicken broth
Pepper and salt to taste	

Directions:

Pierce your spaghetti squash with a knife in many places. Keep it in a baking dish. Cook in your microwave for 12-minutes on high heat. Turn the spaghetti halfway through. Set aside. Cut it in half along the length. Remove the fibers and seeds. Twist the strands out with a fork. Keep in a bowl. Heat your nonstick skillet over medium temperature. Apply cooking spray lightly. Add the chicken. Cook while stirring occasionally. Transfer chicken to a bowl once done. Keep it aside. Now bring down the heat to medium. Add the coconut oil and olive oil. Include the shallots. Cook for 3-minutes. Stir the rosemary, garlic, oregano, and thyme in. Cook for another minute while stirring. Now stir the chicken broth in. Let your mixture simmer for a couple of-minutes. Include your cooked chicken and spaghetti squash in the skillet. Toss with your sauce. Add the parsley and Parmesan. Toss once more.

Nutritional Information: Calories 295 Carbs 12g Fat 15g Protein 28g Sugar 5g Fiber 3g Sodium 557mg

353. Shrimp-Lime Bake with Zucchini and Corn

Prep Time: 12-minutes | Total time: 32-minutes | Yield: 4-servings

Ingredients:

1 tbsp. extra-virgin olive oil	2 small zucchinis, cut into ¼-inch dice
1 c. frozen corn kernels	2 scallions, thinly sliced
1 tsp. salt	½ tsp. ground cumin
½ tsp. chipotle chili powder	1 lb. peeled shrimp, thawed if necessary
1 tbsp. finely chopped fresh cilantro	Zest and juice of 1 lime

Directions:

Preheat the oven to 400°F. Grease the baking sheet with oil. On the baking sheet, combine the zucchini, corn, scallions, salt, cumin, and chili powder and mix well. Arrange in a single layer. Add the shrimp on top. Roast within 15 to 20-minutes. Put the cilantro and lime zest and juice, stir to combine, and serve.

Nutritional Information: Calories: 184 Fat: 5g Carbs: 11g Sugar: 3g Fiber: 2g Protein: 26g Sodium: 846mg

354. Lemon And Garlic Scallops

Prep Time: 12-minutes | Total time: 17-minutes | Yield: 4-servings

Ingredients:

1 tbsp. olive oil	1 and ¼ lbs. dried scallops
2 tbsps. all-purpose flour	¼ tsp. sunflower seeds
4-5 garlic cloves, minced	1 scallion, chopped
1 pinch of ground sage	1 lemon juice
2 tbsps. parsley, chopped	

Directions:

Place a non-stick skillet overheat. Add the oil. Then allow it to heat up. Take a medium-sized bowl and add scallops alongside sunflower seeds and flour. Place the scallops in the skillet and add scallions, garlic, and sage Sauté for 3-4-minutes until they show an opaque texture. Stir in lemon juice and parsley. Remove heat and serve hot!

Nutritional Information: Calories: 151 Fat: 4g Carbohydrates: 10g Protein: 18g

355. Pita Pizza

Prep Time: 17-minutes | Total time: 27-minutes | Yield: 2-servings

Ingredients:

Marinara sauce (.5 cup)	Low-carb pita (1)
Cheddar cheese (2 oz.)	Peperoni (14 slices)
Roasted red peppers (1 oz.)	

Directions:

Program the oven temperature setting to 450° Fahrenheit. Slice the pita in half and place it onto a foil-lined baking tray. Rub with a little oil and toast for one to two-minutes. Pour the sauce over the bread. Sprinkle using the cheese and other toppings. Bake until the cheese melts (5 min.). Cool thoroughly.

Nutritional Information: Net Carbohydrates: 4 g |Protein: 13 g | Fats: 19 g |Calories: 250

356. Simple Mushroom Chicken Mix

Prep Time: 5-minutes | Total time: 23-minutes | Yield: 2-servings

Ingredients:

2 Tomatoes, chopped	½ lb. Chicken, cooked and mashed
1 c. Broccoli, chopped	1 tbsp. Butter
2 tbsp. Mayonnaise	½ c. Mushroom soup
Salt and Pepper, to taste	1 Onion, sliced

Directions:

Once cooked, put the chicken into a bowl. Mix the mayo, mushroom soup, tomatoes, onion, broccoli, and salt and pepper in a separate bowl. Add the chicken. Grease a round baking tray with butter. Put the mixture in a tray. Inside the instant pot, add in two cups of water and place the trivet inside. Place the tray on top. Seal the lid, press Manual, and cook for 14-minutes on High pressure. When ready, do a quick release.

Nutritional Information: Calories 561, |Protein 28.5g, | Net Carbs 6.3g, |Fat 49.5g

357. Roasted Vegetables with White Beans and Sweet Potatoes

Prep Time: 15-minutes | Total time: 40-minutes | Yield: 4-servings

Ingredients:

2 small, sweet potatoes, dice	½ red onion, cut into ¼-inch dice
1 medium carrot, peeled and thinly sliced	4 oz. green beans, trimmed
¼ c. extra-virgin olive oil	1 tsp. salt
¼ tsp. freshly ground black pepper	1 can (15½ oz.) of white beans, well rinsed and dried
1 tbsp. minced or grated lemon zest	1 tbsp. chopped fresh dill

Directions:

Preheat the oven to 400°F. Combine the sweet potatoes, onion, carrot, green beans, oil, salt, and pepper on a large, rimmed baking sheet and mix to combine well. Arrange in a single layer. Roast till the vegetables is pretty tender, this will take about 25-minutes. Add the white beans, lemon zest, and dill, mix well and serve.

Nutritional Information: Calories: 315 Fat: 13g Carbs: 42g Sugar: 5g Fiber: 13g Protein: 10g Sodium: 632mg

358. Braised Leeks, Cauliflower, and Artichoke Hearts

Prep Time: 12-minutes | Total time: 22-minutes | Yield: 4-servings

Ingredients:

2 tbsp. coconut oil	2 garlic cloves, chopped
1 ½ c. artichoke hearts	1 ½ c. chopped leeks
1 ½ c. cauliflower flowerets	

Directions:

In a skillet, warm oil at medium-high heat temperature. Put the garlic and sauté for one minute. Add the vegetables and constantly stir until the vegetables are cooked. Serve with roasted chicken, fish, or pork.

Nutritional Information: Calories 111|Total Fat 7g|Saturated Fat 1g|Total Carbs 12 |Net Carbs 8g

359. Broccoli and Tilapia

Prep Time: 4-minutes | Total time: 18-minutes | Yield: 2-servings

Ingredients:

6 oz. of tilapia, frozen	1 tbsp. of almond butter
1 tbsp. of garlic, minced	1 tsp. of lemon pepper seasoning
1 c. of broccoli florets, fresh	

Directions:

Preheat your oven to 350 degrees Fahrenheit. Add fish in aluminum foil packets. Arrange broccoli around fish. Sprinkle lemon pepper on top. Close the packets and seal. Bake for 14-minutes. Take a bowl, add garlic and almond butter, mix well, and keep the mixture on the side. Remove the packet from the oven and transfer it to a platter. Place almond butter on top of the fish and broccoli, serve and enjoy!

Nutritional Information: Calories: 362 Fat: 25g Net Carbohydrates: 2g Protein: 29g

360. Walnut Encrusted Salmon

Prep Time: 12-minutes | Total time: 26-minutes | Yield: 34-servings

Ingredients:

½ c. walnuts	2 tbsps. stevia
½ tbsp. Dijon mustard	¼ tsp. dill
2 Salmon fillets (3 oz. each)	1 tbsp. olive oil
Sunflower seeds and pepper to taste	

Directions:
Preheat your oven to 350 degrees F. Add stevia, mustard, walnut into a food processor, then process till you accrue desired consistency. Place a frying pan on medium heat. Add oil and let it heat up. Add salmon and sear for 3-minutes. Add walnut mix and coat well. Transfer your coated salmon into a baking sheet, then bake in the oven for 8-minutes. Serve and enjoy!
Nutritional Information: Calories: 373 Fat: 43g Carbohydrates: 4g Protein: 20g

361. Minty Lamb Stew

Prep Time: 11-minutes | Total time: 1 hour 56-minutes | Yield: 4-servings

Ingredients:

3 c. orange juice	½ c. mint, chopped
Salt and black pepper to the taste	2 lbs. lamb shoulder, boneless and cubed
3 tbsps. olive oil	1 carrot, chopped
1 yellow onion, chopped	1 celery rib, chopped
1 tbsp. ginger, grated	28 oz. canned tomatoes, crushed
1 tbsp. garlic, minced	1 c. apricots, dried and halved
½ c. mint, chopped	15 oz. canned chickpeas, drained
6 tbsps. Greek yogurt	

Directions:
Heat up a pot with 2 tbsps. Of oil using medium-high heat, then add in the meat and brown for 5-minutes. Add the carrot, onion, celery, garlic, and ginger, stir and sauté for 5-minutes more. Add the remaining ingredients except for the yogurt, bring to a simmer, and cook using medium heat for about 1 hour 30-minutes. Divide the stew into bowls, top each serving with the yogurt and serve.
Nutritional Information: Calories 355, | fat 14.3, | fiber 6.7, | carbs 22.6, | protein 15.4

362. Braised Kale

Prep Time: 11-minutes | Total time: 26-minutes | Yield: 3-servings

Ingredients:

2 to 3 tbsp. water	1 tbsp. coconut oil
½ sliced red pepper	2 stalk celeries (sliced to ¼-inch thick)
5 c. of chopped kale	

Directions:
Heat a pan over medium heat. Add coconut oil and sauté the celery for at least five-minutes. Add the kale and red pepper. Add a tbsp. of water. Let the vegetables wilt for a few-minutes. Add a tbsp. of water if the kale starts to stick to the pan. Serve warm.
Nutritional Information: Calories 61 Saturated Fat 1g | Total Carbs 3g | Net Carbs 2g | Protein 1g

363. Tasty Roasted Broccoli

Prep Time: 7-minutes | Total time: 27-minutes | Yield: 4-servings

Ingredients:

4 c. broccoli florets	1 tbsp. olive oil
Sunflower seeds and pepper to taste	

Directions:
Preheat your oven to 400 degrees F. Add broccoli in a zip bag alongside oil and shake until coated. Add seasoning and shake again. Spread broccoli out on the baking sheet, bake for 20-minutes. Let it cool and serve.
Nutritional Information: Calories: 62 Fat: 4g Carbohydrates: 4g Protein: 4g

364. Scallops with Mushroom Special

Prep Time: 16-minutes | Total time: 36-minutes | Yield: 2-servings

Ingredients:

1 lb. Scallops	2 Onions, chopped
1 tbsp. Butter	2 tbsp. Olive oil
1 c. Mushrooms	Salt and Pepper, to taste
1 tbsp. Lemon juice	½ c. Whipping Cream
1 tbsp. chopped fresh Parsley	

Directions:
Heat the oil on Sauté. Add onions, butter, mushrooms, salt, and pepper. Cook for 3 to 5-minutes. Add the lemon juice and scallops. Lock the lid and set it to Manual mode. Cook for 15-minutes on High pressure. When ready, do a quick pressure release and carefully open the lid. Top with a drizzle of cream and fresh parsley.
Nutritional Information: Calories 312, | Protein 31g, | Net Carbs 7.3g, | Fat 10.4g

365. Blackened Chicken Breast

Prep Time: 11-minutes | Total time: 26-minutes | Yield: 2-servings

Ingredients:

2 chicken breast halves, skinless and boneless	1 tsp. thyme, ground
2 tsp. of paprika	2 tsp. olive oil
½ tsp. onion powder	

Directions:

Combine the thyme, paprika, onion powder, and salt together in your bowl. Transfer the spice mix to a flat plate. Rub olive oil on the chicken breast. Coat fully. Roll the chicken pieces in the spice mixture. Press down, ensuring that all sides have the spice mix. Keep aside for 5-minutes. In the meantime, preheat your air fryer to 360 degrees F. Keep the chicken in the air fryer basket. Cook for 8-minutes. Flip once and cook for another 7-minutes. Transfer the breasts to a serving plate. Serve after 5-minutes.

Nutritional Information: Calories 424 Carbs 3g Fat 11g Protein 79g Sugar 1g Fiber 2g Sodium 516mg

---

366. Cajun Jambalaya Soup

Prep Time: 16-minutes | Total time: 56-minutes | Yield: 6-servings

Ingredients:

1 lb. large shrimp, raw and deveined	4 oz. chicken, diced
¼ c. Frank's red-hot sauce	2 c. okra
3 tbsps. Cajun seasoning	2 bay leaves
½ head cauliflower	1 large can organic, diced
1 large onion, chopped	2 cloves garlic, diced
5 c. chicken stock	4 peppers

Directions:

Take a heavy-bottomed pot and add all ingredients except cauliflower. Place it over on high heat. Mix well and let them boil. Once boiled, lower the heat to simmer Simmer for 30-minutes. Rice the cauliflower in your blender. Stir inside the pot, then simmer for about 5-minutes. Serve and enjoy!

Nutritional Information: Calories: 143 Fat: 3g Carbohydrates: 14g Protein: 18g

---

367. Feta and Cauliflower Rice Stuffed Bell Peppers

Prep Time: 11-minutes | Total time: 31-minutes | Yield: 3-servings

Ingredients:

1 green Bell Pepper	1 red Bell Pepper
1 yellow Bell Pepper	½ c. Cauliflower rice
1 c. Feta cheese	1 Onion, sliced
2 Tomatoes, chopped	1 tbsp. black Pepper
2-3 Garlic clove, minced	3 tbsp. Lemon juice
3-4 green Olives, chopped	3-4 tbsp. Olive oil
Yogurt Sauce:	1 clove Garlic, pressed
1 c. Greek Yogurt	kosher Salt, to taste
the juice from 1 Lemon	1 tbsp. fresh dill

Directions:

Grease the Instant Pot with olive oil. Make a cut at the top of the bell peppers near the stem. Place feta cheese, onion, olives, tomatoes, cauliflower rice, salt, black pepper, garlic powder, and lemon juice into a bowl; mix well. Fill up the bell peppers with the feta mixture and insert them in the Instant Pot. Set on Manual and then cook on high pressure for about 20-minutes. When the timer beeps, allow the pressure to release naturally for 5-minutes, then do a quick pressure release. To prepare the yogurt sauce, combine garlic, yogurt, lemon juice, salt, and fresh dill.

Nutritional Information: Calories 388, |Protein 13.5g, |Net Carbs 7.9g, |Fat 32.4g

---

368. Taco Casserole

Prep Time: 11-minutes | Total time: 31-minutes | Yield: 8-servings

Ingredients:

Ground turkey or beef (1.5 to 2 lb.)	Taco seasoning (2 tbsp.) Shredded cheddar cheese (8 oz.)
Salsa (1 cup) Cottage cheese (16 oz.)	

Directions:

Heat the oven to reach 400° Fahrenheit. Combine the taco seasoning and ground meat in a casserole dish. Bake it for 20-minutes. Combine the salsa and both kinds of cheese. Set aside for now. Carefully transfer the casserole dish from the oven. Drain away the cooking juices from the meat. Break the meat into small pieces and mash with a potato masher or fork. Sprinkle with cheese. Bake inside an oven for about 20-minutes more until the top is browned.

Nutritional Information: Net Carbohydrates: 6 g |Protein: 45 g | Fats: 18 g |Calories: 367

---

369. Dijon Salmon with Green bean Pilaf

Prep Time: | Total time: 30-minutes | Yield: 4-servings

Ingredients:

1 ¼ lb. wild salmon, skinned and cut into pieces	3 tsp. extra virgin olive oil
1 tsp. garlic, minced	¾ tsp. salt
2 tsp. hummus	2 tsp. wholegrain mustard
½ tsp. ground pepper	12 oz. thin green beans, pre-trimmed

1 lemon, zested, and cut into wedges	2 tsp. pine nuts
1(8 oz.) package, pre-cooked brown rice	2 tsp. water
Fresh parsley, chopped	

Directions:

Preheat your oven up to 425°F and line a baking sheet with parchment paper. Brush the salmon with 1 tbsp. of the oil and place it on the baking sheet. Using a mortar and a pestle, mash the garlic and salt to form a paste. Transfer 1 tbsp. of the garlic paste to a bowl, then add hummus, ¼ tbsp. of pepper, and mix to combine. Spread the seasoning mixture on top of the salmon. Roast the salmon for about 8-minutes. Meanwhile, using a skillet, heat up the remaining heat on medium heat. Add the green beans, lemon zest, pine nuts, the remaining garlic paste, and pepper to the skillet. Cook the green beans as you stir for about 4-minutes. Reduce the heat to medium and add rice and water to the green beans. Cook the rice for 3-minutes. Transfer salmon to a serving platter, then sprinkle parsley. Serve the salmon with green bean pilaf and lemon wedges.

Nutritional Information: Calories 442 Total fat 25g Carbs 22g Protein 32g

370. Pan-Seared Halibut with Citrus Butter Sauce

Prep Time: 11-minutes | Total time: 26-minutes | Yield: 3-servings

Ingredients:

4 (5 oz.) halibut fillets, each about 1 inch thick	Sea salt
Freshly ground black pepper	¼ c. butter
2 tsp. minced garlic	1 shallot, minced
1 tbsp. freshly squeezed lemon juice	1 tbsp. freshly squeezed orange juice
2 tsp. chopped fresh parsley	2 tbsps. olive oil

Directions:

Pat your fish dry using paper towels, then lightly season the fillets with salt and pepper. Set aside on a paper towel–lined plate. Melt butter using a small sized saucepan over medium heat. Sauté the garlic and shallot until tender, about 3-minutes. Whisk in the lemon juice and orange juice and bring the sauce to a simmer, cooking until it thickens slightly, about 2-minutes. Remove sauce from heat, then stir in the parsley; set aside. Place a large skillet over medium-high heat and add the olive oil. Panfry the fish until lightly browned and just cooked through, turning them over once, about 10-

minutes in total. Serve the fish immediately with a spoonful of sauce for each.

Nutritional Information: Calories: 319 | Fat: 26g | Protein: 22g | Carbohydrates: 2g | Fiber: 0g

371. Spicy Chicken Vegetable Soup

Prep Time: 11-minutes | Total time: 36-minutes | Yield: 4-servings

Ingredients:

1 lb. chicken, skinless	1 tsp. basil, dried
1 small onion, diced	1 can tomatoes, diced
2 c. vegetable, frozen	3 bay leaves
1 garlic clove, minced	1 and ½ c. sweet potatoes, cubed
½ tsp. red chili pepper flakes	1 jar spicy tomato sauce
½ tsp. of sea salt	2 c. chicken broth

Directions:

Add all ingredients in your Dutch oven, mix them well. Season with salt and pepper. Simmer for 15-minutes. Then cook 10-minutes. Serve warm and enjoy!

Nutritional Information: Calories: 279 Fat: 11g Carbohydrates: 18g Protein: 27g

372. Banana and Peanut Butter Detox

Prep Time: 11-minutes | Total time: 11-minutes | Yield: 1 serving

Ingredients:

1/2 banana, frozen and fresh	2 tbsps. almond butter
1/4 c. dandelion green	1 c. beet greens
1/2 c. almond milk	6 ice cubes

Directions:

Add all ingredients to your blender. Blend it you attain a smooth and creamy mixture. Serve chilled and enjoy!

Nutritional Information: Calories: 366 Fat: 20g Carbohydrates: 44g Protein: 10g

373. Creamy Cauliflower Parsnip Mash

Prep Time: 6-minutes | Total time: 30-minutes | Yield: 5-servings

Ingredients:

1 Medium-Sized Cauliflower	2 Parsnips
2 Tbsp. Extra Virgin Olive Oil	1/2 Tbsp. Salt
1/2 Tbsp. Lemon Juice	1 Tbsp. Black Pepper
5/6 Roasted Garlic Cloves	

Directions:
Cut the vegetables into small pieces. Boil the vegetables for 10 to 15-minutes at medium temperature until fork-tender. Drain the water and mash them in a blender. Add the remaining ingredients with the mash and blend until the mixture is smooth as butter. Add water and add salt if needed making sure that the batter isn't too thick or runny and serve.
Nutritional Information: Calories: 72 Carbohydrates: 12 g Fat: 0.8 g Protein: 3.7 g

374. Spinach Tomatoes Mix

Prep Time: 4-minutes | Total time: 14-minutes | Yield: 2-servings

Ingredients:

2 tbsp. Butter	1 Onion, chopped
2 cloves Garlic, minced	1 tbsp. Cumin powder
1 tbsp. Paprika	2 Tomatoes, chopped
2 c. Vegetable broth	1 small bunch of Spinach, chopped
Cilantro for garnishing	

Directions:
Melt the butter on Sauté mode. Add onion, garlic, and cumin powder, paprika, and vegetable broth; stir well. Add in tomatoes and spinach. Seal the lid, press Manual, and cook on High pressure for 10-minutes.
When ready, do a quick pressure release.
Nutritional Information: Calories 125, |Protein 7.7g, |Net Carbs 8.3g, |Fat 5.5g

375. Baked Tilapia with Rosemary and Pecan

Prep Time: 11-minutes | Total time: 28-minutes | Yield: 4-servings

Ingredients:

1/3 c. of whole-wheat panko breadcrumbs	1/3 c. raw pecans, chopped
½ tsp. of agave nectar	2 tsp. of rosemary, chopped
1 pinch of cayenne pepper	1-1/2 tsp. of olive oil
¼ lb. tilapia fillets, 4 pieces	1 egg white
1/8 tsp. of salt	

Directions:
Preheat your oven to 350 degrees F. Stir together the breadcrumbs, pecans, agave, rosemary, cayenne pepper, and salt in a baking dish. Pour the olive oil. Toss and coat the mixture. Bake for 7-minutes. Now turn up the temperature to 400 degrees F. Apply cooking spray on a glass baking dish. Whisk your egg white in a dish. Dip your fish inside the egg and then into your pecan mix. One fish fillet at a time. Coat each side lightly.

Keep the fish fillets in your baking dish. Keep the remaining pecan mix on the fillets. Bake for 10-minutes.
Nutritional Information: Calories 244 Carbs 7g Fat 12g Protein 27g Sugar 1g Fiber 2g Sodium 153mg

376. Walnut Rosemary Crusted Salmon

Prep Time: 11-minutes | Total time: 26-minutes | Yield: 4-servings

Ingredients:

2 tsp. Dijon mustard	1 minced garlic clove
¼ tsp. lemon zest	1 tsp. lemon juice
1 tsp. fresh rosemary, chopped	½ tsp. honey
½ tsp. kosher salt	¼ tsp. crushed red pepper
3 tsp. whole-wheat panko breadcrumbs	3 tsp. walnuts, finely chopped
1 tsp. extra virgin olive oil	1 lb. salmon fillet, skinless
Olive oil cooking spray	Chopped fresh parsley
Lemon wedges	

Directions:
Preheat oven up to 420°F and line a rimmed baking sheet with parchment paper, then set aside. Mix the mustard, garlic, lemon zest, lemon juice, rosemary, honey, salt, and red pepper in a bowl until well combined. In another bowl, mix the breadcrumbs, walnuts, and olive oil. Place the salmon on the baking sheet and spread the mustard mixture over the fillet. Sprinkle the salmon with the breadcrumbs mixture and press them over the salmon to adhere. Coat the salmon with the cooking spray. Bake, the salmon for about 12-minutes. Transfer your salmon to a serving platter, then sprinkle the parsley. Serve the salmon with lemon wedges.
Nutritional Information: Calories   222 Total fat 12g Carbs 4g Protein 24g

377. Roasted Cauliflower and Potato Curry Soup

Prep Time: 21-minutes | Total time: 51-minutes | Yield: 8
Ingredients:

2 tsp. ground coriander	2 tsp. ground cumin
1 ½ ground cinnamon	1 ½ ground turmeric
1 ¼ tsp. salt	¾ tsp. ground pepper
1/8 tsp. cayenne pepper	1 cauliflower head, cut into florets
2 tsp. extra virgin olive oil	1 chopped onion
1 c. diced carrot	3 minced garlic cloves
11/2 tsp. fresh ginger, grated	1 fresh jalapeno peppers, minced

4 c. low sodium vegetable broth	3 c. russet potatoes, peeled and diced
3 c. sweet potatoes, peeled and diced	2 tsp. lime zest
2 tsp. lime juice	1 (14 oz.) can coconut milk
Fresh cilantro, chopped	

Directions:

Preheat the oven to 410°F. In a bowl, mix the coriander, cumin, cinnamon, turmeric, salt, pepper, and cayenne until well combined. Toss the cauliflower with 1 tbsp. olive oil in a different bowl. Add 1 tbsp. of the seasoning mixture to the cauliflower and toss again. Spread the cauliflower on a rimmed baking sheet in a single layer. Roast cauliflower for about 20-minutes till the edges are browned. Meanwhile, pour the remaining oil into a skillet and heat it over medium heat. Brown the onions and carrots for about 3-minutes. Reduce the heat and cook the carrots for an additional 4-minutes. Stir in garlic, ginger, jalapeno, and the remaining spice mixture to the carrots mixture and cook for 1 minute. Add the broth, potatoes, sweet potatoes, lime zest, and lemon juice to the carrot mixture and let them boil over high heat. Cook the potatoes partially covered over medium heat for 20-minutes. Stir in the milk and the roasted cauliflower to the potatoes curry and allow simmering for 1 minute. Transfer your cauliflower to a serving platter and garnish it with cilantro. This is a good dinner recipe.

Nutritional Information: Calories 272 Total fat 15g Carbs 33g Protein 5g

378. Creamy Broccoli Stew

Prep Time: 11-minutes | Total time: 31-minutes | Yield: 4-servings

Ingredients:

1 c. Heavy Cream	3 oz. Parmesan cheese
1 c. Broccoli florets	2 Carrots, sliced
½ tbsp. Garlic paste	¼ tbsp. Turmeric powder
Salt and black Pepper, to taste	½ c. Vegetable broth
2 tbsp. Butter	

Directions:

Melt butter on Sauté mode. Add garlic and sauté for 30 seconds. Add broccoli and carrots, and cook until soft, for 2-3-minutes. Season with salt and pepper. Stir in the vegetable broth and seal the lid. Cook on Meat/Stew mode for 40-minutes. When ready, do a quick pressure release. Stir in the heavy cream.

Nutritional Information: Calories 239, |Protein 8g, |Net Carbs 5.1g, |Fat 21.4g

379. Garlic Lamb Chops

Prep Time: 35-minutes | Total time: 40-minutes | Yield: 2-servings

Ingredients:

¼ c. olive oil	¼ c. mint, fresh and chopped
8 lamb rib chops	1 tbsp. garlic, minced
1 tbsp. rosemary, fresh and chopped	

Directions:

Add olive oil, mint, and garlic into a bowl and then mix well. Keep a tbsp. of this mixture aside to use later. Toss your lamb chops inside the marinade and let them marinate for about 30-minutes. Preheat the cast-iron skillet using medium-heat. Add the lamb and then cook for 2-minutes per side for medium-rare. Let your lamb rest for a couple of-minutes, then drizzle the remaining marinade. Serve and enjoy!

Nutritional Information: Calories: 566 | Fat: 40g | Carbohydrates: 2g | Protein: 47g | Fiber: 1g

380. Green and Leafy Ginger-Apple Drink

Prep Time: 11-minutes | Total time: 11-minutes | Yield: 1 serving

Ingredients:

1 medium apple, cored	2 medium carrots, chopped
2 large handfuls of baby spinach	1 tbsp. ginger root, freshly grated
8 oz. of water, filtered	

Directions:

Add all ingredients to your blender. Blend it till you attain a smooth and creamy mixture. Serve chilled and enjoy!

Nutritional Information: Calories: 163 Fat: 0.1g Carbohydrates: 40g Protein: 3g

381. Cod and Peas

Prep Time: 11minutes | Total time: 26-minutes | Yield: 4-servings

Ingredients:

10 oz. peas, blanched	1 tbsp. chopped parsley
A drizzle of olive oil	4 cod fillets, boneless
1 tsp. dried oregano	2 oz. veggie stock
2 garlic cloves, minced	1 tsp. smoked paprika
Black pepper and salt	

Directions:

Put the parsley, paprika, oregano, stock, and garlic in your food processor and blend well. Heat up your pan with the oil using medium-high heat, add the cod, season with pepper and salt, then cook for 4-minutes on each side. Add the peas and the parsley, mix, and cook for 5-minutes more. Divide everything between plates and serve.

Nutritional Information: calories 271, fat 4, fiber 6, carbs 14, protein 15

382. Beets with Yogurt

Prep Time: 11-minutes | Total time: 51-minutes | Yield: 3-4-servings

Ingredients:

1 lb. Beets washed	1 lime, zested and juiced
1 c. Plain Full Milk Yogurt	1 clove Garlic, minced
Salt to taste	1 tbsp. Fresh Dill, chopped
1 tbsp. Olive oil to drizzle	Black Pepper to garnish
1 c. Water	

Directions:

Pour the water into the Instant Pot and fit in a steamer basket. Add the beets, seal the lid, secure the pressure valve, and select Manual mode on High Pressure mode for 30-minutes. Once ready, do a natural pressure release for 10-minutes, then quickly release the remaining pressure. Next, remove the beets to a bowl to cool, and then remove the skin. Cut into wedges. Place beets in a dip plate, drizzle the olive oil and lime juice over; set aside. In a bowl, mix garlic, yogurt, and lime zest. Pour over the beets and garnish with black pepper, salt, and dill.

Nutritional Information: Calories 102, |Protein 5.7g, |Net Carbs 8.2g, | Fat 3.8g

383. Gluten-Free Teriyaki Salmon

Prep Time: 17-minutes | Total time: 27-minutes | Yield: 4-servings

Ingredients:

24 oz. salmon steaks	Sauce
¼ c. coconut aminos	1 tsp. olive oil
½ c. lemon juice	1 tbsp. honey
1 tbsp. ginger, minced	1 tsp. garlic, minced
½ c. onions, chopped	¼ tsp. black pepper
1 stalk lemongrass, minced	1 tsp. sesame seeds

Directions:

Preheat oven up to 350F, then line a baking sheet with wax paper. Meanwhile, whisk the sauce ingredients in a mixing bowl until well mixed. Place salmon in a clean dish and then pour over the sauce. Rub the salmon with the seasoning until well covered. Refrigerate for at least 20-minutes. Transfer your salmon to the baking sheet you had prepared and bake for 12-minutes or until cooked through. Serve the salmon with sautéed veggies or salad of choice.

Nutritional Information: Calories 408 Total Fat 24 g Carbs 8 g Protein 39 g

384. Delicious Creamy Crab Meat

Prep Time: 6-minutes | Total time: 16-minutes | Yield: 3-servings

Ingredients:

1 lb. Crabmeat	½ c. Cream cheese
2 tbsp. Mayonnaise	Salt and Pepper, to taste
1 tbsp. Lemon juice	1 c. Cheddar cheese, shredded

Directions:

Mix mayo, cream cheese, salt and pepper, and lemon juice in a bowl. Add in crab meat and make small balls. Place the balls inside the pot. Seal the lid and press Manual. On high pressure, cook for 10-minutes. When you are done, let the pressure release naturally for about 10-minutes. Sprinkle the cheese over and serve!

Nutritional Information: Calories 443, |Protein 41g, |Net Carbs 2.5g, |Fat 30.4g

385. Scallops Stew

Prep Time: 11-minutes | Total time: 31-minutes | Yield: 4-servings

Ingredients:

2 leeks, chopped	2 tbsps. olive oil
1 tsp. chopped jalapeno	2 tsp. chopped garlic
A small pinch of black pepper and salt	¼ tsp. ground cinnamon
1 carrot, chopped	1 tsp. ground cumin
1½ c. chopped tomatoes	1 c. veggie stock
1 lb. shrimp, peeled and deveined	1 lb. sea scallops
2 tbsps. chopped cilantro	

Directions:

Heat up a pot using the oil over medium-heat, add garlic and leeks, stir, and cook for 7-minutes. Add jalapeno, salt, pepper, cayenne, carrots, cinnamon, and cumin, stir, and cook for 5 more-minutes. Add tomatoes, stock, shrimp, and scallops stir, cook for 6 more minutes, divide into bowls, sprinkle cilantro on top, and serve.

Nutritional Information: Calories 251, Fat 4, Fiber 4, Carbs 11, Protein 17

386. Broccoli Rice with Mushrooms

Prep Time: 6-minutes | Total time: 38-minutes | Yield: 3-servings

Ingredients:

2 tbsp. Olive oil	1 small Red Onion, chopped
1 Carrot, chopped	2 c. Button Mushrooms, chopped
½ Lemon, zested and juiced	Salt to taste
Pepper to taste	2 cloves Garlic, minced
½ c. Broccoli rice	½ c. Chicken Stock
5 Cherry Tomatoes	Parsley Leaves, chopped for garnishing

Directions:

Set on Sauté. Heat oil and cook the carrots and onions for 2-minutes. Stir in mushrooms and cook for 3-minutes. Stir in pepper, salt, lemon juice, garlic, and lemon zest. Stir in broccoli and chicken stock. Drop the tomatoes over the top, but don't stir. Seal lid, and then cook on High pressure for 10-minutes. Once ready, do a natural pressure release for 4-minutes, then quickly release the remaining pressure. Sprinkle with parsley and stir evenly.

Nutritional Information: Calories 160, |Protein 6g, |Net Carbs 10g, |Fat 2g

387. Squash Spaghetti with Bolognese Sauce

Prep Time: 6-minutes | Total time: 16-minutes | Yield: 3-servings

Ingredients:

1 large Squash, cut into 2, and seed pulp removed	2 c. Water
Bolognese Sauce to serve	

Directions:

Place the trivet and add the water. Add in the squash, seal the lid, select Manual and cook on High Pressure for 8-minutes. Once ready, quickly release the pressure. Carefully remove the squash; use two forks to shred the inner skin. Serve with Bolognese sauce.

Nutritional Information: Calories 37, |Protein 0.9g, |Net Carbs 7.8g, |Fat 0.4g

388. Celery Root Hash Browns

Prep Time: 11-minutes | Total time: 21-minutes | Yield: 4-servings

Ingredients:

4 tbsp. coconut oil	½ tsp sea salt
2 to 3 medium celery roots	

Directions:

Scrub the celery root clean and peel it is using a vegetable peeler. Grate the celery root in a manual grater.

In a skillet, add oil and heat it over medium heat. Place the grated celery root on the skillet and sprinkle with salt. Let it cook for 10-minutes on each side or until the grated celery turns brown. Serve warm.

Nutritional Information: Calories 160| Fat 14g|Saturated Fat 3g | Carbs 10g|Net Carbs 7g Protein 1.5g

389. Chai Tea Drink

Prep Time: 6-minutes | Total time: 7-minutes | Yield: 1 serving

Ingredients:

1 c. almond milk	1 tbsp. honey
1 c. boiling water	¼ tsp. cacao powder
1 green tea bag	

Directions:

Take a large mug, add a tea bag and hot water. Leave it for 5-minutes. Discard tea bag and stir in cacao powder and honey. Mix them well. Stir in cold almond milk Serve and enjoy!

Nutritional Information: Calories: 216 Fat: 8g Carbohydrates: 29g Protein: 8g

390. Tamari Steak Salad

Prep Time: 17-minutes | Total time: 27-minutes | Yield: 2-servings

Ingredients:

1 large bunches salad green	4 oz. beefsteak
½ red bell pepper, diced	4 cherry tomatoes, cut into halves
2 radishes, sliced	2 tbsps. olive oil
¼ tbsp. fresh lemon juice	1 oz. gluten-free tamari sauce
Salt as needed	

Directions:

Marinate steak in tamari sauce. Make the salad by adding bell pepper, tomatoes, radishes, salad green, oil, salt, and lemon juice to a bowl and toss them well.

Grill your steak to attain the desired doneness and transfer steak on top of the salad platter. Let it sit for 1 minute and cut it crosswise. Serve and enjoy!

Nutritional Information: Calories: 500 | Fat: 37g | Carbohydrates: 4g | Protein: 33g | Fiber: 2g |

391. Zucchini Noodles in Garlic and Parmesan Toss

Prep Time: 7-minutes | Total time: 22-minutes | Yield: 4-servings

Ingredients:

3 large Zucchinis, spiralized	2 tbsp. Olive oil
3 cloves Garlic, minced	1 Lemon, zested and juiced
Salt to taste	Black Pepper to taste
5 Mint Leaves, chopped	6 tbsp. Parmesan Cheese, grated

Directions:

Set on Sauté. Heat the oil, and add lemon zest, garlic, and salt. Stir and cook for 30 seconds. Add zucchini and pour lemon juice over. Coat the noodles quickly but gently with the oil. Cook for 10 seconds, press Cancel. Sprinkle the mint leaves and cheese over and toss gently.

Nutritional Information: Calories 15, |Protein 10g, | Net Carbs 2g, |Fat 2g

392. Tropical Fruit Parfait

Prep Time: 11-minutes | Total time: 21-minutes | Yield: 1 serving

Ingredients:

1 tbsp. toasted sliced almonds	¼ c. plain soy yogurt
½ c. of fruit combination cut into ½-inch cubes (pineapple, mango, and kiwi	

Directions:

Prepare fresh fruit by peeling and slicing into ½-inch cubes. Place cubed fruit in a bowl and top with a dollop of soy yogurt. Garnish with sliced almonds and if desired, refrigerate for an hour before.

Nutritional Information: Calories: 119 Fat: 21g Carbohydrates: 25g Protein: 9g Sugar: 12g Fiber: 7g

393. Creamy Chicken Salad

Prep Time: 11-minutes | Total time: 41-minutes | Yield: 4-servings

Ingredients:

1 lb. Chicken Breast	2 Avocados
2 Garlic Cloves	3 tbsps. Minced Lime Juice
1/3 c. Onion	1 Minced Jalapeno Pepper
A dash Minced Salt	1 tbsp. Cilantro
A dash Pepper	

Directions:

You will want to start this recipe off by prepping the stove to 400. As this warms up, get out your cooking sheet and line it with paper or foil. Next, it is time to get out the chicken. Go ahead and layer the chicken breast up with some olive oil before seasoning to your liking. When the chicken is all set, you will want to line them along the surface of your cooking sheet and pop it into the oven for about twenty-minutes. By the end of twenty-minutes, the chicken should be cooked through and taken out of the oven for chilling. Once it's cool enough, cool to handle, you may either dice or shred your chicken, dependent upon how you like your chicken salad. Now that your chicken is all cooked, it is time to assemble your salad! You can begin this process by adding everything into a bowl and mashing down the avocado. Once your ingredients are mended to your liking, sprinkle some salt over the top and serve.

Nutritional Information: Fats: 20g |Carbs: 4g |Proteins: 25g

394. Mushroom & Cauliflower Risotto

Prep Time: 6-minutes | Total time: 16-minutes | Yield: 4-servings

Ingredients:

1 Grated head of cauliflower	1 c. Vegetable stock
9 oz. Chopped mushrooms	2 tbsps. Butter
1 c. Coconut cream	

Directions:

Pour the stock into a saucepan. Boil and set aside. Prepare a skillet with butter and sauté the mushrooms until golden. Grate and stir in the cauliflower and stock. Simmer and add the cream, cooking until the cauliflower is al dente. Serve.

Nutritional Information: Net Carbohydrates: 4 g |Protein: 1 g | Fats: 17 g |Calories: 186

395. Spicy Pork Chops

Prep Time: 4 hours and 10-minutes | Total time: 4 hours 25-minutes | Yield: 2-servings

Ingredients:

¼ c. lime juice 2 pork rib chops	1/2 tbsp. coconut oil, melted
1/2 garlic cloves, peeled and minced	1/2 tbsp. chili powder
1/2 tsp. ground cinnamon	1 tsp. cumin
Salt and pepper to taste	1/4 tsp. hot pepper sauce
Mango, sliced	

Directions:

Take a bowl and mix in lime juice, oil, garlic, cumin, cinnamon, chili powder, salt, pepper, hot pepper sauce. Whisk well. Add pork chops and toss. Keep it on the side, and let it refrigerate for 4 hours. Preheat your grill to medium and transfer pork chops to the preheated grill. Grill for 7-minutes, flip and cook for 7-minutes more. Divide between serving platters and serve with mango slices. Enjoy!

Nutritional Information: Calories: 200 | Fat: 8g | Carbohydrates: 3g | Protein: 26g | Fiber: 1g |

396. Lemony Mussels

Prep Time: 6-minutes | Total time: 11-minutes | Yield: 4-servings

Ingredients:

1 tbsp. extra virgin olive oil	2 minced garlic cloves
2 lbs. scrubbed mussels	Juice of one lemon

Directions:

Put some water in a pot, add mussels, bring a boil over medium heat, cook for 5-minutes, discard unopened mussels, and transfer them with a bowl. Mix the oil with garlic and freshly squeezed lemon juice in another bowl, whisk well, and add over the mussels, toss, and serve. Enjoy!

Nutritional Information: |Calories: 140|Fat: 4 g|Carbs:8 g|Protein:8 g| Sugars:4g|Sodium:600 mg

397. Healthy Halibut Fillets

Prep Time: 6-minutes | Total time: 16-minutes | Yield: 2-servings

Ingredients:

2 Halibut fillets	1 tbsp. Dill
1 tbsp. Onion powder	1 c. Parsley, chopped
2 tbsp. Paprika	1 tbsp. Garlic powder
1 tbsp. Lemon Pepper	2 tbsp. Lemon juice

Directions:

Mix lemon juice, lemon pepper, garlic powder, paprika, parsley, dill, and onion powder in a bowl. Pour the mixture into the Instant pot and place the halibut fish over it. Seal the lid, press Manual mode, and cook for 10-minutes on High pressure. When ready, do a quick pressure release by setting the valve to venting.

Nutritional Information: Calories 283, |Protein 22.5g, |Net Carbs 6.2g, |Fat 16.4g

398. Tender salmon in mustard sauce

Prep Time: 11-minutes | Total time: 31-minutes | Yield: 2-servings

Ingredients:

5 tbsps. Minced dill Pepper.	2/3 c. sour cream
	2 tbsps. Dijon mustard
1 tsp. garlic powder	5 oz. salmon fillets
2-3 tbsps. Lemon juice	

Directions:

Mix sour cream, mustard, lemon juice, and dill. Season the fillets with pepper and garlic powder. Arrange the salmon on a baking sheet skin side down and cover with the prepared mustard sauce. Bake for 20-minutes at 390°F.

Nutritional Information: Calories: 318, Fat: 12 g, Carbs: 8 g, Protein: 40.9 g, Sugars: 9 g

399. Faux Beet Risotto

Prep Time: 7-minutes | Total time: 22-minutes | Yield: 2-servings

Ingredients:

4 Beets, tails, and leaves removed	2 tbsp. Olive oil
1 big head of Cauliflower, cut into florets	4 tbsp. c. Full Milk
2 tsp Red Chili Flakes	Salt to taste
Black Pepper to taste	½ c. Water

Directions:

Pour the water into the Instant Pot and fit a steamer basket. Place the beets and cauliflower in the basket. Seal lid, and then cook on High Pressure mode for 4-minutes. Once ready, do a natural pressure release for 10-minutes, then quickly release the pressure. Remove steamer basket containing the veggies and discard water. Remove the beets' peels. Place veggies back in the pot, add salt, pepper, and flakes. Mash with a potato masher. Hit Sauté and cook the milk for 2-minutes. Stir frequently. Dish onto plates and drizzle with oil.

Nutritional Information: Calories 153, | Protein 3.6g, |Net Carbs 2.5g, | Fat 9g

400. Shrimp and Vegetable Curry

Prep Time: 6-minutes | Total time: 16-minutes | Yield: 4-servings

Ingredients:

1 sliced onion	3 tbsps. of olive oil
2 tsp. of curry powder	1 c. of coconut milk
1 cauliflower	1 lb. shrimp tails

Directions:

Add the onion to your oil. Sauté to make it a bit soft. Steam your vegetables in the meantime. Add the curry seasoning, coconut milk, and spices if you want once the onion has become soft. Cook for 2-minutes. Include the shrimp. Cook for 5-minutes. Serve with steamed vegetables.

Nutritional Information: Calories 491 Carbs 11g Fat 39g Protein 24g Sugar 3g Fiber 5g Sodium 309mg

401. Vegetarian Faux Stew

Prep Time: 5-minutes | Total time: 30 minute | Yield: 3-servings

Ingredients:

1 ½ c. Diced Tomatoes	4 cloves Garlic
1 tsp Minced Ginger	1 tsp Turmeric
1 tsp Cayenne Powder	2 tsp Paprika
Salt to taste	1 tsp Cumin Powder
2 c. Dry Soy Curls	1 ½ c. Water
3 tbsp. Butter	½ c. Heavy Cream
¼ c. Chopped Cilantro	

Directions:

Place the tomatoes, water, soy curls, and all spices in the Instant Pot. Seal the lid, secure the pressure valve and select Manual mode on High Pressure mode for 6-minutes. Once ready, do a natural pressure release for 10-minutes. Select Sauté, add the cream and butter. Stir while crushing the tomatoes with the back of the spoon. Stir in the cilantro and serve.

Nutritional Information: Calories 143, |Protein 4g, |Net Carbs 2g, |Fat 9g

402. Turmeric Rice Bowl with Garam Masala Root Vegetable and chickpeas

Prep Time: 26-minutes | Total time: 56-minutes | Yield: 4-servings

Ingredients:

Rice	2 ½ c. of water
1 c. brown basmati rice, cleaned and rinsed	½ c. raisins
2 tsp. extra virgin olive oil	2 tsp. onion powder
1 tsp. ground turmeric	½ tsp. ground cinnamon
½ tsp. ground black pepper	¼ tsp. kosher salt
Vegetables and Chickpeas	4 tsp. coconut oil
2 (15 oz.) can chickpeas	2 tsp. garam masala
2 c. roasted root vegetables	2 tsp. honey
½ tsp. kosher salt	½ tsp. ground pepper
4 tsp. lemon juice	4 tsp. low-fat plain yogurt
Chopped mint, parsley, and cilantro	

Directions:

Combine all the rice ingredients in a saucepan and bring the rice to a boil. Cook covered at a reduced heat for 20-minutes until all the water is absorbed. Meanwhile, using a skillet heat up oil on medium heat. Stir in the chickpeas to the skillet and cook for 5-minutes.

Stir in the garam masala to the chickpeas and cook for 1 minute. Add the root vegetables, honey, salt, and pepper to the skillet and cook while stirring for 4-minutes. Stir the lemon juice into the vegetable mixture and remove from heat. Allow the rice to stand covered for 10-minutes. Serve chickpeas over rice and then top with yogurt.Garnish the rice with mint, parsley, and cilantro.

Nutritional Information: Calories 671 Total fat 13g Carbs 107g Protein 16g

403. Broccoli Bites

Prep Time: 17-minutes | Total time: 26-minutes | Yield: 4-servings

Ingredients:

2 eggs, beaten	¼ c. parmesan cheese, grated
2 c. broccoli florets	1½ c. cheddar cheese, grated
Salt and pepper, to taste	

Directions:

Add broccoli to the food processor and pulse until crumbly. Mix broccoli and the remaining ingredients in a large bowl. Make small balls from the mixture and arrange them on a baking sheet. Let it refrigerate for 30-minutes. Preheat Air Fryer to attain 360 degrees F. Transfer balls to air fryer cooking basket and cook for 12-minutes. Serve and enjoy!

Nutritional Information: Calories: 234, | Fat: 17g, | Carbs: 4g, |Fiber: 1g, |Net Carbs: 2g, |Protein: 16g

404. Cauliflower Mac & Cheese

Prep Time: 17-minutes | Total time: 37-minutes | Yield: 4-servings

Ingredients:

1 head Cauliflower	3 tbsps. Butter
¼ c. Unsweetened almond milk	¼ c. Heavy cream
1 c. Cheddar cheese	

Directions:

Using a pretty sharp knife, slice your cauliflower into small florets. Shred the cheese. Prepare the oven to reach 450° Fahrenheit. Cover the baking pan using a layer of parchment baking paper or foil. Add two tbsps. Of butter to a pan and melt. Add the florets, butter, salt, and pepper together. Place the cauliflower on the baking pan and roast for 10 to 15-minutes. Warm up the rest of the butter, milk, heavy cream, and cheese in the microwave or double boiler. Pour the cheese over the cauliflower and serve.

Nutritional Information: Net Carbohydrates: 7 g|Protein: 11 g | Fats: 23 g |Calories: 294 g

405. Stuffed Chicken Breasts
Prep Time: 32-minutes | Total time: 1 hour | Yield: 4-servings
Ingredients:

1 tbsp. butter	¼ c. chopped sweet onion
½ c. goat cheese, at room temperature	¼ c. Kalamata olives, chopped
¼ c. chopped roasted red pepper	2 tbsps. chopped fresh basil
4 (5 oz.) chicken breasts, skin-on	2 tbsps. extra-virgin olive oil

Directions:
Preheat the oven to 400°F. Melt butter using medium heat and then add onions in a small sized skillet. Sauté till tender, about 3-minutes. Transfer onion into a medium sized bowl and add the olives, cheese, basil, and red. Stir till well blended and then refrigerate for about 30-minutes. Cut a horizontal pocket into every chicken breast, and then stuff them evenly using the filling. Secure each chicken breast side with toothpicks. Place a large sized ovenproof skillet over medium-high heat and add the olive oil. Brown your chicken on both sides, about 10-minutes in total. Place skillet in an oven and roast until the chicken is just cooked through, about 15-minutes. Remove the toothpicks and serve.
Nutritional Information: Calories: 389 |Fat: 30g |Protein: 25g |Carbohydrates: 3g |Fiber: 0g

406. Tilapia with Asparagus and Acorn Squash
Prep Time: 16-minutes | Total time: 46-minutes | Yield: 4-servings
Ingredients:

2 tbsps. extra-virgin olive oil	1 medium acorn squash, seeded and thinly sliced or in wedges
1 lb. asparagus, with woody, ends trimmed, cut into 2-inch pieces	1 large shallot, thinly sliced
1 lb. tilapia fillets	½ c. white wine
1 tbsp. chopped fresh flat-leaf parsley	1 tsp. salt
¼ tsp. freshly ground black pepper	

Directions:
Preheat the oven to 400°F. Grease the baking sheet with oil. Arrange the squash, asparagus, and shallot in a single layer on the baking sheet. Roast within 8 to 10-minutes. Put the tilapia and add the wine. Sprinkle with parsley, salt, and pepper. Roast within 15-minutes. Remove, then let rest for 5-minutes, and serve.
Nutritional Information: Calories: 246 Fat: 8g Carbs: 17g Sugar: 2g Fiber: 4g Protein: 25g Sodium: 639mg

407. Fennel & Figs Lamb
Prep Time: 11-minutes | Total time: 51-minutes | Yield: 2-servings
Ingredients:

6 oz. lamb racks	1 fennel bulbs, sliced
Salt	pepper, to taste
1 tbsp. olive oil	2 figs, cut in half
1/8 c. apple cider vinegar	1/2 tbsp. swerve

Directions:
Take a bowl and add fennel, figs, vinegar, swerve, oil, and toss. Transfer to baking dish. Season with salt and pepper. Bake it for 16-minutes at 400 degrees F. Season lamb with salt, pepper, and transfer to a heated pan over medium-high heat. Cook for a few-minutes. Add lamb to the baking dish with fennel and bake for 20-minutes. Divide between plates and serve. Enjoy!
Nutritional Information: Calories: 230 | Fat: 3g | Protein: 10g | Fiber: 2g | Net Carbohydrates: 3g

408. Mediterranean Mushroom Olive Steak
Prep Time: 11-minutes | Total time: 25-minutes | Yield: 2-servings
Ingredients:

1/2 lb. boneless beef sirloin steak, ¾ inch thick, cut into 4 pieces	1/2 large red onion, chopped
1/2 c. mushrooms	2 garlic cloves, thinly sliced
2 tbsps. olive oil	1/4 c. green olives, coarsely chopped
1/2 c. parsley leaves, finely cut	

Directions:
Place large sized skillet over medium heat. Add oil and let it heat up. Add beef, then cook till both sides are well, remove beef and drain fat. Add the rest of the oil to the skillet and heat it. Add garlic, onions, and then cook for 2-3-minutes. Stir well. Add olives, mushrooms and then cook till mushrooms are thoroughly done. Return the beef to skillet and lower heat to medium. Cook for 3-4-minutes (covered). Stir in parsley. Serve.
Nutritional Information: Calories: 386 | Fat: 30g | Protein: 21g | Fiber: 5g | Net Carbohydrates: 6g

409. Bacon Burger Cabbage Stir Fry
Prep Time: 11-minutes | Total time: 31-minutes | Yield: 10 serving
Ingredients:

Ground beef (1 lb.)	Bacon (1 lb.) Small onion (1)

Minced cloves of garlic (3)	Cabbage (1 lb./1 small head)

Directions:

Dice the bacon and onion. Combine the beef and bacon in a wok or large skillet. Prepare it until done and store it in a bowl to keep warm. Mince the onion and garlic. Toss both into the hot grease. Slice and toss in the cabbage and stir-fry until wilted. Blend in the meat and combine. Sprinkle with pepper and salt as desired.

Nutritional Information: Net Carbohydrates: 4.5 g | Protein: 32 g | Fats: 22 g | Calories: 357

410. Creamed Savoy Cabbage

Prep Time: 6-minutes | Total time: 22-minutes | Yield: 3-servings

Ingredients:

2 medium Savoy Cabbages, finely chopped	2 small Onions, chopped
2 c. Bacon, chopped	2 ½ c. Mixed Bone Broth, see recipe above
¼ tsp Mace	2 c. Coconut Milk
1 Bay Leaf	Salt to taste
3 tbsp. Chopped Parsley	

Directions:

Set on Sauté. Add the bacon crumbles and onions; cook until crispy. Add bone broth and scrape the bottom of the pot. Stir in bay leaf and cabbage. Cut out some parchment paper and cover the cabbage with it.

Seal the lid, select Manual mode, and cook on High Pressure for 4-minutes. Once ready, press Cancel and quickly release the pressure. Select Sautee, stir in the milk and nutmeg. Simmer for 5-minutes, add the parsley.

Nutritional Information: Calories 27, | Protein 4g, | Net Carbs 3.1g, | Fat 3g

411. Clean Salmon with Soy Sauce

Prep Time: 11-minutes | Total time: 41-minutes | Yield: 2

Ingredients:

2 Salmon fillets	2 tbsp. Avocado oil
2 tbsp. Soy sauce	1 tbsp. Garlic powder
1 tbsp. fresh Dill to garnish	Salt and Pepper, to taste

Directions:

To make the marinade, thoroughly mix the soy sauce, avocado oil, salt, pepper, and garlic powder into a bowl. Dip salmon in the mixture and place in the refrigerator for 20-minutes. Transfer the contents to the Instant pot. Seal, set on Manual, and cook for 10-minutes

on high pressure. When ready, do a quick release. Serve topped with the fresh dill.

Nutritional Information: Calories 512, | Protein 65g, | Net Carbs 3.2g, | Fat 21g

412. Ambrosial Avocado & Salmon Salad in Lemon-Dressed Layers

Prep Time: 10-minutes | Total time: 10-minutes | Yield: 4-servings

Ingredients:

For the Avocado & Salmon Salad:

6 oz wild salmon	1 pc avocado, pitted, peeled, and diced
2 c. loosely packed salad greens	½ c. Monterey Jack cheese, reduced-fat, shredded
¾ c. tomato, chopped	1 Tbsp lemon juice, freshly squeezed

For the Lemon Dressing:

1 Tbsp. lemon juice, freshly squeezed	1 Tbsp. olive oil, extra-virgin
1 tsp. honey	1/8 tsp. Kosher or sea salt
1/8 tsp. black pepper	½ tsp Dijon mustard
4 units jars	

Directions:

Combine and whisk all the dressing ingredients, excluding the olive oil, in a small mixing bowl. Mix well. Drizzle gradually with the oil into the dressing mixture and keep whisking while pouring. Pour the dressing to distribute evenly into each jar. Distribute uniformly into each jar similar amounts of the following ingredients in this order: diced tomatoes, cheese, avocado, salmon, and lettuce. Secure each jar with its lid and chill the jars in the fridge until ready for serving.

Nutritional Information: Calories: 267 Cal Fat: 7.4 g Protein: 16.6 g Carbs: 38.1 g Fiber: 4.8 g

413. Vegetable and Papillae

Prep Time: 6-minutes | Total time: 22-minutes | Yield: 3-servings

Ingredients:

4 small Carrots, widely julienned	¼ tsp Black Pepper
A pinches salt	1 clove Garlic, crushed
2 tbsp. Butter	2 slices Lemon
1 tbsp. Chopped Thyme	1 tbsp. Oregano
1 tbsp. Chopped Parsley	17-inch Parchment Paper

Directions:

Add all ingredients, except lemon slices and butter, to a bowl and toss. Place the paper on a flat surface, and then add the mixed ingredients at the center of the paper. Put the lemon slices on top and drop the butter over. Wrap it up nicely. Pour 1 cup of water in and lower the trivet with a handle. Put the veggie pack on the trivet, seal the lid, and cook on High Pressure for 2-minutes. Once ready, do a quick release. Carefully remove the packet and serve veggies in a wrap on a plate.

Nutritional Information: Calories 60, |Protein 3g, |Net Carbs 1g, |Fat 3g

414. Zucchini and Lemon Herb Salmon

Prep Time: 16-minutes | Total time: 36-minutes | Yield: 4-servings

Ingredients:

2 tbsps. of olive oil	4 chopped zucchinis
2 tbsps. of lemon juice	2 tbsps. of agave nectar
2 garlic cloves, minced	1 tbsp. of Dijon mustard
½ tsp. oregano, dried	½ tsp. Dill, dried
¼ tsp. rosemary, dried	¼ tsp. thyme, dried
4 salmon fillets	2 tbsps. parsley leaves, chopped
Ground black pepper and kosher salt to taste	

Directions:

Preheat your oven to 400 degrees F. Apply cooking spray on your baking sheet lightly. Whisk the lemon juice, brown sugar, dill, garlic, Dijon, rosemary, thyme, and oregano in a bowl. Season with pepper and salt to taste. Set aside. Keep the zucchini on your baking sheet in one single layer. Drizzle some olive oil. Season with pepper and salt. Add the fish in one layer. Brush each fillet with your herb mix. Keep in the oven. Cook for 17-minutes. Garnish with parsley and serve.

Nutritional Information: Calories 355 Carbs 15g Fat 19g Protein 31g Sugar 12g Fiber 2g Sodium 132mg

415. Miso Salmon and Green Beans

Prep Time: 11-minutes | Total time: 36-minutes | Yield: 4-servings

Ingredients:

1 tbsp. sesame oil	1 lb. green beans, trimmed
1 lb. skin-on salmon fillets, cut into 4 steaks	¼ c. white miso
2 tsp. gluten-free tamari or soy sauce	2 scallions, thinly sliced

Directions:

Preheat the oven to 400°F. Grease the baking sheet with oil. Put the green beans, then the salmon on top of the green beans, and brush each piece with the miso. Roast within 20 to 25-minutes. Drizzle with the tamari, sprinkle with the scallions and serve.

Nutritional Information: Calories: 213 Fat: 7g Carbs: 13g Sugar: 3g Fiber: 5g Protein: 27g Sodium: 989mg

416. Sheet Pan Steak with Brussels sprouts And Red Wine

Prep Time: 11-minutes | Total time: 31-minutes | Yield: 4-servings

Ingredients:

1 lb. rib-eye steak	1 tsp. salt
¼ tsp. freshly ground black pepper	1 tbsp. unsalted butter
½ red onion, minced	8 oz. Brussels sprouts, trimmed and quartered
1 c. red wine	Juice of ½ lemon

Directions:

Preheat the broiler on high. Massage the steak with salt and pepper on a large, rimmed baking sheet. Broil until browned, 2 to 3-minutes per side. Turn off and heat-up the oven to 400°F. Put the steak on one side of the baking sheet and add the butter, onion, Brussels sprouts, and wine to the other side. Roast within 8-minutes. Remove, and let rest for 5-minutes. Sprinkle with the lemon juice and serve.

Nutritional Information: Calories: 416 Fat: 27g Carbs: 8g Sugar: 2g Fiber: 3g Protein: 22g Sodium: 636mg

417. Chicken Lemon Piccata

Prep Time: 11-minutes | Total time: 31-minutes | Yield: 4-servings

Ingredients:

2 chicken breasts, skinless & boneless	2 tbsps. dairy-free margarine
1-1/2 tbsps. whole wheat flour	¼ tsp. salt
¼ tsp. white pepper	1/3 c. white wine, dry
2 tbsps. olive oil	¼ c. lemon juice
1/3 c. chicken stock, low-sodium	¼ c. minced Italian parsley
¼ c. capers, drained	Pepper and salt to taste

Directions:

Cut in half each chicken breast. Spread your flour on a plate thinly. Season with pepper and salt. Dredge the breast slices lightly in your seasoned flour. Set aside. Heat your sauté pan over medium temperature. Add the breast slices to your pan when you see the oil simmering. Cook for 3 to 4-minutes. Turn over the chicken slices. Take out the slices. Set aside. Add wine to the pan. Stir. Scrape up browned bits from the bottom. Now add the chicken stock and lemon juice. Go to high heat. Boil till you have a thick sauce. Bring down the heat. Stir the parsley and capers in. Add back the breast slices to your pan. Rewarm.

Nutritional Information: Calories 227 Carbohydrates 3g Fat 15g Fiber 1g Sugar 0g Protein 20g

418. Tilapia Delight

Prep Time: 6-minutes | Total time: 16-minutes | Yield: 4-servings

Ingredients:

4 Tilapia fillets	4 tbsp. Lemon juice
2 tbsp. Butter	2 Garlic cloves
½ c. Parsley	Salt and Pepper, to taste

Directions:

Melt butter on Sauté, and add garlic cloves, parsley. Season with salt and pepper; stir well. Cook for 2 to 3-minutes. Then, add tilapia and lemon juice and stir well. Seal the lid and set it on Manual mode. Cook for 10-minutes on High pressure. When the timer beeps, allow the pressure to release naturally, for 5-minutes.

Nutritional Information: Calories 135, |Protein 23.7g, |Net Carbs 1.3g, |Fat 4.4g

419. Garlic Salmon with Cheese

Prep Time: 17-minutes | Total time: 30-minutes | Yield: 4-servings

Ingredients:

½ c. Asiago cheese	2 tbsps. lemon juice, freshly squeezed
2 tbsps. butter	2 tsp. minced garlic
1 tsp. chopped basil, fresh	1 tsp. chopped oregano, fresh
4 (5 oz.) salmon fillets	1 tbsp. olive oil

Directions:

Preheat your oven to attain 350°F. Line a parchment paper to your baking sheet and set it aside. Add in the Asiago cheese, butter, basil, garlic, lemon juice, and oregano using a bowl. Pat the salmon dry using a towel and set the fillets on your prepared baking sheet with the skin-side down. Evenly divide topping between your fillets and spread across the fish with the use of a knife. Drizzle the olive oil to the fish and bake for about 12-minutes until the topping turns golden in color and your fish is just cooked through. Serve.

Nutritional Information: Calories: 358 |Fat: 27.8g |Protein: 25g |Carbohydrates: 2g |Fiber: 0g

420. Escarole, Pineapple, and Apple Smoothie

Prep Time: 11-minutes | Total time: 12-minutes | Yield: 1 serving

Ingredients:

2 c. pineapple, cubed	2 apples, cored
8 oz. almond milk	1 head escarole lettuce
1 stalk celery	

Directions:

Add all ingredients to your blender. Blend till you attain a smooth and creamy mixture. Serve chilled.

Nutritional Information: Calories: 466 Fat: 8g Carbohydrates: 103g Protein: 8g

421. Sesame-Tamari Baked Chicken with Green Beans

Prep Time: 11-minutes | Total time: 56-minutes | Yield: 4-servings

Ingredients:

1 lb. green beans, trimmed	4 bone-in, skin-on chicken breasts
2 tbsps. honey	1 tbsp. sesame oil
1 tbsp. gluten-free tamari or soy sauce	1 c. chicken or vegetable broth

Directions:

Preheat your oven to attain 400°F. Arrange the green beans on a large, rimmed baking sheet. Put the chicken, skin-side up, on top of the beans. Drizzle with honey, oil, and tamari. Add the broth. Roast within 35 to 40 min. Remove and let it cool off for about 5-minutes before you serve.

Nutritional Information: Calories: 378 Fat: 10g Carbs: 19g Sugar: 10g Fiber: 4g Protein: 54g Sodium: 336mg

422. Blackened Tilapia

Prep Time: 9-minutes | Total time: 18-minutes | Yield: 2-servings

Ingredients:

1 c. cauliflower, chopped	1 tsp. red pepper flakes
1 tbsp. Italian seasoning	1 tbsp. garlic, minced
6 oz. tilapia	1 c. English cucumber, chopped with peel
2 tbsps. olive oil	1 sprig dill, chopped
1 tsp. stevia	3 tbsp. lime juice
2 tbsp. Cajun blackened seasoning	

Directions:

Take a bowl and add the seasoning ingredients (except Cajun). Add a tbsp of oil and whip. Pour dressing over cauliflower and cucumber. Brush fish with olive oil on either side. Take a skillet and grease it well with 1 tbsp. of olive oil. Press Cajun seasoning on both sides of the fish. Cook fish for 3-minutes per side. Serve with vegetables and enjoy!

Nutritional Information: Calories: 530 | Fat: 33g | Net Carbohydrates: 4g | Protein: 32g | Fiber: 2g |

423. Chicken Curry with Tamarind & Pumpkins

Prep Time: 11-minutes | Total time: 46-minutes | Yield: 4-servings

Ingredients:

1 tsp. of olive oil	8 chicken thighs, boneless & skinless, trimmed
1 onion, chopped	¾ tsp. pepper, ground
½ tsp. of salt	2 c. pumpkins, diced
3 garlic cloves, minced	¼ lb. tamarind, pulped
1-1/2 tsps. coriander, ground	1-1/2 tsps. of curry powder
1-1/2 tsps. cumin, ground	¼ c. parsley, minced
1-1/4 c. chicken broth, fat-free	Pepper and salt to taste

Directions:

Season your chicken thighs (both sides) with half of the pepper and salt. Heat your nonstick skillet over medium temperature. Apply cooking spray lightly. Add the chicken. Cook each side for 2-minutes. Transfer to a plate. Heat olive oil in a skillet. Add the garlic and onions. Cook for 3-minutes. Stir together the curry powder, pumpkin, tamarind, cumin, coriander, chicken broth, ¼ tsp. pepper, and ¼ tsp. salt in your skillet. Boil the mixture and reduce heat to medium. Let it simmer for 12-minutes. Stir occasionally. Include the chicken. Cook covered for 15-minutes. Cook uncovered for 10-minutes. Stir the parsley in.

Nutritional Information: Calories 757 Carbs 52g Fat 29g Protein 86g Sugar 16g Fiber 8g Sodium 750mg

424. Fish Tacos with Cabbage Slaw

Prep time: 15 – 20-minutes | Total time: 20 – 25-minutes | Yield: 4-servings

Ingredients:
For the slaw:

4 c. shredded cabbage	½ tsps. kosher salts
1 small sized carrot, grated	3 medium sized scallions, sliced thinly
1 jalapeno pepper, minced and seeded	1 tbsp. freshly squeezed lime juice
2 tbsps. mayonnaise	1 garlic clove, minced
Honey (optional)	Black pepper freshly ground

For the fish:

1/3 c. all-purpose flour	1 tsp. kosher salt
¼ tsp. freshly ground pepper	1/4 tsp. smoked paprika
1 ½ lbs. snapper, tilapia, or sole	2 tbsps. vegetable oil

Directions:
For the slaw:

Place cabbage inside a colander and sprinkle some salt. Squeeze and massage the cabbage with your hand to release its liquid and begin wilting. Place in another bowl and let it drain for about 15-minutes.
Squeeze off the excess water off the cabbage and transfer it to a larger bowl. Add scallions, jalapeno, and carrots. Toss to mix them up. Add in mayonnaise, garlic, and lime juice, then toss again to mix. Taste and season using pepper and salt to taste.

The fish:
Combine pepper, paprika salt, and flour in a shallow container. Pat the fish dry using paper towels, then dredge it in the flour mixture till it is evenly coated.
Heat oil using a heavy pan over medium high heat to bring it to a shimmer. Add in the fish in one layer, work in batches if needed. Cook them undistributed till they turn golden brown on the bottom. Using a flat spatula, flip the fish carefully, they might fall apart a bit but do not worry about this. Continue cooking till the second side turns golden brown, and the fish is opaque, and it flakes apart quickly in the thickest parts. Transfer the fish onto a thin plate and lakes onto large chunks. Keep them warm. Heat corn tortillas one at a time using a heavy and dry pan until they turn soft and warm. Wrap them up using a clean kitchen towel. Serve with tortillas, avocado, slaw, salsa, and lime.

Nutritional information: Calories: 663 | Fat: 22.5 g | carbs: 69.1g | Sugars: 10.6g | Protein: 47.6 g |

425. Turmeric-Ginger Chickpea Stew

Prep time: 5-minutes | Total time: 55-minutes | Yield: 4-6-servings

Ingredients:

¼ c. olive oil	4 cloves garlic, chopped
1 large yellow onion, chopped	1 (2 inches) piece of ginger, chopped finely
Black pepper and kosher salt	1 ½ tsp. ground turmeric
1 tsp. red pepper flakes	2 (15 oz) cans of well drained and rinsed chickpeas

2 (15 oz.) cans of full-fat coconut milk	2 c. veggies
1 bunch swiss chard, kale, stems removed and torn into bite sizes	1 c. mint leaves
Yogurt (optional)	

Directions:

Heat ¼ c. of oil in a large pot using medium heat. Add in garlic, ginger, and onion. Season using pepper and salt, let them cook while occasionally stirring till the onions turn translucent, and then start to brown a little around the edges. Add in 1 ½ tsps. of turmeric, 1 tsp. of red pepper flakes and chickpeas. Season using pepper and salt. Cook while occasionally stirring to ensure the chickpeas sizzle and fry a bit in the oil and spices till they start to break down and get a bit browned and crisp. Remove about one cup of chickpeas and set aside to garnish. Crush the remaining chickpeas slightly using a spatula or a wooden spoon to release their starchy insides. Add in coconut milk and stock, season using pepper and salt. Bring the mixture to simmer, scraping up any bits that might form on the bottom part of your pot. Cook while occasionally stirring till the stew thickens. If you want a thicker stew, keep simmering till you gain your desired consistency. Add in greens and stir to ensure they are submerged into the liquid. Cook till they soften and wilt. Season again using pepper and salt. Divide among set bowls and top using mint, a sprinkle of red pepper flakes, a drizzle of olive oil, and reserved chickpeas. Serve alongside yogurt and enjoy!

Nutritional information: Calories 626 | Fat: 44 g| Saturated fat: 29 g | Carbs: 48g | Dietary fiber: 12 g

426. Lemon-Artichoke Risotto

Prep time: 11-minutes | Total time: 46-minutes | Yield: 4-servings

Ingredients:

1.5 c. carnaroli rice or Arborio	6 c. veggie stock warm
½ c. leek or onion	1 batch of marinated artichoke hearts
¼ c. dry white wine	2 tbsps. salted butter
2 tbsps. extra virgin olive oil	1 organic lemon, zested and juiced
¼ c. mascarpone cheese or Parmigiano-Reggiano (optional)	4 tbsps. fresh thyme and basil leaves
1 pinch sea salt	Black pepper, freshly cracked, to taste

Directions:

For the marinated artichoke hearts: Use a medium sized bowl to whisk together olive oil with lemon juice, salt, and garlic. Add in the oregano, lemon zest, and thyme, and then stir well to combine the mixture. Season to taste using black pepper, red pepper, and salt. Slice the artichoke hearts into quarters or halves. Add into the bowl containing marinade. Give the mixture a gentle toss to coat all over. Taste to adjust seasoning appropriately. Transfer to a container that has a lid and refrigerates for at least 2 hours.

Next step:

Heat up the veggie stock and season to your preferred taste. Melt 1 tbsp. of olive oil and butter using a skillet over medium low heat. Add on leeks and onion and let them sauté together till translucent. Next, stir in the risotto rice and toss to coat in oils. Toast for a minute, then add in white wine. When the wine is almost fully absorbed, start adding in the stock a ladleful at a time while still maintaining a constant gentle simmer. Ensure you stir well each time you add more stock and do not let the rice dry out completely before adding more liquid. The risotto should be done in about 30-minutes, once the grains are all done, they still have a slight bite onto them, and they are not mushy. Remove them from the heat, and then stir in the pureed artichoke hearts, parmesan cheese, and 1 tbsp. of the remaining butter. Add more warm stock, not much though, 2 tbsp. of lemon juice and stir again, then cover using a lid and let it sit for about 3-minutes. Divide the meal between 4 plates and then serve with the reserved artichoke hearts on top, black pepper, drizzled olive oil, and fresh thyme plus and basil

Nutritional information: Calories: 142 | Carbs: 4g | Fat: 12 g | Saturated fat: 4g | Sugar: 3g

427. Chipotle Chickpea Taco Bowls

Prep time: 11-minutes | Total time: 35-minutes | Yield: 5-servings

Ingredients:

For the Quinoa:

1 c. tri-colored quinoa	3 c. vegetable broth, low sodium
½ tsp. sea salt	

For the chipotle chickpea:

3 (15 oz) cans cooked chickpeas, rinsed, and dried	2 tsp. olive oil
2 tsp. Chili powder	½ tsp. Chipotle chili powder
½ tsp. Sea salt	½ tsp. ground cumin
¼ garlic powder	

For the toppings:

2 c. romaine lettuce, chopped	1 (15 oz) can of low sodium rinsed and dried black beans.
10 oz. grape tomatoes, sliced	¼ c. fresh cilantro, chopped
2 limes, sliced into wedges	3 green onions, sliced
2 avocados, well diced	¼ c. plain Greek yogurt

Directions:

For the baked chipotle chickpeas:

Preheat oven to 3500 F and line a rimmed baking sheet with parchment paper. Set this aside first. Place rinsed chickpeas onto a clean kitchen towel and let them drain. When completely dried off, transfer onto a large mixing bowl. Add chili powder, olive oil, cumin, chipotle chili powder, garlic powder, sea salt. Toss this mixture thoroughly using a spoon to make sure the chickpeas are coated evenly. Transfer seasoned chickpeas onto the prepared baking sheet in a layer that's even. Bake the chickpeas for 20 – 25-minutes, shaking the pan halfway through the baking time till the chickpeas are heated thoroughly, and they start to become crunchy. Remove chickpeas from the oven, and then let them cool off.

For the Quinoa:

With the chickpeas still in the oven, combine the uncooked quinoa with the low sodium veggie broth and sea salt in a saucepan, bring them to boil. Cover and let them simmer for about 20-minutes till the water is completely absorbed. Fluff using a fork and set aside to cool off

For assembling the vegetarian Taco Bowls:

Add the quinoa into one quarter of the meal prepared containers. Next to the quinoa, add grape tomatoes, sliced, spicy, chipotle chickpea, fresh chopped lettuce, and rinsed and drained black beans. Top the mixture off using diced avocado, cilantro, wedge lime, and a little Greek yogurt. Seal up the container and place it inside a fridge for up to 5 days

Nutritional information: Calories: 312 | Fat: 11g | Carbohydrates: 38g | Protein: 12 g | Fiber: 10g

428. Stuffed Portobello Mushrooms

Prep time: 11-minutes | Total time: 46-minutes | Yield: 4-servings

Ingredients:

4 large size Portobello mushrooms	1 tbsp. olive oil
½ medium sized onions, chopped	4 garlic cloves, minced
½ medium sized green bell pepper, chopped	2 c. spinach, chopped
4 cocktail tomatoes, chopped	¼ c of goat cheese, crumbled
¼ tsp. salt	¼ tsp. pepper
1 tbsp. hot sauce	½ c. breadcrumbs
½ c. mozzarella cheeses, shredded	

Directions:

Preheat your oven to 4000 F. Remove mushroom stems carefully. Reserve and chop the stems for stuffing. Place the mushroom stems onto a baking pan side down. Bake them for about 15-minutes till the water leaks out of them. Remove the stems from the oven using a paper towel to soak up any excess water. Set aside. Using an oven, heat your olive over medium heat. Add garlic and chopped onion, then sauté for some-minutes till the onion is translucent. Add spinach and green pepper into the skillet and let the mixture cook for a couple of-minutes or up until the spinach wilts. Add tomatoes, goat cheese, mushroom stems, salt, pepper, breadcrumbs, and hot sauce. Stir and let them cook for some-minutes. Stuff the mushrooms with the mixture equally. Top using mozzarella cheese. If you are using smaller mushrooms, this mixture should be enough for at least 8 mushrooms. Bake until the cheese melts, this takes approximately 10-minutes

Nutritional information: Calories: 221 | Carbs: 20g | Protein: 13g | Fiber: 5g | Saturated fat: 5g |

429. Easy Bean Veggie Burgers

Prep time: 18-minutes | Total time: 28-minutes | Yield: 6 burgers

Ingredients:

2 (15-oz) cans of black beans, rinsed & drained	3 garlic cloves, cut roughly
½ c. rolled oats	½ c. fresh cilantro
1 large beaten egg	2 tsp. ground cumin
¼ tsp. cayenne pepper	1 ½ tsp. dried oregano leaves
½ tsp. kosher salt	1/3 c. chopped red onion
½ lime juice, about 1 tbsp.	1 tbsp. extra virgin olive oil or canola oil

Directions:

Place about 2/3 of the black beans onto a food processor with the cilantro, garlic, and oats. Process for at least 25 seconds or up until the mixture sticks together, forming a paste, it should not be completely smooth. Transfer the black bean mixture into a large size mixing bowl.

Add the remaining black beans and the remaining ingredients, excluding the oil. Mix using a spatula. Shape into 6 patties, each measuring about ¾ inches thick. Heat a large size non-stick skillet using medium heat. Add oil and swirl to spread. Cook every patty for 4-5-minutes per side without crowding the cooking pan. You can work on the patties in batches for better results, add more oil in between the batches.

Nutritional information: Calories: 164 | Carbs: 25g | Protein: 9g | Fiber: 6g | Saturated fat: 0.8 g

430. Cherries and Quinoa

Prep time: 11-minutes | Total time: 31-minutes | Yield: 8-servings

Ingredients:

1 ¾ c. uncooked quinoa	2 tbsps. And 2 tsp. extra virgin olive oil, divided
3 tbsps. shallots, finely chopped	2 c. water
1/3 c. dry white wine	½ tsp. salt
3 tbsps. lemon juice, fresh	¼ tsp. pepper, freshly ground
½ c. sweet cherries, dried and chopped	½ c. dry roasted pistachios, chopped
¼ c. fresh mint, chopped	¼ c. fresh parsley, chopped

Directions:

Rinse and drain the quinoa. Heat 2 tsp. of oil in a large size saucepan over medium high heat. Add shallots into the pan: Sauté for 2-minutes or till tender. Add 2 c. of water, wine, and salt into the pan, let them boil. Add quinoa, cover, reduce the heat and let it simmer for 15-minutes or till all the liquid has been well absorbed and the quinoa is tender. Remove from heat and let the meal cool off slightly. Combine the remaining 2 tbsps. of lemon juice, pepper, and olive oil in a large bowl and stir using a whisk. Add cherries, quinoas, and the remaining ingredient and toss gently to combine

Nutritional information: Calories: 256 | Fat: 10.3g | Saturated fat: 1.3 g | Carbohydrates: 34g | Fiber: 4.3 g

431. Three-Bean Chili

Prep time: 11-minutes | Total time: 4 hours 21-minutes | Yield: 10-servings

Ingredients:

1 package (20 oz.) 93% lean, grounded turkey	1 (28 oz.) can dice fire-roasted tomatoes
1 (16 oz.) can tomato sauce	1 (15.5 oz.) can pinto beans, drained & rinsed
1(15.5 oz.) can kidney beans, rinsed and drained	1 (15 oz.) can black beans, with reduced sodium rinsed and drained
1 small onion, chopped	1 (4.5 oz.) can have chopped green chilies
2 tbsps. chili powder	1 tbsp. minced garlic
1 tsp. oregano	1 pinch ground cumin

Directions:

Cook while stirring the turkey in a large size skillet till it is completely browned, this takes 7 – 8-minutes, transfer to a slow cooker. Stir tomato sauce, tomatoes, kidney beans, black beans, pinto beans, green chilies, chili powder, onion, oregano, garlic, and cumin with the turkey in a slow-cooker. Cook on high for about 4-hours / cook on low for about 7-hours

Nutritional information: Calories: 238 | Protein: 19.8g | Carbohydrates: 29g | Sodium: 877.8 mg

432. Creamy Avocado Vegetable Burritos

Prep time: 6-minutes | Total time: 27-minutes | Yield: 4-servings

Ingredients:

1 tbsp. olive oil	2 thinly sliced bell peppers
1 onion, sliced thinly	Pepper and salt
½ c. Greek yogurt, plain	Juiced of ½ lime
¼ tsp. chili powder	2 tbsp. chopped cilantro
1 (15 oz.) can rinse pinto beans, dried	4 large sized tortillas, whole wheat
1 c. Monterey jack cheese, grated	2 peeled and pitted avocados, chopped

Directions:

Set a skillet over medium heat. Add in bell peppers and onions and cook, occasionally stirring to soften. Season using pepper and salt to taste. Meanwhile, mix the lime juice, Greek yogurt, cilantro, and chili powder in a bowl Warm the beans using a saucepan using medium low heat for a couple of-minutes. Set tortillas in paper towels and warm in a microwave. Assemble your burritos by spreading ¼ of the yogurt mixture to the center of each tortilla. Add a topping of cheese, avocado, beans, onions, and pepper. Fold up the burritos. Serve.

Nutritional information: Calories: 563 | Carbs: 55g | Proteins: 21g | Fat: 31g | Saturated Fat: 9g |

433. Baked Salmon Cakes

Prep time: 17-minutes | Total time: 26-minutes | Yield: 4-servings

Ingredients:

1 can (7 oz) salmon, flaked and dried	1 tbsp. olive oil

1 egg, beaten	2 chopped green onions
2 c. saltine cracker crumbs, crushed	Lemon pepper

Directions:

Preheat your oven to 200 C. Mix green onions, salmon, egg, 2/3 cup of the cracker crumbs, and olive oil. Add lemon pepper for seasoning. Form 8 patties from the mixture. Use the remaining crumbs to coat your patties, then arrange them on the baking sheet in one layer Bake inside a preheated oven for approximately 10-minutes, turning only once or till both sides turn golden brown.

Nutritional information: Calories: 281 | Protein: 16.4 g | Carbs: 25.5 g | Fat: 12.2g | Sodium: 570.4 mg

434. Turkey Sweet Potato Hash

Prep time: 10-minutes | Total time: 27-minutes | Yield: 4-servings

Ingredients:

1 ½ tbsps. avocado oil	1 medium yellow onion, peeled and diced
2 cloves garlic, minced	1 medium sweet potato, cut into cubes (peeling not necessary)
1/2 lb. lean ground turkey	1/2 tsp. salt
1 tsp. Italian seasoning blend	

Directions:

Attach the oil and allow the oil to heat 1 minute and then add the onion and cook until softened, about 5-minutes. Attach the garlic and cook for an additional 30 seconds. Add the sweet potato, turkey, salt, and Italian seasoning and cook for another 5-minutes.

Nutritional information: Calories: 172 | Fat: 9 g | Protein: 12 g | Fiber: 1 g | Carbs: 10 g Sugar: 3 g

435. Lemon Garlic Turkey Breast

Prep time: 10 | Total time: 27-minutes | Yield: 4-servings

Ingredients:

1 (1 ½ lbs.) boneless, skinless turkey breast	2 tbsps. avocado oil, divided
Zest from 1/2 large lemon	1/2 medium shallot, peeled and minced
1 large clove garlic, minced	1/2 tsp. kosher salt
1/4 tsp. black pepper	

Directions:

Dry the turkey breast with a towel. Cut the turkey breast in half to fit in your Instant Pot. Brush both sides of turkey breast with 1 tablespoon oil. In a small-bowl, mix the lemon zest, shallot, garlic, salt, and pepper together. Massage this mixture onto both sides of the turkey breast. Press the Sauté button and heat the remaining 1 tablespoon oil in the inner pot for 2-minutes. Add the turkey breast and sear it on both sides, about 3-minutes per side. Press the Cancel button. Remove the turkey from the inner pot and place it on a plate. Add 1 cup water to the inner pot and use a spatula to scrape any stuck brown bits. Place steam rack in the pot and the turkey breast on top of it. Slice and serve.

Nutritional information: Calories: 250 | Fat: 9 g | Protein: 40 g | Sodium: 445 mg | Carbs: 1 g | Sugar: 0 g

436. Chicken and Veggie Casserole

Prep time: 6-minutes | Total time: 11-minutes | Yield: 4-servings

Ingredients:

1/3 c. Dijon mustard	1/3 c. organic honey
1 tsp. dried basil	1/4 tsp. ground turmeric
1 tsp. dried basil, crushed	Salt and freshly ground black pepper
13/4 lb. chicken breasts	1 c. fresh white mushrooms, sliced
1/2 head broccoli	

Directions:

Warm the oven to 350 degrees F. Lightly grease a baking dish. In a bowl, merge together all ingredients except chicken, mushrooms, and broccoli. Set chicken in a prepared baking dish and top with mushroom slices. Place broccoli florets around the chicken evenly. Pour 1 / 2 of honey mixture over chicken and broccoli evenly. Bake for approximately twenty-minutes. Now, coat the chicken with the remaining sauce and bake for approximately 10-minutes.

Nutritional information: Calories: 248 kcal | Fat: 9 g | Protein: 40 g | Sodium: 568 mg | Carbs: 190 g

437. Ground Turkey with Veggies

Prep time: 16-minutes | Total time: 27-minutes | Yield: 2-servings

Ingredients:

1 tbsp. sesame oil	1 tbsp. coconut oil
1 lb. lean ground turkey	2 tbsps. fresh ginger, minced
2 minced garlic cloves	1 (16 oz.) bag vegetable mix (broccoli, carrot, cabbage, kale, and Brussels sprouts)
1/4 c. coconut aminos	2 tbsps. balsamic vinegar

Directions:

In a big skillet, heat both oils on medium-high heat. Add turkey, ginger, and garlic and cook approximately 5-6-minutes. Add vegetable mix and cook approximately 4-5-minutes. Stir in coconut aminos and vinegar and cook for about 1 minute. Serve hot.

Nutritional information: Calories: 99 kcal | Fat: 4 g | Protein: 1 g | Sodium: 1,348 mg | Sugar: 7 g. | Fiber: 4 g | Carbs: 16 g

CHAPTER 6:
SEAFOOD RECIPES

438. Salmon Balls
Prep Time: 6-minutes | Total time: 19-minutes | Yield: 2-servings

Ingredients:

Salt and ground black pepper to taste	2 tbsp. water
2 tbsp. lemon juice	½ tsp dried cilantro
½ tsp paprika	½ tsp ginger powder
3 tbsp. coconut oil	½ c. heavy cream
1 garlic clove	1 egg
1 avocado	2 tbsp. keto mayo
1 can of tuna	

Directions:
Drain the salmon, chop it. Mince the garlic clove, peel the avocado. In a bowl, Mix the garlic, egg, mayo, and fish, season with salt, paprika, and ginger, mix well. Make 4 balls of it. Using a skillet, preheat the oil at medium heat. Fry the balls for 4-6-minutes on each side. Meanwhile, put the lemon juice, cilantro, avocado, heavy cream, and 1 tbsp. Of oil in a blender. Pulse well. Serve the balls with the sauce.
Nutritional Information: Carbs: 3,9 g |Fats: 50 g |Protein: 20,1 g |Calories: 555

439. Citrus Salmon on a Bed of Greens
Prep Time: 10-minutes | Total time: 29-minutes | Yield: 4-servings

Ingredients:

¼ c. Extra Virgin Olive Oil, divided	1½ lbs. Salmon
1 tsp. Sea Salt, divided	½ tsp. Freshly ground black pepper, divided
1 Lemon Zest	6 c. Swiss Chard, stemmed and chopped
3 Garlic cloves, chopped	2 Lemon Juice

Directions:
Preheat a huge nonstick skillet at medium-high, heat 2 tbsps. of the olive oil until it shimmers. Season the salmon with ½ tsp. of the salt, ¼ tsp. of pepper, and the lemon zest. Put the salmon in the skillet, skin-side up, and cook until the flesh is opaque for about 7-minutes. Flip the salmon and cook to crisp the skin for at least 3 to 4-minutes. Cover it on a plate using aluminum foil.

Return the skillet to the oven, add the leftover 2 tbsps. of olive oil until it glistens. Augment the Swiss chard and cook for 8-minutes, then whisk until soft. Add the garlic. Cook for 30 seconds, stirring constantly. Sprinkle in the lemon juice, the remaining ½ tsp. of salt, and the remaining ¼ tsp. of pepper—Cook for 2-minutes. Serve the salmon on the Swiss chard.
Nutritional Information: Calories: 363| Fat: 25 | Carbs: 3 |Sugar: 1 |Protein: 34g |Sodium: 662mg

440. Blackened Fish Tacos with Slaw
Prep Time: 14-minutes | Total time: 20-minutes | Yield: 4-servings

Ingredients:

1 tbsp. olive oil	1 tsp. chili powder
2 tilapia fillets	1 tsp. paprika
4 low carb tortillas	

Slaw:

½ c. red cabbage, shredded	1 tbsp. lemon juice
1 tsp. apple cider vinegar	1 tbsp. olive oil
Salt and black pepper to taste	

Directions:
Season the tilapia with paprika and chili powder. Heat the vegetable oil using a skillet over medium heat. Cook your tilapia for about 3-minutes on each side until blackened. Slice into strips. Separate the tilapia among the tortillas. In a bowl, blend all the slaw ingredients and top the fish to serve.
Nutritional Information: Calories: 268 |Fat: 20g |Net Carbs: 3.5g |Protein: 13.8g

441. Tender Creamy Scallops
Prep Time: 16-minutes | Total time: 37-minutes | Yield: 2-servings

Ingredients:

8 fresh sea scallops	4 bacon slices
½ c. grated parmesan cheese	1 c. heavy cream
2 tbsp. ghee butter	Salt and black pepper to taste

Directions:
In a skillet, heat the butter at medium-high heat. Cook the bacon for 5-minutes on both sides till it is crispy.

Place the bacon on a paper-towel to eliminate the excess fat. Sprinkle with more butter as you reduce the heat to medium. Put the parmesan cheese and heavy cream. Season with pepper and salt. Cook for 8-10-minutes on low heat while constantly Whisk till you get a thick sauce. Over medium-high heat, cook the ghee butter in another skillet. In a skillet, add the scallops, season with pepper and salt. Cook each side until golden for about 2-minutes. Dry the scallops on a paper towel. Top with the crumbled bacon and sauce.

Nutritional Information: Carbs: 11 g |Fat: 72,5 g |Protein: 24 g |Calories: 765

442. Gingered Tilapia

Prep Time: 16-minutes | Total time: 22-minutes | Yield: 5-servings

Ingredients:

2 tbsps. coconut oil	5 tilapia fillets
3 garlic cloves, minced	2 tbsps. unsweetened coconut, shredded
4 oz. freshly ground ginger	2 tbsps. coconut aminos
8 scallions, chopped	

Directions:

Heat the coconut oil in a huge skillet at medium heat. Cook the tilapia fillets for about 2-minutes. Flip the side and add ginger, coconut, and garlic and cook for about 1 minute. Put the coconut aminos and let it cook for about 1 minute. Put the scallion and let it cook for another 2-minutes. Serve immediately.

Nutritional Information: |Calories: 135 |Fat: 3g |Carbohydrates: 2g |Protein: 26g

443. Daring Shark Steaks

Prep Time: 36-minutes | Total time: 1 hour 16-minutes | Yield: 2-servings

Ingredients:

2 Shark steak, skinless	2 tbsp. Onion powder
2 tsp. Chili powder	1 Garlic clove, minced
¼ c. Worcestershire sauce	1 tbsp. Ground black pepper
2 tbsp. Thyme, chopped	

Directions:

Mix all the spices and seasonings in a bowl to form a paste before setting it aside. Apply a thin layer of paste on each side of the fish, and wait for chill for 30-minutes Preheat oven to 150°C /325°F/Gas Mark 3. Use parchment paper for baking the fish for 40-minutes, until well cooked. Serve on a whole-grain couscous or bed of quinoa together with your favorite salad.

Nutritional Information: Calories: 112 |Protein: 4.87 g |Fat: 3.65 g |Carbohydrates: 16.78 g

444. Coconut Rice with shrimps in Coconut curry

Prep Time: 12-minutes | Total time: 52-minutes | Yield: 2-3-minutes

Ingredients:

16 oz. Shrimp (deveined)	3 cloves Garlic (chopped)
2 Tsp. Curry powder	¼ c. Scallions (chopped)
15 oz. Coconut milk	1 ½ c. Water
⅛ c. Cilantro (chopped)	2 tbsp. Butter
½ Lime juice	2 tbsp. Ginger (shredded)
1 c. Jasmine rice	Salt and red pepper flakes

Directions:

Melt 1 tbsp. of butter, on medium heat, then add rice and Whisk to coat. Pour 1 cup the water and coconut milk, then cook for 30-minutes until rice is cooked.
Use a large pan to melt butter on medium heat, add ginger, garlic, and scallions, then leave to cook for 3-minutes. Mix curry powder and coconut milk and in a separate bowl. Add the shrimps after the scallions are cooked, then cook till they are pink. Add the curry and coconut mixture and cook, then season accordingly.
Serve rice mixed with cilantro and lime juice alongside the shrimps.

Nutritional Information: Calories: 400 |Protein: 40.46 g |Fat: 18.01 g |Carbohydrates: 29.99 g

445. Coconut Mahi-Mahi Nuggets

Prep Time: 12-minutes | Total time: 22-minutes | Yield: 2-servings

Ingredients:

1 c. avocado oil or coconut oil, plus more as needed	1 lb. frozen mahi-mahi, thawed
2 large eggs	2 tbsps. avocado oil mayonnaise
1 c. almond flour	½ c. shredded coconut
½ lime, cut into wedges	Freshly ground black pepper
Salt	¼ c. Dairy-Free Tartar Sauce

Directions:

Warm a ½ inch deep avocado oil in a skillet at high heat. Use paper towels to Pat the fish to take off any excess water. Put and mix the mayonnaise and eggs in a small bowl. Put and mix the almond flour, coconut in a medium mixing bowl. Season with pepper and salt. Slice the mahi-mahi into nuggets. Mix the egg mixture with fish, then scour in the dry mix. Press into the dry mix to ensure the "breading" sticks well on all sides.

Put the fish in hot oil. Ensure it sizzles upon adding the nuggets. Cook each side for-minutes until crispy and golden. Line a paper towel on a plate and put the cooked nuggets. Then squirt the lime wedges over the nuggets.

Nutritional Information: Calories: 733 | Fat: 53g | Protein: 54g | Carbs: 10g | Fiber: 6g | Net Carbs: 4g

446. Salmon Ceviche

Prep Time: 10-minutes +20 resting time | Total time: 30-minutes | Yield: 4-servings

Ingredients:

1 lb. Salmon, skinless & boneless, cut into bite-size pieces	½ c. Freshly squeezed lime juice
2 Tomatoes, diced	¼ c. Fresh Cilantro Leaves, chopped
1 Jalapeno Pepper, seeded and diced	2 tbsp. Extra Virgin Olive Oil
½ tsp. Sea Salt	

Directions:

Put and whisked the lime juice and salmon in a medium bowl. Let it marinate for 20-minutes. Whisk in the salt, olive oil, jalapeño, cilantro, and tomatoes.

Nutritional Information: Calories: 222 | Fat:14g | Carbs: 3g | Sugar: 2 | Fiber: 1 | Protein: 23 |

447. Salmon and Cauliflower

Prep Time: 12-minutes | Total time: 37-minutes | Yield: 4-servings

Ingredients:

2 tbsps. coconut aminos	1 cauliflower head, florets separated and chopped
4 pieces' salmon fillets, skinless	1 big red onion, cut into wedges
1 tbsp. olive oil	Pinch of sea salt
Pinch black pepper	

Directions:

Put oil all over the salmon in a baking dish. Then season with pepper and salt. Preheat the broiler over medium heat. Cook the salmon for about 5-minutes. Add onion, cauliflower, and coconut aminos. Set salmon in your oven and bake at 400 degrees F for 15-minutes. Divide between plates and serve.

Nutritional Information: Calories 112 | Fat 5 | Fiber 3 | Carbs 8 | Protein 7

448. Honey Crusted Salmon with Pecans

Prep Time: 22-minutes | Total time: 42-minutes | Yield: 6-servings

Ingredients:

3 tbsps. olive oil	3 tbsps. mustard
5 tsp. raw honey	½ c. chopped pecans
6 salmon fillets, boneless	3 tsp. chopped parsley
Salt and black pepper to the taste	

Directions:

Whisk the mustard with oil and honey in a bowl. Then mix the pecans with parsley and whisk in another bowl—season salmon fillets with pepper and salt. Then brush with mustard mixture on a baking sheet. Top with the pecans mix and put them in a 400 degrees F oven to bake for 20 around-minutes. Serve into plates and serve them with a salad. Enjoy!

Nutritional Information: Calories 200 | Fat 10 | Fiber 5 | Carbs 12 | Protein 16

449. Quick Fish Bowl

Prep Time: 11-minutes | Total time: 26-minutes | Yield: 2-servings

Ingredients:

2 tilapia fillets	1 tbsp. olive oil
1 avocado	1 tbsp. ghee butter
1 tbsp. cumin powder	1 tbsp. paprika
2 c. coleslaw cabbage, chopped	1 tbsp. salsa sauce
Himalayan rock salt, to taste	Black pepper to taste

Directions:

Heat the oven to 424F. Using a foil, line a baking sheet. Puree the avocado. Using olive oil, brush the tilapia fillets and season with spices and salt. Grease with the ghee butter and put the fish onto the baking sheet.

Let it bake for 15-minutes, then remove it from the heat. Allow it to cool for 5-minutes. Mix and gently toss the salsa sauce and the coleslaw cabbage in a bowl. Add the mashed avocado, season with pepper and salt

Cut the fish and add to the bowl. Bake for 14-15-minutes. Serve hot.

Nutritional Information: Carbs: 5,2 g | Fat: 24,5 g | Protein: 16,1 g | Calories: 321

450. Her bed Rockfish

Prep Time: 12-minutes | Total time: 32-minutes | Yield: 8-servings

Ingredients:

1 1/2 lbs. rockfish fillets	2 egg whites
1 1/2 tbsps. nonfat milk	1/2 tbsps. canola oil

1 c. nonfat plain yogurt	1 tbsp. lemon juice
1 tbsp. oregano	1 tbsp. fresh parsley, chopped
1 tbsp. pimento, minced	1 tsp. garlic, minced
1 tsp. ground black pepper	6 slices wheat bread, toasted
1/4 c. flaxseed, ground fresh	1/4 c. extra virgin olive oil
1-pint cherry tomatoes, chopped	2 fresh lemons, wedges

Directions:

Use cold water to clean rockfish fillets. Scrape off the skin and eliminate any bones. Using a paper towel, pat dries the fish. Mix lemon juice, canola oil, yogurt, nonfat milk, and egg whites in a medium-sized bowl. Add the following 8 ingredients (oregano-flaxseed) to a food processor and grind them finely. Put in a different dish. In a pan, preheat the olive oil. Initially, soak the fillets in the spice mixture, followed by the yogurt blend, finally, compress the crumbs softly into the fish for the final layer. Put the fillets in preheated olive oil. Flip over the fillets and lower heat — Cook for 15 to 20-minutes more. Complete with tomatoes and lemon wedges.

Nutritional Information: Calories: 178 |Protein: 19.62 g|Fat: 8.96 g |Carbohydrates: 4.73 g

451. Seasoned Catfish

Prep Time: 15-minutes | Total time: 38-minutes | Yield: 4-servings

Ingredients:

4 catfish fillets	2 tbsps. Italian seasoning
Salt and ground black pepper	1 tbsp. olive oil
1 tbsp. fresh parsley, chopped	

Directions:

Arrange the Crisp Basket and grease Cook in the pot of Ninja Foody. Close the Ninja Foody with a crisping lid and select Air Crisp. Set the temp to 400 degrees F for about 5-minutes. Press Start/Stop to begin preheating. Rub the fish fillets with black pepper, salt, and seasoning munificently, and then cover with oil. After preheating, open the lid. Put the catfish fillets in the Cook & Crisp Basket. Close the Ninja Foody with a lid and select Air Crisp. Increase the heat to 400°F for 20-minutes. Press Start/Stop to begin cooking. Flip the fish fillets once halfway through. Serve hot with the garnishing of parsley.

Nutritional Information: Calories: 205|Fats: 14.2g|Carbohydrates 0.8 proteins: 17.7g

452. Cheesy Tuna Pasta

Prep Time: 12-minutes | Total time: 31-minutes | Yield: 2-4-servings

Ingredients:

2 c. arugula	1/4 c. chopped green onions
1 tbs. red vinegar	5 oz. Drained canned tuna
1/4 tsp. black pepper	2 oz. cooked whole-wheat pasta
1 tbsp. olive oil	1 tbsp. grated low-fat parmesan

Directions:

Prepare the pasta in unsalted water. Drain and set aside. In a large-sized bowl, thoroughly mix the black pepper, pasta, arugula, oil, vinegar, green onions, and tuna. Toss well and top with the cheese. Serve.

Nutritional Information: Calories: 566.3 | Fat: 42.4 g | Carbs: 18.6 |Sugars: 0.4 g |Protein: 29.8 g

453. Grilled fish tacos

Prep Time: 11-minutes | Total time: 21-minutes | Yield: 8-servings

Ingredients:

1 lb. Mahi-mahi fillets	2 tbsps. canola oil
2 tbsps. omega-3-rich margarine	Juice of 1 lime
1 tsp. salt, divided	1 tsp. chili powder
1/2 tsp. crushed red pepper	1/2 tsp. garlic powder
1/2 tsp. oregano	1/2 tsp. ground cumin
2 mangoes	1/4 c. cilantro, chopped
8 wheat flour tortillas	

Directions:

Whisk together one tsp of salt, lime juice, margarine, canola oil, and the residual dried spices In a medium-sized bowl. Ad the fish to the mixture. Cover and allow it to marinate for 45-minutes in the fridge. Then, peel mangoes and cut them into cubes. Mix with remaining salt and cilantro. Preheat oven to medium-high. Remove your fish from the refrigerator. Cook on your grill for 3-minutes on each side. Put tortillas on the grill and heat for 10 to 15 seconds on both sides. Fill with mango topping and fish fillets.

Nutritional Information: Calories: 231 |Protein: 13.99 g|Fat: 17.04 g |Carbohydrates: 6.02 g

454. Grilled Salmon with Caponata

Prep Time: 12-minutes | Total time: 37-minutes | Yield: 4-servings

Ingredients:

¼ c. good-quality olive oil, divided	1 onion, chopped
2 celery stalks, chopped	1 tbsp. minced garlic
2 tomatoes, chopped	½ c. chopped marinated artichoke hearts
¼ c. pitted green olives, chopped	¼ c. cider vinegar
2 tbsps. chopped pecans	4 (4 oz.) salmon fillets
Freshly ground black pepper for seasoning	2 tbsps. chopped fresh basil

Directions:

Make the caponata. Warm 3 tbsp. Olive oil in a big skillet at moderate heat. Add the garlic, celery, onion, and sauté until they are soft, for 4-minutes. Whisk in the pecans, vinegar, olives, artichoke hearts, and tomatoes. Add the mixture to a boil, lower the heat to low, and simmer until the liquid reduces for about 7-minutes. Set aside. Grill the fish. Warm the oven to medium-high heat. Dry fish with paper towels, then cover it with the residual 1 tbsp—olive oil and lightly season with black pepper. Grill the salmon, turning once for about 8-minutes until well cooked. Serve. Share the salmon into four plates, top with the caponata, and serve instantly with fresh basil.

Nutritional Information: |Calories: 348| Fat: 25g| Carbs: 7g|Fiber: 3g |Sodium: 128mg|Protein: 24g

455. Easy Crunchy Fish Tray Bake

Prep Time: 12-minutes | Total time: 32-minutes | Yield: 4-servings

Ingredients:

600g frozen crumbed whiting fish fillets	1/2 small red onion
2 x 250g punnets tomatoes	2 zucchinis
180g baby stuffed peppers	1 tbsp. parmesan
2 tsp. oregano leaves	1 lemon, cut into wedges

Directions:

Preheat the oven to 400F. Apply oil to a large preparing plate. Add the fish fillets to the prepared dish. Spread the parmesan and oregano over the fish. Add stuffed peppers, tomatoes, and zucchini to the plate. Spread the onion rings on top. Season properly. Spray with olive oil. Heat until the fish is cooked through and brilliant. Split the vegetables and fish among plates & present with the lemon and rocket wedges.

Nutritional Information: Calories: 346 |Protein: 3.67 g|Fat: 2.8 g |Carbohydrates: 81.77 g

456. Shrimp with Spicy Spinach

Prep Time: 12-minutes | Total time: 27-minutes | Yield: 4-servings

Ingredients:

¼ c. Extra Olive Oil. divided	1½ lb. Peeled Shrimp
1 tsp. Sea Salt, divided	4 c. Baby Fresh Spinach
6 Garlic cloves, minced	½ c. Freshly Squeezed Orange Juice
1 tbsp. Sriracha Sauce	⅛ tsp. Freshly ground black pepper

Directions:

Heat 2 tbsps. of the olive oil until it shimmers in a huge nonstick skillet. Add the shrimp and ½ tsp. salt. Cook it for about 4-minutes while stirring. Cook until pink. Put the shrimp on a plate, tent with an aluminum foil to keep it hot, and set aside. Return the skillet to the grill and heat the other 2 tbsps. Of olive oil until it shimmers. Add the spinach. Cook for 3-minutes, stirring. Add the garlic. Cook for 30 seconds, stirring constantly. Mix the pepper, remaining ½ tsp. of salt, Sriracha, and orange juice in a small bowl. Add the mixture to the spinach and allow to cook for around 3-minutes. Serve it with spinach.

Nutritional Information: Calories: 317| Fat: 16| Carbs: 7g|Sugar: 3|Fiber: 1g|Protein: 38g|

457. Seafood Paella

Prep Time: 11-minutes | Total time: 27-minutes | Yield: 2-servings

Ingredients:

Lemon juice	4 units pre-cooked whole prawn
Chilies to decorate	½ packet of chopped parsley
500g mussel	200g of frozen pea
400g of pre-cooked shrimp	Black pepper to taste
Salt to taste	Turmeric (2 packets) dissolved in 1.2 liters of fish stock
400g squid in rings	400g of sliced cooked octopus
400g of the pump or par-boiled rice	½ chopped red peppers
½ chopped yellow pepper	½ chopped green peppers
4 whole cloves garlic + 2 cloves minced garlic in shell	1 chopped onion
Extra virgin olive oil	

Directions:
In olive oil, sauté rice, peppers, garlic, and onion. Add half the broth, the squid, and the octopus. Adjust pepper and salt. Let the liquid dry. Then add more broth while caring for the rice point. Add the shrimp and the pea when the stock is almost dehydrated. Add the mussels and parsley. Put peppers on top for prawns and garnish. Cook while covered for 15-minutes Finish with lemon juice and olive oil.

Nutritional Information: Calories: 1468 | Protein: 177.19 g | Fat: 28.65 g | Carbohydrates: 115.89 g

458. Shrimp and Corn

Prep Time: 7-minutes | Total time: 17-minutes | Yield: 4-servings

Ingredients:

1 lb. shrimp, peeled and deveined	2 garlic cloves, minced
1 c. corn	½ c. veggie stock
1 bunch parsley, chopped	Juice of 1 lime
2 tbsps. olive oil	Pinch of sea salt
Pinch of black pepper	

Directions:
Preheat the pan with the oil on medium-high heat, then put the corn and the garlic and cook for 2-minutes. Mix the shrimp with the other ingredients, cook everything for 8-minutes, and share and serve between plates.

Nutritional Information: Calories: 343 | Protein: 29.12 g | Fat: 10.97 g | Carbohydrates: 34.25 g

459. Popcorn Shrimp

Prep Time: 7-minutes | Total time: 27-minutes | Yield: 2-servings

Ingredients:

2 eggs, whisked	Peeled 1/2 lb. (225 g) small shrimp,
6 Tbsps. (36 g) Cajun seasoning	6 Tbsps. (42 g) coconut flour
Coconut oil for frying	

Directions:
In a saucepan, preheat the coconut oil (use enough coconut oil so that it's 1/2 inch deep) or deep fryer. In a large bowl, put the whisked eggs, and mix the coconut flour and seasoning in another large bowl. Add the shrimp into the whisked eggs and whisk until each shrimp is coated. Then take out the shrimp and put it in the seasoning bowl. Coat the shrimp in the seasoning mixture and coconut flour. Take the coated shrimp and put it in the hot oil to fry till golden. (You must deep fry the shrimp). Remove shrimp using a slotted spoon and dry the excess oil using paper towels. Repeat the same process for all shrimps (change the oil if there are too many solids in it). Give it 10-minutes to cool

Nutritional Information: Calories: 390 | Fat: 23 g | Net Carbohydrates: 3 g | Protein: 30 g

460. Citrus & Herb Sardines

Prep Time: 7-minutes | Total time: 22-minutes | Yield: 2-servings

Ingredients:

10 Sardines, scaled and clean	2 Whole Lemon zest
Handful-Flat leafy parsley, chopped	2 Garlic cloves, finely chopped
Pinch of Black Pepper	8 Cherry Tomatoes, halved (optional)
1/2 can Butterbeans or Chickpeas, drained and rinsed	1 can Tomato, chopped, (optional)
3 tbsp. Olive oil	1/2 c. Black Olives (pitted and halves)

Directions:
Put the lemon zest to the sliced parsley (keep a pinch for garnishing) and half of the sliced garlic, ready for later. Put a huge frying pan on the hob, then heat on high. Once the oil is hot, lay the sardines flat on the pan. Sauté each side for 3-minutes until they turn golden. Set on a plate to cool. Cook the remaining garlic for 1 min until softened. Combine with the tin of sliced tomatoes, mix, and let bubble for around 5-minutes. Whisk in butter beans, fresh tomatoes, and chickpeas and heat well. Dip your sardines in parsley/lemon dressing, then set to your pan to cook for 4 extra-minutes. Serve alongside parsley and garnished with the extra lemon zest.

Nutritional Information: Calories: 493 | Protein: 24.16 g | Fat: 35.67 carbohydrates: 20.92 g

461. Crab Stuffed Salmon

Prep Time: 12-minutes | Total time: 42-minutes | Yield: 8-servings

Ingredients:

2 lbs. Salmon (wider filet works best)	2 tbsp. Butter (melted)
2 tsp. Lemon zest	Black pepper
Sea salt	Crab Filling:
½ big onion (chopped)	1 tbsp. Lemon juice
1 tsp. Old Bay seasoning	2 cloves Garlic (minced)
2 tbsp. Fresh parsley (chopped)	2 tbsp. Mayonnaise
8 oz. Lump crab meat	

Directions:

Preheat your oven to 400°F. Coat a baking sheet using foil or parchment paper. In a pan at moderate heat, sauté onion for approximately 7-10-minutes, until translucent and browned (or cook longer to caramelize if you wish). Mix mayonnaise, parsley, Old Bay seasoning, lemon juice, and garlic in a separate bowl. Mix in the sautéed onion. Cautiously fold in the lump crab meat without breaking up the lumps. Put the salmon fillet on the baking sheet. Organize the crab mixture along the length down the middle of the salmon. Beginning from the thinner sides of the filet, fold over the long way. Mix lemon zest with melted butter and brush onto your salmon lightly dusted with black pepper and salt. Bake for a minimum of 16-20-minutes until the fish flakes easily using a fork. Drizzle with additional fresh parsley. Cut crosswise into individual filets to serve.

Nutritional Information: Calories: 243, Fat: 13g, Carbohydrates: 1g, Protein: 29g

462. Tilapia and Red Sauce

Prep Time: 11-minutes | Total time: 30-minutes | Yield: 4-servings

Ingredients:

4 tilapia fillets, boneless	A pinch of salt and black pepper
2 tbsps. avocado oil	1 tbsp. lemon juice
2 spring onions, minced	½ c. chicken stock
¼ c. tomato passata	1 tsp. garlic powder
1 tsp. oregano, dried	1 c. roasted red peppers, chopped
10 oz. canned tomatoes and chilies, chopped	

Directions:

Press sauté on the instant pot. Add oil and onions. Cook for about 2-minutes. Add in the remaining ingredients except for fish. Simmer for an additional 8-minutes. Add in the fish and close. Cook for 10-minutes on high. Naturally, release pressure for about 10-minutes. set in plates and enjoy.

Nutritional Information: Calories 184 | Fat: 2.2 | Fiber: 1.6 | Carbs: 1.9 | Protein: 22.2

463. Swordfish with Pineapple and Cilantro

Prep Time: 12-minutes | Total time: 32-minutes | Yield: 4-servings

Ingredients:

1 tsp. Salt.	1 tbsp. coconut aminos
¼ c. chopped fresh cilantro	2 minced garlic cloves
¼ tsp. Ground black pepper.	2 tbsps. Chopped fresh parsley
2 lbs. sliced swordfish	1 tbsp. coconut oil
1 c. fresh pineapple chunks	

Directions:

Preheat the oven to 400F. Grease a baking tray with coconut oil. Mix cilantro, coconut aminos, garlic, pineapple, parsley, pepper, swordfish, and salt. Set the dish to the oven and allow it to bake for about 20-minutes.

Nutritional Information: Calories: 444 | Protein: 47.53 g | Fat: 20.32 carbohydrates: 16.44 g

464. Cucumber Ginger Shrimp

Prep Time: 7-minutes | Total time: 17-minutes | Yield: 1 serving

Ingredients:

10-15 large shrimp/prawns	1 sizeable, sliced cucumber, into 1/2-inch round
1 tsp. (1 g) fresh ginger, grated	Salt to taste
Coconut oil	

Directions:

In a frying pan, add 1 Tbsp. coconut oil and heat on medium heat. Add in cucumber and ginger and sauté for 3-minutes. Mix in the shrimp and cook until they become pink and opaque. Sprinkle with salt to taste.

Nutritional Information: Calories: 25 | Fat: 16 g | Net Carbohydrates: 4 g | Protein: 20 g

465. Spicy Kingfish

Prep Time: 15-minutes | Total time: 25-minutes | Yield: 2-servings

Ingredients:

½ tsp. ground turmeric	1 garlic clove, minced
1 lime wedge	1 tbsp. fresh lime juice
1 tbsp. olive oil	1 tsp. cumin seeds
1 tsp. dried unswee10ed coconut	1 tsp. fennel seeds
1 tsp. peppercorns	10 curry leaves
1½ tsps. fresh ginger, grated finely	4 (4 oz.) kingfish steaks
Salt, to taste	

Directions:

Heat a cast-iron frying pan on low heat. Put in coconut, cumin seeds, fennel seeds, peppercorns, and curry leaves and cook, constantly stirring for approximately one minute. Take off from the heat and cool to room temperature. In a spice grinder, put in the spice mixture and turmeric and grind rill powdered finely. Move the mixture to a big container with ginger, garlic, salt, and lime juice and mix thoroughly. Put in fish fillets and cat with the mixture uniformly. Put in your fridge to marinate for approximately three hours. In a huge nonstick frying pan, warm oil on moderate heat. Put the fish fillets and cook for three to 5-minutes per side or till the desired doneness. Move onto a paper towel-lined plate to drain. Serve with lime wedges.

Nutritional Information: Calories: 592, Protein: 67.03 g, Fat: 34.55 g, Carbohydrates: 4.91 g

466. Herbed Coconut Milk Steamed Mussels

Prep Time: 11-minutes | Total time: 25-minutes | Yield: 4

Ingredients:

2 tbsps. coconut oil	½ sweet onion, chopped
2 tsp. minced garlic	1 tsp. Grated fresh ginger
½ tsp. turmeric	1 c. coconut milk
Juice of 1 lime	1½ lbs. fresh mussels, scrubbed and debearded
1 scallion, finely chopped	2 tbsps. chopped fresh cilantro
1 tbsp. chopped fresh thyme	

Directions:

Sauté the aromatics. In a huge skillet, warm the coconut oil. Add the onion, garlic, ginger, turmeric, and sauté until they have softened for about 3-minutes. Add the liquid. Mix in the coconut milk, lime juice, then bring the mixture to a boil. Steam the mussels. Put the mussels to the skillet, cover, and steam until the shells are open, about 10-minutes. Take the skillet off the heat and throw out any unopened mussels. Add the herbs. Whisk in the scallion, cilantro, and thyme. Serve. Divide the mussels and the sauce into 4 bowls and serve them immediately.

Nutritional Information: Calories: 319|Fat: 23g| Carbs: 8g| Fiber: 2g |Sodium: 395mg| Protein: 23g

467. Cod with Ginger

Prep Time: 10-minutes | Total time: 25-minutes | Yield: 4-servings

Ingredients:

2 tbsp. Extra Virgin Olive Oil	4 (6 oz.) Cod Fillets
1 tbsp. Grated fresh ginger	1 tsp. Sea Salt, divided
¼ tsp. Freshly ground black pepper	5 Garlic cloves, minced
¼ c. Fresh Cilantro Leaves, chopped	

Directions:

In a huge nonstick skillet at medium-high heat, heat the olive oil until it shimmers. Season the cod with ginger, ½ tsp. of the salt, and the pepper. Put it in the hot oil, then cook for at least 4-minutes per side until the fish is opaque. Take off the cod from the pan and set it aside on a platter tented with aluminum foil. Put back the skillet to the heat and add the garlic. Cook for 30 seconds, stirring constantly. Cook for 5-minutes, stirring occasionally. Whisk in the cilantro over the cod.

Nutritional Information: Calories: 41| Fat: 2g| Carbs: 33 |Sugar: 1g |Fiber: 8 |Protein: 50g |

468. Mozzarella Fish

Prep Time: 5-minutes | Total time: 15 – 20-minutes | Yield: 6-8-servings

Ingredients:

2 lbs. of bone gold sole	Salt and pepper to taste
½ tsp. dried oregano	1 c. grated mozzarella cheese
1 large fresh tomato, sliced thinly	

Directions:

Excellent source of cooking the butter. Organize a single layer of trout. Add salt, pepper, and oregano. Top with sliced cheese slices and tomatoes. Cook, covered, for 10 to 15-minutes at 425°F.

Nutritional Information: Calories: 156 |Fat: 6g |Net Carbs: 5g |Protein: 8g

469. Curry Tilapia and Beans

Prep Time: 5-minutes | Total time: 25-minutes | Yield: 4-servings

Ingredients:

1 c. canned red kidney beans, drained	1 tbsp. olive oil
1 tbsp. parsley, chopped	2 tbsps. green curry paste
4 tilapia fillets, boneless	Juice of ½ lime

Directions:

Warm a pan with the oil on moderate heat, put the fish, and cook for 5-minutes on each side. Put the remaining ingredients, toss lightly, cook on moderate heat for about 10-minutes more, split between plates before serving.

Nutritional Information: Calories 271, Fat: 4, Fiber: 6, Carbs: 14, Protein: 7

470. Salmon and Roasted Peppers

Prep Time: 5-minutes | Total time: 30-minutes | Yield: 4-servings

Ingredients:

1 c. red peppers, cut into strips	4 salmon fillets, boneless
¼ c. chicken stock	2 tbsps. olive oil
1 yellow onion, chopped	1 tbsp. cilantro, chopped
Pinch of sea salt	Pinch black pepper

Directions:

Warm a pan with the oil on medium-high heat; add the onion and sauté for 5-minutes. Put the fish and cook for at least 5-minutes on each side. Add the rest of the ingredients, introduce the pan in the oven, and cook at 390 degrees F for 10-minutes. Divide the mix between plates and serve.

Nutritional Information: Calories 265 | Fat 7 | Fiber | Carbs 1 | Protein 16

471. Mexican Salad with Mahi-Mahi

Prep Time: 20-minutes | Total time: 1-hour 35-minutes | Yield: 4-servings

Ingredients:

1 lb. Ground beef	Pepper (as desired)
Salt (as expected)	Hot pepper sauce (as desired)
5 tsp. Chili powder	5 tbsp. Cumin, ground
25 c. Cilantro, chopped	1 clove Garlic, crushed
2 tbsp. Agave sweetener	1 tbsp. Lemon juice
2 tbsp. Lime juice	5 c. Coconut oil
1 Red onion, chopped	10 oz. Corn kernels, frozen
1 Red bell pepper, frozen	1 Green bell pepper, chopped
32 oz. Mahi-mahi	

Directions:

In a serving bowl, Mix the red onion, frozen corn, bell peppers and mix well. In a smaller separate bowl, Mix the pepper, cumin, cilantro, hot pepper sauce, garlic, salt, sugar, lemon juice, lime juice, and coconut oil and whisk well. Pour the dressing over the salad, toss well to coat, cover the salad with plastic wrap, chill in the refrigerator, and serve chilled. Before serving, Season the fish as desired. Add the coconut oil to a pan before placing the pan on the stove over a medium heat burner. Add in the fish and let it cook for approximately 5-minutes on each side.

Nutritional Information: Calories: 709 | Protein: 39.23 g | Fat: 47.12 g | Carbohydrates: 36.61 g

472. Sherry and Butter Prawns

Prep Time: 5-minutes | Total time: 10-minutes | Yield: 4-servings

Ingredients:

1 ½ lb. king prawns, peeled and deveined	2 tbsps. dry sherry
1 tsp. dried basil	1/2 tsp. mustard seeds
1 ½ tbsps. fresh lemon juice	1 tsp. cayenne pepper, crushed
1 tbsp. garlic paste	1/2 stick butter, at room temperature

Directions:

Whisk the dry sherry with cayenne pepper, garlic paste, basil, mustard seeds, lemon juice, and prawns. Let it marinate for 1 hour in your refrigerator. In a frying pan, melt the butter over medium-high flame, basting with the reserved marinade. Sprinkle with salt and pepper to taste.

Nutrition294 Calories | 14.3g Fa | 3.6g Carb | 34.6g Protei | 1.4g Fiber

473. Fish Sandwich

Prep Time: 10-minutes | Total time: 20-minutes | Yield: 4-servings

Ingredients:

1 lb. quartered Salmon fillet	2 tsp. Cajun seasoning
1 pitted Avocado, peeled	2 tbsp. Mayonnaise
4 Wheat rolls	1 c. Arugula
2 Plum tomatoes, sliced thin	5 c. Red onion, sliced thin
2 tbsp. Coconut oil	

Directions:

Coat the grill in coconut oil before ensuring it is heated to high heat. Coat the fish using the seasoning before adding it to the grill and let it cook for approximately 3-minutes on each side. Mash the avocado before blending it with the mayonnaise and spreading on the rolls before serving. Season as required, serve hot and enjoy.

Nutritional Information: Calories: 389 | Protein: 26.88 g Fat: 26.27 g | Carbohydrates: 12.21 g

474. Amberjack Fillets with Cheese Sauce

Prep Time: 10-minutes | Total time: 20-minutes | Yield: 4-servings

Ingredients:

6 amberjack fillets	1/4 c. fresh tarragon chopped

2 tbsps. olive oil, at room temperature	Sea salt, to taste
Ground black pepper, to taste	For the Sauce:
1/3 c. vegetable broth	3/4 c. double cream
1/3 c. Romano cheese, grated	3 tsp. butter, at room temperature
2 garlic cloves, finely minced	

Directions:
In a non-stick frying pan, warm the olive oil until sizzling. Once hot, fry the amberjack for about 6-minutes per side or until the edges turn opaque. Sprinkle them with salt, black pepper, and tarragon. Reserve. To make the sauce, melt the butter in a saucepan over moderately high heat. Sauté the garlic until tender and fragrant or about 2-minutes. Add in the vegetable broth and cream and continue to cook for 5 to 6-minutes more heat off. Whisk in the Romano cheese and continue stirring in the residual heat for a couple of-minutes more.
Nutritional Information: 285 Calories | 20.4g Fat | 1.2g Carbs | 23.8g Protein | 0.1g Fiber

475. Shrimp and Beets

Prep Time: 10-minutes | Total time: 20-minutes | Yield: 4-servings

Ingredients:

1 lb. shrimp, peeled and deveined	2 tbsps. avocado oil
2 spring onions, chopped	2 garlic cloves, minced
1 beet, peeled and cubed	1 tbsp. lemon juice
Pinch of sea salt	Pinch of black pepper
1 tsp. coconut aminos	

Directions:
Warm a pan with the oil on medium-high heat, add the spring onions and the garlic and sauté for 2-minutes. Add the shrimp and the other ingredients, toss, cook the mix for 8-minutes, divide into bowls and serve.
Nutritional Information: Calories 281 | Fat 6 | Fiber 7 | Carbs 11 | Protein 8

476. Salmon in Dill Sauce

Prep Time: 10-minutes | Total time: 2-hours 10-minutes | Yield: 6-servings

Ingredients:

2 c. water	1-c. homemade chicken broth
2 tbsps. fresh lemon juice	¼ c. fresh dill, chopped
6 salmon fillets	1 tsp. cayenne pepper
Salt and ground black pepper	

Directions:
In the pot of Ninja Foody, mix the water, broth, lemon juice, lemon juice, and dill. Organize the salmon fillets on top, skin side down, and sprinkle with cayenne pepper, salt black pepper. Close the Ninja Foody with a crisping lid and select Slow Cooker. Set on Low for 1-2 hours. Press Start/Stop to begin cooking. Serve hot.
Nutritional Information: Calories: 16 | Fats: 7.4 | Carbohydrates 1.6 g | Protein: 23.3g

477. Quick Shrimp Moqueca

Prep Time: 10-minutes | Total time: 20-minutes | Yield: 4-servings

Ingredients:

600g Shrimp Peeled and Clean	Salt to taste
Juice of 2 lemons	Braised olive oil
2 chopped purple onions	4 cloves garlic, minced
3 chopped tomatoes	1 chopped red pepper
1 chopped yellow pepper	1 c. tomato passata
200ml of coconut milk	2 finger peppers
2 tbsps. palm oil	Chopped cilantro to taste

Directions:
In a container, arrange shrimp, season with salt and lemon juice, and set aside. In a hot pan, arrange olive oil and sauté onion and garlic. Add the chopped tomatoes and sauté well. Add the peppers and the tomato passata. Let it cook for a few-minutes. Add coconut milk, mix well. Add the shrimp to the sauce. Finally, add the finger pepper, palm oil, and chopped coriander. Serve with rice and crumbs.
Nutritional Information: Calories: 426 | Protein: 46.15 g | Fat: 15.46 g | Carbohydrates: 26.26 g

478. Haddock with Swiss Chard

Prep Time: 15-minutes | Total time: 25-minutes | Yield: 1 serving

Ingredients:

2 tbsps. coconut oil, divided	2 minced garlic cloves
2 tsp. fresh ginger, grated finely	1 haddock fillet
Salt, to taste	Freshly ground black pepper, to taste
2 c. Swiss chard, chopped roughly	1 tsp. coconut aminos

Directions:
In a skillet, put 1 tbsp. Of coconut oil, then melt it on medium heat. Add garlic and ginger and sauté for

about 1 minute. Add haddock fillet and sprinkle with salt and black pepper. Cook for at least about 3-5-minutes per side or till the desired doneness. Meanwhile, in another skillet, melt the remaining coconut oil on medium heat. Add Swiss chard and coconut aminos and cook for about 5-10-minutes. Serve the salmon fillet over Swiss chard.

Nutritional Information: Calories: 486 | Protein: 39.68 g | Fat: 34.34 g | Carbohydrates: 5.57 g

479. Stuffed Trout

Prep Time: 20minutes | Total time: 1 hour 35-minutes | Yield: 4-servings

Ingredients:

1 c. chicken broth	1/2 c. quinoa
2 tbsps. omega-3-rich margarine	1 yellow onion, finely dices
1 c. (100 g) mushrooms, sliced	2 tsp. dehydrated tarragon
Salt and pepper	1 c. cherry tomatoes, chopped
2 tbsps. lemon juice	2 tbsps. canola oil
2 whole lake trout	2 tbsps. flour

Directions:

In a pan, Put the chicken broth on to simmer. Mix the quinoa, cover, and decrease the heat to low — Cook for 45 to 60-minutes. Preheat the oven to 400°F and proceed to line a baking tray with parchment paper. To make the stuffing, melt margarine in a wide pan over medium heat. Sauté the onions and mushrooms till tender. Season by including tarragon, and salt, and pepper. Mix cherry tomatoes and sauté 1 to 2-minutes further, mixing continually. Take off the heat and mix with cooked quinoa. Add in lemon juice and stir. Spray the canola oil covering the trout. In a bowl, blend flour, salt, and pepper. Glaze the interior and exterior of the trout with the flour batter. Stuff the trout with the stuffing blend. Cook uncovered for 10-minutes per inch of trout.

Nutritional Information: Calories: 342 | Protein: 18.76 g | Fat: 19.1 g | Carbohydrates: 24.38 g

480. Sole with Vegetables

Prep Time: 10-minutes | Total time: 25-minutes | Yield: 4-servings

Ingredients:

4 tsp. divided extra-virgin olive oil	1 thinly sliced and divided carrot
Salt	Lemon wedges
½ c. divided vegetable broth	5 oz. sole fillets
2 sliced and thinly divided shallots	Ground black pepper
2 tbsps. divided snipped fresh chives	1 thinly sliced and divided zucchini

Directions:

Preheat the oven to about 375 F. Separate the aluminum foil into medium-sized pieces. Put a fillet on one half of the aluminum foil piece and add seasonings. Add shallots, zucchini, and ¼ each of the carrots on top of the fillet. Sprinkle with 1 ½ tsp. of chives. Drizzle 2 tbsp. Of broth and a tbsp. of olive oil over the fish and vegetables. Seal to make a packet and put the packet on a large baking tray. Repeat for the rest of the ingredients and make more packets. Put the sheet in a preheated oven and bake the packets for 15-minutes. Peel back the foil and put the contents with the liquid onto a serving plate. Garnish with lemon wedges before serving.

Nutritional Information: Calories: 130 | Protein: 9.94 g | Fat: 7.96 g Carbohydrates: 4.92 g

481. Potato Dumpling with Shrimp

Prep Time: 15-minutes | Total time: 1-hour 5-minutes | Yield: 6-8-servings

Ingredients:

500g of pink potatoes	1 egg
salt to taste	1 tbsp. chopped parsley
½ packet of chopped cilantro	black pepper to taste
10 units of clean giant tailed shrimp	2 tbsps. flour + flour for handling and breading
3 tbsps. palm oil frying oil	4 lemon juice

Directions:

Put the potato to cook for 40-minutes. When very tender, remove from heat, let cool, and mash potatoes already peeled. Add the egg and mix well, season with salt and parsley and add the flour. Set aside in the fridge for 2 hours. Make small transverse cuts on the belly of the shrimp without cutting to the end. Season the shrimp with black pepper, salt, chopped coriander, palm oil, and lemon juice. Leave marinating for 15-minutes. Take a portion of the potato flour dough in your hands and shape around a shrimp leaving the tail out. Rinse flour again and fry in hot oil until golden.

Nutritional Information: | Calories: 159 | Protein: 6.95 g | Fat: 8.42 g | Carbohydrates: 14.48 g

482. Fast Fish Pie

Prep Time: 15-minutes | Total time: 1-hour | Yield: 4-servings

Ingredients:

2 slices prosciutto	1 c. frozen peas
2 sheets frozen puff pastry	600g firm white fish fillets
1/2 bunch dill	1 tbsp. cornflour
350g cauliflower	1 lemon
1 Coles Australian Free-Range Egg	1 tbsp. sesame seeds

Directions:

Preheat broiler to 400°F. Spot the cauliflower, prosciutto, fish, peas, lemon pizzazz, dill & cornflour in an enormous bowl. Season. Delicately hurl until very much consolidated. Move the blend to a 6-c — round pie dish. Cut 1 good baking sheet into 3 strips — brush 2 adjacent edges of residual baked good sheet with egg. Spot 1 baked good strip, somewhat covering, over each edge, squeezing delicately to make an enormous square. Brush sides of the pie dish with the use of egg. Spot pastry over fish blend, squeezing into the edge of the plate. Overlay overabundance baked good inwards. Brush the baked good with egg. Utilize a sharp blade to cut 3 cuts in the focal point of the baked good. Sprinkle with sesame seeds. Bake the pie until the baked good is brilliant darker & puffed. Slice into wedges to serve.

Nutritional Information: Calories: 364 | Protein: 35.95 g | Fat: 20.51 g | Carbohydrates: 8.57 g

483. Pan-Seared Scallops with Lemon-Ginger Vinaigrette

Prep Time: 10-minutes | Total time: 17-minutes | Yield: 4-servings

Ingredients:

2 tbsps. extra virgin olive oil	1 1/2 lbs. sea scallop
1/2 tsp. sea salt	1/8 tsp. freshly ground black pepper
1/4 c. lemon ginger vinaigrette	

Directions:

In a big nonstick skillet at medium-high heat, heat the olive oil until it shimmers. Flavor the scallops with pepper and salt and add them to the skillet. Cook per side until just opaque. Serve with the vinaigrette set over the top.

Nutritional Information: Calories 280, Fat 16, Carbs 5 g, Sugar 1 g, Fiber 0 g, Protein 29 g, Sodium 508 mg

484. Seared Ahi Tuna

Prep Time: 10-minutes | Total time: 25-minutes | Yield: 2-servings

Ingredients:

1 tsp. lime juice	1 green onion (scallion) thinly sliced, reserve a few slices for garnish
1 clove garlic, minced	1 tbsp. of grated fresh ginger
2 tbsp. soy sauce	2 tbsp. dark sesame oil
2 (4 oz. each) ahi tuna steaks (3/4-inch thick)	

Directions:

Begin by preparing the marinade. Put the sesame oil, soy sauce, fresh ginger, minced garlic, green onion, and lime juice in a small bowl. Mix well. Put tuna steaks into a sealable Ziploc freezer bag and pour marinade over the top of the tuna. Seal bag and shake or massage with hands to coat tuna steaks well with marinade. Bring the bag in a bowl in case of breaks and Put tuna in the refrigerator to marinate for at least 10-minutes. Put a large non-stick skillet over medium-high to high heat. Let the pan heat for 2-minutes. When hot, remove tuna steaks from the marinade and lay them in the pan to sear for 1-1½-minutes on each side. Remove tuna steaks from the pan and cut them into ¼-inch thick slices. Garnish with a sprinkle of sliced green onion. Serve immediately.

Nutritional Information: Calories: 213 | Protein: 4.5 g | Fat: 19.55 g | Carbohydrates: 5.2 g

485. Souvlaki Spiced Salmon Bowls

Prep Time: 10-minutes | Total time: 30-minutes | Yield: 4-servings

Ingredients:
For the Salmon:

¼ c. good-quality olive oil	¼ tsp. Freshly ground black pepper
½ tsp. sea salt	1 tbsp. balsamic vinegar
1 tbsp. minced garlic	1 tbsp. smoked sweet paprika
2 tbsps. chopped fresh oregano	4 (4 oz.) salmon fillets
Juice of 1 lemon	

For the Bowls:

½ c. cut Kalamata olives	½ c. sour cream
1 big tomato, chopped	1 cucumber, diced
1 red bell pepper, cut into strips	1 yellow bell pepper, cut into strips

1 zucchini, cut into ½-inch strips along the length	2 tbsps. good-quality olive oil
6 oz. feta cheese, crumbled	

Directions:

To make the Salmon:

Marinate the fish. Put and mix the olive oil, lemon juice, oregano, garlic, vinegar, paprika, salt, and pepper in a moderate-sized container. Put the salmon and turn to coat it thoroughly with the marinade. Cover the container and let the salmon sit marinating for 15 to 20-minutes. Grill the fish. Preheat the grill to moderate-high heat and grill the fish until thoroughly cooked, four to 5-minutes per side. Set the fish aside on a plate.

To make the Bowls:

Grill the vegetables. In a moderate-sized container, put the oil, red and yellow bell peppers, and zucchini. Grill the vegetables, flipping over once, until they are mildly charred and soft, approximately 3-minutes per side. Assemble before you serve. Split the grilled vegetables between four bowls. Top each container with cucumber, tomato, olives, feta cheese, and sour cream. Put 1 salmon fillet on top of every container and serve instantly.

Nutritional Information: Calories: 553, Fat: 44g Carbs: 10g , Fiber: 3g, Sodium: 531mg , Protein: 30g

486. Crab Salad Cakes

Prep Time: 10-minutes | Total time: 15-minutes | Yield: 4-servings

Ingredients:

½ tsp. Black pepper	½ tsp. Salt
1 tbsp. Extra virgin coconut oil	½ c. Swiss cheese, shredded
2 Hot sauce, dashes	¼ tsp. Old Bay seasoning
1 tbsp. Mayonnaise	4 tsp. Lemon juice
1 Scallion, chopped	¼ c. Red bell pepper, chopped
1/3 c. Celery, chopped	8 oz. Crabmeat
4 asparagus spears, sliced	

Directions:

Pace the rack high in the oven and heat your broiler. Microwave the asparagus in a covered bowl with 1 tsp. Water for 30 seconds. Mix the seasonings as desired and the mayonnaise, lemon juice, scallion, bell pepper, celery, and crab. For the results into 4 patties and top with the cheese. Broil the patties for 3-minutes.

Nutritional Information: Calories: 310 |Protein: 28.19 g|Fat: 12.45 g|Carbohydrates: 24.34 g

487. Simple Founder in Brown Butter Lemon Sauce

Prep Time: 10-minutes | Total time: 20-minutes | Yield: 4-servings

Ingredients:

For the Sauce:

½ c. unsalted grass-fed butter, cut into pieces	Juice of 1 lemon
Sea salt for seasoning	Freshly ground black pepper for seasoning

For the Fish:

4 (4 oz.) boneless flounder fillets	Sea salt for seasoning
Freshly ground black pepper for seasoning	¼ c. almond flour
2 tbsps. good-quality olive oil	1 tbsp. chopped fresh parsley

Directions:

To make the Sauce:

Brown the butter. In a medium saucepan at medium heat, cook the butter, stirring it occasionally, until it is golden brown, at least 4-minutes. Finish the sauce. Remove the saucepan from the heat and then whisk in the lemon juice. Spice the sauce with salt and pepper and set it aside.

To make a Fish:

Season the fish. Pat the fish, fillets dry, then spice them lightly with salt and pepper. Spoon the almond flour onto a plate, then roll the fish fillets through the flour until lightly coated. Cook the fish. In a large skillet at medium-high heat, warm the olive oil. Add the fish fillets and fry them until they are crispy and golden on both sides, 2 to 3-minutes per side. Serve. Moved the fish to a serving plate and drizzled it with the sauce. Top with the parsley and serve it hot.

Nutritional Information: Calories: 389| Fat: 33g| Carbs: 1g|Fiber: 0g |Sodium: 256mg | Protein: 22g

488. Thai Chowder

Prep Time: 10-minutes | Total time: 30-minutes | Yield: 6-servings

Ingredients:

3 c. 98 % fat-free chicken broth	10 small red potatoes, diced
3 cobs fresh sweet corn	3/4 c. coconut milk
1/2 tsp. fresh ginger, diced	1 tsp. dried lemongrass
1 tsp. green curry paste	1/2 c. cabbage, chopped
4 (5 oz.) tilapia fillets	2 tbsps. fish sauce

3/4 c. fresh shrimp, cleaned, with tails on	3/4 c. bay scallops
3/4 c. cilantro, chopped	

Directions:

In a saucepan, boil chicken stock at high heat until it reaches a simmer. Decrease temperature and add the cabbage, ginger, coconut milk, lemongrass, sweet corn, lemongrass, curry paste, and potatoes — cover and cook for 15-minutes. Firstly, Mix fish fillets with the fish sauce, and cook for about 6-minutes. Secondly, add the shrimp. Then cook for an extra 2 to 3-minutes. Finally, add the scallops and cook until the scallops are opaque in color. Serve with cilantro.

Nutritional Information: Calories: 761 | Protein: 33.25 g | Fat: 5.34 g | Carbohydrates: 150.45 g

489. Tilapia with Spicy Dijon Sauce

Prep Time: 10-minutes | Total time: 15-minutes | Yield: 4-servings

Ingredients:

1 tbsp. butter, room temperature	2 chili peppers, deveined and minced
1 c. heavy cream	1 tsp. Dijon mustard
1 lb. tilapia fish, cubed	Sea salt, to taste
Ground black pepper, to taste	1 c. white onions, chopped
1 tsp. garlic, pressed	1/2 c. dark rum

Directions:

Toss the tilapia using pepper, salt, garlic, onions, rum, and chili peppers. Let it marinate for about 2-hours in your refrigerator. Melt the butter in a grill pan over moderately high-heat. Sear the fish in hot-butter, basting using the reserved marinade. Add in the mustard with the cream and then continue to cook until everything is thoroughly cooked, for 2 to 3-minutes.

Nutritional Information: 228 Calories | 13g Fat | 6.5g Carbs | 13.7g Protein | 1.1g Fiber

490. Trout with Chard

Prep Time: 10-minutes | Total time: 25-minutes | Yield: 4-servings

Ingredients:

½ c. vegetable broth	2 bunches of sliced chard
4 boneless trout fillets	Salt
1 tbsp. extra-virgin olive oil	2 minced garlic cloves
¼ c. golden raisins	Ground black pepper
1 chopped onion	1 tbsp. apple cider vinegar

Directions:

Preheat the oven to about 3750F. Add seasonings to the trout. Add olive oil to a pan, then heat. Add garlic and onion, then sauté for 3-minutes. Add chard to sauté for 2 more-minutes. Add raisins, broth, and cedar vinegar into the pan. Layer a topping of trout-fillets. Cover the pan and place it in the preheated oven for 10-minutes. Serve and enjoy.

Nutritional Information: Calories: 284 | Protein: 2.07 g | Fat: 30.32 g | Carbohydrates: 3.49 g

491. Spicy herb catfish

Prep Time: 10-minutes | Total time: 35-minutes | Yield: 4-servings

Ingredients:

For the spice mixture:

1/4 c. coriander seeds	1/2 tsp. cumin seeds
1/2 tbsp. ground red pepper	1/2 tsp. crushed cardamom
1 tbsp. raw sugar	1 tbsp. kosher salt
1 tsp. ground black pepper	1 lemon quartered

For the garnish:

4 (6 oz.) catfish fillets	Several sprigs of fresh cilantro
1 medium tomato	Canola oil spray
1/2 c. flaxseed, freshly ground	

Directions:

Preheat oven to 350°F. Put the spice blend ingredients into a mixing bowl and Mix well. Put the mixture inside a pie pan. Clean and pat dry the catfish fillets. Fill a second pie pan halfway with ground flaxseed. Dredge the fillets in the spice mixture first, then in the flaxseed. Spray the baking sheet with canola oil and set it aside. Cook the fillets for 18-minutes on a baking sheet. Boil the stock juices for 6-minutes more. Pour the juices over the fillets and garnish with cilantro, a tomato slice, and a lemon quarter.

Nutritional Information: Calories: 208 | Protein: 13.5 g | Fat: 12.65 g | Carbohydrates: 13.66 g

492. Shrimp Pie

Prep Time: 10-minutes | Total time: 40-minutes | Yield: 8-servings

Ingredients:

250g of flour	200g of cold butter
1 tsp. salt	3 tbsp. water
2 tbsp. olive oil	2 cloves garlic,
400g shrimp	1 tomato

2 tbsp. coconut milk	1 minced finger pepper
1/4 c. sour cream	2 tbsp. chopped cilantro
1 gem	

Directions:

Set the flour in a bowl and add the diced butter. Knead with fingertips until crumbly. Attach salt and, gradually, water until it turns into dough. Secure with plastic and refrigerate for 1 hour. Warm the frying pan, sprinkle with olive oil, and brown the garlic and prawns. Attach the tomatoes, sauté for a couple of-minutes, add coconut milk and pepper and cook for another two-minutes. Flavor with salt, and by adding the cream, turn off the heat and add the cilantro. Set aside to cool. To open the dough in portions and cover the pancakes, stuff with the shrimp, and cover with a dough circle. Set with the yolk and bake in the preheated oven at 180 degrees for about 30-minutes or until golden brown.

Nutritional Information: Calories: 248, Fat: 9 g, Protein: 40 g, Sodium: 568 mg

493. Spicy Salmon Tempura Roll

Prep Time: 10-minutes | Total time: 10-minutes | Yield: 8-servings

Ingredients:

½ avocado, cut into strips	½ tbsp. Sirach
1 tbsp. mayonnaise	1/4 English cucumber, julienned
1/4 tsp. ground ginger	20 grams pork rinds or cracklings
4 oz. canned wild salmon	Nori sheet
Pickled ginger (not necessary)	Sesame seeds (not required)
Soy sauce (not required)	Wasabi (not required)

Directions:

Put in salmon, mayonnaise, Siracha, and ginger in a container and Whisk until well blended. Put pork-rinds in a plastic bag and crush until you get big crumbs.

Put a nori sheet on your work surface with the glossy side down. Mix pork rind crumbs into the salmon mixture. Position salmon/pork rind mixture and veggies on the nori, minimum an inch away from the edge closest to you. Roll the nori around the filling firmly, tucking the edge under as you go. Spread a little amount of water on the rest of the "rough" side of the nori and go ahead with rolling to bind together and create a uniform roll. Cut in half, then continue to slice every portion in half until you get 8 pieces. Decorate using sesame seeds, soy sauce, wasabi, or pickled ginger. Serve.

Nutritional Information: Calories: 243, Fat: 14g, Carbohydrates: 6g, Protein: 23g

494. Manhattan-Style Salmon Chowder

Prep Time: 10-minutes | Total time: 25-minutes | Yield: 4-servings

Ingredients:

¼ c. Extra Virgin Olive Oil	1 Red Bell Pepper, Chopped
1 lb. Skinless Salmon. Pin Bones removed, chopped into ½ inch	2 (28 oz.) Cans Crushed Tomatoes, 1 Drained, 1 undrained
6 c. No salt added chicken broth	2 c. diced (1/2 inch) Sweet Potato
1 tsp. Onion Powder	½ tsp. Sea Salt
¼ tsp. Freshly Ground Black Pepper	

Directions:

Add the salmon and red bell pepper. Cook for at least 5-minutes, occasionally stirring, until the fish is opaque, and the bell pepper is soft. Whisk in the tomatoes, chicken broth, sweet potatoes, onion powder, salt, and pepper. Put to a simmer, and then lower the heat to medium heat. Cook for at least 10-minutes, occasionally stirring, until the sweet potatoes are soft.

Nutritional Information: Calories: 570 | Fat: 42 | Carbs: 55g | Sugar: 12g | Fiber: 16g | Protein: 41g |

495. Quick Chermoula Fish Parcels

Prep Time: 15-minutes | Total time: 45-minutes | Yield: 4-servings

Ingredients:

Chermoula	Baby rocket
100g roasted red capsicum	Lemon wedges
400g can chickpeas	1/2 small red onion
4 x 150grams firm, skinless white fish fillets	1/4 c. olive-oil
2 garlic cloves	1 long red chili
3/4 c. parsley leaves	3/4 c. coriander leaves
1 1/2 tsp. ground cumin	2 tbsps. lemon juice

Directions:

Preheat a grill barbecue/hotplate on low, warm heat. Consolidate chickpeas, capsicum, & onion in a bowl. Make Chermoula. Join all fixings in a bowl—season with salt & pepper. Cut four 30-cm-long pieces of foil. Each one should be topped with a 15-centimeter piece of heating paper. Chickpea blend separation amid scraps of paper Serve with fish on top. 13 chermoula spooned over fish Overlap the paper and foil edges to wrap the fish, scrunching the foil at the top to seal. Spot fish separates a foil heating plate—spot plate on the grill—spot plate on the grill barbeque. Cook with the hood closed until the fish is cooked through. Put fish divides serving plates. Cautiously open. Shower fish with remaining chermoula. Serve it.

Nutritional Information: |Calories: 316 |Protein: 9.82 g|Fat: 18.27 g |Carbohydrates: 30.9 g

496. Sesame-Tuna Skewers

Prep Time: 10-minutes | Total time: 25-minutes | Yield: 6-servings

Ingredients:

¼ tsp. Ground black pepper.	½ tsp. Ground ginger.
¾ c. sesame seeds	1 tsp. Salt
2 tbsps. toasted sesame oil	6 oz. cubed thick tuna steaks
Cooking spray	

Directions:

Preheat your oven to approximately 400 degrees F. Coat a rimmed baking tray using cooking spray. Soak 12 wooden skewers in water. In a small mixing container, mix pepper, ground ginger, salt, and sesame seeds. In another container, toss the tuna with sesame oil. Push the oiled cubes into a sesame seed mixture and put the cubes on each skewer. Put the skewers on a readily readied baking tray and put the tray into the preheated oven. Bake for about 12-minutes and turn once. Serve and enjoy.

Nutritional Information: Calories: 196, Protein: 14.47 g, Fat: 15.01 g, Carbohydrates: 2.48 g

497. Chili Shrimp and Pineapple

Prep Time: 10-minutes | Total time: 20-minutes | Yield: 4-servings

Ingredients:

1 lb. shrimp, peeled and deveined	2 tbsps. chili paste
Pinch of sea salt	Pinch of black pepper
1 tbsp. olive oil	1 c. pineapple, peeled and cubed
½ tsp. ginger, grated	2 tsp. almonds, chopped
2 tbsps. cilantro, chopped	

Directions:

Warm a pan using the oil on medium-high heat, add the ginger and the chili paste, Whisk and cook for 2-minutes. Add other ingredients with the shrimp. Toss and then cook the mix for 8-minutes more, divide into bowls, and serve.

Nutritional Information: |Calories 261 | Fat 4|Fiber 7|Carbs 15|Protein 8

498. Shrimp Risotto

Prep Time: 10-minutes | Total time: 25-minutes | Yield: 4-servings

Ingredients:

14 oz. shrimps, peeled and deveined	12 oz. cauli rice
4 button mushrooms	½ lemon
4 stalks green onion	3 tbsp. ghee butter
2 tbsp. coconut oil	Salt and black pepper to taste

Directions:

Preheat the oven to 400F. Put a layer of cauliflower rice on a sheet pan, season with salt and spices; sprinkle the coconut oil over it. Bake in the oven for 10-12-minutes Cut the green-onion and slice up the mushrooms. Remove the rind from the lemon. Heat the ghee-butter over medium heat in a skillet. Add the shrimps and season it; then sauté for about 5-6-minutes. Top the cauliflower rice with shrimp, sprinkle the green onion over it.

Nutritional Information: Carbs: 9,2 g |Fat: 26,2 g |Protein: 25 g |Calories: 363

499. Crispy Fish Stick

Prep Time: 10-minutes | Total time: 20-minutes | Yield: 4-servings

Ingredients:

¼ c. Dairy-Free Tartar Sauce	½ c. grated Parmesan cheese
½ c. ground pork rinds	½ tsp. Chili powder
½ tsp. chopped fresh parsley	1 c. almond flour
1 c. avocado oil or other cooking oil, plus more as required	1 lb. frozen cod, thawed
2 big eggs	2 tbsps. avocado oil mayonnaise
Freshly ground black pepper	Salt

Directions:

Heat the avocado-oil in a frying-pan at high-heat. The oil should be about half an inch deep, so adjust the amount of oil based on your pan's size. Pat the dry fish using paper-towels to remove any surplus water. In a small container, put the eggs and mayonnaise, then whisk. Put the Parmesan, almond flour, pork rinds, chili powder, and parsley in another container and mix thoroughly. Sprinkle with salt and pepper. Chop the cod into strips. Place the fish into the egg-mixture, then dredge in the dry mix. Push the strips into the dry mixture so that the "breading" sticks well on all sides. Put in 3 to 4 fish sticks at a time to the hot oil. Cook until crunchy and golden, for a minimum of 2-minutes on each side. Put the cooked fish sticks on a paper towel-lined plate while you continue to fry the remaining fish sticks. Serve with tartar sauce.

Nutritional Information: Calories: 402, Fat: 30g, Protein: 30g, Carbohydrates: 3g, Fiber: 1g

---

500. Grilled Calamari

Prep Time: 10-minutes | Total time: 15-minutes | Yield: 4-servings

Ingredients:

2 lbs. calamari tubes and tentacles, cleaned	½ c. good-quality olive oil
Zest and juice of 2 lemons	2 tbsps. chopped fresh oregano
1 tbsp. Minced garlic	¼ tsp. Sea salt
⅛ tsp. freshly ground black pepper	

Directions:
Prepare the calamari. Score the top-layer of the calamari tubes about 2 inches apart. Marinate the calamari. Whisk the lemon zest, olive oil, lemon juice, oregano, garlic, salt, and pepper in a large bowl. Add the calamari & toss to coat it well, then put it in the refrigerator to marinate for about 30-minutes to 1-hour. Grill the calamari. Preheat, then grill to high-heat and grill the calamari, turning once, for about 3-minutes total, until it's lightly charred and tender. Serve. Divide the calamari between 4 plates and then serve it hot.

Nutritional Information: Calories: 455 | Fat: 30g | Carbs: 8g | Fiber: 1g; | Protein: 35g

---

501. Sweet Crab Cakes

Prep Time: 15-minutes | Total time: 25-minutes | Yield: 4-servings

Ingredients:

1 lb. cooked lump crab-meat, drained and picked over	¼ c. shredded unsweetened coconut
1 tbsp. Dijon mustard	1 scallion, finely chopped
¼ c. minced red bell pepper	1 egg, lightly beaten
1 tsp. lemon zest	Pinch cayenne pepper
3 tbsps. coconut flour	3 tbsps. coconut oil
¼ c. Classic Aioli	

Directions:
Making the crab cakes:
In a medium bowl, mix the crab, mustard, coconut, scallion, red bell pepper, egg, lemon zest, and cayenne until

it holds together. Form the mixture into eight equal patties about ¾ inch thick. Chill. Put the patties on a plate, cover the container using plastic wrap, and chill them in the refrigerator for around 1 hour to 12 hours. Coat the patties. Spread the coconut flour on a plate. Dip each cake in the flour until it is lightly coated. Cook. Warm the coconut oil in a large skillet at a medium-heat. Fry the crab-cake patties, turning them just once until golden and cooked through, about 5-minutes per side. Serve. Put two crab cakes on each of four plates and serve with the aioli.

Nutritional Information: Calories: 370 | Fat: 24g | Carbs: 12g | Fiber: 6g | Protein: 26g

---

502. Pumpkin Shrimp

Prep Time: 20-minutes | Total time: 1-hour 30-minutes | Yield: 4-6-servings

Ingredients:

1 average pumpkin	1kg medium shrimp
1 white onion	3 cloves of garlic
2 cans of peeled tomatoes	1 box of sour cream
1 c. of curd	salt
Aluminum paper	

Directions:
Cut the lid off the pumpkin and wrap in foil. Then bake at 180 degrees for 15-minutes. Remove from oven, remove seeds, and then return to oven for another 40-minutes at 180 degrees. Sauté the chopped onion in a pan. When the onion is golden, add the garlic and sauté until the aroma is released. Add the peeled tomato cans—Cook for 15-minutes over medium heat. Add water if it dries too fast. Add the cream & 1/2 cup of curd when the tomato is well-crushed. Let it reduce until thickened — season using salt. In a skillet with olive oil, cook the prawns over high-heat. Add to the sauce when it becomes golden. Remove the pumpkin from the oven, pass the rest of the cream cheese on the inner walls, and place the shrimp sauce inside.

Nutritional Information: Calories: 218 | Protein: 29.55 g | Fat: 5.94 g | Carbohydrates: 10.65 g

---

503. Rockfish Curry

Prep Time: 15-minutes | Total time: 45-minutes | Yield: 8-servings

Ingredients:

2 lb. rockfish	¾ tsp. ground turmeric, divided
Salt, to taste	2 tbsps. coconut oil
12 pearl onions, halved	2 medium red onions, sliced thinly

2 Serrano peppers halved	40 small leaves, divided
1 (½-inch) piece fresh ginger, minced	Freshly ground black pepper, to taste
¼ c. water	1½ (14 oz.) cans coconut milk, divided
1 tsp. apple cider vinegar	

Directions:

In a bowl, season the fish with ¼ tsp. of turmeric and salt and keep aside. Melt coconut oil in a big skillet on medium heat. Add red onions, pearl onions, ginger, Serrano peppers, and 20 curry leaves and sauté for about 15-minutes. Add ginger, the rest of the turmeric, salt, and black pepper, and sauté for about 2-minutes. Please put half of the mixture into a bowl and then keep aside. Add the rest of the fish fillets, curry leaves, water, and 1 can of coconut milk and cook for about 2-minutes. Now cook, covered for about 5-minutes. Add apple cider vinegar and the remaining half can of coconut milk and cook for about 3-5-minutes or thoroughly. Serve hot with the reserved onion mixture.

Nutritional Information: Calories: 331 |Protein: 24.72 g | Fat: 18.38 g | Carbohydrates: 18.83 g

504. Tuna Steaks with Shirataki Noodles

Prep Time: 10-minutes | Total time: 30-minutes | Yield: 4-servings

Ingredients:

1 red bell pepper, seeded and halved	1 pack (7 oz.) miracle noodle angel hair
3 c. water	4 tuna steaks
Salt and black pepper to taste	Olive oil for brushing
2 tbsps. pickled ginger	2 tbsps. chopped cilantro

Directions:

Based on the package instructions, cook the shirataki rice: Rinse the shirataki noodles with running cold water in a colander. Put a pot of salted water to a boil; blanch the noodles for 2-minutes. Drain and move to a dry skillet over medium heat. Dry roast for a few-minutes until opaque. Grease a grill's grate using a cooking spray and preheat it on medium heat. Spice the red bell pepper and tuna with salt and black pepper, brush with olive oil, and grill covered. Cook both for at least 3-minutes on each side. Moved to a plate to cool. Dice bell pepper with a knife. Arrange the noodles, tuna, and bell pepper into the serving plate.
Top with pickled ginger and garnish with cilantro.
Serve with roasted sesame sauce.

Nutritional Information: Calories: 310 |Fat: 18.2g | Net Carbs: 2g | Protein: 22g

505. Cod Curry

Prep Time: 10-minutes | Total time: 35-minutes | Yield: 4-servings

Ingredients:

4 cod fillets, boneless	½ tsp. mustard seeds
Salt and black pepper to the taste	2 green chilies, chopped
1 tsp. freshly grated ginger	1 tsp. Curry powder
¼ tsp. ground cumin	4 tbsps. olive oil
1 small red onion, chopped	1 tsp. ground turmeric
¼ c. chopped parsley	1½ c. coconut cream
3 garlic cloves, minced	

Directions:

Heat a pot with half of the oil over medium heat. Add mustard seeds and cook for 2-minutes. Add ginger, onion, garlic, turmeric, curry powder, chilies, and cumin, whisk and cook for 10-minutes more. Add coconut milk, salt, and pepper, then stir. Bring to a boil, cook for 10-minutes, and take off the heat. Place another pan using the oil remaining over medium heat, add fish, and then cook for 4-minutes. Transfer the fish on top of the curry mix, toss gently, then cook for 6 more-minutes. Divide between plates, sprinkle the parsley on top and serve. Enjoy!

Nutritional Information: Calories 210, Fat 14, Fiber 7, Carbs 6, Protein 16

506. Special Oysters

Prep Time: 10-minutes | Total time: 10-minutes | Yield: 4-servings

Ingredients:

½ tsp. ginger; grated	1 c. tomato juice
1 Serrano chili pepper; chopped.	1/4 c. cilantro; chopped.
1/4 c. olive oil	1/4 c. scallions; chopped.
1/4 tsp. garlic; minced	12 oysters; shucked
2 tbsps. ketchup	Juice from 1 lime
Juice from 1 orange	Juice of 1 lemon
Salt to the taste.	Zest from 1 lime
Zest from 1 orange	

Directions:

In a container, mix lemon juice, orange juice, orange zest, lime juice and zest, ketchup, chili pepper, tomato juice, ginger, garlic, oil, scallions, cilantro, and salt whisk thoroughly. Ladle this into oysters and serve them.

Nutritional Information: Calories: 100, Fat: 1 Fiber: 0, Carbohydrates: 2, Protein: 5

507. Fish Cakes
Prep Time: 2-hour 30-minutes | Total time: 2-hours 40-minutes | Yield: 4-servings

Ingredients:

4 tbsp. Whole wheat flour	oz. Shrimp
9 oz. Tuna	½ c. Bread crumbs
1 tbsp. Italian seasoning	2 Chili pepper, seeded
6 Basil leaves	1 Egg
5 Sun-dried tomatoes, chopped	4 cloves Garlic
½ Onion	6 oz. Scallops
4 tbsp. Coconut oil	

Directions:

Coat a pan in 1 T oil and put it on the stove above a burner turned to a high/medium heat. Add in the scallops and let them cook until they are entirely white.
In a food processor, mix in 1 T coconut oil, the egg, tomatoes, garlic, and onion before adding the seasoning, chilies, basil, parsley, and medium setting process.
Add in the shrimp, scallops, and tuna and process on a low setting. Add in the breadcrumbs and keep processing until everything binds together. Make the results into patties before adding them to a plate and placing them in the refrigerator for at least 2 hours. Coat a pan in the remaining oil and put it on the stove above a burner turned to medium heat. Cook the patties in the pan until both sides have turned a golden brown.
Nutritional Information: Calories: 396 | Protein: 35.52 g | Fat: 19.68 g | Carbohydrates: 22.73 g

508. Healthy Fish Nacho Bowl
Prep Time: 13-minutes | Total time: 33-minutes | Yield: 20-minutes

Ingredients:

500g fish fillets, white	400g red cabbage
3 green shallots	1 tbsp. yogurt
1 tbsp. olive oil	50g gluten-free corn chips
200g halved cherry tomatoes	2-3 tsp. gluten-free chipotle seasoning
1 chopped avocado	1/3 c. fresh coriander leaves
1 juiced lime, rind finely grated	

Directions:

Using a bowl, mix the fish, stew powder/chipotle flavoring & 2 tsp. Oil. Shred your cabbage in a nourishment processor that has a cutting connection. Move to a huge bowl alongside the tomato, lime skin, yogurt, 2 tbsps. Lime juice, 2 shallots, & the rest of the oil. Hurl well to consolidate. Heat a huge non-stick skillet over high warm. Cook your fish as you turn until simply cooked through. Move to a serving plate. Meanwhile, consolidate the coriander, avocado, the rest of the shallot & 1 tbsp. remaining lime squeeze in a small bowl. Divide your fish, cabbage blend, corn chips & guacamole among bowls. Add sprinkles of the additional coriander & accompany with extra lime wedges.
Nutritional Information: Calories: 388 | Protein: 28.17 g | Fat: 16.64 g | Carbohydrates: 35.72 g

509. Squid Rings with Potato and Spinach
Prep Time: 10-minutes | Total time: 25-minutes | Yield: 3-servings

Ingredients:

1 lb. fresh spinach, torn	1 lb. squid rings, frozen
1 tsp. dried rosemary, crushed	1 tsp. garlic paste
1 tsp. sea salt	2 c. cauliflower, roughly chopped
2 tbsp. lemon juice	2 thyme sprigs, fresh
4 tbsp. extra virgin olive oil	

Directions:

Put squid rings in a deep container and pour in enough warm water to immerse. Allow it to sit for a while. Moved to a big colander and drain. Set aside. Set the instant pot and grease the inner pot with 2 tbsp of olive oil. Push the "Sauté" button, then put garlic paste and rosemary. Stir-fry for a minute, then put in the spinach. Sprinkle with salt and cook for a minimum of 3-4-minutes or until wilted. Take off the spinach from the pot and save it for later. Put the rest of the oil in the pot and heat up on the "Sauté" mode. Put chopped cauliflower, making a uniform layer. Top with squid rings and squeeze of lemon juice and optionally some olive oil to taste. Sprinkle with salt, put in thyme sprigs, and pour in one cup of water (or fish stock). Secure the lid, then set the steam release handle to the "Sealing" position. Push the "Fish" button, then set the timer for 9-minutes. When you hear the cooker's end signal, gently move the pressure valve to the "Venting" position to release the pressure. Open the pot and mix in the spinach. Optionally, put some more garlic powder or dried thyme. Serve instantly.
Nutritional Information: Calories 353, Fats 21.5g, Net Carbohydrates: 8.9g, Protein: 29.3g, Fiber: 5g

510. Poached Halibut and Mushrooms

Prep Time: 5-minutes | Total time: 35-minutes | Yield: 8-servings

Ingredients:

1/8 tsp. sesame oil	2 lbs. halibut, cut into bite-sized pieces
1 tsp. Fresh lemon juice	½ tsp. soy sauce
4 c. mushrooms, sliced	¼ c. water
Salt and pepper to taste	¾ c. green onions

Directions:

Put a heavy-bottomed pot on the medium-high fire. Add all ingredients and mix well. Cover and bring to a boil. Once boiling, lower the fire to a simmer. Cook for 25-minutes. Adjust seasoning to taste. Serve and enjoy.

Nutritional Information: Calories: 217 | Fat 15.8 | Carbs: 1.1 g | Protein: 16.5 | Fiber: 0.4 g

511. Sesame Ginger Salmon

Prep Time: 10-minutes | Total time: 30-minutes | Yield: 2-servings

Ingredients:

2 tbsp. White wine	2 tsp. Sesame oil
1 tbsp. Rice vinegar	2 tbsp. Keto-friendly soy sauce substitute
1 tbsp. Sugar-free ketchup	1 tbsp. Fish sauce – Red Boat
1-2 tsp. Minced ginger	1-10 oz. Salmon fillet

Directions:

Mix all fixings in a plastic canister with a tight-fitting lid (omit the ketchup, oil, and wine for now). Marinade them for approximately 1o to 15-minutes. On the stovetop, prepare a frying pan using the high-heat temperature setting. Pour in the oil. Put in the fish when it's hot, skin side down. Brown each side for three to 5-minutes. Pour in the marinated juices to the pan to simmer when the fish is flipped. Position the fish on two dinner plates. Pour in the wine and ketchup to the pan and simmer for 5-minutes until it's reduced. Serve with a vegetable.

Nutritional Information: Calories: 370, Net Carbohydrates: 2.5 g, Total Fat: Con10t: 24 g, Protein: 33 g

512. Crispy Tilapia

Prep Time: 15-minutes | Total time: 29-minutes | Yield: 4-servings

Ingredients:

¾ c. pork rinds, crushed	1 packet dry ranch-style dressing mix
2½ tbsps. olive oil	2 organic eggs
4 tilapia fillets	

Directions:

Arrange the greased Cook & Crisp Basket in the pot of Ninja Foody. Close the Ninja Foody with a crisping lid and select Air Crisp. Set the temp to 355 degrees F for 5-minutes. Press "Start/Stop" to begin preheating. In a shallow bowl, beat the eggs. Add the pork rinds, ranch dressing, and oil to another bowl and mix until a crumbly mixture. Put the fish fillets into the egg, then coat with the pork rind mixture. After preheating, open the lid. Arrange the tilapia fillets in the prepared Cook & Crisp Basket in a single layer. Close the Ninja Foody with a crisping lid and select Air Crisp. Set the temperature to 350°F for 14-minutes. Press Start/Stop to begin cooking. Serve hot.

Nutritional Information: Calories: 304 | Fats: 16.8 | Carbohydrates 0.4 | Proteins: 38g

513. Rosemary-Lemon Cod

Prep Time: 5-minutes | Total time: 15-minutes | Yield: 4-servings

Ingredients:

1 Lemon Juice	½ tsp. Sea Salt
½ tsp. Ground black pepper, or more to taste	1 tbsp. Fresh Rosemary Leaves, chopped
1½ lbs. Cod, Skin, and Bone Removed, cut into 4 fillets	2 tbsp. Extra Virgin Olive Oil

Directions:

In a huge nonstick skillet at medium-high heat, heat the olive oil until it shimmers. Season the cod with rosemary, pepper, and salt. Place the fish in the skillet. Then cook for about 3 - 5-minutes per side until opaque. Pour the lemon juice over the cod fillets and cook for 1 minute.

Nutritional Information: Calories: 24 | Fat: 9g | Carbs: 1g | Sugar: 1g | Fiber: 1g | Protein: 39g |

514. Orange and Maple-Glazed Salmon

Prep Time: 15-minutes | Total time: 30-minutes | Yield: 4-servings

Ingredients:

2 Orange Juice	1 Orange Zest
¼ c. Pure maple syrup	2 tbsp. Low Sodium Soy Sauce
1 tsp. Garlic Powder	4 4-6 oz. Salmon Fillet, Pin bones removed

Directions:

Preheat the oven to 400°F. Whisk the orange juice and zest, maple syrup, soy sauce, and garlic powder in a

small, shallow dish. Put the salmon pieces, flesh-side down, into the dish. Let it marinate for 10-minutes. Transfer the salmon, skin-side up, to a rimmed baking sheet and bake for about 15-minutes until the flesh is opaque.
Nutritional Information: Calories: 297 | Fat: 11 | Carbs: 18g | Sugar: 15g | Fiber: 1g | Protein: 34 |

515. Balsamic Scallops
Prep Time: 5-minutes | Total time: 15-minutes | Yield: 4-servings

Ingredients:

1 lb. sea scallops	4 scallions, chopped
2 tbsps. olive oil	1 tbsp. balsamic vinegar
1 tbsp. cilantro, chopped	A pinch of salt and black pepper

Directions:
Warm a pan with the oil on medium-high heat, add the scallops, the scallions, and the other ingredients, toss, cook for 10-minutes. Divide into bowls and serve.
Nutritional Information: Calories 300 | Fat 4 | Fiber 4 | Carbs 14 | Protein 17

516. Bacon and Jalapeno Wrapped Shrimp
Prep Time: 10-minutes | Total time: 30-minutes | Yield: 2-servings

Ingredients:

6 thin bacon slices	¼ c. shredded pepper jack cheese
Freshly ground black pepper	Salt
12 large shrimp, deveined, butterflied, tail-on	4 seedless jalapeño peppers, and cut into 3 to 4 long strips each

Directions:
Preheat the oven to 350°F. On a baking sheet, arrange the jalapeño strips in a single layer and roast for 10-minutes. In a small bowl, season the shrimp with salt and pepper. Remove the jalapeño strips from the oven. Put a strip inside each open butterflied shrimp. Wrap each shrimp with bacon and insert it with a toothpick. Organize in a single layer on a baking sheet. Cook for 8-minutes until the bacon is crispy. Adjust the oven to broil. Sprinkle the cheese on top of the shrimp and broil for about 1 minute until the cheese is bubbling.
Nutritional Information: Calories: 240 | Fat: 16 g | Protein: 21 g | Total Carbs: 3g | Fiber: 1g | Net Carbs: 2g

517. Parsley Tilapia
Prep Time: 15-minutes | Total time: 1-hour 45-minutes | Yield: 6-servings

Ingredients:

6 tilapia fillets	Salt and ground black pepper
½ c. yellow onion, chopped	3 tsp. fresh lemon rind, grated finely
¼ c. fresh parsley, chopped	2 tbsps. unsalted butter, melted

Directions:
Grease the pot of Ninja Foody. Spice the tilapia fillets with salt and black pepper generously. In the prepared pot of Ninja Foody, Put the tilapia fillets. Arrange the onion, lemon rind, and parsley over fillets evenly and drizzle with melted butter. Close the Ninja Foody with a crisping lid and select Slow Cooker. Set on Low for 1½ hours. Press Start/Stop to begin cooking. Serve hot.
Nutritional Information: Calories: 133 | Fats: 4.9g | Carbohydrates: 1.3g | Proteins: 21.3g

518. Wasabi Salmon Burgers
Prep Time: 5-minutes | Total time: 15-minutes | Yield: 1 serving

Ingredients:

1/2 tsp. Honey	2 tbsp. Reduce-salt soy sauce
1 tsp. Wasabi powder	1 Beaten free-range egg
2 can get Wild Salmon, drained	2 Scallion, chopped
2 tbsp. Coconut Oil	1 tbsp. Fresh ginger, minced

Directions:
Mix the salmon, egg, ginger, scallions, and 1 tbsp. Oil in a bowl, mixing well with your hands to form 4 patties. Add the wasabi powder and soy sauce with the honey and whisk until blended in a separate bowl. Heat 1 tbsp. Oil over medium heat in a skillet and cook the patties for 4-minutes on each side until firm and browned. Glaze the top of each patty with the wasabi mixture and cook for another 15 seconds before you serve. Serve with your favorite side salad or vegetables for a healthy treat.
Nutritional Information: Calories: 591 | Protein: 63.52 g | Fat: 34.3 g | Carbohydrates: 3.83 g

519. Fish & Chickpea Stew
Prep Time: 5-minutes | Total time: 15-minutes | Yield: 4-servings

Ingredients:

2 c. fish stock	1 brown onion

400g can tomatoes	4 kale leaves
500g firm white fish fillets	Sliced Coles Bakery Stone
2 garlic cloves	Finely grated parmesan
400g can chickpeas	1 carrot, peeled
Salt & pepper to taste	

Directions:

Spray a skillet with an olive oil shower. Spot over medium-low warm. Include the carrot & onion & cook, mixing until delicate & brilliant. Include garlic & cook, blending until sweet-smelling. Add the chickpeas stock & tomato & to the onion blend in the skillet. Bring to the bubble. Lessen warm to medium-low & stew until the mixture thickens somewhat. Add the kale & fish to the dish & stew until the fish is simply cooked through. Season. Divide the stew among serving bowls. Sprinkle with parmesan & present with the bread.

Nutritional Information: Calories: 1447 | Protein: 42.1 g | Fat: 127.85 g | Carbohydrates: 32.4 g

520. Cod with Bell Pepper

Prep Time: 15-minutes | Total time: 1-hour 45-minutes | Yield: 4-servings

Ingredients:

1 tbsp. fresh rosemary, chopped	1 can sugar-free diced tomatoes
3 garlic cloves, minced	1 bell pepper, seeded and sliced
½ small onion, sliced	¼ c. homemade fish broth
¼ tsp. red pepper flakes	Salt and ground black pepper
1 lb. cod fillets	

Directions:

In the pot of Ninja Foody, add all the ingredients except cod and whisk to combine. Season cod fillets with salt and black pepper evenly. Arrange the cod fillets over broth mixture. Close the Ninja Foody with a crisping lid and select Slow Cooker. Set on High for 1½ hours. Press Start/Stop to begin cooking. Serve hot.

Nutritional Information: Calories: 232 | Protein: 27 g | Fat: 4.1 g | Carbohydrates: 14 g

521. Fish Casserole with Cream Cheese Sauce

Prep Time: 10-minutes | Total time: 45-minutes | Yield: 4-servings

Ingredients:

280 g broccoli	280 g cooked fish
85 g grated Gouda cheese	1 tsp. chopped green onions
1 liter of water	

For the sauce:

119 ml of fat cream	2 tbsp. grated Parmesan cheese
1 tbsp. butter	56.7 g cream cheese
1/4 tsp. chopped garlic	1/8 tsp. Chile
Sea salt and black pepper to taste	

Directions:

Preheat the oven to 350° F. Set all the sauce ingredients into a saucepan and simmer for 3-minutes, stirring occasionally. In another saucepan, bring the water to a boil and cook the broccoli for 3-minutes or until tender. Mash the fish with a fork. Put the broccoli in a casserole dish, put the chopped fish on top, pour the sauce and sprinkle with grated cheese. Bake for at least 20-minutes or until golden brown. Let stand for 5-minutes, sprinkle with chopped green onions and enjoy!

Nutritional Information: Carbohydrates: 9 g | Fats: 36 g | Proteins: 32 g | Calories: 474

522. Shrimp with Cinnamon Sauce

Prep Time: 10-minutes | Total time: 20-minutes | Yield: 4-servings

Ingredients:

2 tbsp. Extra Virgin Olive Oil	1½ lbs. Peeled Shrimp
2 tbsp. Dijon Mustard	1 c. No Salt Added Chicken Broth
1 tsp. Ground Cinnamon	1 tsp. Onion Powder
½ tsp. Sea Salt	¼ tsp. Freshly Ground Black Pepper

Directions:

In a huge nonstick skillet at medium-high heat, heat the olive oil until it shimmers. Add the shrimp. Cook for at least 4-minutes, occasionally stirring, until the shrimp is opaque. Whisk the mustard, chicken broth, cinnamon, onion powder, salt, and pepper in a small bowl. Pour this into the skillet and continue to cook for 3-minutes, stirring occasionally.

Nutritional Information: Calories: 270 | Fat: 11g | Carbs: 4g | Sugar: 1g | Fiber: 1g | Protein: 39g |

523. Roasted Salmon and Asparagus

Prep Time: 5-minutes | Total time: 20-minutes | Yield: 4-servings

Ingredients:

1 lb. Asparagus Spears, trimmed	2 tbsp. Extra Virgin Olive Oil
1 tsp. Sea Salt, divide	1½ lbs. Salmon, cut into 4 fillets

⅛ tsp. freshly ground cracked black pepper	1 Lemon, zest, and slice

Directions:
Preheat the oven to 425°F. Whisk the asparagus with the olive oil, then put ½ tsp. of the salt. Put in a single layer in the bottom of a roasting pan. Season the salmon with the pepper and the remaining ½ tsp. of salt. Put skin-side down on top of the asparagus. Sprinkle the salmon and asparagus with the lemon zest and put the lemon slices over the fish. Roast it in the oven for at least 12 to 15-minutes until the flesh is opaque.

Nutritional Information: Calories: 308 | Fat: 18g | Carbs: 5g | Sugar: 2g | Fiber: 2 | Protein: 36g |

524. Tuna-Stuffed Tomatoes

Prep Time: 10-minutes | Total time: 20-minutes | Yield: 2-servings

Ingredients:

1 medium tomato	1 6oz. can tuna, drained and flaked
2 tbsp. mayonnaise	1 tbsp. Celery, chopped
½ tsp. Dijon mustard	¼ tsp. seasoning salt
Shredded mild cheddar cheese to garnish	

Directions:
Preheat oven to 375°. Wash tomato and cut in half from the stem. Using a tsp., scoop out tomato pulp and seeds until you have two ½" shells remaining. In a small mixing bowl, Mix tuna, mayonnaise, celery, mustard, and seasoning salt. Whisk until well blended. Scoop an equal amount of tuna mixture into each ½ tomato shell. Put on a baking sheet and sprinkle shredded cheddar cheese over the top of each tuna-stuffed tomato shell. Bake for 7 to 8-minutes or until cheese is melted and golden-brown. Serve immediately. Any remaining mixture can be safely stored, covered in the fridge for up to 72 hours.

Nutritional Information: Calories: 175 | Protein: 21.24 g | Fat: 8.79 g | Carbohydrates: 3.04 g

525. Curried Fish

Prep Time: 10-minutes: Total time: 13 – 15-minutes | Yield: 4-servings

Ingredients:

½ tsp. Cayenne pepper, optional	½ tsp. Ground coriander
½ tsp. ground cumin	1 ½ c. basmati rice
1 bell pepper, cored and thinly chopped	1 tbsp. curry powder

1 yellow onion, finely chopped	1/4 c. hot water
1/4 tsp. turmeric	2 big tomatoes, diced
2 tbsps. canola oil	Four 5 oz. fish fillets

Directions:
Put the rice in a pan, put in roughly 3 cups water, then leave to come to its boiling point; then decrease the heat and simmer for about 20-minutes until all the liquid is assimilated. In a different pan, heat canola oil using high heat. Put in the onions and sauté for about 2-minutes. Put in spices and bell pepper, and cook one to two-minutes longer, stirring continually. Put fillets in the pan and spoon seasoning mixture over the top, then mix tomatoes and water to the dish. Once the liquid comes to simmer, turn the heat down and cover. Cook 8 to 10-minutes longer. Serve with rice.

Nutritional Information: Calories: 362, Protein: 14.26 g, Fat: 24.98 g, Carbohydrates: 35.58 g

526. Baked Tomato Hake

Prep Time: 10-minutes | Total time: 30 – 35-minutes | Yield: 4-servings

Ingredients:

½ c. tomato sauce	1 tbsp. olive oil
Parsley	2 sliced tomatoes
½ c. grated cheese	4 lbs. de-boned and sliced hake fish
Salt.	

Directions:
Preheat the oven to 400 0F. Season the fish with salt. In a skillet or saucepan, stir-fry the fish in the olive oil until half-done. Take four foil papers to cover the fish. Shape the foil to resemble containers; add the tomato sauce into each foil container. Add the fish, tomato slices, and top with grated cheese. Bake until you get a golden crust, for approximately 20-25-minutes. Open the packs and top with parsley.

Nutritional Information: Calories: 265 | Fat: 15 g | Carbs: 18 g | Protein: 22 g | Sugars: 0.5 g |

527. Salmon and Shrimp Mix

Prep Time: 5-minutes | Total time: 25-minutes | Yield: 4-servings

Ingredients:

4 salmon fillets, boneless	1 lb. shrimp, peeled and deveined
1 tsp. Cajun seasoning	A pinch of salt and black pepper
2 tbsps. olive oil	Juice of 1 lemon
½ c. chicken stock	2 tbsps. tomato passata

Directions:
Set the instant-pot on Sauté mode, put the oil, heat it, add the rest of the ingredients except the salmon and shrimp and cook for 3-minutes. Add the salmon. Then cook for about 2-minutes on each side. Put the shrimp, set the lid on, and cook on High for 10-minutes. Release the pressure fast for 5-minutes, divide the mix between plates and serve.
Nutritional Information: Calories 393 | Fat: 20 | Fiber: 0.1 | Carbs: 2.2 | Protein: 25

528. Clams with Garlic-Tomato Sauce

Prep Time: 5-minutes | Total time: 25-minutes | Yield: 4-servings

Ingredients:

40 littleneck clams	

For the Sauce:

2 tomatoes, pureed	2 tbsps. olive oil
1 shallot, chopped	Sea salt, to taste
Freshly ground black pepper, to taste	1/2 tsp. paprika
2 garlic cloves, pressed	1/2 lemon, cut into wedges

Directions:
Grill the clams for about 5 to 6-minutes until they are open. In a frying pan, heat the olive oil over moderate heat. Cook the shallot and garlic until tender and fragrant. Whisk in the pureed tomatoes, salt, black pepper, and paprika and continue to cook for an additional 10 to 12-minutes, up to well cooked. Heat off, Whisk to combine. Garnish with fresh lemon wedges.
Nutritional Information: 134 Calories | 7.8g Fat | 5.9g Carbs | 8.3g Protein | 1g Fiber

529. Garlic Crab Legs

Prep Time: 10-minutes | Total time: 30-minutes | Yield: 2-servings

Ingredients:

4 tbsps. butter or ghee	2 tbsps. extra-virgin olive oil
½ lemon, juiced and zested	4 garlic cloves, crushed and minced
2 tsp. Old Bay Seasoning	1 tbsp. red pepper flakes
2 lbs. crab legs	2 tbsps. chopped fresh parsley

Directions:
Preheat the oven to 375°F. Heat a large oven-safe skillet at medium-low heat. Add the butter, olive oil, lemon juice, lemon zest, garlic, Old Bay, and red pepper flakes. Sauté for 2-minutes. Add the crab legs and parsley to the skillet. Spoon the butter mixture over the crab and baste for 3-minutes. Bring the skillet in the oven, then bake for 15-minutes, basting every 5-minutes. Put the crab legs on a platter and pour the butter mixture into a small dish for dipping.
Nutritional Information: Calories: 514 | Total Fat: 38g | Protein: 41g | Carbs: 2g | Fiber: 0g |

530. Ginger & Chili Sea Bass Fillets

Prep Time: 5-minutes | Total time: 15-minutes | Yield: 2-servings

Ingredients:

2 Sea bass fillet	1 tsp. Black pepper
1 tbsp. Extra virgin olive oil	1 tsp Ginger, peeled and chopped
1 Garlic cloves, thinly sliced	1 Red chili, deseeded and thinly sliced
2 Green onions stemmed, chopped	

Directions:
Get a skillet and heat the oil on medium to high heat. Sprinkle black pepper over the Sea Bass and score the fish's skin a few times with a sharp knife. Add the sea bass fillet to the very hot pan with the skin side down. Cook for 5-minutes and turn over. Cook for a further 2-minutes. Remove seabass from the pan and rest. Put the chili, garlic, and ginger and cook for approximately 2-minutes or until golden. Remove from the heat and add the green onions. Scatter the vegetables over your sea bass to serve. Try with a steamed sweet potato or side salad.
Nutritional Information: Calories: 306 | Protein: 29.92 g | Fat: 8.94 g | Carbohydrates: 26.59 g

531. Vietnamese Roll and Tarê

Prep Time: 20-minutes | Total time: 30-minutes | Yield: 4-servings

Ingredients:

1 c. of soy sauce	1 c. of sake baby
1 c. of sugar	6 sheets of rice paper
Warm water	Mint leaves
250g sauteed medium prawns	1 c. carrot cut into sticks
1 c. chopped Japanese cucumber	6 shredded lettuce leaves
1 ½ c. rice noodles prepared per package instructions	

Directions:
Bring the soy sauce, sake, and sugar to medium heat. Whisk from time to time and cook the mixture until it

reduces to ⅓ of the initial amount and obtain a soft syrup consistency. Set aside to cool. Dip the rice leaf in warm water for about 30 seconds or until it softens. Arrange on a flat surface and stuff the center of the rice paper with mint leaves, prawns, carrots, cucumber, lettuce, and pasta. Roll up, cut in half and half again. Repeat the process with the other sheets of rice paper. Serve with taré sauce.

Nutritional Information: Calories: 552 |Protein: 10.54 g |Fat: 20.48 g |Carbohydrates: 82.12 g

532. Garlic Butter Shrimps

Prep Time: 13-minutes | Total time: 29-minutes | Yield: 3-servings

Ingredients:

½ lb. shrimp, peeled and deveined	2 garlic cloves
½ white onion	3 tbsp. ghee butter
1 tsp black pepper	1 lemon (peeled)
Himalayan rock salt to taste	

Directions:

Preheat the oven to 425F. Mince the garlic and onion, cut the lemon in half. Season the shrimps with pink salt and pepper. Slice one-half of the lemon thinly, cut the other half into 2 pieces. Grease a baking dish with butter; Mix the shrimp with the garlic, onion, and lemon slices, put in the baking dish. Bake the shrimps for 15-minutes, stirring halfway through. Remove the shrimps from the oven and squeeze the juice from 2 lemon pieces over the dish.

Nutritional Information: Carbs: 3, 9 g |Fat: 19, 8 g |Protein: 32 g |Calories: 338

533. Salmon and Coconut Mix

Prep Time: 10-minutes | Total time: 30-minutes | Yield: 4-servings

Ingredients:

4 salmon fillets, boneless	3 tbsp. avocado mayonnaise
1 tsp. lime zest, grated	¼ c. coconut cream
¼ c. lime juice	½ c. coconut, unsweetened and shredded
2 tsp. Cajun seasoning	A pinch of salt
Pinch of black pepper	

Directions:

Set the instant-pot on Sauté mode, put the coconut cream and the rest of the ingredients except the fish, mix and cook for at least 5-minutes. Add the fish, set the lid on, and cook on High for at least 10-minutes. Release the pressure for 10-minutes, divide the salmon and sauce between plates and serve.

Nutritional Information: Calories 306 |Fat: 17.5 |Fiber: 1.4 |Carbs: 2.5 |Protein: 25.3

534. Shrimp Scampi

Prep Time: 10-minutes | Total time: 25-minutes | Yield: 4-servings

Ingredients:

¼ c. Extra Olive Oil	1 Onion, Finely Chopped
1 Red Bell Pepper, Chopped	1½ lbs. Shrimp, Peeled, and Tails Removed
6 Garlic Cloves, Minced	2 Lemon Juices
2 Lemon Zest	½ tsp. Sea Salt
⅛ tsp. Freshly Ground Black Pepper	

Directions:

In a huge nonstick skillet on medium-high heat, warm the olive oil until it shimmers. Add the onion and red bell pepper. Cook for about 6-minutes, occasionally stirring, until soft. Add the shrimp and cook for about 5-minutes until pink. Add the garlic. Cook for 30 seconds, stirring constantly. Add the lemon juice and zest, salt, and pepper. Simmer for 3-minutes.

Nutritional Information: |Calories: 345| Fat: 16| Carbs: 10g |Sugar: 3g |Fiber: 1g |Protein: 40g |

535. Tilapia with Parmesan Bark

Prep Time: 4-minutes | Total time: 16-minutes | Yield: 4-servings

Ingredients:

¾ c. freshly grated Parmesan cheese	2 tsp. pepper
1 tbsp. chopped parsley	4 tilapia fillets (4 us)
Lemon cut into pieces	

Directions:

Set the oven to 400° F. Mix cheese in a shallow dish with pepper and parsley and season with salt and pepper. Mix the fish in the cheese with olive oil and flirt. Put on a baking sheet with foil and bake for 10 to 12-minutes until the fish in the thickest part is opaque. Serve the lemon slices with the fish.

Nutritional Information: Calories: 210 |Fat: 9.3g |Net Carbs: 1.3g |Protein: 28.9g

536. Marinated Fish Steaks

Prep Time: 10-minutes | Total time: 25-minutes | Yield: 4-servings

Ingredients:

4 lime wedges	2 tbsps. Lime juice
2 minced garlic cloves	2 tsp. Olive oil

1 tbsp. snipped fresh oregano	1 lb. fresh swordfish
1 tsp. lemon-pepper seasoning	

Directions:

Rinse fish steaks; pat dry using paper towels. Cut into four serving-size pieces, if necessary. Put and Mix lime juice, oregano, oil, lemon-pepper seasoning, and garlic in a shallow dish. Add fish; turn to coat with marinade. Cover & marinate in the refrigerator for about 30-minutes to 1-1/2 hours, turning steaks occasionally. Drain fish, reserving marinade. Put the fish on the greased, unheated rack of a broiler pan. Broil, 4 inches from the heat for at least 8 to 12-minutes or until fish starts to flake when tested with a fork, turning once, and brushing with reserved marinade halfway through cooking. Take off any remaining marinade. Before serving, squeeze the lime juice on each steak.

Nutritional Information: Calories: 240 | Fat: 6 | Carbs: 19 g | Protein: 12 g | Sugars: 3.27 g | Sodium: 325 mg

537. Oven-Baked Sole Fillets

Prep Time: 10-minutes | Total time: 30-minutes | Yield: 4-servings

Ingredients:

2 tbsps. olive oil	1/2 tbsp. Dijon mustard
1 tsp. garlic paste	1/2 tbsp. fresh ginger, minced
1/2 tsp. porcini powder	Salt and ground black pepper, to taste
1/4 c. fresh parsley, chopped	1/2 tsp. paprika
4 sole fillets	

Directions:

Mix the oil, Dijon mustard, garlic paste, ginger, porcini powder, salt, black pepper, and paprika. Rub this mixture all over sole fillets. Put the sole fillets in a lightly oiled baking pan. Bake in the preheated oven at 400 degrees F for about 20-minutes.

Nutritional Information: 195 Calories | 8.2g Fat | 0.5g Carbs | 28.7g Protein | 0.6g Fiber

538. Coconut-Crusted Shrimp

Prep time: 10-minutes | Total time: 16-minutes | Yield: 4-servings

Ingredients:

2 eggs	1 c. unsweetened dried coconut
¼ c. coconut flour	½ tsp. salt
¼ tsp. paprika	Dash cayenne pepper

Dash freshly grounds black pepper	¼ c. coconut oil
1 lb. (454 g) raw shrimp, peeled and deveined	

Directions:

In a small shallow bowl, whisk the eggs. Mix the coconut, coconut flour, salt, paprika, cayenne pepper, and black pepper in another small shallow bowl. Over medium-high heat, heat the coconut-oil in a large skillet. Pat the shrimp dry using a paper-towel. Working one at a time, hold each shrimp by the tail, dip it into the egg mixture, and then into the coconut mixture until coated. Put into the hot skillet. Cook per side for about 1 to 3-minutes. Transfer to a paper towel-lined plate to drain excess oil. Serve immediately.

Nutritional information: Calories: 279 | fat: 20g | protein: 19g | carbs: 6g | fiber: 3g | sugar: 2g |

539. Miso-Glazed Salmon

Prep time: 5-minutes | Total time: 10 – 15-minutes | Yield: 4-servings

Ingredients:

4 (4 oz.) salmon fillets	3 tbsps. miso paste
2 tbsps. raw honey	1 tsp. coconut aminos
1 tsp. rice vinegar	

Directions:

Preheat the broiler. Line a baking-dish with aluminum-foil and put the salmon fillets in it. Whisk together the honey, miso, coconut aminos, and vinegar together in a small bowl. Over the top of each fillet, brush the glaze evenly. Broil for about 5-minutes. The fish is done when it flakes easily. The exact cooking time depends on its thickness. Brush any remaining glaze over the fish, and continue to broil for 5-minutes, if needed.

Nutritional information: Calories: 264 | fat: 9g | protein: 30g | carbs: 13g | fiber: 0g | sugar: 9g |

540. Fresh Tuna Steak and Fennel Salad

Prep time: 15-minutes | Total time: 40-minutes | Yield: 4-servings

Ingredients:

2 (1 inch) tuna steaks	2 tbsps. Olive oil, 1 tbsp. olive oil for brushing
1 tsp. crushed black peppercorns	1 tsp. crushed fennel seeds
1 fennel bulb, trimmed and sliced	½ c. water
1 lemon, juiced	1 tsp. fresh parsley, chopped

Directions:

Coat the fish with oil and then season with peppercorns and fennel seeds. Heat the oil on medium heat and sauté the fennel bulb slices for 5-minutes or light brown. Add the water to the pan and cook for 10-minutes until the fennel is tender. Whisk in the lemon juice and lower the heat to a simmer. Meanwhile, heat another skillet and sauté the tuna steaks for about 2 to 3-minutes each side for medium-rare. (Add 1 minute each side for medium and 2-minutes each side for medium-well). Serve the fennel mix with the tuna steaks on top and garnish with the fresh parsley.

Nutritional information: Calories: 288 | fat: 9g | protein: 44g | carbs: 6g | fiber: 2g | sugar: 3g |

541. Lemon Garlic Shrimp Pasta

Prep time: 30-minutes | Total time: 45-minutes | Yield: 4-servings

Ingredients:

2 bags Miracle Noodle Angel Hair Pasta	2 tbsps. Olive oil
2 tbsps. Butter	4 cloves Garlic
1 lb. Jumbo raw shrimp	Zest of 1 Lemon
½ tsp. Paprika	Fresh basil
Pepper and salt (as desired)	

Directions:

Set the water from the package of noodles and wash them in cold water. Add them to a pot of boiling water for two-minutes. Transfer them to a hot pot over medium heat to remove the excess liquid (dry roast). Set them to the side. Using the same pan, add the oil, butter, and smashed garlic. Cook for a few-minutes – not browned. Divide the lemon into rounds and add them to the garlic, along with the shrimp. Sauté for approximately three-minutes per side. Add the noodles and spices and whisk to blend the flavors.

Nutritional information: Carbohydrates: 3.5 grams | Fat: 21 grams | Protein: 36 grams | Calories: 360

542. Cuttlefish Salad in Sweet and Sour Sauce

Prep time: 10-minutes | Total time: 25-minutes | Yield: 2-servings

Ingredients:

550g fresh cuttlefish	30g raisins
20g pine nuts	80g oil
60g vinegar rose grapes	Salt to taste
Parsley in leaves	1 head radicchio

Directions:

Clean the cuttlefish and blanch in the water; the fins and the weave take longer. Cool and cut into julienne strips. Clean the radicchio and cut it thinly. In a steel bowl, mix cuttlefish, radicchio, raisins, pine nuts, vinegar, oil, salt, and a tsp. of sugar. Leave to marinate and flavor. Serve in a radicchio leaf. Decorate with parsley leaves.

Nutritional information: Calories 1366 | Carbs 166g | Cholesterol 6mg | Fat 67g | Protein 59g | Fiber 41g

543. Ribbons with Thalli and Tuna

Prep time: 10-minutes | Total time: 40-minutes | Yield: 2-servings

Ingredients:

200g ribbons	200g zucchini seeds
100g tuna Callipo reserve gold	2 tbsps. olive oil
pepper	garlic

Directions:

While the pasta is cooking, take the thalli clean, cut into strips, and pass them quickly in boiling water. On a frying pan, make the garlic sweat and then remove it. Add the thalli; turn quickly. Drain the pasta al dente and then add it to the thalli. For another minute, turn-off the heat, add the tuna, and turn over pepper. You can serve.

Nutritional information: Calories: 337 | Fat: 5 g | Protein: 56 g | Sodium: 755 mg | Fiber: 3 g | Carbs: 12 g

544. Smoked Herring Sandwich

Prep time: 15-minutes | Total time: 15-minutes | Yield: 4-servings

Ingredients:

1 (6 oz.) can kipper, drained	1/8 tsp. pepper
1/8 tsp. salt	1 clove garlic, minced
1 tsp. lemon juice	1 tbsp. chopped fresh parsley
1 celery stalk, finely chopped	1 small onion, finely chopped
½ c. reduced-fat mayonnaise	8 lettuce leaves
4 slices of multi-grain bread	

Directions:

Mix pepper, salt, garlic, lemon juice, parsley, celery, onion, and mayonnaise in a medium bowl. Mix well. Add drained kippers and mix well. To assemble the sandwich, cut each slice of bread diagonally to form a triangle. On one slice, add 1 lettuce leaf, slather with 2 tbsp of kipper mixture, top with another lettuce, and cover with another triangular piece of bread. Repeat process to remaining bread slices. Serve and enjoy.

Nutritional Information: Calories 278, Fat 3g, Carbs 11.5g, Protein 15g, Sugar: 2.7g, Fiber 2.5g

545. Steamed Lemon Pepper Salmon

Prep time: 10-minutes | Total time: 30-minutes | Yield: 4-servings

Ingredients:

4 salmon fillets	2 tbsps. olive oil
2 tbsps. soy sauce	1 tsp. lemon juice
Salt and pepper to taste	

Directions:

Put a trivet or steamer basket inside your pot and pour water up to an inch high. Bring to a boil. Place the salmon fillets in a baking-dish that will fit in the Pot. Pour over the rest of the ingredients. Mix well and cover the dish securely with foil. Put the baking dish on the steam rack. Close the lid and steam fish for 15-minutes. Turn off the fire and let fish sit for another 5-minutes. Serve and enjoy.

Nutritional information: Calories 239, Fat 3.3g, Net Carbs 0.6g, Protein 20.2g, Sugar: 0g, Fiber 0.3g

546. Island Style Sardines

Prep time: 10-minutes | Total time:-8 hours 10-minutes | Yield: 4-servings

Ingredients:

2 tbsp. olive oil	1 Roma tomato dice
¼ c. sliced onion	1 clove of garlic, minced
1 tsp. cayenne pepper flakes	½ lb. sardines gutted and scales removed
1 tbsp. lemon juice, freshly squeezed	A dash of rosemary
A dash of sage	Salt and pepper to taste

Directions:

Add all ingredients to a slow-cooker and mix well. Cover & cook on low settings for 8 hours. Adjust seasoning if needed. Serve and enjoy.

Nutritional Information: Calories 195, Saturated Fat 2g, Net Carbs 3g, Protein 15g, Sugar: 2g, Fiber 1g,

547. Steamed Garlic-Dill Halibut

Prep time: 5-minutes | Total time: 30-minutes | Yield: 4-servings

Ingredients:

1 lb. halibut fillet	1 lemon, freshly squeezed
Salt and pepper to taste	1 tsp. garlic powder
1 tbsp. dill weed, chopped	

Directions:

Put a large pot on medium fire and fill up to 1.5-inches of water. Put a trivet inside the pot. Add all ingredients and mix well inside a baking dish that fits well inside your large pot. Cover dish with foil. Put the dish on top of the trivet inside the pot. Cover pot and steam fish for 15-minutes. Let fish rest for at least 10-minutes before removing from pot. Serve and enjoy.

Nutritional information: Calories 270, Fat 0.5g, Net Carbs 1.8g, Protein 47.8g, Sugar: 0g, Fiber 2.1g

548. Rice 'n Tuna Casserole

Prep time: 20-minutes | Total time: 40-minutes | Yield: 6-servings

Ingredients:

2 c. white rice, cooked according to manufacturer's instructions	1 1/3 c. unsweetened almond milk
2 large eggs	3 Tbsps. avocado oil mayonnaise
2 Tbsps. stone-ground mustard	3 cans tuna drained
1 c. low-fat mozzarella cheese divided	

Directions:

In a bowl, whisk well milk, eggs, mayonnaise, 2 cups cheese, and mustard. Whisk in tuna and mix well. Whisk in cooked rice and mix well. Evenly spread in a lightly greased casserole dish. Sprinkle remaining cheese on top and bake in a preheated 400 degrees F oven for 20-minutes. Remove from oven and let it rest for 5-minutes. Serve and enjoy.

Nutritional information: Calories 318, Saturated Fat 5g, Net Carbs 17g, Protein 27g, Sugar: 3g, Fiber 1g

CHAPTER 7:
MEATS RECIPES

549. Spicy Chipotle Chicken

Preparation Time: 10-minutes | Total time: 22-minutes | Yield: 4-servings

Ingredients:

1 lb. chicken breasts, skinless, boneless, and cut into strips	1 tsp. chili powder
1 tsp. ground cumin	A pinch of salt and black pepper
1 tbsp. olive oil	1 red bell pepper, sliced
1 c. halved mushrooms	1 yellow onion, chopped
3 garlic cloves, minced	1 tbsp. chopped chipotles in adobo
1½ tbsps. lime juice	

Directions:

Warm a pan with the oil on medium-high heat and add the chicken. Mix and cook for 3-4-minutes. Add the chili powder, cumin, salt, pepper, bell pepper, mushrooms, onion, garlic, chipotles, and lime juice. Mix and cook for 7-minutes more, divide into bowls, and serve.

Nutritional Information: Calories: 241 | Fat: 4 | Fiber: 7 | Carbs: 14 | Protein: 7

550. Cheesy Bacon-Wrapped Chicken with Asparagus Spears

Preparation Time: 20-minutes | Total time: 40-minutes | Yield: 4-servings

Ingredients:

4 chicken breasts	8 bacon slices
1 lb. (454 g) asparagus spears	2 tbsps. fresh lemon juice
½ c. Manchego cheese, grated	From the cupboard
4 tbsps. olive oil, divided	Salt, to taste
Freshly ground black pepper, to taste	

Directions:

Set the oven to 400ºF. Line a baking-sheet using parchment-paper, then grease with 1 tbsp. Olive oil. Place the chicken breasts in a large-bowl, and sprinkle with salt and black pepper. Toss to Mix well. Wrap every chicken breast with 2 slices of bacon. Put the chicken on the baking sheet, then bake in the preheated oven for 25-minutes or until the bacon is crispy. Preheat the grill to high, then brush with the remaining olive oil. Put the asparagus spears on the grill grate, and sprinkle with salt. Grill for 5-minutes or until fork-tender. Flip the asparagus frequently during the grilling. Transfer the bacon-wrapped chicken breasts to four plates, drizzle with lemon juice, and scatter with Manchego cheese. Spread the hot asparagus spears on top to serve.

Nutritional Information: Calories: 455 | Total fat: 38.1g | Net carbs: 2g | Protein: 26.1g

551. Feta & Bacon Chicken

Preparation Time: 20-minutes | Total time: 30-minutes | Yield: 2-4-servings

Ingredients:

4 oz. bacon, chopped	1 lb. chicken breasts
3 green onions, chopped	2 tbsp. coconut oil
4 oz. feta cheese, crumbled	1 tbsp. parsley

Directions:

Put a pan over medium-heat and then coat using cooking spray. Add in the bacon. Cook until crispy. Remove to paper towels, drain the grease and crumble. To the same pan, add in the oil, cook the chicken breasts for 4-5-minutes, then flip to the other side; cook for an additional 4-5-minutes. Place the chicken breasts inside a baking dish. Put the green onions, set in the oven, turn on the broiler, and cook for 5-minutes at high temperature. Remove to serving plates and serve topped with bacon, feta cheese, and parsley.

Nutritional Information: Calories 45 | Fat 35g | Net Carbs 3.1g | Protein 31.5g

552. Double Cheese Italian Chicken

Preparation Time: 10-minutes | Total time: 30-minutes | Yield: 2-servings

Ingredients:

2 chicken drumsticks	2 c. baby spinach
1 tsp. Italian spice mix	1/2 c. cream cheese
1 c. Asiago cheese, grated	

Directions:

In a saucepan, heat 1 tbsp. Of oil over medium-high heat. Sear the chicken drumsticks for 7 to 8-minutes or until nicely browned on all sides; reserve. Pour in 1/2 cup of chicken bone broth; add spinach and continue to cook for 5-minutes more until spinach has wilted. Add the Italian spice mix, cream cheese, Asiago cheese, and reserved chicken drumsticks; partially cover and cook for 5 more-minutes. Serve warm.

Nutritional Information: 589 Calories | 46g Fat | 5.8g Carbs | 37.5g Protein | 2g Fiber

553. Thyme Pork and Kale

Preparation Time: 10-minutes | Total time: 1-hour | Yield: 4-servings

Ingredients:

2 lb. pork roast, sliced	2 tbsps. olive oil
4 scallions, chopped	2 cored green apples, cut into wedges
1 c. baby kale	A pinch of salt and black pepper
1 tsp. chili powder	1 tbsp. thyme, chopped

Directions:

Mix the roast with the oil, the apples, and the other ingredients, toss and bake at 390 degrees F for 50-minutes in a roasting pan. Divide everything between plates and serve.

Nutritional Information: calories 605, fat 28.8, fiber 3.8, carbs 19.1, protein 65.9

554. Cilantro-Lime Chicken Drumsticks

Preparation Time: 15-minutes | Total time: 2-hours 15-minutes – 3 hours 15-minutes | Yield: 4-servings

Ingredients:

¼ c. fresh cilantro, chopped	3 tbsps. Freshly squeezed lime juice
½ tsp. Garlic powder	½ tsp. Sea salt
¼ tsp. ground cumin	3 lbs. chicken drumsticks

Directions:

Mix the cilantro, lime juice, garlic powder, salt, and cumin to form a paste in a bowl. Put the drumsticks in the slow cooker. Spread the cilantro paste evenly on each drumstick. Cover the cooker and set it too high. Cook for 2 to 3 hours, or until the internal temperature of the chicken reaches 165°F on a meat thermometer and the juices run clear and serve (see Tip).

Nutritional Information: Calories: 417 | Fat: 12g | Carbs: 1g | Sugar: 1g | Fiber: 1g | Protein: 71g |

555. Duck Breast and Blackberries Mix

Preparation Time: 10-minutes | Total time: 35-minutes | Yield: 4-scrvings

Ingredients:

4 duck breasts	2 tbsps. balsamic vinegar
3 tbsps. sugar	Salt and black pepper to taste
1 ½ c. water	4 oz. blackberries
¼ c. chicken stock	1 tbsp. butter
2 tsp. corn flour	

Directions:

Pat dry duck breasts with paper towels score the skin, season with salt and pepper to taste, and set aside 30-minutes. Put breasts skin side down in a pan, heat over medium heat, and cook for 8-minutes. Flip breasts and cook for 30 more seconds.

Transfer duck breasts to a baking dish skin side up, put in the oven at 425 degrees F, and bake for 15-minutes. Pull out the meat from the oven and leave it aside to cool down for 10-minutes before you cut them. Meanwhile, put sugar in a pan, heat over medium heat, and melt it, stirring all the time. Take the pan off the heat, add the water, stock, balsamic vinegar, and blackberries. Heat this mix to medium temperature and cook until sauce is reduced to half. Transfer sauce to another pan, add corn flour mixed with water, heat again, and cook for 4-minutes until it thickens. Add salt and pepper, the butter, and whisk well. Slice the duck breasts, divide between plates, and serve with the berries sauce on top.

Nutritional Information: Calories: 320 | Fat: 15 | Fiber: 15 | Carbs: 16 | Protein: 11

556. Roast with Onions and Potatoes

Preparation Time: 10-minutes | Total time: 1-hour 10-minutes | Yield: 4-servings

Ingredients:

2 lbs. pork roast, sliced	2 sweet potatoes, peeled and sliced
2 tbsps. olive oil	1 tsp. Rosemary, dried
1 tsp. turmeric powder	2 yellow onions, sliced
½ c. veggie stock	A pinch of salt and black pepper

Directions:

In a roasting pan, Mix the pork slices with the sweet potatoes, the onions, and the other ingredients, toss and bake at 400 degrees F for 1 hour. Divide everything between plates and serve.

Nutritional Information: calories 290, fat 4, fiber 7, carbs 10, protein 17

557. Chicken-Bell Pepper Sauté

Preparation Time: 10-minutes | Total time: 40-minutes | Yield: 6-servings

Ingredients:

1 tbsp. olive oil	1 sliced large yellow bell pepper

1 sliced large red bell pepper	3 c. onion sliced cross-wise
6 4-oz skinless, boneless chicken breast halves	Cooking spray
20 Kalamata olives	1/4 tsp. Freshly ground black pepper
1/2 tsp. salt	2 tbsps. finely chopped fresh flat-leaf parsley
2 1/3 c. coarsely chopped tomato	1 tsp. chopped fresh oregano

Directions:

Set your heat to medium-high and put non-stick frying in Put. Warm the oil. Sauté the onions for 8-minutes once the oil is hot. Attach bell pepper and sauté for 10 more-minutes. Attach tomato, salt, and black pepper to cook for about 7-minutes until the tomato juice evaporates. Attach parsley, oregano, and olives to cooking for 2-minutes until heated. Set into a bowl and keep warm. Using a paper towel, wipe the pan and grease with cooking spray. Cook on each of the sides. When cooking the last batch, attach back the previous chicken and onion-bell pepper mixture, then cook. Serve warm and enjoy.

Nutritional Information: Calories: 223, Protein: 28.13 g, Fat: 7.82 g, Carbs: 9.5 g

---

558. Pulled Buffalo Chicken Salad with Blue Cheese

Preparation Time: 10-minutes | Total time: 40-minutes | Yield: 2-servings

Ingredients:

2 boneless, skinless free-range chicken breasts	4 uncured center-cut bacon strips
1/4 c. Buffalo Sauce	4 c. chopped romaine lettuce, divided
1/2 c. blue cheese dressing, divided	1/2 c. crumbled organic blue cheese, divided
1/4 c. chopped red onion, divided	

Directions:

Put a large pot of water to a boil over high heat. Put the chicken breasts in the water, lower the heat, and then simmer until their internal temperature reaches 180°F, about 30-minutes. Take the chicken to a bowl and let it cool for about 10-minutes. On the other hand, crisp the bacon strips in a skillet over medium heat, about 3-minutes per side. Drain the bacon on a paper towel.

Shred the chicken using a fork and tossed it with the buffalo sauce. Divide the lettuce into 2 bowls. Top each with half of the pulled chicken, half of the blue cheese

dressing, blue cheese crumbles, and chopped red onion. Crumble the bacon over the salads and serve.

Nutritional Information: Calories: 843 | Saturated Fat: 14g | Protein: 59g | Fiber: 1g | Net Carbs: 5g

---

559. Baked Fillet Mignon with Potatoes

Preparation Time: 20-minutes | Total time: 1-hour 20-minutes | Yield: 4-servings

Ingredients:

1/4 c. coconut oil	1 lb. of fillet Mignon
1½ c. balsamic vinaigrette	4 big potatoes, peeled and slice into 1" chunks
Garlic	Onion
Salt and pepper to taste	

Directions:

Preheat your oven to 250 degrees Fahrenheit. Rub the fillet mignon with garlic, salt, and pepper. In an iron frying pan on moderate heat, put 1 tbsp. Of coconut oil. Brown the fillet mignon for a couple of-minutes on each side. Set aside to cool. In the same frying pan, put in the remaining coconut oil. Sauté the onion until translucent. Mix in the potatoes and brown them for approximately two-minutes. Set aside. Cube the fillet mignon in the equal size as the potatoes. Put in the potatoes. Toss until the ingredients are blended well. Move to a baking dish. Bake for 45 to an hour.

Nutritional Information: Calories: 770 kcal, Protein: 35.9 g, Fat: 35.97 g, Carbohydrates: 79.16 g

---

560. Pork Chops with Tomato Salsa

Preparation Time: 10-minutes | Total time: 25-minutes | Yield: 4-servings

Ingredients:

4 pork chops	1 tbsp. olive oil
4 scallions, chopped	1 tsp. Cumin, ground
1/2 tbsp. hot paprika	1 tsp. garlic powder
Pinch of sea salt	Pinch of black pepper
1 small red onion, chopped	2 tomatoes, cubed
2 tbsps. lime juice	1 jalapeno, chopped
1/4 c. cilantro, chopped	1 tbsp. lime juice

Directions:

Warm a pan with the oil on medium heat, add the scallions and sauté for 5-minutes. Add the meat, cumin, paprika, garlic powder, salt, and pepper, toss, cook for 5-minutes on each side, and divide between plates.

Mix the tomatoes with the remaining ingredients in a bowl, toss, divide next to the pork chops, and serve.

Nutritional Information: Calories 313 | Fat 23.7 | Fiber 1. | Carbs 5. | Protein 19.2

561. BBQ Chicken Liver and Hearts

Preparation Time: 15-minutes | Total time: 35-minutes | Yield: 4-servings

Ingredients:

bamboo skewers	black pepper
sea salt	1 lb. chicken livers
1 lb. chicken hearts	

Directions:

The liver and hearts defrost and bring to room temperature. The heart's extreme top parts can be evacuated with a sharp blade. Meanwhile, set up the BBQ - we utilize just charcoals; however, you can use gas and bring to prescription/high warm. Presently string the hearts on the sticks, 5 to 7 each, contingent upon their size.

After cleaning the livers, focusing not to break or smash them, lay level on an adaptable barbecuing bushel. Season both liver and hearts with ocean salt and naturally ground dark pepper. The livers will generally stick on the barbecue, effectively break separated currently set on the flame broil, and cook until the ideal doneness comes.

Nutritional Information: Calories 361 | Fat 28g | Carbs 4.5g | Protein 23g

562. Cheesy Ranch Chicken

Preparation Time: 10-minutes | Total time: 30-minutes | Yield: 4-servings

Ingredients:

2 chicken breasts	1/2 tbsp. ranch seasoning mix
4 slices bacon, chopped	1/2 c. Monterey-Jack cheese, grated
4 oz. Ricotta cheese, room temperature	

Directions:

Preheat your oven to 360 degrees F. Rub the chicken with ranch seasoning mix. Heat a saucepan over medium-high flame. Now, sear the chicken for about 8-minutes. Lower the chicken into a lightly greased casserole dish. Top cheese and bacon and bake in the preheated oven for about 10-minutes until hot and bubbly. Serve with freshly snipped scallions, if desired.

Nutritional Information: 295 Calories | 19.5g Fat | 2.9g Carbs | 25.5g Protein | 0.4g Fiber

563. Chicken in Pita Bread

Preparation Time: 10-minutes | Total time: 20-minutes | Yield: 4-servings

Ingredients:

½ tsp. coarsely ground black pepper	1 lb. Ground chicken
1 ½ tsps. chopped fresh oregano	1 tbsp. olive oil
½ c. plain low-fat yogurt	2 tsp. Divided grated lemon rind
4 pieces of 6-inch halved pitas	2 c. shredded lettuce
½ c. chopped green onions	½ c. diced tomato
Two lightly beaten large egg whites	1 tbsp. Greek seasoning blend

Directions:

Mix egg whites, Greek seasoning, a tbsp. Lemon rind, green onions, and black pepper. Separate into 8 parts and mold each into ¼ inch thick patty. Adjust your heat to medium-high. Set a non-stick skillet in. Put and fry patties until browned. Lower the heat to medium. Then, cover the skillet to cook for 4 more-minutes. Set up a small bowl and Mix yogurt, oregano, and a tbsp. of lemon rind. Spread the mixture on the pita and add ¼ cup lettuce and a tbsp of tomato.

Nutritional Information: Calories: 421 kcal | Protein: 29.72 g | Fat: 23.37 g | Carbohydrates: 23.26 g

564. Pork with Carrots

Preparation Time: 10-minutes | Total time: 1-hour 10-minutes | Yield: 4-servings

Ingredients:

1 lb. pork meat, cubed	2 carrots, sliced
2 tbsps. avocado oil	1 yellow onion, chopped
A pinch of black pepper with salt	¼ tsp. smoked paprika
½ c. tomato sauce	

Directions:

Heat a pan with the oil over medium-high heat, add the onion and the meat, and brown for 10-minutes. Add the rest of the ingredients, toss, put the pan in the oven and bake at 390 degrees F for 50-minutes. Divide everything between plates and serve.

Nutritional Information: calories 300, fat 7, fiber 6, carbs 12, protein 20

565. Tomato & Cheese Chicken Chili

Preparation Time: 5-minutes | Total time: 30-minutes | Yield: 2-4-servings

Ingredients:

1 tbsp. butter	1 tbsp. olive oil
1 lb. chicken breasts, skinless, boneless, cubed	½ onion, chopped
2 c. chicken broth	2 c. tomatoes, chopped
2 oz. tomato puree	1 tbsp. chili powder

1 tbsp. cumin	1 garlic clove, minced
1 habanero pepper, minced	½ c. mozzarella cheese, shredded
Salt and black pepper to taste	

Directions:

Season the chicken using salt and pepper. Set a large pan at medium heat and add the chicken; cover it with water and bring it to a boil. Cook until no longer pink, for 10-minutes. Transfer the chicken to a flat surface to shred with forks. In a pot, pour in the butter and olive oil and set over medium heat. Sauté onion and garlic until transparent for 5-minutes. Whisk the chicken, tomatoes, cumin, habanero pepper, tomato puree, broth, and chili powder. Adjust the seasoning and let the mixture boil. Reduce heat to simmer for about 10-minutes. Top with shredded cheese to serve.

Nutritional Information: Calories: 322 | Fat: 16.6g | Net Carbs: 6.2g | Protein: 29g

566. Turkey Crust Meats

Preparation Time: 15-minutes | Total time: 50-minutes | Yield: 4-servings

Ingredients:

1/2 lb. ground turkey	2 slices Canadian bacon
1 tomato, chopped	1 tbsp. pizza spice mix
1 c. Mozzarella cheese, grated	

Directions:

Mix the ground turkey and cheese; season with salt and black pepper and mix until everything is well combined. Press the mixture into a foil-lined baking pan. Bake in the preheated oven at 380 degrees F for 25-minutes. Top the crust with Canadian bacon, tomato, and pizza spice mix. Continue to bake for a further 8-minutes. Let it rest for a few-minutes before slicing and serving. Bon appétit!

Nutritional Information:360 Calories | 22.7g Fat | 5.9g Carbs | 32.6g Protein | 0.7g Fiber

567. Middle Eastern Shish Kebab

Preparation Time: 10-minutes | Total time: 30-minutes | Yield: 5-servings

Ingredients:

2 lbs. chicken tenders, cut into bite-sized cubes	1/2 c. ajar
1 tbsp. mustard Turkish spice mix	1/2 c. tomato sauce

Directions:

Put chicken tenders with the remaining ingredients in a ceramic dish. Cover and let it marinate for 4 hours in your refrigerator. Thread chicken tenders onto skewers and put them on the preheated grill until golden brown on all sides, approximately 15-minutes. Serve immediately and enjoy!

Nutritional Information:274 Calories | 10.7g Fat | 3.3g Carbs | 39.3g Protein | 0.8g Fiber

568. Bacon-Wrapped Chicken with Cheddar Cheese

Preparation Time: 10-minutes | Total time: 4-hours 10-minutes | Yield: 6-servings

Ingredients:

2 large chicken-breasts, each cut into 6-pieces	6 slices of streaky-bacon, each cut in half widthways
4 garlic cloves, crushed	½ c. Cheddar cheese, grated
From the cupboard:	1 tbsp. olive oil
Salt, to taste	Freshly ground black pepper, to taste

Directions:

Grease the insert of the slow-cooker using olive oil. Wrap each piece of the chicken- breast with each half of the bacon slice, and arrange them in the slow-cooker. Sprinkle the chicken breast with salt, garlic, salt, and black pepper. Place the lid, and then cook on low for about 4 hours. Set your oven to 350 degrees F (180 degrees C). Transfer the cooked bacon-wrapped chicken to a baking-abolish, then scatter with cheese. Cook in the preheated oven for about 5-minutes or until the cheese melts. Take it off from the oven. Then serve warm.

Nutritional Information: Calories: 308 | Fat: 20.8g | Fiber: 1g | Net carbs: 2.9g | Protein: 26.1g

569. Moroccan Turkey Tagine

Preparation Time: 15-minutes | Total time: 7-hours 15-minutes – 8 hours 15-minutes | Yield: 4-servings

Ingredients:

4 c. boneless, skinless turkey breast chunks	1 (14 oz.) can diced tomatoes
1 (14 oz.) can chickpeas, drained	2 large carrots, finely chopped
½ c. dried apricots	½ red onion, chopped
2 tbsps. raw honey	1 tbsp. tomato paste
1 tsp. garlic powder	1 tsp. ground turmeric
½ tsp. sea salt	¼ tsp. ground ginger
¼ tsp. ground coriander	¼ tsp. paprika
½ c. water	2 c. broth of choice

Freshly ground black pepper	

Directions:

In your slow cooker, Mix the turkey, tomatoes, chickpeas, carrots, apricots, onion, honey, tomato paste, garlic powder, turmeric, salt, ginger, coriander, paprika, water, and broth, and season with pepper. Gently whisk to blend the ingredients. Cover the cooker & set it to low heat. Cook for about 7 to 8 hours and serve.

Nutritional Information: Calories: 428 | Fat: 5 | Carbs: 46g | Sugar: 15g | Fiber: 8g | Protein: 49g |

570. Capocollo and Garlic Chicken

Preparation Time: 10-minutes | Total time: 50-minutes | Yield: 5-servings

Ingredients:

2 lbs. chicken drumsticks, skinless and boneless, butterflied	10 thin slices of capocollo
1 garlic clove, peeled and halved	Coarse sea salt, to taste
Ground black pepper, to taste	1/2 tsp. smoked paprika

Directions:

Over the surface of chicken drumsticks, rub the garlic halves. Season with salt, paprika, and black pepper. Put a slice of capocollo on each chicken drumstick and roll them up, secure with kitchen twine. Bake in the oven for about 30 - 35-minutes until your chicken starts to brown at 410 degrees F. Bon appétit!

Nutritional Information:485 Calories | 33.8g Fat | 3.6g Carbs | 39.2g Protein | 1g Fiber

571. Chimichurri Turkey

Preparation Time: 15-minutes | Total time: 7-8 hours + 15-minutes | Yield: 4-servings

Ingredients:

1 (3 lbs.) whole, boneless turkey breast	2 c. Chimichurri Sauce (double the recipe)
½ c. broth of choice	

Directions:

Put the turkey in the slow cooker. Pour on the sauce and broth. Cover the slow cooker & set it to low and then cook for about 6 to 7 hours, or until the turkey's internal temperature reaches 165°F on a meat thermometer and the juices run clear and serve.

Nutritional Information: Calories: 776 | Fat: 59g | Carbs: 14g | Sugar: 4g | Fiber: 6 | Protein: 60g

572. Apple Pork Raisins

Preparation Time: ten-minutes | Total time: 45-minutes | Yield: 4-servings

Ingredients:
Salsa:

¼ c. finely chopped sweet onion	½ c. dried raisins
½ tsp. (shredded or grated) fresh ginger	1 tsp. olive oil
2 apples, peeled, cored, and diced	Pinch sea salt

Chops:

1 tbsp. olive oil	1 tsp. garlic powder
1 tsp. ground cinnamon	4 (4 oz.) boneless center-cut pork chops, trimmed and patted dry
Freshly ground black pepper, to taste	Salt to taste

Directions:

In a frying pan or deep cooking pan, warm the oil on the medium stove flame. Put in the onions and ginger, whisk the mixture, and cook while stirring until tender for approximately 2-3-minutes. Mix in the apples and raisins. Sauté for approximately 4-5-minutes. Flavor it with sea salt and set it aside. Coat the pork chops on each side with garlic powder, cinnamon, sea salt, and pepper. In a frying pan or deep cooking pan, warm the oil on the medium stove flame. Put in the chops and cook, while stirring, until it becomes uniformly brown. Serve the chops with apple salsa.

Nutritional Information: Calories 384, Fat: 27g, Carbohydrates: 11g, Fiber: 2g, Protein: 26g

573. Chinese-Orange Spiced Duck Breasts

Preparation Time: 4-minutes | Total time: 24-minutes | Yield: 2-servings

Ingredients:

2 Pak or Bok Choy plants leaves separated	1 Orange-Zest and Juice (Reserved the wedges)
1 tsp. Cloves	1 tsp. Cinnamon
2 tsp. Ginger, grated	3 Cloves garlic, minced
1 White onion, sliced	2 Duck breasts, skin removed
1 tsp. EXTRA Virgin olive oil	

Directions:

Slice the duck breasts into strips. Add to a dry, hot pan, cooking on each side for about 5-7 minutes or until cooked through to your liking. Remove to one side.

Add olive oil to a clean pan. Sauté the onions using the garlic, ginger, and the rest of the spices for 1-minute. Put the juice & zest of the orange. Go ahead to sauté for about 3-5-minutes. Add the duck and bok choi and heat through until wilted, and the duck is piping hot. Serve and garnish with the orange segments.

Nutritional Information: Calories: 267 kcal | Protein: 36.58 g | Fat: 11.1 g | Carbohydrates: 3.31 g

574. Coconut-Curry-Cashew Chicken

Preparation Time: 15-minutes | Total time: 7-8 hour + 15-minutes | Yield: 4-servings

Ingredients:

1½ c. Chicken Bone Broth	1 (14 oz.) can full-fat co-conut milk
1 tsp. garlic powder	1 tbsp. red curry paste
1 tsp. Sea salt	½ tsp. Freshly ground black pepper
½ tsp. coconut sugar	2 lbs. boneless, skinless chicken breasts
1½ c. unsalted cashews	½ c. diced white onion

Directions:

Mix the broth, coconut milk, garlic powder, red curry paste, salt, pepper, and coconut sugar in a bowl. Whisk well. Place the cashews, chicken, and onion in the slow cooker. Pour the coconut milk mixture on top. Cover the cooker and set it to low. Cook for about 7 to 8 hours, or until the internal temp of the chicken reaches 165 degrees F on a meat thermometer and the juices run clear. Use a fork to shred the chicken. Mix it into the cooking-liquid. Also, if you want, remove the chicken from the broth and chop it with a knife into bite-size pieces before returning it to the slow cooker. Serve.

Nutritional Information: Calories: 714 | Fat: 43g | Carbs: 21g | Sugar: 5g | Fiber: 3g | Protein: 57g |

575. Cipollini & Bell Pepper Chicken Souvlaki

Preparation Time: 5-minutes | Total time: 17-minutes | Yield: 2-4-servings

Ingredients:

2 chicken breasts, cubed	2 tbsp. olive oil
2 cloves garlic, minced	1 red bell pepper, cut into chunks
8 oz. small Cipollini	½ c. lemon juice
Salt and black pepper to taste	1 tsp rosemary leaves to garnish
2 to 4 lemon wedges to garnish	

Directions:

Thread the chicken, bell pepper, and Cipollini onto skewers and set aside. Mix half of the oil, garlic, salt,

black pepper, and lemon juice in a bowl, and add the chicken skewers. Cover the bowl. And then marinate the chicken for about 2 hours in the refrigerator. Preheat a grill to high heat and grill the skewers for 6-minutes on each side. Remove and serve garnished with rosemary leaves and lemons wedges.

Nutritional Information: Calories 363 | Fat 14.2g | Net Carbs 4.2 | Protein 32.5g

576. Cheesy Mexican-Style Chicken

Preparation Time: 10-minutes | Total time: 35-minutes | Yield: 6-servings

Ingredients:

1-½ lb. chicken-breasts, cut into bite-sized cubes	2 ripe tomatoes, pu-reed
4 oz. sour cream	6 oz. Cotija cheese, crumbled
1 Mexican chili pepper, finely chopped	

Directions:

Preheat your oven to 390 degrees F. In a saucepan, heat 2 tbsps. Of olive oil over medium-high heat. Cook the chicken-breasts for about 10-minutes, frequently stirring to ensure even cooking. Then, add in Mexican chili pepper and cook until it has softened. Add in the pu-reed tomatoes and continue to cook, partially covered, for 4 to 5-minutes — season with the Mexican spice mix. Transfer the mixture to a lightly greased baking dish. Top with sour cream and Cotija cheese. Bake in the preheated oven for about 15-minutes or until hot and bubbly. Enjoy!

Nutritional Information:354 Calories | 23.2g Fat | 6g Carbs | 29.3g Protein | 0.6g Fiber

577. Cajun Chicken & Prawn

Preparation Time: 5-minutes | Total time: 40-minutes | Yield: 2-servings

Ingredients:

2 Free-range Skinless Chicken breast, chopped	1 Onion, chopped
1 Red pepper, chopped	2 Garlic cloves, crushed
10 Fresh or frozen prawn	1 tsp. Cayenne powder
1 tsp. Chili powder	1 tsp. Paprika
1/4 tsp. Chili powder	1 tsp. Dried oregano
1 tsp. Dried thyme	1 c. Brown or wholegrain rice
1 tbsp. Extra Virgin olive oil	1 can Tomatoes, chopped

2 c. Homemade chicken stock	

Directions:

Place all the herbs and spices together in a bowl, then mix to form your Cajun spice mix. Grab a large pan and add the olive oil, heating on medium heat. Add the chicken and brown each side for around 4-5-minutes. Put to one side. Add the onion to the pan and fry until soft. Add the garlic, prawns, Cajun seasoning, and red pepper to the pan and cook for around 5-minutes or until prawns become opaque. Add the brown rice along with the chopped tomatoes, chicken, and chicken stock to the pan. Cover the pan and allow to simmer for around 25-minutes or until the rice is soft. Serve and enjoy!

Nutritional Information: Calories: 557 kcal | Protein: 18.96 g | Fat: 12.34 g | Carbohydrates: 93.28 g

578. Spicy Pulled Chicken Wraps

Preparation Time: 15-minutes | Total time: 6- 8 hours + 15-minutes | Yield: 4-servings

Ingredients:

1 romaine lettuce head	1 1/2 tsp. ground cumin
1 1/2 c. low-fat, low-sodium chicken broth	1 tsp. paprika
1 tsp. garlic powder	1 lb. skinless, deboned chicken breasts
2 tsp. chili powder	

Directions:

In a slow cooker, put all the ingredients except lettuce and gently Whisk to combine. Set the slow cooker on low. Cover and cook for about 6-8 hours. Unsecure the slow cooker and transfer the breasts to a large plate. With a fork, shred the breasts. Serve the shredded beef over lettuce leaves.

Nutritional Information: Calories: 150, Fat: 3.4 g, Carbs: 12 g, Protein: 14 g, Sugars: 7 g

579. Slow Cooker Chicken Cacciatore

Preparation Time: 15-minutes | Total time: 25-minutes | Yield: 4-servings

Ingredients:

¼ c. good-quality olive oil	4 (4 oz.) boneless chicken breasts, each cut into three pieces
1 onion, chopped	2 celery stalks, chopped
1 c. sliced mushrooms	2 tbsps. minced garlic
1 (28 oz.) can sodium-free diced tomatoes	½ c. tomato paste
1 tbsp. dried basil	1 tsp. Oregano, dried

⅛ tsp. red pepper flakes	

Directions:

Brown the chicken. In a skillet at medium-high heat, warm olive oil. Add the chicken breasts and brown them, turning them once, about 10-minutes in total. Cook in the slow cooker. Put the chicken in the slow cooker and Whisk in your onion, celery, mushrooms, garlic, red pepper flakes, tomato paste, basil, oregano, and tomatoes. Cook it on high for approximately 3 to 4 hours or low for 6 to 8 hours, until the chicken is fully cooked and tender. Serve. Divide the chicken and sauce between four bowls and serve it immediately.

Nutritional Information: Calories: 383 | Fat: 26g | Fiber: 4g Net carbs: 7g | Sodium: 116mg | Protein: 26g

580. Pan-Fried Chorizo Sausage

Preparation Time: 5-minutes | Total time: 20-minutes | Yield: 4-servings

Ingredients:

16 oz. smoked turkey chorizo	1 ½ c. Asiago cheese, grated
1 tsp. oregano	1 tsp. basil
1 c. tomato puree	4 scallion stalks, chopped
1 tsp. garlic paste	Sea salt, to taste
Ground black pepper, to taste	1 tbsp. dry sherry
1 tbsp. extra-virgin olive oil	2 tbsps. fresh coriander, roughly chopped

Directions:

In a skillet, put oil and heat it over moderately high heat. Now, brown the turkey chorizo, crumbling with a fork for about 5-minutes. Add in the other ingredients, except for cheese; continue to cook for 10-minutes more or until cooked through.

Nutritional Information:330 Calories | 17.2g Fat | 4.5g Carbs | 34.4g Protein | 1.6g Fiber

581. Chicken Pie with Bacon

Preparation Time: 20-minutes | Total time: 55-minutes | Yield: 24-servings

Ingredients:

3 tbsps. butter	1 onion, chopped
4 oz. bacon, sliced	1 carrot, chopped
3 garlic cloves, minced	Salt and black pepper, to taste
¾ c. crème fraîche	½ c. chicken stock
1 lb. chicken breasts, cubed	2 tbsps. yellow mustard
¾ c. cheddar cheese, shredded	Dough

1 egg	¾ c. almond flour
3 tbsps. cream cheese	1 ½ c. mozzarella cheese, shredded
1 tsp onion powder	1 tsp garlic powder
Salt and black pepper, to taste	

Directions:

Sauté the onion, garlic, black pepper, bacon, and carrot in melted butter for 5-minutes. Add in the chicken and cook for 3-minutes. Whisk in the crème fraîche, black pepper, salt, mustard, and stock, and cook for 7-minutes. Add in the cheddar cheese and set aside.

In a bowl, Mix the mozzarella cheese with the cream cheese and heat in a microwave for 1 minute. Whisk in garlic powder, salt, flour, black pepper, onion powder, and egg. Knead the dough well, split it into 4 pieces, and flatten each into a circle. Set the chicken mixture into 4 ramekins, top each with a dough circle, and cook in the oven at 370 F for 25-minutes.

Nutritional Information: Calories 563 | Fat 44.6g | Net Carbs 7.7 | Protein 36g

582. Pork with Spiced Zucchinis

Preparation Time: 10-minutes | Total time: 50-minutes | Yield: 4-servings

Ingredients:

2 lbs. pork stew meat, roughly cubed	2 zucchinis, sliced
2 tbsps. olive oil	1 tsp. nutmeg, ground
1 tsp. cinnamon powder	1 tsp. cumin, ground
2 tbsps. lime juice	2 garlic cloves, minced
A pinch of black pepper with sea salt	

Directions:

In a roasting pan, Mix the meat with the zucchinis, the nutmeg, and the other ingredients, toss and bake at 390 degrees F for 40-minutes. Divide everything between plates and serve.

Nutritional Information: calories 200, fat 5, fiber 2, carbs 10, protein 22

583. Paprika Chicken & Pancetta in a Skillet

Preparation Time: 20-minutes | Total time: 30-minutes | Yield: 2-servings

Ingredients:

1 tbsp. olive oil	5 pancetta strips, chopped
1/3 c. Dijon mustard	Salt and black pepper, to taste
1 onion, chopped	¼ tsp sweet paprika

2 chicken breasts, skinless and boneless	1 c. chicken stock
2 tbsps. oregano, chopped	

Directions:

In a bowl, Mix the paprika, black pepper, salt, and mustard. Sprinkle this mixture the chicken breasts and massage. Heat a skillet over medium heat; whisk in the pancetta, cook until it browns, for about 3-4-minutes, and remove to a plate. To the pancetta fat, add olive oil and cook the chicken breasts for 2-minutes per side. Put in the stock black pepper, pancetta, salt, and onion. Sprinkle with oregano and serve.

Nutritional Information: Calories 323 | Fat 21g | Net Carbs 4.8g | Protein 24.5g

584. Avocado-Orange Grilled Chicken

Preparation Time: 10-minutes | Total time: 22-minutes | Yield: 4-servings

Ingredients:

1 thinly sliced small red onion	1 tbsp. honey
2 tbsps. chopped cilantro	4 pieces of 4-6oz boneless, skinless chicken breasts
Salt	1 c. low-fat yogurt
1/4 c. fresh lime juice	1 deseeded avocado, peeled and chopped
2 peeled and sectioned oranges	Pepper
1/4 c. minced red onion	

Directions:

Set up a mixing bowl and merge yogurt, minced red onion, cilantro, and honey. Attach chicken into the mixture and marinate for half an hour. Set grate and preheat the grill to medium-high heat. Set the chicken aside and add seasonings. Grill for 6-minutes on each side. Set the avocado in a bowl. Attach lime juice and toss avocado to coat well. Attach oranges, thinly sliced onions, and cilantro into the bowl with avocado and merge well. Serve avocado dressing alongside grilled chicken.

Nutritional Information: Calories: 216, Protein: 8.83 g, Fat: 11.48 g, Carbs: 21.86 g

585. Chicken & Cheese Filled Avocados

Preparation Time: 10-minutes | Total time: 10-minutes | Yield: 2-servings

Ingredients:

2 avocados	¼ c. mayonnaise

1 tsp dried thyme	2 tbsp. cream cheese
2 tbsp. lemon juice	Salt and black pepper, to taste
1 tsp paprika	½ tsp garlic powder
½ tsp onion powder	¼ tsp cayenne pepper
Salt and black pepper, to taste	1 ½ c. cooked chicken, shredded

Directions:
Halve the avocados and scoop the insides. Put the flesh in a bowl, then add in the chicken, Whisk in the remaining ingredients. Fill the avocado cups with chicken mixture and serve.

Nutritional Information: Calories 518 | Fat 41.6 | Net Carbs 5.3gProtein 23.2g

586. Duck Breast with Apricot Sauce
Preparation Time: 10-minutes | Total time: 30-minutes | Yield: 4-servings

Ingredients:

4 duck breasts, boneless	Salt and black pepper to taste
¼ tsp. Cinnamon, ground	¼ tsp. coriander, ground
5 tbsps. apricot preserving	3 tbsps. chives, chopped
2 tbsps. parsley, chopped	A drizzle of olive oil
3 tbsps. apple cider vinegar	2 tbsps. red onions, chopped
1 c. apricots, chopped	¾ c. blackberries

Directions:
Season duck breasts with salt, pepper, coriander, and cinnamon, put them on a preheated grill pan over medium-high heat, cook for 2-minutes, flip them, and cook for 3-minutes more. Flip duck breasts again. Add 3 tbsps. Apricot preserving, cook for 1 minute, transfer them to a cutting board, leave aside for 2-3-minutes, and slice. Heat a pan over medium heat, add vinegar, onion, 2 tbsps. Apricot preserving, apricots, blackberries, and chives, Whisk and cook for 3-minutes. Divide sliced duck breasts between plates and serve with apricot sauce drizzled on top.

Nutritional Information: Calories: 275 | Fat: 4 | Fiber: 4 | Carbs: 7 | Protein: 12

587. Chicken with Fennel
Preparation Time: 10-minutes | Total time: 18-minutes | Yield: 4-servings

Ingredients:

1 ¼ lb. chicken cutlets	1 ½ tsp. smoked paprika

A pinch of salt and black pepper	3 tbsps. olive oil
1 fennel bulb, sliced	¾ c. fennel fronds
1/3 c. red onion, sliced	1 avocado, peeled, pitted, and sliced
2 tbsps. lemon juice	

Directions:
Warm a pan with 1 tbsp. Olive oil on medium-high heat temperature, add the chicken, season with salt, pepper, and smoked paprika, and cook for 4-minutes on each side. Divide between plates. In a bowl, mix the rest of the oil with the fennel, fennel fronds, onion, avocado, and lemon juice. Toss the salad and put next to the chicken, then serve. Enjoy!

Nutritional Information: Calories: 288 | Fat: 4 | Fiber: 6 | Carbs: 12 | Protein: 7

588. Winter Chicken with Vegetables
Preparation Time: 5-minutes | Total time: 35--minutes | Yield: 2-servings

Ingredients:

2 tbsp. olive oil	2 c. whipping cream
1 lb. chicken breasts, chopped	1 onion, chopped
1 carrot, chopped	2 c. chicken stock
Salt and black pepper, to taste	1 bay leaf
1 turnip, chopped	1 parsnip, chopped
2 tsp fresh thyme, chopped	

Directions:
Heat a pan at medium heat and warm the olive oil. Sauté the onion for 3-minutes, pour in the stock, carrot, turnip, parsnip, chicken, and bay leaf. Put to a boil, and simmer for 20-minutes. Add in the asparagus and cook for 7-minutes. Discard the bay leaf, Whisk in the whipping cream, adjust the seasoning, and scatter it with fresh thyme to serve.

Nutritional Information: Calories 483 | Fat 32.5g | Net Carbs 6.9g | Protein 33g

589. Spiced Ground Beef
Preparation Time: 10-minutes | Total time: 32-minutes | Yield: 5-servings

Ingredients:

2 tbsps. coconut oil	2 whole cloves
2 whole cardamoms	1 (2-inch) piece cinnamon stick
2 bay leaves	1 tsp. cumin seeds
2 onions, chopped	Salt, to taste

1/2 tbsp. garlic paste	1/2 tbsp. fresh ginger paste
1 lb. lean ground beef	11/2 tsp. fennel seeds powder
1 tsp. ground cumin	11/2 tsp. red chili powder
1/8 tsp. ground turmeric	Freshly ground black pepper, to taste
1 c. coconut milk	1/4 c. water
1/4 c. fresh cilantro, chopped	

Directions:

In a sizable pan, warm oil on medium heat. Attach cloves, cardamoms, cinnamon sticks, bay leaves, and cumin seeds and sauté for about 20-a a few seconds. Add onion and 2 pinches of salt and sauté for about 3-4-minutes. Attach garlic-ginger paste and sauté for about 2-minutes. Attach beef and cook for about 4-5-minutes, entering pieces using the spoon. Secure and cook for approximately 5-minutes. Whisk in spices and cook, stirring for approximately 2-21/2-minutes.

Set in coconut milk and water and cook for about 7-8-minutes. Flavor with salt and take away from heat. Serve hot using the garnishing of cilantro.

Nutritional Information: Calories: 216, Protein: 8.83 g, Fat: 11.48 g, Carbs: 21.86 g

590. Cheesy Pinwheels with Chicken

Preparation Time: 10-minutes | Total time: 40-minutes | Yield: 2-servings

Ingredients:

2 tbsp. ghee	1 garlic, minced
1/3 lb. chicken breasts, cubed	1 tsp creole seasoning
1/3 red onion, chopped	1 tomato, chopped
½ c. chicken stock	¼ c. whipping cream
½ c. mozzarella cheese, grated	¼ c. fresh cilantro, chopped
Salt and black pepper, to taste	4 oz. cream cheese
5 eggs	A pinch of garlic powder

Directions:

Season the chicken with creole seasoning. Heat a pan at medium heat and warm 1 tbsp. Ghee. Put chicken and cook per side for 2-minutes; remove to a plate. Melt the rest of the ghee and Whisk in garlic and tomato; cook for 4-minutes. Return the chicken to the pan and pour in stock; cook for 15-minutes. Put in whipping cream, red onion, salt, mozzarella cheese, and black pepper; cook for 2-minutes. Mix the cream cheese with garlic powder, salt, eggs, and black pepper in a blender, and

pulse well. Put the mixture into a lined baking sheet, and then bake for 10-minutes in the oven at 320 F. Allow the cheese sheet to cool down. Put on a cutting board, roll, and slice into medium slices. Organize the slices on a serving plate and top with chicken mixture. Sprinkle with cilantro to serve.

Nutritional Information: |Calories 463| Fat 36.4g| Net Carbs 6.3g| Protein 35.2g

591. Cinnamon Pork Mix

Preparation Time: 10-minutes | Total time: 1-hour 10-minutes | Yield: 4-servings

Ingredients:

2 lbs. pork stew meat, cubed	2 tbsps. olive oil
1 yellow onion, chopped	2 avocados, peeled, pitted, and sliced
1 tbsp. chili powder	Salt and black pepper to the taste
1 tsp. Cumin, ground	½ tsp. cinnamon powder
A pinch of cayenne pepper	½ c. vegetable stock
½ c. parsley, chopped	

Directions:

Heat a pan with the oil over medium-high heat, add the onion and the meat, and brown for 10-minutes, stirring often. Add the avocados and the other ingredients toss, introduce the pan in the oven and bake at 390 degrees F for 50-minutes. Divide the mix between plates.

Nutritional Information: calories 300, fat 7, fiber 6, carbs 12, protein 18

592. Balsamic Pork and Peaches

Preparation Time: 10-minutes | Total time: 55-minutes | Yield: 4-servings

Ingredients:

2 peaches, cubed	1 c. red cabbage, shredded
2 lbs. pork stew meat, cubed	2 tbsps. olive oil
4 scallions, chopped	1 tbsp. balsamic vinegar
A pinch of salt and black pepper	1 tbsp. cilantro, chopped

Directions:

Heat a pan with the oil over medium-high heat, add the scallions and the meat, and brown for 10-minutes.

Add the peaches and the other ingredients, toss, and cook over medium heat for 35-minutes. Divide everything between plates and serve.

Nutritional Information: calories 260, fat 5, fiber 4, carbs 12, protein 14

593. Slow Cooker Chicken Fajitas

Preparation Time: 15-minutes | Total time: 7-8 hours + 15-minutes | Yield: 4-servings

Ingredients:

1 (14.5 oz.) can diced tomatoes	1 (4 oz.) can Hatch green chills
1½ tsps. garlic powder	2 tsp. chili powder
1½ tsps. ground cumin	1 tsp. paprika
1 tsp. sea salt	Juice of 1 lime
Pinch cayenne pepper	Freshly ground black pepper
1 red bell pepper, seeded and sliced	1 green bell pepper, seeded and sliced
1 yellow bell pepper, seeded and sliced	1 large onion, sliced
2 lbs. boneless, skinless chicken breast	

Directions:

In a medium bowl, put together the diced tomatoes, chiles, garlic powder, chili powder, cumin, paprika, salt, lime juice, and cayenne, season with black pepper, then mix. Pour half the diced tomato mixture into the bottom of your slow cooker. Layer half the red, green, and yellow bell peppers and half the onion over the tomatoes in the cooker. Put the chicken on top of the peppers and onions. Cover the chicken with the remaining red, green, and yellow bell peppers and onions. Pour the remaining tomato mixture on top. Cover the cooker. Then set it to low heat. Cook for around 7 to 8 hours, or until the internal temperature of the chicken reaches 165°F on a meat thermometer and the juices run clear and serve.

Nutritional Information: Calories: 310| Fat: 5g| Carbs: 19g|Sugar: 7g|Fiber: 4g|Protein: 46|

594. Easy Chicken Tacos

Preparation Time: 5-minutes | Total time: 32-minutes | Yield: 4-servings

Ingredients:

1 lb. ground chicken	1 ½ c. Mexican cheese blend
1 tbsp. Mexican seasoning blend	2 tsp. butter, room temperature
2 small-sized shallots, peeled and finely chopped	1 clove garlic, minced
1 c. tomato puree	1/2 c. salsa
2 slices bacon, chopped	

Directions:

In a saucepan, put butter, then melt in over a moderately high flame. Now, cook the shallots until tender and fragrant. Then, sauté the garlic, chicken, and bacon for about 5-minutes, stirring continuously and crumbling with a fork. Add the Mexican seasoning blend. Fold in the tomato puree and salsa; continue to simmer for 5 to 7-minutes over medium-low heat; reserve.

Line a baking pan with wax paper. Put 4 piles of the shredded cheese on the baking pan and gently press them down with a wide spatula to make "taco shells." Bake in the preheated oven at 365 degrees F for 6 to 7-minutes or until melted. Allow these taco shells to cool for about 10-minutes.

Nutritional Information:535 Calories|33.3g Fat|4.8g Carbs|47.9g Protein|1.9g Fiber

595. Healthy Turkey Gumbo

Preparation Time: 5-minutes | Total time: 2-hours 5-minutes | Yield: 1 serving

Ingredients:

1 Whole Turkey	1 Onion, quartered
A stalk of Celery, chopped	3 Cloves garlic, chopped
1/2 c. Okra	1 can chopped tomatoes
1 tbsp. Extra virgin olive oils	1-2 Bay leaves
Black pepper to taste	

Directions:

Take the first four ingredients and add 2 cups of water in a stockpot, heating on high heat until boiling. Lower the heat and simmer for 45-50-minutes or until turkey is cooked through. Remove the turkey and strain the broth. Grab a skillet, heat the oil on medium heat, and brown the rest of the vegetables for 5-10-minutes. Whisk until tender, and then add to the broth. Add the tomatoes and turkey meat to the broth and stir. Add the bay leaves and continue to cook for an hour or until the sauce has thickened. Season with black pepper and enjoy.

Nutritional Information: Calories: 261 kcal|Protein: 11.72 g|Fat: 12.91 g |Carbohydrates: 28.33 g

596. Basil Pork and Pine Nuts

Preparation Time: 10-minutes | Total time: 55-minutes | Yield: 4-servings

Ingredients:

2 lbs. pork roast, sliced	¼ c. basil, chopped
1 tbsp. pine nuts, toasted	1 tbsps. garlic, minced
2 tbsps. olive oil	¼ c. vegetable stock
A pinch of salt and black pepper	1 tsp. coriander, ground
1 tsp. onion powder	

Directions:
Mix the basil in a blender with the pine nuts and the other ingredients except for the roast and the stock and pulse well. Put the roast slices on a baking dish, add the stock and the basil mix, toss, and bake at 390 degrees F for 45-minutes. Divide everything between plates and serve.

Nutritional Information: calories 270, fat 6 g , fiber 5g , carbs 13 g , protein 18 g

597. Nacho Chicken Casserole

Preparation Time: 15-minutes | Total time: 40-minutes | Yield: 6-servings

Ingredients:

1 medium Jalapeño pepper	1.75 lbs. Chicken thighs
Pepper and salt (to taste)	2 tbsps. Olive oil
1 ½ tsp. Chili seasoning	4 oz. Cheddar cheese
4 oz. Cream cheese	3 tbsps. Parmesan cheese
1 c. Green chilies and tomatoes	¼ c. Sour cream
1 pkg. Frozen cauliflower	

Directions:
Warm the oven to reach 375° Fahrenheit. Slice the jalapeño into pieces and set them aside. Cutaway the skin and bones from the chicken. Chop it and sprinkle it using pepper and salt. Prepare in a skillet using a portion of olive oil on the med-high temperature setting until browned. Mix in the sour cream, cream cheese, and ¾ of the cheddar cheese. Whisk until melted and combined well. Put in the tomatoes and chilies. Whisk then put it all to a baking dish. Cook the cauliflower in the microwave. Blend in the rest of the cheese with the immersion blender until it resembles mashed potatoes. Season as desired. Spread the cauliflower concoction over the casserole and sprinkle with the peppers. Bake approximately 15 to 20-minutes.

Nutritional Information: Calories: 426 |Net Carbs: 4.3 g |Total Fat Content: 32.2 g|Protein: 31 g

598. Chili & Lemon Marinated Chicken Wings

Preparation Time: 5-minutes | Total time: 17-minutes | Yield: 2-4-servings

Ingredients:

3 tbsp. olive oil	1 tsp coriander seeds
1 tsp xylitol	1 lb. wings
Juice from 1 lemon	½ c. fresh parsley, chopped
2 garlic cloves, minced	1 red chili pepper, chopped
Salt and black pepper, to taste	Lemon wedges, for serving
½ tsp cilantro	

Directions:
Using a bowl, Whisk together lemon juice, xylitol, garlic, salt, red chili pepper, cilantro, olive oil, and black pepper. Put in the chicken wings and toss well to coat. Refrigerate for 2 hours. Preheat grill over high heat. Add the chicken wings and grill each side for 6-minutes. Serve the chicken wings with lemon wedges.

Nutritional Information: Calories 223|Fat 12g|Net Carbs 5.1g|Protein 16.8g

599. Red Pepper and Mozzarella-Stuffed Chicken Caprese

Preparation Time: 10-minutes | Total time: 50-minutes | Yield: 2-servings

Ingredients:

2 tbsps. olive oil	2 butterflied chicken breasts
10 basil leaves, fresh	black pepper
1 (8 oz.) ball mozzarella cheese, sliced into 4 slices	1 c. Red Peppers, roasted
2 tbsps. Italian seasoning	Sea salt

Directions:
Preheat your oven to attain 400 degrees F. Line a parchment paper on a rimmed baking sheet. To the inside of each chicken breast, set in 5 basil leaves and 2 mozzarella slices. Divide red peppers equally and set them to your 2 breasts. Sprinkle with Italian seasoning, black pepper, and salt. Close the breasts to ensure the fillings are enveloped. Set your breasts to your prepared baking sheet and allow to bake for 40-minutes until well cooked. Serve while hot.

Nutritional Information: Calories: 539| Saturated Fat: 5g|Protein: 63g | Fiber: 1g |Net Carbs: 3g

600. Pork with Thyme Sweet Potatoes

Preparation Time: 10-minutes | Total time: 45-minutes | Yield: 4-servings

Ingredients:

2 sweet potatoes, cut into wedges	4 pork chops
3 spring onions, chopped	1 tbsp. thyme, chopped
2 tbsps. olive oil	4 garlic cloves, minced
Pinch of sea salt	Pinch black pepper
½ c. vegetable stock	½ tbsp. chives, chopped

Directions:
In a roasting pan, Mix the pork chops with the potatoes and the other ingredients, toss gently, and cook at 390

degrees F for 35-minutes. Divide everything between plates and serve.

Nutritional Information: Calories 210 | Fat 12.2 | Fiber 5.2 | Carbs 12 | Protein 10

601. Delightful Teriyaki Chicken Under Pressure

Preparation Time: 5-minutes | Total time: 25-minutes | Yield: 8-servings

Ingredients:

1 c. Chicken Broth	¾ c. Brown Sugar
2 tbsp. ground Ginger	1 tsp Pepper
3 lbs. Boneless and Skinless Chicken Thighs	¼ c. Apple Cider Vinegar
¾ c. low-sodium Soy Sauce	20 oz. canned Pineapple, crushed
2 tbsp. Garlic Powder	

Directions:

Mix each and every ingredient together, except the chicken. Add the chicken meat and turn to coat. Seal the lid, press POULTRY, and cook for 20-minutes at High. Do a quick pressure release by turning the valve to an "open" position.

Nutritional Information: Calories 352 | Carbs 31g | Fat 11g | Protein 31g

602. Cauliflower Lamb Meal

Preparation Time: five-minutes | Total time: 25-minutes | Yield: 4-servings

Ingredients:
Mash:

½ tsp. Garlic powder	½ tsp. salt
1 big head cauliflower, cut into florets	Dash cayenne pepper

Lamb:

½ tsp. freshly ground black pepper	1 tsp. dried rosemary
1 tsp. salt	2 (8 oz.) grass-fed lamb fillets
2 tbsps. avocado oil	

Directions:

In cooking (you can also use a deep cooking pan), put in the cauliflower and water to immerse it. Heat it over the medium stove flame. Boil and cook for about ten-minutes. Drain water and move the cauliflower to a food processor (or blender). Put in the ghee, garlic powder, salt, and cayenne pepper. Blend until smooth.
Spice the lamb with pepper and salt. In a frying pan or deep cooking pan, warm the oil on the medium stove flame. Put in the lamb, rosemary, and cook, while stirring, until it becomes uniformly brown for 8-ten-minutes. Cut the lamb into coins and serve with the cauliflower mash.

Nutritional Information: Calories 294, Fat: 17g, Carbohydrates: 11g, Fiber: 3g, Protein: 36g

603. Ground Beef with Cabbage

Preparation Time: 10-minutes | Total time: 25-minutes | Yield: 6-servings

Ingredients:

1 tbsp. olive oil	1 onion, sliced thinly
2 tsp. fresh ginger, minced	4 garlic cloves, minced
1 lb. lean ground beef	1½ tbsps. fish sauce
2 tbsps. fresh lime juice	1 small head of purple cabbage, shredded
2 tbsps. peanut butter	½ c. fresh cilantro, chopped

Directions:

In a huge skillet, warm oil on medium heat. Add onion, ginger, and garlic and sauté for about 4-5-minutes. Add beef and cook for approximately 7-8-minutes, getting into pieces using the spoon. Drain off the extra liquid in the skillet. Whisk in fish sauce and lime juice and cook for approximately 1 minute. Add cabbage and cook around 4-5-minutes or till the desired doneness. Whisk in peanut butter and cilantro and cook for about 1 minute. Serve hot.

Nutritional Information: Calories: 402 | Fat: 13g | Carbohydrates: 21g | Fiber: 10g | Protein: 33g

604. Tuscan Chicken Sauté

Preparation Time: 10-minutes | Total time: 45-minutes | Yield: 4-servings

Ingredients:

1 lb. boneless chicken breasts, each cut into three pieces	Sea salt for seasoning
Freshly ground black pepper for seasoning	3 tbsps. olive oil
1 tbsp. minced garlic	¾ c. chicken stock
1 tsp. Dried oregano	½ tsp. dried basil
½ c. heavy (whipping) cream	½ c. shredded Asiago cheese
1 c. fresh spinach	¼ c. sliced Kalamata olives

Directions:

Prepare the chicken. Pat the chicken, breasts dry, and lightly season them with salt and pepper. Sauté the chicken. In a large skillet over medium-high heat, warm the olive oil. Add the chicken and sauté until it is golden brown and just cooked through, about 15-minutes in total. Transfer the chicken to a plate and set it aside. Make the sauce. Put the garlic to the skillet, then sauté until it's softened for about 2-minutes. Whisk in the chicken stock, oregano, and basil, scraping up any browned bits in the skillet. Bring to a boil & reduce the heat to low and simmer until the sauce is reduced by about one-quarter, about 10-minutes. Finish the dish. Whisk in the cream, Asiago, and simmer, stirring the sauce frequently, until it has thickened about 5-minutes. Put back the chicken to the skillet along with any accumulated juices. Whisk in the spinach and olives and simmer until the spinach is wilted for about 2-minutes. Serve. Divide the chicken and sauce between four plates and serve it immediately.

Nutritional Information: Calories: 483 | Fat: 38g | Fiber: 1g; | Net carbs: 3g | Sodium: 332mg | Protein: 31g

605. Pork and Brown Rice

Preparation Time: 10-minutes | Total time: 50-minutes | Yield: 4-servings

Ingredients:

1 lb. pork stew meat, cubed	2 tbsps. avocado oil
1 yellow onion, chopped	1 c. brown rice
3 c. vegetable stock	2 tsp. sweet paprika
1 tsp. fennel seeds, crushed	A pinch of salt and black pepper
1 tbsp. parsley, chopped	

Directions:

Heat a pan with the oil over medium-high heat, add the onion and the meat, and brown for 10-minutes.

Add the rest of the ingredients, toss, cook over medium heat for 30-minutes more, divide between plates and serve.

Nutritional Information: calories 440, fat 13.9, fiber 3.2, carbs 40.6, protein 37.4

606. Blue Cheese Buffalo Chicken Balls

Preparation Time: 10-minutes | Total time: 28-minutes | Yield: 4-6-servings

Ingredients:

1 lb. free-range ground chicken	1 large free-range egg, lightly beaten
1 c. shredded organic mozzarella cheese	½ c. crumbled organic blue cheese
¼ c. chopped celery	2 tbsps. water
1 tsp. Onion powder	½ tsp. Sea salt
½ tsp. freshly ground black pepper	1 recipe Buffalo Sauce

Directions:

Preheat the oven to 450°F. Line a baking pan with parchment paper. Put and mix the chicken, egg, mozzarella, blue cheeses, celery, water, onion powder, salt, and pepper in a large bowl. Mix the ingredients well using your hands. Make 20 meatballs into a mixture, then put them inside the baking-pan as you do. Bake for about 18-minutes until the internal temp reaches 165 degrees F. On the other hand, warm the buffalo sauce in a medium saucepan over low heat. When the meatballs are done, toss them in the warm sauce and serve.

Nutritional Information: Calories: 340 | Saturated Fat: 6g | Protein: 44g | Fiber: 0g | Net Carbs: 2g

607. Beef with Asparagus & Bell Pepper

Preparation Time: 15-minutes | Total time: 28-minutes | Yield: 4-5-servings

Ingredients:

1 bunch asparagus, trimmed and halved	1 red bell pepper, seeded and cut
1/8 tsp. ground ginger	1/8 tsp. red pepper flakes, crushed
1 lb. flank steak, trimmed and sliced thinly	2 tbsps. olive oil, divided
2 tsp. arrowroot powder	3 tbsps. coconut aminos
3 tbsps. water	4 garlic cloves, minced
Freshly ground black pepper, to taste	

Directions:

Mix garlic, coconut aminos, red pepper flakes, crushed, ground ginger, and black pepper in a container. Keep aside. Cook the asparagus inside a pan of boiling-water for approximately 2-minutes. Drain and wash under cold water. In a substantial frying pan, heat 1 tbsp. Of oil on moderate to high heat. Put in beef and Whisk fry for about four-minutes. With a slotted spoon, move the beef to a container. In a similar frying pan, heat the remaining oil on moderate heat. Put in asparagus and bell pepper and Whisk fry for roughly 2-3-minutes.

In the meantime, in the container, Mix water and arrowroot powder. Mix beef, garlic, and arrowroot mixture, and cook for about four-minutes or preferred thickness.

Nutritional Information: Calories: 399, Fat: 17g Carbohydrates: 27g, Fiber: 8g, Protein: 35g

608. Pork and Cumin Pinto Beans

Preparation Time: 10-minutes | Total time: 1-hour 10-minutes | Yield: 4-servings

Ingredients:

2 lbs. pork stew meat, roughly cubed	1 c. canned pinto beans, drained and rinsed

4 scallions, chopped	2 tbsps. olive oil
1 tbsp. chili powder	2 tsp. cumin, ground
A pinch of black pepper and sea salt	2 garlic cloves, minced
1 c. vegetable stock	Handful parsley, chopped

Directions:

Heat a pan with the oil over medium-high heat, add the scallions and the garlic and sauté for 5-minutes. Add the meat and then brown for about 5-minutes more. Add the beans and the other ingredients, toss, introduce the pan in the oven and cook everything at 380 degrees F for 50-minutes. Divide the mix between plates and serve.

Nutritional Information: calories 291, fat 4, fiber 10, carbs 15, protein 24

609. Chicken & Apple Cider Chili

Preparation Time: 15-minutes | Total time: 7-8 hours + 15-minutes | Yield: 4-servings

Ingredients:

3 c. chopped cooked chicken (see Basic "Rotisserie" Chicken)	1 medium onion, chopped
1 (15 oz.) can diced tomatoes	3 c. Chicken Bone Broth or store-bought chicken broth
1 c. apple cider	2 bay leaves
1 tbsp. extra-virgin olive oil	2 tsp. garlic powder
1 tsp. chili powder	1 tsp. sea salt
½ tsp. ground cumin	¼ tsp. ground cinnamon
Pinch cayenne pepper	Freshly ground black pepper
¼ c. apple cider vinegar	

Directions:

In your slow cooker, Mix the chicken, onion, tomatoes, broth, cider, bay leaves, olive oil, garlic powder, chili powder, salt, cumin, cinnamon cayenne, and season with black pepper. Cover the cooker. Then set it to low heat. Cook for 7 to 8 hours. Remove and discard the bay leaves. Whisk in the apple cider vinegar until well blended and serve.

Nutritional Information: Calories: 469| Fat: 8g| Carbs: 46g | Sugar: 13g | Fiber: 9g | Protein: 51g |

610. Delicious Roasted Duck

Preparation Time: 10-minutes | Total time: 5-hours | Yield: 4-servings

Ingredients:

| 1 medium duck | 1 celery stalk, chopped |

2 yellow onions, chopped	2 tsp. thyme, dried
8 garlic cloves, minced	2 bay leaves
¼ c. parsley, chopped	A pinch of salt and black pepper
One tsp. herbs de Provence	

For the sauce:

1 tbsp. tomato paste	1 yellow onion, chopped
½ tsp. sugar	3 c. water
1 c. chicken stock	1 ½ c. black olives, pitted and chopped
¼ tsp. herbs de Provence	

Directions:

In a baking dish, arrange thyme, parsley, garlic, and 2 onions. Add duck, season with salt, 1 tsp. Herbs de Provence and pepper. Put in the oven at 475 degrees F and roast for 10-minutes. Cover the dish, reduce heat to 275 degrees F, and roast duck for 3 hours and 30-minutes. Meanwhile, heat a pan over medium-heat, add 1 yellow onion, Whisk, and cook for 10-minutes. Add tomato paste, stock, sugar, ¼ tsp. Herbs de Provence, olives, and water, cover, reduce heat to low, and cook for 1 hour. Transfer duck to a work surface, carve, discard bones, and divide between plates. Drizzle the sauce all over and serve right away.

Nutritional Information: Calories: 254 | Fat: 3 | Fiber: 3 | Carbs: 8 | Protein: 13

611. Adobo Lime Chicken Mix

Preparation Time: 10-minutes | Total time: 50-minutes | Yield: 6-servings

Ingredients:

6 chicken thighs	Salt and black pepper to the taste
1 tbsp. olive oil	Zest of 1 lime
1½ tsps. chipotle peppers in adobo sauce	1 c. sliced peach
1 tbsp. lime juice	

Directions:

Warm a pan with the oil on medium-high heat and add the chicken thighs. Season with salt and pepper, then brown for 4-minutes on each side and bake in the oven at 375 degrees F for 20-minutes. In your food processor, mix the peaches with the chipotle, lime zest, and lime juice, then blend and pour over the chicken. Bake for 10-minutes more, divide everything between plates and serve. Enjoy!

Nutritional Information: Calories: 309 | Fat: 6 | Fiber: 4 | Carbs: 16 | Protein: 15

612. Ground Beef with Cashews & Veggies

Preparation Time: 15-minutes | Total time: 30-minutes | Yield: 4-servings

Ingredients:

1½ lb. lean ground beef	1 tbsp. garlic, minced
2 tbsps. fresh ginger, minced	¼ c. coconut aminos
Salt, to taste	Freshly ground black pepper, to taste
1 medium onion, sliced	1 can water chestnuts, drained, and sliced
1 large green bell pepper, sliced	½ c. raw cashews, toasted

Directions:

Heat a nonstick skillet on medium-high heat. Add beef and cook for about 6-8-minutes, breaking into pieces with all the spoons. Add garlic, ginger, coconut aminos, salt, and black pepper and cook for approximately 2-minutes. Put the vegetables and cook for about 5-minutes or till the desired doneness. Whisk in cashews and immediately remove from heat. Serve hot.

Nutritional Information: Calories: 452 | Fat: 20g | Carbohydrates: 26g | Fiber: 9g | Protein: 36g

613. Pork with Scallions and Cauliflower

Preparation Time: 10-minutes | Total time: 8 hours 10-minutes | Yield: 4-servings

Ingredients:

2 lbs. pork roast, sliced	4 scallions, chopped
2 garlic cloves, minced	1 yellow onion, chopped
2 tbsps. olive oil	1 c. cauliflower florets
½ c. vegetable stock	A pinch of salt and black pepper
A pinch of red chili pepper flakes	

Directions:

In your slow cooker, mix the pork roast with the scallions, the garlic, and the other ingredients, toss, put the lid on and cook on Low for 8 hours. Divide everything between plates and serve.

Nutritional Information: calories 556, fat 29, fiber 1.7, carbs 6, protein 65.8

614. Basil Chicken Sauté

Preparation Time: ten-minutes | Total time: 25-minutes | Yield: 2-servings

Ingredients:

1 chicken breast, minced or chopped minuscule	1 chili pepper, diced (not necessary)
1 c. basil leaves, finely chopped	1 Tbsp. tamari sauce
2 cloves garlic, minced	2 Tbsps. avocado or coconut oil to cook in
Salt, to taste	

Directions:

Put in oil to a frying pan and sauté the garlic and pepper. Then put in the minced chicken and sauté until the chicken is cooked. Put in the tamari sauce and salt to taste. Put in in the basil leaves and mix it in.

Nutritional Information: Calories: 320, Fat: 24 g, Net Carbohydrates: 2 g, Protein: 24 g

615. Hidden Valley Chicken Dummies

Preparation Time: 15-minutes | Total time: 45-minutes | Yield: 4 serving

Ingredients:

2 tbsps. Hot sauce	½ c. melted butter
Celery sticks	2 packages Hidden Valley dressing dry mix
3 tbsps. Vinegar	12 chicken drumsticks
Paprika	

Directions:

Preheat the oven to 350 degrees F. Rinse and pat dry the chicken. In a bowl, blend the dry dressing, melted butter, vinegar, and hot sauce. Whisk until combined. Put the drumsticks in a large plastic baggie, pour the sauce over the drumsticks. Massage the sauce until the drumsticks are coated. Put the chicken in a single layer on a baking dish. Sprinkle with paprika. Bake for 30-minutes, flipping halfway. Serve with crudité or salad.

Nutritional Information: Calories: 155 | Fat: 18 g | Carbs: 96 g | Protein:15 g | Sugars: 0.7 g |

616. Chicken Piccata

Preparation Time: 15-minutes | Total time: 45-minutes | Yield: 4-servings

Ingredients:

4 boneless, skinless chicken breasts	1 c. ground almond meal
1/4 c. grated Parmesan cheese	1/2 tsp. Dijon mustard
1 yellow onion, chopped	1 tsp. of sea salt
1/2 tsp. ground black pepper	4 tbsps. olive oil
4 tbsps. organic unsalted butter	1/2 c. organic, gluten-free chicken broth
3 tbsps. lemon juice	2 tbsps. capers
3 tbsps. organic butter	1/4 c. fresh parsley, chopped

Directions:
Mix the almond meal, cheese, mustard, salt, and pepper spread the mixture on a shallow dish. Wash the pounded chicken breasts in water and shake off the excess. Dredge the chicken in the flour mixture. Add tbsps. Of butter in a large saucepan over high heat, add the olive oil. Cook chicken in butter and oil for approximately 3-4-minutes on each side until golden brown. Put the cooked chicken on a serving dish and cover to keep warm. Whisk in the chicken broth, lemon juice, and capers, scraping up any brown bits in the pan. Add the chicken broth, lemon juice, and capers to the skillet, stirring and scraping up any brown bits in the skillet. Simmer until the sauce is reduced and reaches a light syrup consistency. Reduce heat to low and Whisk in remaining butter. Spoon the sauce over the chicken breasts and top with chopped parsley. Serve with lemon slices or wedges.
Nutritional Information: Calories: 357 kcal | Protein: 4.51 g | Fat: 35.73 g | Carbohydrates: 6.16 g

617. Turkey Breast with Fennel and Celery
Preparation Time: 10-minutes | Total time: 25-minutes | Yield: 3-servings

Ingredients:

2 lbs. Boneless and Skinless Turkey Breast	1 c. Fennel Bulb, chopped
1 c. celery with leaves, chopped	2 ¼ c. Chicken Stock
¼ tsp Pepper	¼ tsp Garlic Powder

Directions:
Throw all ingredients in your pressure cooker. Give it an excellent Whisk and seal the lid. Press PRESSURE COOK/MANUAL and cook for 15-minutes at High. Do a quick pressure release. Shred the turkey with two forks.
Nutritional Information: Calories 272 | Carbs 7g | Fat 4g | Protein 48g

618. Allspice Pork Mix
Preparation Time: 10-minutes | Total time: 1-hour 10-minutes | Yield: 4-servings

Ingredients:

2 tbsps. olive oil	2 lbs. pork stew meat, cubed
1 tsp. cumin, ground	1 tbsp. sage, chopped
1 yellow onion, chopped	1 c. vegetable stock
A pinch of salt and black pepper	1 tsp. Chili pepper flakes, dried
½ tsp. allspice, ground	

Directions:
Heat a pan with the oil over medium-high heat, add the onion and the meat, and brown for 10-minutes. Add the rest of the ingredients, toss, introduce in the oven and bake at 390 degrees F for 50-minutes. Divide everything between plates and serve.
Nutritional Information: calories 261, fat 4, fiber 7, carbs 12, protein 18

619. Traditional Hungarian Gulyás
Preparation Time: 10-minutes | Total time: 1-hour 20-minutes | Yield: 4-servings

Ingredients:

1/2 c. celery ribs, chopped	1 ripe tomato, pureed
1 tbsp. spice mix for goulash	2 (1 oz.) slices bacon, chopped
1/2 lb. duck legs, skinless and boneless	

Directions:
Heat a heavy-bottomed pot over the medium-high flame; then, fry the bacon for about 3-minutes. Whisk in the duck legs and continue to cook until they are nicely browned on all sides. Shred the meat and discarded the bones. Set aside. In the pan drippings, sauté the celery for about 3-minutes, stirring with a wide spatula. Add in pureed tomatoes and spice mix for goulash; add in the reserved bacon and meat. Pour over two cups of chicken broth or water into the pot.
Put heat to medium-low, cover, and simmer for 50-minutes more or until everything is cooked thoroughly. Serve warm and enjoy!
Nutritional Information: 363 Calories | 22.3g Fat | 5.1g Carbs | 3.2g Protein | 1.4g Fiber

620. Turnip Greens & Artichoke Chicken
Preparation Time: 5-minutes | Total time: 35-minutes | Yield: 2-servings

Ingredients:

4 oz. cream cheese	2 chicken breasts
4 oz. canned artichoke hearts, chopped	1 c. turnip greens
¼ c. Pecorino cheese, grated	½ tbsp. Onion powder
½ tbsp. garlic powder	Salt and black pepper, to taste
2 oz. Monterrey Jack cheese, shredded	

Directions:
Line a baking dish using parchment paper and put it in the chicken breasts. Season with black pepper and salt.

Set in the oven at 350 F and bake for 35-minutes. Mix the artichokes with onion powder, Pecorino cheese, salt, turnip greens, cream cheese, garlic powder, and black pepper in a bowl. Take off the chicken from the oven, cut each piece in half, divide the artichokes mixture on top, spread with Monterrey cheese, and bake for 5 more-minutes.

Nutritional Information: Calories 443 | Fat 24.5g | Net Carbs 4.2g | Protein 35.4g

621. Balsamic-Glazed Turkey Wings

Preparation Time: 15-minutes | Total time: 7 – 8 hours + 15-minutes | Yield: 4-servings

Ingredients:

1¼ c. balsamic vinegar	2 tbsps. raw honey
1 tsp. garlic powder	2 pounds' turkey wings

Directions:

In a bowl, put together the vinegar, honey, and garlic powder, then mix. Put the wings in the bottom of the slow cooker and pour the vinegar sauce on top.
Cover the cooker. Set it to low heat, and then cook for about 7 to 8 hours. Baste the wings with the sauce from the bottom of the slow cooker and serve.

Nutritional Information: Calories: 501 | Fat: 25g | Sugar: 7g | Fiber: 0g | Protein: 47g |

622. Spicy Almond Chicken Strips with Garlic Lime Tartar Sauce

Preparation Time: 10-minutes | Total time: 20-minutes | Yield: 4-servings

Ingredients:
Chicken sticks:

1 ½ lb. chicken breast, cut into 1x5-inch pieces	2 organic free-range eggs, whisked
1/2 c. blanched almond flour	1/2 tsp. ground cayenne pepper
1/4 c. dried basil	3 cloves garlic, finely chopped
1 tsp. salt	1/4 tsp. freshly ground black pepper
1/2 c. coconut oil	

Garlic Lime Tartar Sauce:

1 c. mayonnaise	1 tsp. garlic powder
2 tbsps. lime juice	1 1/2 tbsp. dill pickle relish
1 tbsp. dried onion flakes	1/2 tsp. salt

Directions:
Whisk together each ingredient for the tartar sauce until well-combined. Chill for at least30-minutes until serving. Whisk eggs in a medium bowl. Mix almond flour, cayenne pepper, basil, garlic, salt, and pepper in another bowl. Dip chicken strips in egg, then flour mixture; coat well and Put sticks on a plate. Heat some coconut oil in a saucepan over medium-high heat. Add half of the chicken strips and cook for 2-3-minutes on each side until well-browned. Leave enough room around chicken strips so that they aren't overcrowded. Drain sticks on paper towels on a plate. Heat another 1/4 cup coconut oil and cook the remaining half of the chicken strips. Serve with the prepared Garlic Lime Tartar Sauce.

Nutritional Information: Calories: 1092 kcal | Protein: 94.15 g | Fat: 75.01 g | Carbohydrates: 7.5 g

623. Turkey Ham and Mozzarella Pate

Preparation Time: 10-minutes | Total time: 10-minutes | Yield: 6-servings

Ingredients:

4 oz. turkey ham, chopped	2 tbsps. fresh parsley, roughly chopped
2 tbsps. flaxseed meal	4 oz. mozzarella cheese, crumbled
2 tbsps. sunflower seeds	

Directions:
Thoroughly Mix the ingredients, except for the sunflower seeds, in your food processor. Spoon the mixture into a serving bowl and scatter the sunflower seeds over the top.

Nutritional Information: 212 Calorie | 18.8g Fat | 2g Carbs | 10.6g Protein | 1.6g Fiber

624. Nutty Pesto Chicken Supreme

Preparation Time: 10-minutes | Total time: 40-minutes | Yield: 2-servings

Ingredients:

2 Free ranges skinless chicken/ turkey breasts	1 bunch of fresh basil
1/2 c. raw spinach	1 c. Crashed macadamias/almonds/walnuts or a combination
2 tbsp. Extra virgin olive oil	1/2 c. low-fat hard cheese (optional)

Directions:
Set the oven to 350°F. Get the chicken breasts and use a meat pounder to 'thin' each breast into a 1cm thick escalope. Reserve a handful of the nuts before adding the rest of the ingredients and a little black pepper to a blender or pestle and mortar and blend until smooth (you can leave this a little chunky for a rustic feel if you wish). Add a little water if the pesto needs loosening.

Coat the chicken in the pesto. Bake for at least 30-minutes in the oven or until chicken is completely cooked through. Top each chicken escalope with the remaining nuts and Put under the broiler for 5-minutes for a crispy topping to complete.

Nutritional Information: Calories: 2539 kcal | Protein: 444.61 g | Fat: 71.66 g | Carbohydrates: 5.99 g

625. Pork with Olives

Preparation Time: 10-minutes | Total time: 50-minutes | Yield: 4-servings

Ingredients:

1 yellow onion, chopped	4 pork chops
2 tbsps. olive oil	1 tbsp. sweet paprika
2 tbsps. balsamic vinegar	1/4 c. Kalamata olives
1 tbsp. cilantro, chopped	A pinch of Sea Salt
A pinch of black pepper	

Directions:

Warm a pan with the oil on medium heat; add the onion and sauté for 5-minutes. Attach the meat and brown for a further 5-minutes. Set the rest of the ingredients, toss, cook over medium heat for 30-minutes, divide between plates and serve.

Nutritional Information: Calories: 280, Fat: 11 g, Fiber: 6 g, Carbs: 10 g, Protein: 21 g

626. Oregano Pork Pan

Preparation Time: 10-minutes | Total time: 50-minutes | Yield: 4-servings

Ingredients:

1 tbsp. olive oil	2 spring onions, chopped
2 lbs. pork stew meat, cut into strips	1 zucchini, cubed
1 red bell pepper, cut into strips	1 green bell pepper, cut into strips
2 tomatoes, cubed	1 tsp. coriander, ground
1 tsp. oregano, dried	A pinch of salt and black pepper
1 tsp. ginger, grated	

Directions:

Heat a pan with the oil over medium-high heat, add the spring onions, ginger, and the meat, and brown for 10-minutes stirring from time to time. Add the rest of the ingredients, toss, cook over medium heat for 30-minutes more, divide between plates and serve.

Nutritional Information: calories 270, fat 3, fiber 6, carbs 8, protein 15

627. Spicy & Creamy Ground Beef Curry

Preparation Time: 15-minutes | Total time: 47-minutes | Yield: 4-servings

Ingredients:

1-2 tbsps. coconut oil	1 tsp. black mustard seeds
2 sprigs curry leaves	1 Serrano pepper, minced
1 large red onion, chopped finely	1 (1-inch) fresh ginger, minced
4 garlic cloves, minced	1 tsp. ground coriander
1 tsp. ground cumin	½ tsp. ground turmeric
¼ tsp. red chili powder	Salt, to taste
1 lb. lean ground beef	1 potato, peeled and chopped
3 medium carrots, peeled and chopped	¼ c. water
1 (14 oz.) can coconut milk	Salt, to taste
Freshly ground black pepper, to taste	Chopped fresh cilantro for garnishing

Directions:

In a big pan, melt coconut oil on medium heat. Add mustard seeds and sauté for about thirty seconds. Add curry leaves and Serrano pepper and sauté for approximately half a minute. Add onion, ginger, and garlic and sauté for about 4-5-minutes. Add spices and cook for about 1 minute. Add beef and cook for about 4-5-minutes. Whisk in potato, carrot, and water and provide with a gentle simmer. Simmer, covered for around 5-minutes. Whisk in coconut milk and simmer for approximately fifteen-minutes. Whisk in salt and black pepper and remove from heat. Serve hot while using garnishing of cilantro.

Nutritional Information: Calories: 432 | Fat: 14g | Carbohydrates: 22g | Fiber: 8 | Protein: 39g

628. BBQ Chicken Zucchini Boats

Preparation Time: 10-minutes | Total time: 25 – 30-minutes | Yield: 4-servings

Ingredients:

3 Zucchini halved	1 lb. cooked Chicken breast
½ c. BBQ sauce	1/3 c. Shredded Mexican cheese
1 Avocado, sliced	½ c. Halved cherry tomatoes
¼ c. Diced green onions	3 tbsps. Keto-friendly ranch dressing
Also Needed: 9x13 casserole dish	

Directions:

Set the oven to reach 350° Fahrenheit. Using a knife, cut the zucchini in half. Discard the seeds. Make the boat by carving out of the center. Put the zucchini flesh side up into the casserole dish. Discard and cut the skin and bones from the chicken. Shred and add the chicken in with the barbeque sauce. Toss to coat all the chicken entirely. Fill the zucchini boats with the mixture using about .25 to .33 cups each. Sprinkle with Mexican cheese on top. Bake for approximately 15-minutes. (If you would like it tenderer, bake for an additional 5 to 10-minutes to reach the desired tenderness.) Remove from the oven. Top it off with avocado, green onion, tomatoes, and a drizzle of dressing. Serve.

Nutritional Information: Calories: 212 | Net Carbs: 9 g | Total Fat Content: 11 g | Protein: 19 g

629. Italian Meatballs in Asiago Sauce

Preparation time: 15-minutes | Total time: 30-minutes | Yield: 3-servings

Ingredients:

1 tsp. Italian spice mix	1/2 lb. ground beef
1 egg	3 oz. Asiago cheese, grated
1/4 c. mayonnaise	

Directions:

In a mixing bowl, thoroughly Mix Italian slice mix, beef, and egg. Mix until everything is well combined. Roll the mixture into meatballs. In another bowl, mix Asiago cheese and mayonnaise. Heat 1 tbsp. Of olive oil in a frying pan over moderate heat. Then, sear the meatballs for about 5-minutes, turning them occasionally to ensure even cooking. Bon appétit!

Nutritional Information: 458 Calories; 35.8g Fat; 4.3g Carbs; 28.2g Protein; 0.2g Fiber

630. Parsley Pork and Artichokes

Preparation Time: 10-minutes | Total time: 45-minutes | Yield: 4-servings

Ingredients:

2 tbsp. balsamic vinegar	1 c. canned artichoke hearts, drained
2 tbsp. olive oil	2 lb. pork stew meat, cubed
2 tbsp. parsley, chopped	1 tsp. cumin, ground
1 tsp. turmeric powder	2 garlic cloves, minced
Pinch of sea salt	Pinch black pepper

Directions:

Warm a pan with the oil on medium heat, add the meat, and brown for 5-minutes. Add the artichokes, the vinegar, and the other ingredients, toss, cook over medium heat for 30-minutes, divide between plates and serve.

Nutritional Information: Calories 260 | Fat 5 | Fiber 4 | Carbs 11 | Protein 20

631. Cheesy Chicken Sun-Dried Tomato Packets

Preparation Time: 15-minutes | Total time: 55-minutes | Yield: 4-servings

Ingredients:

1 c. goat cheese	½ c. chopped oil-packed sun-dried tomatoes
1 tsp. Minced garlic	½ tsp. Dried basil
½ tsp. dried oregano	4 (4 oz.) boneless chicken breasts
Sea salt for seasoning	Freshly ground black pepper for seasoning
3 tbsps. olive oil	

Directions:

Preheat the oven. Set the oven temperature to 375°F. Prepare the filling. Put the goat cheese, sun-dried tomatoes, garlic, basil, and oregano in a medium bowl, then mix until everything is well blended. Stuff the chicken. Make a horizontal-slice in the center of each chicken-breast to make a pocket, making sure not to cut through the sides or ends. Spoon one-quarter of the filling into each breast, folding the skin and chicken meat over the slit to form packets. Secure the packets with a toothpick. Season the breasts lightly with pepper and salt. Brown the chicken. In a large oven-safe skillet, warm the olive oil over a medium-heat. Add the breasts and sear them, turning them once, until they are golden, about 8-minutes in total. Bake the chicken. Bring the skillet into the oven and bake the chicken for 30-minutes or until it's cooked through. Serve. Remove the toothpicks. Divide the chicken into 4 plates and serve them immediately.

Nutritional Information: Calories: 388 | Fat: 29g | Fiber: 1g; Net carbs: 3g | Sodium: 210mg | Protein: 28g

632. Pork with Corn and Peas

Preparation Time: 10-minutes | Total time: 50-minutes | Yield: 4-servings

Ingredients:

2 lbs. pork stew meat, cut into strips	½ c. corn
½ c. green peas	2 tbsps. olive oil
½ c. yellow onion, chopped	3 tbsps. coconut aminos
½ c. vegetable stock	A pinch of salt and black pepper

Directions:

Heat a pan using the oil over medium heat, add the meat and the onion, and brown for 10-minutes. Add the corn and the other ingredients, toss, cook over medium heat for 30-minutes more, divide between plates, and serve.

Nutritional Information: calories 250, fat 4, fiber 6, carbs 9.7, protein 12

633. Slow Cooker Jerk Chicken

Preparation Time: 10-minutes | Total time: 5-hours 10-minutes | Yield: 4-servings

Ingredients:

chicken drumsticks and 8 chicken wings	4 tsp. (20 g) salt
4 tsp. (9 g) paprika	1 tsp. (2 g) cayenne pepper
2 tsp. (5 g) onion powder	2 tsp. (3 g) dried thyme
2 tsp. (4 g) white pepper	2 tsp. (6 g) garlic powder
1 tsp. (2 g) black pepper	

Directions:

Put all the spices in a bowl, then mix to make a run for the chicken. Wash the chicken meat in cold water briefly. Put the washed chicken meat into the bowl with the rub, and rub the spices onto the meat thoroughly, including under the skin. Put each piece of chicken covered with the spices into the slow cooker (no liquid required). Set the slow cooker on medium heat and cook for 5 hours or until the chicken meat falls off the bone.

Nutritional Information: Calories: 480 | Fat: 30 g | Net Carbohydrates: 4 g | Protein: 45 g

634. Pork and Creamy Leeks

Preparation Time: 10-minutes | Total time: 1 hour 5-minutes | Yield: 4-servings

Ingredients:

2 lbs. pork stew meat, cubed	3 leeks, sliced
2 tbsps. olive oil	1 tsp. black peppercorns
1 tbsp. parsley, chopped	2 c. coconut cream
1 tsp. Rosemary, dried	A pinch of black pepper and salt

Directions:

Heat a pan using the oil over medium heat, add the leeks and the meat, and brown for 5-minutes. Add the rest of the ingredients, toss, put the pan in the oven and bake at 390 degrees F for 50-minutes. Divide everything into bowls and serve.

Nutritional Information: calories 280, fat 5, fiber 7, carbs 12, protein 18

635. Avocado Pineapple Pork

Preparation Time: ten-minutes | Total time: 50-minutes | Yield: 4-servings

Ingredients:

(ground) black pepper and salt to taste	¼ c. cilantro, chopped
1 mango, chopped	1 lb. pork, ground
1 tbsp. olive oil	1 tsp. chili powder
1 tsp. cumin	1 tsp. garlic powder
2 avocados, pitted, peeled, and chopped	8 oz. canned pineapple, crushed
Juice of 1 lime	

Directions:

In a frying pan or deep cooking pan, warm the oil on the medium stove flame. Put the pork and cook, while stirring, until it becomes uniformly brown. Put in the garlic, cumin, chili powder, salt, and pepper, Whisk cook for 7-8-minutes. Put in the pineapple, mango, avocados, lime juice, cilantro, salt, and pepper; stir-cook for five-minutes. Split between serving plates before you serve.

Nutritional Information: Calories 238, Fat: 6g, Carbohydrates: 12g, Fiber: 7g, Protein: 17g

636. Slow Turkey

Preparation Time: 15-minutes | Total time: 4-hours 45-minutes | Yield: 4-6-servings

Ingredients:

Olive oil (1 tablespoon)	Cumin (2 tablespoons)
Garlic powder (1/2 teaspoon)	Turkey broth (5 cups)
Canned tomatoes (3 ½ cups, diced)	Cooked Turkey (2 cups, chopped)
Red Onion (1/2, diced)	Oregano (1/2 tablespoon)
Parsley (1 tablespoon)	Tomato paste (3/4 cup)
Bell peppers (2, diced)	Avocado
Cilantro	

Directions:

Set cooker on low and put in all ingredients and stir. Cook for 8 hours. Serve topped with avocado and cilantro.

Nutritional Information: Calories 122 Fat 5 g Saturated Fat 0.5 g Carbohydrates 9.3 g Protein 4.6 g

637. Cumin Pork and Beans

Preparation Time: 10-minutes | Total time: 1 hour 10-minutes | Yield: 4-servings

Ingredients:

2 lbs. pork stew meat, roughly cubed	1 c. canned pinto beans, drained and rinsed

4 scallions, chopped	2 tbsps. olive oil
1 tbsp. chili powder	2 tsp. cumin, ground
A pinch of salt and black-pepper	2 garlic cloves, minced
1 c. vegetable stock	Handful parsley, chopped

Directions:

Heat a pan with the oil over medium-high heat, add the scallions and the garlic and sauté for 5-minutes. Add the meat and brown for 5-minutes more. Add the beans and the other ingredients, toss, introduce the pan in the oven and cook everything at 380 degrees F for 50-minutes. Divide the mix between plates and serve.

Nutritional Information: calories 291, fat 4, fiber 10, carbs 15, protein 24

638. Flying Jacob Casserole

Preparation Time: 15-minutes | Total time: 35 – 40-minutes | Yield: 6-servings

Ingredients:

1 pc Grilled Chicken	2 tbsp. Butter
225 g Diced bacon	250 g Mushrooms
475 ml Cream	125 ml hot chili sauce
1 tsp. Seasoning curry	Salt and black pepper to taste
Salad	175 g Spinach
2 pcs Tomato	

Directions:

Preheat the oven to 400 ° F. Chop the mushrooms into small pieces, then fry in oil with bacon. Salt and pepper to taste. Separate the chicken meat from the bones and chop it into small pieces. Put these pieces of chicken in a mold for baking, oiled. Add mushrooms and bacon. Beat the cream until soft peaks. Put chili sauce, curry, and salt, and pepper to taste. Pour the chicken into the resulting mixture. Bake in the oven for at least 20-25-minutes until the dish gets a pleasant golden color. Serve with salad.

Nutritional Information: Carbohydrates: 11 g | Fats: 80 g | Proteins: 40 g | Calories: 912

639. Caraway and Dill Pork

Preparation Time: 10-minutes | Total time: 55-minutes | Yield: 4-servings

Ingredients:

2 lbs. pork meat, cubed	1 yellow onion, chopped
2 tbsps. olive oil	1 c. vegetable stock
1 tsp. caraway seeds	A pinch of salt and black pepper
2 tbsps. dill, chopped	

Directions:

Heat a pan using the oil over medium heat, add the onion and sauté for 5-minutes. Add the meat & brown for about 5-minutes more. Add the remaining ingredients, toss, cook over medium heat for 35-minutes, divide between plates, and serve.

Nutritional Information: calories 300, fat 12.8, fiber 6, carbs 12, protein 16

640. Asian Saucy Chicken

Preparation Time: 10-minutes | Total time: 25-minutes | Yield: 4-servings

Ingredients:

1 tbsp. sesame oil	4 chicken legs
2 tbsps. brown erythritol	1/4 c. spicy tomato sauce

Directions:

Heat the sesame oil in a wok at medium-high heat. Fry the chicken until golden in color, reserve. Add in erythritol and spicy tomato sauce and bring the mixture to a boil. Then, immediately reduce the heat to medium-low. Let it simmer for about 10-minutes until the sauce coats the back of a spoon. Add the chicken back to the wok. Continue to cook until the chicken is sticky and golden, or about 4-minutes. Enjoy!

Nutritional Information: 367 Calories | 14.7g Fat | 3.5g Carbs | 51.2g Protein | 1.1g Fiber

641. Super Sesame Chicken Noodles

Preparation Time: 10-minutes | Total time: 20-minutes | Yield: 2-servings

Ingredients:

2 Free-range skinless chicken breasts, chopped	1 c. Rice/Buck-wheat noodles such as Japanese Udo
1 Carrot, chopped	1/2 orange juiced
1 tsp. Sesame Seed	2 tsp. Coconut Oil
1 Thumb size piece of ginger, minced	1/2 c. Sugar snap peas

Directions:

Warm 1 tsp oil on medium heat in a skillet. Sauté the chopped chicken breast for about 10-15-minutes or until cooked through. While cooking the chicken, Put the noodles, carrots, and peas in a pot of boiling water for about 5-minutes. Drain. Mix the ginger, sesame seeds, 1 tsp oil, and orange juice to make your dressing in a bowl. Once the chicken is cooked and noodles are cooked and drained, add the chicken, noodles, carrots, and peas to the dressing and toss. Serve warm or chilled.

Nutritional Information: Calories: 168 kcal | Protein: 5.31 g | Fat: 8.66 g | Carbohydrates: 19.34 g

642. Exquisite Pear and Onion Goose

Preparation Time: 15-minutes | Total time: 35-minutes | Yield: 8-servings

Ingredients:

2 c. Chicken Broth	1 tbsp. Butter
½ c. slice Onions	½ tsp Pepper
¼ tsp Garlic Powder	3 Pears, peeled and sliced
1 tsp Cayenne Pepper	2 tbsp. Balsamic Vinegar
1 ½ lb. Goose, chopped into large pieces	

Directions:

Melt the butter on sauté. Add the goose and cook until it becomes golden on all sides. Transfer to a plate. Add the onions and cook for 2-minutes. Return the goose to the cooker. Add the rest of the ingredients, whisk well to Mix, and seal the lid. Select PRESSURE COOK/MANUAL mode and set the timer to 18-minutes at High Pressure. Do a quick pressure release. Serve and enjoy!

Nutritional Information: Calories 313 | Carbs 14g | Fat 8g | Protein 38g

643. Ground Beef & Veggies Curry

Preparation Time: 15-minutes | Total time: 51-minutes | Yield: 6 – 8-servings

Ingredients:

2-3 tbsps. coconut oil	1 c. onion, chopped
1 garlic clove, minced	1 lb. lean ground beef
1½ tbsps. curry powder	1/8 tsp. ground ginger
1/8 tsp. ground cinnamon	1/8 tsp. ground turmeric
Salt, to taste	2½-3 c. tomatoes, chopped finely
2½-3 c. fresh peas shelled	2 sweet potatoes, peeled and chopped

Directions:

In a sizable pan, melt coconut oil on medium heat.
Add onion and garlic and sauté for around 4-5-minutes. Add beef and cook for about 4-5-minutes. Add curry powder and spices and cook for about 1 minute.
Whisk in tomatoes, peas, and sweet potato and bring to your gentle simmer. Simmer covered approximately 25-minutes.

Nutritional Information: Calorie: 432 | Fat: 16g | Carbohydrates: 21g | Fiber: 11g | Protein: 36g

644. Cashew Chicken Curry

Preparation Time: 15-minutes | Total time: 40-minutes | Yield: 4-servings

Ingredients:

1 c. Cauliflower	2 large fresh tomatoes
1 medium Red onion	2 c. Cucumber
2 tbsps. Coconut oil	1 tbsp. & ½ tsp. Yellow curry powder - divided
Sea salt & Black pepper (as desired)	2/3 c. Roasted and salted cashews
1. lb Breasts of chicken, 4 small	1 large Egg white

For the Garnish:

Freshly chopped fresh mint	Minced fresh cilantro

Also Needed: Food processor & Rimmed baking sheet

Directions:

Chop the cauliflower into florets and quarter the tomatoes. Roughly chop the onion and thinly slice the cucumber into halves. Take off the skin and bones from the chicken. Heat the oven to 425° Fahrenheit. Toss the quartered tomatoes, cauliflower florets, and onion into a mixing container. Melt the coconut oil and sprinkle using 1.5 tsp of curry powder. Mix until well. Prepare on a baking sheet in one layer. Dust with pepper and salt to your liking. Add the rest of the curry powder and cashews into a food processor. Pulse leaving a few chunks for texture. Pat to remove the moisture from the chicken breasts using a paper towel. Put the egg white and cashews into two shallow plates. Dredge the chicken through the egg white. Shake off any excess and press into the cashews. Flip and lightly press the other side into the cashews. Put the chicken breast onto a small cooling rack that fits your sheet pan (one with legs is preferred, so it sits over the veggies). Continue the process with the remaining chicken. Place the cooling rack over a sheet-pan (over the top of the veggies). Bake the chicken to reach an internal temperature of 165° Fahrenheit (14-15 min.). Once it's done, toss the fresh cucumbers onto the pan. Garnish with mint and cilantro.

Nutritional Information: Calories: 364 | Net Carbs: 14 g | Total Fat Content: 18 g | Protein: 34 g

645. Dark Chocolate Chicken

Preparation Time: 10-minutes | 4 hours 10-minutes – 6 hour 10-minutes | Yield: 6-servings

Ingredients:

Chicken breasts (2lbs, skinned)	Ghee (2 tablespoons)

Garlic (4 cloves, crushed)	Sweet Onion (1, chopped)
Chipotles (5, chopped)	Tomatoes (7, seeds removed and diced)
Dark chocolate (2 ½ oz)	Cumin (1 teaspoon)
Chili powder- guajillpo (1/2 teaspoon)	Cinnamon (1/2 teaspoon)
Jalapeno (chopped)	Cilantro (chopped)
Avocado (chopped)	

Directions:
Season chicken with pepper. Heat a pan and add ghee. Place the chicken into the pan and then brown all over. Remove from pan and put into slow cooker. Return pan to flame and sauté onion and garlic. Add cooked onion and garlic to chicken inside the pot. Add the ingredients remaining to the range except for cilantro, jalapeno, and avocado. Set pot to low and cook for 4-6 hours until chicken can be pulled apart. Serve topped with jalapeno, cilantro, and avocado.

Nutritional Information: Calories 625.2 Fat 42.3 g Saturated Fat 11.5 g Carbohydrates 27.4 g Protein 48.4 g

---

646. Baked Chicken Meatballs - Habanero & Green Chili

Preparation Time: 10-minutes | Total time: 35-minutes | Yield: 15-servings

Ingredients:

1 lb. ground chicken	1 poblano pepper
1 habanero pepper	1 jalapeno pepper
1/2 c. cilantro	1 tbsp. vinegar
1 tbsp. olive oil	salt to taste

Directions:
Preheat broiler to 400 degrees Fahrenheit. Join chicken, minced peppers, cilantro, salt, and vinegar in an enormous blending bowl with your hands. Structure 1-inch meatballs with the blend. Coat every meatball with olive oil. At that point, Put on a rimmed heating sheet or meal dish. Heat for 25-minutes

Nutritional Information: Calories 54 | Fat 3g | Carbs 5g | Protein 5g

---

647. Mustard Pork Mix

Preparation Time: 10-minutes | Total time: 45-minutes | Yield: 4-servings

Ingredients:

2 shallots, chopped	1 lb. pork stew meat, cubed
2 garlic cloves, minced	2 tbsps. olive oil
¼ c. Dijon mustard	2 tbsps. chives, chopped
1 tsp. cumin, ground	1 tsp. Rosemary, dried

Pinch of sea salt	Pinch black pepper

Directions:
Warm a pan with the oil on medium-high heat, add the shallots and sauté for 5-minutes. Put the meat and brown for a further 5-minutes. Put the rest of the ingredients, toss, and cook on medium heat for 25-minutes more. Divide the mix between plates and serve.

Nutritional Information: Calories 280 | Fat 14.3 | Fiber 6 | Carbs 11.8 | Protein 17

---

648. Pork with Mushrooms and Cucumbers

Preparation Time: 10-minutes | Total time: 35-minutes | Yield: 4-servings

Ingredients:

2 tbsps. olive oil	½ tsp. oregano, dried
4 pork chops	2 garlic cloves, minced
Juice of 1 lime	¼ c. cilantro, chopped
Pinch of sea salt	Pinch black pepper
1 c. white mushrooms, halved	2 tbsps. balsamic vinegar

Directions:
Warm a pan with the oil on medium heat, add the pork chops, and brown for 2-minutes on each side.
Put the rest of the ingredients, toss, cook on medium heat for 20-minutes, divide between plates and serve.

Nutritional Information: Calories 220 | Fat 6 | Fiber 8 | Carbs 14.2 | Protein 20

---

649. Pork with Lemongrass

Preparation Time: 10-minutes | Total time: 40-minutes | Yield: 4-servings

Ingredients:

4 pork chops	2 tbsps. olive oil
2 spring onions, chopped	A pinch of salt and black pepper
½ c. vegetable stock	1 stalk lemongrass, chopped
2 tbsps. coconut aminos	2 tbsps. cilantro, chopped

Directions:
Warm a pan with the oil on medium-high heat, add the spring onions and the meat, and brown for 5-minutes. Add the other ingredients, toss, and cook everything over medium heat for 25-minutes. Divide the mix between plates and serve.

Nutritional Information: Calories 290 | Fat | Fiber 6 | Carbs 8 | Protein 14

650. Skillet Chicken with Brussels Sprouts Mix

Preparation Time: 10-minutes | Total time: 25-minutes | Yield: 4-servings

Ingredients:

1½ lbs. chicken thighs, skinless and boneless	1 tbsp. olive oil
2 tsp. chopped thyme	A pinch of salt and black pepper
¼ c. walnuts, chopped	2 tablespoons. balsamic vinegar
1 garlic clove, minced	½ red onion, sliced
1 apple, cored and sliced	12 oz. Brussel sprouts, shredded

Directions:

Warm a pan with the oil using medium-high heat, then add the chicken thighs, season with pepper, salt, and thyme. Cook both-sides for about 5-minutes each and transfer to a bowl. Heat the pan again over medium-heat, add the onion, apple, sprouts, and garlic. Toss the mix and cook for approximately 5-minutes. Add vinegar to the pan and return the chicken as well. Add the walnuts, toss, cook for 1-2-minutes more, divide between plates, and serve. Enjoy!

Nutritional Information: Calories: 211 | Fat: 4 | Fiber: 7 | Carbs:13 | Protein: 8

651. Spinach Chicken Cheesy Bake

Preparation Time: 25-minutes | Total time: 45-minutes | Yield: 6-servings

Ingredients:

6 chicken breasts, skinless and boneless	1 tsp. mixed spice seasoning
Pink salt and black pepper to season	2 loose c. baby spinach
3 tsp. olive oil	4 oz cream cheese, cubed
1 ¼ c. shredded mozzarella cheese	4 tbsps. water

Directions:

Preheat oven to 375F. Season chicken with spice mix, salt, and black pepper. Pat with your hands to have the seasoning stick on the chicken. Put in the casserole dish and layer spinach over the chicken. Mix the oil with cream cheese, mozzarella, salt, black pepper, and Whisk in the water for a tbsp. At a time. Pour the mixture over the chicken and cover the pot with aluminum foil. Bake for at least 20-minutes, take off the foil, and continue cooking for 15-minutes until a nice golden-brown color is formed on top. Take out and allow sitting for 5-minutes. Serve warm with braised asparagus.

Nutritional Information: Calories: 340 | Fat: 30.2g | Net Carbs: 3.1g | Protein: 15g

652. Beef Stuffed Cabbage

Preparation Time: 20-minutes | Total time: 1-hour 35-minutes | Yield: 6-8-servings

Ingredients:

½ tsp. garlic powder	1 ½ c. gluten-free tomato sauce
1 c. cooked brown rice	1 medium head cabbage
1 organic, free-range egg	1 lb. ground beef
1 tbsp. apple cider vinegar	1 tbsp. dried parsley flakes
1 tbsp. raw honey	2 celery stalks with leaves

Directions:

Put high heat in a hotpot, put in 2 quarts of water and cabbage, and bring to its boiling point for fifteen-minutes, or until outer leaves are soft. Drain the cabbage and let it cool completely. Use a paring knife to remove the outer core of the cabbage. Mix the beef, rice, egg, parsley flakes, garlic powder, and celery in a large container. Fill the center of each cabbage leaf with 1/3 cup of the beef mixture. Fold sides over, tucking in the sides of the leaf. Pile up the stuffed cabbage leaves in a big pot on moderate to low heat, placing the bigger leaves on the bottom. Put in the tomato sauce, Vinegar, honey, and enough water to immerse. Simmer for an hour or until cabbage is super soft. Put in tomato sauce as required.

Nutritional Information: Calories: 208 kcal, Protein: 19.22 g, Fat: 10.05 g, Carbohydrates: 10.6 g

653. Honey Chicken Tagine

Preparation Time: 60-minutes | Total time: 1-hour 25-minutes | Yield: 12-servings

Ingredients:

1 tbsp. extra virgin olive oil	1 tsp. ground coriander
1 tbsp. Minced fresh ginger	½ tsp. ground pepper
2 thinly sliced onions	12-oz. seeded and roughly chopped kumquats
14-oz. vegetable broth	1/8 tsp. Ground cloves
½ tsp. salt	1 ½ tbsps. honey
1 tsp. ground cumin	2 lbs. boneless, skinless chicken thighs
4 slivered garlic cloves	15-oz rinsed chickpeas
¾ tsp. ground cinnamon	

Directions:

Preheat the oven to about 3750F. Put a heatproof casserole on medium heat and heat the oil. Add onions to sauté for 4-minutes. Add garlic and ginger to sauté for 1 minute. Add coriander, cumin, cloves, salt, pepper, and cloves seasonings. Sauté for a minute. Add kumquats, broth, chickpeas, and honey, then bring to a boil before turning off the heat. Set the casserole in the oven while covered. Bake for 15-minutes as you Whisk at a 15-minute interval. Serve and enjoy

Nutritional Information: Calories: 586 kcal | Protein: 15.5 g | Fat: 40.82 g | Carbohydrates: 43.56 g

---

654. Almond Chicken Cutlets

Preparation Time: 10-minutes | Total time: 25-minutes | Yield: 4-servings

Ingredients:

2 eggs	½ tsp. garlic powder
1 c. almond flour	1 tbsp. chopped fresh oregano
4 (4 oz.) boneless skinless chicken breasts, pounded to about ¼ inch thick	¼ c. good-quality olive oil
2 tbsps. grass-fed butter	

Directions:

Bread the chicken. Whisk together the eggs, garlic powder in a medium bowl, and set it aside. Whisk together the almond flour and oregano and set the plate next to the egg mixture. Pat the chicken breasts to dry using paper towels and dip them into the egg mixture. Remove excess egg, then roll the chicken in the almond flour until they are coated. Fry the chicken. In a large skillet over medium-high heat, warm the olive oil and butter. Add the breaded chicken breasts and fry them, turning them once until they are cooked through, crispy, golden brown, and 14 to 16-minutes in total. Serve. Put one cutlet on each of the four plates and serve them immediately.

Nutritional Information: Calories: 328 | Saturated fat: 4g | Fiber: 0g | Net carbs: 5g | Protein: 28g

---

655. Keto Chicken Enchiladas

Preparation Time: 10-minutes | Total time: 35-minutes | Yield: 6-servings

Ingredients:

2 c. gluten-free enchilada sauce	Chicken
1 tbsp. Avocado oil	4 cloves Garlic (minced)
3 c. Shredded chicken (cooked)	¼ c. Chicken broth
¼ c. fresh cilantro (chopped)	12 Coconut tortillas
3/4 c. Colby jack cheese (shredded)	¼ c. Green onions (chopped)

Direction:

Warm oil at medium to high heat in a large pan. Add the chopped garlic and cook until fragrant for about a minute. Add rice, 1 cup enchilada sauce (half the total), chicken, and coriander. Simmer for 5-minutes.

In the meantime, heat the oven to 3750 F. Grease a 9x13 baking dish. In the middle of each tortilla, Put ¼ cup chicken mixture. Roll up and put seam side down in the baking dish. Pour the remaining cup of enchilada sauce over the enchiladas. Sprinkle with shredded cheese. Bake for 10 to 12-minutes. Sprinkle with green onions.

Nutritional Information: Calories: 349 vFat: 19g | Net Carbs: 9g | Protein: 31g

---

656. Minty Pork and Almonds

Preparation Time: 10-minutes | Total time: 50-minutes | Yield: 4-servings

Ingredients:

4 pork chops	1 c. mint leaves
2 tbsps. balsamic vinegar	1 tbsp. almonds, chopped
2 tbsps. olive oil	2 garlic cloves, minced
Salt and black pepper to the taste	¼ tsp. red pepper flakes

Directions:

Mix the mint with the vinegar and the other ingredients except the pork chops and pulse well in a blender. Heat a pan with the mint mix over medium heat, add the pork chops, toss, introduce in the oven and bake at 390 degrees F for 40-minutes. Divide everything between plates and serve.

Nutritional Information: calories 260, fat 6 fiber 1, carbs 8, protein 23

---

657. Duck Stew Olla Tapaha

Preparation Time: 15-minutes | Total time: 45-minutes | Yield: 3-servings

Ingredients:

1 red bell pepper, deveined and chopped	1 lb. duck breasts, boneless, skinless, and chopped into small chunks
1/2 c. chayote, peeled and cubed	1 shallot, chopped
1 tsp. Mexican spice mix	

Directions:

In a clay pot, heat 2 tsp. Of canola oil over a medium-high flame. Sauté the peppers and shallot until softened for about 4-minutes. Add in the remaining ingredients; pour in 1 ½ cups of water or chicken bone broth. Once your mixture starts boiling, reduce the heat to medium-low. Let it simmer, partially covered, for 18 to 22-minutes, until cooked through. Enjoy!

Nutritional Information: 228 Calorie | 9.5g Fa | 3.3g Carb | 30.6g Protein | 1g Fiber

658. Citrus Beef with Bok Choy

Preparation Time: 15-minutes | Total time: 26-minutes | Yield: 4-servings

Ingredients:

For Marinade:

2 minced garlic cloves	1 (1-inch piece fresh ginger, grated
1/3 c. fresh orange juice	½ c. coconut aminos
2 tsp. fish sauce	2 tsp. Sriracha
1¼ lb. sirloin steak, sliced thinly	

For Veggies:

2 tbsp. coconut oil, divided	3-4 wide strips of fresh orange zest
1 jalapeño pepper, sliced thinly	1 tbsp. Arrowroot powder
½ lb. Bok choy, chopped	2 tsp. sesame seeds

Directions:

Put garlic, ginger, orange juice, coconut aminos, fish sauce, and Sriracha for the marinade in a big bowl, then mix. Put the beef and coat with marinade. Marinate by placing it in the fridge for a couple of hours. In a skillet, warm oil on medium-high heat. Add orange zest and sauté for approximately 2-minutes. Take off the beef from a bowl, reserving the marinade. In the skillet, add beef and increase the heat to high. Whisk fry for at least 2-3-minutes or till browned. With a slotted-spoon, transfer the beef and orange strips right into a bowl. Wipe out the skillet with a paper-towel. In a similar skillet, heat the remaining oil on medium-high heat. Add jalapeño pepper and Whisk fry for about 3-4-minutes. Meanwhile, add arrowroot powder in reserved marinade and Whisk to mix. In the skillet, add marinade mixture, beef, and Bok choy and cook for about 1-2-minutes. Serve hot with garnishing of sesame seeds.

Nutritional Information: Calories: 39 | Fat: 11 | Carbohydrates: 20 | Fiber: 6g | Protein: 34g

659. Turkey Chili

Preparation Time: 5-minutes | Total time: 35-minutes | Yield: 2-servings

Ingredients:

1 oz. jalapeno pepper	1 oz. red bell pepper (or other colors)
3 oz. zucchini	1 ½ tbsp. olive oil
5 oz. ground turkey	1 c. water or as needed
1 ½ oz. cauliflower rice	1 ½ tbsps. sour cream
4 tbsps. Shredded cheddar cheese	¼ tsp. pepper
1 tsp. paprika	1/3 tsp. onion powder or garlic powder (optional)
¼ tsp. ground cumin (optional)	Salt to taste

Directions:

Chop the red bell pepper, jalapeno pepper, and zucchini into smaller, bite-sized pieces. Feel free to slice jalapeno pepper into larger pieces if you want to avoid them and control the spiciness in your mouth later.

Take a large stewing pot, add the olive oil, and put it on medium heat. Put the ground turkey and cook it until it becomes brown. Use a spatula to break it up.

Mix bell pepper, jalapeno, and zucchini with turkey. Put a cover on your pot and let your mixture cook on low heat for approximately 5-minutes or until you see that vegetables become slightly softer. Season everything and add water. Whisk the chili. Cover your pot once again and bring your mixture to a simmer. Continue to Whisk it for about 10 more-minutes. Add the cauliflower rice. Remove the cover and keep cooking at low heat. Fill approximately ½ of a cup with the liquid you remove from the pot. Put it into a clean bowl and mix it with the sour cream. Bring the thickened liquid back to the pot. Whisk your ingredients once again and let your chili simmer for 5 more-minutes to concentrate a little more. While serving this meal, fill 2 bowls and top each of those with 2 tbsps. of cheddar cheese.

Nutritional Information: Calories: 378 | Fiber: 2g | Net Carbs: 4,3g | Fat: 30g | Protein: 23g

660. Chili Pork Pan

Preparation Time: 10-minutes | Total time: 1-hour 10-minutes | Yield: 4-servings

Ingredients:

2 lbs. pork stew meat, cubed	2 tbsps. olive oil
½ c. vegetable stock	1 yellow onion, chopped
1 tbsp. ginger, grated	2 tbsps. balsamic vinegar
A pinch of black-pepper and salt	½ tsp. chili powder

Directions:

Heat a pan using the oil over medium-heat, add the onion and the ginger and sauté for 5-minutes. Add the meat and other ingredients, toss, cook over medium heat for 45-minutes more, divide between plates.

Nutritional Information: calories 280, fat 7.8, fiber 8, carbs 12, protein 15.6

661. Chicken Parmigiana

Preparation Time: 15-minutes | Total time: 41-minutes | Yield: 4-servings

Ingredients:

1 large organic egg, beaten	½ c. of superfine blanched almond flour
¼ c. Parmesan cheese, grated	½ tsp. Dried parsley
½ tsp. Paprika	½ tsp. garlic powder
Salt and ground black pepper, as required	4 -6 oz. grass-fed boneless, skinless chicken breasts, pounded into a ½-inch thickness
¼ c. olive oil	1½ c. marinara sauce
4 oz. mozzarella cheese, thinly sliced	2 tbsps. fresh parsley, chopped

Directions:

Preheat the oven to 375 degrees F. Add the beaten egg into a shallow dish. Put the almond flour, Parmesan, parsley, spices, salt, and black pepper in another shallow dish and mix well. Dip each chicken-breast into the beaten-egg and then coat with the flour mixture.

In a deep-skillet, heat the oil over medium-high heat and fry the chicken breasts for about 3-minutes per side. Using a slotted spoon, moved the chicken breasts onto a paper towel-lined plate to drain. At the bottom of a casserole, put about ½ cup of marinara sauce and spread evenly. Arrange the chicken breasts over marinara sauce in a single layer. Top with the other marinara sauce, followed by mozzarella cheese slices. Bake for about at least 20-minutes or until done completely. Take off from the oven and serve hot with the garnishing of fresh parsley.

Nutritional Information: Calories: 542 Net Carbs: 5.7g | Fiber: 3.3g | Protein: 54.2g | Fat: 33.2g

662. Pesto & Mozzarella Chicken Casserole

Preparation Time: 10-minutes | Total time: 35 – 40-minutes | Yield: 8-servings

Ingredients:

Cooking oil (as needed)	2 lbs. Grilled & cubed chicken breasts
8 oz. Cubed mozzarella	8 oz. Cream cheese
8 oz. Shredded mozzarella	½ c. Pesto
½ c. Heavy cream	

Directions:

Warm the oven to 400° Fahrenheit. Spritz a casserole dish with a spritz of cooking oil spray. Mix the pesto, heavy cream, and softened cream cheese. Add the chicken and cubed mozzarella into the greased dish.

Sprinkle the chicken using the shredded mozzarella. Bake for 25-30-minutes.

Nutritional Information: Calories: 451 | Net Carbs: 3 g | Total Fat Content: 30 g | Protein: 38 g

663. Greek Chicken Stefano

Preparation Time: 10-minutes | Total time: 45-minutes | Yield: 2-servings

Ingredients:

2 oz. bacon, diced	1 tsp. poultry seasoning mix
2 vine-ripe tomatoes, pureed	3/4 lb. whole chicken, boneless and chopped
1/2 medium-sized leek, chopped	

Directions:

Cook the bacon in the preheated skillet over medium-high heat. Fold in the chicken and continue to cook for 5-minutes more until it is no longer pink; set aside.

In the same skillet, sauté the leek until it has softened or about 4-minutes. Whisk in the poultry seasoning mix and 2 cups of water or chicken broth. Now, decrease the heat to medium-low and go ahead to simmer for 15 to 20-minutes. Add in tomatoes along with the reserved meat. Continue to cook for a further 13-minutes or until cooked through. Bon appétit!

Nutritional Information: | 352 Calories | 14.3g Fat | 5.9g Carbs | 44.2g Protein | 2.4g Fiber

664. Vodka Duck Fillets

Preparation Time: 5-minutes | Total time: 20-minutes | Yield: 4-servings

Ingredients:

1 tbsp. lard, room temperature	4 duck fillets
4 green onions, chopped	Salt and cayenne pepper, to taste
1 tsp. mixed peppercorns	1 ½ c. turkey stock
3 tbsps. Worcestershire sauce	2 oz. vodka
1/2 tsp. ground bay leaf	1/2 c. sour cream

Directions:

Melt the lard in a skillet that is preheated over medium-high heat. Sear the duck fillets, turning once, for 4 to 6-minutes. Now, add the remaining ingredients, except for the sour cream, to the skillet. Cook, partially covered, for a further 7-minutes. Serve warm, garnished with sour cream. Bon appétit!

Nutritional Information: 351 Calories | 24.7g Fat | 6.6g Carbs | 22.1g Protein

665. Chicken Divan

Preparation Time: 15-minutes | Total time: 45-minutes | Yield: 4-servings

Ingredients:

1 can mushroom soup	½ lb. de-boned and skinless cooked chicken pieces
1 c. grated extra sharp cheddar cheese	½ c. water
1 c. cooked and diced broccoli pieces	1 c. croutons

Directions:

Preheat the oven to 350∘F. In a large pot, heat the soup and water. Add the chicken, broccoli, and cheese. Mix thoroughly. Pour into a greased baking dish. Put the croutons over the mixture. Bake until the casserole is bubbling & the croutons are golden brown, for about 30-minutes.

Nutritional Information: Calories: 38 | Fat: 22 g | Carbs: 10 g | Protein: 25 g | Sodium: 475 mg

666. Champion Chicken Pockets

Preparation Time: 5-minutes | Total time: 5-minutes | Yield: 4-servings

Ingredients:

¼ c. shredded carrot	¼ c. plain low-fat yogurt
1 ½ c. chopped cooked chicken	¼ c. chopped pecans or walnuts
¼ c. bottled reduced-fat ranch salad dressing	2 halved whole wheat pita bread rounds
½ c. chopped broccoli	

Directions:

In a bowl, put together yogurt and ranch salad dressing, then mix. Put then Mix chicken, broccoli, carrot, and, if desired, nuts in a medium bowl. Pour yogurt mixture over chicken; toss to coat. Spoon chicken mixture into pita halves.

Nutritional Information: Calories: 384 | Fat: 11.4 g | Carbs: 7.4 g | Protein: 59.3 g | Sodium: 368.7 mg

667. Stuffed Chicken with Sauerkraut and Cheese

Preparation Time: 10-minutes | Total time: 45-minutes | Yield: 4-servings

Ingredients:

5 chicken cutlets	1 c. Romano cheese, shredded
2 garlic cloves, minced	5 Italian peppers, deveined and chopped
5 tbsps. sauerkraut, for serving	

Directions:

Spritz a baking pan with 1 tbsp of olive oil. Brush the chicken with another tbsp. of olive oil. Season the chicken with the Italian spice mix. You can spread Dijon mustard on one side of each chicken cutlet if desired. Divide the garlic, peppers, and Romano cheese between chicken cutlets; roll them up. Bake at 360°F for 25 to 33-minutes until nicely brown on all sides. Serve with the sauerkraut and serve. Bon appétit!

Nutritional Information: 376 Calories | 16.7g Fat | 5.8g Carbs | 47g Protein | 1g Fiber

668. Meatloaf with a Sweet Sticky Glaze

Preparation Time: 1 hour | Total time: 2 hours 10-minutes | Yield: 2-servings

Ingredients:

3/4 lb. ground chuck	1/4 c. flaxseed meal
2 eggs, beaten	1/2 c. tomato sauce with garlic and onion
1 tsp. liquid monk fruit	

Directions:

Mix the ground chuck, flaxseed meal, and eggs, season with salt and black pepper. In a separate mixing bowl, Mix the tomato sauce and liquid monk fruit; add 1 tsp. Of mustard and whisk until well combined. Spoon the mixture into the foil-lined loaf pan and smooth the surface. Bake in the preheated oven at 365 degrees F for about 25-minutes. Spoon the tomato mixture on top of the meatloaf and continue to bake for a further 25-minutes or until thoroughly cooked. Allow your meatloaf to rest for 10-minutes before slicing and. Bon appétit!

Nutritional Information: 517 Calories; 32.3g Fat; 8.4g Carbs; 48.5g Protein; 6.5g Fiber

669. Smoked Beef Sausage Bake with Broccoli

Preparation Time: 45-minutes | Total time: 2-hours 25-minutes | Yield: 4-servings

Ingredients:

1 red bell pepper, thinly sliced	2 shallots, chopped
1 c. broccoli, broken into florets	4 smoked beef sausages, sliced
1 green bell pepper, thinly sliced	2 tbsps. fresh parsley, roughly chopped
2 garlic cloves, minced	1/2 tsp. ground bay leaf
Salt and black pepper, to taste	1 tsp. marjoram

6 eggs, whisked	

Directions:

Begin by preheating your oven to 3700F. Heat a non-stick skillet using a moderate flame; now, Heat the sausage for 3-minutes, stirring regularly. Include the peppers, shallots, broccoli, and garlic; continue cooking for about 5-minutes. Season with marjoram, salt, pepper, and ground bay leaf. Move the sausage mixture to a previously greased baking dish. Pour the whisked eggs over it. Bake for 35-minutes. Enjoy garnished with fresh parsley.

Nutritional Information: Calories 289, Protein 19.8g Fat 19.7g Carbs 6.3g Sugar 2.4g

670. Basic "Rotisserie" Chicken

Preparation Time: 15-minutes | Total time: 6 – 8 hours + 15-minutes | Yield: 6-servings

Ingredients:

½ medium onion, cut	1 (4-5 lb.) whole chicken
1 tsp. chili powder	1 tsp. dried thyme leaves
1 tsp. garlic powder	1 tsp. paprika
1 tsp. sea salt	Freshly ground black pepper
Pinch cayenne pepper	

Directions:

Mix the garlic powder, chili powder, paprika, thyme, salt, and cayenne in a small container. Flavor it with black pepper and whisk again to blend. Rub the spice mix all over the exterior of the chicken. Put the chicken in the cooker with the cut onion sprinkled around it.
Secure the lid of your cooker and set it to low. Cook for a minimum of six to eight hours, or until the internal temperature reaches 165°F on a meat thermometer and the juices run clear before serving.

Nutritional Information: Calories: 862, Fat: 59g, Carbs: 7g, Sugar: 6g, Protein: 86g

671. Pancetta & Cheese Stuffed Chicken

Preparation Time: 15-minutes | Total time: 40-minutes | Yield: 2-servings

Ingredients:

4 slices pancetta	2 tbsp. olive oil
2 chicken breasts	1 garlic clove, minced
1 shallot, finely chopped	2 tbsp. dried oregano
4 oz. mascarpone cheese	1 lemon, zested
Salt and black pepper to taste	

Directions:

Warm the oil in a small skillet, then sauté the garlic and shallots for 3-minutes. Whisk in salt, black pepper, and lemon zest. Transfer to a bowl and let it cool. Whisk in the mascarpone cheese and oregano. Score a pocket in each chicken's breast, fill the holes with the cheese mixture and cover it with the cut-out chicken. Wrap each breast with two pancetta slices and secure the ends with a toothpick. Set the chicken on a greased baking sheet and cook in the oven for 20-minutes at 380 F.

Nutritional Information: Calories 643 | Fat 44.5g | Net Carbs 6.2g | Protein 52.8g

672. Beef with Carrot & Broccoli

Preparation Time: 15-minutes | Total time: 29-minutes | Yield: 4-servings

Ingredients:

Salt, to taste	1 pound of beef-sirloin steak, sliced into thin strips
2 medium garlic cloves, minced	2 tbsps. coconut oil, divided
¼ c. chicken broth	2 tsp. fresh ginger, grated
1 tbsp. Ground flax seeds	½ tsp. Red pepper flakes, crushed
¼ tsp. freshly ground black pepper	1 large carrot, peeled and sliced thinly
2 c. broccoli florets	1 medium scallion, sliced thinly

Directions:

In a skillet, warm 1 tbsp. of oil on medium-high heat. Put garlic and sauté for approximately 1 minute. Add beef and salt and cook for at least 4-5-minutes or till browned. Using a slotted spoon, transfer the beef to a bowl. Take off the liquid from the skillet. Put together broth, ginger, flax seeds, red pepper flakes, and black pepper, then mix in a bowl. In the same skillet, warm remaining oil on medium heat. Put the carrot, broccoli, and ginger mixture, then cook for at least 3-4-minutes or desired doneness. Mix in beef and scallion, then cook for around 3-4-minutes.

Nutritional Information: Calories: 41 | Fat: 13g | Carbohydrates: 28g | Fiber: 9g | Protein: 35g

673. Boozy Glazed Chicken

Preparation Time: 5-minutes | Total time: 1-hour | Yield: 4-servings

Ingredients:

2 pounds chicken drumettes	2 tbsps. ghee, at room temperature
Sea salt, to taste	Ground black pepper, to taste
1 tsp. Mediterranean seasoning mix	2 vine-ripened tomatoes, pureed

3/4 c. rum	3 tbsps. coconut aminos
A few drops of liquid Stevia	1 tsp. chili peppers, minced
1 tbsp. minced fresh ginger	1 tsp. ground cardamom
2 tbsps. fresh lemon juice, + wedges for serving	

Directions:

Toss the chicken with the melted ghee, salt, black pepper, and Mediterranean seasoning mix until well coated on all sides. In another bowl, thoroughly Mix the pureed tomato puree, rum, coconut aminos, Stevia, chili peppers, ginger, cardamom, and lemon juice. Pour the tomato mixture over the chicken drumettes; let it marinate for 2 hours. Bake inside the preheated-oven for about 45-minutes, at 410 degrees F. Add in the reserved marinade and put under the preheated broiler for 10-minutes.

Nutritional Information: 307 Calories | 12.1g Fat | 2.7g Carbs | 33.6g Protein | 1.5g Fiber

674. Lemon-Garlic Chicken with Caramelized Onions

Preparation Time: 10-minutes | Total time: 1-hour 15-minutes | Yield: 2-servings

Ingredients:

3 tbsp. extra-virgin olive oil	3 tbsp. freshly squeezed lemon juice
2 tbsp. minced garlic	1 tsp. Sea salt, plus additional for seasoning
¼ tsp. Freshly ground black pepper	¼ tsp. Paprika
⅛ tsp. red pepper flakes	2 large boneless, skinless free-range chicken breasts
1 yellow onion, quartered	¼ c. Golden Ghee, melted

Directions:

In. a medium bowl or a zipper-top plastic bag, Mix the olive oil, lemon juice, garlic, salt, black pepper, paprika, and red pepper flakes. Put the chicken, then coat it in the marinade. Cover the bowl or seal the bag, then marinate the chicken in the fridge for at least 1 hour, or overnight if possible. Preheat the oven to 350°F. Dice 1 of the onion quarters and cut the remaining 3 quarters into large chunks. Put the larger chunks of onion across the bottom of cast-iron or ovenproof skillet.

Put the scatter of the diced onion above. Put on the top the onion with the ghee. Put the marinated chicken breasts, then spoon the remaining marinade at the chicken. Season the dish with a sprinkle of sea salt.

Bake the chicken until its internal temperature reaches at least 165°F, about 65-minutes. Serve hot.

Nutritional Information: Calories: 803 | Saturated Fat: 23g | Protein: 53g | Fiber: 5g | Net Carbs: 9g

675. Turkey & Sweet Potato Chili

Preparation Time: 15-minutes | Total time: 4 – 6 hours + 15-minutes | Yield: 4-servings

Ingredients:

1 tbsp. extra-virgin olive oil	1 lb. ground turkey
3 c. sweet potato cubes	1 (28 oz.) can diced tomatoes
1 red bell pepper, diced	1 (4 oz.) can Hatch green chiles
½ medium red onion, diced	2 c. broth of choice
1 tbsp. freshly squeezed lime juice	1 tbsp. chili powder
1 tsp. garlic powder	1 tsp. cocoa powder
1 tsp. ground cumin	1 tsp. Sea salt
½ tsp. ground cinnamon	Pinch cayenne pepper

Directions:

In your slow cooker, Mix the olive oil, turkey, sweet potato cubes, tomatoes, bell pepper, chiles, onion, broth, lime juice, chili powder, garlic powder, cocoa powder, cumin, salt, cinnamon, and cayenne. Using a large spoon, break up the turkey into smaller chunks to Mix with the other ingredients. Cover the cooker. Set to low heat and cook for about 4 - 6 hours. Whisk the chili well, continue to break up the rest of the turkey, and serve.

Nutritional Information: Calories: 38 | Fat: 12 | Carbs: 38 | Sugar: 9g | Fiber: 6g | Protein: 30g |

676. Berry Chops Dinner

Preparation Time: ten-minutes | Total time: 25-minutes | Yield: 4-servings

Ingredients:

(ground) black pepper and salt to taste	½ c. balsamic vinegar
½ tsp. thyme, dried	1 tsp. cinnamon powder
12 oz. blackberries	2 lbs. pork chops
2 tbsps. water	

Directions:

Spice the pork chops with salt, pepper, cinnamon, and thyme. Heat a cooking pot; put in the blackberries, and heat on moderate heat. Put in the vinegar, water, salt, and pepper, whisk the mix. Simmer for three to five-minutes and take it off the heat. Brush the pork-chops using half of the blueberry mix. Preheat your grill and grill the chops on moderate heat for about six-minutes on each side. Split the pork chops between serving plates, top with the remaining blackberry sauce. Serve warm.

Nutritional Information: Calories 286, Fat: 6g, Carbohydrates: 11g, Fiber: 6g, Protein: 22g

677. Almond Cinnamon Beef Meatballs

Preparation Time: 10-minutes | Total time: 35-minutes | Yield: 8-servings

Ingredients:

½ c. fresh parsley, minced	1 ½ tsp. dried oregano
1 c. almond flour	1 medium onion, grated
1 tsp. cinnamon	1 tsp. garlic, minced
1 tsp. pepper	2 lbs. ground beef
2 tsp. cumin	2 tsp. salt
3 eggs	

Directions:

Set the oven to 400 F. Put all together ingredients into the mixing container and whisk until well blended. Make small meatballs from the mixture, put them on a greased baking tray, and bake for about twenty-minutes. Serve and enjoy.

Nutritional Information: Calories 325, Fat: 16 g, Carbs: 6 g, Sugar: 2 g, Protein: 40 g,

678. Curry Chicken Lettuce Wraps

Preparation Time: 15-minutes | Total time: 25-minutes | Yield: 5-servings

Ingredients:

2 Minced garlic cloves	¼ c. Minced onion
1 lb. Chicken thighs – skinless & boneless	2 tbsp. Ghee
1 tsp. Black pepper	2 tsp. Curry powder
1.5 tsp. Salt	Keto-friendly sour cream (as desired - count the carbs)
5-6 Lettuce leaves	1 c. Riced cauliflower

Directions:

Mince the garlic and onions. Set aside for now. Pull out the bones and skin from the chicken and dice them into one-inch pieces. On the stovetop, add 2 tbsp. of ghee to a skillet and melt. Toss in the onion and sauté until browned. Fold in the chicken and sprinkle with garlic, pepper, and salt. Cook for eight-minutes. Whisk in the remainder of the ghee, riced cauliflower, and curry. Whisk until well mixed. Prepare the lettuce leaves and add the mixture. Serve with a dollop of cream.

Nutritional Information: Calories: 554 | Net Carbs: 7 g | Total Fat Content: 36 g | Protein: 50 g

679. Lebanese Chicken Kebabs and Hummus

Preparation Time: 10-minutes + 1 hour marinate | Total time: 1 hour 45-minutes | Yield: 4-servings

Ingredients:
For the Chicken:

1 c. Lemon Juice	8 Garlic cloves, minced
1 tbsp. Thyme, finely chopped	1 tbsp. Paprika
2 tsp. ground cumin	1 tsp. Cayenne pepper
4 Free-range skinless chicken breasts, cubed	4 Metal kebabs skewers
Lemon wedges to garnish	

For the Hummus:

1 can Chickpeas/ 1 c. dried (soaked overnight)	2 tbsp. Tahini paste
1 Lemon juice	1 tsp. Turmeric
1 tsp. Black pepper	2 tbsp. Olive oil

Directions:

Whisk the lemon juice, garlic, thyme, paprika, cumin, and cayenne pepper in a bowl. Skewer the chicken cubes using kebab sticks (metal). Baste the chicken per side with the marinade, covering for as long as possible in the fridge (the lemon juice will tenderize the meat and means it will be more suitable for the anti-inflammatory diet). When ready to cook, set the oven to 400°F/200 °C/Gas Mark 6 and bake for 20-25-minutes or until chicken is thoroughly cooked through. Prepare the hummus by putting the ingredients into a blender and whizzing up until smooth. If it is a little thick and chunky, add a little water to loosen the mix. Serve the chicken kebabs garnished with lemon wedges and hummus on the side.

Nutritional Information: Calories: 576 kcal | Protein: 61.66 g | Fat: 18.55 g | Carbohydrates: 42.07 g

680. Pork and Cumin Zucchinis

Preparation Time: 10-minutes | Total time: 50-minutes | Yield: 4-servings

Ingredients:

2 lbs. pork stew meat, roughly cubed	2 zucchinis, sliced
2 tbsps. olive oil	1 tsp. nutmeg, ground
1 tsp. cinnamon powder	1 tsp. cumin, ground
2 tbsps. lime juice	2 garlic cloves, minced
A pinch of black-pepper & sea salt	

Directions:

In a roasting pan, Mix the meat with the zucchinis, the nutmeg, and the other ingredients, toss and bake at 390

degrees F for 40-minutes. Divide everything between plates and serve.
Nutritional Information: calories 200, fat 5, fiber 2, carbs 10, protein 22

681. Tarragon Pork Roast

Preparation Time: 10-minutes | Total time: 1-hour 10-minutes | Yield: 4-servings

Ingredients:

2 lbs. pork loin roast, sliced	1 tbsp. tarragon, chopped
A pinch of salt and black pepper	4 garlic cloves, chopped
1 tsp. red pepper, crushed	¼ c. olive oil

Directions:
In a roasting pan, Mix the roast with the tarragon and the other ingredients, toss, and bake at 390 degrees F for 1 hour. Divide the mix between plates and serve.
Nutritional Information: calories 281, fat 5, fiber 7, carbs 8, protein 10

682. Orange Chicken Legs

Preparation Time: 10-minutes | Total time: 8-hours 10-minutes | Yield: 4-servings

Ingredients:

Zest of 1 orange	Juice of 1 orange
¼ c. red vinegar	A pinch of salt and black pepper
4 chicken legs	5 garlic cloves, minced
1 red onion, cut into wedges	7 oz. canned peaches halved
½ c. chopped parsley	

Directions:
Mix the orange zest with the orange juice, vinegar, salt, pepper, garlic, onion, peaches, and parsley in a slow cooker. Add the chicken, toss, cover, and cook on Low for 8 hours. Divide between plates and serve. Enjoy!
Nutritional Information: Calories: 251 | Fat: 4 | Fiber: 8 | Carbs: 14 | Protein: 8

683. Chicken Frittata with Asiago Cheese and Herbs

Preparation Time: 10-minutes | Total time: 40-minutes | Yield: 4-servings

Ingredients:

1 lb. chicken breasts, chopped into small strips	4 slices of bacon
1 c. Asiago cheese, shredded	6 eggs
1/2 c. yogurt	

Directions:
Preheat an oven-proof skillet. Then, fry the bacon until crisp and reserve. Then, cook the chicken for about 8-minutes or until no longer pink in the pan drippings. Add the reserved bacon back to the skillet. In a mixing dish, thoroughly Mix the eggs and yogurt, season with the Italian spice mix. Pour the egg mixture over the chicken and bacon. Top cheese and bake in the pre-heated oven at 380 degrees F for 22-minutes until hot and bubbly. Let it sit for 1-2-minutes before slicing and serving. Bon appétit!
Nutritional Information: 484 Calories | 31.8g Fat | 5.8g Carbs | 41.9g Protein | 0.7g Fiber

684. Tangy Chicken with Scallions

Preparation Time: 10-minutes | Total time: 50-minutes | Yield: 4-servings

Ingredients:

3 tbsps. butter, melted	1 lb. chicken drumettes
1 garlic clove, sliced	1 tbsp. fresh scallions, chopped

Directions:
Arrange the chicken drumettes on a foil-lined baking pan. Brush with melted butter. Add in the garlic. Spice with salt and black pepper to taste. Bake in the pre-heated oven at 400 degrees F for about 30-minutes or until internal temperature reaches about 165 degrees F. Serve garnished with scallions and enjoy!
Nutritional Information: 209 Calories | 12.2g Fat | 0.4g Carbs | 23.2g Protein | 1.9g Fiber

685. Chili Chicken Kebab with Garlic Dressing

Preparation Time: 7-minutes | Total time: 17-minutes | Yield: 2 – 4-servings

Ingredients:
Skewers

2 tbsp. olive oil	3 tbsp. soy sauce, sugar-free
1 tbsp. ginger paste	2 tbsp. swerve brown sugar
Chili pepper to taste	2 chicken breasts, cut into cubes

Dressing

½ c. tahini	1 tbsp. parsley, chopped
1 garlic clove, minced	Salt and black pepper to taste
¼ c. warm water	

Directions:
To make the marinade:
In a small bowl, Put and mix the soy sauce, ginger paste, brown sugar, chili pepper, and olive oil. Put the chicken in a zipper bag, pour the marinade over, seal,

and shake for an even coat. Marinate in the fridge for 2 hours. Preheat a grill to high heat. Thread the chicken on skewers and cook for 10-minutes, with three to four turnings golden brown. Transfer to a plate.

Mix the tahini, garlic, salt, parsley, and warm water in a bowl. Serve the chicken skewers topped with the tahini dressing.

Nutritional Information: Calories 410 | Fat 32gvNet Carbs 4.8gvProtein 23.5g

686. Slow Cooked Meatballs

Preparation Time: 10-minutes | Total time: 4 – 6 hours + 10-minutes | Yield: 4 – 6-servings

Ingredients:

1lb. Veggie mince	½ c. White Onion, chopped
1 tbsp. Italian seasoning	1 tbsp. Garlic, diced
3 ½ Tomatoes, crushed	1 lb. Turkey sausage
¼ c. Almond flour	1 tbsp. Basil

Directions:

Mix each of the ingredients in a big bowl, excluding tomatoes. Roll into balls and oil slow cooker. Put meatballs into the cooker and pour tomatoes along with more seasonings on top of meatballs. Set on high heat and cook for about 4-hours. Serve with salad or other preferred side dishes.

Nutritional Information: Calories 141.7 Fat 7.5 g Saturated Fat 2.4 g Carbohydrates 4.3 g Protein 8.6 g

687. Lemon & Garlic Chicken Thighs

Preparation Time: 15-minutes | Total time: 7 – 8 hours + 15-minutes | Yield: 4-servings

Ingredients:

2 c. chicken broth	1½ tsps. garlic powder
1 tsp. sea salt	Juice and zest of 1 large lemon
2 pounds boneless skinless chicken thighs	

Directions:

Pour the broth into the slow cooker. Put the garlic powder, salt, lemon juice, and lemon zest in a small bowl, then stir. Baste each chicken thigh with an even coating of the mixture. Put the thighs along the bottom of the slow cooker. Cover the cooker and set it to low. Cook for around 7 to 8 hours, or until the internal temperature of the chicken reaches 165°F on a meat thermometer and the juices run clear and serve.

Nutritional Information: Calories: 29 | Total Fat: 14g | Total Carbs: 3g | Protein: 43g | Sodium: 1,017mg

688. Roasted Chicken

Preparation Time: 60-minutes | Total time: 2-hours | Yield: 8-servings

Ingredients:

½ tsp. thyme	3 lbs. whole chicken
1 bay leaf	3 garlic cloves
4 tbsps. Coarsely chopped orange peel	½ tsp. Black pepper
½ tbsp. salt	

Directions:

Put the chicken under room temperature for about 1 hour. Using paper towels, pat dries the inside and outside of the chicken. Preheat the oven to 4500F as soon as you start preparing the chicken seasoning. Mix thyme, salt, and pepper in a small bowl. Wipe inside using 1/3 of the seasoning. Inside the chicken, put the garlic, citrus peel, and bay leaf. Tuck the tips of the wing and tie the legs together. Spread the rest of the seasoning all over the chicken and put it on a roasting pan. Put in the oven to bake for 60-minutes at 1600F. Set aside to rest for 15-minutes. Cut up the roasted chicken and serve. Enjoy.

Nutritional Information: Calories: 201 kcal | Protein: 35.48 g | Fat: 5.36 g | Carbohydrates: 0.5 g

689. Apricot Chicken Wings

Preparation Time: 15-minutes | Total time: 1-hour to 1-hour 15-minutes | Yield: 3-4-servings

Ingredients:

1 medium jar apricot preserve	1 package Lipton onion dry soup mix
1 medium bottle Russian dressing	2 lbs. chicken wings

Directions:

Preheat the oven to 350°F. Rinse and pat dry the chicken wings. Bring the chicken wings on a baking pan, single layer. Bake for 45 – 60-minutes, turning halfway. In a medium bowl, Mix the Lipton soup mix, apricot preserve, and Russian dressing. Once the wings are cooked, toss with the sauce until the pieces are coated. Serve immediately with a side dish.

Nutritional Information: Calories: 162 | Fat: 17 g | Carbs: 76 | Protein: 13 g | Sugars: 11 g |

690. Baked Pork Chops with Cashew

Preparation Time: ten-minutes | Total time: 35-minutes | Yield: 4-servings

Ingredients:

½ c. cashew meal	1 tsp. chipotle chili powder

1/3 c. sunflower seeds, minced	1½ tsp. smoked paprika
2 eggs, whisked	2 tsp. garlic powder
4 pork chops	A pinch of salt and black pepper

Directions:

Mix the cashew meal with sunflower seeds, garlic powder, salt, pepper, paprika, and chili powder in a container. Immerse the pork chops in whisked eggs, then in cashew mix, put them on a lined baking sheet, and bake at 400 degrees F for about twenty-five-minutes. Split between plates before you serve.

Nutritional Information: Calories 251, Fat: 12, Fiber: 4, Carbs: 7, Protein: 16

691. Buffalo Pizza Chicken

Preparation Time: 5-minutes | Total time: 10 – 11-minutes | Yield: 5-servings

Ingredients:

Vegetable cooking spray	2 c. deli-roasted whole chicken, chopped
½ c. hot sauce, buffalo-style	1 (16 oz.) package Italian pizza crust, prebaked
1 c. Provolone cheese, shredded	¼ c. blue cheese, crumbled

Directions:

Coat the grill with the spray and put it on the grill. Preheat your grill to attain 350° F (medium heat). Spread the hot sauce to the crust, and pizza, provolone cheese, and chicken. Put the crust on the cooking grate directly. Grill at 350° F (medium heat) for 4 min, covered with the grill lid. While covered using the grill top, rotate 1-quarter turn pizza and grill for 5 to 6 min or until heated thoroughly. Serve right away.

Nutritional Information: Calories: 365 | Fat: 11g | Net Carbs: 42g | Protein: 24g

692. Keto Tacos with Bacon Sauce

Preparation Time: 30-minutes | Total time:1-hour 10-minutes | Yield: 4-servings

Ingredients:

1 ½ c. ground beef	2 jalapeno peppers, minced
2 Campari tomatoes, crushed	1/2 tsp. ground cumin
6 slices bacon, chopped	2 tsp. champagne vinegar
1/2 tsp. onion powder	1/2 tsp. celery salt
1 ½ c. Cotija cheese, shredded	Salt and ground black pepper, to taste
1/2 c. bone broth	3 tbsps. tomato paste

Directions:

Preheat your oven to 390 degrees F. Spritz a baking pan with the aid of a nonstick cooking spray. Spread 6 (six piles of Cotija cheese on the baking pan; bake for about 15-minutes; let taco shells cool down for some-minutes. In a nonstick skillet, brown the beef for the duration of about 4 to 5-minutes, crumbling with a spatula. Include crushed pepper, tomatoes, salt, celery salt, onion powder, and ground cumin. Heat until everything is cooked through. Now, make the sauce by cooking the bacon for 2 to 3-minutes, stirring continually. Include the remaining ingredients and heat until everything comes together. After the above, assemble your tacos. Share the meat mixture among 6 taco shells: top with the bacon sauce. Bon appétit!

Nutritional Information: Calories 258, Protein 16.3g, Fat 19.3g, Carbs 5g, Sugar 2.9g

693. Beef with Zucchini Noodles

Preparation Time: 15-minutes | Total time: 24-minutes | Yield: 4-servings

Ingredients:

1 tsp. fresh ginger, grated	2 medium garlic cloves, minced
1/4 c. coconut aminos	2 tbsps. fresh lime juice
11/2 lb. NY strip steak, trimmed and sliced thinly	2 medium zucchinis, spiralized with Blade C
Salt, to taste	3 tbsps. essential olive oil
2 medium scallions, sliced	1 tsp. red pepper flakes, crushed
2 tbsps. fresh cilantro, chopped	

Directions:

In a big bowl, merge ginger, garlic, coconut aminos, and lime juice. Add beef and coat with marinade generously. Refrigerate to marinate for approximately 10-minutes. Set zucchini noodles over a large paper towel and sprinkle with salt. Keep aside for around 10-minutes. In a big skillet, warm oil on medium-high heat. Attach scallion and red pepper flakes and sauté for about 1 minute. Attach beef with marinade and Whisk fry for around 3-4-minutes or till browned. Add zucchini and cook for approximately 3-4-minutes. Serve hot.

Nutritional Information: Calories 1366, Carbs 166g, Cholesterol 6mg, Fat 67g, Protein 59g, Fiber 41g

694. Turkey and Potatoes with Buffalo Sauce

Preparation Time: 10-minutes | Total time: 30-minutes | Yield: 2-servings

Ingredients:

3 tbsps. Olive Oil	4 tbsp. Buffalo Sauce
1 lb. Sweet Potatoes, cut into cubes	½ c. Water
1 Onion, diced	½ tsp Garlic Powder
1 ½ lb. Turkey Breast, cut into pieces	

Directions:

Heat 1 tbsp. Of olive oil on SAUTÉ mode at High. Stir-fry onion in hot oil for about 3-minutes. Whisk in the remaining ingredients. Seal the lid, set it to PRESSURE COOK/MANUAL mode for 20-minutes at high pressure. When cooking is over, do a quick pressure release by turning the valve to an "open" position.

Nutritional Information: Calories 377 | Carbs 32g | Fat 9g | Protein 14g

695. Coconut Pork and Spring Onions

Preparation Time: 10-minutes | Total time: 50-minutes | Yield: 4-servings

Ingredients:

2 green onions, chopped	2 lbs. pork stew meat, roughly cubed
2 endives, shredded	4 garlic cloves, minced
1 c. cherry tomatoes, cubed	A pinch of salt and black pepper
¾ c. coconut cream	

Directions:

In a roasting pan, Mix the pork meat with the endives and the other ingredients, toss, and cook at 390 degrees F for 40-minutes. Divide everything between plates and serve.

Nutritional Information: calories 261, fat 11, fiber 1, carbs 8, protein 18

696. Pork with Spring Onions and Grapes

Preparation Time: 10-minutes | Total time: 50-minutes | Yield: 6-servings

Ingredients:

2 lbs. pork stew meat, cubed	2 spring onions, chopped
1 c. grapes, halved	2 tbsps. Olive oil
¼ tsp. Coriander, ground	¼ tsp. smoked paprika
¼ c. coconut aminos	A pinch of black pepper and salt

Directions:

Heat a pan with the oil, add the onions and the meat, and brown for 10-minutes over medium heat. Add the remaining ingredients, toss, cook over medium heat for 30-minutes more, divide between plates and serve.

Nutritional Information: calories 574, fat 29, fiber 0.5, carbs 7.6, protein 66.7

697. Tarragon Chicken with Roasted Balsamic Turnips

Preparation Time: 10-minutes | Total time: 1-hour | Yield: 2-4-servings

Ingredients:

1 lb. chicken thighs	2 lb. turnips, cut into wedges
2 tbsp. olive oil	1 tbsp. balsamic vinegar
1 tbsp. tarragon	Salt and black pepper, to taste

Directions:

Set the oven to 400°F, then grease a baking dish with olive oil. Cook turnips in boiling water for 10-minutes, drain and set aside. Add the chicken and turnips to the baking dish. Sprinkle with tarragon, black pepper, and salt. Roast for 35-minutes. Remove the baking dish, drizzle the turnip wedges with balsamic vinegar and return to the oven for another 5-minutes.

Nutritional Information: Calories: 383 | Fat: 26g | Net Carbs: 9.5g | Protein: 21.3g

698. Ground Beef with Greens & Tomatoes

Preparation Time: 15-minutes | Total time: 30-minutes | Yield: 4-servings

Ingredients:

1 tbsp. organic olive oil	½ of white onion, chopped
2 garlic cloves, chopped finely	1 jalapeño pepper, chopped finely
1 lb. lean ground beef	1 tsp. ground coriander
1 tsp. Ground cumin	½ tsp. Ground turmeric
½ tsp. Ground ginger	½ tsp. Ground cinnamon
½ tsp. ground fennel seeds	Salt, to taste
Freshly ground black pepper, to taste	8 fresh cherry tomatoes, quartered
8 collard greens leave, stemmed, and chopped	1 tsp. fresh lemon juice

Directions:

In a huge skillet, warm oil on medium heat. Put onion and sauté for approximately 4-minutes. Add garlic and jalapeño pepper and sauté for around 1 minute. Add beef and spices and cook for approximately 6-minutes, breaking into pieces while using a spoon. Whisk in tomatoes and greens and cook, stirring gently for about 4-minutes. Whisk in lemon juice and take away from heat.

Nutritional Information: Calories: 432 | Fat: 16g | Carbohydrates: 27g | Fiber: 12g | Protein: 39g

699. Home-Style Chicken Kebab

Preparation Time: 10-minutes | Total time: 20-minutes | Yield: 2-servings

Ingredients:

2 Roma tomatoes, chopped	1 lb. chicken thighs, boneless, skinless, and halved
2 tbsps. olive oil	1/2 c. Greek-style yogurt
1 ½ oz. Swiss cheese, sliced	

Directions:

Put the chicken thighs, yogurt, tomatoes, and olive oil in a glass storage container. You can add mustard seeds, cinnamon, and sumac if desired. Cover then Put in the fridge to marinate for 3 to 4 hours. Thread the chicken thighs onto skewers, creating a thick log shape. Grill the kebabs over medium-high heat for 3 or 4-minutes on each side. Use an instant-read thermometer to check the doneness of the meat; it should read about 165 degrees F. Top with the cheese; continue to cook for 4-minutes or until cheesy is melted. Enjoy!

Nutritional Information: |498 Calories|23.2g Fat|6.2g Carbs|61g Protein|1.7g Fiber

700. Tangy Barbecue Chicken

Preparation Time: 15-minutes | Total time: 3 – 4 hours + 15-minutes | Yield: 4-servings

Ingredients:

2 c. Tangy Barbecue Sauce with Apple Cider Vinegar	4- 5 (2 lb.) boneless, skinless chicken breasts

Directions:

In your slow cooker, Mix the chicken and barbecue sauce. Whisk until the chicken breasts are well coated in the sauce.

Cover the cooker and set it to high. Cook for about 3 to 4 hours / until the internal temperature of the chicken reaches 165°F on a meat thermometer and the juices run clear.

Shred the chicken with a fork, mix it into the sauce, and serve.

Nutritional Information: Calories: 41 | Total Fat: 13g | Total Carbs: 22 | Sugar: 12 | Fiber: 0 | Protein: 51 | Sodium: 766mg

CHAPTER 8:
SNACKS AND SIDES RECIPES

701. Spiced Nuts
Preparation Time: 10-minutes | Total time: 20 – 25-minutes | Yield: 2-servings

Ingredients:

1 c. almonds	½ c. walnuts
¼ c. pumpkin seeds	¼ c. sunflower seeds
½ tsp. ground cumin	1 tsp. ground turmeric
¼ tsp. red pepper flakes	¼ tsp. garlic powder

Directions:
Warm the oven to 350°F (180°C). In a medium-bowl, Whisk all the ingredients together until well combined. Split the nuts out onto a rimmed baking sheet and bake for 10 to 15-minutes, stirring once or twice halfway through, or until the nuts are lightly browned and fragrant. Let the nuts cool for 5 to 10-minutes before serving.

Nutritional Information: calories: 179 fat: 16.2g protein: 6.1g carbs: 6.8g fiber: 3.1g sugar: 1.0g

702. Lemon Garlic Red Chard
Preparation Time: 10-minutes | Total time: 17-minutes | Yield: 4-servings

Ingredients:

1 tbsp. avocado oil	1 small yellow onion, peeled and diced
1 bunch red chard, leaves, and stems chopped and kept separate (about 12 oz.)	3 cloves garlic, minced
¾ tsp. salt	Juice from ½ medium lemon
1 tsp. lemon zest	

Directions:
Put the oil in the inner pot and allow it to heat for 1 minute. Add the onion and chard stems and sauté for 5-minutes. Put the garlic and sauté for another 30 seconds. Put the chard leaves, salt, and lemon juice and Whisk to combine. Turn off. Cook again within 60 seconds. Scoop the chard mixture into a serving bowl and top with lemon zest.

Nutritional Information: Calories 57Fat: 3g Protein: 2g Sodium: 617mg Fiber: 2g Carbohydrates: 6g

703. Low Cholesterol-Low Calorie Blueberry Muffin
Preparation Time: 10-minutes | Total time: 35-minutes | Yield: 12-servings

Ingredients:

1 c. blueberries, fresh	2 tbsps. melted margarine
2 tsp. baking powder	1 ½ c. flour, all-purpose
1 egg white	½ c. skim milk or non-fat milk
1 tbsp. coconut oil	½ c. white sugar
Pinch of salt	

Directions:
Set the oven to 205C. Grease a 12-cup muffin pan using oil. In a small bowl, Put the blueberries. Add ¼ cup of the flour and mix it. Set aside. In another bowl, whisk the egg white and the coconut oil. Add the melted margarine. In a separate bowl, mix all together with the dry ingredients and sift. Sift again over the egg white mixture. Mix to moisten the flour. The flour should look lumpy, so do not overmix. Fold in the blueberries. Separate the blueberries so that each scoop will have blueberries. Scoop the mixture into the muffin pans. Fill only up to two-thirds of the pan. Bake for 25-minutes or until the muffin turns golden brown.

Nutritional Information: Calories: 114 kcal | Protein: 2.66 gFat: 5.34 g | Carbohydrates: 14.25 g

704. White Fish Ceviche with Avocado
Preparation Time: 20-minutes | Total time: 20-minutes | Yield: 6-servings

Ingredients:

Juice of 5 limes	Juice of 8 lemons
1 lb. (454 g) fresh wild white fish, cut into ½-inch cubes	1 tsp. minced fresh ginger
3 cloves garlic, minced	1 c. minced red onions
½ c. minced fresh cilantro	1 tsp. Himalayan salt
1 tsp. ground black pepper	½ medium Hass avocado, peeled, pitted, and diced

Directions:
Mix the lime juice and lemon juice in a large bowl, then dunk the fish cubes in the mixture, press so the fish is

submerged in the juice. Cover the bowl in plastic and refrigerate for at least 40-minutes. Meanwhile, Mix the ginger, garlic, onions, cilantro, salt, and ground black pepper in a small bowl. Whisk to mix well. Remove the fishbowl from the refrigerator, then sprinkle with the powder mixture. Toss to coat well. Spread the diced avocado over the ceviche and serve immediately.

Nutritional Information: Calories: 159 Fat: 4.9g Protein: 19.0g Carbs: 11.6g Fiber: 2.0g Sodium: 677mg

705. Easy Peasy Ginger Date

Preparation Time: 20-minutes | Total time: 30-minutes | Yield: 8-servings

Ingredients:

¾ c. Dates	1 tsp. Ground ginger
1 or 1 ½ c. Almonds or almond flour	¼ c. Almond milk

Directions:

Prep oven by preheating it to 350°F. If you're using fresh almonds, put them through a blender to turn them into almond flour. Blitz for 2-minutes or so until it looks and feels smooth. Don't blitz for too long, or you might end up making nut butter. Now that you have your almond powder, please put it in a bowl and set it aside. Pour the dates and almond milk into the blender and pulse for 5-minutes. If it doesn't resemble a paste, pulse for another 2-minutes. Pour in the ground ginger and almond flour. Pulse for 3 to 4-minutes to mix. Place the mixture into a baking-dish and bake for about 20-minutes. Remove from the oven. Then leave it to cool before cutting into bits. Serve or store.

Nutritional Information: Calories: 55 kcal Protein: 1.24 g Fat: 0.99 g Carbohydrates: 11.24 g

706. Clove Artichokes

Preparation time: 10-minutes | Total time: 35-minutes | Yield: 4-servings

Ingredients:

4 artichokes, trimmed and halved	4 tbsps. avocado oil
1 tbsp. garlic powder	1 tbsp. ground clove

Directions:

Rub the artichokes with garlic powder and ground clove. Sprinkle them with avocado oil.Put the artichokes in the oven and bake at 365F for 25-minutes.

Nutritional Information: 107 calories, 5.9g protein, 20.4g carbs, 2.4g fat, 10.1g fiber, 0mg

707. Parmesan Endive

Preparation time: 5-minutes | Total time: 20-minutes | Yield: 4-servings

Ingredients:

1 lb. endives, trimmed	3 oz. Parmesan, grated
1 tbsp. Olive oil	½ tsp. cayenne pepper

Directions:

Sprinkle the endives with olive oil and cayenne pepper and put them in the tray. Bake the endives for 10-minutes at 365F. Then top the endives with Parmesan and cook for 5-minutes more.

Nutritional Information: 118 calories, 8.3g protein, 4.7g carbohydrates, 8.3g fat, 3.6g fiber, 15mg

708. Cottage Cheese with Apple Sauce

Preparation Time: 5-minutes | Total time: 5-minutes | Yield: 2-servings

Ingredients:

5-6 tbsps. Cottage cheese	½ tsp. cinnamon powder
2-3 tbsps. applesauce or more if required	

Directions:

Divide the cottage cheese into 2 bowls. Spread applesauce over the cottage cheese. Sprinkle ¼ tsp. Cinnamon powder on each and serve.

Nutritional Information: Calories: 79 kcal|Protein: 8.09 g|Fat: 3.45 g |Carbohydrates: 3.92 g

709. Flourless & Flaky Muffin Munchies

Preparation Time: 25-minutes | Total time: 45-minutes | Yield: 4-servings

Ingredients:

½-c. quick oats or quinoa flakes, loosely packed	¾-tsp baking powder
¼-tsp salt	1/8-tsp baking soda
1-pc medium mashed banana, very ripe	1-c. white beans, cooked
¼-c. peanut butter or allergy-friendly substitution	2-tsp pure vanilla extract
A handful of pinch cinnamon, shredded coconut, crushed walnuts, mini chocolate chips, etc. (optional)	¼-c. pure maple syrup or honey

Directions:

Preheat the oven to 350 F. Line 8-muffin cups with glassine. Mix all the ingredients in your blender. Blend to a smooth consistency. Pour the mixture into the muffin cups at 2/3 full. Put the cups in the oven and bake for 20-minutes. Allow the muffins to sit and cool for 20-minutes.

Nutritional Information: Calories: 119 Fat: 3.9g Protein: 8.9g Sodium: 102mg Net Carbs: 11.9g

710. Homemade Guacamole

Preparation Time: 10-minutes | Total time: 10-minutes | Yield: 4-servings

Ingredients:

2 ripe avocados, peeled, pitted, and cubed	2 garlic cloves, finely minced
Juice of 1 lime	½ red onion, minced
2 tbsps. chopped fresh cilantro leaves	½ tsp. sea salt

Directions:

Put the avocados, garlic, lime juice, red onion, cilantro, and sea salt in a medium bowl. Lightly mash them using the back of a fork until a uniform consistency is achieved. Serve chilled.

Nutritional Information: Calories: 214 Fat: 19.9g Protein: 2.1g Carbs: 10.8g | Fiber: 7.3g Sugar: 1.0g

711. Bell Pepper Veggie Wraps

Preparation Time: 10-minutes | Total time: 10-minutes | Yield: 4-servings

Ingredients:

6 c. chopped red bell pepper	4 c. chopped tomatoes
2 tsp. salt	1 small avocado
½ c. flaxseed, ground	

Directions:

Blend peppers, tomatoes, and salt. Add avocado and continue blending. Add flaxseed. Spread over parchment paper on a dehydrator tray into a thin layer. Shape as tortillas. Dehydrate at 109 degrees F for 5-6 hrs. Then flip over for 4 hours. Wraps should be dry but still very pliable.

Nutritional Information: Calories: 524 kcal Protein: 15.05 g Fat: 33.86 g Carbohydrates: 48.94 g

712. Coconut Quinoa with Turmeric Spice

Prep time: 10-minutes | Total time: 35-minutes | Yield: 4-servings

Ingredients:

1 c. quinoa	2 c. water
1 c. coconut milk	1 tsp. ground turmeric

Directions:

Using a bowl, mix the first 3 ingredients. Add turmeric. Cook your meal on low heat for approximately 25-minutes.

Nutritional Information: 296 calories, 7.4g protein, 31g carbs, 16.9g fat, 4.4g fiber, 0mg sodium

713. Boiled Okra and Squash

Preparation Time: 5-minutes | Total time: 10-minutes | Yield: 1 serving

Ingredients:

½ c. of okra, cut in 1" cubes	½ c. of squash, sliced in 1" cubes
1 clove garlic, minced	Salt to taste
2/3 c. fish stock or vegetable stock, you may use plain water as well	

Directions:

Boil the liquid in high heat. Add the okra and squash. Bring to a boil. Add the garlic. Reduce the heat and simmer for at least 5-minutes or until the squash is tender. Add salt to taste and serve hot.

Nutritional Information: Calories: 117 | Protein: 8.2 g | Fat: 6.25 g | Carbohydrates: 7.82 g

714. Lemony Ginger Cookies

Preparation Time: 15-minutes + 30-minutes chill time | Total time: 55/ 57minutes | Yield: 25-servings

Ingredients:

1/2 c. arrowroot flour	1 1/2 c. stevia
3/4 tsp. salt	1/2 tsp. baking soda
1 1/2 c. coconut butter, softened	3 inches of ginger root, peeled and diced
1 tsp. nutritional yeast	Zest of 1 lemon
2 tsp. vanilla	

Directions:

Set the oven to 350F, then line two or three cookie sheets with parchment paper. Mix the arrowroot flour, stevia, salt, soda, and yeast in a bowl. In another bowl, put the remaining ingredients and mix well. Put in the dry ingredients gradually until well combined. If the dough is too soft, put an additional 1 to 2 tbsps of arrowroot powder. The dough will stiffen when chilled, so be careful. Wrap the dough in parchment and press it flat. Chill for 30-minutes. Take a chunk of the chilled dough and flatten it between two pieces of parchment until it is 1/8 inch thick. Dust with a little arrowroot powder and cut into shapes. Put on baking sheets about 1 inch apart and bake for 10 to 12-minutes. Cool on cookie sheets for 15-minutes before removing.

Nutritional Information: Calories: 112 kcal Protein: 0.44 g Fat: 11.3 g Carbohydrates: 2.49 g

715. Parmesan Asparagus

Preparation time: 10-minutes | Total time: 25-minutes | Yield: 4-servings

Ingredients:

3 oz Parmesan, grated	2 tbsps. olive oil

1 bunch asparagus, trimmed and halved	

Directions:

Line the baking tray with baking paper. Put the asparagus in the tray in one layer and sprinkle it with Parmesan and olive oil. Bake the asparagus at 385F for 15-minutes.

Nutritional Information: 142 calories, 8.3g protein, 3.4g carbs, 11.6g fat, 1.4g fiber, 15mg cholesterol

716. Rosemary Black Beans

Preparation time: 10-minutes | Total time: 10-minutes | Yield: 4-servings

Ingredients:

1 tbsp. avocado oil	2 c. drained & rinsed canned black beans
1 tbsp. dried rosemary	1 tbsp. lemon juice
1 onion, sliced	

Directions:

Mix black beans with dried rosemary and lemon juice. Add onion and avocado oil. Shake the meal nicely.

Nutritional Information: 350 calories, 21.4g protein, 63.9g carbs, 2g fat, 15.9g fiber, 7mg sodium

717. Carrot and Pumpkin Seed Crackers

Preparation Time: 10-minutes | Total time: 25-minutes | Yield: 4-servings

Ingredients:

1 1/3 c. pumpkin seeds	½ c. packed shredded carrot (about 1 carrot)
3 tbsps. Chopped fresh dill	¼ tsp. sea salt
2 tbsps. extra-virgin olive oil	

Directions:

Pre-heat the oven to 350-degrees F (180 degrees C). Line a baking sheet with parchment paper. Ground the pumpkin seeds inside a food-processor, then add the carrot, dill, salt, and olive oil to the food processor and pulse to mix well. Pour them into the prepared baking-sheet, and then shape the mixture into a rectangle with a spatula. Line a sheet of parchment paper over the rectangle, and then flatten the rectangle to about 1/8 inch thick with a rolling pin.

Remove the parchment paper-lined over the rectangle, then score it into 40 small rectangles with a sharp knife. Arrange the baking sheet in the preheated oven and bake for 15-minutes or until golden browned and crispy. Transfer the crackers to a large plate and allow them to cool for a few-minutes before serving.

Nutritional Information: Calories: 130 Fat: 11.9g Protein: 5.1g Carbs: 3.8g Fiber: 1.0g Sugar: 0

718. Peach Dip

Preparation Time: 10-minutes | Total time: 10-minutes | Yield: 2-servings

Ingredients:

½ c. nonfat: yogurt	1 c. peaches, chopped
A pinch of cinnamon powder	A pinch of nutmeg, ground

Directions:

In a bowl, Mix the yogurt while using the peaches, cinnamon, and nutmeg. Whisk and divide into small bowls and serve.

Nutritional Information: Calories: 165Fat: 2gFiber: 3gCarbs: 14gProtein: 13g

719. Oregano Green Beans

Preparation time: 10-minutes | Total time: 25-minutes | Yield: 4-servings

Ingredients:

1 lb. green beans, trimmed and halved	1 c. of water
1 tbsp. dried oregano	1 tsp. chili powder
1 tbsp. almond butter	

Directions:

Bring the water to a boil. Add green beans and boil them for 10-minutes. Then transfer the green beans to the bowl and add dried oregano, chili powder, and almond butter. Whisk the meal nicely.

Nutritional Information: 65 calories, 3.1g protein, 9.9g carbohydrates, 2.6g fat, 5g fiber

720. Party-Time Chicken Nuggets

Preparation Time: 10-minutes | Total time: 35-minutes | Yield: 6-servings

Ingredients:

2 (6 oz.) grass-fed skinless, boneless chicken breasts	2 large organic eggs
1½ c. of blanched almond flour	½ c. tapioca flour
½ tsp. of paprika	½ tsp. of onion powder
½ tsp. of garlic powder	Salt, to taste
Freshly ground black pepper, to taste	

Directions:

Preheat the oven to 400 degrees F, then grease a large baking sheet. With a rolling pin, roll the chicken breasts to an even thickness. Cut each breast into bite-sized pieces. In a shallow dish, crack the eggs and beat well. In another shallow dish, mix flours and spices. Dip the chicken nuggets in beaten eggs. Then roll in flour

mixture completely. Arrange the nuggets onto the prepared baking sheet in a single layer. Bake for about 10-12-minutes, flipping once after 5-minutes.
Nutritional Information: Calories: 238 | Fat: 12.5g | Carbs: 11.8g | Protein: 4.1g | Fiber: 2.1g

721. Berry Energy bites

Preparation Time: 10-minutes | Total time: 10-minutes | Yield: 6-servings

Ingredients:

½ c. of coconut flour	1 tsp. of cinnamon
1 tbsp. of coconut sugar	¼ c. of dried blueberries
½ - 1 c. of almond milk	

Directions:
Put together the coconut flour, cinnamon, coconut sugar, and blueberries in a huge mixing bowl, and mix well. Add the almond milk slowly until a firm dough is formed. Form into bite-sized balls and refrigerate for 30-minutes so they can harden up. Store leftovers in the refrigerator.
Nutritional Information: Dietary Fiber: 1g | Net Carbs: | Protein: 5g | Total Fat: 12g | Calories: 87

722. Carrot Sticks with Avocado Dip

Preparation Time: 10-minutes | Total time: 10-minutes | Yield: 6-servings

Ingredients:

1 large avocado, pitted	6 oz. shelled edamame
½ c. cilantro, tightly packed	½ onion
Juice of one lemon	2 tbsps. olive oil
1 tbsp. of chili-garlic sauce or chili sauce	Salt and pepper

Directions:
Put the edamame, cilantro, onion, and chili sauce in a blender or food processor. Pulse it to chop and mix the ingredients. Add the avocado and lemon juice. Gradually add the olive oil as you blend. Transfer to a jar. Scoop 2 spoons and serve with carrot sticks.
Nutritional Information: Calories: 154 kcal | Protein: 5.16 g | Fat: 11.96 g | Carbohydrates: 8.44 g

723. Paleo Ginger Spiced Mixed Nuts

Preparation Time: 5-minutes | Total time: 45-minutes | Yield: 8-servings
Ingredients:

1 tsp. Grated fresh ginger	2 Large Egg,
Egg whites	½ tsp. Vietnamese cinnamon
½ tsp. Fine Sea salt	Coconut oil spray

2 c. Mix nuts, pumpkin seeds, raw almonds, goji berries, Cashew, etc.	

Directions:
Prepare the oven by preheating to 250°F. Whisk egg whites in a bowl until it gets fluffy. Pour in sea salt, grated ginger, and Vietnamese cinnamon. Whisk until it's one large mix. Pour in the mixed nuts and Whisk to mix. Coat the parchment-lined baking sheet with coconut oil spray and spread the nut mixture across the baking sheet. Let it bake for about 20-minutes, rotate the sheet then bake for an additional 20-minutes. Take off the baking sheet from the oven and leave to cool. Once it's completely cool and hard, break them into bits with clean hands. Serve or store.
Nutritional Information: Calories: 212 kcal Protein: 6.92 g Fat: 17.3 g Carbohydrates: 10.05 g

724. Celery Spread

Preparation time: 10-minutes | Total time: 10-minutes | Yield: 2-servings

Ingredients:

6 celery stacks, chopped	3 tbsps. tomato sauce
¼ c. avocado mayonnaise	Salt and black pepper to the taste
½ tsp. garlic powder	

Directions:
Mix the celery with mayo, tomato sauce, black pepper, salt, and garlic powder in a bowl. Whisk well and divide into bowls and serve. Enjoy!
Nutritional Information: calories 100, fat 12, fiber 3, carbs 1, protein 6

725. Buckwheat Crackers

Preparation Time: 10-minutes | Total time: 10-minutes | Yield: 4-servings

Ingredients:

1½ c. raw buckwheat groats sprouted 2 days and rinsed	1 small bell pepper
½ zucchini	1 c. of young coconut meat. (This requires 1-2 young coconuts)
½ tsp. Unrefined salt.	1 tsp. dried basil (optional)
¼ tsp. dried oregano (optional)	

Directions:
Pulse buckwheat groats in the food processor. The groats should be coarsely chopped and not overly processed. Put the processed groats into a large bowl.

Quarter the bell pepper and cut zucchini into smaller pieces before placing it into the processor. In the food processor, pulse the bell pepper and zucchini into finely chopped pieces (doing your best not to puree the mixture) and add it to the bowl when done. Process coconut meat very thoroughly and add it to the bowl. Mix all ingredients well. Spread onto dehydrator trays lined with parchment paper. Dehydrate at 109 degrees F for about 18 hours. Crackers should be dehydrated without a hint of moisture or softness. Use in Put of bread for lunch. Top with avocado slices and a pinch of salt.
Nutritional Information: calories: 268 kcal Protein: 6.21 g Fat: 14.25 g Carbohydrates: 33.7 g

726. Flaxseed Crackers
Preparation Time: 10-minutes | Total time: 10-minutes | Yield: 3-servings

Ingredients:

2 c. flax seeds (soaked for 1-2 hours in 2 c. of water)	1/3 C. red bell pepper, chopped finely
2/3 C. sun-dried tomatoes	1/3 C. chopped finely fresh cilantro or basil,
1 ¼ c. tomatoes, diced	1 clove garlic, minced
Pinch cayenne	1 tsp. unrefined salt

Directions:
Put bell pepper, cilantro, sun-dried tomatoes, tomatoes, cayenne, garlic, and salt into the food processor and process until pureed. Transfer contents into a large-bowl. Then mix in the flax-seeds. Spread mixture onto a dehydrator sheet and dehydrate at 109 degrees F for about 18 hours.
Nutritional Information: calories: 1774 kcal Protein: 65.67 g Fat: 145.63 g Carbohydrates: 86.04 g

727. Dried Dates & Turmeric Truffles
Preparation Time: 15-minutes | Total time: 15-minutes | Yield: 4-servings

Ingredients:

1/3 c. walnuts	½ c. rolled oats
1 Tbsp turmeric powder + more for rolling	¼ tsp black pepper
¾ c. dates pitted	

Directions:
Whisk in all the ingredients, excluding the dates in a food processor. Blend until thoroughly combined. Add the dates gradually until forming into the dough. Shape and roll balls from the mixture. Roll each ball with the other turmeric powder until coating fully. Store the truffles in an airtight jar until ready to serve.

Nutritional Information: Calories: 95 Fat: 3.1g Protein:4.7g,Sodium:62mg Dietary Fiber: 2g Carbs: 11.8g

728. Banana Ginger Bars
Preparation Time: 10-minutes | Total time: 50-minutes | Yield: 5-servings

Ingredients:

2 large ripe bananas, peeled and mashed	1 c. coconut flour
1/3 c. coconut oil	1/3 c. raw honey
6 eggs, pasture-raised	1 tbsp. grated fresh ginger
2 tsp. cinnamon powder	1 tsp. ground cardamom powder
1 tsp. baking soda	2 tsp. apples cider vinegar

Directions:
Preheat the oven to 3500F. Grease a baking dish. In a food processor, mix the bananas, coconut flour, coconut oil, honey, eggs, ginger, cinnamon, and cardamom. Pulse until smooth. Put the baking soda plus apple cider vinegar last and quickly blend. Pour into the prepared pan. Bake within 40-minutes. Allow cooling before slicing.
Nutritional Information: Calories 364 Total Fat 26g Total Carbs 23g Protein 12g Sugar 12g Fiber: 1g

729. Soft Flourless Cookies
Preparation Time: 10-minutes | Total time: 35-minutes | Yield: 4-servings

Ingredients:

¾ c. of shredded unsweetened coconut	1 peeled large banana
Pinch of ground cinnamon	¼ tsp. of organic vanilla extract

Directions:
Set the oven to 350F. Line a cookie sheet with a large, greased parchment paper. In a large food processor, put all ingredients and pulse until well-combined. Spoon the mixture onto the prepared cookie-sheet. With your hands, flatten the cookies slightly.
Bake for at least 25-minutes or till golden brown.
Nutritional Information: Calories: 68 | Fat: 9.5g | Carbs: 11.8g | Protein: 5.1g | Fiber: 2.1g

730. Mexican Veggie Meat
Preparation Time: 10-minutes | Total time: 10-minutes | Yield: 4-servings

Ingredients:

2 c. sunflower seeds, soaked 8 hours and rinsed	5 c. zucchini, shredded

1/2 c. onion, minced	1 c. celery, minced
1/2 c. homemade chili powder	1/4 c. lemon juice
1 tsp. unrefined salt	2 garlic cloves, crushed

Directions:
Use a food processor to process sunflower seeds into flour. In a large bowl, mix with other ingredients. Spread the mixture onto two dehydrator sheets lined with parchment paper. Dehydrate at 109 degrees F for 5 hours (or until it reaches your desired consistency).
Nutritional Information: calories: 2132 Protein: 80.1 g Fat: 163.49 g Carbohydrates: 153.89 g

731. Green Bean Snack
Preparation time: 10-minutes | Total time: 8-hours 10-minutes | Yield: 8-servings

Ingredients:

1/3 c. coconut oil, melted	5 lbs. green beans
Salt to the taste	1 tsp. garlic powder
1 tsp. onion powder	

Directions:
In a bowl, mix green beans with coconut oil, salt, garlic, and onion powder. Put them in your dehydrator and dry them for 8 hours at 135 degrees. Serve cold as a snack. Enjoy!
Nutritional Information: calories 100, fat 12, fiber 4, carbs 8, protein 5

732. Mandarin Cottage Cheese
Preparation Time: 5-minutes | Total time: 5-minutes | Yield: 1 serving

Ingredients:

1/2 c. low-fat cottage cheese	1/2 c. canned mandarin oranges
1 1/2 tbsps. slivered almonds	

Directions:
Put the cottage cheese in a bowl. Drain the mandarin oranges, Put them atop the cottage cheese, and sprinkle with almonds.
Nutritional Information: Calories: 360 kcal Protein: 26.24 g Fat: 21.37 g Carbohydrates: 15.22

733. Cardamom Roasted Apricots
Preparation Time: 10-minutes | 35 – 40-minutes | Yield: 4-servings

Ingredients:

20 fresh apricots, pitted and quartered	2 tbsps. coconut oil
1/8 tsp. cardamom (optional)	

Directions:
Pre-heat the oven to 350-degrees F (180 degrees C). Toss the apricots with the coconut oil and cardamom (if desired) in a baking dish until well coated. Roast in the preheated oven for about 25 to 30-minutes, stirring once or twice during cooking, or until the apricots begin to caramelize. Let the apricots cool for 5 to 10-minutes before serving.
Nutritional Information: Calories: 141, Fat: 8.2g, Protein: 2.0g, Carbs: 18.9g, Fiber: 3.1g, Sugar: 11.7g

734. Lime Brussels Sprouts
Preparation time: 10-minutes | Total time: 30-minutes | Yield: 4-servings

Ingredients:

2 lbs. Brussels sprouts, trimmed and halved	1 tbsp. olive oil
2 tbsps. lime juice	1 tsp. lime zest, grated
1 tsp. ground paprika	

Directions:
Mix Brussel sprouts with olive oil, lime juice, lime zest, and ground paprika. Put the vegetables in line with the baking paper tray and bake for 20-minutes at 365F.
Nutritional Information: 130 calories, 7.8g protein, 21g carbs, 4.3g fat, 8.8g sodium, 895mg potassium.

735. Blueberry Curd
Preparation Time: 10-minutes | Total time: 25-minutes | Yield: 4-servings

Ingredients:

2 tbsps. lemon juice	2 tbsps. sunflower oil
1 tbsp. chicory root powder	12 oz. blueberries
2 tbsps. Flax meal mixed with 4 tbsps. water	

Directions:
Mix the blueberries with lemon juice, oil, chicory powder, and flax meal in a small pot. Bring to a boil over medium-heat and then cook for about 15-minutes. Divide into bowls and serve cold. Enjoy!
Nutritional Information: calories 113, fat 8, fiber 4, carbs 12, protein 1

736. Cabbage Bowl
Preparation time: 10-minutes | Total time: 30-minutes | Yield: 4-servings

Ingredients:

4 c. white cabbage	1 c. tomatoes, diced
2 tbsps. olive oil	2 c. of water
1 tsp. dried parsley	

Directions:
Mix white cabbage with tomatoes in the saucepan. Add water, dried parsley, and olive oil. Close the lid and simmer the meal on medium heat for 20-minutes.
Nutritional Information: 86 calories, 1.3g protein, 5.8g carbohydrates, 7.2g fat, 2.3g fiber

737. Turmeric Coconut Flour Muffins

Preparation Time: 5-minutes | Total time: 30-minutes | Yield: 8-servings

Ingredients:

½ c. Unsweetened coconut milk	¾ c. & 2 tbsp. Coconut flour
1 tsp. Vanilla extract	6 large Whole eggs
½ tsp. Baking soda	½ tsp. Ginger powder
Pepper and salt	2 tsp. Turmeric
1/3 c. Maple syrup	

Directions:
Preheat the oven to 350F.Prepare 8 muffin tins with muffin liners. In a mixing-bowl, whisk the maple syrup, eggs, milk, and vanilla extract together until the egg begins to form bubbles. Combine the coconut-flour, turmeric powder, pepper, baking soda, ginger powder, and salt in a separate-bowl. Whisk the dry ingredient into the wet mixture until it is completely combined and thick. Spoon out the batter into the prepared muffin tins. Leave it to bake until it looks golden, for about 25-minutes. Let the muffins cool for 1-2-minutes before transferring them to a rack.
Nutritional Information: Calories: 143 kcal Protein: 6.18 g Fat: 8 g Carbohydrates: 11.8 g

738. Mini Pepper Nachos

Preparation Time: 5-minutes | Total time: 15-minutes | Yield: 8-servings

Ingredients:

1 c. Tomato, chopped	1 tbsp. Chili powder
1 c. Cheddar cheese, shredded	1 tsp. Cumin, ground
16 oz. Mini peppers, seeded, halved	1 tsp. Garlic powder
16 oz. Ground beef	1 tsp. Paprika
½tsp. Red pepper flakes	½ tsp. Salt
½ tsp. Oregano	½ tsp. Pepper

Directions:
Mix seasonings together in a bowl. On medium heat, brown the meat, be sure all the clumps are broken up. Mix in the spices and continue to sauté until the seasoning has gone through all the meat. Heat the oven to 400F. Put the peppers in a single line. They can touch.

Coat with the beef mix. Sprinkle with cheese. Bake for at least 1--minutes / until cheese has melted. Pull out of the oven and top with the toppings.
Nutritional Information: Calories: 240 kcal | Protein: 11.01 g | Fat: 18.2 g | Carbohydrates: 9.49 g

739. Cado Choco Cake

Preparation Time: 10-minutes | Total time: 35-minutes | Yield: 8-servings

Ingredients:

1pc large avocado	1tsp vanilla extract
½c. maple syrup	½c. applesauce, unsweetened
3pcs large eggs	1tsp baking soda
½c. cocoa powder, unsweetened and Dutch-processed	½c. coconut flour
¼tsp sea salt	

Directions:
Preheat your oven to 350°F. Grease a baking pan with coconut oil. Mix the avocado, vanilla, syrup, and applesauce in your food processor. Blend until thoroughly combined. Transfer the mixture into a large mixing-bowl. Whisk in the eggs. Add the baking soda, cocoa powder, coconut flour, and sea salt. Mix well until thoroughly combined. Add the butter to the baking pan. Put the pan in the oven. Bake for 25-minutes. Allow cooling for 20-minutes before cutting the cake into 16 squares.
Nutritional Information: Calories: 253 Fat: 8.4g Protein: 12.6g Sodium: 245mg Net Carbs: 31.6g

740. Massaged Kale Chips

Preparation Time: 5-minutes | Total time: 25-minutes | Yield: 2-servings

Ingredients:

4 c. kale, stemmed, rinsed, drained, torn into 2-inch pieces	2 tbsps. extra-virgin olive oil
1 tsp. sea salt	2 tbsps. apple cider vinegar

Directions:
Warm the oven to 350°F (180°C). Mix all the ingredients in a large bowl. Whisk to mix well. Gently massage the kale leaves in the bowl for 5-minutes or until wilted and bright. Put the kale on a baking sheet. Bake inside the oven for 20-minutes or until crispy. Toss the kale halfway through. Remove the kale from the oven and serve immediately.
Nutritional Information: calories: 138 fat: 13.8g protein: 1.4g carbs: 2.9g fiber: 1.2g sugar: 3g

741. Berry Delight

Preparation Time: 15-minutes | Total time: 15-minutes | Yield: 6-servings

Ingredients:

1 c. of fresh organic blueberries	1 c. of fresh organic raspberries
1 c. of fresh organic blackberries	¼ c. of raw honey
1 tbsp. of cinnamon	

Directions:

Mix all the berries in a large bowl, add in the honey, and gently stir. Sprinkle with cinnamon.

Nutritional Information: Carbohydrates: 20g | Dietary Fiber: 3g | Protein: 1g | Fat: 0g | Calories: 78

742. Kale Chips

Preparation Time: 5-minutes | Total time: 20-minutes | Yield: 8-servings

Ingredients:

1 bunch kale leaves	1 tbsp. organic olive oil
1 tsp. smoked paprika	A pinch of black pepper

Directions:

Spread the kale leaves over a baking sheet, add black pepper, oil, and paprika. Toss and put inside the oven and bake at 350 degrees F for a quarter-hour. Divide into bowls and serve to be a snack.

Nutritional Information: Calories: 177Fat: 2gFiber: 4gCarbs: 13gProtein: 6g

743. Pecan and Spice Stuffed Apple Bake

Preparation Time: 10-minutes | Total time: 2 hours 10-minutes | Yield: 5 apples

Ingredients:

5 apples, cored	½ c. water
½ c. crushed pecans	¼ tsp. ground cloves
1 tsp. Ground cinnamon	¼ tsp. Ground cardamom
½ tsp. ground ginger	¼ c. melted coconut oil

Directions:

Peel a thin strip off the top of each apple. Pour the water in the slow cooker, then arrange the apples in the slow cooker, upright. Mix the remaining ingredients in a small bowl. Whisk to mix well. Spread the mixture on the tops of the apples, then put the slow cooker lid on and cook on high for 2 hours or until the apples are tender. Allow cooling for 15-minutes, gently remove the apples from the slow cooker, and serve warm.

Nutritional Information: (1 apple) calories: 216; fat: 11.6g; protein: 0g; carbs: 30.1g; fiber: 6.2g;

744. Toasted Pumpkin Seeds

Preparation Time: 5-minutes | Total time: 35-minutes | Yield: 2-4-servings

Ingredients:

1 to 2 c. pumpkin seeds	Water
1 tsp. salt Sea salt	1/2 tsp. extra virgin olive oil

Directions:

Put seeds in a saucepan and cover with water. Add salt. Bring it to a boil and boil for 10-minutes. Simmer uncovered for 10 more-minutes. These-servings the seeds very crispy when baked. Drain the seeds and pat dry using a paper towel. Cover a baking sheet with parchment paper and spread out the seeds in a single layer. Dust with salt, then bake in an oven at 325F for at least 10-minutes, stirring halfway through. Cool, then store in an airtight container.

Nutritional Information: Calories: 192 kcal Protein: 10.41 g Fat: 16.23 g Carbohydrates: 4.34 g

745. Steamed Cauliflower

Preparation Time: 5-minutes | Total time: 7-minutes | Yield: 6-servings

Ingredients:

1 large head cauliflower, cored and cut into large florets	2 c. water

Directions:

Put two cups of water into the inner pot. Put a steam rack inside. Put the cauliflower inside a steamer basket and put the basket on the steam rack, steam within 2-minutes. Carefully remove the steamer basket and serve.

Nutritional Information: Calories: 34 Fat: 0g Protein: 3g Sodium: 41mg Fiber: 3g Carbs: 7g Sugar: 3g

746. Garlic Chili Edamame

Preparation Time: 5-minutes | Total time: 20-minutes | Yield: 4-servings

Ingredients:

1 lb. Edamame – 1 lb.	½ tsp. Sesame seed oil – 0.5 tsp.
2 tbsps. Extra virgin olive oil – 2 tbsps.	3 cloves Garlic, minced – 3 cloves
2 tbsps. Chili paste – 2 tbsps. Sea salt – 1 tsp.	Date paste – 1 tsp.

Directions:

Head a large skillet over medium-high heat and wait for it to warm up before adding in your edamame.

Allow your edamame to sear undisturbed until the bottom sides are charred, and then give them a light stir. Let the pods cook this way until both sides are charred and tender. Remove the edamame from the skillet and set it aside. Reduce the stove's heat to medium and then add the garlic, allowing it to toast for about thirty seconds. Add the remaining ingredients, stirring together until combined, and then add back to the charred edamame. Cook the edamame in the sauce for a minute or two before removing it from the heat and serving warm.

Nutritional Information: Calories: 187 kcal, Protein: 13.16 g, Fat: 9.7 g, Carbohydrates: 15.38 g

747. Butternut Squash Fries

Preparation Time: 20-minutes | Total time: 1-hour | Yield: 4-servings

Ingredients:

1 large butternut squash, deseeded, peeled, and cut into fry-size pieces, about 3 inches long and ½ inch thick	3 fresh rosemary sprigs, stemmed and chopped (about 1½ tablespoons)
¾ tsp. sea salt 2 tbsps. Coconut oil	

Directions:

Warm the oven to 190 degrees C (375 degrees F). Line a baking sheet with parchment paper. Put the butternut-squash in a large-bowl, then drizzle with coconut oil and sprinkle with salt. Toss to coat well. Arrange the butternut squash pieces in a single layer on the prepared baking sheet. Bake in the preheated oven for 40-minutes or until golden brown and crunchy. Flip the zucchini fries at least three times during the cooking and top the fries with rosemary sprigs halfway through. Transfer the fries to a cooling-rack and allow them to cool for a few-minutes. Serve warm.

Nutritional Information: Calories: 191 Fat: 6.8g Protein: 3.0g Carbs: 34.1g Fiber: 7.2g Sugar: 5.9g

748. Beef Bites

Preparation Time: 10-minutes | Total time: 25-minutes | Yield: 4-servings

Ingredients:

1 tbsp. lime juice	2 tbsps. avocado oil
1-lb. beef stew meat, cubed	2 garlic cloves, minced
1 c. beef stock	

Directions:

Start by adding oil and meat to a cooking pan, then sauté for 5-minutes. Whisk in remaining ingredients

and mix well. Cover the pot's lid and cook for 30-minutes on medium heat. Serve fresh and enjoy.

Nutritional Information: Calories 142 Fat 8.4 g Carbs 3.4 g Sugar 1 g Fiber 0.8 g Protein 4.1 g

749. Simple Coconut Pancakes

Preparation Time: 10-minutes | Total time: 15-minutes | Yield: 8-servings

Ingredients:

4 eggs	1 c. coconut milk, plus additional as needed
1 tbsp. pure maple syrup	1 tsp. vanilla extract
1 tbsp. melted coconut oil	½ c. coconut flour
1 tsp. Baking soda	½ tsp. sea salt

Directions:

Whisk together the eggs, coconut milk, maple syrup, vanilla, and coconut oil in a large bowl. Whisk to mix well. Mix the baking soda, salt, and coconut flour in a separate bowl. Whisk to mix well. Make a well at the center of the coconut-flour mixture, then pour the egg mixture into the well. Whisk to mix well until smooth and no lump. Grease a nonstick skillet with coconut oil, then heat over medium-high heat until shimmering. Divide the batter, pour ½ cup of batter into the skillet, and cook for 5-minutes or lightly browned. Flip halfway through the cooking time. Repeat with the remaining batter. Transfer the pancakes to four plates and serve immediately.

Nutritional Information: calories: 192 fat: 10.6g protein: 9.1g carbs: 14.9g fiber: 6.5g sugar: 5.7g

750. Cucumber Rolls Hors D'oeuvres

Preparation Time: 20-minutes | Total time: 20-minutes | Yield: 8-10-servings

Ingredients:

4 normal cucumbers	

For the avocado spread:

½ c. capers	1 tsp. Himalayan pink salt
¼ c. fresh dill, finely chopped	½ c. fresh parsley + extra to garnish, finely chopped
5-6 ripe avocadoes, peeled, pitted, mashed	Freshly cracked pepper to taste

Directions:

Peel the cucumbers and cut thin slices along the length on a mandolin slicer. Put the cucumber slices on your countertop. To make the avocado spread: Add all the ingredients of avocado spread into a bowl and mix until well combined. Spread the avocado mixture evenly and thinly on the cucumber slices. Start rolling from one of the shorter-ends to the other end and Put on a serving platter with its seam side facing down. Repeat the above step with the remaining cucumber slices. Serve immediately as the cucumbers tend to get soggy after a while.

Nutritional Information: Calories: 227 kcal | Protein: 3.77 g | Fat: 19.88 g | Carbohydrates: 12.99 g

751. Spicy Kale Chips

Preparation time: 10-minutes | Total time: 1-hour 40-minutes | Yield: 10-servings

Ingredients:

2 c. cashews, soaked and drained	1 bunch kale, trimmed and leaves separated
Salt and black pepper to the taste	3 tbsps. avocado oil
Juice of 1 lemon	2/3 c. jarred roasted peppers
1 tsp. Italian seasoning	¼ tsp. chili powder
½ tsp. garlic powder	

Directions:

In your food processor, mix cashews with peppers, oil, lemon juice, Italian seasoning, chili powder, garlic powder, salt, and pepper and blend very well. In a bowl, mix kale leaves with cashews, mix and massage well. Spread them on a lined baking-sheet. Bake at 400degrees F in the oven for 1 hour. Flip and cook Spicy Kale Chips for 30-minutes more, then allow to cool. Serve the chips cold. Enjoy!

Nutritional Information: calories 126, fat 7, fiber 2, carbs 9, protein 7

752. Chewy Choco Chip Cookies

Preparation Time: 15-minutes | Total time: 25-minutes | Yield: 6-servings

Ingredients:

¾-c. almond butter	½-c. coconut sugar
¼-c. cocoa powder	2-tsps vanilla extract
1-pc egg	1-tsp baking soda
¼-tsp salt	½-c. chocolate chips
A dash of sea salt (optional)	

Directions:

Preheat your oven to 350°F. In the meantime, use parchment paper to line two baking trays. Mix the almond butter, coconut sugar, vanilla, and cocoa powder in a medium-sized bowl. Whisk the egg and egg yolk in another bowl. Add the egg mixture to the almond butter mixture. Mix well until combined thoroughly. Add the baking soda, salt, and chocolate chips. Whisk well until

thoroughly combined. Form balls from the dough and put six balls on each tray. Put the trays in the oven. Bake for 10-minutes. Let the cookies cook for 5-minutes as they continue to cook in the tray. Sprinkle over with a dash of sea salt, if desired.

Nutritional Information: Calories: 226 Fat: 7.5g Protein: 11.3g Sodium: 154mg Net Carbs: 28.2g

753. Frozen Blueberry Yogurt Bites

Preparation Time: 10-minutes | Total time: 10-minutes | Yield: 2-servings

Ingredients:

2 c. plain whole-milk yogurt	1 banana
½ c. fresh blueberries	1 tbsp. raw honey

Directions:

Line a baking-sheet with a piece of wax paper. Pulse the banana, yogurt, blueberries, and honey in a blender until smooth and creamy. Transfer the smooth mixture to a large resealable plastic bag with the corner snipped off. Squeeze the mixture into quarter-sized dots onto the prepared baking sheet. Transfer to the freezer to freeze until solid. Store leftovers in an airtight container in the freezer.

Nutritional Information: Calories: 91 Fat: 3.1g Protein: 3.0g Carbs: 12.8g Fiber: 1.0g Sugar: 10.0g

754. Turmeric Muffins

Preparation Time: 10-minutes | Total time: 35-minutes | Yield: 8 muffins

Ingredients:

¾ c. + 2 tbsp. Coconut Flour	6 Eggs, large & preferably pastured
½ tsp. Ginger Powder	½ c. Coconut Milk, unsweetened
Dash of Salt & Pepper	1/3 c. Maple Syrup
½ tsp. Baking Soda	1 tsp. Vanilla Extract
2 tsp. Turmeric	

Directions:

Preheat the oven to 350 degrees F. After that, mix eggs, vanilla extract, milk, maple syrup, and milk in a large mixing bowl until combined well. Mix turmeric, coconut flour, ginger powder, baking soda, pepper, and salt in another bowl. Now, gradually Whisk in the coconut flour mixture to the milk mixture until you get a smooth batter. Then, pour the smooth mixture into a paper-lined muffin pan while distributing it evenly. Finally, bake them for 20 to 25-minutes or until slightly browned at the edges. Allow the muffins to cool completely.

Tip: They are freezer friendly and stay good for one month.
Nutritional Information: Calories: 220 Cal Proteins: 1.1 g Carbohydrates: 2.1 g Fat: 1.2 g

755. Almonds and Blueberries Yogurt Snack

Preparation Time: 10-minutes | Total time: 10-minutes | Yield: 2-servings

Ingredients:

1 ½ c. nonfat Greek yogurt	20 almonds, chopped
1 c. blueberries	

Directions:
Take 2 bowls and add ¾ cup yogurt into each bowl. Divide the blueberries among the bowls and stir. Sprinkle half the almonds in each bowl and serve.
Nutritional Information: Calories: 223 kcal | Protein: 6.57 g | Fat: 9.45 g | Carbohydrates: 30.82 g

756. Balsamic Onion Snack

Preparation time: 10-minutes | Total time: 20-minutes | Yield: 4-servings

Ingredients:

1 lb. pearl onions, peeled	A pinch of salt and black pepper
½ c. water	4 tbsps. balsamic vinegar
1 tbsp. coconut flour	

Directions:
In a small pot, whisk the water with vinegar and coconut flour. Bring to a simmer over medium heat. Add the pearl onions, toss, cook for 10-minutes, Drain the liquid, divide into bowls, and serve as a snack. Enjoy!
Nutritional Information: calories 100, fat 9, fiber 4, carbs 11, protein 6

757. Cayenne Pepper Green Beans

Preparation time: 10-minutes | Total time: 30-minutes | Yield: 4-servings

Ingredients:

1 tsp. cayenne pepper	1 lb. green beans, trimmed and halved
1 tbsp. avocado oil	2 c. of water

Directions:
Bring the water to a boil. Then add the green-beans. Cook them for 10-minutes. Then remove water and add avocado oil and cayenne pepper. Roast the vegetables for 2-3-minutes on high heat.
Nutritional Information: 41 calories, 2.2g protein, 8.5g carbohydrates, 0.7g fat, 4.1g fiber, 11mg sodium

758. After's Apple Cinnamon Chips

Preparation Time: 20-minutes | Total time: 2-hours 50-minutes | Yield: 3-servings

Ingredients:

3 pcs large apples, cored, rinsed, and drained	¾ tsp cinnamon, ground

Directions:
Preheat your oven to 200°F. Line two baking pans with parchment paper. Using a very sharp knife / a mandolin, slice the apples horizontally into 1/8-inch-thick rounds. Assemble the slices in a single layer on the baking pans. Sprinkle over with the cinnamon. Put the pans in the upper and lower racks of the oven and then bake for 1 hour. Switch positions of the pans on the upper and lower racks. Bake for another hour, or until a single chip becomes crispy when set at room temperature for 3-minutes. Switch off the oven and allow the chips to sit in the oven for an hour while cooling down for additional crispiness.
Nutritional Information: Calories 65 Fat 2.1g Protein: 3.2g Sodium: 2mg Dietary Fiber: 5g Net Carbs: 8.2g

759. Garlic Cashew "Hummus"

Preparation Time: 20-minutes | Total time: 20-minutes | Yield: 1 serving

Ingredients:

1 c. raw cashews, soaked in filtered water for 15-minutes and drained	¼ c. filtered water Pinch cayenne pepper
2 garlic cloves	1 tbsp. extra-virgin olive oil
1 tsp. freshly squeezed lemon juice	2 tsp. Coconut aminos
½ tsp. Ground ginger	¼ tsp. sea salt

Directions:
Put all the ingredients inside a blender and blend together until completely mixed. You'll need to stop the blender occasionally to scrape down the sides. Serve immediately or refrigerate to chill for at least 2 hours for the best flavor.
Nutritional Information: calories: 111 fat: 8.7g protein: 3.0g carbs: 5.2g fiber: 0.7g sugar: 5.9g

760. Almond Yogurt, Berry, and Walnut Parfait

Preparation Time: 10-minutes | Total time: 10-minutes | Yield: 2-servings

Ingredients:

2 c. plain unsweetened almond yogurt	2 tbsps. honey

1 c. fresh raspberries	1 c. fresh blueberries
½ c. walnut pieces	

Directions:
Mix the yogurt & honey in a bowl. Whisk to mix well, then pour half of the honey yogurt in a large glass. Top the honey yogurt with berries, then top the berries with the remaining honey yogurt. Spread the walnut pieces on top and serve immediately.
Nutritional Information: Calories: 504 Fat: 22.1g Protein: 22.9g Carbs: 56.0g | Fiber: 8.1g Sugar: 16.2g

761. Easy Eggplant Spread
Preparation time: 10-minutes | Total time: 10-minutes | Yield: 6-servings

Ingredients:

2 lbs. eggplant, baked, peeled, and chopped	A pinch of salt and black pepper
4 tbsps. olive oil	4 garlic cloves, chopped
Juice of 1 lemon	¼ c. black olives, pitted
1 tbsp. sesame paste	

Directions:
Mix the eggplant with salt, pepper, oil, garlic, lemon juice, olives, and sesame paste in a blender. Blend until smooth, then divide into bowls and serve. Enjoy!
Nutritional Information: calories 165, fat 11, fiber 4, carbs 8, protein 5

762. Cauliflower Puree
Preparation time: 10-minutes | Total time: 35-minutes | Yield: 4-servings

Ingredients:

1 lb. cauliflower florets	1 c. coconut cream
1 oz. Parmesan, grated	

Directions:
Mix cauliflower with coconut cream and simmer the mixture for 10-minutes. Then mash it using the potato-masher and mix it with parmesan.
Nutritional Information: 189 calories, 5.9g protein, 9.6g carbs, 15.9g fat, 4.2g fiber, 5mg sodium

763. Cumin Zucchini Spread
Preparation time: 10-minutes | Total time: 10-minutes | Yield: 5-servings

Ingredients:

4 c. chopped zucchini	¼ c. olive oil
Salt and black pepper to the taste	4 garlic cloves, minced
¾ c. tahini	½ c. lemon juice
1 tbsp. ground cumin	

Directions:
Mix zucchini with salt, pepper, oil, lemon juice, garlic, tahini, and cumin in your blender. Pulse until smooth, then divide into small bowls and serve. Enjoy!
Nutritional Information: calories 110, fat 5, fiber 3, carbs 6, protein 7

764. Lemon Carrots
Preparation time: 10-minutes | Total time: 35-minutes | Yield: 4-servings

Ingredients:

1 lemon	1 lb. carrot, peeled, chopped
1 tsp. ground cinnamon	1 tbsp. olive oil

Directions:
Mix the carrots with ground cinnamon and olive oil. Put the carrot in the baking tray. Then squeeze the lemon juice over the carrots. Bake the carrots at 385F for 25-minutes.
Nutritional Information: 82 calories, 1.1g protein, 13g carbs, 3.6g fat, 3.5g fiber, 78mg sodium

765. Almond and Honey Homemade Bar
Preparation Time: 15-minutes + 30-minutes' fridge time | Total time: 1 hour | Yield: 8-servings

Ingredients:

A ¼ c. of almonds	1 c. oats
¼ c. sunflower seeds	1/3 c. currants
1 tbsp. flaxseeds	1/3 c. apricots (dried and chopped)
1/3 c. raisins (chopped)	1 tbsp. sesame seeds
1 c. whole-grain puffed cereal (unsweetened)	¼ c. almond butter
¼ c. honey	1/8 tsp salt
¼ c. sugar (or another sweetener to your taste in adjusted amount)	½ tsp. vanilla extract

Directions:
Preheat the oven to 350 degrees Fahrenheit. Put a baking paper into an 8-inch pan or coat it with cooking spray/oil. Mix the almonds, oats, and seeds and spread the mixture on a rimmed baking sheet. Bake the mixture until you notice that the oats are lightly toasted (for about 10-minutes). Transfer the mixture to a bowl. Add cereal, raisins, currants, and apricots to the bowl.
Toss well to combine. Mix honey, almond butter, vanilla, salt, and sugar in a saucepan. Heat over medium heat. Whisk frequently for 2-5-minutes until you see light bubbles. Immediately you notice the bubbles, pour the mixture over the dry mixture with apricots

and oats you prepared previously. Mix well with a spatula. There mustn't be any dry spots. Transfer the new mixture to the previously prepared pan. Press it to the pan to make a firm and flat layer. Refrigerate for 30-minutes. Cut the layer into eight equal bars or squares, to your taste. Consume immediately or refrigerate for up to seven days. You can store these energy bars in the freezer as well (for long-term storage). Wrap them in stretch plastic folium and store them at –16 to –18 degrees.

Nutritional Information: Calories: 213 kcal Protein: 6.92 g Fat: 9.59 g Carbohydrates: 32.33 g

766. Candied Dates

Preparation Time: 5-minutes | Total time: 5-minutes | Yield: 2-servings

Ingredients:

4 pitted Medjool dates	2 tbsps. of peanut butter
2 tbsps. of dark cocoa nibs	

Directions:

Slice the pitted dates in half and spread half a tbsp of peanut butter on each date. Top each date with half a tbsp of dark cocoa nibs. Divide the candied dates between two plates and enjoy!

Nutritional Information: Carbohydrates: 20g | Dietary Fiber: 3g | Protein: 5g | Fat: 12g | Calories: 187

767. Turmeric Gummies

Preparation Time: 5-minutes | Total time: 4-hours 15-minutes | Yield: 4-servings

Ingredients:

6 tbsp. Maple syrup	3 ½ c. Water
8 tbsp. Unflavored gelatin powder	1 tsp. Ground turmeric
¼ tsp. Ground pepper	

Directions:

Mix the ground turmeric, maple syrup, and water in a pot set over medium heat. Whisk constantly for 5-minutes before removing from heat and pouring in the gelatin powder. Whisk with a wooden spoon to dissolve the gelatin. Put back the pan on the heat and whisk for another 2-minutes. Turn off the heat and take the mixture to a deep bowl that you will seal with plastic wrap right after. Refrigerate the mixture for about 4 hours. It should be firm now, cut into small squares, and served or stored.

Nutritional Information: Calories: 123 kcal Protein: 2.15 g Fat: 1.56 g Carbohydrates: 25.67 g

768. Date Dough & Walnut Wafer

Preparation Time: 15-minutes | Total time: 33-minutes | Yield: 8-servings

Ingredients:

1½-c. oats (divided)	6-pcs Medjool dates, pitted and sliced into quarters
½-c. coconut, unsweetened	½-tsp baking soda
¼-tsp sea salt	½-c. walnuts
2-Tbsps ground flaxseed	1-pc egg
¼-c. coconut oil	For the Date Layer:
18-pcs Medjool dates pitted	1-tsp lemon juice
½-tsp sea salt	

Directions:

Preheat your oven to 325°F. Line a baking pan with parchment paper. Pulse a cup of oats in your food processor until forming a flour consistency. Add in the dates, coconut, baking soda, and sea salt. Pulse again until the dates entirely break up. Add the remaining oats and walnuts, and pulse until the nuts break but are still chunky. Add the flaxseed, egg, and oil. Pulse the mixture further until thoroughly combined. Set aside ½-cup of the date mixture to use as a topping later. Press down the remaining mix to an even layer in the pan. Rinse your food processor and add all the data layer ingredients. Pulse the mixture until the dates entirely break up and take on a light caramel color.

With wet hands, press the mixture down, smoothing it on the date mixture. Crumble and sprinkle the reserved date mixture over the top. Put the pan in the oven. Bake for 18-minutes. Allow the water to cool completely before slicing into 16 pieces.

Nutritional Information: Calories: 203 Fat: 6.7g Protein: 10.1g Sodium: 76mg Carbs: 28.3g

769. Protein-Packed Croquettes

Preparation Time: 10-minutes | Total time: 15-minutes | Yield: 12-servings

Ingredients:

¼ c. plus 1 tbsp. of olive oil, divided	½ c. of thawed frozen peas
2 minced garlic cloves	1 c. of cooked quinoa
2 large peeled and mashed boiled potatoes	Freshly ground black pepper, to taste
Salt, to taste	¼ tsp. of ground turmeric
½ tsp. of paprika	2 tsp. of ground cumin
¼ c. of chopped fresh cilantro leaves	

Directions:
In a frying pan, heat 1 tbsp. of oil on medium heat. Add peas and garlic and sauté for about 1 minute. Transfer the peas mixture into a large bowl. Put remaining ingredients, then mix till well combined. Make equal sized oblong shaped patties from the mixture. In a huge skillet, warm the remaining oil on medium-high heat. Add croquettes in batches and fry for about 4-minutes per side.
Nutritional Information: Calories: 165 | Fat: 12.5g | Carbs: 10. 8g | Protein: 5.1g | Fiber: 3.1g

770. Quinoa Tortillas

Preparation Time: 10-minutes | Total time: 10-minutes | Yield: 4-servings

Ingredients:

2 medium potatoes, un-peeled	1 c. arrowroot powder, plus more for rolling
1 c. sprouted quinoa flour	1 ½ tsps. flaxseed, ground
1 ½ tsps. guar gum	1 tsp. unrefined salt

Directions:
Put whole potatoes into a steamer basket and saucepan with approximately 1 inch of water at the bottom of the saucepan. Cover the saucepan. Bring water to a boil and then lower heat to simmer until tender, about 20-minutes. Drain fluid and remove potatoes from the saucepan. Cut potatoes so that they fill a measuring cup and measure 1½ cup to use for the recipe. Place the potatoes in a food-processor with the remaining ingredients and process until a dough is formed. The dough should not be sticky; add quinoa flour until the dough is soft, pliable, and does not stick to your hands.
When the dough is well blended, spoon it into your hand and form into small balls, approximately 2 inches in diameter
Use a tortilla-press to press the dough ball into a flat tortilla. If no tortilla press is available, roll the dough into thin circles, dusting lightly with arrowroot flour to prevent sticking. Put the tortillas in heated cast iron or ceramic skillet for about 1 minute, turn over with a spatula, and toast until lightly golden brown on both sides. Use them as you would use a tortilla or taco.
Nutritional Information: calories: 650 kcal Protein: 22.47 g Fat: 6.69 g Carbohydrates: 127.77 g

771. Cilantro Brussels Sprouts

Preparation time: 10-minutes | Total time: 30-minutes | Yield: 4-servings

Ingredients:

2 tbsps. olive oil	1 lb. Brussels sprouts, trimmed and halved
¼ c. fresh cilantro, chopped	1 tbsp. lemon juice

Directions:
Line the baking tray with baking paper. Then mix Brussel sprouts with cilantro, lemon juice, and olive oil. Put the vegetables in the tray in one layer and bake at 385F for 20-minutes.
Nutritional Information: 110 calories, 3.9g protein, 10.4g carbs, 7.4g fat, 4.3g fiber, 451mg potassium.

772. Buttered Banana Chickpea Cookies

Preparation Time: 10-minutes | Total time: 22-minutes | Yield: 8-servings

Ingredients:

15 oz. chickpeas, rinsed and drained	½ c. creamy peanut butter
1 pc small banana, very ripe	2 tsp vanilla extract
1/3 c. coconut sugar	2 Tbsps ground flaxseed
1 tsp baking powder	¼ tsp salt
¼ tsp cinnamon	1/3 c. chocolate chips

Directions:
Preheat your oven to 350F. Grease a baking pan with cooking spray. Whisk in all the ingredients except the chocolate chips in your blender. Blend the batter for two-minutes or until turning into a smooth consistency. Whisk in the chocolate chips. Spoon the batter to form cookies. Put the cookies in the pan and bake for 12-minutes.
Nutritional Information: Calories: 372 Fat: 12.4g Protein: 18.6g Dietary Fiber: 11.6g Net Carbs: 46.5g

773. Bruschetta

Preparation Time: 10-minutes | Total time: 30-minutes | Yield: 5-servings

Ingredients:

10 slices Bread, whole-grain	4 tsp. Extra virgin olive oil, divided
¼ tsp. Sea salt	2 cloves Garlic, minced
1 tbsp. Balsamic vinegar	1/3 c. Basil, fresh, chopped
¼ c. Parmesan, grated	8 Roma tomatoes, seeded and diced
¼ tsp. Black pepper, ground	

Directions:
In a mixing dish, prepare the topping for your bruschetta by combining the tomatoes, Parmesan, basil, garlic, sea salt, balsamic, one tsp. of olive oil, and black pepper. Once combined, cover the kitchen mixing dish,

and put it in the fridge to marinate while you move on to the next step. Heat a grill pan for the bruschetta over medium heat on your stovetop, or you can use a gas grill to medium heat or a charcoal grill until the coals have paled in color. While your grill heats, slice each slice of bread in half so that you are left with twenty small pieces rather than ten large ones. Using a pastry brush, use the remaining tbsp of olive oil to brush over the bread slices on both sides. Grill both sides of the bruschetta bread, until toasted with visible grill marks, and then remove it, add your chilled brochette toppings, and serve immediately.

Nutritional Information: Calories: 91 kcal, Protein: 4.6 g, Fat: 2.51 g, Carbohydrates: 13.88 g

774. Saucy Brussels sprouts and Carrots

Preparation Time: 15-minutes | Total time: 27-minutes | Yield: 4-servings

Ingredients:

1 tbsp. coconut oil	12 oz. Brussels sprouts, cut in half and tough ends removed
12 oz. carrots (about 4 medium), peeled, ends removed, and cut into 1" chunks	¼ c. fresh lime juice
¼ c. apple cider vinegar	½ c. coconut amino
¼ c. almond butter	

Directions:

Sauté the Brussels sprouts and carrots and sauté until browned, about 5–7-minutes. While the vegetables are browning, make the sauce. Mix the lime juice, vinegar, coconut amino, and almond butter in a small bowl.
Pour the sauce over the vegetables—Cook within 6-minutes. Serve.

Nutritional Information: Calories: 216 Fat: 11g Protein: 6g Sodium 738mg Fiber: 6g Carbs: 22g Sugar: 5g

775. Simple Mango Salsa

Preparation time: 10-minutes | Total time: 10-minutes | Yield: 4-servings

Ingredients:

1 avocado, pitted, peeled, and cubed	2 c. cubed mango
¼ c. chopped cilantro	½ c. chopped red onion
2 tbsps. olive oil	Salt and black pepper to the taste
Juice of 1 lime	A pinch of red pepper flakes

Directions:

In a bowl, mix avocado with mango, onion, and cilantro. Add olive oil, salt, pepper, lime juice, and pepper flakes, then toss to coat and serve as a snack. Enjoy!

Nutritional Information: calories 100, fat 3, fiber 4, carbs 8, protein 9

776. Purple Cabbage Salad with Quinoa and Edamame

Preparation Time: 5-minutes | Total time: 7-minutes | Yield: 8-servings

Ingredients:

½ c. dry quinoa	1 (10 oz.) bag frozen shelled edamame
1 c. vegetable broth	¼ c. reduced-sodium tamari
¼ c. natural almond butter	3 tbsps. toasted sesame seed oil
½ tsp. pure stevia powder	1 head purple cabbage, cored and chopped

Directions:

Put the quinoa, edamame, and broth in the inner pot of your Instant Pot. Cook within 2-minutes. Whisk the tamari, almond butter, sesame seed oil, and stevia in a small bowl. Set aside. Fluff the quinoa using a fork, and then transfer the mixture to a large bowl. Allow the quinoa and edamame to cool, and then add the purple cabbage to the bowl and toss to combine. Put the dressing and toss again. Serve.

Nutritional Information: Calories 220 Fat: 11g Protein: 10g Sodium: 313mg Fiber 7g Carbs 21g Sugar 5g

777. Coco Cherry Bake-less Bars

Preparation Time: 10-minutes | Total time: 10-minutes | Yield: 6-servings

Ingredients:

1 c. old-fashioned oats	1/3 c. ground flaxseed
1/3 c. coconut, unsweetened and shredded	3 scoops vanilla plant-based protein powder
½ c. almond butter	¼ c. pure maple syrup
1 Tbsp almond milk	1 Tbsp vanilla extract
1/3 c. dried cherries or cranberries	

Directions:

Line a loaf pan with parchment paper. Whisk in the first four ingredients in your blender. Blend until the mixture becomes powdery. Transfer the mixture to a mixing bowl. Add in all the remaining ingredients. Mix well until thoroughly combined. Put the mixture in the pan, and press down onto a uniformly flat surface. Freeze for 30-minutes before slicing into six bars.

Nutritional Information: Calories: 193 Fat: 6.4g Protein: 9.6g Sodium: 200mg Net Carbs: 24.1g

778. Chia Cashew Cream

Preparation Time: 2 hours and 5-minutes | Total time: 2 hours 5-minutes | Yield: 1 serving

Ingredients:

2-Tbsps chia seeds	2-Tbsps hemp hearts
2-Tbsps maple syrup or a dash of liquid stevia	¾-c. cashew milk
¼-tsp vanilla powder A pinch of cinnamon	¼-c. quinoa, cooked

Directions:

Mix all the ingredients in a jar. Mix well until thoroughly combined. Cover the jar and refrigerate for 2 hours. To serve, top with your desired toppings.

Nutritional Information: Calories: 258 Fat: 8.6g Protein: 12.9g Dietary Fiber: 2g Net Carbs: 32.2g

779. Lentil and Mushrooms Cakes

Preparation time: 10-minutes | Total time: 20-minutes | Yield: 8-servings

Ingredients:

2 tsp. freshly grated ginger	1 c. chopped yellow onion
1 c. minced mushrooms	1 c. canned red lentils, drained and rinsed
1 sweet potato, grated	¼ c. chopped parsley
1 tbsp. curry powder	¼ c. chopped cilantro
2 tbsps. coconut flour	1 tbsp. olive oil

Directions:

Place the lentils inside a bowl and mash them well using a potato masher. Add the onion, ginger, mushrooms, potato, curry powder, parsley, cilantro, and flour to the bowl with the lentils. Whisk well and shape medium cakes out of this mix. Heat a pan with the oil over medium-high heat, add the cakes and cook them for about 5-minutes on each side. Serve as an appetizer while warm. Enjoy!

Nutritional Information: calories 142, fat 4, fiber 3, carbs 8, protein 8

780. Avocado and Egg Sandwich

Preparation Time: 10-minutes | Total time: 10-minutes | Yield: 2-servings

Ingredients:

1 avocado (ripe)	1 egg, organic
½ lime juice	2 slices of who wheat, seed bread
2 radishes	Black pepper – to your taste
A pinch of salt (sea or Himalayan)	1 scallion
Mixed seeds – to your choice	

Directions:

Peel the avocado. Boil the egg. Cut the radishes into thin slices. Dice the scallion. Mix lime juice, salt, and avocado in a bowl. Mash the mixture thoroughly. Spread the mixture onto the bread. Add some radish. Put soft-boiled eggs on top. Add some scallion, seeds, and pepper.

Nutritional Information: Calories: 342 kcal | Protein: 12.36 g | Fat: 22.99 g | Carbohydrates: 26.54 g

781. Buckwheat Waffles

Preparation Time: 15-minutes | Total time: 27-minutes | Yield: 4-servings

Ingredients:

1½ c. buckwheat flour	½ c. brown rice flour
1 tsp. baking soda	2 tsp. Baking powder
½ tsp. sea salt	1 egg
2 tsp. vanilla extract	1 tbsp. pure maple syrup
1½ c. almond milk	1 c. water
Coconut oil for greasing the waffle iron	

Directions:

Mix the baking soda, flours, baking powder, and salt in a bowl. Whisk to mix well. Whisk together the egg, vanilla, maple syrup, almond milk, and water in a separate bowl. Pour the egg-mixture into the flour-mixture and keep stirring until a smooth batter forms. Let the batter stand for 10-minutes. Preheat the waffle iron & grease with coconut-oil. Pour the batter in the waffle iron to cover ¾ of the bottom. Cook for 10 to 12-minutes or until golden brown and crispy. Flip the waffle halfway through the cooking-time. The cooking-time will vary depending on the waffle iron you use. Serve the waffles immediately.

Nutritional Information: Calories: 281 Fat: 3.6g Protein: 9.3g Carbs: 54.9g Fiber: 6.1g Sugar: 7.1g

782. Roasted Beets

Preparation Time: 10-minutes | Total time: 45 to 55-minutes | Yield: 6-servings

Ingredients:

2 and a ½ lbs. of beets, peeled and diced	1 tbsp. of coconut oil, melted
1 tsp. of salt	

Directions:

Preheat the oven to 400°F. Spread the beets onto a baking sheet and drizzle with melted coconut oil. Add salt and mix well. Roast the beets in the oven for 35-45-minutes until the beets are soft.

Nutritional Information: Carbohydrates: 5g | Dietary Fiber: 2g | Protein: 5g | Total Fat: 12g | Calories: 57

783. Pecan and Lime Cheesecake

Preparation Time: 10-minutes | Total time: 10-minutes | Yield: 10-servings

Ingredients:

1 c. coconut flakes	20 oz. mascarpone cheese, room temperature
1 ½ c. pecan meal	1/2 c. xylitol
3 tbsps. key lime juice	

Directions:

Mix the pecan meal, 1/4 cup of xylitol, and coconut flakes in a mixing bowl. Press the crust into a parchment-lined spring form pan. Freeze for 30-minutes. Now, beat the mascarpone cheese with 1/4 cup of xylitol with an electric mixer. Beat in the key lime juice; you can add vanilla extract if desired. Spoon the filling onto the prepared crust. Allow it to cool in your refrigerator for about 3 hours. Bon appétit!

Nutritional Information: Calories: 296Fat: 20gCarbs: 6gProtein: 21gFiber: 3.7g

784. Steamed Purple Sweet Potatoes

Preparation Time: 5-minutes | Total time: 45-minutes | Yield: 4-servings

Ingredients:

4 purple sweet potatoes, whole and unpeeled

Directions:

Put in a steamer basket. Steam until thoroughly cooked, approximately 40-minutes.

Nutritional Information: Energy (calories): 762 kcal Protein: 45.18 g Fat: 9.25 g Carbohydrates: 160.03 g

785. Choco Chia Cherry Cream

Preparation Time: 4-hours 5-minutes | Total time: 4 hours 5-minutes | Yield: 4-servings

Ingredients:

1½ c. almond milk	¼ c. chia seeds, powdered
3 Tbsps raw cacao, powdered	2 Tbsps pure maple syrup or honey
½ c. sliced and pitted cherries, + extra for plating	

Additional toppings: extra raw cacao nibs, cherries, and 70% or higher dark chocolate shavings

Directions:

Whisk in all the ingredients, excluding the cherries in a mason jar. Mix well until thoroughly combined. Refrigerate overnight or for 4 hours. When ready to serve, divide the pudding equally among four serving plates. Top each plate with cherries. Garnish with the additional toppings.

Nutritional Information: Calories: 502 Fat: 16.7g Protein: 25.1g Sodium: 68mg Net Carbs: 62.7g

786. Creamy Artichoke Spread

Preparation time: 10-minutes | Total time: 45-minutes | Yield: 6-servings

Ingredients:

2 garlic cloves, minced	Juice of ½ lemon
1 c. veggie stock	1 lb. baby artichokes, trimmed and stems cut off
1 c. coconut cream	A pinch of salt and black pepper

Directions:

In a small pot, mix the artichokes with the stock, salt, and pepper. Whisk and bring to a simmer over medium heat. Simmer for 35-minutes, transfer to a blender, add the garlic, lemon juice, and cream, and pulse well. Divide into bowls and serve. Enjoy!

Nutritional Information: calories 150, fat 2, fiber 3, carbs 8, protein 5

787. Café-style Fudge

Preparation Time: 10-minutes | Total time: 10-minutes | Yield: 6-servings

Ingredients:

1 tbsp. instant coffee granules	4 tbsps. confectioners' Swerve
4 tbsps. cocoa powder	1 stick butter
1/2 tsp. vanilla extract	

Directions:

Beat the butter and Swerve at low speed. Add cocoa powder, instant coffee granules, and vanilla and continue to mix until well combined. Spoon the batter into a foil-lined baking sheet. Refrigerate for 2 to 3 hours.

Nutritional Information: Calories: 144Fat: 15.5gCarbs: 2.1gProtein: .8gFiber: 1.1g

788. Vegetable Nuggets

Preparation Time: 10-minutes | Total time: 35-minutes | Yield: 24-servings

Ingredients:

¼ tsp. Black Pepper	2 c. Cauliflower Florets

1 Egg, large & pastured	2 c. Broccoli Florets
½ c. Almond Meal	1 c. Carrots, chopped coarsely
¼ tsp. Salt	1 tsp. Garlic, minced
½ tsp. Turmeric, grounded	

Directions:

To make these tasty nuggets, you first need to preheat the oven to 400 degrees F. Next, Put broccoli, turmeric, cauliflower, black pepper, carrots, sea salt, and turmeric in a food processor. Pulse them for a minute or until you get a finely grounded mixture. Then, Whisk in the almond meal and egg into it and pulse them again until mixed. Now, transfer the veggie-almond mixture to a large mixing bowl. Scoop out the mixture with a tbsp. And make circular discs with your hands. After that, Put the discs on the parchment paper-lined baking sheet. Finally, bake them for 20 to 25-minutes while flipping them once.

Tip: Serve it along with homemade ranch sauce.

Nutritional Information: Calories: 220 Cal Proteins: 1.1g Carbohydrates: 2.1g Fat: 1.2g

789. Turmeric Chickpea Cakes

Preparation Time: 20-minutes | Total time: 50-minutes | Yield: 8-servings

Ingredients:

2 small onions, minced	2 cans (15oz.) chickpeas, rinsed, drained
Freshly ground pepper to taste	1 tsp. cayenne pepper, to taste (optional)
4 cloves garlic, minced	4 tbsps. cornstarch
1 tsp. salt or to taste	2 tsp. turmeric powder
8-10 tbsps. chickpea flour	Avocado dipping sauce to serve
½ c. fresh parsley, minced	Grapeseed oil to fry

Directions:

Put a skillet over medium heat. Add a little oil. When the oil is heated, put onion and garlic and sauté until translucent. Turn off the heat and cool completely.

Add chickpeas into the food processor bowl and process until very finely chopped. Add the onion mixture, salt, pepper, cayenne pepper, and turmeric powder and pulse again until well combined. Transfer into a bowl. Add parsley and mix well. Make small balls of the mixture (of about 1-inch diameter) and shape them into patties. Put chickpea flour on a plate. Put a nonstick pan over medium heat. Add a little oil and swirl the pan so that the oil spreads. Dredge the patties in the chickpea flour and Put a few on the pan. Cook in batches. Cook until the underside is golden brown. Flip, then cook the other side till it's golden brown. Repeat steps 6-8 to fry the remaining patties. Serve with avocado dipping sauce.

Nutritional Information: Calories: 154 kcal | Protein: 7.32 g | Fat: 2.85 g | Carbohydrates: 25.43 g

790. Stuffed Mushrooms

Preparation time: 10-minutes | Total time: 30-minutes | Yield: 5-servings

Ingredients:

¼ c. avocado mayonnaise	1 tsp. garlic powder
1 small yellow onion, chopped	24 oz. white mushroom caps
Salt and black pepper to the taste	1 tsp. curry powder
¼ c. coconut cream	1 c. shrimp, cooked, peeled, deveined, and chopped

Directions:

In a bowl, whisk the mayo with garlic powder, onion, salt, pepper, curry powder, coconut cream, and shrimp. Stuff the mushrooms with this mix and arrange them on a baking sheet. Cook in the oven at 350 degrees F for 20-minutes. Arrange on a platter and serve. Enjoy!

Nutritional Information: calories 204, fat 10, fiber 3, carbs 7, protein 11

791. Sweet Potato and Celery Root Mash

Preparation Time: 5-minutes | Total time: 25 – 30-minutes | Yield: 4-servings

Ingredients:

2 c. chopped sweet potatoes	2 c. chopped celery root, scrubbed, trimmed, and peeled
2 tbsps. almond butter	1 tsp. Freshly squeezed lemon juice
½ tsp. salt	Pinch cayenne pepper

Directions:

Place a steamer basket in a large-saucepan with 1 to 2 inches of filtered water. Put the sweet potatoes and celery root in the steamer basket. Cover and steam over medium heat for about 20 to 25-minutes until fork-tender. Transfer them to a blender or food processor, along with the almond butter, lemon juice, sea salt, and cayenne pepper. Blend until completely smooth. Serve.

Nutritional Information: calories: 109 fat: 4.6g protein: 2.4g carbs: 14.6g fiber: 2.6g sugar: 1.0g

792. Baked Sweet Peppers

Preparation time: 15-minutes | Total time: 35-minutes | Yield: 4-servings

Ingredients:

4 sweet peppers, trimmed, seeded	2 tbsps. olive oil
1 tbsp. minced garlic	1 tbsp. lemon juice

Directions:

Put the sweet peppers in the oven and bake them at 375F for 20-minutes. When the time is over, remove the peppers from the heat and peel. Chop the peppers and put them in the bowl. Add olive oil, minced garlic, and lemon juice. Whisk the meal.

Nutritional Information: 102 calories, 1.4g protein, 9.8g carbs, 7.3g fat, 1.7g fiber, 4mg sodium

793. Cereal Chia Chips

Preparation Time: 10-minutes | Total time: 40-minutes | Yield: 10-servings

Ingredients:

¼-c. rolled oats, gluten-free	½-c. white quinoa, un-cooked
¾-c. pecans, chopped	2-Tbsps chia seeds
2-Tbsps coconut sugar	A pinch of sea salt (optional)
2-Tbsps coconut oil	½-c. maple syrup

Directions:

Preheat your oven to 325°F. Line a baking pan with parchment paper. Whisk in the first six ingredients in a mixing bowl. Mix well until thoroughly combined. Set aside. Pour the oil and syrup into a small saucepan. Put over medium-low heat. Heat the mixture for 3-minutes, stirring occasionally. Fold in the dry ingredients; Whisk well to coat thoroughly. Pour the mixture into the baking pan and spread to an even layer using a spoon.

Put the pan in the oven. Bake for 15-minutes. Turn the pan around to cook evenly. Bake for 8-10-minutes until the mixture turns golden brown. Allow cooling entirely before breaking the chips into bite-size pieces.

Nutritional Information: Calories: 157 Fat: 5.2g Protein: 7.8g S Sodium: 25mg Net Carbs: 19.6g

794. Crunchy Roasted Chickpeas

Preparation Time: 5-minutes | Total time: 25-minutes | Yield: 2-servings

Ingredients:

4 c. cooked (or canned) chickpeas, rinsed, drained, and dried well	2 tbsps. extra-virgin olive oil
1 tsp. garlic powder	1 tsp. salt
Freshly ground black pepper, to taste	

Directions:

Preheat the oven to 400ºF (205ºC). Spread the chickpeas out in an even layer on a rimmed baking sheet. Use olive oil to drizzle and then toss to coat well. Bake in the preheated oven for 20-minutes, stirring the chickpeas halfway through the cooking until browned and crunchy. Remove from the oven to a large bowl. Season with garlic powder, salt, and pepper, and then serve.

Nutritional Information: Calories: 151, Fat: 4.9g, Protein: 6.0g, Carbs: 20.8g, Fiber: 6.1g, Sugar: 3.9g

795. Baked Veggie Turmeric Nuggets

Preparation Time: 10-minutes | Total time: 35-minutes | Yield: 24-servings

Ingredients:

2 c. Broccoli florets	¼ tsp. Sea salt
2 c. Cauliflower florets	1 tsp. Minced garlic
½ c. Almond meal	1 c. Chopped carrots
½ tsp. Turmeric powder	1 sizeable Whole egg
¼ tsp. Black pepper powder	

Directions:

Prep oven by preheating to 400°F. Get a parchment-lined baking sheet ready. Pour cauliflower, turmeric, broccoli, carrots, black pepper, garlic, and sea salt in the blender and blitz until it's smooth. Pour in the egg and almond meal and mix until it's incorporated. Pour the paste into a mixing bowl. Scoop out a bit onto your hand and form a circular disc. Put this disc on the baking sheet and repeat the process until the mixing bowl is empty. Slide into the oven. Then bake for at least 15-minutes on one before flipping and baking for 10-minutes on the other-side. You can serve with Paleo ranch sauce and enjoy!

Nutritional Information: Calories: 12 kcal Protein: 0.88 g Fat: 0.52 g Carbohydrates: 1.12 g

796. Energetic Oat Bars

Preparation Time: 10-minutes | Total time: 35-minutes | Yield: 6-servings

Ingredients:

½ c. of gluten-free rolled oats	2 tbsp. of flax seeds
1 tbsp. of sunflower seeds	1 tbsp. of chopped walnuts
2 tbsp. of raisins	¾ c. fresh blueberries
1 peeled and mashed banana	2 tbsp. of pitted and chopped finely dates
1 tbsp. of fresh pomegranate juice	

Directions:

Set the oven to 350F. Lightly oil an 8-inch baking dish. In a huge mixing bowl, put all ingredients and mix till well combined. Put the mixture into the prepared baking dish evenly. Bake for about 25-minutes. Take off from the oven, then cool. Using a knife, divide the bars into the size of your desired pieces, then serve.

Nutritional Information: Calories: 88 | Fat: 12.5g | Carbs: 11.8g | Protein: 5.1g | Fiber: 2.8g

797. Spicy Roasted chickpeas

Preparation Time: 10-minutes | Total time: 50-minutes | Yield: 6-servings

Ingredients:

2 (15 oz.) cans chickpeas, drained & rinsed	1 tsp. paprika
1 tsp. Turmeric	¼ tsp. cayenne pepper
2 tsp. coconut oil, melted	

Directions:

Set the oven to 425°F. Line a baking sheet using paper towels, then put the chickpeas on them and use more paper towels to take off the excess water in the chickpeas. Remove all the paper towels. Put the oil and spices into the chickpeas and mix well. Roast your chickpeas for 40-minutes, stirring every 10-minutes. Once the chickpeas are done, take them off from the oven and let them completely cool.

Nutritional Information: Carbohydrates: 15g | Dietary Fiber: 3g | Protein: 5g | Fat: 12g | Calories: 177

798. Delectable Cookies

Preparation Time: 20-minutes | Total time: 35 – 40-minutes | Yield: 6-servings

Ingredients:

1 c. of almonds	1 1/3 c. of almond flour
¼ c. of arrowroot flour	1 tbsp. of coconut flour
1 tsp. ground turmeric	Salt, to taste
Freshly ground black pepper, to taste	1 organic egg
¼ c. of olive oil	3 tbsp. of raw honey
1 tsp. of organic vanilla extract	

Directions:

In a food processor, put the almonds and pulse till chopped roughly. Transfer the chopped almonds to a large bowl. Put the flours and spices and mix well. In another bowl, put the remaining ingredients, then beat till well combined. Put the flour mixture into the egg mixture and mix till well combined. Arrange a plastic wrap over the cutting board. Put the dough over the cutting board. Using your hands, pat into about a 1-inch-thick circle. Gently cut the circle into 6 wedges. Set the scones onto a cookie sheet in a single layer. Bake for about 15-20-minutes.

Nutritional Information: Calories: 335 | Fat: 27.7g | Carbs: 17.6g | Protein: 9g | Fiber: 4.8g

799. Flavorsome Almonds

Preparation Time: 10-minutes | Total time: 25-minutes | Yield: 8-servings

Ingredients:

2 c. of whole almonds	3 tbsp. of raw honey
1 tsp. of extra-virgin olive oil	1 tbsp. of filtered water
½ tsp. of chili powder	½ tsp. of ground cinnamon
¼ tsp. of ground cumin	¼ tsp. of cayenne pepper
Salt, to taste	

Directions:

Preheat the oven to 350 degrees F. Arrange the almonds onto a large, rimmed baking sheet in a single layer. Roast for about 10-minutes. Meanwhile, in a microwave-safe bowl, add honey and microwave on Hugh for about 30 seconds. Remove from microwave and Whisk in oil and water. In a small bowl, mix all spices. Remove the almonds from the oven, add them into the bowl of honey mixture, and Whisk to Mix well. Transfer the almond mixture onto the baking sheet in a single layer. Sprinkle with spice mixture evenly. Roast for about 3-4-minutes. Take off from the oven and keep aside to cool completely before serving. You can preserve these roasted almonds in an airtight jar.

Nutritional Information: Calories: 168 | Fat: 12.5g | Carbs: 11.8g | Protein: 5.1g | Fiber: 3.1g

800. Sweet Quinoa

Preparation time: 10-minutes | Total time: 30-minutes | Yield: 4-servings

Ingredients:

1 c. pears, chopped	1 c. quinoa
3 c. of water	1 tbsp. almond butter

Directions:

Mix water with quinoa and cook it on low heat for 10-minutes. Then add pears and almond butter. Whisk the meal and cook it for 10-minutes.

Nutritional Information: 209 calories, 7.3g protein, 34.8g carbs, 5g fat, 5g fiber, 40mg sodium

801. Turmeric Mushrooms

Preparation time: 10-minutes | Total time: 30-minutes | Yield: 4-servings

Ingredients:

1 lb. mushrooms, sliced	1 tbsp. ground turmeric
½ c. cilantro, chopped	1 tbsp. olive oil
3 garlic cloves, diced	

Directions:

Mix mushrooms with ground turmeric, cilantro, and garlic. Put the mixture in the saucepan, add olive oil, and cook the meal on medium heat for 20-minutes. Whisk the mushrooms from time to time.

Nutritional Information: 64 calories, 3.9g protein, 5.6g carbohydrates, 4g fat, 1.6g fiber

802. Chewy Blackberry Leather

Preparation Time: 15-minutes | Total time: 5 – 6 hours + 15-minutes | Yield: 8-servings

Ingredients:

2 c. of fresh blackberries	1 tbsp. of fresh mint leaves
1 tsp. of ground cinnamon	1/8 tsp. of fresh lemon juice
¼ c. of raw honey	

Directions:

Set the oven to 170F. Line baking sheet with parchment paper. In a food processor, put all ingredients and pulse till smooth. Take the mixture onto the prepared baking sheet and smooth the top with the back of a spoon.
Bake for about 5-6 hours. Cut the leather into equal-sized strips. Now, roll each rectangle to make fruit rolls.

Nutritional Information: Calories: 48 | Fat: 12.5g | Carbs: 11.8g | Protein: 5.1g | Fiber: 2.1g

803. Sesame Spread

Preparation time: 10-minutes | Total time: 10-minutes | Yield: 6-servings

Ingredients:

1 c. tahini sesame seed paste	Salt and black pepper to the taste
1 c. veggie stock	½ c. lemon juice
1 tbsp. chopped cilantro	½ tsp. ground cumin
3 garlic cloves, chopped	

Directions:

Put the sesame seed paste with salt, pepper, lemon juice, stock, cilantro, cumin, and garlic into a food processor. Pulse well, divide into bowls and serve as a party spread. Enjoy!

Nutritional Information: calories 120, fat 12, fiber 2, carbs 11, protein 5

804. Basil Peppers Dip

Preparation Time: 10-minutes | Total time: 25-minutes | Yield: 2-servings

Ingredients:

3 shallots, minced	1 and ½ lbs. mixed peppers, roughly chopped
¼ c. chicken stock	1 tbsp. olive oil
2 tbsps. basil, chopped	

Directions:

Start by sautéing shallots with oil in a pan, then sauté for 2-minutes. Whisk in remaining ingredients and mix well. Cover the pot's lid and cook for 13-minutes on medium heat. Use an immersion blender to blend the pepper mixture until smooth. Serve fresh and enjoy.

Nutritional Information: Calories 199 Fat 17.4 g Carbs 9.9 g Sugar 1.5 g Fiber 4.3 g Protein 6.4 g

805. French Toast Sticks

Preparation Time: 10-minutes | Total time: 20-minutes | Yield: 2-servings

Ingredients:

½ tsp. ground nutmeg	1 tsp. vanilla extract
1 tsp. cinnamon	¼ c. almond milk
4 slices bread, sliced into sticks	

Directions:

Line your air-fryer basket with parchment-paper. Preheat your air-fryer to 360-degrees F. Mix all ingredients except bread sticks in a bowl. Dip bread sticks into the mixture. Air fry for 5-minutes. Flip and cook for another 5-minutes.

Nutritional Information: Calories: 134 kcal, Protein: 3.81 g, Fat: 1.92 g, Carbohydrates: 24.17 g

806. Simple Garlic-Roasted Chickpeas

Prep time: 5-minutes | Total time: 25-minutes | Yield: 4-servings

Ingredients:

4 c. cooked (or canned) chickpeas, rinsed, drained, and thoroughly dried with paper towels (be careful not to crush them)	2 tbsps. extra-virgin olive oil
1 tsp. salt	1 tsp. garlic powder
Freshly ground black pepper, to taste	

Directions:

Preheat the oven to 400°F (205°C). Spread the chickpeas evenly on a rimmed baking sheet and coat them with

olive oil. Bake for 20-minutes, stirring halfway through. Transfer the hot chickpeas to a large bowl. Toss with the salt and garlic powder, season with pepper. Store leftovers in a sealed container or bag at room temperature; they'll remain crispy for 1 to 2 days.
Nutritional Information: Calories: 150 | fat: 5g | protein: 6g | carbs: 21g | fiber: 6g | sugar: 3g |

807. Avocado with Tomatoes and Cucumber
Preparation Time: 10-minutes | Total time: 10-minutes | Yield: 2-servings

Ingredients:

2 avocados	1 cucumber
4 Roma tomatoes	½ red onion
1/8 c. parsley	¼ c. cilantro
¼ c. olives – to your choice	1 lemon
1 Tbsp. turmeric	Salt and pepper – to your taste

Directions:
Dice the tomatoes, cucumber, avocado, and olives. Slice the cilantro, parsley, and onion. Add the above ingredients into a bowl. Squeeze the lemon juice, then add to the vegetables. Add olive oil, turmeric, salt, and pepper. Toss well. Consume immediately after adding lemon juice and olive oil. If you prefer to consume the salad later, add the dressing immediately before consuming it.
Nutritional Information: Calories: 480 kcal | Protein: 11.57 g | Fat: 35.27 g | Carbohydrates: 39.77 g

808. Lemony Berry Gummies
Preparation Time: 5-minutes | Total time: 15-minutes | Yield: 24 gummies

Ingredients:

1 c. frozen or fresh berries of choice	½ c. freshly squeezed lemon juice
3 tbsps. raw honey	¼ c. filtered water
¼ c. gelatin powder	

Directions:
Purée the berries, lemon juice, honey, and water in a blender. Transfer the purée to a small saucepan and heat over medium heat until it warms. Add the gelatin powder and continue Whisking for 5-minutes until well combined. Pour the mixture into a mini muffin tin and freeze until the mixture gels, about 15-minutes. Serve immediately or refrigerate for up to 1 week.
Nutritional Information: Calories: 67 Fat: 0g Protein: 4.1g Carbs: 13.2g Fiber: 1.0g Sugar: 11.9g

809. Sautéed Kale
Preparation time: 10-minutes | Total time: 30-minutes | Yield: 4-servings

Ingredients:

4 c. kale, chopped	1 c. coconut cream
2 oz. walnuts, chopped	1 tsp. dried sage

Directions:
Mix kale with coconut cream in the saucepan. Add walnuts and dried sage. Close the lid and cook the meal on medium heat for 20-minutes.
Nutritional Information: 259 calories, 6.8g protein, 11.8g carbohydrates, 22.7g fat, 3.4g fiber

810. Energy Dates Balls
Preparation Time: 10-minutes | Total time: 35-minutes | Yield: 7-servings

Ingredients:

1 c. of toasted almonds	1 c. of pitted and chopped dates
¼ c. of fresh lemon juice	½ c. of shredded sweetened coconut

Directions:
Line a large baking-sheet using parchment-paper. Keep it aside. In a food-processor, add almonds and pulse till chopped coarsely. Add dates and lemon juice and pulse till a soft dough form. Make equal-sized balls from the mixture. In a shallow, dish Put shredded coconut. Roll the balls in shredded coconut evenly. Put the balls onto the baking sheet in a single layer. Refrigerate to set completely before serving.
Nutritional Information: Calories: 148 | Fat: 14.5g | Carbs: 11.8g | Protein: 5.1g | Fiber: 2.1g

811. Chia Pudding with Cashews and Cherries
Preparation Time: 10-minutes | Total time: 10-minutes | Yield: 4-servings

Ingredients:

2 c. almond milk	½ c. chia seeds
1 tsp. vanilla extract	¼ c. pure maple syrup
½ c. chopped cashews, divided	1 c. frozen no-added-sugar pitted cherries, thawed, juice reserved, divided

Directions:
Mix the almond milk, chia seeds, vanilla, and maple syrup in a bowl. Whisk to mix well. Refrigerate overnight. Divide the almond milk mixture into four bowls, then serve with cashews and cherries on top.
Nutritional Information: calories: 271 fat: 13.9g; protein: 7.1g; carbs: 37.8g; fiber: 6.2g; sugar: 15.0g;

812. Baked Broccoli

Preparation time: 10-minutes | Total time: 40-minutes | Yield: 4-servings

Ingredients:

2 lbs. broccoli, roughly chopped	2 tbsps. olive oil
1 tbsp. cayenne pepper	

Directions:

Line the baking tray with baking paper. Put the broccoli in the tray and sprinkle with olive oil and cayenne pepper. Bake the broccoli for 30-minutes at 355F.

Nutritional Information: 141 calories, 6.5g protein, 15.8g carbs, 8g fat, 6.3g fiber, 745mg potassium.

813. Amazing Apricot Bites

Prep time: 5-minutes | Total time: 5-minutes | Yield: 4-servings

Ingredients:

1 c. dried apricots, finely chopped	1 c. raw walnuts or pecans, finely chopped
½ c. desiccated coconut	1 tbsp. honey

Directions:

Mix the ingredients to form a sticky dough. Shape into 8 bite-size balls with the palms of your hands. Cover and then refrigerate for at least 2 hours to set. Serve or wrap for later.

Nutritional information: Calories: 334 | fat: 22g | protein: 6g | carbs: 34g | fiber: 5g | sugar: 16g |

814. Mashed Avocado with Jicama Slices

Prep time: 15-minutes | Total time: 15-minutes | Yield: 4-servings

Ingredients:

2 ripe avocados, pitted	1 scallion, sliced
2 tbsps. Chopped fresh cilantro	½ tsp. ground turmeric
Juice of ½ lemon	1 tsp. Salt
¼ tsp. freshly ground black pepper	1 jicama, peeled and cut into ¼-inch-thick slices

Directions:

In a small bowl, Mix the scooped-out avocado, the scallion, cilantro, turmeric, lemon juice, salt, and pepper. Mash the ingredients together until well mixed and still slightly chunky. Serve with the jicama slices.

Nutritional information: Calories: 270 | fat: 20g | protein: 3g | carbs: 24g | fiber: 15g | sugar: 4g |

815. Spinach and Kale Breaded Balls

Prep time: 15-minutes | Total time: 45-minutes | Yield: 4-servings

Ingredients:

2 c. frozen or fresh spinach, thawed and chopped	1 c. frozen or fresh kale, thawed and drained
½ c. onion, finely chopped	1 garlic clove, finely chopped
3 tbsps. extra virgin olive oil	2 free-range eggs, beaten
½ tsp. Ground thyme	½ tsp. Rubbed dried oregano
½ tsp. dried rosemary	1 c. dry 100% wholegrain breadcrumbs
½ tsp. dried oregano	1 tsp. ground black pepper

Directions:

Preheat oven to 350ºF (180ºC). Line a baking sheet with parchment paper. Mix the olive oil and eggs in a bowl, add spinach, garlic, onions, and toss to coat. Add the rest of the ingredients, mixing to blend. Use the palms of your hands to roll into 1-inch balls and arrange them onto the baking sheet. Bake for 15-minutes, and then flip the balls over. Continue to bake for another 15-minutes or until they're golden brown. Serve and enjoy!

Nutritional information: Calories: 262 | fat: 14g | protein: 10g | carbs: 26g | fiber: 4g | sugar: 3g |

816. Creamy Polenta

Prep time: 8-minutes | Total time: 53-minutes | Yield: 4-servings

Ingredients:

1 c. polenta	1 ½ c. water
2 c. chicken stock	½ c. cream
1/3 c. Parmesan, grated	

Directions:

Put polenta in the pot. Add water, chicken stock, cream, and Parmesan. Mix up polenta well. Then preheat the oven to 355 degrees F. Cook polenta in the oven for 45-minutes. Mix up the cooked meal with the help of the spoon carefully before serving.

Nutritional Information: Calories 208, Fat 5.3, Fiber 1, Carbs 32.2, Protein 8

817. Crispy Corn

Prep time: 8-minutes | Total time: 13-minutes | Yield: 3-servings

Ingredients:

1 c. corn kernels	1 tbsp. Coconut flour

½ tsp. salt	3 tbsps. Canola oil
½ tsp. Ground paprika	¾ tsp. chili pepper
1 tbsp. water	

Directions:

In the mixing bowl, mix corn kernels with salt and coconut flour. Add water and mix up the corn with the help of the spoon. Pour canola oil into the skillet and heat it. Add corn kernels mixture and roast it for 4-minutes. Whisk it from time to time. When the corn kernels are crunchy, transfer them to the plate and dry with the help of the paper towel. Add chili pepper and ground paprika. Mix up well.

Nutritional Information: Calories 179, Fat 15, Fiber 2.4, Carbs 11.3, Protein 2.1

818. Whole Grain Porridge

Prep time: 15-minutes | Total time: 25-minutes | Yield: 2-servings

Ingredients:

¾ c. oats	1 tbsp. flax meal
2 tsp. Goji berries	½ tsp. Vanilla extract
¼ tsp. Ground cinnamon	¼ tsp. ground ginger
2 tbsps. honey	1 c. of water
¼ c. quinoa	

Directions:

Pour water into the pan. Then bring it to a boil. Add quinoa, ground ginger, cinnamon, vanilla extract, flax meal, and oats. Whisk well. Bring the mixture to boil and add goji berries. Close the lid and let the porridge rest for 15-minutes. Then add honey and transfer it to the serving plates.

Nutritional Information: Calories 303, Fat 4.6, Fiber 6.6, Carbs 58.5, Protein 8.9

819. Salmon Salsa

Prep time: 10-minutes | Total time: 22-minutes | Yield: 2-servings

Ingredients:

2 salmon fillets, boneless	½ c. chopped yellow onion
4 tsp. olive oil	1 tsp. Greek seasoning
1 tsp. minced garlic	1 green bell pepper, chopped
½ c. canned tomato salsa	2 tbsps. kalamata olives, pitted and chopped
¼ c. vegetable stock	Salt and black pepper to the taste

Directions:

Heat a pan with half of the oil over medium heat, add bell pepper, garlic, Greek seasoning, and onion; whisk and cook for 5-minutes. Add stock, olives, and salsa, toss, cook for 3-4-minutes more and transfer to the bowl. Heat the same pan with the rest of the oil over medium heat, add fish, season with salt and pepper, cook for 2-minutes on each side, transfer to a cutting board, cut into medium cubes, and put them in a baking dish. Add the salsa, toss, bake in the oven at 425 degrees F for 6-minutes, divide into bowls and serve cold as an appetizer. Enjoy!

Nutritional Information: Calories 170, Fat 5, Fiber 2, Carbs 7, Protein 7

820. Chicken Bites

Prep time: 10-minutes | Total time: 20-minutes | Yield: 2-servings

Ingredients:

½ c. almond flour	1 egg
2 tbsps. garlic powder	2 chicken breasts, cubed
Salt and black pepper to the taste	½ c. coconut oil

Directions:

In a bowl, mix garlic powder with flour, salt, and pepper and stir. In another bowl, whisk the egg well. Dip the chicken breast pieces in the egg mix, then in the flour mix. Heat a pan using the oil over medium-heat, then drop chicken pieces into the hot pan. Cook them for 5-minutes on each side, divide them into bowls and serve as a snack. Enjoy!

Nutritional Information: Calories 60, Fat 3, Fiber 2, Carbs 6, Protein 7

821. Avocado And Jalapeno Salsa

Prep time: 10-minutes | Total time: 10-minutes | Yield: 4-servings

Ingredients:

1 small red onion, chopped	2 avocados, pitted, peeled, and chopped
3 jalapeno peppers, chopped	Salt and black pepper to the taste
2 tbsps. cumin powder	2 tbsps. lime juice
½ tomato, chopped	

Directions:

Mix the onion with the avocados, jalapenos, salt, pepper, cumin, lime juice, and tomato in a bowl. Divide into smaller bowls and serve. Enjoy!

Nutritional Information: Calories 120, Fat 2, Fiber 2, Carbs 7, Protein 4

822. Farro Salad with Arugula

Prep time: 10-minutes | Total time: 45-minutes | Yield: 2-servings

Ingredients:

1/2 c. farro	1 1/2 c. chicken stock
1 tsp. salt	1/2 tsp. ground black pepper
2 c. arugula, chopped	1 cucumber, chopped
1 tbsp. lemon juice	1/2 tsp. olive oil
1/2 tsp. Italian seasoning	

Directions:

Mix farro, salt, and chicken stock and transfer the mixture to the pan. Secure the lid and boil it for 35-minutes. Meanwhile, set all remaining ingredients in the salad bowl. Chill the farro and add it to the salad bowl too. Mix up the salad well.

Nutritional information: Calories 92 | Fat 2.3 g | Fiber 2 g | Carbs 15.6 g | Protein 3.9 g

823. Roasted Curried Cauliflower

Prep time: 5-minutes | Total time: 35-minutes | Yield: 4-servings

Ingredients:

1 large head cauliflower, cut into florets	1 tsp. curry powder
1 1/2 tbsp. olive oil	1 tsp. cumin seeds
1 tsp. mustard seeds	3/4 tsp. salt

Directions:

Preheat your oven to 375°F . Grease a baking sheet with cooking spray. Take a bowl and put all ingredients. Toss to coat well. Arrange the vegetable on a baking sheet. Roast for 30-minutes. Serve and enjoy!

Nutritional information: Calories: 67 | Fat: 6 g | Carbs: 4 g | Protein: 2 g

824. Tangy Turmeric Flavored Florets

Prep time: 10-minutes | Total time: 1 hour 5-minutes | Yield: 1 serving

Ingredients:

1 cauliflower head, chopped into florets	1 tbsp. olive oil
1 tbsp. turmeric	A pinch of cumin
A dash of salt	

Directions:

Set the oven to 400F. Set all the ingredients in a baking pan. Mix well until thoroughly combined. Secure the pan with foil. Roast for 40-minutes. Remove the foil cover. Then roast for extra for 15-minutes.

Nutritional information: Calories: 90 | Fat: 3 g | Protein: 4.5 g | Sodium: 87 mg | Total carbs: 16.2 g

825. Oven Crisp Sweet Potato

Prep time: 10-minutes | Total time: 30-minutes | Yield: 2-servings

Ingredients:

1 medium-sized sweet potato, raw	1 tsp. sugar
1 tsp. coconut oil	

Directions:

Preheat the oven to 160 degrees C. Divide the sweet potato into thin chips or strips. Wash and pat dry. Drizzle the coconut oil over the potatoes. Toss until all chips are coated. Set in an oven baking sheet. Bake for 10-minutes. Take out the crispy sweet potatoes. Sprinkle with sugar and serve.

Nutritional information: Calories: 123 | Protein: 4.23 g | Fat: 5.39 g | Carbs: 14.63 g

826. Black Bean Cakes

Prep time: 1 hour 20-minutes | Total time: 2 hours 20-minutes | Yield: 8-servings

Ingredients:

4 c. water	2 c. dried black beans, picked over and rinsed, soaked overnight, and drained
8 cloves garlic, chopped	1/2 tsp. salt
1/2 c. chopped fresh cilantro	2 tbsps. olive oil

Directions:

In a big size saucepan over high heat, mix the black beans and water. Bring to a boil. Reduce heat to low, partially cover, and simmer until beans are tender, about 60 to 70-minutes. Drain well. In a big bowl, mash the beans and garlic. Add the cilantro and salt. Form 8 cakes with the mixture. Move to a plate and refrigerate for about 1 hour. In a large nonstick skillet, heat olive oil over medium heat. Add cakes and cook, turning once, until lukewarm and outside is slightly crisp, about 5-minutes. Serve immediately.

Nutritional information: Calories 196, Protein 10g, Carbohydrates 30g, Fat 4g Sodium 156 mg

827. Chinese-Style Asparagus

Prep time: 10-minutes | Total time: 25-minutes | Yield: 4-servings

Ingredients:

1/2 tsp. sugar	1 1/2 lbs. fresh asparagus, woody ends removed and cut into 1 1/2-inch length
1/2 c. water	1 tsp. reduced-sodium soy sauce

Directions:

In a big saucepan, heat the water, sugar, and soy sauce over high heat. Cook to the boiling, then add the asparagus. Reduce heat and simmer until asparagus is crisp and tender, about 3-4-minutes. Move to a serving plate and serve immediately.

Nutritional information: Calories 24, Protein 2g, Carbohydrates 4g, Fat 0g Sodium 76 mg

828. Watermelon Tomato Salsa

Prep time: 10-minutes | Total time: 10-minutes | Yield: 16-servings

Ingredients:

4 yellow tomatoes, seedless and chopped	A pinch of black pepper
1 c. watermelon, seedless and chopped	1/3 c. red onion, chopped
2 jalapeno peppers, chopped	1/4 c. cilantro, chopped
3 tbsps. lime juice	

Directions:

In a bowl, mix tomatoes with watermelon, onion, and jalapeno. Add cilantro, lime juice, and pepper, toss, divide between plates and serve as a side dish.

Nutritional information: Calories 87, Fat 1g, Carbohydrates 4g, Protein 7g Sodium: 112mg

829. Creamy Cucumber Mix

Prep time: 10-minutes | Total time: 10-minutes | Yield: 2-servings

Ingredients:

1 big cucumber, peeled and chopped	1 small red onion, chopped
4 tbsps. non-fat yogurt	1 tsp. balsamic vinegar

Directions:

In a bowl, mix the onion with cucumber, yogurt, and vinegar, toss, divide between plates and serve as a side dish.

Nutritional information: Calories 90, Carbohydrates 7g, Protein 5g, Fat 1g, Sodium 38mg.

CHAPTER 9:
DESSERTS RECIPES

830. Anti-Inflammatory Apricot Squares

Preparation Time: 20-minutes | Total time: 20-minutes | Yield: 8-servings

Ingredients:

1 c. shredded coconut, dried	1 tsp. vanilla extract
1 c. apricot, dried	1 c. macadamia nuts, chopped
1 c. apricot, chopped	1/3 c. turmeric powder

Directions:

Place all ingredients in your food processor. Pulse until smooth. Place the mixture into a square pan and press evenly. Serve chilled and enjoy!

Nutritional Information: Calories: 201 | Fat: 15g | Carbohydrates: 17g | Protein: 3g

831. Chocolate Bananas

Preparation Time: 5-minutes | Total time: 20-minutes | Yield: 4-servings

Ingredients:

3 Bananas, large & cut into thirds	12 oz. Dark Chocolate
1 tbsp. Coconut Oil	

Directions:

Melt the chocolate with coconut-oil in a double boiler for 3 to 4-minutes till you get a smooth and glossy mixture. Keep the popsicles at the end of each of the bananas by inserting them. Then, immerse the chocolate into the warm chocolate mixture. Shake off the excess chocolate and put them on parchment paper. Sprinkle with the topping of your choice. Place them in the freezer for some hours or until set. You can use topping like chopped pistachios or unsweetened chocolate sprinkles etc.

Nutritional Information: Calories: 427Kcal | Proteins: 5.9g | Carbohydrates: 80g | Fat: 15.6g

832. Chocolate Covered Strawberries

Preparation Time: 15-minutes | Total time: 15-minutes | Yield: 24-servings

Ingredients:

16 oz. milk chocolate chips	2 tbsps. shortening
1 lb. fresh strawberries with leaves	

Directions:

In a bain-marie, melt chocolate and shorter, occasionally stirring until smooth. Hold them by the toothpicks and immerse the strawberries in the chocolate mixture. Put toothpicks on the top of the strawberries. Turn the strawberries and put the toothpick in the Styrofoam so that the chocolate cools.

Nutritional Information: Calories: 205 | Fat: 16g | Carbohydrates: 32g | Protein: 6g

833. Cookie Dough Bites

Preparation Time: 10-minutes | Total time: 15-minutes | Yield: 2-servings

Ingredients:

¼ c. Almond Flour	¼ c. Chocolate Chips, dairy-free & sugar-free
½ c. Almond Butter or any nut butter	½ tsp. Salt
1 ½ c. Chickpeas, cooked	1 tsp. Vanilla Extract
2 tbsp. Maple Syrup	

Directions:

First, put all the ingredients, excluding the chocolate chips, in a high-speed blender for about three-minutes or until you get a thick, smooth mixture. After this, move the mixture to a moderate-sized container. Next, fold the chocolate chips into the batter. Check for sweetness and put in more maple syrup if required. Serve and enjoy.

Nutritional Information: Calories: 373 Kcal, Protein: 12.6g, Carbohydrates: 59.1g, Fat:10g

834. Thar She' Salts Peanut Butter Cookies

Preparation Time: 15-minutes | Total time: 15-minutes | Yield: 9-servings

Ingredients:

1 c. raw almonds	½ c. peanut butter (creamy and unsalted)
1 c. pitted Medjool dates	1 ¼ tsp. vanilla extract
Sea salt as needed	

Directions:
Take a food processor and add almonds, peanut butter, vanilla, dates and blend the whole mixture until a dough-like texture comes (should take a few-minutes). If you want, add some more peanut butter to make the dough sticker. Form balls using the dough and press down using a fork to create a crisscross pattern. Sprinkle salt generously. Serve immediately.
Nutritional Information: Calories: 214 |Fat: 16g| Carbohydrates: 32g| Protein: 6g

---

835. Oats, flaxseeds, and banana smoothie
Preparation Time: 10-minutes | Total time: 10-minutes | Yield: 1 serving

Ingredients:

½ c. of ice	1 tsp. honey
2 tsp. flaxseeds	¼ c. 100% whole grain rolled oats
1/2 c. Greek Yogurt, plain	½ c. almond milk
½ banana, peeled	¼ c. kale, shredded and stems discarded

Directions:
Add all ingredients to a blender. Blend until smooth and creamy. Serve and enjoy.
Nutritional Information: Carbs 54g Protein 11g Sugar: 14g Fiber 8g Calories 305 Fat 10g

---

836. Mango, Cucumber and Spinach Smoothie
Preparation Time: 10-minutes | Total time: 10-minutes | Yield: 1 serving

Ingredients:

1 c. water	1 c. orange juice, fresh
3 c. baby spinach	1 c. frozen mango, cubed and deseeded
2 apples, cored and chopped roughly	1 cucumber, ends removed and chopped roughly

Directions:
Add all ingredients to a blender. Blend until smooth and creamy. Serve and enjoy.
Nutritional Information: Calories 455 Fat 2g Carbs 111g Protein 8g Sugar: 21g Fiber 15g Sodium 90mg

---

837. Easiest Pressure-Cooked Raspberry Curd
Preparation Time: 10-minutes plus 1 hour in the fridge | Total time: 1 hour 35-minutes | Yield: 5-servings

Ingredients:

12 oz. Raspberries	2 tbsp. Almond Butter
Juice of ½ Lemon	1 c. Packed Brown Sugar
2 Egg Yolks	

Directions:
Mix the raspberries, sugar, & lemon juice in your Instant Pot. Close the lid and cook for a 1 on MANUAL mode. Release the pressure naturally for 5-minutes. Puree the raspberries and discard the seeds. Whisk the yolks in a bowl. Mix the yolks with the hot raspberry puree. Pour the mixture into your pot. Cook with the lid off for a minute on SAUTÉ mode. Whisk in the butter and cook for a couple more-minutes, until thick. Transfer to a container with a lid. Refrigerate for at least an hour before serving.
Nutritional Information: Calories 249, Carbohydrates 48.4 g, Fiber 4.6 g, Fat 6.8 g, Protein 1.8 g

---

838. Milk Dumplings in Sweet Cardamom Sauce
Preparation Time: 10-minutes | Total time: 30-minutes | Yield: 20-servings

Ingredients:

6 c. Water	2 ½ c. Packed Brown Sugar
3 tbsps. Lime Juice	6 c. Almond Milk
1 tsp. ground Cardamom	

Directions:
Put the milk in a pot inside your Instant Pot and bring it to a boil. Whisk in the lime juice. The solids should start to separate. Pour the milk through a cheesecloth-lined colander. Drain as much liquid as you possibly can. Put the paneer on a smooth surface. Form a ball and then divide it into 20 equal pieces. Pour the water into your pressure cooker and bring it to a boil. Add the sugar and cardamom and cook until dissolved. Shape the dumplings into balls, and put them in the syrup. Close the lid and cook on MANUAL mode for about 4-5-minutes. Let it cool, and then refrigerate till you're ready to serve.
Nutritional Information: Calories 134, Carbohydrates 28.7 g, Fiber 0 g, Fat 1.5 g, Protein 2.4 g

---

839. Lemon Vegan Cake
Preparation Time: 10-minutes | Total time: 20-minutes | Yield: 3-servings

Ingredients:

1 c. of pitted dates	2-1/2 c. pecans
1-1/2 c. agave	3 avocados, halved & pitted
3 c. cauliflower rice, prepared	1 lemon juice and zest

½ lemon extract	1-1/2 c. pineapple, crushed
1-1/2 tsp. vanilla extract	Pinch of cinnamon
1-1/2 c. of dairy-free yogurt	

Directions:
Line your baking sheet with parchment paper. Pulse the pecans in your food processor. Add the agave and dates. Pulse for a minute. Transfer this mix to the baking sheet. Wipe the bowl of your processor. Bring together the pineapple, agave, avocados, cauliflower, lemon juice, and zest in your food processor. Get a smooth mixture. Now add the lemon extract, cinnamon, and vanilla extract. Pulse. Pour this mix into your pan on the crust. Refrigerate for 5 hours minimum.
Take out the cake. Then keep it at room temperature for 20-minutes. Take out the cake's outer ring. Whisk together the vanilla extract, agave, and yogurt in a bowl. Pour on your cake.

Nutritional Information: Calories 688 |Carbohydrates 100g |Fat 28g |Protein 9g |Sugar 17g

840. Citrus Cauliflower Cake

Preparation Time: 5-hours 30-minutes | Total time: 5 hours 30-minutes | Yield: 10-servings

Ingredients:
For the Crust:

2½ c. pecan nuts	1 c. dates pitted
2 Tbsps maple syrup or agave	

For the Filling:

3-pcs avocados halved and pitted	3-c. cauliflower, riced
1½-c. pineapple, crushed	¾-c. maple syrup or agave
1-pc lemon, zest, and juice	A pinch of cinnamon
½-tsp lemon extract	½-tsp pure vanilla extract
For the Topping:	3-Tbsps maple syrup or agave
1-tsp pure vanilla extract	1½-c. plain coconut yogurt

Directions:
For the Crust:
Line a baking tray with parchment paper. Set the outer ring of a 9-inch spring-form pan onto the baking tray. Pulse the pecans in your food processor to a finely ground texture. Add the remaining crust ingredients, and pulse further until the mixture holds together. Transfer and press the mixture to an even layer in the baking tray.

For the Filling:
Wipe the bowl of your food processor, and add in the avocado, cauliflower, pineapple, syrup, lemon zest, and juice. Process the mixture to a smooth consistency. Add the cinnamon and the lemon and vanilla extracts. Pulse until thoroughly combined. Pour the mixture over the crust. Put the tray in your freezer overnight or for 5 hours. Take the cake out from your freezer, and let it sit at room temperature for 20-minutes. Remove the outer ring.

For the Topping:
Whisk in all the topping ingredients in a mixing bowl. Pour the mixture over the cake and spread evenly.

Nutritional Information: Calories: 667 Fat: 22.2g Protein: 33.3g Dietary Fiber: 4.8g Net Carbs: 78.3g

841. Spiced Pumpkin Smoothie

Preparation Time: 10-minutes | Total time: 10-minutes | Yield: 1 serving

Ingredients:

Ice, optional	Pinch of nutmeg
½ tsp. ginger	1 tsp. cinnamon
1 small frozen banana	½ c. pureed pumpkin
1 tbsp. chia seeds	¼ c. rolled oats
1 c. almond milk	

Directions:
Overnight or for an hour, soak chia seeds and oats in almond milk. This will give your smoothie a finer consistency. Then, Put all the ingredients in your food processor and blend ingredients until you get a smooth consistency.

Nutritional Information: Calories 348 Fat 11g Carbs 61g Protein 15g Sugar: 12g Fiber 9g Sodium 109mg

842. Peanut Butter Bars

Preparation Time: 5-minutes | Total time: 55-minutes | Yield: 6-servings

Ingredients:

1 c. Whole Wheat Flour	1 ½ c. Water
1 Egg	1/3 c. powdered Peanut Butter
1/3 c. Peanut Butter softened	½ c. Almond Butter, softened
1 c. Oats	½ c. Packed Brown Sugar
½ tsp. Baking Soda	½ tsp. Salt

Directions:
Grease a spring form pan and line it with parchment paper. Beat the eggs, powdered peanut butter, softened peanut butter, salt, white sugar, and brown sugar.

Fold in the oats, flour, and baking soda. Press the batter into the pan. Cover the pan with a paper towel and then with a piece of aluminum foil. Pour the water inside the pressure-cooker and lower the trivet. Put the pan inside and close the lid. Cook for 35-minutes on MANUAL mode. Release the pressure naturally. Wait for about 15-minutes before inverting onto a plate and cutting into bars.

Nutritional Information: Calories 561, Carbohydrates 61 g, Fiber 1.50 g, Fat 18 g, Protein 8 g

843. Hot Chocolate

Preparation Time: 5-minutes | Total time: 10-minutes | Yield: 2-servings

Ingredients:

¼ tsp. Turmeric	½ tsp. Cinnamon
1 tbsp. Coconut Oil	1 tbsp. Honey, raw
2 c. Almond Milk	2 tbsp. Cocoa Powder, unsweetened

Directions:

To start with, bring the almond milk to its boiling point in a deep cooking pan on moderate heat. Now, bring this mixture to a simmer and then mix in the cocoa powder. Next, spoon in the turmeric powder and cinnamon to it. Mix thoroughly. Next, put in honey to it, and once blended well, put in the coconut oil. Give the drink a good Whisk until everything comes together. Serve instantly.

Nutritional Information: Calories: 150 Kcal, Protein: 2.1g, Carbohydrates: 15.2g, Fat: 11.1gm

844. Spicy Popper Mug Cake

Preparation Time:5-minutes | Total time: 10-minutes | Yield: 2-servings

Ingredients:

¼ tsp. Sunflower seeds	½ a jalapeno pepper
½ tsp. baking powder	1 bacon, cooked and cut
1 big egg	1 tbsp. almond butter
1 tbsp. cashew cheese	1 tbsp. flaxseed meal
2 tbsps. almond flour	

Directions:

Take a frying pan, then Put it on moderate heat. Cook the cut bacon until it has a crispy texture. In a microwave-safe container, combine all of the stated ingredients and clean the sides. Microwave for 75 seconds, making sure your microwave is set to maximum power. Remove the cup and slam it on a surface to remove the cake. Decorate using a bit of jalapeno and serve!

Nutritional Information: Calories: 429, Fat: 38g, Carbohydrates: 6g, Protein: 16g

845. Fruit Cobbler

Preparation Time: 10-minutes | Total time: 30-minutes | Yield: 8-servings

Ingredients:

1 Tsp. Coconut Oil	¼ C. Coconut Oil, Melted
2 C. Peaches, Fresh & Sliced	2 C. Nectarines, Fresh & Sliced
2 Tbsps. Lemon Juice, Fresh	¾ C. Rolled Oats
¾ C. Almond Flour	¼ C. Coconut Sugar
½ Tsp. Vanilla Extract, Pure	1 Tsp. Ground Cinnamon
Dash Salt	Filter Water for Mixing

Directions:

Start by heating your oven to 425F. Get out a cast-iron skillet, coating it with a tsp. of coconut oil. Mix your lemon juice, peaches, and nectarines in the skillet. Get out a food processor, mixing your almond flour, oats, coconut sugar, and remaining coconut oil. Add your cinnamon, vanilla, and salt, pulsing until the oat mixture resembles a dry dough. If you need more moisture, add filtered water a tbsp. At a time, and then break the dough into chunks, spreading it across the fruit. Bake for twenty-minutes before serving warm.

Nutritional Information: Protein: 4 Grams | Fat: 12 Grams | Carbs: 15 Grams

846. Berry Parfait

Preparation Time: 10 min | Total time: 20-minutes | Yield: 5-servings

Ingredients:

7oz / 200g almond butter	3.5oz / 100g Greek yogurt
14oz / 400g mixed berries	2 tsp honey

Directions:

Mix the Greek yogurt, butter, and honey until it's smooth. Add a layer of berries and a layer of the mixture in a glass until it's full. Serve immediately

Nutritional Information: Calories: 394 |Fat: 18g| Carbohydrates: 35g| Protein: 8g

847. Raw Black Forest Brownies

Preparation Time: 2 hours and 10-minutes | Total time: 2 hours 10-minutes | Yield: 6-servings

Ingredients:

¼ tsp. salt	½ c. almonds, chopped
½ c. dates pitted	1 ½ c. cherries, pitted, dried, and chopped
1 c. raw cacao powder	2 c. walnuts, chopped

Directions:
Put all ingredients in a food processor. Pulse until small crumbs are formed. Push the brownie batter in a pan. Freeze for a couple of hours. Slice before you serve and enjoy!

Nutritional Information: Calories: 294, Fat: 18g, Carbohydrates: 33g, Protein: 7g

848. Rum Butter Cookies

Preparation Time: 10-minutes + chilling time | Total time: 15-minutes | Yield: 12-servings

Ingredients:

½ c. coconut butter	½ c. confectioners' Swerve
1 stick butter	1 tsp. rum extract
4 c. almond meal	

Directions:
Melt the coconut butter and butter. Mix in the Swerve and rum extract. Afterward, put in the almond meal and mix to blend. Roll the balls and put them on a parchment-lined cookie sheet. Keep in your fridge until ready to serve.

Nutritional Information: 400 Calories 40g, Fat: 4.9g, Carbs: 5.4g, Protein: 2.9g

849. Papaya Smoothie

Preparation Time: 5-minutes | Total time: 5-minutes | Yield: 2-servings

Ingredients:

250ml Golden Milk	200gm Ripe Papaya Puree
1/8 Tbsp. Cinnamon Powder	1 C. Frozen Banana (Chopped)
1 C. Plain Yoghurt	1 Tbsp. Lemon Juice

Directions:
Blend everything and serve.

Nutritional Information: Calories: 224.5 kcal Carbs: 33.7 g Fat: 7.7g Protein: 6.9 g

850. Coconut and Chocolate Cream

Preparation Time: 2 hours | Total time: 2 hours | Yield: 4-servings

Ingredients:

½ tsp. cinnamon powder	1 c. dark chocolate, chopped and melted
1 tsp. vanilla extract	2 c. coconut milk
2 tbsps. ginger, grated	2 tbsps. honey

Directions:
Throw all the ingredients into a blender and blend. Split into bowls and store in the refrigerator for about two hours before you serve.

Nutritional Information:, Calories: 200 , Fat: 3 , Fiber:5 , Carbohydrates: 12 , Protein: 7

851. Pomegranate-Avocado Smoothie

Preparation Time: 10-minutes | Total time: 10-minutes | Yield: 1 serving

Ingredients:

½ c. spinach	½ c. ice
½ tsp. vanilla extract	½ tbsp. honey
½ c. Pomegranate Juice	¼ c. Greek Yogurt
½ Avocado, peeled	

Directions:
Add all ingredients to a blender. Blend until smooth and creamy. Serve and enjoy.

Nutritional Information: Calories 295 Fat 15g Carbs 36g Protein 7g Sugar: 17g Fiber 7g Sodium 46mg

852. Coconut Butter Fudge

Preparation Time: 10-minutes | Total time: 10-minutes | Yield: 6-servings

Ingredients:

¼ tsp. of salt	1 c. of coconut butter
1 tsp. of pure vanilla extract	2 tbsps. of raw honey

Directions:
Start by lining an 8 x 8-inch baking dish using parchment paper. Melt the coconut butter, honey, and vanilla using low heat. Put the mixture into the baking pan, and Put in your fridge for about two hours before you serve.

Nutritional Information: Carbohydrates: 6g, Fiber: 0g, Protein: 0g, Total Fat: 36g, Calories: 334

853. Creamy & Chilly Blueberry Bites

Preparation Time: 2-hours 5-minutes | Total time: 2 hours 5-minutes | Yield: 2-servings

Ingredients:

1 pint blueberries	2 tsp lemon juice
8 oz. vanilla yogurt	

Directions:
Coat the blueberries with lemon juice and yogurt in a mixing bowl. Toss carefully without squishing the berries. Scoop out each of the coated berries and Put them on a baking sheet lined with parchment paper. Put the sheet in your freezer for two hours before serving.

Nutritional Information: Calories: 394 Fat: 13.1g Protein: 19.7g Sodium: 164mg Carbs: 42.9g

854. Easy Peach Cobbler

Preparation Time: 5-minutes | Total time: 25-minutes | Yield: 6-servings

Ingredients:

¼ brown rice flour	¼ c. coconut palm sugar, divided
¼ c. extra virgin olive oil	¼ c. ground flaxseeds
½ c. gluten-free oats	½ tsp. cinnamon
¾ c. chopped pecans	5 organic peaches, pitted and chopped

Directions:

Preheat your oven to 3500F. Grease the bottom of 6 ramekins. In a container, mix the peaches, ½ of the coconut sugar, cinnamon, and pecans. Distribute the peach mixture into the ramekins. In the same container, Mix the oats, flaxseed, rice flour, and oil. Put in the rest of the coconut sugar. Mix until a crumbly texture is formed. Top the mixture over the peaches. Put for about twenty-minutes.

Nutritional Information: Calories 26, Fat: 11g, Carbohydrates: 28g, Protein: 10g, Sugar: 12g, Fiber: 6g

855. Strawberry Granita

Preparation Time: ten-minutes | Total time: 20-minutes | Yield: 8-servings

Ingredients:

¼ tsp. Balsamic vinegar	½ tsp. lemon juice
1 c. of water	2 lb. strawberries, halved & hulled
Agave to taste	Just a small pinch of salt

Directions:

Wash the strawberries in water. Keep in a blender. Put in water, agave, balsamic vinegar, salt, and lemon juice. Pulse multiple times so that the mixture moves. Blend until smooth. Pour into a baking dish. The puree must be 3/8 inch deep only. Put in your fridge, the dish uncovered till the edges start to freeze. The center must be slushy. Whisk crystals from the edges lightly into the center. Whisk thoroughly to mix. Chill till the granite is nearly fully frozen. Scrape loose the crystals like before and mix. Put in your fridge once more. Using a fork, Whisk 3-4 times till the granite has become light.

Nutritional Information: Calories 72, Carbohydrates: 17g, Fat: 0g, Sugar: 9g, Fiber: 2g, Protein:

856. Fruit Salad

Preparation Time: 10-minutes | Total time: 30-minutes | Yield: 2-3-servings

Ingredients:

½ of 1 Watermelon, chopped into small pieces	1 Pineapple, cut into small pieces
Dash of Turmeric	4 Strawberries, chopped
1 Red Papaya, cut into small pieces	1 tsp. Ginger, freshly grated
1 Pomegranate, small	

Directions:

To start with, Put all the fruits in a large-sized bowl. After that, spoon in the turmeric and ginger over the fruits. Toss well and serve.

Tip: Instead of ginger, you can use cinnamon or clove.

Nutritional Information:Calories: 118Kcal | Proteins: 1.6g | Carbohydrates: 36.6g | Fat: 0.5g

857. Caramelized Pears

Preparation Time: 20-minutes | Total time: 25-minutes | Yield: 5-servings

Ingredients:

1 Tsp. Cinnamon	2 Tbsp. Honey, Raw
1 Tbsp. Coconut Oil	4 Pears, Peeled, Cored & Quartered
2 C. Yogurt, Plain	¼ C. Toasted Pecans, Chopped
1/8 Tsp. Sea Salt	

Directions:

Get out a large skillet, and then heat the oil over medium-high heat. Add in your honey, cinnamon, pears, and salt. Cover, and allow it to cook for four to five-minutes. Whisk occasionally, and your fruit should be tender. Uncover it, and allow the sauce to simmer until it thickens. This will take several-minutes. Soon your yogurt into four dessert bowls. Top with pears and pecans before serving.

Nutritional Information:Calories: 290 | Protein: 12 Grams | Fat: 11 Grams | Carbs: 41 Grams

858. Strawberry Ice Cream

Preparation Time: 5-minutes | Total time: 10-minutes | Yield: 2 – 3-servings

Ingredients:

1 Banana, frozen & cut	1 c. Strawberries, frozen
1 tsp. Vanilla extract	2 tbsp. Coconut Milk

Directions:

Begin by placing strawberries and bananas in a high-speed blender and blending it for two to three-minutes. While you blend, spoon in the coconut milk and the vanilla extract. Carry on blending until the mixture is thick and smooth. Serve the ice cream instantly since it does not keep well in the freezer.

Nutritional Information: Calories: 78 Kcal, Protein: 1g, Carbohydrates: 13.6g, Fat:2.7g

859. Apple Fritters

Preparation Time: 15-minutes | Total time: 25-minutes | Yield: 4-servings

Ingredients:

1 apple, cored, peeled, and chopped	1 c. all-purpose flour
1 egg	½ c. cashew milk
1-1/2 tsp. of baking powder	2 tbsps. of stevia sugar

Directions:

Preheat your air-fryer to 175 degrees C or 350 degrees F. Keep parchment paper at the bottom of your fryer. Apply cooking spray. Mix ¼ cup sugar, flour, baking powder, egg, milk, and salt in a bowl. Mix well by stirring. Sprinkle 2 tbsps. of sugar on the apples. Coat well. Mix the apples into your flour mixture. Use a cookie scoop and drop the cakes with it to the air fryer basket's bottom. Now air fry for 5-minutes. Flip the cakes once and fry for another 3-minutes. They should be golden.

Nutritional Information: Calories 348 |Carbohydrates 14g |Fat 18g |Protein 9g |Sugar 13g

860. Mediterranean Rolled Baklava with Walnuts

Preparation Time: 20-minutes | Total time: 50-minutes | Yield: 12-servings

Ingredients:

2 c. Walnuts	1 Lemon zest
1 c. Cream of wheat or plain breadcrumbs	8 sheets Thawed phyllo dough
3 tbsp. Sugar	1/3 c. Milk
3 sticks Melted Unsalted butter	

Syrup:

1 medium Lemon	3 c. Granulated sugar
3 c. Water	

Directions:

Mix 3 cups of sugar, 3 cups of water, and lemon slices in a pan and leave to boil. Lower the heat, then let it simmer until the sugar completely dissolves. It should take 15-minutes. You should have a nice smooth syrup now. Now leave it to cool for a bit. Chop the walnuts in a blender into bits using short pulses. Pour the walnuts in a bowl along with the cream of wheat, lemon zest, and 4 tbsps. of sugar. Whisk in milk and set aside. Now, preheat your oven to 375°F. Spread out the phyllo dough and fit it into a baking pan. Trim off the edges

that don't fit with scissors. Cover the remaining phyllo sheets while you work so they don't dry out. Put a sheet on a clean flat surface and glaze with melted butter. Do this for all the sheets until it's finished. Arrange the walnut mixture on one side of the sheets and roll them up like you're trying to make a sausage. Do this for all the sheets and walnuts. Arrange the walnut rolls on an ungreased baking pan and glaze with the leftover butter. Bake for about 45-minutes. It's ready when it looks golden. Turn off the oven, then pull out the baking pan. Drizzle syrup over the baklava, making sure the syrup gets everywhere. Bring back the baking pan into the oven, then leave to sit for 5-minutes. Take off from the oven and leave it to cool for a few hours. Slice the rolls into tiny bits and serve.

Nutritional Information: Calories: 488 kcal| Protein: 4.49 g| Fat: 36.89 g| Carbohydrates: 38.21 g

861. Spiced Tea Pudding

Preparation time: 10-minutes | Total time: 20-minutes | Yield: 3-servings

Ingredients:

1 can coconut milk	½ c. coconut flakes
1 c. almond milk	1 tsp. nutmeg
1 tbsp. Ground cinnamon	½ tsp. cloves
1 tsp. allspice	1 tbsp. Raw honey
tsps. ground ginger	1 tsp. Cardamom
tbsps. pumpkin seeds	1 ½ c. berries
1 tbsp. chia seeds	1 tsp. green tea powder

Directions:

Puree tea powder with coconut milk, almond milk, cinnamon, coconut flakes, nutmeg, allspice, cloves, honey, cardamom, and ginger in your blender, then divide into bowls. Heat a pan over medium heat, add berries until bubbling, then transfer to your blender and pulse well. Divide the berries into the bowls with the coconut milk mix, top with chia seeds and pumpkin seeds and serve.

Nutritional Information: Calories 150, Fat 6, Fiber 5, Carbs 14, Protein 8

862. Flourless Sweet Potato Brownies

Preparation Time: 10-minutes | Total time: 40-minutes | Yield: 9-servings

Ingredients:

¼ c. Unsweetened Cocoa powder	½ c. Almond butter
½ c. Cooked sweet potato	½ tsp. Baking soda
1 Whole big egg	2 tsp. Vanilla extract
3 tbsp. Dairy-free chocolate chips, optional.	6 tbsp. Honey

Directions:

Prep the oven by pre-heating to 350 degrees F. Coat a baking pan using parchment paper, leaving a few extra inches on the sides to make it easier to discard or remove. Blend all the ingredients, excluding the chocolate chips, until you get a super smooth and tender batter. Move the creamy batter to your readied baking pan and use a spatula to spread it around, so it looks almost even. Slide it in your oven, then bake for thirty-minutes or until a knife inserted into the pan comes out clean. Remove from the oven. Then let cool in the pan for fifteen-minutes before putting it on a wire rack. If you decide to use the chocolate chip topping, put the chips in a microwave-safe dish and heat until it completely melts. Remove from the microwave and sprinkle over the brownies. Serve or store!

Nutritional Information: Calories: 171 kcal, Protein: 5.17 g, Fat: 9.28 g, Carbohydrates: 20.01 g

863. Paleo Raspberry Cream Pie

Preparation Time: 20-minutes | Total time: 20-minutes | Yield: 12-servings

Ingredients:

For the crust:

1 ½ tbsp. Maple syrup	Pinch Salt
½ c. Unsweetened shredded coconut	1 tsp. Vanilla extract
1 c. Roasted or salted cashews	

Raspberry filling:

¾ c. Unrefined coconut oil	1 ½ c. Roasted or salted cashews
½ c. & 1 tbsp. Maple syrup	¼ c. & 2 tsp. Fresh lemon juice
¼ c. Coconut cream from the top solid part of a can of coconut milk that has been refrigerated overnight	2 tsp. Vanilla extract
3 c. fresh raspberries	Pinch Salt

Directions:

Prepare 12 biscuit dishes, line them with biscuit liners, and put them away. Make the hull. Set a dish over medium hotness and the coconut and whisk until it's toasted. Stay by the dish since coconuts will quite often consume without any problem. Transfer the toasted coconuts to a bowl and pass them on to cool for 5-minutes or something like that. Honestly, this toasting step isn't fundamental. However, it adds fantastic character to the outside. To make the outside, put every fixing in a blender and heartbeat at the most minimal speed until the blend gets all clumpy. Likewise, don't beat for a

long time, or you may wind up with glue. To know whether it's prepared, put a touch of the combination on your fingers and squeeze. If it gets clumpy, you're on target. If not, add a little water and heartbeat at the least speed for additional-minutes. Scoop the blend into the lined tins utilizing your fingers to pack the combination firmly inside the dish. Put the dish to refrigerate while you get to make the filling. In a little pot set over low hotness, Whisk in every one of the fixings until the oil and coconut cream softens totally. Clean the blender utilizing a paper towel and pour in the filling. Pulse at rapid for like 60 seconds or until it's smooth. The main clusters we can excuse are the raspberry seeds. Drizzle a fourth of the filling over the highest point of each covering. There ought to be additional filling; you can store and utilize that in another dish. Put the covered biscuits in the ice chest to cool. This will require a couple of hours, similar to 6 hours, so put it in the cooler if you don't possess the energy for that. To serve, pass on them to thaw out for 80-minutes or until clearly rich.

Nutritional Information: Calories: 565 kcal | Protein: 7.74 g | Fat: 43.72 g | Carbohydrates: 42.72 g

864. Green Tea Pudding

Preparation time: 6 hours and 5-minutes | Total time: 6 hours 5-minutes | Yield: 4-servings

Ingredients:

2 tbsps. coconut milk	1 c. coconut cream
3 tbsps. Hot water	½ tsp. green tea powder

Directions:

Mix green tea powder with hot water in a bowl, whisk well and then cool down. Add milk and cream, Whisk and pour into a container. Keep in the freezer for 6 hours before serving frozen. Enjoy!

Nutritional Information: Calories 210, Fat 9, Fiber 5, Carbs 10, Protein 7

865. Easy Street Sweet Corn

Preparation Time: 10-minutes | Total time: 13-minutes | Yield: 6-servings

Ingredients:

Juice of 2 Limes	1 c. grated Parmesan Cheese
6 Ears Sweet Corn	2 c. Water
6 tbsp. Plain Yogurt	½ tsp. Garlic Powder
1 tsp. Chili Powder, optional	

Directions:

Pour the water into your Instant Pot. Put the corn in a steamer basket and inside the pot. Close the lid and cook for 3-minutes on MANUAL mode. Mix the

remaining ingredients, except the cheese, in a bowl. Release the pressure quickly and let it cool for a couple of minutes. Remove the husks from the corn and brush them with the mixture. Top with parmesan and enjoy.
Nutritional Information: Calories 130, Carbohydrates 16 g, Fiber 2.4 g, Fat 5 g, Protein 9 g

866. Sweet Strawberry Sorbet

Preparation Time: 5-minutes | Total time: 5-minutes | Yield: 3-servings

Ingredients:

1 lb strawberries, frozen	1 c. Orange juice or 1-c. coconut water

Directions:

Process the strawberries in your food processor for 2-minutes or until the fruit turns into flakes. Pour the orange juice, and process it further into a smooth frozen puree. To serve, you may present it either as a chilled soft dessert or as sorbet, frozen after an hour and 45-minutes. You can also serve it like a Popsicle by pouring the soft serve into Popsicle molds and freezing over-night.
Nutritional Information: Calories: 86 Fat: 2.3g Protein: 5.3g Dietary Fiber: 9.6g Net Carbs: 10.7g

867. Poached Pears with Orange, Cinnamon, and Ginger

Preparation Time: 10-minutes | Total time: 22-minutes | Yield: 4-servings

Ingredients:

4 Pears cut in half	1 tsp. powdered Ginger
1 tsp. Nutmeg	1 c. Orange Juice
2 tsp. Cinnamon	1/3 c. Coconut Sugar

Directions:

Mix the juice and spices in your Instant Pot. Put the pears on the trivet. Close the lid and cook for 7-minutes on MANUAL mode on high pressure. Release the pressure naturally after 5-minutes. Put the pears onto a serving plate. Pour the juice over and serve.
Nutritional Information: Calories 170.4, Carbohydrates 43.7 g, Fiber 5.2 g, Fat 0.6 g, Protein 1.1 g

868. Pumpkin Ice Cream

Preparation Time: 15-minutes | Total time: 15-minutes | Yield: 6-servings

Ingredients:

½ c. of dates (pitted and chopped)	½ tsp. of ground cinnamon
½ tsp. of vanilla flavor	1 (15 oz.) can think of sugar-free pumpkin puree
1 ½ tsp. of pumpkin pie spice	2 (14 oz.) cans of unsweetened coconut milk
Pinch of salt	

Directions:

Mix all ingredients in a high-speed blender and pulse. Move the puree to an airtight container and freeze for roughly 1-2 hours. Move the frozen puree to an ice-cream maker and process following the manufacturers. Return the ice cream to the airtight container and freeze for approximately 1-2 hours before serving.
Nutritional Information:, Calories: 373 , Fat: 31.9g , Carbs: 24.7g , Sugar: 12.2g , Protein: 4.2g

869. Raspberry Gummies

Preparation Time: 5-minutes | Total time: 20-minutes | Yield: 6-servings

Ingredients:

¼ c. grass-fed gelatin	¾ c. cold water
1 c. frozen raspberries	3 tbsps. raw honey

Directions:

Pour water into a blender followed by frozen raspberries. Puree and move them to a deep cooking pan on moderate heat. Put in honey and gelatin. Whisk. Reduce the heat, then whisk constantly for five-minutes. Put the mixture on a baking dish or molds and Put in your fridge for 60-minutes or until it firms. If you used a baking dish, chop the gelatin into squares. Pop the gelatin out with the molds.
Nutritional Information: Total Carbohydrates: 9g, Fiber: 1g, Protein: 5g, Total Fat: 9g, Calories: 96

870. Raspberry Diluted Frozen Sorbet

Preparation Time: 10 min | Total time: 30-minutes | Yield: 4-servings

Ingredients:

14oz / 400g frozen raspberry	4 fly oz. / 50g almond milk
1 tsp honey	Mint

Directions:

Put the almond milk and raspberry in a mixer till it's smooth, and leave the consistency in the freezer for 20-minutes. When serving, please put them in ice cream bowls and serve with mint on top.
Nutritional Information: Calories: 224 |Fat: 16g| Carbohydrates: 22g| Protein: 4g

871. Wild Berry Smoothie

Preparation Time: 5-minutes | Total time: 5-minutes | Yield: 2-servings

Ingredients:

350g Frozen Wild Berries	200g Sour Yoghurt
1 tbsp. Brown Sugar	4/5 Ice Cubes

Directions:

Blend everything. Serve with berries.

Nutritional Information: Calories: 334 kcal Carbs: 34 g Fat: 4.3 g Protein: 1.2 g

872. Refreshing Raspberry Jelly

Preparation Time: 10-minutes+ 1 hour freezing | Total time: 1 hour 40-minutes | Yield: 4-servings

Ingredients:

¼ c. of water	1 tbsp. of fresh lemon juice
2 lbs. of fresh raspberries	

Directions:

In a moderate-sized pan, put in raspberries and water on low heat and cook for approximately 8-ten-minutes until done completely. Put in lemon juice and cook for approximately 30-minutes, stirring once in a while. Turn off the heat and put the mixture into a sieve. Position a strainer over a container. Through strainer, strain the mixture by pushing using the backside of a spoon. Put the mixture into a blender, then pulse till a jelly-like texture is formed. Move into serving glass bowls and Put in your fridge for a minimum of 1 hour.

Nutritional Information: Calories: 119, Fat: 1.5g, Carbohydrates: 27.2, Protein: 2.8g, Fiber: 14.8g

873. Roasted Bananas

Preparation Time: 2-minutes | Total time: 9-minutes | Yield: 1 serving

Ingredients:

1 banana, sliced into diagonal pieces	Avocado oil cooking spray

Directions:

Take parchment paper and line the air fryer basket with it. Preheat your air fryer to 190 degrees C or 375 degrees F. Keep your slices of banana in the basket. They should not touch. Apply avocado oil to mist the slices of banana. Cook for 5-minutes. Take out the basket. Flip the slices carefully. Cook for 2 more-minutes. The slices of banana should be caramelized and brown. Take them out from the basket.

Nutritional Information: Calories 234 |Carbohydrates 16g |Fat 28g |Protein 9g |Sugar 12g

874. The Most Elegant Parsley Soufflé Ever

Preparation Time: 5-minutes | Total time: 11-minutes | Yield: 5-servings
Ingredients:

1 fresh red chili pepper, chopped	1 tbsp. fresh parsley, chopped
2 tbsps. coconut cream	2 whole eggs
Sunflower seeds to taste	

Directions:

Preheat the oven to 390 degrees F. Almond butter 2 soufflé dishes. Put the ingredients to a blender and mix thoroughly. Split batter into soufflé dishes and bake for about six-minutes. Serve and enjoy!

Nutritional Information: Calories: 108 Fat: 9g, Carbohydrates: 9g Protein: 6g

875. Pineapple Banana-Oat Smoothie

Preparation Time: 10-minutes | Total time: 10-minutes | Yield: 1 serving

Ingredients:

5-6 ice cubes	¼ tsp. coconut extract
½ c. diced pineapple, fresh frozen	½ banana, frozen
1 container of 5.3oz nonfat Greek yogurt	¼ c. quick-cooking oats
1 c. almond milk	

Directions:

In a microwave-safe cup, microwave on high for 2.5-minutes the 1 cup almond milk and ¼ cup oats. Once oats are cooked, add 2 ice cubes to cool it down quickly and mix. Then pour the rest of the ingredients in a blender and puree until the mixture is smooth and creamy and the slightly cold cooked oats.

Nutritional Information: Calories 255 Saturated Fat 2g Net Carbs 41g Protein 14g Sugar: 13g Fiber 4g

876. Creamy Frozen Yogurt

Preparation Time: 10-minutes + 2-3 hours freezing | Total time: 2-3 hours + 10-minutes | Yield: 3-servings

Ingredients:

½ c. of coconut yogurt	½ c. of unsweetened almond milk
1 tbsp. of raw honey	1 tsp. of fresh mint leaves
1 tsp. of organic vanilla extract	2 peeled, pitted and chopped medium avocados
2 tbsp. of fresh lemon juice	

Directions:

Throw all the ingredients into a blender apart from mint leaves and pulse till creamy and smooth. Put into an airtight container, then freeze for a minimum of 2-three hours. Take off from the freezer and keep aside for about fifteen-minutes. With a spoon, whisk thoroughly. Top with fresh mint leaves before you serve.

Nutritional Information: Calories: 105, Fat: 1.3g, Carbohydrates: 20.3g, Protein: 2.8g, Fiber: 1.4g

877. Spiced Carrot Smoothie

Preparation Time: 10-minutes | Total time: 10-minutes | Yield: 1 serving

Ingredients:

1 c. spinach, optional	½ tsp. ground cinnamon
½ tsp. vanilla extract	1 banana, frozen
1 c. carrot, peeled and halved	1 c. almond milk
3 tbsp. raisins	

Directions:

Add all ingredients to a blender. Blend until smooth and creamy. Serve and enjoy.

Nutritional Information: Calories 274 Fat 3g Carbs 53g Protein 11g Sugar: 18g Fiber 8g

878. Oatmeal Chocolate Cookies

Preparation Time: 10-minutes | Total time: 25-minutes | Yield: 2-servings

Ingredients:

¼ c. Whole Wheat Flour	¼ c. Oats
1 tbsp. Olive Oil	2 tbsp. Packed Brown Sugar
½ tsp. Vanilla Extract	1 tbsp. Honey
2 tbsp. Coconut Milk	2 tsp. Coconut Oil
1/8 tsp. Sea Salt	3 tbsp. Bittersweet Chocolate Chips

Directions:

Mix each of the ingredients in a large bowl. Line a baking pan with parchment paper. Make lemon-sized cookies out of the mixture and flatten them onto the lined pan. Add some water to your Instant Pot and lower the trivet. Add the baking pan to your pot. Cook for 15-minutes on MANUAL mode on high pressure. Release the pressure quickly, carefully open the lid and serve warm.

Nutritional Information: Calories 412, Carbohydrates 59 g, Fiber 1 g, Fat 20 g, Protein 6 g

879. Sherbet Pineapple

Preparation Time: 20-minutes | Total time: 20-minutes | Yield: 4-servings

Ingredients:

1 (8 oz.) pineapple chunks	1/3 c. orange marmalade
¼ tsp. ground ginger	¼ tsp. vanilla extract
1 (11 oz.) can orange sections	2 c. pineapple, lemon, or lime sherbet

Directions:

Drain the pineapple, ensure you reserve the juice. Take a medium-sized bowl and add pineapple juice, ginger, vanilla, and marmalade to the bowl. Add pineapple chunks, drained mandarin oranges as well. Toss well and coat everything. Free them for 15-minutes and allow them to chill. Spoon the sherbet into 4 chilled stemmed sherbet dishes. Top each of them with a fruit mixture. Enjoy!

Nutritional Information: Calories: 204 |Fat: 17g| Carbohydrates: 32g| Protein: 6g

880. Berry Red Smoothie

Preparation Time: 10-minutes | Total time: 10-minutes | Yield: 1 serving

Ingredients:

2 tbsp. cocoa powder	2 dried and pitted dates, sliced
1 c. almond milk	1 frozen banana
4 medium hulled strawberries	¾ c. raw red beets

Directions:

Add all ingredients to a blender. Blend until smooth and creamy. Serve and enjoy.

Nutritional Information: Calories 377 Fat 10g Carbs 69 Protein 13g Fiber 11g Sodium 188mg

881. Crème Caramel Coconut Flan

Preparation Time: 10-minutes | Total time: 30-minutes | Yield: 4-servings

Ingredients:

2 Eggs	7 oz. Condensed Coconut Milk
½ c. Coconut Milk	1 ½ c. Water
½ tsp. Vanilla	1 c. Packed Brown Sugar

Directions:

Put a pan with a heavy bottom in your Instant Pot. Put the sugar in the pan. Cook until a caramel is formed. Divide the caramel between 4 small ramekins. Pour the water into the pressure cooker and lower the trivet. Beat the rest of the ingredients together and divide them between the ramekins. Cover them using aluminum foil and place them in the pot. Close the lid and cook for 5-minutes on MANUAL mode. Release the pressure naturally for 10-minutes.

Nutritional Information: Calories 107.8, Carbohydrates 16.5 g, Fiber 0 g, Fat 3.3 g, Protein 3.3 g

882. Almond and Pear Smoothie

Preparation Time: 10-minutes | Total time: 10-minutes | Yield: 1 serving

Ingredients:

2-3 dates, optional	¼ tsp. ground cinnamon
1 tbsp. unsalted almond butter	½ c. almond milk
½ pear, deseeded	1 banana, frozen

Directions:

Add all ingredients to a blender. Blend until smooth and creamy. Serve and enjoy.

Nutritional Information: Calories 341 Fat 11g Saturated Fat 0.8g Net Carbs 53g Protein 6g Sugar: 17g

883. Citrus Strawberry Granita

Preparation Time:15-minutes | Total time: 15-minutes | Yield: 4-servings

Ingredients:

¼ c. of raw honey	¼ lemon
1 grapefruit (peeled, seeded, and sectioned)	12 oz. of fresh strawberries, hulled
2 oranges (peeled, seeded, and sectioned)	

Directions:

Put strawberries, grapefruit, oranges, and lemon in a juicer and extract juice according to the manufacturer's instructions. Put 1½ cups of the veggie juice and honey into a pan and cook on moderate heat for five-minutes while stirring constantly. Remove it from heat and put it into the rest of the juice. Set aside for roughly thirty-minutes. Move the juice mixture into an 8x8-inch glass baking dish.Freeze for 4 hours while scraping after every thirty-minutes.

Nutritional Information:, Calories: 145 , Fat: 0.4g , Carbs: 37.5g , Sugar: 12.4g , Protein: 1.7g

884. Yummy Fruity Ice-Cream

Preparation Time: 20-minutes + 3-4 hours freezing | Total time: 3-4 hours + 20-minutes | Yield: 4-servings

Ingredients:

½ c. of coconut cream	½ peeled and cut small banana
1 c. fresh strawberries, hulled and cut	2 tbsp. of shredded coconut

Directions:

In a powerful blender, put it all together with the ingredients and pulse till smooth. Put it into an ice cream maker, then process following the manufacturer's directions. Now, move into an airtight container. Freeze to set for minimum 3-4 hours, stirring after every thirty-minutes.

Nutritional Information: Calories: 103, Fat: 8.2g, Carbohydrates: 8.2g, Protein: 1.2g, Fiber: 2g

885. Mint Chocolate Chip Ice-cream

Preparation Time: 5-minutes | Total time: 5-minutes | Yield: 2-servings

Ingredients:

2 Frozen overripe bananas	Pinch Spirulina or any natural food coloring, optional.
3 tbsp. Chocolate chips or sugar-free chocolate chips	1/8 tsp. Pure peppermint extract
½ c. raw cashews or coconut cream, optional.	Pinch Salt

Directions:

Mint or imitation peppermint won't be a substitute for this. Use pure peppermint extract and pour it all at once because a drop is more potent than you realize, so add slowly. Peel and cut the bananas first. Put the slices in a Ziplock bag, then freeze. For the ice cream, put all the ingredients in a blender and pulse. You can skip the chocolate chips and just add them after blending. It'll turn out delicious either way. Serve as soon as it's ready or freeze until it's firm enough, then serve!

Nutritional Information: Calories: 250 kcal| Protein: 6.13 g| Fat: 24.37 g | Carbohydrates: 7.72 g

886. Pressure Cooked Cherry Pie

Preparation Time: 15-minutes | Total time: 33-minutes | Yield: 6-servings

Ingredients:

1 9-inch double Pie Crust	2 c. Water
½ tsp. Vanilla Extract	4 c. Cherries pitted
¼ tsp. Almond Extract	4 tbsp. Quick Tapioca
1 c. Packed Brown Sugar	A pinch of Salt

Directions:

Add water to the Instant-Pot and Put the steam rack on top. Mix the cherries with tapioca, sugar, extracts, and salt. Place one pie-crust on the bottom of a lined spring-form pan. Spread the filling over. Top with the other crust. Put the pan on the steam rack. Seal the lid and cook for 18-minutes on MANUAL mode on high pressure. Wait for 10-minutes before releasing the pressure quickly. Carefully remove the top so that any condensation doesn't drip on the pie, then carefully remove the pan using oven mitts or tongs. Let it cool for at least 5-minutes before serving.

Nutritional Information: Calories 393, Carbohydrates 70.6 g, Fiber 1.6 g, Fat 12 g, Protein 2 g

887. Glorious Blueberry Crumble

Preparation Time: 10-minutes | Total time: 40-minutes | Yield: 6-servings

Ingredients:

½ c. of softened coconut oil	½ tsp. of ground cinnamon
1 c. of almond meal	1 c. of toasted and finely crushed almonds
2 tbsp. of coconut sugar	4 c. of fresh blueberries

Directions:

Set the oven to 350F then lightly, grease a pie dish. In a huge container, Mix all ingredients apart from blueberries. Split half of the almond mixture at the bottom of the prepared pie dish. Put blueberries over almond mixture uniformly. Top with the rest of the almond mixture uniformly. Bake for a minimum of 30-minutes or till the top becomes golden brown. Serve warm.

Nutritional Information: Calories: 411, Fat: 34.3g, Carbohydrates: 24.9g, Protein: 7.4g, Fiber: 6.4g

888. Tropical Fruit Crisp

Preparation Time: 10-minutes | Total time: 25-minutes | Yield: 6-servings

Ingredients:

For the Filling:

1 big mango (cut into chunks)	1 big pineapple (cut into pieces)
1/8 tsp. of ground cinnamon	1/8 tsp. of ground ginger
2 tbsps. of coconut oil	2 tbsps. of coconut sugar

For the Topping:

¾ c. of almonds	½ tsp. of ground allspice
½ tsp. of ground cinnamon	½ tsp. of ground ginger
1/3 c. of unsweetened coconut, shredded	

Directions:

Preheat your oven to 375 degrees F. To make the filling: Melt the coconut-oil in a pan on medium-low heat and cook the coconut sugar for a couple of-minutes while stirring. Place in the rest of the ingredients, then cook for a minimum of five-minutes. Stir. Take away the contents from heat and move it to a baking dish. For the topping: Mix each ingredient for topping in a mixer and pulse until a coarse meal forms. Put the topping over the filling. Bake for a minimum of fifteen-minutes or until the top becomes golden brown.

Nutritional Information: Calories: 265, Fat: 12.4g, Carbs: 38g, Sugar: 23.3g, Protein: 4.3g, Sodium: 17mg

889. Full Coconut Cake

Preparation Time: 5-minutes | Total time: 50-minutes | Yield: 4-servings

Ingredients:

3 eggs, yolks, and whites separated	¾ c. Coconut Flour
½ tsp. Coconut Extract	1 ½ c. warm Coconut Milk
½ c. Coconut Sugar	2 tbsp. melted Coconut Oil
1 c. Water	

Directions:

Beat the whites until soft form peaks. Beat in the egg-yolks along with the coconut sugar. Whisk in coconut extract and coconut oil. Gently fold in the coconut flour. Line a baking dish and pour the batter inside. Cover with aluminum foil. Pour the water inside your Instant Pot. Put the container in the pressure cooker. Close the lid and cook for 45-minutes in MANUAL mode. Do a quick pressure release. Serve and enjoy.

Nutritional Information: Calories 350, Carbohydrates 47 g, Fiber 7.5 g, Fat 14.1 g, Protein 7.5 g

890. Turmeric Milkshake

Preparation Time: 5-minutes | Total time: 5-minutes | Yield: 2-servings

Ingredients:

1 tbsp. of ground flaxseeds	1 tsp. of turmeric
2 c. of unsweetened almond milk	2 frozen bananas
2 tbsps. of raw cocoa powder	3 tbsps. of raw honey

Directions:

Mix all ingredients into a high-speed blender, and blend until the desired smoothness is achieved. Split between two serving glasses, and enjoy straight away.

Nutritional Information: Total Carbohydrates: 74g Fiber: 7g, Protein: 4g, Total Fat: 6g, Calories: 334

891. Grilled Peaches

Preparation Time: 10-minutes | Total time: 20-minutes | Yield: 6-servings

Ingredients:

¼ c. of walnuts, chopped	½ c. of coconut cream
1 tsp. of organic vanilla extract	3 medium peaches (halved and pitted)
Ground cinnamon	

Directions:

Preheat the grill on moderate to low heat. Grease the grill grate. Position the peach slices on the grill with the cut-side down. Grill each side for three to five-minutes or until the desired doneness is attained. In the meantime, mix coconut cream with vanilla extract in a container. Beat until the desired smoothness is achieved. Scoop the whipped cream over each peach half. Top with walnuts and drizzle with cinnamon. Serve instantly.

Nutritional Information:, Calories: 110 , Fat: 8g , Carbohydrates: 8.8g , Sugar: 7.8g , Protein: 2.4g

892. Fried Pineapple Slice

Preparation Time:10-minutes | Total time: 18-minutes | Yield: 8-servings

Ingredients:

¼ c. of coconut oil	¼ c. of coconut palm sugar
¼ tsp. of ground cinnamon	1 fresh pineapple (peeled and slice into big slices)

Directions:

Warm a huge cast-iron frying pan on moderate heat. Put in oil and sugar and cook until the coconut oil has melted while stirring constantly. Put the pineapple slices into two batches and cook for roughly 1-2-minutes. Flip the medial side and cook for approximately one minute. Carry on cooking for one more minute. Repeat the steps with the rest of the slices. Drizzle with cinnamon before you serve.

Nutritional Information:, Calories:138,Fat: 7g , Carbs: 20.9g , Sugar: 12.7g , Protein: 0.6g , Sodium: 15mg

893. Almond Butter Balls Vegan

Preparation Time: 10-minutes | Total time: 10-minutes | Yield: 4-servings

Ingredients:

12 dates, pitted and diced	1/3 c. of unsweetened shredded coconut
2 and a ½ tbsp. of almond butter	

Directions:

Take a bowl and add dates, almond butter, and coconut. Mix well. Use the mixture to form small balls. Store them in your fridge and chill them. Enjoy!

Nutritional Information: Calories: 62 Cal |Fats: 3 g | Carbohydrates: 8 g|Protein: 1 g

894. Pure Avocado Pudding

Preparation Time: 3 hours | Total time: 3 hours | Yield: 4-servings

Ingredients:

¼ tsp. cinnamon	¾ c. cocoa powder
1 c. almond milk	1 tsp. vanilla extract
2 avocados, peeled and pitted Walnuts, chopped for serving	2 tbsps. stevia

Directions:

Put in avocados to a blender and pulse well. Put in cocoa powder, almond milk, stevia, vanilla bean extract and pulse the mixture well. Put into serving bowls, then top with walnuts.Chill for two to three hours and serve!

Nutritional Information: Calories: 221, Fat: 8g, Carbohydrates: 7g, Protein: 3g

895. Fennel and Almond Bites

Preparation Time: 10-minutes + 3 hours freezing time | Total time: 3 hours 35-minutes | Yield: 10-servings

Ingredients:

¼ c. almond milk	¼ c. of cocoa powder
½ c. almond oil	1 tsp. fennel seeds
1 tsp. vanilla extract	A pinch of sunflower seeds

Directions:

Take a container and mix the almond oil and almond milk. Beat until the desired smoothness is achieved and shiny by using an electric beater. Whisk in the remaining ingredients. Take a piping bag and pour it into a parchment paper-lined baking sheet. Freeze for around three hours and stored in your refrigerator

Nutritional Information: Total Carbohydrates: 1g, Fiber: 1g, Protein: 1g, Fat: 20g

896. Fall-Time Custard

Preparation Time: 15 -minutes | Total time: 1 hour 15-minutes | Yield: 6-servings

Ingredients:

¼ tsp. of ground ginger	1 c. of canned pumpkin
1 c. of coconut milk	1 tsp. of ground cinnamon
1 tsp. of organic vanilla extract	2 organic eggs
2 pinches of freshly grated nutmeg	8-10 drops of liquid stevia
Pinch of salt	

Directions:

Preheat your oven to 350 degrees F. In a big container, put together pumpkin and spices, then mix. In another container, set in the eggs and beat thoroughly. Place the rest of the ingredients, then whisk till well blended.

Put egg mixture into pumpkin mixture and mix till well combined. Move the mixture to 6 ramekins. Position the ramekins in a baking dish. Add sufficient water in the baking dish about two-inch high around the ramekins. Bake for approximately 1-hour or till a toothpick inserted in the middle comes out clean.

Nutritional Information: Calories: 131 , Fat: 11.1g , Carbohydrates: 6.1g , Protein: 3.3g , Fiber: 2.3g

897. Almond Cookies

Preparation Time: 15 min | Total time: 30-minutes | Yield: 12-servings

Ingredients:

Salt	½ tsp honey
½ tsp vanilla	1.7oz / 50g coconut butter
3.5oz / 100g tahini	1tsp baking powder
1tsp baking soda	14oz / 400g non-wheat flour

Directions:

Mix the baking powder, salt, soda, flour together. Mix tahini and coconut butter and add 2 tbsp. Water in the same bowl. Add honey, vanilla to the tahini mixture and blend it well with a mixer. Preheat your oven (180C/356F) and put a baking sheet on it. Add 24 tbsps. The mixture onto the baking sheet and let it bake in the oven for 11-15-minutes. Let it get cold a little bit and serve.

Nutritional Information: Calories: 114 |Fat: 16g| Carbohydrates: 22g| Protein: 6g

898. Berry-Banana Yogurt

Preparation Time: 10-minutes | Total time: 10-minutes | Yield: 1 serving

Ingredients:

½ banana, frozen fresh	1 container 5.3ounes Greek yogurt, non-fat
¼ c. quick-cooking oats	½ c. blueberries, fresh and frozen
1 c. almond milk	¼ c. collard greens, chopped
5-6 ice cubes	

Directions:

Take a microwave-safe cup and add 1 cup almond milk and ¼ cup oats. Put the cups into your microwave on high for 2.5-minutes. When oats are cooked and 2 ice cubes to cool. Mix them well. Add all ingredients to your blender. Blend it until it gets a smooth and creamy mixture. Serve chilled and enjoy!

Nutritional Information: Calories: 379| Fat: 10g |Carbohydrates: 63g| Protein: 13g

899. Dark Chocolate Granola Bars

Preparation Time: 10-minutes | Total time: 35-minutes | Yield: 12-servings

Ingredients:

¼ c. dark cocoa powder	¼ c. of flaxseed
½ c. dark chocolate chips	1 c. of walnuts
1 c. tart cherries, dried	1 tsp. of salt
1 tsp. of vanilla	2 c. buckwheat
2 eggs	2/3 c. honey

Directions:

Preheat the oven to 350 degrees F. Line with cooking sprays your baking pan. Pulse together the flaxseed, salt, tart cherries, wheat, and walnuts in a food processor. Everything must be chopped fine. Mix the honey, eggs, vanilla, and cocoa powder in a container. Put the wheat mix in your container. Whisk to blend well. Include the chocolate chips. Whisk once more. Then pour this mixture into a baking-dish. Drizzle some chocolate chips and tart cherries. Bake for about twenty-five-minutes. Allow cooling before you serve.

Nutritional Information: Calories 364, Carbs: 37g, Fat: 20g, Protein: 6g, Sugar: 14g, Fiber: 4g

900. Blueberry Crisp

Preparation Time: 5-minutes | Total time: 35-minutes | Yield: 4-servings

Ingredients:

¼ c. pecans, chopped	1 c. buckwheat
½ tsp. ginger	1 tsp. of cinnamon
2 tbsps. Olive oil	¼ tsp. nutmeg
1 lb. blueberries	1 tsp. of honey

Directions:

Preheat your oven to 350 degrees F. Grease your baking dish. Whisk together the pecans, wheat, oil, spices, and honey in a bowl. Add the berries to your pan. Layer the topping on your berries. Bake for 30-minutes at 350 F.

Nutritional Information: Calories 348 |Carbohydrates 40g |Fat 28g |Protein 9g |Sugar 18g

CHAPTER 10: MEAL PLAN

BREAKFAST	LUNCH	DINNER	SNACK
1ST WEEK			
Root Vegetable Egg Casserole	Pineapple Three Bean Salad	Mushroom Pork Chops	Peach Dip
Huevos Rancheros	Instant Pot Black Beans	Roasted Tofu and Greens	Easy Peasy Ginger Date
Healthy Zucchini Stir Fry	Quinoa with Apricots	Easy Shrimp	Lemon Garlic Red Chard
Healthy Breakfast Chocolate Donuts	Tzatziki Dip with Cauliflower	Parmesan and Lemon Fish	Blueberry Muffin
Banana with Cashew Toast	Curried Shrimp and Vegetables	Brie-Packed Smoked Salmon	White Fish Ceviche with Avocado
Power Pancakes	Shrimp Cakes	Lemonade Broccoli	Clove Artichokes
Tuna & Sweet Potato Croquettes	Simple Brown Rice	Spicy Keto Chicken Wings	Cottage Cheese with Apple Sauce
2ND WEEK			
Oat Porridge with Cherry & Coconut	Italian Halibut Chowder	Anti-Inflammatory Turmeric Gummies	Homemade Guacamole
Savory Pancake Blast	Anti-Inflammatory Buddha Bowl	Steamed Artichokes	Bell Pepper Veggie Wraps
Oats with Berries	Simply Sautéed Flaky Fillet	Cheesy Ham Quiche	Oregano Green Beans
Golden Milk	Curried Beef Meatballs	Mexican Cod Fillets	Celery Spread
Spinach Fritters	Pumpkin Spiced Almonds	Chicken Marrakesh	Berry Energy bites
Anti-Inflammatory Crepes	Potato Mash	Italian Stuffed Peppers	Carrot Sticks with Avocado Dip

Spiced Morning Chia Pudding	Lemony Trout	Peas Soup	Flaxseed Crackers
3RD WEEK			
Berry Coconut Porridge	Lime Cod Mix	Steamed fish balls	Banana Ginger Bars
Bake Apple Turnover	Chili Snapper	Especial Glazed Salmon	Soft Flourless Cookies
Maple Oatmeal	Kale Salad	Nutty Pina Colada	Green Bean Snack
Breakfast Burgers with Avocado Buns	Sheet Pan Rosemary Mushrooms	Vanilla Turmeric Orange Juice	Mandarin Cottage Cheese
Anti-Inflammatory Muffins	Clean Eating Egg Salad	Vegan and Mediterranean Mango and Bean stew	Lime Brussels Sprouts
Ginger Turmeric Shake Meal	Air Fryer Salmon	Lemon And Garlic Scallops	Mini Pepper Nachos
Anti-Inflammatory Breakfast Oatmeal	Carrot Bread	Minty Lamb Stew	Cado Choco Cake

CHAPTER 11: CONVERSION UNITS OF MEASURE

CONVERSION UNITS OF VOLUME

AMERICAN SYSTEM	OTHER UI	METRIC SYSTEM
drop	1/76 teaspoon	0.0649 milliliters
teaspoon	76 drops o 1/3 tablespoon	4.9288 milliliters
tablespoon	3 teaspoons	14.786 milliliters
cup	16 tablespoons o 1/2 pint	0.2366 liters
pint	2 cups	0.4732 liters
quart	4 cups o 2 pints	0.9463 liters
gallon	128 ounces o 8 pints	3.7853 liters

CONVERSION UNITS OF WEIGHT

AMERICAN SYSTEM	OTHER UI	METRIC SYSTEM
grain	1/7000 pound (libbra)	64.799 milligrams
dram	1/16 ounce (oncia)	1.7718 grams
ounce	16 drams	28.350 grams
pound	16 ounces (once)	453.6 grams
ton (short)	2,000 pounds (libbre)	907.18 kilograms
ton (long)	2,240 pounds (libbre)	1016 kilograms

OVEN TEMPERATURE

(Degrees F / Degrees C)

250 Degrees F = 120 Degrees C

275 Degrees F = 140 Degrees C

300 Degrees F = 150 Degrees C

325 Degrees F = 160 Degrees C

350 Degrees F = 180 Degrees C

375 Degrees F = 190 Degrees C

400 Degrees F = 200 Degrees C

425 Degrees F = 220 Degrees C

450 Degrees F = 230 Degrees C

475 Degrees F = 240 Degrees C

500 Degrees F = 260 Degrees C

When you know this ...	... multiply by ...	... to get this
teaspoons (tsp or tsps)	4.93	milliliters
tablespoons (tbsp or tbsps)	14.79	milliliters
fluid ounces (fl. oz.)	29.57	milliliters
cups	236.59	milliliters
cups	0.236	liters
ounces	28.35	grams

CHAPTER 12: RECIPE INDEX

Adobo Lime Chicken Mix   166
After's Apple Cinnamon Chips   200
Air Fryer Salmon 73
Allspice Pork Mix 168
Almond and Honey Homemade Bar 201
Almond and Pear Smoothie   226
Almond Breaded Chicken Goodness   100
Almond Butter and Berry Sandwiches   84
Almond Butter Balls Vegan   229
Almond Butter-Banana Smoothie   29
Almond Chicken Cutlets   177
Almond Cinnamon Beef Meatballs 183
Almond Cookies 230
Almond Mascarpone Dumplings   66
Almond Scones   32
Almond Syrup with Greek Yogurt Parfait   50
Almond Yogurt, Berry, and Walnut Parfait   200
Almonds and Blueberries Yogurt Snack   200
Amazing Apricot Bites   212
Amazing Pesto Egg   44
Amberjack Fillets with Cheese Sauce   131
Ambrosial Avocado & Salmon Salad in Lemon-Dressed Layers   114
Anti-Inflammatory Apricot Squares 216
Anti-Inflammatory Berry Smoothie 37
Anti-Inflammatory Breakfast Oatmeal   52
Anti-Inflammatory Buddha Bowl   67
Anti-Inflammatory Crepes 26
Anti-Inflammatory Muffins   30
Anti-Inflammatory Porridge   35
Anti-Inflammatory Turmeric Gummies   94
Appetizing Quinoa Breakfast Stew 51
Apple and Tomato Dipping Sauce   81
Apple Bread   60
Apple Bruschetta with Blackberries and Almonds 34
Apple Cinnamon Steel Cut Oats   37
Apple Fritters   222
Apple Muesli   55
Apple Omelet   49
Apple Pork Raisins   156

Apple, Ginger, and Rhubarb Muffins   34
Apricot Chicken Wings   185
Asian Beef Short Ribs   86
Asian Saucy Chicken   173
Avocado and Egg Sandwich   205
Avocado And Jalapeno Salsa   213
Avocado Cup with Egg   21
Avocado Eggs with Balsamic Vinegar   45
Avocado Pineapple Pork   172
Avocado Toast with Spinach Leaves 51
Avocado with Tomatoes and Cucumber   211
Avocado-Orange Grilled Chicken   159
Awesome Breakfast Parfait   44
Bacon and Jalapeno Wrapped Shrimp   143
Bacon Burger Cabbage Stir Fry   113
Bacon Cheeseburger   100
Bacon-Wrapped Chicken with Cheddar Cheese 155
Bake Apple Turnover   28
Bake Chicken Top-up with Olives, Tomatoes, And Basil   71
Baked Broccoli   211
Baked Butternut Squash Rigatoni 57
Baked Chicken Meatballs - Habanero & Green Chili   175
Baked Eggs with Portobello Mushrooms   32
Baked Fillet Mignon with Potatoes 153
Baked Pork Chops with Cashew   185
Baked Salmon Cakes   120
Baked Sweet Peppers   207
Baked Tilapia with Rosemary and Pecan   106
Baked Tomato Hake   145
Baked Veggie Turmeric Nuggets   208
Balsamic Chicken and Vegetables   59
Balsamic Onion Snack   200
Balsamic Pork and Peaches   161
Balsamic Scallops 143
Balsamic-Glazed Turkey Wings   169
Banana and Peanut Butter Detox   105
Banana Baked Oatmeal   28
Banana Date Porridge   46
Banana Ginger Bars   194
Banana Pancake Bites   30
Banana Steel Oats   33

Banana with Cashew Toast   22
Basic "Rotisserie" Chicken 181
Basil Chicken Sauté   167
Basil Peppers Dip 210
Basil Pork and Pine Nuts   162
BBQ Chicken Liver and Hearts   154
BBQ Chicken Zucchini Boats   170
Beef and Broccoli Stir-Fry 76
Beef Bites   198
Beef Stuffed Cabbage   176
Beef with Asparagus & Bell Pepper 165
Beef with Carrot & Broccoli   181
Beef with Zucchini Noodles   186
Beet and Cherry Smoothie 36
Beets Gazpacho 56
Beets with Yogurt   108
Bell Pepper Veggie Wraps 191
Berry Chops Dinner   182
Berry Coconut Porridge   27
Berry Delight   197
Berry Energy bites   193
Berry Parfait   219
Berry Red Smoothie   226
Berry-Banana Yogurt   230
Black Bean and Mango Lettuce Wraps   84
Black Bean Cakes 214
Blackened Chicken Breast 103
Blackened Fish Tacos with Slaw   123
Blackened Tilapia 116
Blue Cheese Buffalo Chicken Balls   165
Blue Cheese, Fig and Arugula Salad 33
Blueberry & Cashew Waffles   28
Blueberry Crisp   230
Blueberry Curd   195
Blueberry Hemp Seed Smoothie   22
Blueberry Vanilla Quinoa Porridge 45
Blueberry-Bran Breakfast Sundae   36
Boiled Okra and Squash   191
Boozy Glazed Chicken   181
Braised Kale   103
Braised Leeks, Cauliflower, and Artichoke Hearts   102
Breakfast Burgers with Avocado Buns   29
Breakfast Cherry Muffins 35
Breakfast Corn Salad   54
Breakfast Pitas   24
Breakfast Sausage and Mushroom Casserole   27

Breakfast Shakshuka 20
Breakfast Spinach Mushroom Tomato Fry Up 24
Breakfast Stir Fry 21
Brie-Packed Smoked Salmon 94
Broccoli and Tilapia 102
Broccoli Bites 112
Broccoli Rice with Mushrooms 109
Broiled Lamb Chops 85
Broiled White Sea Bass 89
Brown Rice and Chicken Mix 65
Brown Sugar Cinnamon Oatmeal 22
Bruschetta 203
Brussels Sprouts and Paprika Chicken Thighs 87
Buckwheat Crackers 193
Buckwheat Ginger Granola 33
Buckwheat Pancakes with Vanilla Almond Milk 48
Buckwheat Waffles 205
Buffalo Pizza Chicken 186
Buttered Banana Chickpea Cookies 203
Buttered Sprouts 80
Butternut Squash Fries 198
Cabbage Bowl 195
Cabbage Orange Salad with Citrusy Vinaigrette 69
Cabbage with Apple 62
Cado Choco Cake 196
Café-style Fudge 206
Cajun Chicken & Prawn 157
Cajun Jambalaya Soup 104
Candied Dates 202
Capellini Soup with Tofu and Shrimp 76
Capocollo and Garlic Chicken 156
Caramelized Pears 221
Caramelized Pork Chops 63
Caraway and Dill Pork 173
Cardamom Roasted Apricots 195
Carrot and Pumpkin Seed Crackers 192
Carrot Bread 73
Carrot Cake Overnight Oats 20
Carrot Salad 80
Carrot Sticks with Avocado Dip 193
Cashew Chicken Curry 174
Cauliflower and Chorizo 36
Cauliflower Lamb Meal 164
Cauliflower Mac & Cheese 112
Cauliflower Puree 201
Cauliflower Steaks with Tamarind and Beans 82
Cauliflower Tikka Masala with Chickpeas 94
Cayenne Pepper Green Beans 200
Celery Root Hash Browns 109
Celery Spread 193

Cereal Chia Chips 208
Chai Tea Drink 109
Champion Chicken Pockets 180
Cheddar and Chive Souffles 41
Cheesy Bacon-Wrapped Chicken with Asparagus Spears 151
Cheesy Chicken Sun-Dried Tomato Packets 171
Cheesy Ham Quiche 95
Cheesy Hemp Seeds and Flax Muffins 50
Cheesy Mexican-Style Chicken 157
Cheesy Pinwheels with Chicken 161
Cheesy Ranch Chicken 154
Cheesy Tuna Pasta 126
Cherries and Quinoa 120
Cherry Smoothie 19
Chewy Blackberry Leather 210
Chewy Choco Chip Cookies 199
Chia Cashew Cream 205
Chia Pudding with Cashews and Cherries 211
Chicken & Apple Cider Chili 166
Chicken & Cabbage Platter 78
Chicken & Cheese Filled Avocados 159
Chicken and Veggie Casserole 121
Chicken Bacon Quesadilla 83
Chicken Bites 213
Chicken Breasts and Mushrooms 58
Chicken Chili 73
Chicken Curry with Tamarind & Pumpkins 117
Chicken Divan 180
Chicken Frittata with Asiago Cheese and Herbs 184
Chicken in Pita Bread 154
Chicken Lemon Piccata 115
Chicken Marrakesh 96
Chicken Meatball Soup 82
Chicken Muffins 31
Chicken Parmigiana 179
Chicken Pasta Parmesan 87
Chicken Piccata 167
Chicken Pie with Bacon 158
Chicken with Fennel 160
Chicken with Herb Parmesan Spaghetti Squash 101
Chicken-Bell Pepper Sauté 152
Chickpea Stuffed Butternut Squash 68
Chili & Lemon Marinated Chicken Wings 163
Chili Chicken Kebab with Garlic Dressing 184
Chili Pork Pan 178
Chili Shrimp and Pineapple 138
Chili Snapper 72
Chimichurri Turkey 156

Chinese-Orange Spiced Duck Breasts 156
Chinese-Style Asparagus 214
Chipotle Chickpea Taco Bowls 118
Choco Chia Cherry Cream 206
Choco-Banana Oats 49
Chocolate Bananas 216
Chocolate chip 83
Chocolate Covered Strawberries 216
Choco-Nana Pancakes 36
Cilantro Brussels Sprouts 203
Cilantro Pancakes 41
Cilantro-Lime Chicken Drumsticks 152
Cinnamon Flaxseed Breakfast Loaf 43
Cinnamon Granola 54
Cinnamon Pork Mix 161
Cinnamon-Apple Granola with Greek Yogurt 37
Cipollini & Bell Pepper Chicken Souvlaki 157
Citrus & Herb Sardines 128
Citrus Beef with Bok Choy 178
Citrus Cauliflower Cake 218
Citrus Salmon on a Bed of Greens 123
Citrus Strawberry Granita 227
Clams with Garlic-Tomato Sauce 146
Classic Guacamole Dip 61
Clean Eating Egg Salad 73
Clean Salmon with Soy Sauce 114
Clove Artichokes 190
Coco Cherry Bake-less Bars 204
Coconut & Banana Cookies 47
Coconut Almond Granola 37
Coconut and Chocolate Cream 220
Coconut and Cinnamon Bowl 46
Coconut and Cinnamon Pancakes 31
Coconut Butter Fudge 220
Coconut Chicken Curry with Cauliflower Rice 70
Coconut Chocolate Oatmeal 23
Coconut Flakes and Almond Pancakes 43
Coconut Mahi-Mahi Nuggets 124
Coconut Pork and Spring Onions 187
Coconut Quinoa with Turmeric Spice 191
Coconut Rice with Berries 53
Coconut Rice with shrimps in Coconut curry 124
Coconut Turkey Mix 89
Coconut-Crusted Shrimp 148
Coconut-Curry-Cashew Chicken 157
Coco-Tapioca Bowl 25
Cod and Peas 107
Cod Curry 140
Cod with Bell Pepper 144
Cod with Ginger 130

Cold Oatmeal with Apple and Cinnamon 52
Cookie Dough Bites 216
Cornmeal Grits 75
Cottage Cheese with Apple Sauce 190
Crab Salad Cakes 135
Crab Stuffed Salmon 128
Creamed Savoy Cabbage 114
Creamy & Chilly Blueberry Bites 220
Creamy Artichoke Spread 206
Creamy Avocado Vegetable Burritos 120
Creamy Broccoli Stew 107
Creamy Cauliflower Parsnip Mash 105
Creamy Chicken Breast 89
Creamy Chicken Salad 110
Creamy Cucumber Mix 215
Creamy Frozen Yogurt 225
Creamy Polenta 212
Creamy Queso Dip 77
Creamy Sweet Potato Mash 57
Crème Caramel Coconut Flan 226
Crepes with Coconut Cream & Strawberry Sauce 23
Crispy Cheese-Crusted Fish Fillet 75
Crispy Chicken Fingers 48
Crispy Corn 212
Crispy Fish Stick 138
Crispy Tilapia 142
Crunchy Roasted Chickpeas 208
Cucumber Bites 27
Cucumber Ginger Shrimp 129
Cucumber Rolls Hors D'oeuvres 198
Cumin Pork and Beans 172
Cumin Zucchini Spread 201
Curried Beef Meatballs 67
Curried Fish 145
Curried Shrimp and Vegetables 63
Curry Chicken Lettuce Wraps 183
Curry Tilapia and Beans 130
Cuttlefish Salad in Sweet and Sour Sauce 149
Dairy-Free Antioxidant Yogurt Parfait 35
Daring Shark Steaks 124
Dark Chocolate Chicken 174
Dark Chocolate Granola Bars 230
Date Dough & Walnut Wafer 202
Delectable Cookies 209
Delicious Creamy Crab Meat 108
Delicious Roasted Duck 166
Delightful Teriyaki Chicken Under Pressure 164
Dijon Salmon with Green bean Pilaf 104
Dill Haddock 64
Double Cheese Italian Chicken 151
Dried Dates & Turmeric Truffles 194

Duck Breast and Blackberries Mix 152
Duck Breast with Apricot Sauce 160
Duck Stew Olla Tapaha 177
Easiest Pressure-Cooked Raspberry Curd 217
Easy Bean Veggie Burgers 119
Easy Chicken Tacos 162
Easy Crunchy Fish Tray Bake 127
Easy Eggplant Spread 201
Easy Peach Cobbler 221
Easy Peasy Ginger Date 190
Easy Roasted Carrots 80
Easy Shrimp 92
Easy Stir-Fried Chicken 87
Easy Street Sweet Corn 223
Edamame Omelet 56
Egg Casserole with Kale 39
Egg Porridge 18
Energetic Oat Bars 208
Energy Dates Balls 211
Escarole, Pineapple, and Apple Smoothie 116
Especial Glazed Salmon 98
Exquisite Pear and Onion Goose 174
Fall-Time Custard 229
Farro Salad with Arugula 213
Fast Fish Pie 134
Faux Beet Risotto 111
Fennel & Figs Lamb 113
Fennel and Almond Bites 229
Feta & Bacon Chicken 151
Feta and Cauliflower Rice Stuffed Bell Peppers 104
Fish & Chickpea Stew 143
Fish Cakes 141
Fish Casserole with Cream Cheese Sauce 144
Fish Sandwich 131
Fish Tacos with Cabbage Slaw 117
Flavorsome Almonds 209
Flaxseed Crackers 194
Flourless & Flaky Muffin Munchies 190
Flourless Sweet Potato Brownies 222
Flying Jacob Casserole 173
French Toast Sticks 210
Fresh Tuna Steak and Fennel Salad 148
Fried Coconut Shrimp with Asparagus 69
Fried Pineapple Slice 229
Frozen Blueberry Yogurt Bites 199
Fruit Bowl with Yogurt Topping 97
Fruit Cobbler 219
Fruit Salad 221
Fruit-and-Seed Breakfast Bars 53
Fruity Bowl 34
Fruity Muffins 57
Full Coconut Cake 228

Garlic Butter Shrimps 147
Garlic Cashew "Hummus" 200
Garlic Chili Edamame 197
Garlic Crab Legs 146
Garlic Lamb Chops 107
Garlic Salmon with Cheese 116
Ginger & Chili Sea Bass Fillets 146
Ginger Turmeric Shake Meal 30
Gingerbread Buckwheat Cereal 46
Gingerbread Oatmeal Breakfast 38
Gingered Cauliflower Rice 76
Gingered Tilapia 124
Ginger-Turmeric Carrot Soup 85
Glorious Blueberry Crumble 228
Gluten-Free Crepes 26
Gluten-Free Pineapple Burgers 93
Gluten-Free Teriyaki Salmon 108
Golden Milk 25
Granola 24
Grapefruit-Pomegranate Salad 69
Greek Chicken Stefano 179
Greek Turkey Burgers with Tzatziki 74
Green and Leafy Ginger-Apple Drink 107
Green Bean Snack 195
Green Smoothie Bowl 38
Green Soup 60
Green Tea Pudding 223
Grilled Avocado Sandwich 74
Grilled Calamari 139
Grilled fish tacos 126
Grilled Peaches 228
Grilled Salmon and Zucchini with Mango Sauce 65
Grilled Salmon with Caponata 126
Ground Beef & Veggies Curry 174
Ground Beef with Cabbage 164
Ground Beef with Cashews & Veggies 167
Ground Beef with Greens & Tomatoes 187
Ground Turkey with Veggies 121
Haddock with Swiss Chard 132
Ham and Veggie Frittata Muffins 48
Hash Browns 42
Healthy and Tasty Vanilla Crepes 51
Healthy Breakfast Chocolate Donuts 21
Healthy Chicken Marsala 72
Healthy Fish Nacho Bowl 141
Healthy Halibut Fillets 111
Healthy Turkey Gumbo 162
Healthy Zucchini Stir Fry 21
Hearty Beef and Bacon Casserole 59
Hearty Pineapple Oatmeal 38
Her bed Rockfish 125
Herb and Avocado Omelet 19

Herb Butter Scallops 77
Herbed Coconut Milk Steamed Mussels 130
Hibiscus Ginger Gelatin 93
Hidden Valley Chicken Dummies 167
Homemade Guacamole 191
Home-Style Chicken Kebab 188
Honey Chicken Tagine 176
Honey Crusted Salmon with Pecans 125
Honey Ginger Shrimp Bowls 69
Honey Mustard Grilled Pork 91
Honey Pancakes 40
Honey-Roasted Chicken Thighs with Carrots 100
Hot Chocolate 219
Hot Tuna Steak 81
Huevos Rancheros 18
Instant Banana Oatmeal 39
Instant Pot Black Beans 57
Irish Style Clams 78
Island Style Sardines 150
Italian Calamari 71
Italian Halibut Chowder 66
Italian Meatballs in Asiago Sauce 171
Italian Stuffed Peppers 96
Kale Chips 197
Kale Salad 72
Keto Chicken Enchiladas 177
Keto Salmon Tandoori with Cucumber Sauce 63
Keto Tacos with Bacon Sauce 186
Keto Zoodles with White Clam Sauce 64
Lamb Burger on Arugula 86
Lebanese Chicken Kebabs and Hummus 183
Leek and Chard Frittata 68
Lemon & Garlic Chicken Thighs 185
Lemon And Garlic Scallops 101
Lemon Buttery Shrimp Rice 75
Lemon Carrots 201
Lemon Garlic Red Chard 189
Lemon Garlic Shrimp Pasta 149
Lemon Garlic Turkey Breast 121
Lemon Onion Mash 79
Lemon Tuna 82
Lemon Vegan Cake 217
Lemonade Broccoli 94
Lemon-Artichoke Risotto 118
Lemon-Caper Trout with Caramelized Shallots 62
Lemon-Garlic Chicken with Caramelized Onions 182
Lemon-Mint Green Tea 99
Lemony Berry Gummies 211
Lemony Ginger Cookies 191
Lemony Mackerel 61

Lemony Mussels 111
Lemony Trout 71
Lentil and Mushrooms Cakes 205
Lentil Stew 59
Lime Brussels Sprouts 195
Lime Cod Mix 71
Lime Shrimp and Kale 90
Lovely Pumpkin Oats 38
Low Cholesterol-Low Calorie Blueberry Muffin 189
Mackerel Bombs 79
Mandarin Cottage Cheese 195
Mango & Avocado Salad 75
Mango Granola 39
Mango, Cucumber and Spinach Smoothie 217
Manhattan-Style Salmon Chowder 137
Maple Oatmeal 29
Maple Toast and Eggs 61
Marinated Fish Steaks 147
Mashed Avocado with Jicama Slices 212
Massaged Kale Chips 196
Meatloaf with a Sweet Sticky Glaze 180
Mediterranean Frittata 47
Mediterranean Mushroom Olive Steak 113
Mediterranean Pork 91
Mediterranean Rolled Baklava with Walnuts 222
Mediterranean toast 31
Mexican Cod Fillets 96
Mexican Salad with Mahi-Mahi 131
Mexican Veggie Meat 194
Middle Eastern Shish Kebab 155
Milk Dumplings in Sweet Cardamom Sauce 217
Mini Pepper Nachos 196
Mint Chocolate Chip Ice-cream 227
Minty Lamb Stew 103
Minty Pork and Almonds 177
Miso Salmon and Green Beans 115
Miso-Glazed Salmon 148
Morning Bowl 42
Morning Scrambled Turkey Eggs 41
Moroccan Turkey Tagine 155
Mozzarella Fish 130
Mushroom & Cauliflower Risotto 110
Mushroom Crepes 45
Mushroom Frittata 54
Mushroom Pork Chops 91
Mustard Pork Mix 175
Nacho Chicken Casserole 163
No Cook Overnight Oats 25
No-Bake Frittata 27
No-Bake Turmeric Protein Donuts 47
Nutty Pesto Chicken Supreme 169

Nutty Pina Colada 99
Oat Porridge with Cherry & Coconut 23
Oatmeal Chocolate Cookies 226
Oatmeal Pancakes 46
Oatmeal-Apple sauce Muffins 28
Oats with Berries 24
Oats, flaxseeds, and banana smoothie 217
Omega-3 Chocolate Chia Hemp Pudding 53
Omega-3-rich Cold Banana Breakfast 46
Onion Bacon Pork Chops 61
Open Avocado Tuna Melts 81
Open-Faced Garden Tuna Sandwich 87
Orange and Maple-Glazed Salmon 142
Orange Chicken Legs 184
Oregano Green Beans 192
Oregano Pork Pan 170
Oven Crisp Sweet Potato 214
Oven-Baked Sole Fillets 148
Oven-Poached Eggs 31
Overnight Coconut Chia Oats 39
Overnight Muesli 38
Paleo Ginger Spiced Mixed Nuts 193
Paleo Raspberry Cream Pie 223
Pancetta & Cheese Stuffed Chicken 181
Pan-Fried Chorizo Sausage 158
Pan-Seared Halibut with Citrus Butter Sauce 105
Pan-Seared Scallops with Lemon-Ginger Vinaigrette 134
Papaya Smoothie 220
Paprika Chicken & Pancetta in a Skillet 159
Parmesan and Lemon Fish 93
Parmesan Asparagus 191
Parmesan Endive 190
Parmesan-Crusted Halibut with Asparagus 81
Parsley Pork and Artichokes 171
Parsley Tilapia 143
Party-Time Chicken Nuggets 192
Pasta With Spinach, Garbanzos, And Raisins 88
Peach Dip 192
Peanut Butter Bars 218
Peanut Butter-Banana Muffins 35
Peas Soup 97
Pecan and Lime Cheesecake 206
Pecan and Spice Stuffed Apple Bake 197
Pepper Steak Taco 85
Pepperoni Pizza Loaf 78
Perfect Barley Porridge 47

Pesto & Mozzarella Chicken Casserole 179

Pineapple Banana-Oat Smoothie 225

Pineapple Ginger Smoothie 32

Pineapple Three Bean Salad 56

Pita Pizza 101

Poached Eggs 45

Poached Halibut and Mushrooms 142

Poached Pears with Orange, Cinnamon, and Ginger 224

Pomegranate-Avocado Smoothie 220

Popcorn Chicken 78

Popcorn Shrimp 128

Pork and Brown Rice 165

Pork and Creamy Leeks 172

Pork and Cumin Pinto Beans 165

Pork and Cumin Zucchinis 183

Pork Chops with Tomato Salsa 153

Pork with Carrots 154

Pork with Corn and Peas 171

Pork with Lemongrass 175

Pork with Mushrooms and Cucumbers 175

Pork with Olives 170

Pork with Scallions and Cauliflower 167

Pork with Spiced Zucchinis 159

Pork with Spring Onions and Grapes 187

Pork with Thyme Sweet Potatoes 163

Potato Dumpling with Shrimp 133

Potato Mash 70

Power Pancakes 49

Pressure Cooked Cherry Pie 227

Protein-Packed Croquettes 202

Pulled Buffalo Chicken Salad with Blue Cheese 153

Pumpkin & Banana Waffles 49

Pumpkin Ice Cream 224

Pumpkin Is for More than Just Pie 19

Pumpkin Quinoa Porridge 31

Pumpkin Shrimp 139

Pumpkin Spiced Almonds 68

Pure Avocado Pudding 229

Purple Cabbage Salad with Quinoa and Edamame 204

Puttanesca-Style Greens and Beans 58

Quick Burrito 36

Quick Chermoula Fish Parcels 137

Quick Fish Bowl 125

Quick Shrimp Moqueca 132

Quinoa & Pumpkin Porridge 41

Quinoa Bowls Avocado Egg 53

Quinoa Tortillas 203

Quinoa with Apricots 62

Raisin Bran Muffins 68

Raisins and Cranberry Granola 50

Raspberry Diluted Frozen Sorbet 224

Raspberry Gummies 224

Ratatouille 76

Raw Black Forest Brownies 219

Red Pepper and Mozzarella-Stuffed Chicken Caprese 163

Refreshing Raspberry Jelly 225

Ribbons with Thalli and Tuna 149

Rice 'n Tuna Casserole 150

Roast with Onions and Potatoes 152

Roasted Bananas 225

Roasted Beets 205

Roasted Brussels Sprouts & Sweet Potato 66

Roasted Cauliflower and Potato Curry Soup 106

Roasted Chicken 185

Roasted Curried Cauliflower 214

Roasted Pumpkin Seeds 21

Roasted Salmon and Asparagus 144

Roasted Summer Squash & Fennel Bulb 74

Roasted Tofu and Greens 91

Roasted Vegetables with Polenta 92

Roasted Vegetables with White Beans and Sweet Potatoes 102

Rockfish Curry 139

Romesco Sauce with Vegetables and Sheet-Pan Chicken 99

Root Vegetable Egg Casserole 18

Rosemary Black Beans 192

Rosemary Garlic Lamb Chops 64

Rosemary Roasted Pork with Cauliflower 71

Rosemary-Lemon Cod 142

Rum Butter Cookies 220

Salmon and Cauliflower 125

Salmon and Coconut Mix 147

Salmon and Roasted Peppers 131

Salmon and Shrimp Mix 145

Salmon and Sweet Potato Mix 75

Salmon Balls 123

Salmon Burgers 47

Salmon Cakes 79

Salmon Ceviche 125

Salmon in Dill Sauce 132

Salmon Salsa 213

Salsa Chicken Bites 97

Salsa Chicken 89

Saucy Brussels sprouts and Carrots 204

Sautéed Kale 211

Sautéed Shrimp Jambalaya Jumble 60

Sautéed Veggies on Hot Bagels 24

Savory Bread 42

Savory Breakfast Pancakes 26

Savory Pancake Blast 23

Savory Veggie Muffins 44

Savory White bean soup 83

Scallops Stew 108

Scallops with Mushroom Special 103

Scrambled Eggs with Smoked Salmon 20

Seafood Paella 127

Seared Ahi Tuna 134

Seared Tuna with Vinaigrette and Salad 65

Seasoned Catfish 126

Sesame Ginger Salmon 142

Sesame Spread 210

Sesame Wings with Cauliflower 59

Sesame-Tamari Baked Chicken with Green Beans 116

Sesame-Tuna Skewers 138

Sheet Pan Rosemary Mushrooms 73

Sheet Pan Steak with Brussels sprouts And Red Wine 115

Sheet Pan Turkey Breast with Golden Vegetables 100

Sherbet Pineapple 226

Sherry and Butter Prawns 131

Shirataki Pasta with Avocado and Cream 32

Shrimp and Beets 132

Shrimp and Corn 128

Shrimp and Vegetable Curry 111

Shrimp Cakes 63

Shrimp Pie 136

Shrimp Risotto 138

Shrimp Scampi 147

Shrimp with Cinnamon Sauce 144

Shrimp with Linguine 98

Shrimp with Spicy Spinach 127

Shrimp-Lime Bake with Zucchini and Corn 101

Simple Brown Rice 66

Simple Carrots Mix 74

Simple Coconut Pancakes 198

Simple Founder in Brown Butter Lemon Sauce 135

Simple Garlic-Roasted Chickpeas 210

Simple Mango Salsa 204

Simple Mushroom Chicken Mix 102

Simple Steel-Cut Oats 53

Simply Sautéed Flaky Fillet 67

Skillet Chicken with Brussels Sprouts Mix 176

Slow Cooked Meatballs 185

Slow Cooker Chicken Cacciatore 158

Slow Cooker Chicken Fajitas 162

Slow Cooker Jerk Chicken 172

Slow Turkey 172

Smoked Beef Sausage Bake with Broccoli 180

Smoked Herring Sandwich 149

Soft Flourless Cookies 194

Sole with Vegetables 133
Souvlaki Spiced Salmon Bowls 134
Special Oysters 140
Spiced Broccoli, Cauliflower, and Tofu with Red Onion 93
Spiced Carrot Smoothie 226
Spiced Ground Beef 160
Spiced Morning Chia Pudding 26
Spiced Nuts 189
Spiced Popcorn 33
Spiced Pumpkin Smoothie 218
Spiced Tea Pudding 222
Spicy & Creamy Ground Beef Curry 170
Spicy Almond Chicken Strips with Garlic Lime Tartar Sauce 169
Spicy baked fish 93
Spicy Cauliflower Rice 66
Spicy Chicken and Cauliflower 70
Spicy Chicken Vegetable Soup 105
Spicy Chipotle Chicken 151
Spicy Ginger Crepes 33
Spicy herb catfish 136
Spicy Kale Chips 199
Spicy Keto Chicken Wings 94
Spicy Kingfish 129
Spicy Marble Eggs 44
Spicy Pineapple Smoothie 34
Spicy Popper Mug Cake 219
Spicy Pork Chops 110
Spicy Pulled Chicken Wraps 158
Spicy Ramen Soup 76
Spicy Roasted chickpeas 209
Spicy Salmon Tempura Roll 137
Spicy Tuna Rolls 95
Spinach Almond Tortilla 92
Spinach and Artichoke Egg Casserole 30
Spinach and Blackberries Smoothie 54
Spinach and Kale Breaded Balls 212
Spinach Avocado Smoothie 42
Spinach Breakfast 48
Spinach Chicken Cheesy Bake 176
Spinach Fritters 25
Spinach Salad with Walnuts and Strawberry 88
Spinach Tomatoes Mix 106
Squash Spaghetti with Bolognese Sauce 109
Squash with Broccoli 54
Squid Rings with Potato and Spinach 141
Steamed Artichokes 95
Steamed Cauliflower 197
Steamed fish balls 97
Steamed Garlic-Dill Halibut 150
Steamed Lemon Pepper Salmon 150
Steamed Purple Sweet Potatoes 206

Stir-Fried Mushrooms and Beef 86
Strawberries and Cream Trifle 56
Strawberry Granita 221
Strawberry Ice Cream 221
Strawberry Yogurt treat 19
Strawberry-Oat-Chocolate Chip Muffins 43
Stuffed Chicken Breasts 113
Stuffed Chicken with Sauerkraut and Cheese 180
Stuffed Mushrooms 207
Stuffed Portobello Mushrooms 119
Stuffed Trout 133
Sun-Dried Tomato Garlic Bruschetta 19
Super Sesame Chicken Noodles 173
Sweet Cherry Almond Chia Pudding 52
Sweet Crab Cakes 139
Sweet Onion and Egg Pie 59
Sweet Potato and Celery Root Mash 207
Sweet Potato Cranberry Breakfast bars 29
Sweet Quinoa 209
Sweet Strawberry Sorbet 224
Sweetened Brown Rice 77
Swiss Chard and Spinach with Egg 20
Swordfish with Pineapple and Cilantro 129
Taco Casserole 104
Tamari Steak Salad 109
Tangy Barbecue Chicken 188
Tangy Chicken with Scallions 184
Tangy Turmeric Flavored Florets 214
Tarragon Chicken with Roasted Balsamic Turnips 187
Tarragon Pork Roast 184
Tasty Grilled Asparagus 82
Tasty Roasted Broccoli 103
Tempeh and Root Vegetable Bake 98
Tempeh Wraps with Avocado and Veggies 84
Tender Creamy Scallops 123
Tender salmon in mustard sauce 111
Thai Chowder 135
Thar She' Salts Peanut Butter Cookies 216
The Almond Breaded Chicken Goodness 95
The Most Elegant Parsley Soufflé Ever 225
Three-Bean Chili 120
Thyme Pork and Kale 152
Tilapia and Red Sauce 129
Tilapia Delight 116
Tilapia with Asparagus and Acorn Squash 113

Tilapia with Parmesan Bark 147
Tilapia with Spicy Dijon Sauce 136
Toasted Pumpkin Seeds 197
Tofu Scramble with Veggies 50
Tofu, Chickpeas, and veggie bowl 84
Tomato & Cheese Chicken Chili 154
Tomato and Avocado Omelet 32
Tomato Bruschetta with Basil 39
Traditional Hungarian Gulyás 168
Tropical Carrot Ginger and Turmeric Smoothie 52
Tropical Fruit Crisp 228
Tropical Fruit Parfait 110
Trout with Chard 136
Tuna & Sweet Potato Croquettes 22
Tuna Steaks with Shirataki Noodles 140
Tuna-Stuffed Tomatoes 145
Turkey & Sweet Potato Chili 182
Turkey and Potatoes with Buffalo Sauce 186
Turkey and Quinoa Stuffed Peppers 86
Turkey Breast with Fennel and Celery 168
Turkey Burgers 18
Turkey Chili 178
Turkey Crust Meats 155
Turkey Ham and Mozzarella Pate 169
Turkey Sweet Potato Hash 121
Turkey with Thyme and Sage Sausage 55
Turmeric Chickpea Cakes 207
Turmeric Coconut Flour Muffins 196
Turmeric Gummies 202
Turmeric Milkshake 228
Turmeric Muffins 199
Turmeric Mushrooms 209
Turmeric Protein Donuts 34
Turmeric Rice Bowl with Garam Masala Root Vegetable and chickpeas 112
Turmeric-Ginger Chickpea Stew 117
Turnip Greens & Artichoke Chicken 168
Tuscan Chicken Sauté 164
Tzatziki Dip with Cauliflower 62
Vanilla Turmeric Orange Juice 99
Vegan and Mediterranean Mango and Bean stew 99
Vegan Coconut Chickpea Curry 97
Vegan Mushrooms in Broth 96
Vegan Sweet Potato and Corn Chowder 85
Vegan-Friendly Banana Bread 42
Vegetable and Chicken Stir Fry 98
Vegetable and Papillae 114
Vegetable Nuggets 206
Vegetarian Faux Stew 112
Veggie Balls 40

Veggie Sushi 88
Vietnamese Roll and Tarê 146
Vodka Duck Fillets 179
Waffles 29
Walnut and Banana Bowl 19
Walnut Encrusted Salmon 102
Walnut Rosemary Crusted Salmon 106
Warm Chia-Berry Non-dairy Yogurt 55
Warm Oatmeal with Ginger and Honey
  51
Wasabi Salmon Burgers 143
Watermelon Tomato Salsa 215
White Bean Chili 58

White Fish Ceviche with Avocado 189
Whitefish Curry 77
Whole Grain Porridge 213
Wild Berry Smoothie 224
Winter Chicken with Vegetables 160
Wonderful Breakfast Salad with Grape-
fruit, Oranges, and Berries 52
Yogurt Cheese and Fruit 61
Yogurt, Berry, and Walnut Parfait 55
Yummy Fruity Ice-Cream 227
Yummy Parfait with Yogurt, Berry, and
Walnut 52
Yummy Steak Muffins 42

Zesty Zucchini & Chicken in Classic Santa
Fe Stir-Fry 80
Zucchini and Carrot Combo 20
Zucchini and Lemon Herb Salmon 115
Zucchini Bread 64
Zucchini Noodles in Garlic and Parmesan
Toss 110
Zucchini Pancakes 40
Zucchini Pasta with Avocado Sauce 92
Zucchini Zoodles with Chicken 88

Made in the USA
Las Vegas, NV
08 March 2022

45282184R00133